How To Build a
Killer Street Machine

By Jefferson Bryant

motorbooks

First published in 2010 by Motorbooks, an imprint of MBI Publishing Company, 400 First Avenue North, Suite 300, Minneapolis, MN 55401 USA

Motorbooks titles are also available at discounts in bulk quantity for industrial or sales-promotional use. For details write to Special Sales Manager at MBI Publishing Company, 400 First Avenue North, Suite 300, Minneapolis, MN 55401 USA.

To find out more about our books, join us online at www.motorbooks.com.

ISBN-13: 978-0-7603-3549-9

Editor: Chris Endres
Creative Director: Michele Lanci-Altomare
Design Manager: Jon Simpson
Designer: Danielle Smith

Printed in China

On the cover: The 1969 Chevrolet Camaro is perhaps the most popular street machine platform ever. Equally adaptable to street, road course, or drag strip, the Camaro is a versatile performer.

Inset: The author's 1971 Buick Gran Sport convertible went through an extensive build. You can follow its progress on the pages of this book.

On the title page: With up to 690 available horsepower from its supercharged DOHC V-8, the limited-edition Gene Winfield Anaconda is one of the highest-end (and meanest) street machines on the road today.

On the contents page: Mustangs of all eras make great street machine material. They will accept nearly any engine Ford has built and have tremendous aftermarket support, meaning parts are plentiful and affordable.

About the author: Jefferson Bryant is an avid gearhead whose career began in the car audio industry, though his passion was not to be constrained there for long. Jefferson lives, eats, and breathes muscle cars and hot rods. He has built many street machines since constructing his first, a 1979 Buick Regal. As an automotive journalist, he regularly contributes to *MuscleCar Enthusiast*, *Car Craft*, *Hot Rod*, *Mustang Enthusiast* and many more publications. His most recent project is a 1971 Buick GS convertible, featured in this book. Jefferson resides in Stillwater, Oklahoma.

Contents

Acknowledgments

I thank my wife, Ammie, and my children, Jason, Josie, and Ben, for being so understanding and helpful during the intense process of writing books.

Special thanks go out to all who helped with the preparation of this book: DynoTech Engineering, Comp Cams, Schwartz Performance, Red Line Auto Sports, Street and Performance, TCI, FAST, GM Performance Parts, Global West, QA1, Air Ride Technologies, Stainless Steel Brakes, Power Brakes Service, Classic Performance Parts, Ramsey and Son Automotive, Auto Meter, Painless Performance, Centerline, BF Goodrich, Kumho, Foose Wheels, Magnuson, Nitrous Express, Nano Nitrous, and all of the other manufacturers included in the book.

I also thank Kyle Ambrose, Justin Johnson, Toby Ramsey, Jordan Lewis, Chris Franklin, Steven Marshall, Juston Martin, Fred and Kim, Corey and the rest of the Murfin clan, Gary Lette, and Greg McMeans for all their help with the projects featured in this book.

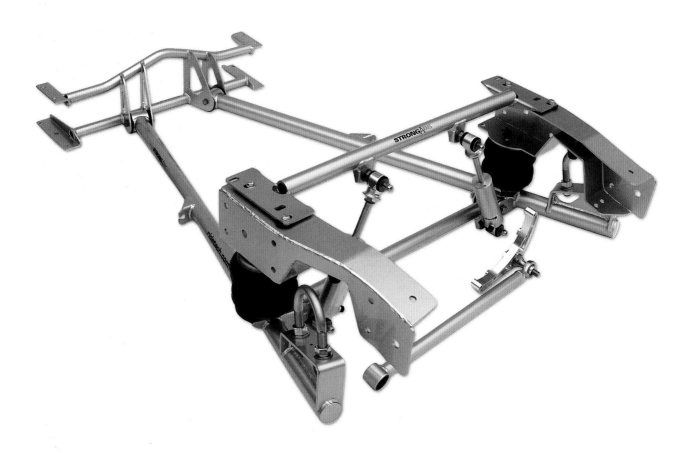

Introduction

Building a street machine is a serious undertaking that requires months of hard work, planning, and a variety of skills. Writing a book on that process is just as difficult. I have put together information about what I think are the most critical areas for building all types of street machines, not just the typical muscle car–era makes and models, to help you plan and build your street machine.

Inside this book, you will find detailed information on key processes, such as engine and transmission swaps, suspension design and modification, and bodywork. Every street machine is built differently and is an expression of the builder's personality. With that, I have written about each process and the technology involved in a way that will benefit builders of all makes and models, not just a select few.

Throughout the history of hot rods, street machines, and customs, the technology used to build these vehicles has changed. In the early days, there was no aftermarket; each builder had to come up with parts and tools to modify the cars themselves. As the sport grew, so did the industry, and companies like Edelbrock, Holley, and Comp Cams were built, usually on a foundation in sanctioned racing. Today the performance aftermarket is full of different companies peddling similar products. This book will show what to look

for and what to avoid so you can make the right choices for your project. From bumper to bumper, *How to Build a Killer Street Machine* gives you the specialized knowledge to build your car and end up with the results you want.

The world of automotive crafting has many pitfalls. The best way to avoid these issues is with proper planning. Inside, you will find a comprehensive guide to help you put your ideas and thoughts on paper and give you a working plan to keep your build on track. From restomod to full-on pro street or pro touring, a plan is the key to a successful build, and this book will help you do that.

Even if you are not building a street machine from the ground up, this book provides the building blocks you need. Detailed chapters on suspension, frames, braking, bodywork, power-adders, and even wheel and tire technology give you critical information for every build.

I hope you enjoy the book and have a successful build. While many builders want to do it all themselves, sometimes the best plan includes help from others. If you have never built an engine before, you might want some help. Spraying paint for the first time usually results in a not-so-good paint job. Know your limitations and seek professional help when needed. Above all else, have fun!

Chapter 1
The Car

Practically any car built after 1948 can be considered street machine fodder. Whether it is a coupe, sedan, wagon, or even a truck, just about anything can be built into a street machine. Building a street machine is less about what you started with and more about what the finished vehicle represents. Some cars simply lend themselves toward the street machine vibe more than others. Any traditional muscle car projects the essence of a street machine in stock form, while your basic family wagon might not look the part at first glance. Take the same classic family wagon, drop the suspension, shave the door handles, slap on some new paint, hop up the engine, and suddenly you have a street machine. Finding the right project is not an easy task. There are so many cars to choose from that it may seem impossible to sift through them all. You need to figure out what kind of street machine you want, and then you can start looking.

There are the requisite classic street machines, models that will always be favored by builders. These include the Camaro/Firebird (any year), Chevelle, Mustang (Mustang IIs are excluded here for "traditional" purposes), and the Mopar muscle cars. Any traditional muscle car lends itself to street machining readily. Soaring prices and increasing scarcity, however, are forcing builders to reconsider performing heavy modifications upon these cars. Paying $30,000 for a clean classic muscle car and then building it into a street machine might not be the best idea. Then again, many of these cars have been driven hard their entire lives and show it. Most of the hard-to-find cars were higher-priced versions of average midlevel cars. The GTO was based on the LeMans, the 442 on the Cutlass, and so on. If the looks of the muscle car are what you want, you can usually find a base model with which to build a project car.

Though 12 years separate the production of this 1967 Camaro and Tri-Five Chevy, both are classic street machines.

The street rod classification covers any car originally built before 1949, like this Model A. These cars are not typically used for street machine projects.

STYLING

While a modified muscle car is almost always referred to as a street machine, other vehicles are not so defined. As time progressed, the styling of the cars from Detroit changed, and popular methods and styles of customizing these cars changed as well. How people refer to the style of a car often depends on how you built it. The most common labels are hot rod, custom, street rod, street machine, traditional hot rod, low rider, muscle car, pro street, and pro touring. Each label has a core group of makes and models that easily fit within the confines of that moniker, but many are often used interchangeably. Let's discuss each.

Street Rod

The street rod is any car built before 1948 that has been modernized in some fashion. That is the definition as per the National Street Rod Association (NSRA). If you have a newer car, you can't enter it in an NSRA show. In the past, all NSRA shows required shiny paint–no primer, patina, or rust buckets. This has changed somewhat, and most

NSRA-style shows now have at least a section for low-buck primed rods.

Hot Rod

Often interchanged with street rod, a hot rod is a car that was built before 1948 and has been updated or hot rodded. A bigger, more powerful engine, lowered suspension, and a custom interior are common modifications. Most people consider the term *hot rod* to be more of an overall term, referring to just about any car that has been modified. I tend to agree, particularly in respect to adding power.

Traditional Hot Rod

This is a tricky one. Terms like *rat rod* are thrown around (see next page), much to the chagrin of many die-hard rodders. Traditional hot rodding, to the younger rodders, is about living a somewhat glorified old-school 1950s lifestyle. A traditional hot rod is built using 1960s and earlier parts and using 1960s and earlier techniques. You won't find an EFI system on a traditional 1928 T-bucket; this car would most likely be powered by a flathead Ford, or even a straight six.

In case you have not seen one, this is rat rod. While some don't like the moniker, there is a difference between a rat rod and a traditional hot rod. Rat rods use any parts that can be scrounged to become roadworthy; these cars are stripped-down, barebones rides. A traditional hot rod uses only 1960s and earlier parts and design as a rule.

The low rider is typically a full-size car from the 1960s through the early 1980s that has been dropped to the ground, typically with either hydraulic or air suspension.

Rat Rod

Though inclusion of this category might put some readers off, it is a viable term. For lack of a better term, a rat rod is basically a pile of rust that runs and drives. Old parts, new parts, it does not matter. This category represents a large group of newer builders who want to have fun and not spend much money. These cars usually have no interior and no paint, just some sort of body on some sort of frame with some sort of engine.

Custom

This group is a little broader. A custom usually means a car (or truck) built between 1949 and the mid-1960s. A custom has unique paint, typically with some sort of graphics, such as flames, scallops, or pinstripes, or additives like pearl or metal flake. Customs are almost always lowered, and often the top has been chopped. Performance is not the goal here; an engine swap may have taken place, but these cars are usually cruised, not raced.

Low Rider

Another cruiser style, the low rider, is low and slow. Stock or mildly modified engines move these behemoths around the boulevard. As the name states, these cars are dropped to the ground as low as they can go and still move. Using adjustable suspension systems like air bags or hydraulics, they often sit on the ground when fully lowered. Low riders are usually built from bigger models, as the idea is to fill them with your buddies (and girls) and go cruising, not racing. Four-door cars are quite common. Just about any car built in this fashion is considered a low rider.

Muscle Car

Most people consider the 1964 GTO to be the first real muscle car, though Chrysler had a few earlier offerings that fit the definition. The commonly accepted time frame for a muscle car is 1964 through 1972, when the EPA and insurance restrictions shifted the priorities of automotive manufacturers away from performance. A two-door, small (Mustang) to midsize (Chevelle) car with a factory big-block, usually accompanied by a styling package, is the original narrowly defined muscle car. Nowadays, the term is applied more loosely; just about any small to midsize V-8-powered two-door car that was built between 1964 and 1972 can be considered a muscle car.

Pro Street

The traditional pro-street car is designed to look like a Pro Stock drag car in street-legal trim. These cars are typically fitted with "big 'n littles" (large tires, often drag slicks or circle-track tires, in the back with skinny front tires), huge hood scoops or cowl induction hoods, lowered front suspension (sometimes with a lifted rear suspension), obnoxious graphic paint schemes, and heavily modified interiors. The interior of a pro-streeter usually has a roll cage (a roll bar at the least), race seats, five-point harnesses, and other race-oriented appointments. Many times the engine sticks out of the hood with a tunnel ram intake or supercharger. The biggest drawback of the pro-street movement of the mid-1970s through the early 1990s was that these cars were mostly about the look and not about actual performance. A tunnel ram looks really cool, but low- to mid-range performance—the most important range for a street car—really suffered. Typically trailered to car shows, the pro-street car was all show and no go. In the last 15 years or so, the pro-street trend has faded out. The remaining pro-street cars have shifted focus from form to function, often competing at events like "The World's Fastest Street Car" and other specialty street-legal drag race competitions.

Just because it is not a typical street machine doesn't mean that it can't be one. This 1978 Mercury has been chopped about 8 inches, lowered with air ride suspension, and given a proper flame job. The stock 460 motor was beefed up, and the exhaust was run out to the lakes pipes.

Pro Touring

When pro street died, pro touring was born. A pro-touring car is built to perform, and not just in a straight line. Pro touring is form closely following function. Large billet-aluminum wheels (17 to 20 inches in diameter) are used at the rear, while slightly smaller (15- to 18-inch) wheels are fitted to the front, usually wrapped in low-profile (45–35 series), high-performance rubber. Paint is smooth and clean, with only the bare minimum of decals or graphics applied; those used are usually stock or similar to stock designs, such as a hockey stripe for a Camaro or a hood bird for a Trans Am. A pro-touring car is likely built with a modified stock engine or crate motor, often retrofitted with fuel injection. Many pro-touring cars use late-model engine swaps, such as Ford mod motors or GM LS-series (Gen III and IV) engines. Because these cars are all about enhancing the driving experience, the interiors are often updated with air conditioning, quality upholstery, good tunes, and electronic gauges.

A pro-touring car must have a modified suspension. This cannot be overlooked, as the point of building this style of car is performance and handling. The stance is lowered at least 2 inches front and rear, often with coil-over shocks or even high-performance air suspension. Disc brakes at all four corners are required as well. Many pro-touring–inspired track events are held for these cars, such as the Year One autocross events held several times each year at car shows across the country.

Whether you want your street machine to fit a specific mold, or you want to be truly unique and stand out from the crowd, it's up to you. Build what you want, how you want it. The best thing about building a street machine is that it does not matter what you start with. If your dream car is out of your price range, there are other options. Two-door cars have always been the most popular for street machines, but if the one you want simply costs too much or you can't find one, consider the four-door version. While some models were never made in four-door models, like the Camaro or the Mustang, many were. In fact, looking outside traditional realms is where many of the best cars are found. Using an off-brand car, even a European make, can make for an exciting project where flexing your imagination is encouraged.

Once you have an idea of what you want to start with, it is time to start looking. The Internet is a vast resource, allowing you to search far and near for the car you desire. However, in the days before the Internet, project cars were found the old-fashioned way, through newspapers, bargain posts, swap meets, and the ol' shoe-leather express. Research is your best friend when purchasing a new project. Understanding exactly what you are looking at and typical prices for that particular model is important in order to get the best deal.

The traditional street machine is generally a compact or midsize car from the 1960s through the 1970s. This Chevy Vega has the pro-street look, with a blown engine (protruding through the hood no less), big 'n littles, and candy flamed paint.

Pro-touring street machines are quickly becoming the fastest-growing segment of the hobby. A pro-touring street machine was once a classic vehicle that would rarely see serious street time, but now some have turned into reliable daily drivers using modern technology and components, with all the creature comforts of a contemporary vehicle. Though most pro-touring cars are not used for daily transport, they are often used for cross-country road trips.

One of the key ingredients of a pro-touring car is the fuel-injected engine. This Camaro has been retrofitted with an LT-1 from a 1996 Camaro.

Doing what all street machines are intended to do, make tires turn to smoke, Fred Murfin of Red Line Auto Sports shows off his 1969 Camaro SS pro-touring convertible. This car has been road-tripped to shows all over the Southwest.

The interior of a pro-touring car is critical. While the interior on the Red Line Camaro looks stock, all of the seat foam was custom-formed for better comfort and wrapped in custom stock-style upholstery.

Cruising is what building a street machine is all about. Sure, many street machines see a fair amount of drag strip action, but the bulk of a street machine's life is spent on the boulevard.

Later-model cars, like this 1996 Chevy Impala SS, are great street machine fodder as well. With a modern fuel-injected engine, overdrive transmission, and updated styling, these cars are just waiting to be plucked for a street machine makeover.

Sites like eBay and craigslist contain countless possibilities for a new street machine project, but they are certainly not the only options. Many times, a car may bring much more than it is worth (at least to you) on eBay, and the ridiculous amount of scammers found on craigslist make it difficult to skim through the junk to find the gold. This is where the specialty websites are so great. If you are looking for a particular brand or model, search out sites that cater to it.

Sites like V8Buick.com or AllFordMustangs.com offer more than just information and chat; many have classified sections where you can find vehicles and parts.

Going one step further, sites such as RedLineAutoSports .com and SmokyHillRestoration.com offer sales brokering for classic cars. Some offer restoration services as well. Chances are you can find what you want through these shops, although you can expect to pay a slight premium for their services.

RED LINE AUTO SPORTS: MUSCLE CAR SPECIALISTS

Muscle cars and their survival are key to Fred and Kim Murfin's business. Proprietors of Red Line Auto Sports in Wilson, Oklahoma, and open since 1994, Red Line builds top-shelf muscle cars and sells them to the highest bidder.

"We specialize in nice drivers that are collectable and fun to drive," Kim Murfin said, "muscle cars that the average working person can afford, a car with a good paint job that probably won't have the original motor, and that's okay." Many of Red Line's customers want to re-create memories of the car that they had in high school that was sold to get a family car. Red Line does not stop with clean, collectable survivor cars, though. Red Line is also a full-service restoration shop.

In just the past few years, Red Line's restoration skills have been featured in numerous magazines and books, garnering much-deserved attention on the national level. "We have spent the last fifteen years working our tails off to build a reputation that is second to none in this field, providing top-quality cars for enthusiasts all over the world," Fred told us during our visit.

Many of the vehicles Red Line sells are done so via the Internet, and the company recommends anyone doing the same secure a vehicle inspection.

"It's always best for the customer to come and take a look; we have many customers who fly in and drive the car home," Fred Murfin said. "You can also send someone to inspect the vehicle. A second set of eyes is always a good idea, even if you come and look the car over yourself."

Any time you purchase a vehicle via the Internet, be wary of deposits and how the seller handles them. Red Line only accepts deposits once the vehicle is definitely sold. The deposit is generally based on the amount of time it will take to complete the transaction and take delivery of the vehicle. Payments for vehicles are typically made by wire transfer or certified or personal checks. Cash in hand is accepted as well. Red Line does charge a small processing fee on every car, but there are no hidden charges or fees, just the price you agreed on for the vehicle and the $99 process fee. Title and registration are the responsibility of the purchaser. Once the purchase is made, the vehicle can be stored for up to 30 days for free before shipment. Red Line highly suggests acquiring insurance for the vehicle as soon as the purchase is made, because once the vehicle is sold, it is no longer covered under its insurance policy.

While the classified sections in many papers are shrinking, specialty publications like *Old Car Trader* and *Hemmings Motor News* are running strong. Your local bargain post paper is another great source. You might not see what you want at first look, but it could take you to a place where you will.

These publications also print ads for salvage yards, auctions, and swap meets. Swap meets are another great place to find a new project. Most vendors at swap meets really don't want to haul cars back home afterward. This means that if the price is not right and the owner won't budge enough, he or she may be more willing to move on the price if the car is still there later in the day or weekend. Buying the car at the right price is a concern for any builder, especially on a full-tilt project.

One of the best places to find a new project is while cruising the back roads. Most of the project cars in this book were discovered on backwoods trips. These cars are generally the best bargains, as the owners usually just want them gone. Sometimes you can even get a car for free. (I've done it many times.) When you come across a barn or field find, often it was parked because of a minor problem. On several occasions I have swapped out the plugs and added some fresh gas to a barn find, and it fired right up. When you do come across a vehicle you may be interested in, talk to the owner of the property first before you start snooping around the car; you wouldn't want to get shot or arrested for trespassing, now would you?

The biggest problem with many project cars, especially field or barn finds, is the paperwork. Usually the title is long gone. The last owner might have passed away and the vehicle just sat for 30 years, being handed down with the property over the years. Most states have a process for procuring a title for such vehicles. This is the same process that salvage yards and wrecking services use for possessory liens to allow them to sell unclaimed vehicles. (Wrecker services are another good source for project vehicles.) Most states do not require you to have a license or permit to file, but some states restrict who can file for a possessory lien.

The little trucks are big in the street machine scene as well. This small-block Chevy-powered S10 was built in the pro-street style, with massive power and slicks.

Any discussion on street machines would be deficient if muscle trucks were left out. A large segment of the street machine aftermarket, classic trucks are street machines in utilitarian guise. The ubiquitous 1967–1972 Chevy and GMC trucks make up the most popular models, but any truck has street machine potential.

Powered by a late-model Gen III Vortec engine, this Cheyenne-packaged C10 built by Street and Performance turns heads and smokes tires at will.

Don't forget the non-muscle car–era cars, either. Wagons like this 1961 Mercury Comet are making a big comeback in popularity, and there is something to be said about a street machine that is different.

Restomods like this 1971 Buick GS convertible take up the middle ground between restorations and fully customized street machines. This GS has been built with all the high-performance goodies like tubular suspension, automatic overdrive, and lots of power, but the exterior is all stock, with the exception of custom Foose wheels.

If you can't find that perfect car, or if everything you find is full of rust and you would rather start fresh, you might be able to just pick up the phone and order a new body for certain makes and models. Dynacorn, Year One, Goodmark, and other companies are now offering brand-new bodies for your building pleasure. For everything from Tri-Five Chevys and first-generation Camaros to Mustangs and trucks, brand-new steel bodies can be found. Other companies, such as Factory Five Racing and many others, build fiberglass bodies for everything from T-buckets and Model A's to Ferrari and AC Cobras. The options for a new body are increasingly interesting.

Chapter 2
The Plan

Once you have chosen the car you want to build, it is time to lay out the plan. Most build projects fail because the project was not fully planned, or the plan was not followed. (This is where many of the best projects are purchased at great loss to the seller; don't be a victim of the same problem.) A proper plan, taking in to account budgetary restraints and your own skill level, makes for a better final result. Any build needs to be planned out, from major projects to the simplest

of builds; this is the only way you can keep on track. That is not to say the plan can't change; most build plans progress along the way, as the builder's budget and skill level increases or, depending on the length of the build, as the styles change. What is cool and progressive now might not be in 10 years.

Don't start writing your build plan by focusing on the smallest details. This will just get you bogged down in the process.

Take some photos of the vehicle, including the following:

- *Front/rear*—This is mostly self-explanatory, but take several shots, one standing up looking slightly down at the hood and one kneeling down, kind of a roadkill-eye view. Repeat for the rear.
- *Front/rear three-quarters*—These are the best shots for any car. You get the side and the front from a good angle to reveal the lines of the car. Take both driver- and passenger-side three-quarter shots. A three-quarter is taken using an imaginary line from the camera lens through the leading edge of the fender, running across the hood to the opposite hood corner. Set the camera with the lens level with the roof; this yields a good overall view of the car. The rear three-quarters tells a different story. Use the same guidelines, but imagine the line from the rear corner of the rear glass to the opposite corner. For trucks, line up your camera to align the closest bed corner with the opposite bed corner.

Taking several pictures of the car before starting the project is critical when creating a plan for the build. A simple straight-on shot from an upright position is needed.

A second front shot from a lower perspective gives a better look at the grille and nose of the car.

The rear view is taken as shown here. A second shot from ground level is helpful as well.

There are two styles of three-quarter shot. This one shows a little more front grille than side.

The wider three-quarter shot shown here is more helpful for renderings and planning body mods. These shots are good for designing paint schemes as well.

The rear three-quarter is another critical wide body shot. A good, low-angle shot like this tells more about the body lines than a roof-level shot.

- *Profile*—Both driver- and passenger-side shots, with the camera level or slightly above the roofline.
- *Engine bay*—Shoot the engine bay with the hood up (or off, if that's the case), using good lighting and the lens framing just the engine bay. Don't waste lens space on the tops of the fenders if you can help it; you want to capture as much detail as possible. If the engine is in the car, shoot the front and both sides.

- *Interior*—The inside of the car requires a few more pictures. The dash, front and rear seats, and the door panels should be photographed. Open the door and roll down the window. Keep the opposing door shut. Flip (or slide) the front seats over to shoot the rear seats. Get as much detail as you can here. Shoot the door panels while kneeling at the door level with the door open.

Avoid shots like this, where the background takes over the car. You want the car to be the main subject of the shot, not the background.

The profile shot shows the entire vehicle's side in one frame. Having other vehicles or objects in the background does not really matter for these working pictures, as long as it does not detract from seeing the car fully.

Shooting the engine bay often requires positioning the vehicle so that the sun lights the area under the hood. In this shot, the sun is above the car, so you have bad shadows.

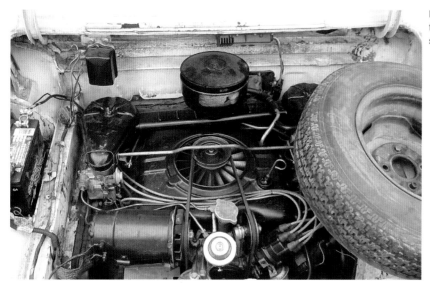

In this shot of the same car, the car was repositioned so that the sun lit up the entire area. This is a Corvair, and the spare is carried over the engine.

Even if the front sheet metal is off the car or the engine is out, you need to take an engine bay shot. This shot illustrates how much room the firewall has for things like power boosters and A/C components.

• *Trunk*—Clean out the trunk and shoot it. Take out all of the accessories such as the spare tire, jack, and so on. You want the empty trunk for the reference shots. If you have it, set up the stock spare and jack for a stock trunk reference shot as well. This will give you an idea of how much space you have with and without the spare and accessories.

Keep these pictures handy at all times. If you are using film, have duplicates made (maybe even have a set blown up for easy reference) and keep a set in the garage. If you are using digital images, print a couple of sets and put them in a folder or three-ring binder so you can reference the stock vehicle. This is also a good idea for the disassembly process. Take pictures of everything and log everything in the folder. This way you will have a photographic log of how each part came off, which will help you put it back together. This is a must for builds where the entire car is disassembled.

Once you have the stock pictures, you can sit down and lay out the things you know you want. This is a basic outline of the vehicle. Do not go into details like "brand X coil-over shocks with 1,200-pound springs and Torrington bearing washers." Simply list "coil-over shocks." The details will come later. Once you have created the basic outline, you can get into more detail as you break down each section of the car.

Interiors are difficult to capture all in one shot. This shot of the dash does not tell much about the seats, doors, or floors.

In this slightly wider shot, the dash and front seats are in clear view. This is what you need for a good, clean interior reference photo.

A straight seat shot can be helpful in planning the seat upholstery design if you are going to stray from stock.

This shot of a 1951 Ford shoebox shows the dash, tattered seat, and the general state of condition of the interior.

A kneeling position is best for shooting the door panels. With the door open you get a full shot. Shooting the door panel through the car does not give you a good reference.

The trunk is a necessary shot too. If you are planning changes like wheel tubs or a serious stereo system, try placing rulers in the trunk for reference or simply mark up the photo with correct measurements later.

Do not forget the trouble spots. Every car has them; you want to keep these areas in mind when laying out the plan. If you have a picture of each trouble area, you won't forget one.

One of the best ways to get a look at what the car will look like once it is done is to draw (or have drawn) a rendering. Many artists offer these services for builders. It is not as costly as you might think. You don't have to hire Thom Taylor or Chip Foose to draw your car, even though that would be really cool. Instead, you might hit up a teacher at your local art or technical school. There is likely to be a starving student who would love to draw up some renderings using your plan outlines as the guide. A little cash goes a long way here; you can have several done to compare different elements for a good price.

Even if you are not an outstanding artist, you don't have to pay somebody to do this for you. If you want to give it a shot yourself (or help guide the person you hired), there are several ways that you can make your own renderings. In the digital age, Photoshop and other programs make it fairly easy to manipulate photos. This software might take some time to learn, but the results can be quite good. If you prefer hand drawings (they make great office or garage art too), this can be done for basically nothing. Tape a photo or printed image to a large window, and then lay a piece of white copy paper over the image. Carefully trace the lines of the vehicle.

Every plan should have a rendering. This simple line drawing of the car lays out the graphics and suspension modifications. Kyle Ambrose of KA Cars and Stripes designed the *Koolvair* for us.

If you want to take on the renderings yourself, or give your artists a head start (which makes it cheaper), take a clean side shot like this one and print it out.

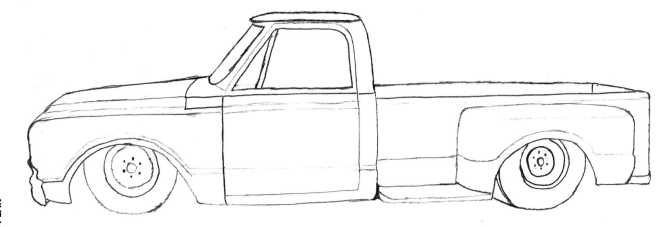

Place the printed photo under a piece of tracing paper or plain white copy paper and tape them together on a window. The sun will shine through both layers, allowing you to simply trace the outline like this. Scan or copy the image so you can create and compare several designs.

If you are planning on lowering the car, you can adjust the paper to accommodate a lowered stance or leave the wheels off all together; you can always add them later. If you do copy the wheel shapes, just the silhouette is needed, unless you are planning on keeping the wheels in the photo. All you are looking for is the basic outline, body lines, and door shapes; everything else can be added later. If you are planning to put roll pans in place, leave the bumpers off. It's the same for shaved door handles and the like.

Once you have the basic outline, scan it to your computer or make some copies. This way you can draw up several versions without having to make new tracings. Keep the original for reference and to make more copies. You can provide this image to your artist as well, which he or she will

likely appreciate. There is even a website that offers blank renderings of quite a few makes and models. The website is V8Renderings.com, and for a small fee, you can order a blank rendering for your model, ready to be modified.

Use colored pencils to color your rendering. Be as flashy as you want; just keep your artistic skills in mind. This is a great way to play with the look of the project without spending any real money.

There are two types of build plan: the dream plan and the reality plan. While anyone would love to build and own a $150k street machine, in reality most of us can't afford that and don't have the skills needed to build a car on that level. That doesn't mean you can't plan some of those high-buck aspects into your build. Creating the dream plan will help

The final rendering of the shop truck turned out nice. Kyle Ambrose added full color to this one, complete with 22-inch wheels and the laid-out suspension.

you figure out the reality plan. Some elements of the mega-buck plan can be done on a budget at home with careful planning and research. What used to be considered a costly modification, like shaved door handles, is really a simple process that just about anybody can do. You might not be able to afford a $15K LS7 crate motor, but searching the salvage yards for a wrecked late-model Corvette or GTO might turn up an LS3 for a few thousand dollars.

Overestimating your skills is one of the biggest pitfalls a builder can make. Do not be afraid to ask for help or seek a professional in areas of the build where you are not experienced. You can easily burn a lot of time and some serious money breaking parts, and risk life and limb, if the install is not up to par. If you want a tube chassis but have

never built one, seek professional advice or look at purchasing a ready-made or pre-designed chassis for your first build. Certain things can be replaced, but if the chassis fails cruising down the road, you have major problems.

If there is any adage that holds true in building a car it is this: "Plan your work and work your plan." Make concessions in your plan for alterations. Most builds evolve over time, but don't think this gives you permission to go off half-cocked and start building. This always costs more in terms of time and money than working from a set build plan. The build plan is the most important feature of any project. If you want the car to turn out right, plan it right. Too many finished cars leave their owners with a few regrets that could have easily been rectified with proper planning.

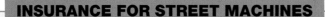

INSURANCE FOR STREET MACHINES

Protecting your street machine after it is finished is too often overlooked by many builders. At some point in every car owner's life, he or she will be faced with an accident. The question is how good your insurance is. Standard insurance, the type you would use for your daily driver is not designed to cover your muscle car. Most insurance companies only offer standard full-coverage policies to vehicles 10 years old or newer, unless you have maintained full coverage on the vehicle, under the same policy, before it hit the 10-year mark. Most muscle car owners do not fit in that category.

For most classic car owners, that means purchasing a policy from a reputable specialty insurance company. With the growing popularity of classic cars, the field of specialty insurance providers has grown rapidly. Simply Google "collector car insurance" and your screen will be flooded with websites. Uncovering which is best for you is the key. We spoke with representatives from several leading collector car insurance providers to help you narrow the field.

There are several specific terms you need to consider when looking at a collector car policy:

Agreed value or actual value: Most standard vehicle policies are actual value, meaning the car is valued at the base market value minus depreciation. That would not be sufficient to cover a collector car. Most collector car insurance policies are agreed value, which means the owner and the insurance company have settled on a specific monetary value that is guaranteed in the event the vehicle is wrecked or stolen.

Prohibitive mileage or unlimited: There are two types of mileage: restricted and unlimited. American Collectors Insurance offers a policy with a 5,000-mile pleasure use limit, while others have as little as 2,500 annual mileage limits. Unlimited-mileage policies have no mileage restriction. Grundy Worldwide's collector policies feature unlimited mileage for hobby use.

Usage: This one divides collector car policy providers. Most providers require the covered vehicle to be of restricted use, meaning you can't drive it to work or to the grocery store. If you do and get in an accident, it might not be covered. Some policies are hobby-use only, meaning parades and car shows. Other policies are more open, including limited pleasure usage. This is a big one if you like to drive your car to work occasionally. The larger providers, such as Hagerty Insurance, are flexible in the usage restrictions. "We want our customers to be able to enjoy their cars without worry," said McKeel Hagerty, CEO of Hagerty Insurance. It is important to check with each provider for details on their specific requirements.

Garage-kept vehicles: All collector car policies require the vehicle to be stored in a garage. Most request photos of the garage to verify you have one. Leaving the vehicle outside one night won't terminate the policy, but it is agreed that the vehicle should be stored inside most of the time.

Modified or original: Some providers restrict coverage to vehicles that are wholly original with no modifications. This type of policy is great for a 100 percent restored car, but most of us don't have those in our garages. If your car has had a few upgrades over the years, make sure you look for the right policy.

Age of the vehicle: Some providers have age restrictions and classifications for collector cars. For CWG's Collector Car Insurance Group, muscle cars are considered to be original and unchanged vehicles 1968 through 20 years old. That would make a 1977 Firebird a muscle car, but a 1965 GTO would be classified as a classic. The quotes are determined in part by vehicle class, so that must be considered.

Wrecks are no laughing matter, especially when someone is seriously hurt. A 50-year-old unlicensed, intoxicated man plowed his 1983 Toyota into the stopped Z/28 at more than 70 miles per hour. There no skid marks at all; he never even touched the brakes. The four people in the Camaro walked away, but the driver of the truck was not so lucky. He died at the scene.

THE PLAN

This restored 1969 Z/28 was in perfect condition in early March 2007. One week after its completion, that all changed. Good thing the owner had the foresight to get full coverage during the build.

The driver of the other car did not have insurance, leaving the Camaro owners to rely on their own policy. The car was hit so hard that the center console popped loose from the floor when the entire floorpan buckled. Amazingly enough, the rear window did not break.

There are a few regional and standard insurance companies that offer collector car insurance. In Oklahoma, Oklahoma Farm Bureau Insurance has a collector car program that offers agreed value (based on a certified appraisal) and has no restrictions, meaning you could drive it to work or to run errands. This policy costs more, with prices like traditional policies, but, depending on your situation, it may make sense for you.

In the growing field of specialty insurers, there are those that offer some unique programs to set themselves apart. Grundy Worldwide, the first collector car insurance provider, now offers some programs typically only seen in standard policies. New options include spare parts, trip interruption, and towing and labor costs for new policyholders. Grundy even offers auto show medical reimbursement in the event you become ill at a car show. Hagerty Insurance offers the only nationwide flatbed roadside assistance service, which guarantees a flatbed truck in the event you need it.

One interesting fact we found during our research is that many of the companies not only offer automobile insurance, but also collectibles insurance. This type of insurance covers many items such as gasoline globes, automobilia, and other irreplaceable collectibles. Contrary to popular belief, most home owners' insurance policies do not adequately cover high-value collectibles. In the event of a loss, these items would not be covered for their true value. "Even if the homeowners do have all risk coverage, the reimbursement from the insurance company may be based on actual cash value (replacement cost less depreciation) rather than collector market value," said Laura Bergan of American Collectors Insurance. Just like collector car insurance, collectibles insurance claims are paid on an agreed-value basis. American Collectors Insurance provides specific coverage for collectibles, including accidental breakage, theft, fire, windstorm, flood, water damage, and earthquake. If you have even a moderate amount of automobilia, you might want to look into specialized collectibles insurance.

With 70 percent of all new collector policies being for muscle cars, the market is certainly gearing itself toward muscle car owners. Pricing for collector car insurance is substantially less than a standard policy. Hagerty Insurance gave us this example: a 1967 Mustang valued at $30,000 would run $215 to $230 per year. That is a considerable savings over a traditional insurance plan and if anything ever happened to it, you get a check for $30,000. McKeel Hagerty had this to say: "The measure of an insurance policy is not how much premium you pay; it is more about how the policy pays at the time of a claim. You want to be dealing with people who know and understand collector cars." Sounds good to me.

Chapter 3
The Engine

The basic purpose of a street machine is go fast and look good while you are at it. Whether you are revving to eight grand with a turbocharged six-cylinder or pounding the pavement with 1,000 horses of ground-shaking big-block, the engine is the cornerstone of a street machine.

The car you choose to build usually has some say in the type of motor that will power it. A Camaro should never be powered by a Ford engine, just like a Mustang should not have a Chevy 454 between the fenders (though both of these combinations have certainly happened). That said, there are so many different engine configurations that the possibilities are practically endless. From small-blocks and big-blocks to rare and exotic engines, it is the builder's choice.

Every street machine build centers around the powerplant. Modern fuel-injected engines like this LS1 in a 1991 Chevy muscle truck are quickly becoming the most popular swap. Soon, Gen III and IV motors will eclipse the small-block Chevy as the supreme swap engine.

Adding aftermarket fuel injection is always a popular way to go. This Ford 302 is topped with a FAST XFI fuel-injection system. The throttle body is good to 1,000 cfm, plenty enough to feed a big-block. Because the flow of air and fuel is controlled via the ECM, the classic "too much carb" issue is eliminated.

This Buick 350 makes 400 horsepower and 414 foot-pounds. This is the engine that powers the 1971 Buick GS convertible found elsewhere in this book.

Choosing the motor to power your street machine is tricky. You may be partial to a specific model or brand, which makes that decision easy; but if you are open to the possibilities, things get a little hazy.

The key to choosing the engine is the intended application. If you're building a daily driver, a monster motor with a radical camshaft that sounds awesome and provides massive amounts of power is probably not a good idea. Too many builders sideline their beloved street machines because they can't be driven on the street reliably. If you intend to drive the car every day, or across the country on cruise trips, you must keep that in mind when choosing the powerplant. On the other hand, if your goal is to build an amazing street machine that you take to car shows, drag races, and dyno days, you need the engine to perform. A basic motor or budget crate motor might not be the best bet.

BUILDING THE STOCK ENGINE

Many street machine projects already have impressive engines. If the base vehicle is a muscle car, then you can always keep the stock motor, with a little freshening. If the project is not a typical make and model, the stock engine choices are likely less abundant, particularly when it comes to pre-muscle car–era vehicles and European projects. These cars often use odd motors (straight eights, straight sixes, and so on) that do not have as many aftermarket performance options. Niche manufacturers for the specific brands may offer some solutions for some models, but in most cases, a swap may be more appropriate for a street machine. In an effort to separate your build from the crowd, using an off-brand or less popular engine might be a good idea.

Building a straight six, Buick Nailhead, or Cadillac motor sets your car apart from the crowd of Chevys and Fords. Finding performance parts will prove difficult, but the effort will result in wide eyes and confused looks when the hood is open, especially when the engine is really rare or odd. A properly built straight six fitted with a turbocharger can create massive amounts of torque and horsepower to fry the tires and set the boulevard ablaze, much to the delight of onlookers and the chagrin of the guy in the next lane.

If the stock motor just will not do, roll out the cherry picker, yank that wheezy motor, and drop in some new life. If there was a factory option for a larger, more powerful engine, in most cases the provisions for installing that engine are there in the chassis. These swaps are much simpler; the parts are readily available and easily found as used or reproduction parts. Swapping in a later-model engine or an engine of a different brand is more work (sometimes, a lot more work).

31

Every engine must be cooled. While a mechanical fan works just fine, many machines need a little more cooling power. In addition, mechanical fans cause quite a bit of parasitic power loss. There are two ways to mount an electric fan. The fan shown here will work, but it will draw air through only about half of the radiator. *Street and Performance*

This fan from Flex-A-Lite features a built-in shroud, which draws air through the surrounding fins of the radiator to increase the cooling capacity. You can also build a shroud for a custom look.

TRANSPLANTS: FACTORY SWAPS

Research is a must with a factory-style swap, as you need to know all of the differences that the factory put in place for different powerplants. Often, a builder will overlook important safety features that are different from engine to engine. Dropping a big-block V-8 in a V-6 car will seriously increase the nose weight of the car, overpowering the V-6 coil springs, making the car unwieldy and difficult to drive.

Cooling

A straight six has less coolant capacity than a V-8 and is easier to keep cool; therefore, the radiator is typically smaller. Try running an even small-block V-8 on a six-cylinder radiator in the middle of summer and you will see the temperature gauge rise to extreme levels. Know what size of radiator the bigger engine needs, and you will be in good shape.

Suspension

As mentioned earlier, different engines have different weights. Swapping a heavier engine where a lighter engine was changes the suspension's needs. This is not always accurate, however. If the smaller engine was cast iron and you swap in an aluminum block, the new engine may even be lighter than the original.

Braking

It takes more braking capacity to stop a car with 1,000 pounds of big-block than one with 400 pounds of V-6. Some cars were fitted with larger brakes (or discs versus drums) when the bigger engine was installed.

Steering

Bigger engines are often longer and wider than the original engine. You might find that the steering linkage that fit the straight six doesn't clear the big-block.

Transmission

The stock transmission for a four- or six-cylinder in most cases is not going to hold up behind a bigger, more powerful engine. Even the small-block V-8 transmission might be short-lived behind a big-block. Some models (not many, but a few) used different transmission tunnels between the economy engine and the big engine option, particularly trucks.

Rear-end

This is a much-too-often overlooked aspect of an engine swap. The factory rear end for economy engines is often the low-end of the scale. Many factory rear-end housings are split between gear ratios, meaning that just because you have GM corporate 8.5-inch 10-bolt (which is a strong rear end as opposed to the smaller and much weaker 8.2-inch rear end) does not mean you can fit it with whatever gearing you want. Many housings have two gear groups: a highway gearing group and the low-end gearing group. If you have a rear that has smaller gears in it (usually in the low 3:1 range), you can't simply drop 4-series (like 4.11:1) gears in it.

All Gen III and IV engines use serpentine belts. This simplifies the installation of the belt and reduces the parasitic loss of added components. There are many versions of these accessory drives, both OEM and aftermarket. When swapping Gen III and IV motors, the style of accessory drive is critical for engine fit in the chassis.

HOW TO "MOD" A SHOEBOX

THE ENGINE

When it comes to hot rods and customs, from the very beginning, Fords (and Mercs) have been the most popular. The classic Shoebox is certainly no exception. The biggest problem with building a Shoebox, however, is choices for the powertrain. Unless you want to spend hours upon hours fabricating motor and tranny mounts, your engine choices are limited to small-block Chevys, small-block Fords, or rebuilding a flathead. Since we have a penchant for the unusual, we decided to shoehorn a 4.6 Ford mod motor into the Shoebox.

We purchased a running and driving 1996 T-bird with a reasonable amount of miles (120,000), pulled the motor and AODE transmission, and set the rest of the car aside for plundering later. Finding a retrofit wiring harness was pretty simple. A phone call to The Detail Zone got a wiring harness on the way, but when it came to finding motor and transmission mounts, things got sticky. We researched the Internet, combed the forums, and chatted up everyone we could think of, including several Shoebox experts. The answer was always the same: "It can't be done," or "I saw it once but the fabrication level was very advanced; duplicating it would be impossible."

Not to be put off by the naysayers (we're building a rod here, anything is possible), we continued our search just to see if it has been done before and then we had a reply on our post, the H.A.M.B. (www.jalopyjournal.com/forum). We found our answer. Hanksville Hot Rods of Highlands Ranch, Colorado, has not only performed several of these swaps, but sells CNC-plasma-cut and TIG-welded kits to make this swap a simple conversion. The price of the kit is even better, spending less than $300 for both the engine and tranny mounts. This allowed us to perform the entire swap in less than three hours, starting with the motor on the hoist to being bolted in the car, ready to wire.

I pulled a 4.6-liter mod motor out of a 1996 Thunderbird. When pulling a used motor, make sure you get all the sensors, wiring, and computer. I bought the whole car to ensure that all the parts were available. The car had less than 120k on the clock and the transmission had been rebuilt, so I installed it unchanged.

Before the actual install, I spent a day cleaning up the motor. Eleven years of grease and road grime made for some seriously difficult cleaning. I used some Justice Brothers engine degreaser to break up the mess and a power washer to blast it off.

The kit I received from Hanksville Hot Rods was a lot nicer than we expected for the price. All the parts were TIG-welded and painted, and all the required hardware was included.

I test-fit the brackets to engine to check for clearance issues. The oil dipstick needed to be tweaked on the driver's side.

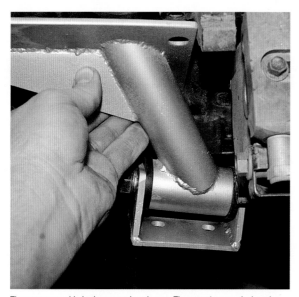

The passenger side had more serious issues. The mounts were designed around a bare motor without air conditioning (A/C). Since this is an Oklahoma car, A/C is a must for summer cruising. The lower portion of the mount won't clear the stock A/C compressor. I fabricated an adapter plate and sent the specs to Hanksville Hot Rods so they can provide them for future customers.

The mounts were bolted to the engine before positioning it between the rails. The kit comes with socket-head cap screws, which make for a nice look, but the lower bolts are a real pain to install.

For the price, you would expect a functional part, but not necessarily a pretty part. What we received from Hanksville Hot Rods was quite beautiful. The welds were perfect, the kit fit better than expected, and they even took the time to test fit an AODE before sending the kit to us. They even made a special adapter bracket just for this application. Before our project, Hanksville sold these kits for 4.6, 5.4, and 6.8 Ford motors and T-56 transmissions, but I wanted to keep the AODE. In the end, the extra bracket was not needed, as I had a different tranny mount than the one they tested; the T-56 mount alone worked for me.

To get many of the 58-plus-year-old bolts out of the original shoebox Ford, they were sprayed with some JB80. Unlike most other penetrating lubricants, JB80 works quickly, foaming up to push its way into locked threads.

With everything ready to go, the motor was lifted and carefully lowered into the car. With the front clip off the car, this was much easier.

With the engine suspended, the lower mounts were removed and a single bolt was placed in the factory slot at the rear of the main crossmember.

Then the motor was set onto the mount and aligned square with the car. A hook pick was used to mark the location for the second bolt hole in the lower mount.

The actual installation was pretty simple and only required minor modifications to the car, considering the obstacles these motors present. One of the main issues with the Shoebox is the rear-steering arrangement and the linkages for that. We are keeping the stock steering components for now, but that creates problems when installing late-model V-8 engines. The Hanksville kit sits the engine a little higher in the car to clear the stock steering components, but the engine still fits under the hood. While the firewall had a good 2 or 3 inches of clearance, the tranny tunnel did not. We had to remove a 2-foot-by-2.5-foot section of the trans tunnel to get adequate clearance. A new tranny cover will be fabricated from 18-gauge sheet metal and screwed into place after the wiring is completed.

I spent the day at Red Dirt Rodz, who performed all the work on this 1951 Ford, and captured the entire process for you. Having seen this project go from being a rat-infested basket case to becoming a proper custom with some modern motivation has been and will certainly continue to be a real treat. The kit from Hanksville Hot Rods saved us a lot of time and money and will allow us to make more mods sooner than expected.

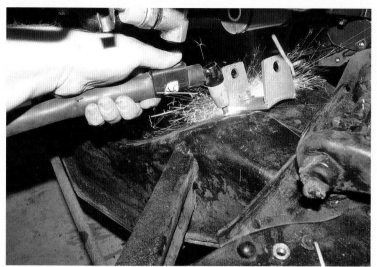

The motor was lifted up again, the lower mount was removed, and the second holes were cut with a plasma cutter. While I could have drilled them, I wanted slots instead of perfect holes to give us a little front-to-back adjustability.

The mounts were then bolted down and the motor set back in the mounts. There is a ton of firewall clearance with this setup, which makes this a simpler swap. The height of the mounts also allows the stock steering components to be used as well.

THE ENGINE

The physical installation is now complete. All that is left is the wiring and exhaust. This installation requires custom headers, which Hanksville Hot Rods also offers.

TRANSPLANTS: LATER MODEL AND AFTERMARKET SWAPS

Swapping in a completely different family of engine complicates things a little. There are a couple of ways of going about swapping later-model (or different-brand) engines into a chassis. The most popular swaps have kits available, taking out all or most of the guesswork. This is nice, but it only applies to the most popular swaps—like GM LS-series engines—into popular makes and models. If you are straying from the path most traveled, then you will have your work cut out for you. It is not that difficult, as long as you are not afraid of hard work and have a modicum of fabrication experience.

The same parameters that apply to the factory-option motor swap apply to this type of swap but in a different fashion. Some of the components that are in the car may work out great with the new engine, depending on what was in the car originally. The more wild the swap, the more components you will have to change. If your project does not have a kit available for the swap you are doing, then you will have to build one. Don't rule out being able to find a swap kit. With some thorough search on the Internet and in magazines, you might surprise yourself and find one. There are quite a few niche shops that build kits for odd swaps. You can easily find a kit to swap a V-8 into a Fiero or an RX-7, and even GM V-8s into BMW chassis, among many others. It just shows that a little research goes a long way.

If you do have to go the custom route, in addition to the aforementioned issues, you will have to consider the following.

Motor Mounts

Without an easy bolt-on part, you will have to fabricate or modify existing motor mounts. While building the actual motor mount is not that difficult, determining the alignment is critical and is not a single-person task. You will need to suspend the motor over the chassis, maintaining it at a correct level and position while taking measurements and making changes. The engine must sit parallel in the chassis, with a slight downward angle to the rear of about 4 degrees for proper alignment. It should be square in the chassis to the frame rails, not to one side or the other, though sometimes there are situations that warrant a slight shift. Even some factory-installed engines are off to one side slightly. Working under a 500-pound engine that is dangling precariously from an engine hoist is not safe. If at all possible, you might want to consider a plastic or foam mock-up engine. These usually weigh less than 50 pounds and are spot-on accurate, with bolt threads where they need to be so that your build can be done safely.

It is important that your engine sits squarely in the chassis and runs parallel with the frame rails and the rest of the drivetrain. This is a critical area. If the engine does not sit square, the transmission will not be square. A misalignment at the front of the engine by a ¼ inch can become 4 or 5 inches at the transmission tail shaft, which would be disastrous. If the engine lies over on its side, even just a few degrees, under heavy cornering you could experience an oil pressure drop should the oil pick-up tube become uncovered. Again, this is a disaster waiting to happen.

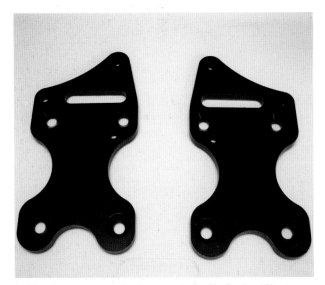

For LS engine swaps, you need motor mount adapters. The Gen III and IV motors use a four-bolt mount instead of the traditional three-bolt SBC mounts. These mounts from Speedhound bolt to a Gen III and IV GM engine and allow a standard motor mount to bolt on.

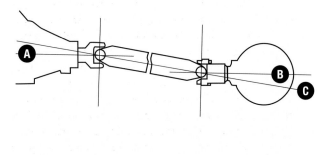

Engine swaps change the factory drivetrain alignment angles. This diagram shows how to measure the alignment. This is done with the transmission in position. *A* is the slip yoke horizontal centerline, and *B* is the rear-end horizontal centerline. *C* represents the angle of the driveshaft. The optimal angle here is 3 degrees each, A to C and B to C; but anywhere between 2 and 5 degrees is acceptable.

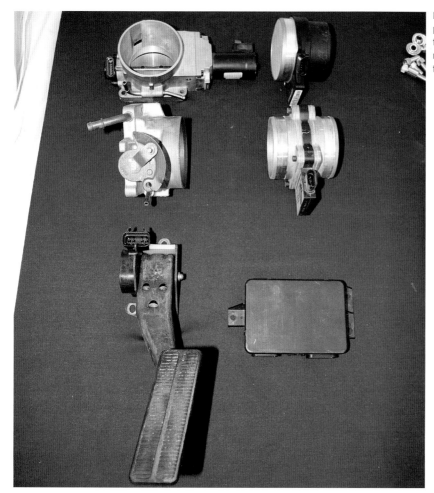

Late-model engines often have drive-by-wire throttle pedals. These systems do not use a throttle cable. Instead, the throttle body is controlled by the computer, which receives (and can override) the electrical input provided by the driver's manipulation of the throttle pedal.

If you are installing an engine with massive amounts of horsepower, you might consider a motor plate. There are two types of motor plates: the front plate and the midplate. Front plates mount to the front of the engine, usually between the block and the water pump. A midplate installs between the back of the engine block and the transmission. Installing a motor plate makes swapping engines easier, as the alignment job is less difficult, and you do not have to fumble around with fabricating frame mounts. The motor plate takes care of all that in one fell swoop. Particularly useful in tube-frame and custom chassis cars, motor plates eliminate engine torque roll, which helps transfer power to the chassis instead of wasting power on rotational force. Really powerful engines can actually twist out of the car using standard rubber-isolated engine mounts, so on some engines a motor plate is required.

Installing an engine with a motor plate is fairly simple. Once the engine is in place and lined up, a pair of simple L-brackets are welded or bolted to the frame, then a bolt is run through the L-bracket and the motor plate. This not only greatly simplifies the installation procedure, but also makes pulling the motor much easier, as the bolts are readily accessible. Using a midplate allows you pull the transmission for service without pulling or otherwise supporting the motor, as the midplate provides the support.

Motor plates do require a little forethought, though. Front plates often require that you space out the pulleys for the accessory drive. A mild steel midplate is usually thin enough that you don't need to adjust the torque converter (which would be done with shims, spacing the converter farther from the flex plate). Aluminum plates are thicker, however, and will require spacing the converter to take up the difference.

A proper fuel system for any engine, stock or otherwise, is critical. The fuel tank must be in good shape and clean, but that is a simple issue. Replacing old, corroded fuel lines seems like a simple task, but it can be a little tricky. If the body is still on the frame, getting the old lines out and the new lines in can be a truly religious experience, in that you will need the patience of Job. At the least, the body mounts need to be loosened and the body gently raised to gain some clearance for the lines. Even though the line may look okay on the outside, the insides of 30-plus-year-old steel lines are bound to be heavily corroded, if not on the verge of rusting through. Replacing the steel hard line is a good idea.

You may get the idea to replace the hard line with rubber hose. While fuel lines are joined with rubber line and many cars use rubber line to run from the frame to the carburetor, running the entire fuel system with rubber line is not a good idea, even if the line has an exterior reinforced with braided steel. The problem with running the entire chassis with rubber line is that over time, the rubber will degrade and collapse, causing myriad issues. Another problem with the rubber hose is that it is more susceptible to damage from road debris. Steel line can take a lot of abuse; rubber line is much more fragile when it comes to rocks and other debris.

There are also considerations for the fuel pump. A stock motor can be fed with a basic mechanical fuel pump, but once you start stepping up the output, the stock fuel pump becomes less adequate. High-performance mechanical fuel pumps are a simple solution to feeding the engine, but an electric fuel pump is the option most chosen.

One tricky point of installing an electric fuel pump is the type of pump you are using. Older diaphragm-style fuel pumps draw fuel through the lines and pump it out the other side. These pumps can be mounted just about anywhere, in many positions, though the best placement is as close to the fuel tank as possible. Many of the newer fuel pumps use a gerotor- or vane-style pump. These pumps rely solely on gravity to feed the input line to the pump, and then the pump pressurizes the fuel line on the output side. There are efficient pumps, but they require the pump to be positioned lower than the fuel tank pickup tube, which can be an issue for some vehicles. Keep this in mind when you are choosing your parts.

Using the stock or rebuilt steel fuel tank is always an acceptable proposition, but in the world of street machines, looks sometimes run a close second to function. A fuel cell may seem a little over the top for a street car, but nothing could be further from the truth. With a lowered stance and low-hanging fuel lines, the stock tank may be in a precarious position. By installing a 15-gallon fuel cell in the trunk or through the trunk, safety prevails, and fuel cells just look cool anyway. When looking at fuel cells, it is important to choose a cell with foam inside. The foam prevents the fuel from sloshing around, and in the event of an accident, the fuel would slowly drip out, rather than spray out.

Another key aspect of a Gen III and IV engine swap is the oil pan. This image depicts the changes made to a cast-aluminum LS1 Camaro/Firebird oil pan to fit into a GM A-body car. *Street and Performance*

Where OE fuel-injection systems leave off, the aftermarket begins. With so many options available, where do you start? One of the better-known manufacturers of comprehensive aftermarket fuel-injection solutions is Fuel Air Spark Technologies, otherwise known as FAST. This company has been building top-shelf fuel-injection solutions for years.

Well-known in racing circles, FAST EFI systems have been proven to work as specified. Many times installing race-oriented products on street cars turns out to be a bad idea; they are great for short blasts down the drag strip, but are not up to the task of daily driving. The FAST XFI is not one of those systems. The XFI EFI system is powerful enough to handle the biggest engines durable enough for regular street driving.

The XFI system offers extreme flexibility for even the most radical engine, something no factory ECM can handle. Where the factory EFI systems can benefit from an XFI ECM, the total system package is designed to work together and power the entire system. The XFI system is not only simple to install, but easy to tune with full access and no preset parameters. The XFI system can support up to 4,600 horsepower, and of course any street machine falls within that range.

The XFI system is compatible with literally any engine, regardless of make. As long as there is a fuel-injection intake available, the XFI system can control it. Each XFI system can be purchased in modules; the ECM, the fuel system, the intake and injectors, the throttle body, and so on. As a complete kit, the XFI system is a plug-and-play unit.

XFI has features like Qwik Tune (up to four programmable tunes available on the fly), nitrous control, and even an optional touchscreen datalogger that can also be used as a digital dashboard.

I put the XFI system to the test on a 1966 Mustang fastback street machine with a freshly built 1999 Ford 302 and 4R70W transmission. The original EFI system turned out to be retrofit unfriendly, so the XFI system was chosen from the sea of aftermarket kits. The results were incredible. Not only did the motor fire right up and run great, but the XFI interfaced with the TCI automatic transmission controller with a single CAN-BUS connection. CAN-BUS is the Controller-Area Network; this is the platform used for microcontrollers in a vehicle to talk to each other and control devices without a master host computer.

The FAST XFI system is available in separate components or as a complete kit. This is a complete kit for a Ford 302. Everything is included: wiring, intake, throttle body, even the fuel pump.

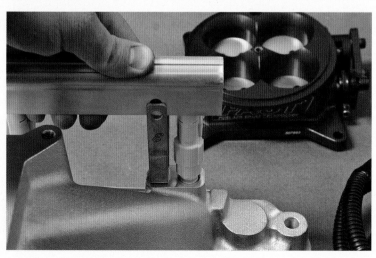

The included intake is an Edelbrock unit that works with the supplied fuel injectors and fuel rails. The rubber O-rings were lubed with a little assembly lube prior to installation. This keeps them from tearing or sticking.

With the intake assembly installed, the engine is ready for plumbing and wiring. Soon the engine bay will be full of hoses and wire harnesses.

The XFI injection uses a return-style fuel system. The hose to the right is the return line, and the one on the left is the feed line. The pressure regulator was mounted to the driver's side inner fender. It is adjustable, but was preset for 40 psi, the suggested level for this system.

We went for the optional FAST Dual-Sync distributor. This unit allows us to choose either a 0-degree or 50-degree timing trigger. Using the 50-degree trigger allows the ECM to control each cylinder individually, but you must have 50-degree timing mark on the balancer.

Once installed in the correct position at TDC according to the instructions, the adjustment is simple. With the key in the run position and the number 1 cylinder at TDC, the distributor is rotated until the cam sensor (to the left) lights up. Then we continued rotating until the crank trigger lights. It is as simple as that.

The throttle body is universal. As such, the throttle linkage arm is long. The arm won't clear a short base air-cleaner as shipped. Trimming is required.

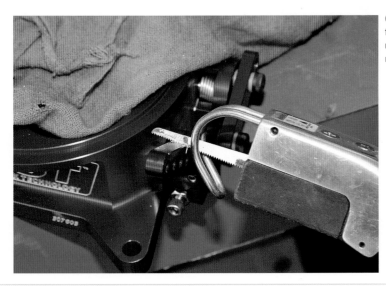

Once we had the arm marked, an air saw was used to cut the excess off. We dressed it with a die-grinder to clean it up. The alloy used in the throttle body is hard; it took five minutes to cut the little arm with a new blade.

The throttle body comes with a new idle air control (IAC) valve. It can only be installed in one clocked position and is held in with two bolts.

The TPS (throttle position sensor) also installs only in one position. The wiring harness simply plugs into place. The throttle body barely clears the intake, so FAST supplies a 1-inch spacer. While this makes everything fit, it also pushes up the throttle body. In order to get the hood to close, a fiberglass Shelby-style hood was ordered for the 1966 Mustang that was receiving this engine.

The XFI system needs an air-temp sensor. This can be mounted in either the intake or the air cleaner. We chose to drill out the air cleaner with a ⅜-inch drill bit.

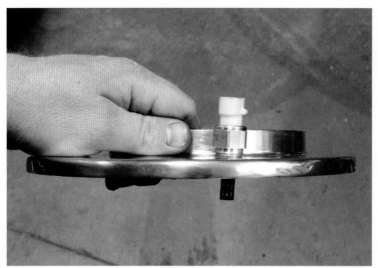

This photo shows the air temp sensor mounted in the air cleaner base once we tapped it. Care must be taken when choosing the location to mount the air temp sensor, as the wiring has to plug in. Mounting it to the rear is a good idea.

FAST sent out a high-pressure Walbro fuel pump as part of the fuel system add-on kit. We had to purchase a variety of AN fittings to make it all integrate with the rest of the fuel system.

The wiring may seem overwhelming, but it isn't. Most of the connections are plug and play; only a few hardwired connections have to be made. Everything is labeled, but the trick is the diagrams, which are included in the software but are not printed. You need to print these beforehand or keep the laptop within arm's reach.

The MAP sensor and MSD Blaster coil were mounted to the firewall to keep things neat and tidy. The MAP sensor requires a short length of vacuum line attached to it. The idea is to keep it as short as possible but with some room to allow for engine flex.

The wiring harnesses plug into the ECM. Some unused wires need to be clipped and grounded to each other, as they may act as an antenna. Doing this at the ECM is a simple process.

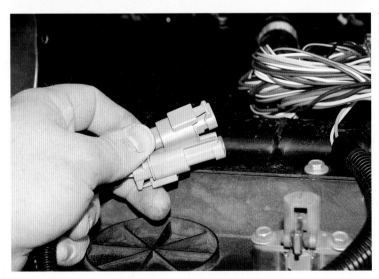

The XFI system uses CAN-BUS protocol for transferring information. This is important for using optional features like the data-logging unit or a transmission controller.

The 302 is backed by a Ford 4R70W overdrive, which requires a transmission computer. A TCI TCU unit was used to hook it all up. Using the CAN-link to connect the XFI ECM and the TCU together allows the two units to send information such as TPS, MAP, and speedometer readings with a single connection.

A lot of the wiring that is included is not needed for many applications. These wires simply need to be cut short and bundled up under the dash.

The XFI ECM was mounted in the glove box. A Masonite panel was cut and covered in carpet for a clean look. The MSD 6AL ignition box and the TCI TCU were mounted in the glove box as well.

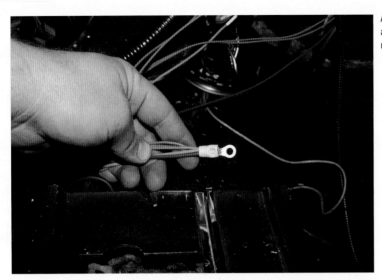

All of the switched power leads were grouped together and run to the ignition switch. The constant-power leads must be wired directly to the battery.

Programming the XFI is fairly simple, but a phone call to the technical support guys at FAST makes it much simpler. They can even remote-tune the system if you have a good Internet connection.

The finished engine fired right up and runs great. With some minor tuning, the engine purrs like a kitten, save for the nice lope of the cam, of course.

Chapter 4
The Transmission

While they may seem a little mundane compared to other components of the typical street machine, the transmission and drivetrain are critical for putting power to the ground. With so many options for street machines, the decisions on what to use can be tough. From an old-school four-speed to a modern electronically controlled five-speed auto, the possibilities are endless.

AUTOMATICS

A healthy stock transmission works great for a restomod street machine. Mild engine modifications typically do not increase power levels enough to require serious transmission mods. That said, most stock transmissions were designed to gently ease into each gear, making for a nice smooth shift. While this is great for a cruiser, put the pedal down and that long, smooth shift becomes a long, slow trip down the drag strip.

There are a lot of options when it comes to upgrading automatic transmissions. One of the best things about automatic transmissions is that they are relatively cheap and easy to rebuild, so you can make them handle the power level you need.

While building the transmission yourself is not as simple as building an engine, it can be done. Transmission rebuilding requires specialized tools and techniques that you probably do not have already. Most builders choose to have a professional performance transmission shop build their transmission. These shops have the necessary know-how and tools, and they also understand the tricks to getting the most out of a transmission. That is not to say that the average tranny shop can't produce a quality high-performance transmission, but you will always get better results when your shop builds high-performance transmissions regularly.

When it comes to selecting a transmission shop, ask around. Ask local racers and those who frequent the cruise spots who they think is the best at building high-performance transmissions in your area. You may find that there simply is not a really good tranny builder in your town. If you are trying to put 500-plus horsepower to the ground with an automatic transmission, you will need a stout transmission, so the choice of builder is crucial. There are several well-known high-performance transmission builders that you can send your tranny to for a quality build. Art Carr Performance

The legendary Powerglide two-speed transmission has been used in drag cars for decades. This Powerglide from TCI is built to handle a lot more than 600 horsepower.

Products and Bowler Transmissions are the top-shelf when it comes to custom transmission building, particularly with overdrive automatics.

When it comes to automatic transmissions, there are three main categories: two-speed, three-speed, and overdrive.

TWO-SPEED

In the early days, there were several two-speed transmissions. GM, Ford, and Chrysler all had two-speed autos.

Ford's Ford-O-Matic is considered by most to be a two-speed, but in reality there are two Ford-O-Matics, the 1950–1958 version and the 1959–1963 version. The older version is actually a three-speed single-range transmission. It always started in second gear, unless Low was manually selected. The later version was a true two-speed automatic used only in economy cars.

Chrysler's Powerflite transmission, built from 1954 through 1961, was the precursor to the Torqueflite three-speed. One of the most unique aspects of the Powerflite was that it could be push-started. Basically the Powerflite was a planetary gearbox with a torque converter. The Ford and Chrysler two-speeds are usable for cruisers, but high-performance use is limited.

The GM two-speeds are a different story. GM made two two-speed transmissions: the Powerglide and the ST300. The ST300, also known as the Jetaway transmission in Oldsmobiles, was built from 1964 to 1969 and used in Buick, Olds, and Pontiac mid- and full-size cars. The ST300 was

a good transmission, but performance parts and even stock rebuild parts are tough to find.

The most popular two-speed transmission by far is the Powerglide. Still in use today for drag cars, the Powerglide was the first economical two-speed auto available, built from 1950 through 1973. This transmission was installed behind everything from economy six-cylinders to small-block V-8s, and even the 409 big-block. The early cast-iron Powerglides did not automatically shift; you either started off in high or you had to shift manually, which was hard on the transmission. Beginning in 1953, the Powerglide was fully automatic. In 1962, the case was switched to aluminum (cast-iron cases were completely gone by 1963) to save weight. Most V-8 Powerglides use a 1.76:1 first gear, while the six-cylinders got a 1.82:1 first gear. High gear is 1:1. These transmissions are quite strong, and when built with aftermarket parts, a Powerglide will easily handle 1,000-plus horsepower with no issues. Another big benefit of the Powerglide is its lack of parasitic drag, meaning it costs less power to run than just about every other automatic transmission. For regular street use, a two-speed transmission is not very efficient. You only have two gears, so you must wrap up the engine and keep the rpm higher for longer periods of time, which costs in terms of gas consumption.

THREE-SPEED

The ever-popular three-speed automatic has been around since automatics came to be. There are popular three-speed autos from each of the big Detroit manufacturers.

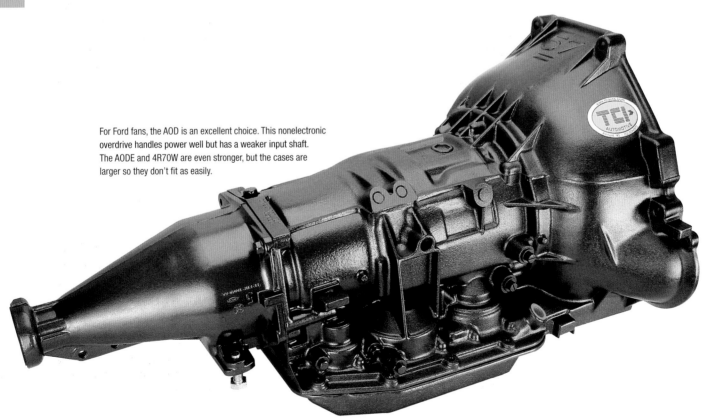

For Ford fans, the AOD is an excellent choice. This nonelectronic overdrive handles power well but has a weaker input shaft. The AODE and 4R70W are even stronger, but the cases are larger so they don't fit as easily.

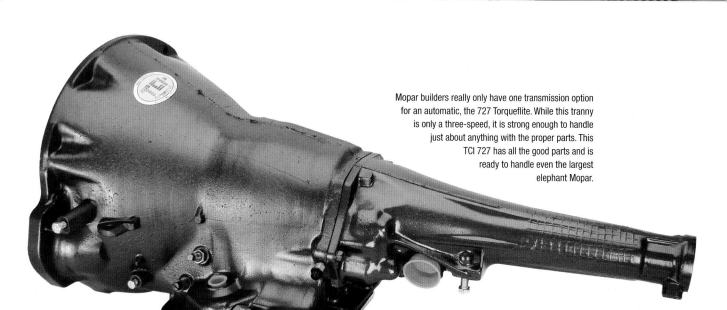

Mopar builders really only have one transmission option for an automatic, the 727 Torqueflite. While this tranny is only a three-speed, it is strong enough to handle just about anything with the proper parts. This TCI 727 has all the good parts and is ready to handle even the largest elephant Mopar.

Ford C4, C6

For Ford, the C4 and C6 transmissions are quite popular. Either transmission can be built to handle higher power levels. For stock setups, the C4 is good to around 400 horsepower. Beefed up, it will handle about 600 horsepower. The C6 transmission was designed for higher torque and horsepower, so it will handle up to about 500 stock but can be built to handle well over 1,000 horsepower.

Chrysler, Torqueflite 727

The main performance transmission for the Mopar group is the 727. For performance Mopar street machines, there is no other automatic transmission to use. Many Mopar builders claim the 727 to be the world's strongest automatic transmission. Installed behind all of the biggest Mopar engines, the 727 can handle just about anything, as long as it is built right.

GM TH350, TH400

Beginning in 1964, GM built the Turbo-Hydramatic 400, or TH400, and introduced the lighter TH350 in 1969. The TH350 was mainly used for small-block V-8s and six-cylinder applications. The TH350 in stock trim is easily capable of handling 400 to 500 horsepower, while the bigger and stouter TH400 can handle a little more. With better internals, either transmission can handle high amounts of horsepower. A built TH350 is easily good to 700, while the TH400 is capable of handling in excess of 1,000 horsepower. The biggest difference between the TH350 and TH400 is the amount of power consumption. The TH350 eats between 18 to 22 percent of the flywheel horsepower; the TH400 consumes 25 to 30 percent. When drag racing, this really counts. An interesting note about the TH400: this transmission has been used as the stock transmission in everything from the highest-powered GM muscle cars to V-12 Ferraris.

Overdrives

While a powerful street machine may be used at the drag strip occasionally, most street machines see much more cruising duty. Where three-speed automatics have a 1:1 third gear, the automatic overdrives have higher ratios beyond 1:1. Adding a fourth gear drops the rpm at cruising speed, yielding higher overall speeds and better gas mileage. This also allows the builder to run lower (higher numerically) rear gears. Most overdrive transmissions have a lockup torque converter, which allows the transmission to effectively eliminate torque converter slippage and be in direct drive with the engine, further increasing efficiency.

While the 700R4 used to be the choice for a non-electronically controlled overdrive automatic, the real solution is the 200-4R. This transmission is much stronger and can handle more power than the weaker 700R4.

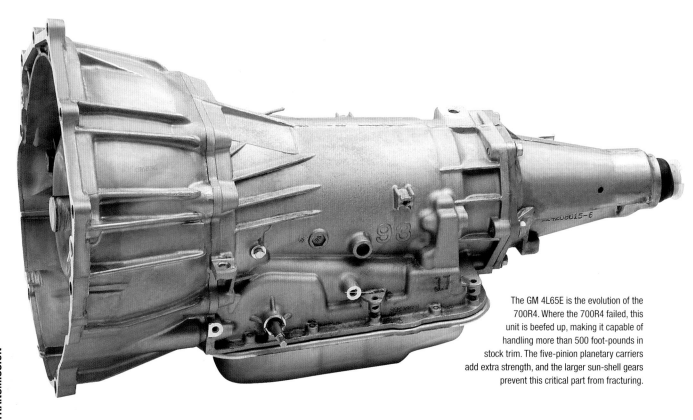

The GM 4L65E is the evolution of the 700R4. Where the 700R4 failed, this unit is beefed up, making it capable of handling more than 500 foot-pounds in stock trim. The five-pinion planetary carriers add extra strength, and the larger sun-shell gears prevent this critical part from fracturing.

The newest high-performance GM cars come with the MYR six-speed automatic. With dual overdrives, these transmissions offer high top speeds and better fuel economy. This is the reason a 400-plus horsepower Corvette gets decent fuel economy.

Ford AOD, AODE, 4R70W

The AOD overdrive transmission was introduced in 1980 as Ford's first overdrive automatic. Based on the FMX platform, the AOD uses a compound six-pinion planetary gear unit instead of the more common two or three planetary carriers used in most other transmissions. Fewer parts means less parasitic loss and less opportunity for failure. The AOD is a strong transmission, as are its descendents, the AODE and 4R70W. The AOD's weak point is the lockup function. The input shaft on the AOD is weak, and under a heavy load, it can snap. This has been eliminated in the AODE and 4R70W, which use an electric clutch in the torque converter to initiate lockup. The later design uses a wider gear set, which is better for pulling power.

Chrysler A500 and A518

For Mopars, there just are not a lot of options. The bulletproof 727 three-speed is the only real performance Chrysler automatic. Beginning in 1988, Mopar began offering the A500 and A518 overdrives. These transmissions do not bolt directly to the B/RB big-block engines; you must use an adapter, which is available from Mopar Performance. The A500 is based on the 904, while the A518 is a derivative of the 727. For serious performance use, the A518 is the way to go. When installing one of these transmissions in a vintage Mopar, serious transmission tunnel modifications are required. In street machines, that may not be an issue, but an aftermarket overdrive kit that mounts to the rear of the 727 may be a better route.

GM 2004R, 700R4, 4L60E

Because General Motors has been the king of high-performance for so long, the company offers more in the way of quality overdrive transmissions as well. Beginning with the 700R4 and 2004R, GM put high-performance overdrives to work. Go back just 10 years, and you will see that the 700R4 was the king of GM overdrives. This transmission was installed in just about every truck and SUV beginning in 1982. The 2004R often has been overlooked, as it was the stock overdrive for six-cylinder and V-8-powered cars. Trucks are heavier; therefore, the 700R4 is better by default, right? Wrong. Ask any drag racer who made the change to a 700R4 how many times he has rebuilt it after blowing up the planetary carriers, warping the drums, and busting sun shell gears.

The 2004R is actually an easier swap into most muscle cars because of its smaller case. It is capable of handling 10-second turbo Buicks in stock trim (not even a rebuild is needed). With just a few tricks, the 2004R can handle massive amounts of power, and thanks to its dual bolt-pattern case, will fit popular Buick, Olds, Pontiac, and Chevy engines.

Moving into the future, GM replaced the 700R4 with the 4L60 and quickly moved to the 4L60E. The 4L60E was introduced in 1993 and 1994 (trucks and SUVs were first, then full-size cars in 1994) and is capable of handling a lot of power. In stock form, the 4L60E can take 500 horsepower without much problem, but add some sticky tires and the planetary gears and sun shell gears become a potential failure point. Aftermarket remedies are easily available. The latest from GM are the six-speed overdrives, which offer extreme power handling at high speed, such as in the LS9-powered ZR1 Corvette, which uses the 6L90.

Because automatic transmissions are actually hydraulic pumps with a gear drive running through them, they generate a lot of heat. Add the torque converter, which is a large, spinning, liquid clutch with a lot of slippage, and you have even more heat. Heat kills a transmission, so proper cooling is necessary.

Transmission coolers come in two main types: stock coolers, which are usually part of the radiator, and aftermarket coolers, which are separately mounted units. If you live in a cold climate and drive the vehicle when the

The torque converter is the only link between the engine and the transmission. From left are the cover, turbine, thrust bearing, stator, thrust bearing, and impeller pump. The converter is a fluid link. There is no solid connection, so there is always an amount of slippage, except in the case of a lock-up converter, which physically locks when activated to create a solid link.

weather is cool, then a radiator-based transmission cooler is a good bet. While heat kills a transmission, they don't like cold either. A radiator-based cooler will maintain a steady transmission fluid temperature, because the radiator also handles the engine coolant. A separate tranny cooler does not have this benefit, and while it may run slightly cooler in the summer months, it will take longer to get to operating temperature in the cooler months. If the transmission is a high-performance unit with a high stall converter, then you will need a better source of cooling, which a separate cooler will handle.

TORQUE CONVERTERS

The torque converter is a fluid coupler. It transmits the engine's output to the transmission input shaft. Unlike a manual transmission, which is disengaged by opening the gap between the flywheel, pressure plate, and clutch, the automatic transmission stays in constant contact with the engine's flex plate. A torque converter also multiplies torque on initial acceleration, to the level of 2:1 or 3:1. This helps get the car moving.

Major components of the converter are the cover, turbine, stator, and impeller pump.

Cover

The cover, or front of the converter, is the outside half of the housing on the engine side of the center weld line. The cover serves to attach the converter to the flywheel (engine) and contain the fluid. While the cover is not actively involved in the converter's performance characteristics, it is important that the cover remain rigid under stress (torsional and thrust stress and the tremendous hydraulic pressure generated by the torque converter internally). Furnace brazing greatly improves the fins' strength. The furnace brazing causes the housing and fins to move and act integrally as one unit. This greatly reduces the amount of flex, which causes fins to bend and break. In addition, the more rigid the fins stay while under pressure, the more consistent the behavior of the torque converter.

In many older cars, transmission swaps require some surgery. Fitting the AODE in this 1951 Ford required the transmission tunnel to be cut away and reshaped. Only an inch of clearance needed to be added.

Turbine

The turbine rides within the cover and is attached to the splines of the input shaft of the transmission. When the turbine moves, the car moves.

Stator

The stator is the "brain" of the torque converter, although the stator is by no means the sole determiner of converter function and characteristics. The stator, which changes fluid flow between the turbine and pump, is what makes a torque converter a torque converter (multiplier) and not strictly a fluid coupler.

With the stator removed, the converter will retain none of its torque multiplying effect. In order for the stator to function properly, the sprag must work as designed: It must hold the stator locked in place while the converter is still in stall mode, with slow relative turbine speed to the impeller pump speed. It must allow the stator to spin with the rest of the converter after the turbine speed approaches the pump speed. This allows for more efficient and less restrictive fluid flow.

The sprag is a one-way mechanical clutch mounted on races that fits inside the stator. The inner race splines onto the stator support of the transmission. The torque multiplier effect means that a vehicle equipped with an automatic transmission and torque converter will output more torque to the drive wheels than the engine is actually producing. This occurs while the converter is in its "stall mode" (when the turbine is spinning considerably slower than the pump) and during vehicle acceleration. Torque multiplication rapidly decreases until it reaches a ratio of 1:1 (no torque increase over crankshaft torque). A typical torque converter will have a torque multiplication ratio in the area of 2.5:1. The main point to remember is that all properly functioning torque converters do indeed multiply torque during initial acceleration. The more drastic the change in fluid path caused by the stator from its "natural" return path, the higher the torque multiplication ratio a given converter will have. Torque multiplication does not occur with a manual transmission clutch and pressure plate. This necessitates the need for heavy flywheels, high numerical gear ratios, and high launch rpm.

Impeller Pump

The impeller pump is the outside half of the converter on the transmission side of the weld line. Inside the impeller pump is a series of longitudinal fins, which drive the fluid around its outside diameter into the turbine. This component is welded to the cover, which is bolted to the flywheel. The size of the torque converter (and pump) and the number and shape of the fins all affect the characteristics of the converter. If long torque converter life is an objective, it is extremely important to reinforce the fins of the impeller pump against fatigue so that the housing does not distort under stress.

The stall speed is the rpm at which a given torque converter has to spin in order for it to overcome a given amount of load and begin moving the turbine. This figure is notated in rpm, that is, 2,500-rpm stall. This figure is derived from two factors: torque output, which varies through the torque curve and is affected by atmosphere, fuel, and engine condition and the vehicle's resistance to acceleration, otherwise known as the load. The entire drivetrain, suspension, vehicle weight, tire and gear size, and even the stiffness of the chassis affect this figure.

Torque converters do not come with a preset stall speed. They are designed to react to the vehicle in a predictable manner across a variable range. You will not get a 2,500-rpm stall every time, but the converter will operate as it is supposed to according to the input and load it is subjected to. For example, at full throttle, the converter will react with more stall, while at lower rpm, it will actually be less.

Choosing a converter with too low a stall can be a problem. When looking at the engine torque curve, it is important to note the relevant range. If you have a converter with a relevant range of 2,000 to 2,600 rpm and the engine in question does not make much torque below 3,000 rpm, then the converter will actually come in below the relevant range (2,000 rpm or less) because of the poor torque range of the engine. Symptoms of not enough stall include: engine stalling when in gear at a stop, low stall speed, hesitation when going to full throttle, and a "bog" when leaving from stop at wide-open throttle.

A torque converter with a too-high stall range will not benefit the vehicle either. You will see this situation most often when the car does not have sufficient gear ratio for the converter stall range or the engine is not capable of the appropriate rpm range (too small a duration camshaft, inadequate valve springs, too low compression, and so on). Symptoms include high rpm required to pull away from stop; soft, mushy accelerator feel when driving at part throttle; transmission and possibly engine overheating; and a pronounced engine rev when you punch the throttle from a cruising speed.

The torque converter is not a singular part; it is part of the entire system. You can get a little help in choosing the right converter for your street machine from the manufacturer.

VALVE BODY

There are many types of valve bodies for the various automatic transmissions. The valve body is the brain of the transmission. This is where the shifts are actually made. This all depends on pressure. For most street machines, the stock valve body is sufficient, as long as it is in good working order. Most shift kits and rebuild kits come with modified springs and valves for changing shift timing and firmness. That said, for some applications, an aftermarket valve body is needed. For overdrive transmissions in engine/tranny swaps, a high-pressure valve body eliminates the need for the TV cable, as the valve body eliminates that circuit. You still need the cable, but only for a kick-down cable. A manual valve body

Manual transmissions use a flywheel, clutch, and pressure plate to couple the engine to the transmission. Stock clutches and pressure plates can handle moderate power increases, but power-adders like nitrous and superchargers often need more clutch. A bigger clutch with better materials, like this Centerforce unit, is a good idea for any street machine.

eliminates all the automatic functions completely. You have to shift the car yourself, but you don't have to use a clutch. These work great for drag-race-only cars but can be a little miserable on the street.

STICK SHIFT

Manual transmissions put the power directly to the drivetrain. While they do not benefit from the torque-multiplication of a converter, they also do not soak up as much horsepower. Because the clutch and flywheel are mechanically linked, there is no slippage, which means better gas mileage.

There are also a few cons for the old gearbox too. Even as recently as 10 to 15 years ago, a typical automatic transmission could not keep up with a moderately experienced stick-shift racer. Even a tuned automatic with all the bells and whistles had too much lag and was not consistent enough for many racers, so they chose to shift it themselves.

Now things are much different. A well-trained driver would have a hard time matching the consistency of an electronically controlled automatic transmission. With the advancements in the components themselves, the transmissions offer much more reliable racing performance and a comfortable trip home, without a heavy pedal to push around. Plus, rebuilding a manual transmission is not easy. The parts are harder to find and many transmission shops shy away from rebuilding manuals. When it comes to street machines with lots of horsepower, however, nothing is cooler than rowing gears.

There are so many different versions of manual transmissions, it would be difficult to cover them all. Even Detroit swapped around manual transmissions, using one brand for this car and another for that car, sometimes building their own, sometimes purchasing already-designed units with specific details from companies such as Borg-Warner and Tremec. The most popular manual transmissions are listed below.

Muncie M21/22

The most popular manual transmission for GM vehicles since the 1960s, the Muncie transmissions were built by GM from 1963 through 1974. The Muncie was most often used behind performance engines. The Muncie is a better transmission than the Saginaw four-speed transmissions and is identified by the seven-bolt side cover and the reverse gear selector on the extension housing. The M22 and M21 are close-ratio transmissions, with the following gear ratios: 1st, 2.2:1; 2nd, 1.64:1; 3rd, 1.28:1; and 4th, 1:1. The wide-ratio version, the M20, is used less as a performance car because the engine speed drops further than the close-ratio versions as determined by the rear differential gearing. Cars with 3.73:1 rear gears or lower (numerically higher) came with the close-ratio

transmission; rear gearing of 3.53:1 or higher (numerically lower) came with the wide-ratio. The M20 has the following ratios: 1st, 2.52:1 or 2.56:1; 2nd, 1.88:1; 3rd, 1.46:1; and 4th, 1:1. The M22 is the extra-heavy-duty version. The M22 is also referred to as the rock-crusher. It gets this name from the straight-cut gears, which produce a whine.

T10/Super T10

Built by Borg-Warner from 1957 through 1974, when it was replaced with the Super T10. These transmissions were used in GM, Ford, and AMC vehicles. The Super T10 is the more desirable unit, as it is stronger. There are several versions for each manufacturer; GM units use a 26-spline input shaft, and most units use a 32-spline TH400 (as in automatic) tail shaft and a 1-inch countershaft diameter.

Available versions of the T10 include the following:

- Ford AS1-T10 short output shaft
- Ford AS2-T10 long output shaft
- GM AS3-T10 Corvette F and A-body cars
- AMC AS40T10 long input shaft
- Aftermarket AS9-T10 "Power Brute" with iron case, nickel gears

The classic close-ratio Muncie M22 and its brothers, the M21 and wide-ratio M20, are the most highly sought-after GM manual transmissions. The M22 gets its name "rock-crusher" not from the tight ratio but from its sound. The gears are cut so they have a loud whine. Identifying the Muncie is simple. The side cover has seven bolts and only the forward gear levers are mounted in the cover. The reverse lever is on the extension housing.

This tranny was sold by Borg-Warner to speed shops as the Power Brute. It can be identified with a small dimple in the side of each gear. They have a low first gear and were primarily for drag racing. Most production versions from 1974 through 1979 had an aluminum case. The Doug Nash 4+3 overdrive was based on the Super T10 for the 1984–1988 Corvette. Borg-Warner sold the Super T10 to Rockland Standard Gear in the mid-1980s, and then it was purchased by Richmond Gear, where it is still produced.

Toploader

The Ford Toploader was introduced in 1964. This side-shaft shifted transmission came in three- and four-speed versions and was Ford's replacement for the Borg-Warner T10. This transmission was used in Ford cars until 1973 but continued production and use in trucks and Jeeps until 1986. In 1977, the Toploader began production under Tremec in Mexico.

T5

The T5 is the most popular Ford manual transmission. This five-speed overdrive manual was used in many cars, everything from Ford cars like the Mustang and Thunderbird to AMCs, Camaros, and Jeeps. There are several versions, each with its own rating. The 1983–1989 T5 is rated for 265 foot-pounds, while the 1990–1993 units can handle 300 foot-pounds. The newest T5, the Ford Super Duty, can handle 330 foot-pounds. The 1994–1995 T5 units have a longer input shaft and require a matching bell housing.

The T5 transmissions use a tail shaft–mounted shifter with no external levers. This slightly complicates swaps but not too much. Another name for the T5 is "World Class T5." All 1983 and later T5s are "World Class" units. The T5 was manufactured by Borg-Warner for Ford. Borg-Warner later became Tremec. The T5 was also used in GM cars. While the ratings only go as high as 330 foot-pounds (for stock units; aftermarket T5 transmissions are rated up to 500 foot-pounds), these factory stock transmissions will live behind sub-500-horsepower motors.

T56

The T56 is the six-speed version of the T5. This transmission was used in GM F-body cars starting in 1993 and in a few Cobra Mustangs here and there, the Dodge Viper, Corvettes, Aston Martin's DB7 and Vanquish, and a few Australian models. Rated at 440 foot-pounds, the T56 is more than capable of handling just about anything a street machine has to offer. There are more than a few variants and several aftermarket versions. The highest-rated T56 is the Tremec

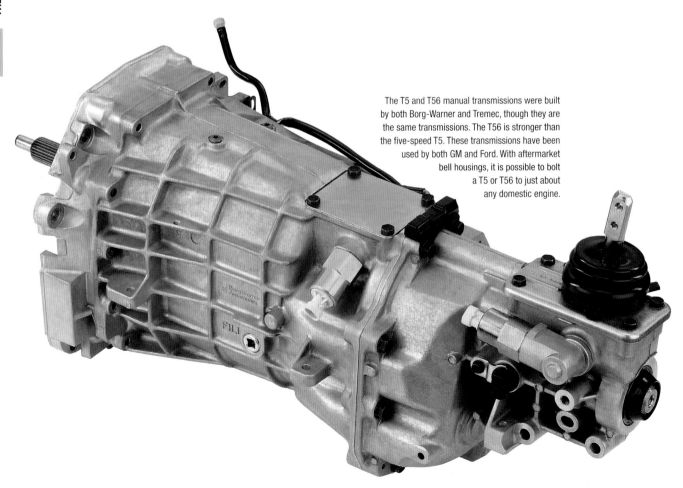

The T5 and T56 manual transmissions were built by both Borg-Warner and Tremec, though they are the same transmissions. The T56 is stronger than the five-speed T5. These transmissions have been used by both GM and Ford. With aftermarket bell housings, it is possible to bolt a T5 or T56 to just about any domestic engine.

TUET-1806, which is rated at 550 foot-pounds. Borg-Warner was bought out by Tremec in 1997. Pre-1998 T56s were Borg-Warner; 1998 and later are Tremec branded. The T56 uses a hydraulic clutch, with the sole exception of the Cobra.

ZF 6

The ZF 6 is a six-speed manual transmission from ZF, a driveline supplier to the OEMs. GM used the ZF S6-40 in the 1989 to 1996 Corvette. Ford uses a ZF 6 in its diesel trucks.

TKO

While the T56 and T5 units were mainly OEM units with some aftermarket versions, the TKO is aftermarket only. This transmission is as suitable for serious racing as it is for a high-powered street cruiser. This tranny uses roller bearing shafts for better performance and less noise. Sixth gear options include .64, .68, and .82 ratios. The .64 is a serious overdrive ratio—good for maintaining speed, but gaining speed with a .64 gear is going to be tough. The .82 ratio is great for racing.

With modular bell housings from Lakewood, Mcleod, and Trans-Dapt, it is possible to swap just about any manual transmission to any engine, as long as you can fit it under the car.

For the older transmissions (T10, ST10, M22, and so on), the old-school manual clutch linkage is suitable. For older cars, the mounting hardware should already be there. If you swap a T56 or TKO, then you have to use a hydraulic clutch. A hydraulic clutch is easier on your leg as it does not take as much pressure to activate, and it takes up less room. A hydraulic setup does not have a series of rods and springs getting in the way. A hydraulic linkage uses a small master cylinder, just like the braking system, and then pumps hydraulic fluid to a specialized throw-out bearing to disengage the clutch.

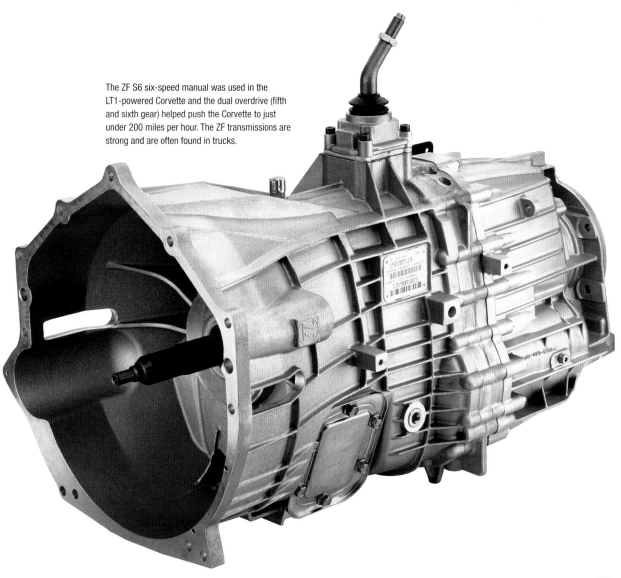

The ZF S6 six-speed manual was used in the LT1-powered Corvette and the dual overdrive (fifth and sixth gear) helped push the Corvette to just under 200 miles per hour. The ZF transmissions are strong and are often found in trucks.

Modern manual transmissions use internal shifters like this. Swapping these transmissions into older cars requires cutting a hole for the shifter, and because the modern cases are larger, the transmission tunnel often needs to be reshaped. This B&M aftermarket Ripper shifter offers a shorter throw than the stock unit. Some aftermarket shifters provide an adjustable shifter position as well.

Manual transmissions require a clutch pedal. These pedals were pulled from a Mustang Cobra, along with the T56 tranny, and were swapped into a 4.6-powered Mustang GT.

Chapter 5
The Drivetrain

DRIVESHAFT

When you hit the throttle, the engine spins the flywheel. The flywheel transfers this energy to the transmission. That energy is transferred to the differential, which turns the tires and puts the power to ground.

The driveshaft is just a simple link between the tranny and the rear end, or at least that is the common view. The fact is while you can't gain horsepower through the driveshaft, you can certainly lose it.

The most important aspect of your driveshaft is who builds it. Building the right driveshaft for the application is critical; any high-performance vehicle should have a driveshaft professionally built by a shop that specializes in high-performance drivelines. If you are going to have a local driveshaft shop build your driveshaft, you need get a few things absolutely straight. Make sure that whoever you have build your driveshaft stands behind it 100 percent. Tell the shop it is for a high-performance application. This means it needs to be held to a higher standard than a stock driveshaft. Ordering a driveshaft over the Internet from a reputable high-performance builder is not only easy but guaranteed.

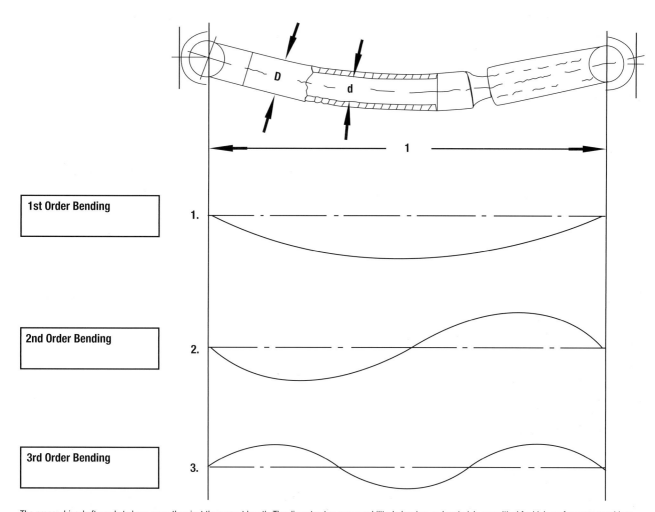

1st Order Bending

2nd Order Bending

3rd Order Bending

The proper driveshaft needs to have more than just the correct length. The diameter, top rpm capability, balancing, and materials are critical for high-performance machines. As the shaft reaches critical speed, it starts to bend, eventually "jump roping" and breaking or twisting. A car can be vaulted into the air by a busted driveshaft, which is quite dangerous.

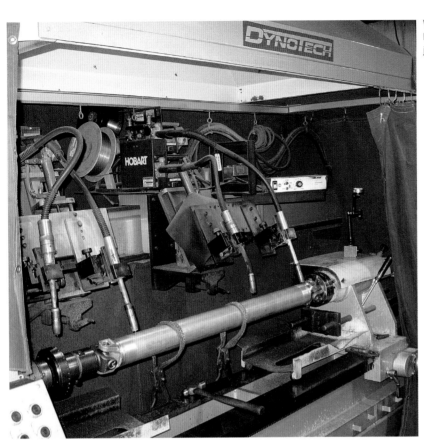

While most local driveshaft shops weld driveshafts by hand, DynoTech uses CNC welders to perform a perfect job every time.

Increasing the power output of any engine has a direct effect on the driveshaft. As the power output goes up, the detrimental effects increase as well. Typically, the factory driveshaft is balanced between 3,000 and 3,500 rpm. As you add power to the engine, the car moves faster, which means the driveshaft spins faster, pushing it beyond the stock balance range. When the driveshaft's rpm goes beyond that range, the suboptimal balance becomes parasitic, eating up horsepower. According to Steve Raymond of DynoTech Engineering, a properly balanced driveshaft can save 3 to 7 horsepower on a chassis dyno. The stock balance on the stock driveshaft is not good enough for anything but a stock engine.

DynoTech Engineering uses Balance Engineering driveshaft balancers, which are considered to be the best in balancing accuracy. Balancing a performance driveshaft to at least 5,000 rpm ensures proper tuning and drastically reduces parasitic loss. Some applications are balanced as high as 7,500 rpm.

The length and diameter of the driveshaft are important to the overall performance of the unit. The most important measurement is the distance from the rear-end pinion yoke to the transmission seal. This must be measured with the car at ride height, and the pinion yoke must be installed. You have to measure the length with the yoke you will use with the driveshaft; changing to a billet pinion yoke can alter the length by as much as ¾ inch. The driveshaft shop builds the shaft with the required slip yoke and run out (the length of splined yoke section that sticks out of the transmission at resting ride height) for the slip yoke using this single measurement, so measure it twice to make sure you have the correct measurement.

Because this measurement must be done at resting ride height, you have to get under the car. The best method is to jack up both ends of the car and use jack stands under the rear end and front suspension to replicate the ride height of the car sitting on the ground. You should be able to do this by ensuring that the stands are all set at the same height. The slightest variation in the suspension can throw off the measurement, resulting in a driveshaft that does not fit. So don't just jack up the rear and leave the front wheels on the ground. For most applications, a run out of 1 inch is more than enough to provide the play needed for suspension travel. Any more than 1 inch is too much. Some transmission shops will try to convince you that 1.5 inches is the required amount, but *do not* buy into it. That much run out could leave you with less than 3 inches of spline section in the transmission, which allows the yoke to wobble on the output shaft, resulting in a heavy vibration at various rpm. The 1-inch rule is the best option according to DynoTech.

The proper length also helps determine the best diameter. Critical speed is the rpm at which the driveshaft becomes unstable and flexes in the middle, causing "jump roping." Critical speed is determined by the length vs. diameter rule; the longer and smaller (diameter) a driveshaft is, the slower its critical speed. Running above critical speed causes excessive vibration, and if the shaft is run at or above critical speed for too long, the unit will fail. Calculating the critical speed incorporates the length, diameter, wall thickness, and the material module of elasticity figures for the shaft into the complex formula shown here.

CRITICAL SPEED CALCULATION

$$\left(\frac{923.44}{\text{Driveshaft Length}} \right) \sqrt{\left(\frac{\text{Module of Elasticity}}{\left(\text{Mat'l Density} \right)\left(100 \right)} \right) \left(10^8 \right) \left(\left(\frac{\text{Tube Dia.}}{2} \right)^2 + \left(\frac{\text{Tube Dia.}}{2} - \text{Wall Thickness} \right)^2 \right)}$$

This is the equation for calculating critical speed for the driveshaft. Module of elasticity of the shaft material is a well-kept secret, though we have managed to get some general numbers.

Each driveshaft must be balanced. This is critical for a proper ride. An unbalanced driveshaft suffers heavy vibration at specific rpm.

The build material of the driveshaft makes a difference in these equations. Factory steel driveshafts are really only suitable for OEM power. Most OEM shafts are rated for no more than 350 foot-pounds of torque or 350 to 400 horsepower. High-performance driveshafts are available in several materials: drawn-over-mandrel (DOM) steel, chrome moly steel, aluminum, and carbon fiber. DOM seamless tubing is stronger than OEM steel and capable of supporting 1,300 foot-pounds and 1,300 horsepower. DOM steel has a higher rpm rating as well. This is a good budget choice for any car where a lighter shaft is not required.

Upgrading to chromoly steel, which is the strongest possible material, is a major step. Pro Stock drag cars run chromoly driveshafts. Heat treating chromoly steel tubing increases torsional strength by 22 percent and increases critical speed by 19 percent. Chromoly steel is heavy, though, which increases the load on the engine. Eliminating weight is important enough that using lighter materials, even if they are not as strong, is sometimes a better choice.

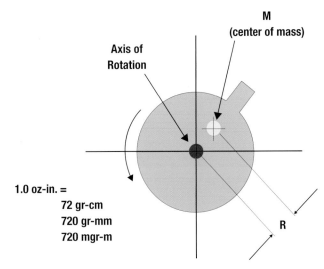

$$1.0 \text{ oz-in.} =$$
$$72 \text{ gr-cm}$$
$$720 \text{ gr-mm}$$
$$720 \text{ mgr-m}$$

Unbalance: U = Mass × Radius

Driveshaft balance is a function of the actual center and the rotational mass center. This diagram illustrates how this works.

DynoTech uses a hydraulic press to insert the ends into the tubes. Each end is designed to handle the stresses of the intended application.

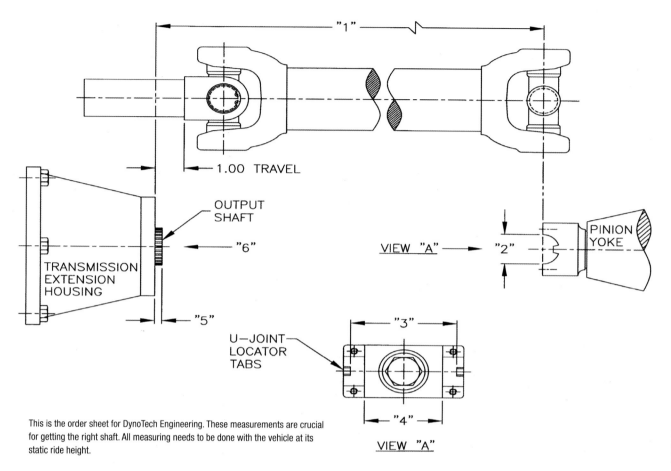

This is the order sheet for DynoTech Engineering. These measurements are crucial for getting the right shaft. All measuring needs to be done with the vehicle at its static ride height.

Aluminum is the most common performance driveshaft material. A lightweight aluminum shaft reduces rotational mass, which in turn decreases parasitic loss. Aluminum driveshafts are quite strong, handling up to 900 foot-pounds and 1,000 horsepower. This is not as much as DOM steel, but if you are making 500 horsepower, the weight savings alone is worth it.

For the ultimate in light weight, there is carbon fiber. Carbon fiber tubes are the most expensive material. Capable of supporting 1,200 foot-pounds and 900 to 1,500 horsepower, carbon fiber is a great choice. Carbon fiber also has an incredibly high torsional strength, which helps lower the shock to the rear end. Carbon fiber shafts do not flex as much either, with a high module of elasticity. A carbon fiber driveshaft combines the highest critical speed factors and its light weight to free up as much as 5 horsepower over a steel driveshaft. When winning margins are tight, 5 horsepower might make the difference.

If you are building a truck or a very long vehicle, a carrier bearing might be necessary. A carrier bearing uses two shorter shafts in place of one long shaft. With a carrier bearing, one half is a stationary unit that only rotates, it does not articulate up

and down with the suspension, like a single-piece driveshaft. It also does not slide in and out of the transmission, the front half of the shaft only spins; it is in a fixed position to the transmission and the carrier unit. The second half uses a slip yoke that slides into the carrier bearing unit and mounts to the differential. Most full-size trucks use carrier bearings to minimize vibrations and reduce the overall diameter of the driveshaft. Two-piece driveshafts are not as strong as one piece units, with twice as many connections and U-joints that can fail. Some smaller cars used two-piece driveshafts from the factory, like the X-frame Biscayne. Swapping these cars to a single-piece shaft is easy and yields excellent results.

The slip yoke and the pinion yoke are crucial points of failure in the driveline. These represent the connection points between the transmission, driveshaft, and differential. When a driveline component fails, all hell breaks loose. The driveshaft for the Buick GS shown here snapped in the middle of the splines. While this type of failure is rare, it does happen. A cast yoke is strong enough to handle around 800 horsepower, depending on the setup. A light car with street tires puts less stress on the driveline than a 2-ton muscle car with a blown big-block and slicks.

The GM 10-bolt has a bad reputation because the 8.2-inch version is not good for anything with a performance motor. The 8.5-inch 10-bolt is much stronger and can handle nearly as much power as a GM 12-bolt rear end.

Phasing the U-joint with the yokes is an area that smaller shops might not pay much attention to. This is where having a pro shop is important. Every rotation where the joint is beyond 0 degrees off axis (as in flat), there is a fourth-order vibration that is very noticeable while driving. This vibration is constant but may be worse at certain rpm. Proper phasing of the yokes to decrease the combined degree of rotation limits this vibration. Phasing is done by the driveshaft builder and is a good point to bring up when ordering the shaft.

No component in the driveline is insignificant. The U-joint is no exception. While load capacity is important, there are other factors to consider. Just about every domestic midsize car uses the 1310-series U-joint. For street machines, the 1350-series joint is ideal. As the series number increases, so does the size of the trunnion (the protruding shafts the caps cover) diameter, which yields more torsional strength. Torsional forces are exerted in rotation. These changes are not to be made lightly; you can't just pop in a bigger series of U-joint. All of the yokes—slip, bolt-on, and weld-in—must match; however, there are crossover U-joints that allow you to run half of one size, half the other. These are good for interim projects and junkyard swaps where the two components don't match up.

The two different body types for U-joints are solid-body and greaseable. The Spicer-style solid-body U-joint does not require periodic greasing and does not have grease Cerk fittings. These units are stronger than the typical greaseable U-joint, as the bodies are solid and not hollow.

REAR ENDS

Rear differentials are the business end of the entire drivetrain. This is where the horizontal rotation gets transferred to the forward motion. There is a lot of stress on the rear differential. Add a significant power increase, and you have a recipe for destruction. There are several options with differential housings.

GM: 10-bolt, 12-bolt

10-Bolt

Long considered a weak rear end, the 10-bolt actually has two variants: the 8.2 and the 8.5. The 8.2 is only good for 400 horsepower maximum; add sticky tires and the axles will snap like matchsticks. The 8.5, however, is good to 1,000 horsepower. The 8.5-inch gear set is only a hair smaller than the classic GM 12-bolt carrier at 8.875 inches, with a difference of only .375 inches. If the car is already fitted with a 10-bolt that is in good shape and you are retaining the stock suspension, there really is no need to swap it. Should you have the weaker 8.2, an 8.5 will likely fit. There are even some 8.5 10-bolts that have bolt-in axles, rather than C-clip-style axles. These are mostly BOP units (Buick, Olds, and Pontiac), but they are fairly rare, found mostly in A-body cars.

12-Bolt

The choice for stout rear-ends in trucks, muscle cars, and full-size cars, the GM 12-bolt is extremely strong. The biggest drawback for the 12-bolt is the C-clips. When a C-clip axle breaks, the axle becomes loose and slides out of the housing, leading to a complete loss of control of the vehicle. If this happens at high speed, it can be fatal. A bolt-in axle attaches to the outer flange on the housing, so in the event of axle breakage, the rest of the axle stays put, allowing the drive to remain in control. There are aftermarket C-clip eliminators to remedy this situation. While original 12-bolt housings are becoming harder and harder to find, the aftermarket is full of them, ready to bolt into just about anything.

Ford: 8.8-inch, 9-inch

8.8-inch

The 8.8 rear end began use in 1980. Ford used the strong rear in everything from full-size Lincolns to Explorers to Fox-bodys and later Mustangs. These rears are just as strong as the GM 12-bolt, with the exception of the axles, and many came with a limited-slip carrier.

The 28-spline axles in the pre-1994 housings are weak and need to be replaced. For the 1994–and later units, Ford upgraded the 8.8 to 31-spline axles with larger axle tubes. As these cars enter the wrecking yards, you have a few more options. The 8.8 also runs C-clips for the axles. These need to be replaced with eliminators for serious performance use.

9-inch

As the main competition for the GM 12-bolt, the 9-inch has a few things going for it. Other than being Ford's strongest differential, built from 1957 and continued for 30 years, the 9-inch has a separate carried third member. This is important because you can carry spares for racing or easily switch out third members on street-strip cars without having to hassle with setting up the gear (gear changes require setting pinion gear depth and gear backlash, which require special tools and expertise). The biggest disadvantage for the 9-inch is that the position of the pinion relative to the ring gear causes the 9-inch to use about 2 to 3 percent more power than the 12-bolt. There are plenty of original 9-inch housings out there, but they are often in trucks and too wide for most cars and require a lot of cutting and welding to fit. The aftermarket offers easy swap-in housings for just about every combination.

The GM 12-bolt is almost impossible to find in the salvage yards nowadays, but aftermarket housings are inexpensive and made to fit just about any car.

Chrysler: 8.75-inch, Dana 60

8.75-inch

These are the main performance rear differentials used in Mopar muscle cars and full-size cars throughout the 1960s and 1970s. The 8.75-inch is capable of handling most high-performance applications. The 8.75 uses symmetrical axles, meaning that you can swap them side to side. They are not uneven like the 9-inch and the Dana 60. Setting up an 8.75 is fairly simple too; just drive the hell out of it.

Dana 60

The Dana 60 is the big boy of them all. This is what many of the highest-powered dragsters use to put thousands of horsepower to the ground. These units are found in the big-block versions of the most popular Mopars of the muscle car era, from 1968 B-bodies to the later E-bodies, and in most of the company's trucks from 1967 through 1978. The truck-sourced Dana 60s are of the full-floater type and need to be changed to the standard flange type for most car applications.

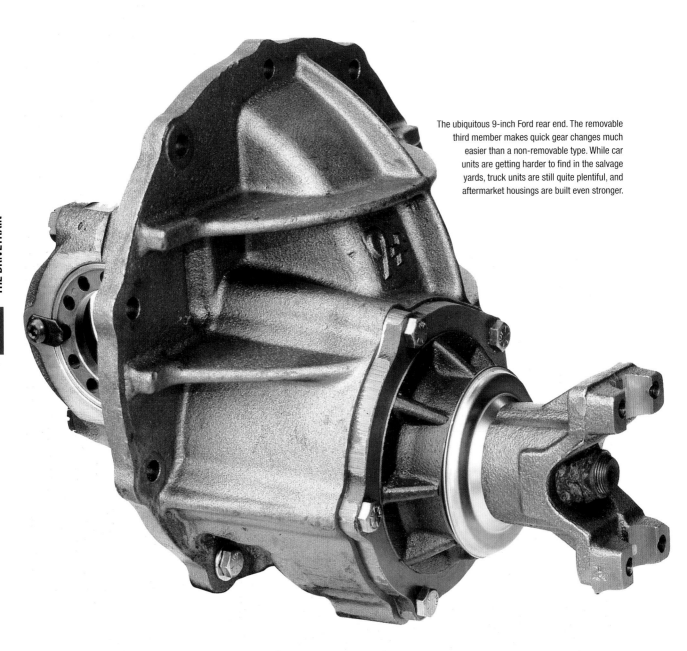

The ubiquitous 9-inch Ford rear end. The removable third member makes quick gear changes much easier than a non-removable type. While car units are getting harder to find in the salvage yards, truck units are still quite plentiful, and aftermarket housings are built even stronger.

Chapter 6
The Chassis

A built motor and high-performance transmission will only get you so far. You have to have a properly set-up chassis to bring it all together. Every vehicle is different and has different chassis requirements. While most street machines run full frames, not all have that luxury. Camaros, Novas, Mustangs, and other unibody cars rely on subframes to support the suspension components. These cars require more work to put serious power to the ground.

Whether or not to modify the stock chassis, run an aftermarket chassis, or build a custom chassis depends on your intended purpose and budget. A basic high-performance streetcar has different chassis needs than a road race or drag strip machine. A street car needs to handle a large spectrum of roads and conditions. A modern, ball-joint, independent front suspension will provide a good base for most cars. Depending on the age of the vehicle, the stock suspension will handle basic street-car duty. The older the car, the less advanced the suspension. Ball joints were not used in most cars until the late 1950s. Understanding the many different components of the chassis and suspension and how they work will help you understand what changes you should make.

There are several styles of frame chassis: ladder, tubular space frame, monocoque (unibody), UltraLight Steel Auto Body (ULSAB) monocoque, and backbone chassis. Each has its advantages and disadvantages.

Ladder frames get their name from the design; they look like a ladder. Most ladder frame rails are C-channel or a derivative thereof. For high-performance applications, boxing the C-channel frame rails increases strength considerably. Boxing is simply closing the open side of the rail with a properly sized piece of steel welded in place.

The underside of a unibody car looks like this. The rear subframe looks similar to full-frame rails, but the metal is thinner and is welded to the floor of the body. Notice the gap between the front and rear subframes (the large section of floorpan in the middle without longitudinal bracing); this is a major weak spot. Adding subframe connectors rectifies that weak spot.

LADDER

This is the most common style of chassis, used since the beginning of automotive manufacturing. Currently the only vehicles that use ladder frames are trucks and SUVs, though there may be a few stragglers out there using ladder frames for cars. A ladder frame is what some call a "full frame," meaning that the body and frame are completely separate entities and can be separated relatively easily. A ladder frame has two large parallel (for the most part) rails connected across the middle with crossmembers. These crossmembers resemble the rungs on a ladder, hence the name. Even though ladder frames have been used since the beginning, there have been a lot of advances in ladder frame technology.

Few people would ever use a Model T frame for anything other than a basic guide to build a stronger version. With only a few weak crossmembers and thin, narrow main rails, the Model T frame is not very strong, even for a lightweight T-bucket. In later model years, the frames became much stronger, using heavier steel and better designs. In the 1950s, X-member ladder frames were common, and they were used through the mid-1960s. An X-member connects the main frame rails with a large X in the center, typically just behind the front body mounts (under the firewall) and connecting to the rear suspension mounts. Many X-member frames use the rear X-member-to-frame-rail junction as the front mount for the rear suspension. This provides a strong connection point. While X-member frames are strong, they limit certain areas that are important for a street machine, namely the size of the driveshaft, transmission options, and how much you can safely lower the vehicle (driveshaft clearance). These issues can be remedied with some forethought.

Ladder frames are quite strong longitudinally, but they are not as good for heavy torsional forces, such as twisting under the power of a supercharged big-block. They are simple and easy to build, which makes them attractive to those needing a custom frame. You can always add torsional strength by tying in a roll cage.

MONOCOQUE

The monocoque, or unibody, chassis has been around for quite a long time, and just about every mass-produced car is built in this style today. One of the first unibody chassis designs came from Ford with the Falcon/Comet platform, which eventually became the Mustang platform.

A unibody design is a one-piece structure that defines and becomes the body shell of the vehicle. These cars incorporate all of the stress members into the body of the car. These chassis are built by welding several sections together, creating the actual one-piece design. The largest structure is the floorpan, which incorporates crossmembers and pickup points for the suspension components. With older designs the roof was often part of the main structure; later designs use a skeleton and all of the outer panels are simply skins welded in place.

The suspension is not part of the chassis structure. The suspension is bolted on using a subframe. The subframe is a separate structure that can be either welded (Mustangs) or bolted (Camaro, Nova) to the main unibody structure.

The rear suspension is typically bolted to the body as well. Some unibody cars, particularly IRS (independent rear suspension) cars, use a separate rear subframe that can be unbolted like the front subframe. The Jaguar XJ6 uses such a design, making this IRS rear suspension ripe for the plucking and integration into a unique street machine. Advantages of the unibody chassis is that they are strong (for a basic street car), with good crash protection, and cheap to manufacture.

You can't really build a custom unibody yourself; it just isn't practical. One of the disadvantages of the unibody chassis is that the early designs are not very good. In particular, the early Mustang and Falcon bodies have a lot of torsional twist when you bolt in a big motor. The main problem here is the lack of upper body strength. There are several fixes for this. Subframe connectors join the front and rear subframes together, simulating a full frame. This gives the car better longitudinal and torsional strength. For additional torsional strength, you need to add a roll bar or roll cage. This helps tie several points of the chassis together and adds an upper strength component to resist twist.

Another weak area on subframe cars is the lack of front end vertical support. A full frame does not have much longitudinal flex; the front and rear ends of the frame are stable. With a unibody, the front suspension can bend at the joint where it meets the body. Adding down bars like these adds rigidity to the entire vehicle. These down bars can also tie into the roll cage, if there is one.

ULSAB MONOCOQUE

Basically the same as the other monocoque, these chassis designs incorporate modern materials, techniques, and processes to make a stronger chassis with less weight. Invented in 1998, the ULSAB designs came about in order to comply with new safety codes. In the early 1990s, the government safety codes for auto manufacturers required that some serious changes be made to the designs in order to comply with safety regulations. This required adding more materials, which added weight. The manufacturers came up with things like hydroforming and sandwich steel and using aluminum in the chassis design.

Hydroforming is a relatively new technique for shaping metal. Typical stamping and pressing require heavy machinery to force the metal into shape. This creates varying thicknesses in the final product, as the corners and edges must be stretched to fit the shape. In order to have the right thickness in the critical areas, the overall thickness of the material must be greater, increasing cost and weight. Hydroforming is different. Instead of using sheet metal, thin metal tubes are formed into the required shapes. The tube is placed in a die for the master shape, and then liquid is pumped into the tube. Once the tube is full, the liquid is pressurized, forcing the tube to expand to fill the tooling. This creates a uniform thickness. The end result is lighter structure that is just as strong, if not stronger than its stamped counterpart.

Sandwich steel is created by placing a thermoplastic (polypropylene) core between two thin sheet metal skins. This combination is up to 50 percent lighter compared with a single piece of sheet metal of the same thickness, without hurting the overall strength. Its excellent rigidity means that it can be used in areas that call for high bending stiffness. Sandwich steel can't be welded, though, so it must be bonded with structural adhesive.

BACKBONE CHASSIS

This style is a little different. Mainly reserved for sports cars, the backbone chassis was invented by Lotus. Based on the animal design, the backbone is just that, like a spine running down the center on the car. The most recognizable vehicles using this style of chassis are the C5 and C6 Corvettes. The backbone centers on the drivetrain. This creates a tight fit for all the chassis components, and it can be built by hand for custom applications. The backbone chassis does not do much for crash protection, so a roll cage would be advised.

TUBULAR SPACE FRAME

When nothing else will do, build a tube frame. The design of choice for NASCAR, NHRA drag cars, and most other purpose-built race cars, the tube frame offers the most versatility and strength. A tube frame chassis can be as simple or complex as you want it, incorporating the roll cage, body mounts, and suspension pickup points. The more complex a tube frame design, the more difficult it is to mount the body, to the point that you have to section the body over the frame like a full-on race car. The materials for a tube frame vary, from 2-by-3 box steel tubing to DOM and chrome moly tubing. Designing a tube frame is only half the battle; the assembly is tricky and should only be left to the experienced builder, as any weak welds could mean disaster.

FRONT SUSPENSION

Modern independent front suspension consists of three basic styles: A-arm/control arm type, strut type, and torsion bar type. Each style has advantages and disadvantages. Changing from one style to another is difficult but not impossible. Key elements for the A-arm style are unequal length A-arms, coil springs, ball joints, and shocks. Strut-style suspensions are different from A-arm suspensions; key elements include struts (large shocks that typically incorporate the spring mount and spindle), lower control arm, lower ball joint, and strut rods. Torsion bar suspensions are different from the two other styles. Key components are similar though, with two control arms (upper and lower), spindles, and ball joints. There is no coil spring. Instead, a large, straight torsion bar is used.

UNEQUAL-LENGTH CONTROL ARMS

For most vintage cars, including muscle cars, the unequal-length control arm suspension was used. This style is still used today on most trucks and SUVs with full frames, with which this style works quite well. The basic design includes a short upper A-shaped arm with a longer lower A-arm. The lower arm mounts to the bottom of the frame or front crossmember and the upper attaches to the top of the frame rail. The unequal length allows the wheels to remain almost perpendicular to the road and clear the fender throughout the suspension travel.

Tubular frames are mostly reserved for race cars, but street machines are not excluded. A tubular frame incorporates the roll cage and body panel mounts in a single structure. This frame is for a drag-strip Corvette.

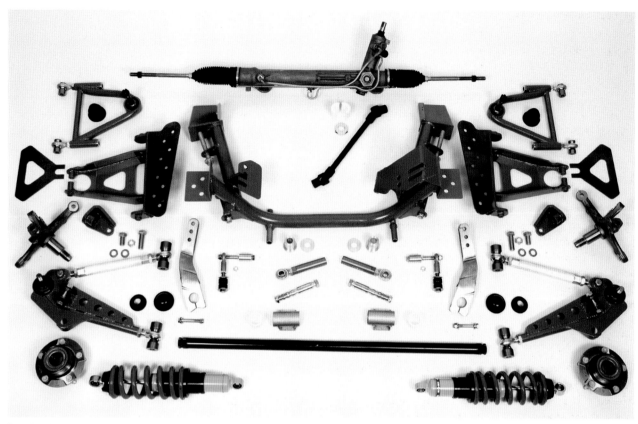

Replacing the subframe is the best way to get the performance you need. Griggs Racing offers these units for all manner of Mustangs, save for the Mustang II. These systems address the problems of the factory suspension and improve handling substantially. The GR-350 kit for the early Mustang allows the removal of the factory shock towers, which yields much more room for big-blocks in the engine bay.

Most A-arm suspensions place the coil spring between the two arms, making use of the space between. Not all unequal-length control arms do this, however, as some systems place the spring above the upper control arm. Regardless of the spring location, ball joints are used to secure the spindles to the A-arms on just about any passenger car and truck built since 1960. Before that, most cars used kingpins, which are still used today for heavy vehicles like buses and commercial trucks. The main drawback of a kingpin is its lack of flexibility. A kingpin mounts horizontally, parallel to the frame, connecting the spindle and the A-arm. These move strictly up and down. While kingpins have excellent vertical strength, an important aspect for a heavy vehicle, this design does not allow for any other movement, which can cause binding. A ball joint is free to move in any direction, allowing for much better handling at all points throughout the suspension travel. Kingpins are also more difficult to service and change.

STRUT STYLE

Unibody cars use this style of suspension almost exclusively. There are certainly variations, but most use a MacPherson-style strut, which has the shock, spring mount, and spindle all in one unit. In MacPherson struts, the lower control arm, which is either an A-arm or a single beam with a separate strut rod support arm, attaches to the bottom of the strut. The top of the strut connects to the strut tower. The lower ball joint in a MacPherson strut system is a follower, meaning that there is no substantial vehicle weight on the joint.

A variation on the strut design is found on the Falcon/Comet/Mustang platform. The original design is similar to the unequal-length control arm suspension, using a short upper A-arm and a single-beam lower control arm with a separate but attached strut rod brace. The two control arms mount to the spindle using ball joints. The spring and shock mount to the top of the upper A-arm. Mustangs use strut towers to support the weight of the body on the springs; these protrude into the engine compartment and can seriously complicate engine swaps. MacPherson strut systems also limit the ability to increase the front tire width, as the strut itself prevents increasing the backspacing, so any increase in wheel width would be to the outside, increasing the possibility of scrubbing the fender. That said, with minor tweaking, this design can handle quite well.

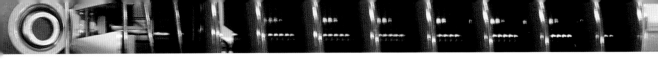

The early Mustang front suspension is okay, but for performance, the stock components lack the stiffness needed for really good handling, especially with big-block weight sitting over it.

Global West's tubular front suspension kit replaces all of the factory components with tubular upper and lower arms, a coil-over shock assembly, and this great looking upper cage. The upper cage is used for the bump stop mount. This system greatly increases handling and offers up to 9 inches of suspension travel.

TORSION BAR

The odd man out is the torsion bar suspension. The overall design is the same as unequal-length controls, but there are no coil springs. Instead, a pair of bars (one per side) are mounted longitudinally to the lower control arm and behind the front suspension to a crossmember behind the motor. As the lower control arm rotates, the torsion bars twist, controlling the amount of rise and fall of the overall suspension. By resisting the movement of the suspension components, they provide a spring effect, just as coil springs do. One unique aspect of torsion bar suspension is that it can be adjusted to raise or lower the vehicle without installing new components. Torsion bar suspensions were fairly popular on Mopars, trucks, and passenger cars throughout the 1960s and 1970s. Some SUVs still use torsion bar suspensions, like the Hummer H3. The biggest problem with torsion bars is the lack of performance upgrades available. Torsion bars are more likely to break, since they rotate and are under constant torsional force. Breaking a torsion bar leaves the vehicle with no suspension at all. At least with a coil spring, you can usually limp home (and coil springs are nowhere near as likely to break).

REAR SUSPENSION

There are quite a few rear suspension designs, several of which are variants of the same basic design. The most common designs are leaf spring, ladder bar, four-link, and independent. Changing rear suspension styles is much simpler than changing the front suspension. The stock rear suspension of just about any street machine project can be bolstered to handle serious power, but drastic changes may be necessary for tuning and performance.

Leaf Springs

The old standby, the use of leaf springs, goes back to the horse-and-carriage days. As with everything, progress and technology make things better. Leaf spring rear suspensions are simple. Most leaf spring suspensions are designed in a similar fashion: a pair of arched spring steel (some cars used fiberglass) leaf packs are mounted longitudinally to the main frame rails or subframe. The front spring eyes are mounted to a spring pocket, while the rears are mounted either in a similar pocket or to a shackle. Shackles are not for raising or lowering a car; they are for tuning. By rotating the shackle angle, you can increase or decrease the spring rate of the leaf springs. Draw a line from the shackle to the opposing spring eye. At 90 degrees, the shackle has no effect, but rotate the shackle to increase the angle and the rate increases. Rotate the angle under 90 degrees, and the rate decreases. Care must be taken, as you can create unsafe conditions with too much or too little spring rate.

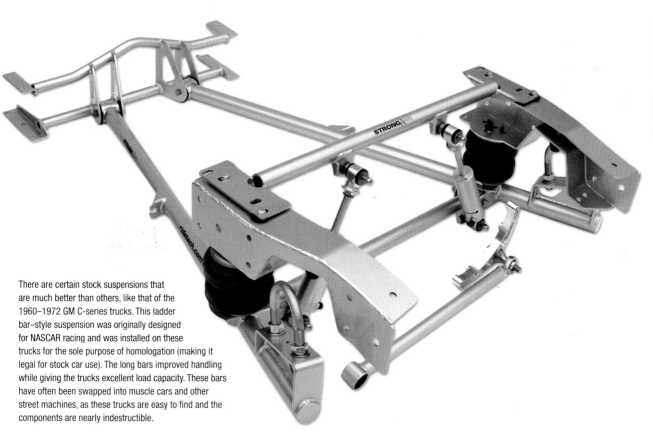

There are certain stock suspensions that are much better than others, like that of the 1960–1972 GM C-series trucks. This ladder bar–style suspension was originally designed for NASCAR racing and was installed on these trucks for the sole purpose of homologation (making it legal for stock car use). The long bars improved handling while giving the trucks excellent load capacity. These bars have often been swapped into muscle cars and other street machines, as these trucks are easy to find and the components are nearly indestructible.

This ladder bar kit from Chassisworks offers adjustability with various mounting positions for the ladder bars at the crossmember, giving it more utility in racing, but simpler tuning than a four-link suspension. The ladder bar system is a great intermediate replacement for leaf springs and is not as complicated as the four-link suspension.

Lowering leaf spring cars is simple though, as long as the rear end is mounted over the leaves. Slip in a pair of lowering blocks (1 to 2 inches will make big difference in stance) and you maintain full suspension travel but with a lowered stance. One of the biggest disadvantages with leaf spring suspension is tuning. While you can tune the spring rate with shackles, changing the instant center is much more difficult, which requires moving the front mounts of the leaf springs to different positions, changing the spring arch, changing rear shackles (longer or shorter), or lowering blocks.

Ladder Bar

Ladder bars come in many different flavors, from stock ladder bar–style setups (as in 1960–1972 Chevy trucks) to full-race setups. Ladder bars use two longitudinally mounted arms that mount forward of the rear end. Stock-style ladder bars typically use coil springs, mounted to either the top of the rear end housing or the bars themselves. To provide lateral location (that is, to control the motion of the rear end from side to side), most stock setups use a Panhard bar, which typically mounts to the top of the rear end housing and to either of the frame rails. Aftermarket ladder bars offer adjustability by providing a variety of pickup points, allowing for tuning changes like instant center. Aftermarket ladders bars are usually sprung with coil-over shocks. The ladder bar is the middle ground between leaf springs and four links.

It provides more adjustability than leaves, but it is not as versatile as a four-link.

Four-Link

The ultimate in solid-axle rear suspensions, the four-link has been used in production cars as well as countless race cars. There are two basic styles of four-link design: parallel and triangulated. A parallel four-link uses four bars, two on each side in a parallel form, over and under the axle tubes. They mount to two plates welded to the tubes. These plates provide several mounting points. The other ends of the bars are welded to a crossmember between the frame rails or to a subframe in unibody cars. Parallel four-links need a lateral location device such as a Panhard bar or Watts link.

Triangulated four-links consist of a pair of lower arms mounted longitudinally, while the upper mars are mounted to a crossmember above the rear end and run inward toward the center of the differential. This eliminates the need for a lateral location device, as the triangulation prevents most lateral movement. Most stock four-link arrangements use the triangulated design, such as 1964–1972 GM A-body muscle cars (Chevelle, Buick GS, Pontiac GTO, and so on). While the stock arrangements are not adjustable, aftermarket replacement components offer adjustability along with stronger materials designs. Aftermarket four-links are sprung with coil-over shocks.

This stock four-link system is on a 1972 GM A-body frame. This a triangulated four-link; note that the upper links are angled inward. This centers the suspension, eliminating the need for a Watts link or Panhard bar.

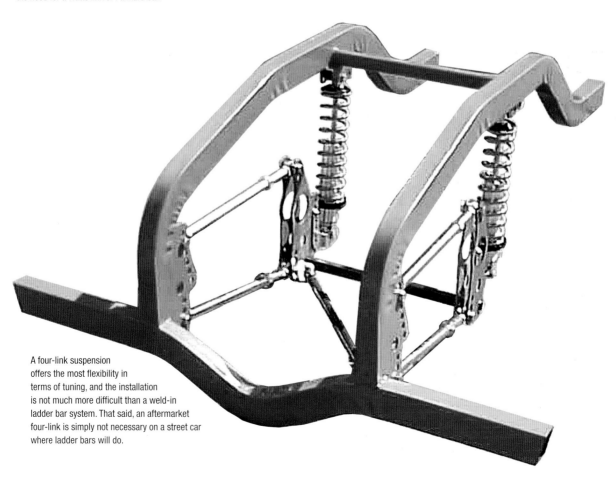

A four-link suspension offers the most flexibility in terms of tuning, and the installation is not much more difficult than a weld-in ladder bar system. That said, an aftermarket four-link is simply not necessary on a street car where ladder bars will do.

Independent

Independent rear suspensions come in many different flavors. Most stock independent rear suspensions use a variation of the unequal-length A-arm design. Some designs use two lower trailing arms with upper A-arms, such as the early Corvette, while other systems use four A-arms mounted laterally. These designs have a universal joint at each end of the axle shafts to allow the tire to run flat on the road throughout the full travel of the suspension. Early swing-axle IRS designs, such as that used in the Corvair, created issues with the rear wheels going into positive camber as they moved, which could cause the driver to lose control of the car and even roll. Swing-axle designs use static-mounted axle shafts fastened to the wheel hub; there is no universal joint. This design keeps the wheel perpendicular to the axle shaft at all times. At full articulation, there is very little tire actually in contact with the ground.

STOCK CHASSIS MODS

If you plan to modify the stock chassis, there are several key aspects to consider. Bolt-on mods, like tubular A-arms and coil-over conversions, make a big difference in handling and add tuning options, while weld-in systems allow custom tweaks into the mix.

Bolt-on mods are available for most popular makes and models. If the car is a muscle car or truck, there will likely be more than a few options in bolt-on mods.

Tubular Control Arms

One of the biggest issues with the stock control arms is strength and reliability. Stamped steel arms flex under hard use, which can actually lead to fatigue and stress cracks. There are modifications that add strength to the stock arms, but this does not fix all the issues. Tubular A-arms are much stronger than stamped steel, which increases the suspension's ability to plant the rear tires. Most tubular systems offer reengineered geometry and adjustability. Most four-link tubular setups feature adjustable upper arms for tuning the pinion angle and instant center, while a few select systems go a little further and have adjustable lowers, allowing even more tuning possibilities.

Coil-Over Shocks

A coil-over shock is similar to a strut, in that the shock body incorporates the spring and its mounts, both top and bottom. The coil-over shock body is adjustable; this allows you to adjust the ride height with reasonable ease.

Most stock coil springs are single-rate springs. This means that each coil of the spring compresses at the same rate. Performance-oriented street cars sometimes can benefit from progressive-rate springs. A progressive spring gradually applies resistive force at an accelerated rate as the suspension compresses. This allows for a smoother ride under normal conditions, but under hard cornering, the spring reacts with more pressure, firming up the ride.

Coil-over shocks come in many different configurations, but the basics are all the same. These are nonadjustable shocks from QA1. The basic components are the shock body, coil spring, washers, upper spring mount, and adjustable lower mounts. This setup uses Torrington bearings between the two washers, which allows the adjustable spring mount to rotate more easily on the compressed spring.

The fully assembled QA1 shock. Once installed, the lower mounting rings are threaded up on the shock body, raising the ride height. It's a good idea to slather on some anti-seize lubricant before assembling the shock to keep the rings from binding up on the body.

Coil-over shocks are a fairly simple conversion for most A-arm suspensions. Many vehicles simply require the existing coil springs and shocks to be removed and the coil-over assembly installed. Other cars, like the Falcon/Mustang strut system, require more work to install a coil-over conversion. Rear coil-overs for most applications require adding a crossmember above the rear-end housing and bolting on the shocks.

Adjustable Shocks

As far as simple upgrades go, adjustable shocks are among the best. Standard gas shocks use simple valving to dampen the compression and rebound (extension) of the suspension at a predetermined rate. More sophisticated shocks contain valving that allows the shock to dampen different rates of wheel travel (and thus shock shaft velocities) differently. For example, sudden bumps in the road cause high shock shaft speeds, while corning and braking forces cause slower speed compression and rebound motions.

An adjustable shock allows the user to set the rate of damping. Adjustable shocks come in several versions, most commonly single- and double-adjustable. Single-adjustable shocks alter rebound and compression together, or may only offer rebound adjustments, while double-adjustable shocks allow the user to fine-tune rebound and compression independently.

Air Ride

A technology that used to only exist for the lowriders and mini-truckers, air ride suspension has come a long way. One of the reasons for this development is Air Ride Technologies. Owner Brett Voelkel is an avid road race enthusiast who wanted to build a better air ride system for muscle cars. Voelkel's 1970 Buick GSX road racer is a prime example. With a full air ride system the car handles much better than stock and has the mean, low look that makes it a killer street machine. Installing the air ride system entails replacing the front coil springs with air bags. The rear suspension is either suspended with air bags just like coil-over shocks, or the bags supplement the leaf springs. There are quite a few different systems, but the basic components are the same. Most air ride systems use Firestone air bags. These bags were originally developed for recreational vehicle leveling systems. A double convoluted air bag (with two defined bulges) rated at 2,500 or 2,600 pounds will support most vehicles and provide a nice ride. Air Ride offers an upgraded version that includes the Shockwave, an air bag integrated into a shock that is capable of supporting the weight of the vehicle. For strut vehicles, there are air bag struts and air cylinder struts. An air cylinder is similar to a hydraulic cylinder, but instead of fluid, air is used to operate the cylinder. Because air will compress, the air cylinder provides a decent ride.

Removing the front suspension is simple for most cars. The most difficult aspect is removing the coil springs. On most ball-joint cars, the process begins with compressing the spring with a jack on the suspension. Always use jack stands under the frame for safety. Once the suspension is under tension, the upper ball joint is removed.

Then the upper A-arms are pulled off. This vehicle, a 1967 Chevy C10 muscle truck, is getting an air ride system with new tubular arms, so all these components were removed as one piece.

Once the upper arm or the ball-joint at the spindle is separated, the jack is slowly lowered, gently taking the tension off the coil spring. Do this too fast and the spring could slip out, becoming a deadly projectile. If you have concerns, you can always use a spring compressor tool to keep the spring compressed while you lower the jack.

The Air Ride Technologies kit came with a mounting plate for the air bag. This mounts to the upper spring pocket and must be drilled. It was clamped in place and the holes were marked and drilled.

The shock mount gets replaced as well. The new mount has a notch that slides into the frame to locate the bracket.

Drilling the frame on one of these old trucks is tough. Each hole took about 5 minutes to drill with a brand new carbide drill bit. Try this with an HSS (high speed steel) or titanium bit and it will either dull quickly or simply break. Lots of cutting oil was used to keep the bit cool.

THE CHASSIS

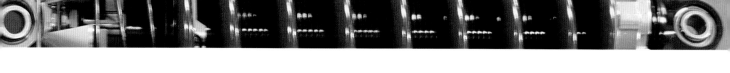

The Air Ride Technologies Strong Arms tubular kit bolted directly to the original upper mounts, using the original hardware.

The air bag, a Firestone 2,600-pound unit, bolts to the upper plate and the fitting was connected with the supplied air line.

The upper plate assembly was then installed to the frame using the supplied bolts. A hole was drilled for the air line to run out the top of the spring perch to keep it out of harm's way.

The new lower tubular A-arm was then bolted to the original mounts using the original U-bolts. Inspect the U-bolts for fatigue before reusing them.

The lower mount was bolted to the lower arm and the spindle was reattached. This truck was also getting a six-lug disc brake conversion from Jamco Suspension, which came with new spindles.

The last step was to trim out a section of the inner fender well for the shock stud. The shock mount positions the shock higher on the frame, making this modification necessary.

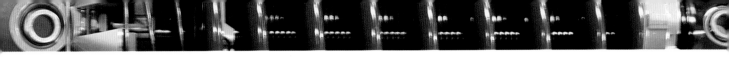

The 1967 Chevy C10 is a departure from your typical muscle truck, using a long step-side bed, as opposed to a short-wide bed. This garners a little extra attention. Here is the front suspension at full ride height.

With the air let out, the truck now sits with the front crossmember nearly on the ground, about 1/4 inch away. If the tires hit the inner fenders when you lower your vehicle, the supplied bump stops can be installed for safety.

Sway Bars

The sway bar helps to control body roll and sway through cornering. Sway bars are made from spring steel, similar to a torsion bar. The steel is formed into a U-shaped bar that mounts to the lower control arm and rides in bushings attached to the frame rails (or subframe). As the suspension moves in the opposite direction to the wheel on the other side, such as in a turn, the bar is twisted, causing it to react with opposing torsional force. This force helps keep the body roll to a minimum. Stock sway bars usually have a small diameter; this is done to apply anti-roll properties while not adding harshness to the ride. Increasing the diameter of the sway bar reduces body roll in a high-performance street machine. Be careful though, because too large of a sway bar will result in a harsh ride and can actually decrease the tire grip on the inside tire in turns on a street-tuned suspension.

Bolt-in rear suspension modifications vary wildly depending on the application and intended use. Leaf springs are more than suitable for street-driven cars and can be used successfully for competitive racing. Bolting on some aftermarket components quickly makes for some serious performance upgrades.

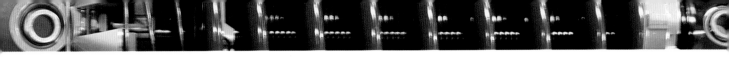THE CHASSIS

82

Watts Link

The Watts link was designed by James Watt (who also invented the steam engine) more than 300 years ago as a centering mechanism for steam engines. Using two parallel arms, a propeller, and a crank bell, the Watts link keeps the rear end housing perfectly centered under the car throughout the suspension travel. Watts links can be used with any suspension system, from leaf springs to four-links. Available as separate systems, or as part of a suspension system, the Watts link is an advanced replacement for the Panhard bar locator. You can also build your own Watts link following the basic design.

Torque Arms

A torque arm suspension is a hybrid of sorts. Typically used to replace leaf springs, the torque arm design mounts between the transmission crossmember and the rear end housing using a crossmember and a bracket to attach to the rear end. The key to a torque arm is the center rotation. A torque arm runs under the driveshaft, centered in the car. The rear end housing is allowed to rotate on the torque arm, yielding excellent lateral stability for straight-line acceleration and centered suspension rotation for better articulation in the corners. The best torque arms use Watts link centering with ladder bar outer supports.

Side-to-side deflection is a serious problem for the rear suspension. The Watts link virtually eliminates the side-to-side movement in any rear suspension. Even a leaf spring suspension has lateral movement that soaks up torque, letting the suspension move to the side instead of putting the power to the ground.

This Watts link is on a 1966 Mustang with the stock leaf springs. The Fays2 Watts link crossmember mounts to the subframe. Then the two horizontal links are mounted to opposite ends of the rear-end housing, a 9-inch Ford in this case. The center links of the bars then connect to the propeller, which is mounted to the Watts link crossmember. Once at ride height, the bars and propeller are adjusted so that the propeller does not bind at full articulation and so the horizontal bars are level at ride height. As the suspension moves up and down, the propeller rotates, keeping the rear end perfectly centered. This car rides like it is on rails. Watts links are perfect for any application—street, drag, or road race.

Ladder Bars

Swapping from leafs to ladder bars is fairly simple. This can be a bolt-on or weld-in installation, depending on a few factors. If you are using the stock rear end housing, then you will have to weld on new mounts for the ladder bars. If you purchase a kit with a new housing, the mounts will already be in place for a simple bolt-in install. Ladder bar kits require coil-over shocks (or air bags) to suspend the cars weight. A Watts link or Panhard bar is also needed.

Pushrod Suspension

Another design in rear coil-over technology is the lay-down style, or pushrod coil-over. These systems place the shock in a semi-horizontal position, allowing for a shorter shock and spring and better control. Rocker arms pivot off of a crossmember to actuate the shocks. By moving these components inboard, you have more room for wheels, tires, and brakes. Currently used on F1, circle track, and many road race cars along with some exclusive sports cars, the pushrod design is popular and efficient.

Full-frame cars are bolted to the frame rails, but if the body were attached solidly to the rails, the ride would be rough. In order to get a better ride, body mount bushings are used. The factory bushings rarely get replaced, usually only when a frame-off build is done. This is a complete polyurethane bushing set from Year One. These won't crush over time like the original rubber bushings.

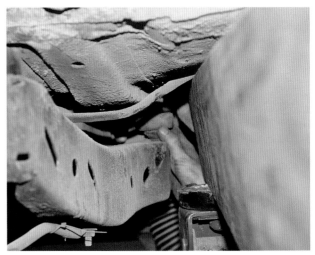

The bushings sit between the frame and the body. Replacing the bushings is dangerous work; properly supporting the body and the frame is critical.

Using a 2x6 and a floor jack, the body was lifted on one side (if the vehicle sits too low to access, it must be lifted and supported with jack stands). All of the mounting bolts must be removed before lifting the body. It's important to keep the other side of the body on the frame. Only lift the body enough to get the bushings out. Full-frame bodies are fragile, and too much twist can permanently tweak the body or even wrinkle the sheet metal.

Use the door gap as a guide. Even with the 2x6 spanning the rocker panel, the top of the door has a larger gap than the bottom. This gap was even before the body was lifted.

Each bushing has a steel insert. This must be removed and cleaned up before reusing it. Getting these out can be tricky. A little penetrating oil goes a long way.

The steel inserts are not available in the aftermarket, so these must be reused. If the insert is not installed, the bushing will get out of shape when the body mounts are tightened. This can cause the mounts to split, ruining them.

Thirty or 40 years of driving wears down the original bushings. The rubber bushing on the right is worthless. The new polyurethane bushing will last much longer.

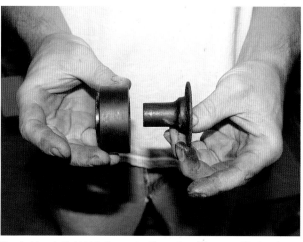

The steel inserts fit right into the new bushings, after a little spray of Eastwood Extreme Chassis Black paint.

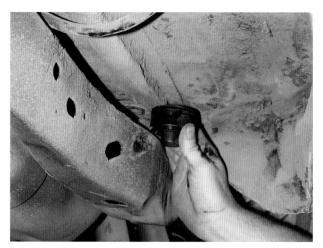

The bushings fit right between the frame and body, like the originals. Again, use extreme caution here. If the body slips, you will lose fingers.

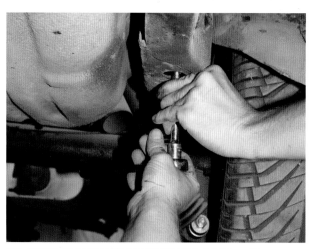

Once all of the mounts are in place, each bolt is replaced and torqued to spec. Check the bolts after the first 100 miles. They tend to loosen over the first few miles.

WELD-IN MODS

Not all weld-in modifications have to feature aftermarket parts. There a lot of things you can do to the stock components to add strength without spending a lot of cash. That said, the stock components are still stock; adjustability in most cases requires aftermarket parts.

Boxing Stock Components

Tubular control arms are expensive and not available for every make and model. Building a street machine on a budget requires making sacrifices. You don't have to have tubular control arms to get more handling performance. Boxing refers to enclosing the stamped areas of a stamped component, simulating a tubular component. Boxing the stock components is a great custom upgrade that does not cost much.

For an A-arm, this would be the underside of the arm. The key to boxing stamped components is to use the same thickness of metal as the stock piece, if possible. If the added material is too thick, you can actually create worse stress points; too thin and the mod is pointless.

Subframes

For some vehicles, the stock suspension simply is not suitable for high-performance use or for the intended purpose. For example, early Mustangs have tight engine compartments, and an overt change to the suspension system may be necessary. There are several options when it comes to subframe swaps.

Mustang II

The traditional subframe swap for most hot rods, the MII suspension is an excellent option for older cars with a straight axle or kingpin front suspension. The MII is not really needed for ball joint, A-arm-suspended cars. Strut-style front suspension cars, like the early Falcon/Comet (1960–1962), have little support in the aftermarket for performance suspension components, so swapping in a Mustang II–style subframe is an option here. The biggest drawback for the MII is that the steering geometry is not very good when it comes to performance. There are modified MII performance suspensions that alleviate this concern, and for a street machine, it would be a good idea to ask a few questions before ordering. MII steering has a tremendous amount of bump steer. When hitting a bump in the road, this causes the car to pull to one side or the other depending on the severity of the bump. The MII is perfectly acceptable for street cars, but for serious race performance, a custom aftermarket solution is best.

Factory Swaps

Another option for early vehicles and for strut cars is to install a factory subframe. This covers everything from factory bolt-on subframes such as Camaro and Nova subframes, to cut-and-splice frame jobs. One of the most popular cut-and-splice swaps is from the 1978–1988 GM G-body. These unequal-length A-arm coil-spring frames can be cut and welded into quite a few other chassis with excellent results. The key to these (and any factory cut-and-splice swap) is to find a close match to the original frame width, inside and outside. Once you have a good match, always cut off more of the donor frame than you need. This ensures you will have plenty of material for achieving just the right fit.

Complete Aftermarket Designs

If all-out performance is what you need, you might consider an aftermarket design. These suspensions are not based on any other factory design using aftermarket parts. These kits are completely new, designed for specific purposes. Considerably more expensive than factory-based systems, a custom design is not for everybody.

Subframe Connectors

Regardless of the style of subframe, unibody cars need subframe connectors for rigidity. Subframe connectors connect the front and rear suspension subframes. This gives the vehicle additional strength and rigidity. Bolt-in subframe connectors do not add much strength; subframe connectors really require welding to provide the most benefit. On the drag strip, unibody cars twist under power because the front and rear subframes are connected only by the floorpans and roof, with not much in between. A full-frame car has a strong chassis to fight the torsional forces of a high-powered motor; the unibody does not. These same issues plague a road racer. Pulling high g's in the corners puts a tremendous amount of stress on the chassis, and the less twist, the better. Adding subframe connectors helps plant the rear tires under heavy acceleration while pushing the front tires into the road in the corners.

FRAMES

Sometimes the stock chassis (or unibody) simply is not up to the task of handling killer street machine power. If you are packing monster power for the drag strip or need to cut corners on the road course, a complete aftermarket chassis might be in order. There are many options when it comes to custom chassis designs. S&W Race Cars offers pre-designed complete chassis systems for many of the most popular makes and models. These chassis kits are pre-cut and ready for assembly in your shop. If you don't trust your welding skills, then a pre-fabricated chassis will work too. Schwartz Performance builds full custom chassis for the most popular muscle cars, including chassis for unibody Mustangs, Camaros, and Novas.

STEERING

Along with the suspension, the steering system requires a little attention. There are two main styles of steering systems: recirculating ball and rack and pinion. Each has its benefits. Both styles have been around since the beginning of automotive manufacture. The rack and pinion was first shown on a Cadillac 1902, while the recirculating ball was first used on a car in 1912.

While factory frames are often suitable, aftermarket frames offer much more flexibility. Schwartz Performance sells custom jig-built frames for the most popular muscle cars, including full frames for unibody cars like Camaros and Mustangs.

Recirculating Ball

The recirculating ball style was used from the beginning of auto manufacture until the mid-1990s, when rack and pinion completely took over. The biggest benefit of recirculating ball steering is the lightweight nature of a nonpower system. These work great for drag cars, but take the car out on the street with some reasonable-width front tires, and the inefficiencies become apparent. This style of steering is sloppy, hard to rebuild, and expensive to replace. Recirculating ball gearboxes, also known as a worm and sector, uses a worm gear (a coil-like gear) interconnected with a sector gear, which is a section of a typical round gear. The worm gear is part of the steering shaft and the sector gear connects to the pitman arm, which rotates as the steering wheel is spun.

The name *recirculating ball* comes from the ball bearings employed in the design. In a recirculating ball design, the steering shaft rides inside a second housing, called the ball nut rack. This section is loaded with tight-fitting ball bearings and is machined inside so that the ball bearings feed in one side and out the other, coiling around the steering shaft. As the shaft rotates, the bearings move the rack, which rotates the sector gear. The ball bearings reduce friction and wear between the gears.

The biggest problem with this design is that over time, the bearings wear down and begin to spread out, which reduces the contact between the two gear sections. Recirculating ball gearboxes, when in good condition, are great for all types of driving, and the lightweight nature of a manual gearbox is perfect for drag strip action. A street machine with a tight recirculating gearbox will be easy to handle and fun to drive, but once things start getting sloppy, they break down quickly. With recirculating ball steering being practically the only design used from the early days throughout the 1980s, particularly in domestic vehicles, most street machine projects are already fitted with this design. The recirculating ball design has many moving parts, as the gearbox and pitman arm rotate, pushing or pulling a drag link (the center connector bar), the opposing idler arm (to keep the other side of the drag link stable) pulls and pushes the tie rods, which attach to each spindle.

Rack and Pinion

A rack-and-pinion gear drive uses a round gear, spun by the steering shaft, which meshes with a flat rack of gear teeth to change rotational motion to linear motion. In automotive steering, the rack-and-pinion gears are sealed in a long housing. The main housing mounts solid to the crossmember. The ends move side to side, pushing and pulling the smaller steering links and tie rods to rotate the spindles. Rack-and-pinion steering is slightly lighter than a recirculating ball system, and the operation is smoother. While mechanical advantage is reduced due to the gearing size, road feel is increased over a traditional gearbox. Some manufacturers of rack-and-pinion units use variable gearing, allowing for a slower application of the steering at higher speeds for stability, but then speeding up the action as the rack extends to full lock.

Retrofitting a rack and pinion to a street machine is a sure-fire way to increase steering feel and ease of turning. Even a manual rack and pinion is easy to operate in a heavy car, whereas a manual gearbox in a larger vehicle is cumbersome. Retrofit kits are available from quite a few companies, including Steeroids, Flaming River, and Unisteer, all for less than $2,000. The trick is getting all of the required components to work together. Mustangs in particular are quite difficult. The rack-and-pinion components are easy to install; the problem is getting headers to clear the rack. Each rack kit is different, and most companies keep a log of what works and what does not with their systems, but step outside the norm, say with a mod motor in a 1966 Fastback, and things may get tough.

Chapter 7
The Brakes

All the power in the world combined with a great-handling chassis and clean body won't mean much if shoddy brakes have you end up wrapped around a tree. The most commonly overlooked aspect of any car build, street machine or otherwise, is the braking system. Adequate braking is the minimum goal; superior braking will make driving the car much more enjoyable and safe to boot. There are many different options when it comes to braking systems. Each has its advantages, and all can be affected by other aspects of the build, such as the engine (vacuum) and power steering (for the pump, but more on that later).

DEFINING THE BRAKING COMPONENTS
The basic braking system consists of several major components, each just as important as the next. The following lists the major components of the entire braking system. Not all of these components are required for every braking system, and some serve a simple utilitarian purpose and are not available in high-performance versions. Components such as the pedal assembly are commonly overlooked, but each of these parts should be looked at and accessed for wear and tear.

BRAKE PEDAL
Everything starts with a brake pedal. The brake pedal is the mechanical link between you and the brakes. It has to be mounted solidly to the firewall or dash bracing. The brake pedal (for most vehicles) operates the master cylinder pushrod below the pivot point, meaning the pushrod pushes into the master cylinder. If the pushrod was mounted above the pivot point, the pushrod would move toward the driver, which would not do anybody any good. Most stock brake pedals are more than adequate to operate the master cylinder. Some cars have an adjustable pushrod, which allows you to adjust the pedal height and the amount of travel for the pushrod.

Stock disc brakes will certainly stop the car, but they are not very trick. You can upgrade your stock rotors and calipers with drilled and slotted rotors and aluminum calipers without going through the entire system.

This Classic Performance Products brake kit, designed for a 1967 Chevy C10 truck, uses Cadillac rear disc brake calipers with a factory-style e-brake. The kit comes with new e-brake cables and simply replaces the original cable that operated the drum brakes. The new cable is a factory unit and connects directly to the factory clip.

Because the rear disc brakes use a rotor that slides over the axle, certain applications require longer wheel studs. This axle for a 1967 Chevy C10 12-bolt needed new studs. With the axle mounted in a vice, the old studs popped right out with a 3-pound sledge.

The new studs, supplied in the brake kit, were driven into the axle using a sledgehammer. An old drum placed below the end of the axle allows you to drive the studs on a solid surface. Once installed, the studs will be pulled into the axle all the way with the wheel on the car when tightening the lug nuts.

BRAKE LIGHT SWITCH

The brake light switch is typically mounted to the swingarm bracket for the brake pedal arm. This is a normally open switch, meaning that the switch is open (off) when the brake pedal is in the fully up position. Once the pedal is pressed, the switch is released to the closed position (on) and the brake lights come on. This switch is normally on the front side of the pedal so that the pedal arm loses contact with the switch as the arm swings away. Some vehicles use a different switch where the arm contacts the switch, but these are not as common.

MASTER CYLINDER

The master cylinder is the force behind the braking system. Whether you are running manual or power-assisted brakes, the master cylinder is the key component. There are several styles of master cylinder, and hundreds if not thousands of individual parts numbers. Stock master cylinders are sufficient for most stock braking systems, even those with some aftermarket upgrades. Once you go beyond basic stock upgrades though, you may find that a stock master is not good enough, the capacity and available pressure may not be adequate. Six-piston calipers, 14-inch rotors, and a full day

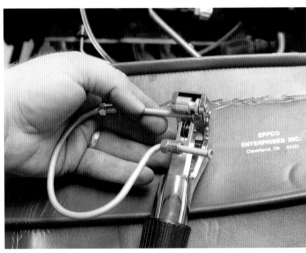

The roll control must be installed in line with the front brake lines. Armed with an assortment of brake line and fittings, a section of 1/4-inch brake line was cut off with a line cutter.

One thing all street machines must be capable of doing is a nasty burn-out. Upgrading the braking system can sometimes hinder the classic "left foot brake, right foot gas" burn-out procedure. A roll control or brake lock allows for easy tire smokage by locking the front brakes while leaving the rear tires free to spin. This roll control from TCI is the perfect solution. They are great for drag racing burn-outs and staging also.

The end was placed in the double flare tool. The edge of the tubing should be level with the die. This is the proper method for creating a double flare.

The die is inserted into the tubing and the assembly is compressed with the press. As the press is tightened, the die rolls the tubing in on itself. Once the press is cranked down hand tight, it is released.

of track time can boil brake fluid in short order. A larger, more efficient aftermarket master would be a good choice. There are single reservoir, dual reservoir (front and rear), and remote reservoir styles.

POWER BOOSTER

If you want consistent braking every time with an easy pedal, adding power assist is the ticket. This area has a lot of options and some pitfalls too. Big-cam engines don't make much vacuum, and vacuum boosters are by far the most common power-assist devices. Vacuum canisters are Band-Aids at best.

They barely function and are depleted after one press of the pedal, leaving you with hard-to-operate brakes. Options such as hydro-boosts, electric assist, and even air brakes can overcome these issues.

PROPORTIONING VALVE

A proportioning valve limits the outgoing pressure in reference to the incoming pressure. Typically used for the rear brakes, these valves keep the rear brakes from locking up before the front brakes. Most stock systems use some sort of proportioning valve, but there is a lot of confusion surrounding these devices.

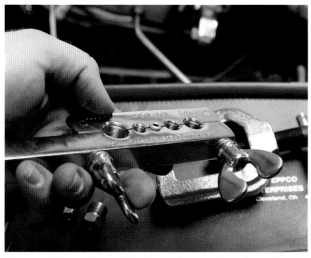

The end result is a mushroomed tube. The press is once again applied and the double flare gets the 45-degree angle that is required for brake lines. The process is repeated for the other side. Don't forget to slide the fittings on before making the other flare.

The finished tube was installed in the roll control device. The fitting should be tightened snug so it doesn't leak, but not too tight to cause the threads in the aluminum body to strip out.

The lines in the car required a little modification as well. The master cylinder fittings needed to be changed, as the roll control had different threads. The flare was trimmed off using a tubing cutter.

Then the fitting was slid on the line. The other fitting was used to make an adapter line for the roll control. This could be done with adapter fittings, but the more connections you have, the more opportunities there are for leaks—and custom lines look better.

The roll control was mounted to the master cylinder and the lines routed. The wiring is simple: Just connect the ground and wire the power to a switch inside the car.

Custom brakes look great on any street machine, and they make a big performance difference. The large 13-inch front and 11-inch rear disc brakes look great on this 1969 GTO Judge convertible.

Quality braking systems are made up of more than just fancy rotors and calipers. Every component in the braking system needs to match and be up to the task of stopping the vehicle. This complete setup from Baer is massive. These six-piston calipers feature three pistons on the inside and three on the outside, putting equal pressure on both sides of the rotor and creating more even wear.

This master cylinder/power booster is designed to be mounted under the floor in vehicles where the original master was frame-mounted. Specifically, this one fits 1948–1951 Ford Shoeboxes. This unit controls front discs with rear drums and includes a proportioning valve. The 10-inch-diameter booster is quite small to fit under the floor. It works for this application but leaves a little to be desired in the power-assist area. You should use the largest vacuum booster you can fit in the car.

For GM muscle car–era vehicles, there were two brass blocks mounted either on the frame or under the master cylinder. All 1968–1972 GM A-body cars had one block installed on the frame, near the firewall. Contrary to popular belief, this is not always a proportioning valve. This is actually just a distribution block, splitting the front brake lines for drum brake cars. If the car was factory-equipped with front disc brakes, the proportioning valve (which looked just like the distribution block, hence the confusion) was mounted on the frame but with a small bracket. The GM-X and F-body cars placed the proportioning valve just below the master cylinder.

A factory proportioning valve could be a system in as many as five parts, including the front and rear bias units, residual valves for drum brakes and a distribution block. Ford and Mopar all had different styles and mounting locations. You only need to use a proportioning valve if the rear brakes lock up on heavy braking. If they don't, then your system is adequately balanced front to rear. Aftermarket adjustable valves are the best option, as this allows you to dial in the system rather than accept somebody else's predetermined pressure variable.

HARD AND FLEX LINES

There are two types of brake line: hard rigid line (usually steel or stainless steel) and rubber high-pressure flex line. You may be tempted to plumb your street machine with all high-pressure flex line, but that would be a huge mistake.

The proportioning valve distributes the amount of braking force front to rear. If the rear brakes lock up before the fronts, the rear will slide out of control, which is not good. The valve limits the hydraulic pressure that goes to the rear brakes, reducing the pressure applied. This unit is a stock-style prop valve, which also serves as a distribution block. It is nonadjustable and more expensive than a universal aftermarket adjustable prop valve.

This is an aftermarket proportioning valve. This valve installs after any distribution blocks, before the rear splitter on the rear-end housing, and is adjustable. I have fitted this valve with a gauge so I can actually measure the line pressure; 600 to 800 psi is perfect for drums. The front brakes in this system are getting more than 2,000 psi from the hydroboost.

Because drum brakes use a simple wheel cylinder to hold the shoes out against a series of springs, as the pressure is reduced, the springs pull the shoes away from the drums. This means that you would have to pump the pedal to get the shoes back to the drums. To eliminate this, a residual valve is used. This one is a 10-pound unit, which is what you want for drum brakes.

Calipers come in many shapes and sizes. This caliper is a three-piston unit from Stainless Steel Brakes. You can see the outline of the three pistons to the right. The three pistons push the inside pad against the rotor while pulling the outer pad against the outer side of the rotor. While more efficient than stock calipers, this style still tends to wear the pads unevenly inside to outside.

Rubber degrades over time with exposure to salt, UV light, gas, oil, and other potential hazards, eventually leading to a pressure expansion and rupture. Even the short flex lines that connect the hard line to the calipers for front and rear disc brake systems have some expansion under pressure, enough that you can see the line expand under heavy pressure.

If the entire system was plumbed in flex hose, you would have incredibly spongy brakes and the chances for a line blow out would be much higher. The hard line helps ensure a constant pressure and removes the flex variable. One exception would be stainless braided Teflon line, which does not expand like rubber hose. Steel is the most common hard line and is the easiest to work with.

WHEEL CYLINDER

For drum brakes, the wheel cylinders operate the brake shoes, clamping on the drums. When a car has been sitting for a while, the wheel cylinders, which are simple cast tubes with rubber seals, tend to spring leaks. Wet lines running down the tires below the cylinder are evidence that you have a leaky wheel cylinder. OEM replacement parts or rebuild kits are the only real options here, as aftermarket parts are uncommon.

DRUMS

Heavy, cast-iron drums fit around the brake shoes, which press against the inside of the drums to provide stopping friction. Drum brakes are inefficient, heavy, and harder to work on than disc brakes, especially in the front. Before disc brakes came about, there were some options such as aluminum drums to reduce weight. Drums are good enough for rear brakes, but front drums are more than a little scary, especially if the car has been upgraded with a bigger engine and more power.

RESIDUAL VALVES

These valves maintain a small amount of pressure in the lines to keep the brakes from backing off too much. Drum brakes have a tendency to shrink back quickly after the brakes are applied because the shoes are being pulled in with springs. Disc brakes usually do not shrink back. The piston only lessens its grab, but it does happen, particularly when the master is mounted level with or below the calipers, such as with a frame-mounted system for 1950s cars.

Two pounds of pressure for discs and 10 pounds of pressure for drums is usually all that is needed to remedy the problem.

CALIPERS

For disc brakes, the caliper is the workhorse. Modern disc brakes came about in 1965 for GM vehicles (Corvette), but they had been around since the 1890s. It was not until the mid-1950s that they became reliable in the form we now know. Most cars after 1973 were fitted with front disc brakes as standard fare. The caliper uses a piston, or a series of pistons, to clamp down on a rotor. Made from either cast iron or machined aluminum, there are many styles or designs of disc brake calipers. While stock calipers work for stock systems, there are many aftermarket options, and aftermarket calipers are required for many rotor upgrades.

The early stock calipers used a large single piston to actuate the brakes. This places the force on one side of the rotor, the other side being static. This tends to result in uneven wear, as the outer side of the rotor is worn thin, while the inner side is like new. Multi-piston calipers use several smaller pistons to spread the load across a larger section of rotor, reducing wear and hot spots that can warp the rotors. Six- and eight-piston calipers go one step further by placing three pistons on either side of the rotor, reducing the one-sided loading that causes uneven rotor wear. This also increases clamping force, as both sides of the rotor are actively pressured.

Choosing the caliper type is not too difficult. While there are many options, the intended use of the caliper is the main consideration. If you plan on late-night cruising and just general driving, you don't really need six-piston calipers. Any autocross or roadracing duty would stipulate more braking power, and therefore you would need to consider a racing brake setup, using multi-piston calipers and big rotors. Stock-style calipers do their job, but the better components you choose, the better braking you will have.

ROTORS

The rotors are mounted between the wheel and the hub or axle. Rotors have two machined surfaces that the pads grip when the brakes are applied. Eventually this surface wears down and the rotors have to be turned and eventually replaced. Stock rotors for earlier cars were solid, and later most front disc rotors gained internal venting ribs to force air between the two outer surfaces for cooling.

Practically all aftermarket rotors use slots, grooves, or drilled holes to add extra cooling to the rotor. A hot rotor warps as it cools, which increases drag and could actually lead to fracturing. There has been a lot of debate in the last few years over drilled versus slotted rotors. Proponents of slotted rotors contend that the sharp edges of drilled rotors crack and split over time, with repeated heating and cooling, leading to the possibility of catastrophic failure. There has been some headway in this issue though, as chamfered edges around the drilled holes has shown to dramatically reduce the possibility of heat cracking. This makes the drilled and slotted rotor a great-looking option, as drilled and slotted rotors stay cooler longer.

The key to choosing rotors is the overall diameter. The larger the rotor, the more surface area there is for clamping force. This is what stops the car. Larger rotors also cool faster because there is more surface area to radiate the heat.

SHOES AND PADS

As the link between the caliper or wheel cylinder and rotor or drum, the brake pads and shoes are quite important. These are regular service items that require replacement, so it is important that you factor this into the price of an upgraded braking system. If the pads cost a couple of hundred dollars, versus $50 for stock pads, that might change your mind on that particular system, as well as availability. There are four main types of brake pads and shoes: semi-metallic, non-asbestos organic (NAO), low-metallic NAO, and ceramic.

Semi-metallic pads contain about 30 to 65 percent metal depending on the formula (which varies widely from brand to brand) and typically includes chopped steel wool or wire, iron powder, copper or graphite mixed with inorganic fillers, and friction modifiers that bond all the ingredients together. These pads are durable and have excellent heat transfer, but also wear down rotors much faster. They tend to be noisy and do not perform well at cold temperatures.

NAO pads are made from fibers such as glass, rubber, carbon, and Kevlar, with filler materials and high-temperature resins. These pads are softer and quieter, but they wear faster and create more dust. This can be an issue for cars with polished and chrome wheels, or any light-colored wheel, as the dust tends to collect on the wheels and can damage the wheel surface if the dust is not washed off regularly.

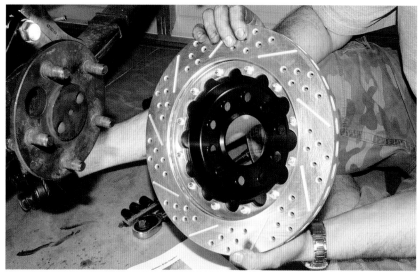

The rotor is just as important as the caliper. These cross-drilled and slotted 13-inch Baer rotors feature chamfered holes to eliminate stress risers, which can lead to cracking, which is bad for brakes. The size of the rotor dictates the size of the wheels. An 11-inch rotor will fill a 15-inch rim. Seventeen-inch or larger rims are required for 13-inch rotors.

Wheel cylinders are simple: two inner cup plungers, a spring, and a pair of outer seals. As long as the cast-iron housing is in good shape and not pitted, rebuilding the wheel cylinders costs much less than buying new ones.

Under the dash, the pedal attaches to the booster or master cylinder via a pushrod. Typically equipped with a U-shaped saddle, the rod is adjustable.

Low-metallic NAO pads are made from an organic formula mixed with smaller amounts, between 10 and 30 percent, of copper or steel to help with heat transfer and provide better braking. These pads are a little noisier than regular NAO pads and create more dust.

Ceramic pads are composed of ceramic fibers, nonferrous filler materials, bonding agents, and potentially small amounts of metal. Ceramic pads are more expensive than other brake pads, but they are cleaner, quieter, and offer excellent braking characteristics without wearing down the rotors.

Which pads you choose is up to you. Consider the overall usage of the car, the conditions you drive in, and what kind of wheels you have. If you have large open wheels, pads that create more dust are going to make your wheels dirtier, but that might not be an issue if you are running stock steel wheels. Ceramic pads are the best, but they cost much more. You need to research the rotors and calipers as well, because not all types of pads are available for all rotors and caliper configurations.

EMERGENCY BRAKE

Do not overlook the e-brake. If your machine is a manual, you must have an e-brake for parking, but all street machines should be properly equipped with an e-brake for braking emergencies. The e-brake is a mechanical rather than a fluid connection to the rear (typically) brakes. Pull the handle and the cable pulls the shoes out (or the piston in disc brakes) to apply the brakes. Aftermarket rear disc conversions are offered in two forms, with an integrated e-brake (most common) or with a separate e-brake caliper. If you leave it off, or don't attach the cable, you will regret it later should the regular braking system fail.

BRAKE FLUID

While most people think that all brake fluid is the same, they would be wrong. There are several versions of brake fluid, from DOT 1 to DOT 5. The most common is DOT 3, though DOT 4 has replaced it in most cases. This glycol-based (just like antifreeze) fluid has a midlevel boiling point and a low moisture content, making it the standard for many years. All glycol-based brake fluid is seriously hazardous to paint.

The advent of synthetic brake fluid changes all that. DOT 5 is a much better brake fluid. DOT 5 does not absorb moisture, it does not eat paint, and it has a much higher boiling point than the glycol-based fluids. The trick to getting optimum performance from DOT 5 is that all of the components must be new, having never been filled with mineral-based fluids. DOT 5 is not compatible with glycol-based fluids. Most issues associated with DOT 5 are because it has been mixed.

Drum brakes are simple in function but complex in setup. A series of springs and levers push brake shoes out toward the drum. All of this operates off the wheel cylinder (center, just above the hole for the axle).

If you are installing a new master cylinder, whether it is a factory replacement or an upgraded unit, it must be bench bled. Most units come with a bleed kit, consisting of a couple of adapter plugs, some tubing, and a tubing clip. If your unit does not come with a kit, you can make one using an old brake line and some clear tubing.

With the tubing adapters plugged into the output ports and the tubing routed to the reservoir, the master cylinder is filled with fluid. The master cylinder must be held level in a vice for this process.

Then, using a screwdriver, the piston is actuated, forcing the air out of the unit, and the fluid is recycled. This is why the clear tubing is important. It allows you to see the bubbles. Once the fluid is air bubble free, you are done.

The cap should be installed and the tubing removed. As long as the piston is not depressed, the master cylinder won't get any air back inside.

The master cylinder should be installed directly to the car, and the brake lines should be installed. You still have to bleed the brake lines, but the master cylinder should be free of air. This process is important. Without a bench bleed, you may never get all of the air out of the unit once it's in the car.

Do not confuse DOT 5 with DOT 5.1, which is an improved formulation of glycol-based fluid. The disadvantage to DOT 5 is that it aerates easily, meaning it takes in air bubbles and may require several bleed jobs to get the brakes just right. Letting the bottle sit for a while before pouring it in and then pouring it slowly is the best method for achieving minimal aeration of DOT 5 fluid.

MODIFYING THE BRAKING SYSTEM

A street machine on any level requires serious braking capability, whether it is a mild restomod or a full-on custom machine. Rebuilding the stock braking system on a mild restomod is okay, but upgrades are always better, even if it is a simple matter of converting from front drums to front discs. Modifying the factory brake system typically consists of basic bolt-on components, such as drilled and slotted rotors, bigger calipers, better master cylinders, and power boosters.

Even though most street machine projects were factory-equipped with drum brakes, they are not efficient. It takes a lot of force to stop the rotation of the wheels because the brake shoes are pushing out against a single surface. There is no clamping force like there is with disc brakes. Additionally, drum brakes do not have good heat dissipation characteristics, unlike disc brakes, and drums are much heavier as well. A street machine by definition has added horsepower, and the faster you go, the longer it takes to stop. For safety reasons, front drum brakes should be replaced on any street machine build. With solid braking power up front, the car will stop much more reliably and be more enjoyable to drive.

DRUMS TO DISC FOR LESS

Drum brakes up front are just not safe. Sure, they technically get the job done, but many a scary moment has been attributed to stock front drums. The problem is that disc brake swap kits cost a fortune. A basic swap kit can cost $700, while the high-end upgrades cost a lot more. These kits usually consist of spindles, brackets, shields, rotors, calipers, and hoses. The basic conversion kits come with stock replacement-style components. This raises the question, "How much would the parts cost at the local parts store?" We set out to answer that question and found the answer a little surprising.

With just a little (and we mean about 10 minutes) of extra work, we were able to convert a 1969 Camaro from stock front drum brakes to stock discs using brand-new stock replacement parts for $321.47, including tax. We sourced all of our parts from the local parts store, all of which were in stock. We didn't even have to wait for shipping.

There is a trick to this swap. All 1969 and later GM drum spindles for cars that had a disc brake option were cast from the factory with a demarcation line on the upper backing plate mount. When a car was optioned for disc brakes, the top mount was machined down about 3/4 inch (this measurement can differ from spindle to spindle). This allows the caliper mount to sit square. This makes the low-buck swap easy. All you have to do is slice off the excess material and go.

Due to manufacturing tolerances, not all spindles require the same amount of trim. To make sure you cut off the right amount, bolt the caliper mount to the spindle and lay the upper portion against the caliper. Then, mark the spindle with a scribe. Using a die-grinder and a cut-off wheel, the mounting boss can then be trimmed (carefully, and making sure it is square) and the rest of the swap can then be completed.

The 1969 and later spindles are threaded all the way through, so no tapping is required. This swap works on earlier spindles as well, but these spindles require drilling and tapping. Still, this is a cheaper way to get better braking.

Contrary to popular belief, there is a much simpler and cheaper way to convert stock drum spindles to disc brakes. This procedure is for 1964–1972 GM cars only, particularly F-, X-, and A-body cars. This is all you need. All of these parts are available from any parts store, with the exception of the caliper mount, which can be found online or at any restoration parts house. The dust shield is optional.

The factory used the same spindle for drum and disc brakes. The main difference is the backing plate mounting tab, which is longer for drum brakes. The factory simply milled this section off in disc brake applications. The hole is already tapped all the way through on 1969 and later versions. Early versions can still be used, but they have to be drilled and tapped.

There is a demarcation line on the spindle, approximately ½ inch back from the tip. It can be tough to see, so it should be marked with a Sharpie. The excess material can be milled off, but that requires removing the spindle and access to a mill. A cut-off wheel works quite well.

The finished cut can be dressed with a die-grinder if needed. It should be smooth, but it does not have to be perfect.

The backing plate and caliper mount line up and bolt right to the spindle. The lower bolt runs through the steering arm; the upper mount bolts to the boss, which was trimmed.

The rubber line installs into the same frame clip mount that was used for the original line.

All told, this entire finished conversion cost less than $350, a far cry from the $600–$800 kits available elsewhere.

Rear drums are a whole other question. The rear brakes are supplemental to the front brakes. They help take the load off the front brakes. When you hit the brakes, the front brakes are applied first in most dual-reservoir braking systems. You can see this action by bench-bleeding a master cylinder. Using clear hoses pushed into the outputs, watch the fluid as you pump the cylinder. Typically, the front brake reservoir pushes fluid before the rear reservoir. Getting to the proper front and rear bias is not easy, but for a street car, this is not nearly as critical as it is for a road race car. There is no perfect ratio for braking bias. It is determined by the weight bias front to rear, the center of gravity, and the wheelbase of the car. You would not want to upgrade to rear discs without upgrading the front drums. If the front already has discs, then adding rear discs would be fine, as long as they are the same size or smaller.

In addition, to upgrade a full-drum car to front and rear discs carries an extra burden of selecting rotor sizes. The front discs should be larger than the rears, *never* the other way around. You can use similar sizes front and rear, such as stock 11-inch fronts and aftermarket 11-inch rear discs, but you must have a proportioning valve to take some braking power away from the rear discs. In many cases, if the front discs are larger, such as a 13-inch front and 11-inch rear, the proportioning valve might not be necessary, though having the ability to tune the amount of rear braking force is beneficial.

Upgrading the rear drums to discs is a personal preference. Obviously, the look is a serious consideration. Rear discs look great on a classic car, while crusty drum brakes hiding behind a shiny polished wheel do not look so hot. The performance aspect is the biggest factor, though. If you are running the car in autocross events, road races, or just like to drive it like you stole it, rear discs are a must. Drag race cars would benefit from the lighter weight of disc brakes, but they are not absolutely required—depending on how fast you are, of course.

There are certain modifications that require upping the ante for the braking system. Larger wheels and tires carry more rolling mass, which means more inertia and therefore more difficulty stopping. A set of 22-inch chrome wheels places the heavy mass farther out from the hub, and cast wheels are heavier than stamped steel wheels. This increases the load on the brakes, leaving you with sluggish, slow brakes that will fail prematurely. Forged wheels, like those manufactured by Centerline, are lighter than cast wheels, so you can get away with a larger wheel and a smaller disc. But there is also an aesthetic issue: Tiny disc brakes behind a big wheel just don't look that good. A 13- or 14-inch rotor fills a fat 20-inch rim, while a stock 11-inch rotor just doesn't quite do it.

The caliper is an issue as well. The stock caliper for most cars is a single-piston unit, where one large piston forces the

Aftermarket disc brake upgrade kits, like this one for a GM A-bodies from Stainless Steel Brakes, range from stock swaps to full-on custom kits. The calipers for this kit were ordered with orange powder coating to match the GTO Judge on which they were installed.

While upgrading front discs is pretty simple, rear disc conversions tend to be a little messier. Some vehicles, specifically Ford 9-inch and GM BOP (Buick, Olds, Pontiac) 10-bolt rear ends, have bolt-in axles, so you don't have to open the case differential. Most other rears use C-clips, which means you have to get messy. The axles are held in place with a drift pin, which is held in place with a small bolt.

With the drift pin removed, the axles push in, and the C-clips drop right out. This is the case for both Posi-Traction (limited-slip) and open differentials.

Rear disc conversions require the axles be removed for the caliper bracket installation. These brackets are usually in two or three pieces and bolt to the axle tubes.

The rotor simply slides over the axle studs and the caliper slides over the rotor, keeping it in place.

Emergency brakes are important for rear disc conversions. Some calipers, particularly in custom upgrades, use simple mechanical levers that must be adapted to the factory e-brake cables, like this unit from Stainless Steel Brakes. A crush ferrule and metal saddle loop were used here to ensure a good connection to the caliper.

pad to the rotor. If you spread the force out, you can get a much better clamping force, which is one of the reasons race cars use six- and eight-piston calipers. The build material is just as important. Cast-iron calipers hold heat much longer than aluminum, putting more heat into the pads, which stresses them. Aluminum calipers dissipate heat much faster, so everything can stay cooler. The piston material is important too. Wilwood uses stainless-steel sleeves for the piston cups to help minimize distortion and heat. This keeps the seals in better condition, increasing the life of the caliper. Piston area,

not caliper size, is the determining factor of clamping force. You get more piston area with three smaller pistons than you can with one larger piston.

That said, the capacity of the caliper must match the cylinder bore of the master cylinder. If you install large six-piston calipers on a small stock master cylinder, you are going to have problems such as running out of fluid during full pedal extension.

If the master cylinder cannot deliver the necessary pressure to the calipers or wheel cylinders, then it is no good.

A set of rear discs, these being 11-inch units, usually fit with 15-inch wheels, provided they are disc-brake wheels (if the car had front discs, they should fit). If you upgrade to larger rotors, the wheel size may need go up too. A 13-inch rotor typically requires 17-inch or larger wheels.

For most street cars with slightly modified braking systems, the stock or stock replacement equivalent is sufficient. For cars that will see road course track time, you may want to look at some other options.

Hard braking, especially on a track where you have to slow down repeatedly from high speeds, generates lots of heat. Heat kills brake components. When the brakes engage, the rotors transfer heat to the calipers, which then transferheat into the fluid. When the fluid starts boiling, you have a serious problem. The boiled fluid eventually makes its way to the master cylinder. This causes the fluid to change to a vapor, which is compressible. With compressible vapor in the system, you get reduced brake pressure and a spongy brake feeling in the pedal. One remedy for this is to use a bypass check valve. A bypass check valve, along with self-bleed lines like the ones from Wilwood, direct a small amount of fluid back to the reservoir with every pedal push. This ensures that fresh, cool fluid circulates through the system, which reduces the chances of boiling the fluid.

If you want a really trick braking set up, there is a new player in the braking game: air brakes. While air brakes have been around for decades on big rigs and heavy-duty machinery, this technology has never been used on performance cars. The increased popularity of air suspension has led to better 12-volt compressors and systems. Power Brakes Services (which also makes high-performance hydroboosts for hot rods and street machines) recently introduced its air-brake system for muscle cars. Using readily available parts, this system provides consistent air pressure to the four-wheel disc brake calipers to stop the vehicle, just like buses and semi-trucks. With the air-brake system, you even get four-wheel emergency braking, which is a great anti-theft feature. While the e-brakes are not meant for long-term storage, they work great for daily use.

Another increasingly popular option is cryogenic treatment of braking components. Cryogenics involves slowly lowering the temperature (usually with liquid nitrogen) of a part until it reaches near absolute zero, the point where all molecular movement ceases. Then the part is slowly raised back to room temperature. This aligns the molecules in a more even pattern, which makes the part stronger and more durable. This is a scientifically proven concept that really works. Many race teams use this process on everything from pistons and rods to rotors and calipers. Test results have shown that cryogenically treated rotors cool up to 35 percent faster and more evenly. Even brake pads last longer when cryogenically treated. Any metal component can be treated cryogenically, even engine parts.

FAST FOX-BODIES NEED BETTER BRAKES

For many Fox-body owners, straight-line performance is the name of the game. Building one of these classic bodies to haul down the quarter is relatively easy, with all the aftermarket support these cars enjoy. They even handle decent out of the box, but what happens at the long end of the track? God forbid it's a short track, and there isn't much room for slowing down. The stock brakes are just not quite enough to slow down an 11-second pony.

There are many different kits available for Fox-body Mustangs and each one has its intended market. For our drag-race–oriented 1992 Mustang, I wanted a lightweight system that required a minimal amount of modifications and would work with the stock wheels. After some Internet research, I came up with the solution from Stainless Steel Brakes Corporation. The SSBC Big Brake front kit offers a cast-iron caliper with a larger piston and beefier, slotted four-lug rotors that easily fit inside the stock 15-inch wheel. This kit uses the stock mounting hardware, keeping the weight the same. SSBC also offered a rear disc kit, which comes complete with rotors, calipers, brackets, and brake lines. The rear kit actually reduced the overall weight of the car, as the heavy drums were eliminated.

The installation for the front kit is simple. It's basically a brake job with no special mods, other than the included braided steel brake line. The rear required a little more effort, as the differential had to be drained and the axles removed. Then the caliper mounts and new splash shield had to be bolted on in place of the original backing plates. The nice thing about the rear calipers is the built-in parking brakes. Using a spring-loaded mechanism, the calipers can be actuated to clamp down on the rotors, just like a factory setup. This is an important component, especially considering this Mustang is a shift-it-yourself model. SSBC even supplies brand-new cables.

The installation took the better part of a day, with about an hour on the fronts and about five hours on the rears. The new pads need to be bedded in before any hard stopping is done. The procedure we use is about 20 to 30 runs of 10-30-10 braking sessions. This means the car is driven to 30, slowed to 10 or so, accelerated to 30, slowed to 10, and so on. This breaks in the pads and establishes the wear pattern that will forever remain for the life of the pads and rotors. After 20 to 30 runs, the car is driven down the highway at a consistent speed with minimal braking. This cools off the brakes. If you don't do this, the brakes will never be as effective as they could be.

The Mustang was tested before and after the upgrade using a Vericom VC3000 data-logging performance meter. This extremely accurate computer measures speed, braking time, braking distance, and g's. The results were impressive and certainly justified the $1,660 total price of both kits. The car was put through its paces in a series of 0-30-0 and 0-60-0 tests. Each test was conducted three times, then the results were averaged to determine the overall performance. In the 0-30-0 testing, the stock Mustang took 2.82 seconds to stop at 63.35 feet, at an average top speed of 31.43 miles per hour. With the new brakes, the car only required 1.98 seconds to stop within 46.36 feet, at an average speed of 31.53 miles per hour. This is a difference of 20 feet and 1 second, more than enough to be the difference between an accident and a near miss. The 0-60-0 testing results were similar. The stock car stopped in 6.37 seconds and 286.51 feet, while the modified Mustang stopped in 5.85 seconds at 197.65 feet. That is almost 100 feet shorter than the stock Mustang, which is substantial in the world of fast braking.

In the end, this 11-second 1992 Mustang has stopping power that is appropriate to its speed down the 1320. This not only makes the car safer on the track, but safer on the street as well. The SSBC kit allowed us to keep the factory look with the stock four-lug wheels and even reduced the weight by a few pounds.

Fox-body Mustangs are among the most popular street machines. These cars make for quick trips down the drag strip, and modifying these machines is relatively inexpensive and simple. Updating the brakes is a necessity, however.

The Stainless Steel Brakes kits include everything needed to complete the installation. Each kit is separate, front and rear, and both came with master cylinders, but you only need to use one.

The car was lifted and the supported with jack stands, then the wheels and rotors were removed, and the spindle was cleaned off.

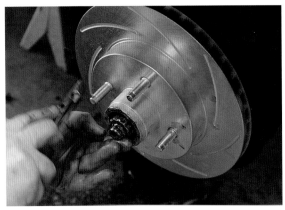

The new slotted rotors, which are not larger in diameter but are thicker, were installed using new bearings. The castle nut was torqued to spec while rotating the rotor back and forth. Then the cotter pin was installed.

The new heavy-duty caliper was installed on the original spindle. This is a big-bore caliper that provides better braking pressure. This is a drag car, so weight is critical. Using this smaller caliper saves weight over a larger braking system, while still decreasing stopping distance versus a stock setup.

The Ford 8.8-inch rear end was opened up and drained of gear oil. This is a C-clip rear; a center pin (shown here coming out of the carrier under the sway bar) must be removed so the axles will slide inward, exposing the C-clips. The pin is held in place with an 8-millimeter bolt.

Then the axles came out. Each axle is a different size, so keep them set apart. Now is a good time to inspect the axles for fatigue, twisting, or stress cracks.

The drum brake backing plates were removed as a single unit. There is no need to disassemble the brakes. While we were at it, the seals and bearings in the rear housing were replaced.

The supplied caliper mounts are left-right specific, so make sure you keep them straight. The mounts go on and are held in place with new hardware.

The backing plate mounts to the caliper bracket. These brackets are powder coated after they are machined. Unfortunately, this means that the coating gets into the threads. Each hole required chasing the threads to remove the coating. You should use a thread chaser-tap for this. A cutting tap can ruin the threads.

The old axles can now be slid back into the housing and the C-clips reinstalled. The rear-end housing should be buttoned back up at this point. See the photo and caption later in this sidebar for a trick you can use to refill the rear end with lubricant.

The calipers bolt on from behind. These rear disc calipers include built-in emergency brakes that mount to the original cables, simplifying the installation.

The finished rear brake installation. The entire process, front and rear, took less than six hours with two people. Expect it to take a couple of hours more if you are working by yourself.

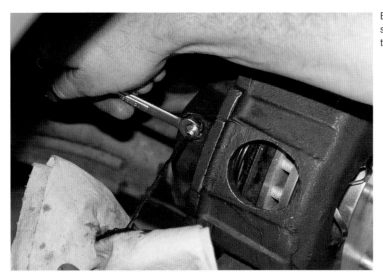

Bleeding the system is a two-man job as well. Always start with the caliper farthest from the master cylinder, typically the right rear, and work to the closest.

Here is a neat trick: The fill hole on the 8.8 rear is damn near impossible to reach with a bottle under the car, making for a serious headache. Instead, use a piece of hose like this air line and run the oil into the housing from the fender.

We tested the system using a Vericom VC3000 data-logging computer. These systems are accurate to a 100th of a second. The feds use these for their own vehicle testing. That's good enough for me.

INCREASE YOUR BRAKING POWER WITH A HYDROBOOST

Probably the most overlooked and undervalued aspect of any car, particularly a high-performance muscle car, is the brake system. When you are focused on making the car go faster, the thought of spending your hard-earned cash on something that makes the car slower just doesn't seem right. The fact of the matter is, the faster and quicker the car is, the better the brakes need to be. But there is more to a good braking system than the brakes themselves. If the system is power-assisted, a few other factors will work their way into to the equation.

It is common knowledge that the bigger an engine's cam profile, the less vacuum it produces. Because power-assist brake systems use vacuum to provide extra braking force, as the engine slows down the vacuum goes away, and so does the assist. This makes it much more difficult to stop the car. The most common fix for this problem is a vacuum canister, which stores vacuum to be used by the braking system when it's needed. The problem with a vacuum, canister is that it is a Band-Aid for a bigger problem. It will work in moderate systems, where the engine still produces a decent amount of vacuum; but a canister does not create vacuum, so an engine with a really big cam or a supercharger won't benefit from a vacuum can.

There are two common fixes for cars that don't build vacuum: an electric vacuum pump or a hydroboost. While the electric pumps work, they are quite noisy and take up a lot of space. The hydroboost is considered the better fix, and it is easier to install. A hydroboost uses the power steering pump to produce the high pressure needed to operate the braking system. If the car is equipped with power steering, the same PS pump can be used.

The pressurized fluid flows from the pump to the hydroboost, pressurizing the system. Then the still-pressurized fluid moves to the gearbox or steering rack, pressurizing that system. Then the low-pressure fluid is returned to the pump and the cycle continues. The flow of the fluid must follow this path, as the steering rack or gearbox takes in pressurized fluid but only outputs a low-pressure stream. The hydroboost is designed to intake high-pressure and output both high-pressure and low-pressure fluid (the unit displaces low-pressure fluid when the brakes are applied and it is using pressure). The hydroboost only uses the high-pressure fluid under braking conditions. Otherwise, it is simply passed through to the steering system. The Power Brake Service Hydroboost I used in the Buick GS has the capability of producing 2,000 psi, much more than the 450 psi a typical stock vacuum-assist booster can provide.

Another benefit of the hydroboost setup is the reserve tank. In the event the engine stalls, the hydroboost unit will provide 60 to 75 percent power to the brakes for the first press of the brakes, then 30 to 40 percent power if the pedal is released and applied again, then another 10 to 20 percent for another application. After that, the reserve is depleted and the system will be in manual mode. This is a safety net that even stock vacuum boosters cannot provide. The reserve tank stores this pressure and only releases it when the brakes are applied after the engine stops running. The second the engine is running again, the tank stores more pressure and the system is ready again.

All of these features make for a great way to restore the power-assist to your brakes. I recently went through the entire process on a 1971 Buick GS project. The GS has a 400-horsepower Buick 350, which uses the largest cam Poston Buick offers for the Buick 350. While it's not the most radical camshaft ever produced, the motor pulls almost no vacuum at idle, making the vacuum-assisted brakes more of a hindrance than a benefit. We installed Power Brake Service's hydroboost unit to fix the problem. Other than a couple of pressure line adapter fit issues, the installation took just a couple of hours and was a breeze. The results were impressive. The pedal is much more firm than the stock system, even before the big cam, and the stopping power is better than ever.

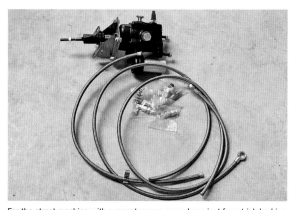

For the street machine with a monster cam, or perhaps just for a trick braking system, the hydroboost provides massive braking power with a smaller footprint than a vacuum booster.

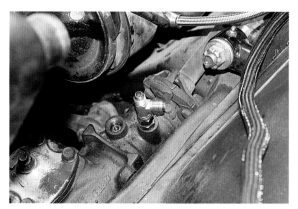

Installing a hydroboost requires splitting the return line for the hydraulic fluid to the power steering pump. This T-fitting installed in the return line at the power steering gearbox does the trick.

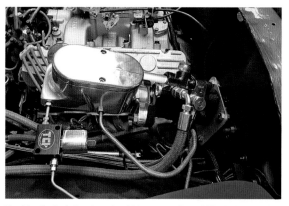

Plumbing the hydroboost requires high-pressure lines. While the kit comes with some stainless steel braided line, the return line in this case (which does not have to be high-pressure) was plumbed with Earl's high-pressure nylon braided hose.

Installing a hydroboost requires a few of the original components. While the hydroboost comes with a new pushrod with which to actuate the brakes, the original saddle mount must be retained to link the rod to the pedal.

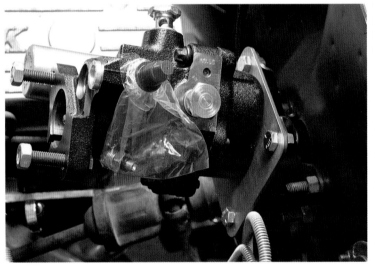

The hydroboost not only makes for much better braking, it also frees up some room under the hood. Each kit comes with a vehicle-specific bracket. If your application is not available, you can always make your own bracket.

Once the hydroboost is on the firewall, the saddle mount is reinstalled on the brake pedal. There is room for adjustment on the pushrod, so you can change the pedal height.

The master cylinder was bench bled and bolted to the hydroboost. As a side note, the hydroboost body is steel, not aluminum. The exposed steel will rust, so you need to paint it.

The pressure lines for the unit do not allow for much room, as the fittings are large and are not adjustable. Your choices are straight, 45- or 90-degree, or use a banjo-fitting. With the Buick 350's headers installed, we barely got it all to fit, but we managed. The lines are braided, so they have a nice flex radius and will withstand a significant amount of heat.

There are several methods of adapting the return lines to the pump. Because this car has power steering, the return line from the hydroboost was simply T'ed to the return fitting on the power steering gearbox. The other method is to weld a second return line to the pump.

With power steering and a hydroboost, the pressurized fluid is first pumped to the hydroboost and then continues on to the gearbox or rack. The fluid maintains pressure, so no loss of power steering occurs. The unit uses banjo fittings for a clean install. Replacements can be tough to find, so don't lose them.

The small canister on the side of the booster is a reserve unit. Unlike other units, this one is not filled with nitrogen. This is a reusable unit. Once pressure is lost via the pump (when the engine dies), the reservoir kicks in and provides full pressure for two braking actions, then diminished pressure for a third action before the reserve pressure is gone.

Hydroboosts require good-quality fluid. Rust and air are the enemies of these systems. We used Royal Purple power steering fluid, which resists aeration and provides excellent lubrication.

Chapter 8
The Body

Bodywork on any vehicle is challenging, but when you are dealing with classic steel, the pitfalls are even deeper. Just because a car looks good with the paint on does not mean the underlying structure is good shape. Too many times an amateur builder or even an unscrupulous seller will mask problems such as collision damage, rust, and poor panel replacement with pounds of body filler. Eventually these poor repair jobs will show through and ruin the car. Quality bodywork does not mean that you have to pay thousands of dollars to a body shop. The keys to good bodywork are patience and cleanliness. If you can manage those two aspects, you should be able to get the body in good enough shape to at least save some serious cash if you decide to use a body shop to finish and paint the car.

RUST

Project cars come in all shapes, sizes, and conditions. You may get lucky and have the perfect street machine in your garage with a straight, rust-free body; however, most of the country has to deal with rust. Combating rust is the bane of most builders' existence, but it does not have to be. Rust requires oxygen and moisture to live; eliminate those two components and your metal will survive. Light or surface rust is the easiest to deal with. Surface rust is very light oxidation on the surface of the metal. Surface rust has not been on the metal long enough to start pitting the metal, so removing it is fairly simple. A medium-grit Scotch-Brite pad will usually knock surface rust out with minimal effort.

Building a street machine often requires pulling the body off the frame. While this can be done with jack stands and about eight buddies, a rotisserie makes it much easier and a one-man job. This AutoTwirler unit even functions as a body stand, engine hoist, and engine stand with the proper optional fittings.

Imagine how easy it is to work on floorpans, rockers, or even the roof with the body raised up or rolled over. Here a 1972 Oldsmobile 442 gets a coating of Al's Liner on the underside to protect the new floors from rust to keep it clean forever. It washes easily and doesn't absorb moisture.

Once you have any type of rust, it is important to understand that it can come back. Treating the metal is required to eliminate the rust. There are quite a few products on the market that are touted as "rust converters." These products vary from brush-on gels to spray-on aerosol cans. In general, these products work for what they are intended for: minor rust. Using them on serious rust will just get you into more trouble later on down the road. Rust converters work by eliminating the open source of oxygen to the rust and converting the damaged metal into black oxide.

The proper way to treat a rusty surface with a converter requires a little hard work. First, any *scale*—the raised portion of surface rust—must be removed by either sanding or using Scotch-Brite pads. This will also remove any dirt or grease. Wiping the area down with a preparation cleaner such as a paint thinner or solvent will help ensure a clean surface. Then the converter is applied and left to dry. Once that is done, the surface is ready for more work, such as using a body filler and primer. Rust converters may or may not be compatible with your primer and paint, so be careful when using these products when they will be exposed. Rust converters work great for less visible areas such as the undercarriage, floorpans, inner fenders, radiator supports, and so on.

As the level of rust rises, you get into more severe treatments. Acid dipping and media blasting are large-scale solutions, while sanding and grinding work great for the small scale. While acid dipping works great and will completely eliminate any rust, dipping requires stripping the body down to just metal, and the chassis must be removed. This is a long way to go for most builders. Media blasting is the next best method of paint and rust removal. There are several types of media blasting available, each with its own pros and cons.

Soda blasting is the jewel of media blasting. Soda blasting uses bicarbonate of soda, otherwise known as baking soda, to strip away unwanted paint and body filler while leaving the underlying surface unharmed. Unlike sand or mixed media, soda blasting is not an abrasive. The soda can only be used once. As the soda crystal impacts the material, there is actually a small explosion. This explosion blows away paint and filler, which is much softer than the metal. The metal is left untouched and in its original form. There is no heat buildup, so the metal doesn't warp.

An alternative method of cleaning metal is soda blasting. Unlike sand blasting, soda blasting does not harm the underlying metal. Soda blasting is safe for any material, and it's virtually impossible to warp metal with it. While soda does not remove rust, it shows you exactly where it begins and what kind of shape the car is in.

Soda blasting can be used on everything from steel and aluminum to wood and fiberglass, all without damaging the substrate surface. With soda, you do not have to remove the trim, glass, or weatherstripping, as soda will not harm those materials. Another benefit of soda is the cleanup. Soda simply washes away, leaving clean metal; all the other media types require a lot of cleanup. You can even store a soda-blasted body inside for months without worrying about surface rust because soda dries the metal. With all the great aspects of soda blasting, the downside is bound to be a fairly big one: soda does not work on rust. Rust is in the metal, and because soda does not affect the metal, the rust does not get removed. Soda works for the paint and filler, but you need a more aggressive media for rusty parts.

Mixed media blasting uses material such as ground corn cob and walnut shells, among others. The benefits here are softer materials that are reusable and less damaging to the underlying substrate. Corn cob and walnut shells are biodegradable, so they won't harm the environment. The

man-made materials—plastic beads, glass beads, and so on—are not biodegradable but also do not generate dust like soda and sand. The cleanup requires a lot of vacuuming, but the media is reusable, so you do not waste much material.

Sandblasting should be your last resort. It is great for spot-cleaning heavy rust, but blasting an entire car is a bad idea. The heat generated by sandblasting along with the pressure can seriously warp thin sheet metal. Forget about sandblasting fiberglass; it would be destroyed in seconds. Sand also doesn't wash away like soda. It has to be vacuumed out, and it will get into every crevice possible. You will never get all of the sand out of the body. Ever.

You can always just spend a couple of weeks sanding and grinding the body to get the old paint off. You will certainly save some money, but you will spend much more time sanding. Whichever method you choose, it is important that you protect the bare metal once the stripping is done. A simple self-etching primer will protect the metal while you complete the bodywork.

Because we are doing a full-on paint job on this car, it was completely disassembled, including door handles, bumpers, locks, mirrors, and all the stainless trim. Here, Toby Ramsey and Jordan Lewis of Ramsey and Son Automotive pull the hefty bumper.

Once down to the metal, the body was searched over, looking for dips, waves, and bumps. You will most likely find lots of dips and few bumps. Each spot was marked with a Sharpie so we can address it later.

Using a pneumatic board sander, Lewis sanded the hood down. A dual-action sander can induce waves into the filler work, so a board sander is best. If you do not have an air-powered unit, large sanding blocks will work.

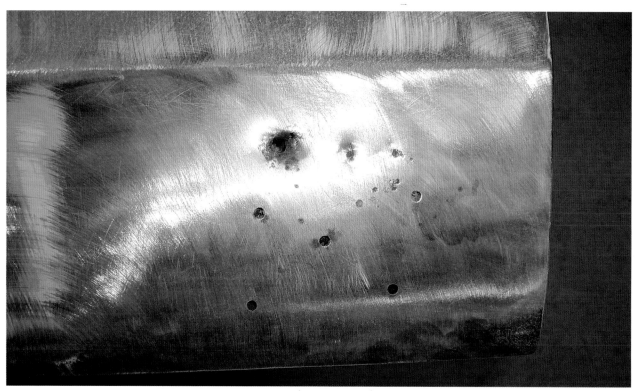

This is why you take everything down to metal. This spot on the trunk lid was not even bubbled up, though it would not have been long before it did. This section was cut away and new steel was stitch welded in place.

The quarter panels had been replaced a few months earlier, so the hard work was done. Block sanding worked out any waves for a laser straight panel.

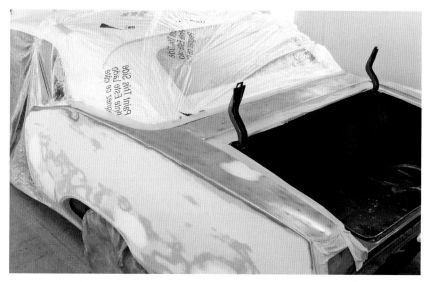

This car was taped off and masked. Because this is a convertible, the top was masked off with plastic sheeting. High-quality tape is a must. Cheap tape will peel when exposed to solvents such as those in paint, leaving residue that can run into the paint, not to mention expose what was taped up in the first place.

The primer was mixed up according to the proper ratios. Hardener and reducer are required for primer, as with all paints.

Once a panel has rust holes, it requires repair. If the rust is not too bad, many times you can simply cut out the damaged area and weld in a small patch panel. If the rust has expanded too far, panel replacement may be required.

Patch panels and full-panel replacement require either welding or bonding. For major body panels, most builders go the weld-in route. Welding on body panels is tricky, though. You must have a good welder, which can be very expensive, and you have to have some skill, otherwise your new quarter panels will have more waves than the Pacific. Bonding uses structural body adhesives, usually an epoxy, that bond to specific substrates, such as metal or fiberglass. You have to use an adhesive that works with your materials. The repairs are simple and do not require a welder, but they do require a lot of drilling and alignment. Most of the auto manufacturers use bonding to glue on the door hinges, fenders, and even frames, so it should be good enough for a 40-year-old street machine. There is a learning curve for both styles of repair.

Before you get to the replacement side of the repair, you have to remove and prepare the bad stuff. There are many ways you can remove a body panel. Fenders unbolt, so that one is easy, but floorpans, rocker panels, and quarter skins are a little trickier. The factory assembled these cars using spot welds, bolts, screws and rivets, and full welds. There is usually a combination of methods used on each panel. How each is removed makes a difference to how the new panel installs.

Rust is the supreme enemy of all vehicles, not just street machines. The problem is that nobody restores a 1978 Citation, but many classic machines are ravaged from the destructive rust. This 1961 Mercury Comet wagon has some Flintstone-esque floorpans.

Using a cut-off wheel, plasma torch, and a spot weld ripper, the bad metal was trimmed away. There were several spot welds that required cutting as well. Notice the leaf spring torque box under the floorpan; care was taken not to damage this area.

The new replacement floorpans from Dearborn Classics were in excellent shape. The new pans were trimmed to match the floor before tossing the old piece in the trash. I used an ESAB Handiplasma 380 for this task.

In order to protect the new metal, it was sprayed with a high-zinc, weld-through coating. This coating prevents the metal from rusting and is formulated to withstand the heat from the welding.

The pans were tack welded in place. This is the first step in the stitch-weld method.

Progressively welding stitches around the pan helps reduce warping and burn through. This is the best method for body panel welding.

The finished stitch weld. While it looks like one continuous weld, it is really hundreds of small welds. While not all of the area gets a full bead, the critical areas around the support member do. Once the welds were dressed with a grinder, all of the seams were coated with seam sealer.

The finished floorpans were sprayed with undercoating on the underside of the car and coated with Al's Liner (a specially formulized body liner similar to truck bed liner) on the topside.

BOLTS, SCREWS, AND RIVETS

Removing a bolt or screw is self-explanatory. Rivets require drilling. When drilling a rivet, make sure to use the smallest possible drill bit you can. You don't want to make the hole any larger than it was if you can avoid it. That will help you get a tight fit for the new rivet.

FULL WELDS

These are pretty simple as well. A grinder or cut-off wheel makes quick work of a weld bead. Use caution not to cut too far, though, as you need to be able to realign the new panel with the rest of the car.

SPOT WELDS

Spot welds can be really tough. First, unless you are on the plug side (the side where weld is made) finding all the spot welds is hard. Look for a small dimple, usually the size of a pencil eraser. Once you have found the spot weld, drill it out. You can use a regular drill bit, but purchasing a spot-weld cutter is your best bet. These bits make it easy to cut away just the spot weld and leave as little damage to the matching side as possible. You can also use a spot weld cutter attachment for an air hammer. These use hammer blows to cut and pop the spot weld free. They are kind of fun too.

If you are working on a door corner, wheelwell, floor, quarter panel, or any number of body sections where you only need to remove a specific section, you will likely need to cut the part. Several tools and methods are available to accomplish this task.

CUT-OFF WHEEL

By far the most common method is the tried-and-true cut-off wheel. The cut-off wheel works great for straight cuts, leaving a nice smooth edge. Where the cut-off wheel suffers is in speed and curves. Large radius curves are not too bad, but a tight turn is almost impossible to cut cleanly with a wheel. Cut-off wheels also take a while to cut, so your arms and back cramp up quickly. The upside is that you probably already have one, and they are cheap if you don't. Cut-off wheels generate a lot of heat, which can warp long flat panels quickly, so be careful.

SHEARS AND NIBBLERS

Shears work great for thin metal (18-gauge and lighter) and cut nice straight lines and large radius curves. They are also good for tighter turns that a cut-off wheel won't make. They jam and bind easily, however, and the air-powered units require a lot of air to run, just like a cut-off wheel. Sheetmetal nibblers come in two types: electric and air-powered. Most of the electric versions are attachments for drills, keeping the cost down. The best parts of a nibbler are that you only need a small hole to start the work, and you can make incredibly tight curves, so trimming away that quarter skin while leaving the emblem mounting holes is easy.

BODY RIPPER

For sheer speed, and maybe a little adrenaline rush, the body ripper is perfect. The body ripper works for straight and curved cuts and surprisingly, contrary to the name, leaves little damage. Most body shops use body rippers to quickly remove the damaged metal and get to the meat of the work. If you are working in a tight area, the body ripper might not be the best, but for floors and quarter panels, it is excellent. The rapid cutting action might create some jagged edges at first, but once you get the hang of it, you will probably like it.

PLASMA TORCH

When absolute precision is necessary, pull out the plasma torch. While most builders don't have access to a plasma torch, the prices are coming down and an inexpensive plasma cutter might be within your reach. Even though plasma uses intense heat to cut the metal, the heat is very focused. The outer areas are not exposed to great level of heat, reducing warpage. Combined with the speed and potential precision, a plasma torch is a handy tool for bodywork.

Once the old panel is out of the way, the remaining metal must be assessed. Is there any underlying rust or body damage in the creases and attachment points? If so, this needs to be addressed before moving on to the next step. Once the area is prepped, the new panel can be trimmed for fit.

There are several methods of fitting panels, but the main types are joint seams and butt seams. Each has their advantages and disadvantages.

While this patch job does not look too bad from here, underneath it is a mess. The previous builder only laid down a few tack welds and didn't even bother to cut away all of the rust. These pans could not be saved. Unfortunately for the buyer, this 1966 Mustang convertible was sold as having new floorpans.

It only took a couple of minutes worth of prying with a screwdriver to remove the repaired pans. Horrible work. This time, the car will be getting the bond-in repair.

JOINT SEAM

A joint seam places one panel behind or on top of another. There are several ways to do this. If you are using the bonding method of repair, you must use the joint seam. For floorpans, simply laying the replacement panel on top of the other is perfectly acceptable. For outer body panels, it is highly suggested that you flange one of the materials, usually the original steel. This allows the new panel to simply sit over the flange, resting flush with the old panel. If the trimming is done right, it leaves a nice area to weld. Flanging also adds a little rigidity to a large flat seam, such as a quarter panel. The main drawbacks for a joint seam are that they typically require a little more body filler (though that depends on who does the work and if you flanged or not), and there is an exposed section behind the panel that may collect debris and lead to future rust. Both of these drawbacks are easily remedied with the proper preparation, which will be discussed shortly.

BUTT SEAM

Some builders rely exclusively on the butt seam, and there are reasons for that. A butt seam places the two materials together edge to edge and requires precision trimming and prep. You can't be sloppy and get a good repair with a butt seam. If you use butt seams and your finished cars look good, then that is a statement to your ability. This type of seam may reduce the amount of body filler needed, though you will always need some amount of filler to make the body smooth. A butt seam is much more difficult to trim, align, and install. Specialized reusable mounting clamps called Cleco pins are needed for a single person to do the job right. Otherwise, at least two persons are required, one to hold the panel in position and another to lay down a few tack welds.

Regardless of the type of seam, the panels require trimming and prepping. Before you actually lay a cutting tool to the metal, you should first place the patch panel to the original metal and make notes of its shape and fit. The next step is trimming away the damaged area. Then trim the patch panel to the car using the same methods. Once the panel is trimmed to fit, it is ready for the prep.

Depending on the method of attachment, the panel must be treated accordingly. In many instances, the backside of the panel is inaccessible after the installation, but the back of the panel requires protection. If you are welding, regular paint just won't suffice. Weld-Thru primer is a specialized high-zinc coating that is designed to withstand the heat of welding. This allows the coating to protect the metal from rust and not flake off during welding. If you use the bonding method, a simple undercoating (on the area not being bonded) will do the trick.

For welding, there are two techniques required for a proper repair: spot welding, to replace the original spot welds and for additional support welds, and stitch welding.

SPOT WELDING

Applying a spot weld is simple. These are used for replacing the original spot welds or adding additional support to welds on layered panels, such as between a floorpan and a support brace. Spot welding requires one panel to have a small hole (¼ inch works great), which lays flat over a solid section of the other panel. Then you simply lay a nice dot of weld. If the weld is exposed, it can be ground smooth.

Bonding requires a clean surface. The entire area was cleaned up with the grinder.

The new pans were trimmed to fit and then placed in the car. Using a drill, the pans were predrilled with the full weight of the builder's body pressing on the pan to keep it in position.

The bonding adhesive requires a mixing tube that will not be reusable because the adhesive cures once mixed. There are several types; this is the universal adhesive.

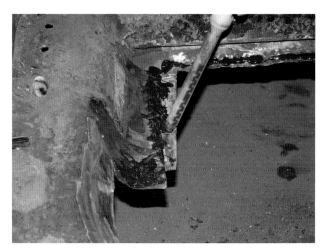

A healthy layer of adhesive was applied to the floorpan. You want plenty of adhesive for the metal to bond with.

The pan was installed on the floor, and the two panels were screwed down using the previously drilled holes.

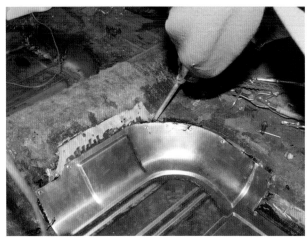

An additional layer of adhesive was applied to the edges of the steel. This acts as an additional bond and a seal for the panels.

Once the adhesive has fully cured, the screws can either be removed and the holes sealed, or the screws can be left in place. The builder of this car chose to grind the heads off and apply seam sealer to the edges for a stock-looking appearance.

STITCH WELDING

Stitch welding is the best method of welding long sections while minimizing warping caused by the heat of welding. A small weld is applied, about the size of a tack weld. Then you move along the seam about 2 to 3 inches before making another similar weld. These small welds are continued until you have reached the end of the seam. Then start back at the beginning and continue the process. By the time you are done, the seam is fully welded and the panel remains straight.

With that said, these techniques are not easy for the beginning welder. They require a lot of practice. If your vehicle needs floorpans, start here and use the pans to practice each technique. By the time you are done, you will know if you are ready for serious bodywork.

The other method of patch panel installation is the bond-in method. While structural bonding has been used for years in new car manufacturing, it is still fairly new and uncommon in restorations. That does not make it any less worthy.

Instead of welding, using structural body adhesive to permanently adhere a replacement floorpan to the rest of the body is a great option. The welding process generates lots of heat, which can warp and distort the metal. While warping is not that big of a deal on floorplans, it is on external panels. Bonding can be used for everything from floors to door skins and quarter panels, all without a welder and with excellent results.

All you need to perform this type of repair are some basic tools you should already have: a grinder, a cut-off wheel, and a drill. One tool you will need that you might not have is the specialized gun used to meter out the adhesive. More than just a basic caulking gun, this gun is heavier duty and fits the special tubes. The adhesive is available in several grades, from universal bonding to structural adhesive and SMC bonding. SMC stands for Sheet Molding Compound, which is what Corvettes and plastic body panels are made from. For floorpans, all you need is the universal adhesive. Brand preference is the only real difference between the varying brands of adhesive, which are available from any body shop supplier.

The entire process of replacing a floorpan using this technique is quick; we had one section done from start to finish in about three hours, minus cure time. The adhesive needs to cure for about 24 hours before moving on to the second half of finishing.

Sometimes you might find that the project vehicle you purchased requires a little more repair than you are capable of doing. This situation requires either selling the car or getting help. Professional bodywork ranges in price depending on the level of expertise in the field and the quality of the work. You need to research your shop. Ask to see examples of their work. If the shop mostly performs collision repair work, as most body shops do, then you might want to go somewhere else. They may even shy away from your job, as they won't make as much money. If you are having trouble finding a reputable shop, ask around the local cruise spot. You will likely find a shop owner or employee who will be able to steer you to right place.

BODY FILLER

With the welding or bonding done, the body filler is next. Do not let anyone tell you that body filler is bad. You must use body filler in order to get a smooth body. There are two types of filler: plastic body filler and body solder.

The 1970s were not kind to muscle cars. The classic aftermarket sunroof ruined many cars. Not only did they look awful, they leaked, which lead to a lot of rust. The owner of this 1972 Challenger wanted the hole filled.

The roof has a gentle compound curve, so flat steel was just not going to work. This was rectified by using an English wheel.

The English wheel uses a larger steel wheel on top and a smaller curved dolly wheel on the bottom. Using different radius dolly wheels and adjusting the pressure, a piece of 16-gauge sheet metal was formed to match the curve of the roof.

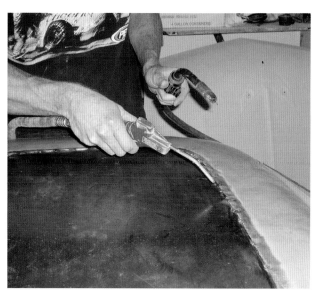

Another trick for welding sheet metal is spot cooling. Using an air gun, each stitch weld was blown with air to cool it down. The roof is particularly thin and easy to warp, so lots of care must be taken here. We want as little filler on the roof as possible.

Once the welding was completed, the underside was sealed with some flexible seam sealer. This keeps out moisture from the vulnerable welds underneath.

From the top, the roof looks as good as new. Very little body filler was needed. Had we used a flat piece of metal, a lot of filler would have been needed.

PLASTIC FILLER

Commonly known as Bondo (which is a brand name), plastic body filler has been around since the early 1960s. Plastic filler has gotten a bad reputation. In the early days of the product, the formulations were not good and the stuff just didn't stick. In addition, plastic filler is a hydrophilic, which means that it absorbs water—not good for sheet metal. These issues have been reconciled with modern formulations. Though bare plastic filler is still absorbent, this isn't a problem once it is primed and painted. Another issue is that too many amateur builders overuse plastic filler, hence the epithet "Bondo bucket." Plastic filler is not bad when used as it was intended. A maximum thickness of ⅛ inch finished filler is suggested, though you will likely add closer to ¼ to ⅜ inch of filler, most of which is sanded off. For heavy filler areas and areas where there is a lot of flex in the panels or rust problems, Duraglas, or fiberglass-reinforced body filler, is a good option, as it will flex and resist moisture.

Body Solder

For custom mods like Frenching, molding tailpipes, and areas where thicker filler is needed, body solder might be considered. Body solder is what was used in the early days of customizing and autobody repair. Commonly referred to as lead, or lead filler, most body solder is made of solid lead. The health hazards of lead created a need for an alternative, which is now available. Lead-free body solder works just like lead, in that it is melted and flowed into place and smoothed with wooden paddles. Lead-free solder, however, maintains a plastic state (the point at which it is malleable) for a wider range of temperature and it melts faster, reducing how much heat you have to put into the metal. In addition, lead-free solder can be sanded, whereas sanding lead solder is really dangerous. Learning to use body solder takes a lot of patience, but the best thing about it is if you screw up, you can just melt it off and start over.

BODY MODS

Building a street machine means making changes that will set it apart from the crowd and make it your own. You can make subtle changes or drastic changes. Subtle modifications such as shrinking bumpers, shaving door handles, and other minor tweaks add definition. The realm of the street machine is full of subtle mods. When an over-the-top engine hangs out of the hood, you don't need radical body modifications to make a statement. Simply shaving the door handles and adding selective badging can make a big statement.

When body filler just won't do the trick, lead solder is the go-to option. Solder is more flexible than plastic filler. It works great for areas like this, the body seam between the quarter panel and the rear deck filler panel on a GM A-body convertible. The factory used lead solder here as well.

Frenching is a classic body modification that works great on street machines, with proper planning, of course. This taillight is from a 1951 Ford Shoebox. The bulbous look is not quite right. The older 1949–1950 Ford taillights look a lot better.

Using the Frenching box from RPPG (formerly Good Times Productions) as a template, the area was marked for cutting.

While the plasma would work here, the smoother the edges the better, so a jigsaw with a metal-cutting blade was used.

The Frenching bucket was pressed in from behind, and then a small body hammer was used to blend the old metal to the bucket.

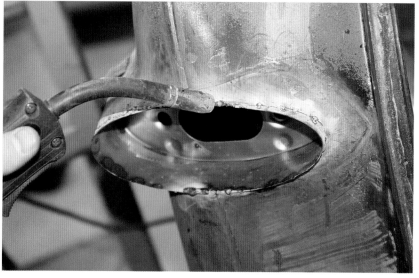

Stitch welds were then placed around the entire perimeter of the bucket. After that, the mod was smoothed out with body filler.

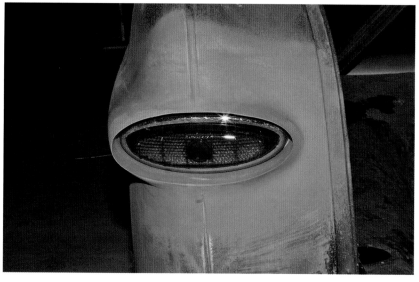

Once the filler was sanded and primed, a 1950 Ford taillight lens was installed.

Major body modifications such as Frenching and reshaping body panels drastically change the overall look of a car, but if they do not blend well, the look will not be good. Making a major change to the body requires a specific vision, and certain modifications do not look good on certain cars. Muscle cars typically do not look good with a chopped top, but that is not to say it can't be done. A subtle reshaping of the roofline can make a striking difference while maintaining a classic look. Older cars and most trucks can take more serious body modifications and look great. Suicide doors on a truck are always unique, but suicide doors on a 1967 Camaro would probably just seem silly.

PAINT

With the body ready for paint, there are some real choices to be made. There are four main types of paint: lacquer, enamel, urethane, and water-based.

One area that is seldom given proper attention is the windshield cowl. Unless it has fallen victim to obvious rust, this area may go untreated for too long, especially when they are covered with chrome trim, as many muscle-car era cars were. The windshield came out so the dash could be painted properly.

With the windshield out, the old seam sealer was busted up to inspect the underlying metal. What was found was a little scary. Under the seam sealer were the beginnings of some real rust.

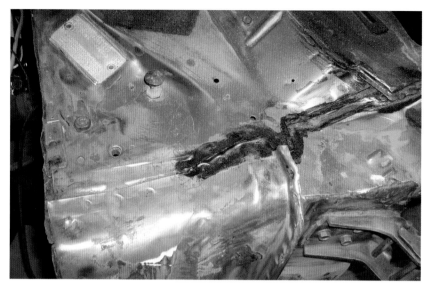

The area was cleaned thoroughly and treated with rust converter. This stuff really works and in an area like this, it is the only real solution for preventing rust where panel replacement is not warranted.

The entire cowl and dash were sanded smooth and prepped for paint. Painting the dash is tough. With the windshield in, it is almost impossible to get it just right.

A quality spray gun is necessary for spraying paint. Siphon feed guns are not used for much other than primer these days. A gravity-feed gun requires less air and wastes much less paint. This is the Concours gun from the Eastwood Company. It has all the features of a full-price professional gun, but it costs a lot less.

The painted dash and cowl look incredible. This paint will last for decades without worries about future rust in the cowl. This is the only way to get the dash this nice. With the hard-to-reach surface rust, the glass has to be removed.

Lacquer-based auto paint was commonly used through the 1960s, and while it is still available, there are certainly much better options. Acrylic lacquer might be illegal in your area. Lacquer paint is inexpensive and easy to apply and achieve quality results. One of the downsides for lacquer paint is that it chips quite easily and does not hold up against sunlight, which will have you respraying after a few years.

Enamel paint dries hard, which is much better than lacquer. Most enamel paints are baked on, which speeds the curing time. The hobbyist can spray enamel in the garage, but enamel paints are not as easy to spray, which means more finish work. There are two types of enamels: single-stage and basecoat/clearcoat.

Urethane paint is the most common (and most expensive) among modern auto paints. Urethanes spray relatively easy and are tough. They last for years with little required maintenance, and they have high UV resistance. Urethane paint is applied as a system, like some enamel paints, and requires reducer and activator. The base color will last for years in a properly stored can, but once activated, the paint will harden within a couple of hours. The reducer is a thinner, allowing the painter to reduce the thickness of the paint for the spray equipment being used. Just like enamel paint, urethane paint comes as single stage and basecoat/clearcoat. Urethane paint is the best system to get metallic, candy, and pearl effects.

The idea of water-based auto paint sounds odd, but this is the latest in paint technology. Initially designed for striping and accent graphic work, water-based paint is now being used to paint entire vehicles. The nontoxic nature of water-based paint is especially helpful for the home-based hobbyist, where spraying highly toxic paint in the garage under your kid's bedroom is not such a good idea. Water-based paint does still require a polyurethane topcoat to protect the paint. While water-based paint is the future for automotive paint, the color choices are still limited. As the technology and formulations grow, the choices for colors will follow suit.

Spraying paint yourself is a tricky business. As mentioned before, spraying highly toxic paint in your garage will work, but you need to take precautions if the garage is attached to the house. It's a good idea to use plastic sheeting to cover all of the windows and doors, and use an exhaust fan to route the fumes out of the garage. Another option is to talk with the local body shops. Many shops will rent out the paint booth for an evening, with supervision, and let you spray your own vehicle.

Once the paint is actually on the car, it must be color sanded. Color sanding removes small layers of paint (or clearcoat if you've applied one) until the surface is smooth. The act of spraying paint creates tiny ripples, which is commonly referred to as orange peel, because it looks bumpy, like the surface of an orange. This must be sanded away to get a smooth, glass-like finish. With a basecoat/clearcoat system, this is relatively simple, 1,200- to 2,000-grit paper on a DA (dual action) orbital sander, using clean water as a lubricant (always use water for color sanding), followed by a good buffing job will get the car looking great. Single-stage paint requires color sanding as well, but because there is no top coat you can more easily accidentally go through the color and hit primer; then you are in trouble.

The last major hurdle for most builds is the paint. For many, this is the biggest task of the entire build; a car just isn't finished until it has shiny paint. The majority of builders regard the paint process as "for pros only," and without the proper equipment, spraying paint yourself may be too much. The nice thing about the entire process is that you get a few shots at spraying primer before you actually lay down the final finish of color.

Before you jump off the deep end and start spraying primer and paint, you have to prepare the car. The final finish will only be as good as the surface it is sprayed on. If the body is rough, there is no point in even spraying primer on it. Even 150-grit scratches can show through the primer. Prepping a car for paint is the most painstaking task and can make all the difference between a best-in-show winner and a 20-footer.

Major body work aside, there is much sanding to do. Once the sanding is done, sand it some more. You can almost not sand it enough. A proper high-quality paint job usually requires taking the car down to the metal. Until you start grinding away paint, you never really know how thick the paint is. Taking the car down to the metal is the only real way of knowing what you are spraying over. In addition, you will often find little trouble spots (that means rust) that were not there before. On our project Buick, there were quite a few pinholes and even a few worse spots that were devoid of all metal, but the paint was not even bubbled up. Had we simply sanded the surface and laid down fresh paint, these spots could have been disastrous in just a few months.

Once the car is sanded down to the bare steel, the real work begins. Body panels are made from stamped steel, which means that even from the factory every car has waves and other defects in the body. If you want laser-straight body panels, these waves and defects must be found. While some you can see, most of the defects are found using your hands. Slowly running your hands over the body, you will find dips, bumps, and ripples. Mark these spots with a Sharpie so you can go back later and work them out, or fill them with body filler.

The mixed primer was strained into the primer gun. You do not want any chunks in the paint can (it happens).

Immediately before the car was sprayed, it was wiped down with degreaser. One wet rag applied the degreaser, and one dry rag wiped it off. You want to work in small areas, about 2 square feet at a time. If the degreaser is left to dry on its own, your paint will have fisheyes, which are a pain.

THE BODY

131

Working out the bumps requires a little hammer and dolly work, and you can work out the dips as well. Small dips and waves can be smoothed over with a little body filler. You may scoff at the thought of Bondo on your prized ride, but there is not a single show car out there that does not have body filler on it. The only way to get a laser-straight body is filler. The trick is to keep the filler as thin a possible. You don't want to goop the filler over a huge dent. It will eventually shrink and crack out. A little here and there is just fine.

Primer is the next step, but you want to make sure you have a clean place to spray. You do not have to have a $10,000 spray booth, but the area you use needs to be clean and secure. If you spray in your garage, lay down some Visqueen plastic sheeting. A sheet on the floor and draped up the walls front and rear will do wonders for keeping the dust out of the primer. The primer stage is not as critical for dust elimination because the primer will be sanded (yup, more sanding) down, but why take chances?

The primer you use is important, as the base must be compatible with the topcoat. Check with your paint store to ensure the primer will match the paint you want. There are varying grades of primer as well. Epoxy primer is designed to etch to the metal, sealing it from oxidation. Often used as an etching primer and a sealer, epoxy primers are hard and durable depending on the brand and formulation. Epoxies do not sand well and do not fill any imperfections. Sealer is used for color holdout (this means that the final color will stay true and not bleed into the underlying coats) and to improve

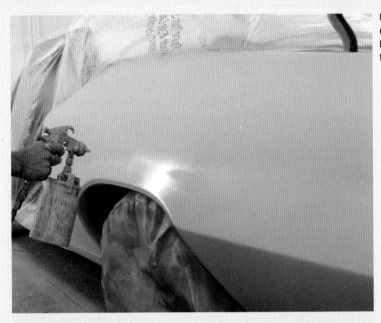

Using a 50 percent overlapping spray pattern, Ramsey laid down the primer. Two medium wet coats were applied. He waited 10 minutes in between to allow the primer to flash, or dry.

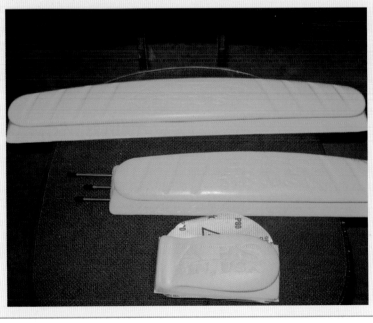

Block sanding requires sanding blocks. These flexible sanding blocks from the Eastwood Company feature steel reinforcement rods. You can increase or decrease the flexibility of the blocks by adding or removing the three rods, letting you get the most out of the block.

THE BODY

132

adhesion. It is usually sprayed over anything other than bare metal. This primer is very thin and not suitable for sanding. That job is left to sanding primer or surfacer, which goes on a little thicker and sands easily. This is important because you never really know what the body looks like until you have a solid color on it. A smooth panel often shows the tiny pinholes and layering that are hard to see when the colors are not even. Each paint system has its own process, so check with the paint shop for further instructions.

Spraying primer should follow the same basic guidelines as spraying paint. For the best coverage, apply the primer in medium-wet coats to avoid runs and use 50 percent overlapping layers. Hold the gun 8 to 10 inches from the body to avoid dry spray, where the liquid actually dries before it hits the body and causes a textured, dull finish. While this does not affect the primer stage as much, if you are planning to spray the color yourself, you might want the practice.

Once everything is in primer, you need to do the final sanding before the paint goes on. This requires block sanding, using hard foam blocks to smooth out the primer and sand out scratches and any other imperfections that will affect the final finish. Sand to 320-grit until the surface is perfectly smooth. Misting a little black spray paint as a guide coat will help you find any low or high spots that need additional attention. Once the block sanding is done, you can rest; the primer will protect the car for a while.

Once everything is blocked, filled, smoothed, and otherwise absolutely perfect, the water and DA come out for the final sanding. You can wet sand by hand with 500-grit and that will be fine. For the GS, Ramsey took it one step further and loaded the DA with 800-grit after hand sanding with 500. This was done right before the car rolled back into the booth for the color.

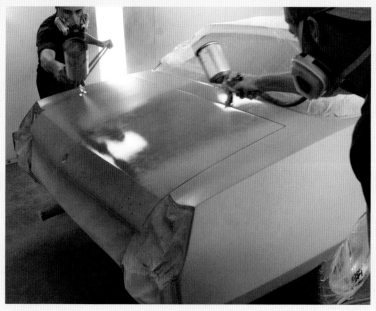

The DuPont Hot Hues "Blue-By-You" paint was mixed according to the proper ratios and filtered in the paint guns as earlier. Using the same overlapping process, the paint was applied in tag-team fashion by Ramsey and Lewis. Every paint has specific instructions as to the right number of coats and flash dry times; consult the manufacturer.

Five coats were applied to the body for a perfectly smooth job. In the next step, three coats of clear were applied. While the instructions specify only two coats, we were planning to color sand the hell out of it, so one coat would literally end up on the floor.

Once the paint had cured, the DA was used to color sand the paint. While it seems crazy to sand fresh paint, this is the only way to get the orange peel out. About 20 hours was spent color sanding the car. First 600-grit, then 1,500, then 2,000-grit, all wet sanded.

The finished product, after the paint was buffed out after color canding. Pictures do not do this paint job justice. Care must be taken when buffing so that the paint does not get burnt.

Chapter 9
The Interior

While the exterior of any street machine is the public view, the interior is just as important. Building a killer-looking car is only half the job. Sure, there is something to be said for a low-buck machine with a huge motor, four-speed, and original interior, but that does not mean it needs to smell. A killer street machine needs a clean interior—original, custom, or otherwise—just as long as it looks good, feels good, and doesn't reek.

Interior work requires a few specialty tools that you are not likely to own already. The main tool you need is a pair of hog ring pliers. These specialty pliers are used to crimp hog rings. Hog rings get their name from their agricultural roots. Hog rings are used to prevent pigs and hogs from rooting. Upholstery hog rings are the same shape, only smaller. Hog rings pierce the upholstery and are usually crimped around the wire or steel seat frames. Some builders prefer double

hog rings for extra holding power, but in reality a double hog ring creates two holes in close proximity to each other. This actually weakens the upholstery, which will lead to premature failure and loose covers. Once crimped, the hog rings are very strong, as you will learn during removal. It is a good idea to have a couple of different hog ring pliers on hand: a straight pair for most of the work and an angled pair for those tight spots where the straight pliers won't fit. Just about every seat cover has a tricky spot.

For custom upholstery, you will need a few more specialty tools, some of which you may already have. Tools like a spray gun, heat gun, air stapler, and upholstery shears are likely already in your toolbox. Other tools, such as an industrial upholstery sewing machine and vinyl tools (for gently stretching vinyl into creases and corners), are probably not in the average shop.

Don't discount the appeal of a stock interior for your street machine. This muscle truck interior has been restored with a touch of restomod style.

On the other side of the spectrum is the custom interior. You can literally spend tens of thousands of dollars on a full-custom interior, but you don't have to. Exotic materials like ostrich, alligator, and even shark skin have been put to good use in custom street machine interiors. These materials are expensive, but you can use faux materials that look like the real thing yet cost a fraction of the real deal.

SPRAY GUN

Not to be confused with rattle-can aerosol spray glue, upholstery adhesive can only be sprayed from an air-powered spray gun. The aerosol glues like 3M Super 77 are good for gluing patterns to vinyl or wood, but do not use this stuff for any real upholstery. A couple of mildly warm days in a car will render aerosol glue useless, and you will have huge mess on your hands. Upholstery glue is sold by the 5-gallon bucket, which is a lot of glue. You could go through 10 cars before you would use 5 gallons of spray glue. Unless you need it, purchase your spray glue in smaller amounts from your local upholstery shop, where you will likely get your vinyl and upholstery materials as well. Most shops will sell you some glue if you bring your own container. A couple of spray gun cups will go pretty far. You should be able to glue up four door panels and have some left over with a single cup, but it is wise to have a little extra on hand.

HOG RING PLIERS

As mentioned earlier hog ring pliers are used to crimp hog rings. There are quite a few options with these relatively simple and single-use tools. The cheap version, which is sometimes supplied with upholstery kits, is okay. They work. The problem with cheap tools is that they are harder to use, not comfortable in your hand, and they don't last long. If you are spending $300 on a seat cover, you should seriously consider spending $30 on a decent set of hog ring pliers. If you need to install a bunch of hog rings and want the ultimate in hog ring technology, go for the air-powered auto ring gun. These hog ring guns use special rings that come glued together, like staples, and are power-crimped.

HEAT GUN

Not so important for seat covers, the heat gun's main use is for vinyl upholstery on door panels and trim. A little heat goes a long way for getting a tight fit around corners and edges on door panels. A $40 heat gun has many uses; this is just one of them. You can use a cheap hair dryer in a pinch. Using heat judiciously is the key. Vinyl burns quickly, so careful heating is important.

AIR STAPLER

If you do any amount of wood work, you probably already have an air nailer or brad gun. This is the equivalent tool for staples. Mostly used for door panels and trim work, short staples are the best to use. The cheap staple guns use large-gauge staples, which damage wood and destroy cardboard. Stock door panels are almost always made with fiberboard or cardboard (think really thick poster board), so you need thin staples. Most upholsterers use no. 7 gauge staples with a ⅜-inch crown. The length depends on the substrate to which you are stapling. An economy stapler that shoots no. 7 staples will run around $100.

SEWING MACHINE

If you plan to sew your own seat covers and door panels, you will need a sewing machine. A typical fabric sewing machine is *not* intended for thick materials like vinyl. If you try to sew heavy vinyl with a standard machine, you will break needles and burn out the motor. You need a quality industrial sewing machine for upholstery work. Although not as cheap as a standard machine, industrial machines can be had for around $500. The keys to a good industrial machine are gear reduction, metal gears, and heavy cast construction. The Mini-Brute light-industrial sewing machine is perfect for the budget upholsterer. Make sure that the machine has a portable base. Otherwise, you will have to have a sewing table with a hole cut into the top for the machine to rest inside.

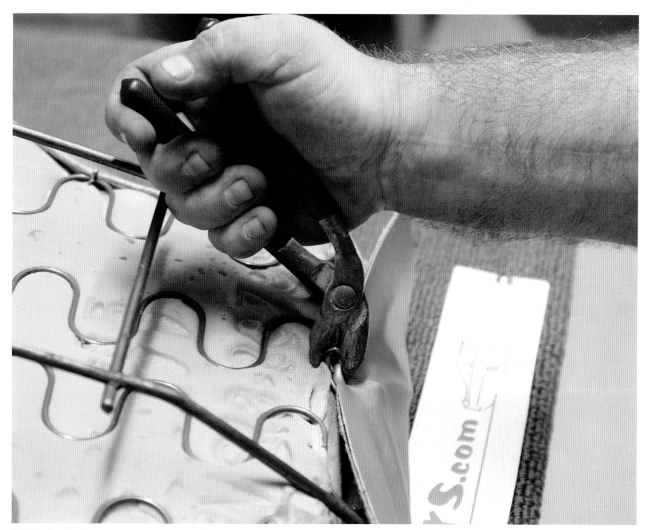

Hog ring pliers like these are used to crimp hog rings. Any seat upholstery work requires these specialized tools.

VINYL TOOLS

Working vinyl into creases and corners is not easy, and you may find it tempting to use a flat-blade screwdriver. The end result will be torn and cut vinyl and a lot of wasted work. Instead, purchase or make your own vinyl tools. Vinyl tools are not expensive and your local upholstery supply will have them on hand. You can use an aluminum plate to cut and shape your own specialty vinyl tools as well.

STOCK

The stock interiors of most economy-level 1960s and 1970s cars (which covers the majority of street machine fodder) are relatively Spartan and simple. This is a good thing when it comes to restoring them. A super-clean stock interior combined with a solid chassis and high-performance drivetrain makes for a truly classic street machine. You can spend the big money where it counts and keep what doesn't need to be changed stock.

Most popular makes and models have a decent aftermarket for restoration upholstery; you can typically find a replacement seat cover for your vehicle and trim level for a decent price. Installing these covers is much simpler than you might think, as long as you take some time and have patience.

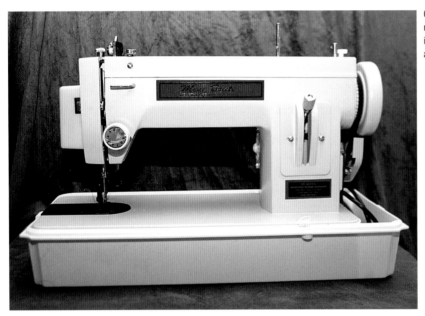

Custom interior work requires an industrial sewing machine. This light-industrial Mini-Brute portable machine includes a base for bench-top use. The gear reduction allows it to sew through six layers of vinyl without stalling.

Working with vinyl is not hard, but you need the right tools. This custom-made vinyl tool allows you to work the vinyl into the creases and corners without damaging it or the substrate.

While a bench seat is not out of the question, most builders prefer bucket seats. Getting bucket seats in a convertible from the factory required a special order in many cases. This 1970 Chevelle had a factory bench, but the owner really wanted Strato-buckets. The main stipulation was that they had to look factory.

The entire interior was removed in preparation for the bucket seat installation. The outer seat mounts work for the buckets, but the center mounts must be welded in place. Anytime sparks are flying, the interior should be removed. All of it.

Using the seat bottom, bolted to the outer mounts for reference, the new inner mounts were positioned and marked for accuracy.

Using a MIG welder, the mounts were welded into place. The floor needs to be clean before the welding begins.

Once the welding was complete, the floor was sprayed with Eastwood's Rust Encapsulator. This coating protects the welds from rusting. All that is left is to bolt in the seats.

Sometimes you get lucky and the interior is in good shape; just a little elbow grease will get it really nice. A quality upholstery cleaner is important. While Armor All looks great, it will actually dry out the vinyl and plastic, which leads to cracking. Instead, a better-quality vinyl and plastic cleaner should be used. Malco makes one of the best cleaners on the market and is an upholstery industry secret.

Malco Vinyl Cleaner will get years of dirt and grime off vinyl upholstery. Another option is to go over the upholstery with a revitalizing cleaner like Meguiar's Quik Out Carpet and Upholstery Cleaner, and a final top coat of protectant. These products do not leave an oily film as Armor All does; they actually soak into the vinyl and add UV protection that actually works.

INTERIOR RESTORATION TIPS AND TRICKS

Not every muscle car is a frame-off restoration candidate. There simply is not enough money floating around for every enthusiast to cruise around in a perfect concours restoration. Besides, a car is only original once. As soon as you stretch on those new seat covers, it is "restored," not original. You say the headliner is torn, the carpet is faded, and the visors are tattered? With a little ingenuity and some basic skills, these issues are remedied quickly and easily.

Headliners are tricky. Most muscle-era cars used spring steel bows and lots of glue to hold the headliner in place. Replacing a shredded headliner is the only solution in many cases, but what if your car just has a small tear or split seam? If the rest of the liner is in good shape, don't spend hours (or days, as it happens) wrestling a headliner when you can spend a few minutes patching up the original with good results. A split seam is more difficult to fix than a small tear, depending on where the split or tear is. A large tear can be patched, simply by sewing in an extra piece of material to the liner. A small tear can be laced together, pulling the tear together. Once laced, you can patch the seam with vinyl repair goo (it works if you follow the directions).

Interior upholstery is sewn with machines. The nature of a sewing stitch uses two threads: the hook and the loop, creating a chain stitch. The hook, the top thread that goes in the needle, is pressed through the material and into the base of the machine, where the bobbin rotates and the loop thread is wrapped around the hook thread and then pulled up through the material. The entire process takes milliseconds and is quite effective—until one of the threads breaks down. Then the entire chain unlocks, and the entire stitch can unravel. This is important to understand because every stitch in your upholstery is done this way. There are locking stitches and other types, but this is how it is done. Stitching a seam in a seat, door panel, or visor is the same, it just takes patience. If you do not have an industrial sewing machine (a regular home sewing machine is not powerful enough, and if it is not yours, the owner will not be happy when you break it), hand stitching is in order. All you need is a needle, some decent thread (three-ply is a minimum; heavy-duty denim thread or upholstery thread is best), and some pliers. Vinyl is thick stuff and pushing a needle can be quite painful when the eye (the part where the thread goes) pushes into your skin, so a pair of needle-nose (no pun intended) pliers makes things much easier.

Faded carpet is probably the easiest task for a quick fix. Sure, replacement carpets are available for a little more than $150, but not all models are available and nothing fits like the original. A can of quality carpet-and-vinyl dye and a vacuum are all that you need for this one. Make sure the carpet is really clean; you don't want to dye any grass into the carpet. If the carpet is nappy, you can use a coarse hair brush to break it up and an electric razor to shave off the fuzzies. Just don't call me when you can't get a close shave the next morning.

As I said, an original interior is only original once. If it is not trashed, try a couple of these tricks to get some extra miles out of it. Spending some time now fixing some stitches here and there may stave off total replacement for quite a while.

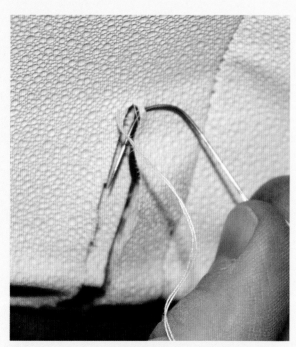

The headliner had split, so we needed to stitch it up. We double threaded a curved needle (you can make one by simply heating a straight needle and bending it). You need to pull off enough thread to get the job done; it is much easier to throw away some thread than to link stitches. Don't tie the thread to the needle. We want strength, so loop the thread, pull the ends together and tie them off. Now you are pulling two layers of thread, increasing the holding power. With the welt pulled away from the headliner, the lacing was started.

The thread was wrapped across the tear into the other side. This is essentially lacing. As the lace is pulled tight, the tear comes together. The finished stitching was then tied off. Simply looping the thread and pulling it tight does the trick. Then the remaining thread was cut away, and the welting was replaced. It is not perfect, but the headliner is not separated and the tear won't get any worse. The stitches can be dressed with vinyl repair gel if you want a little extra protection.

This sun visor looks great, but the sun has disintegrated the thread. New visors are costly, but this one can be repaired with a little labor. The edging was pulled tight so it wrapped up in the curves. Make sure you start where you need the most material. If you stitch up the wrong side and short the edging, you have a problem.

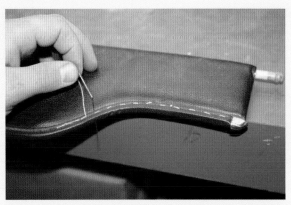

We are not replacing anything other than the thread, so you have the original holes to use as a guide. The needle was threaded through the holes using the pliers to save your skin. Blood, sweat, and tears can be literal here. Just a simple loop stitch is perfect for this task. The original look will come later.

Once you reach the end of the repair area, loop the thread though the last hole and stitch the opposite side. This will give you the chain-stitch look that you want. Once completed, loop the thread under the last stitch. Loop the thread and tie it off. Trim away the excess thread and you are done.

Carpet gets a lot of abuse. Add in some moisture and a convertible top and you get nasty fading. This carpet from a 1971 Buick GS convertible has certainly seen better days, but the weave is good and it isn't matted. It just needs some new color. Starting with a vacuum, the carpet was cleaned up. IA bristle brush helps get the grass and other sticking debris out of the pile.

Starting at the edges, the carpet pad was dyed black. As you go, it gets increasingly difficult to see where you have already sprayed, so a methodical approach is best.

With the entire project dyed, the carpet looks much better. Let the carpet fully dry before putting it back in the car; you don't want to get fresh dye on your upholstery.

RESTOMOD

If the stock bench or buckets just aren't doing it, then maybe a restomod approach would work. In most cases, the idea of a restomod is to keep an original equipment (OE) look, but with some modern touches, such as installing later-model seats and interior trim into an older vehicle. Modern features like heated (and cooled) seats, power options, and better support make new production seats a good choice. Finding newer seats is not too difficult at the salvage yards, and fitting the seats is fairly easy. Nevertheless, matching the upholstery to any existing stock upholstery requires some work. You can replace the remaining stock upholstery with matching OE upholstery to match the seats (the easiest route in most cases), replace the new seat upholstery with a custom-sewn seat cover, or replace it all with custom upholstery. You also must consider updating the door panels and interior trim to match the newer parts.

Headliners are a tricky business. Getting them straight and tight—heck, just getting them to hang right—is tough. This headliner in a 1967 Mustang fastback had seen better days.

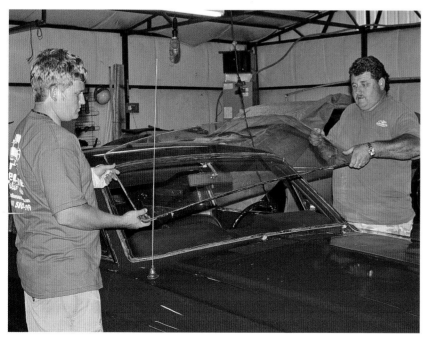

Mustang headliners, like many cars, are held in place at the front by the windshield. So replacing the headliner means removing the glass. Removing glass without breaking it is a 50/50 proposition. We brought in a professional to cut the gasket and pull it loose. Shop owner Fred Murfin and his son, Corey, did the heavy lifting once the glass was loose.

Each bow has a specific order and even hole that it mounts to in the car. As you see here there are several options for the bow. The correct position and bow were marked with corresponding marks so that they will be reinstalled properly.

Most new headliners do not come cut, only sewn. The slots for the bows were hand cut. Don't trim any excess material until the final installation.

Generic contact cement like this is used to hold the edges down. The sides of the headliner are glued in place.

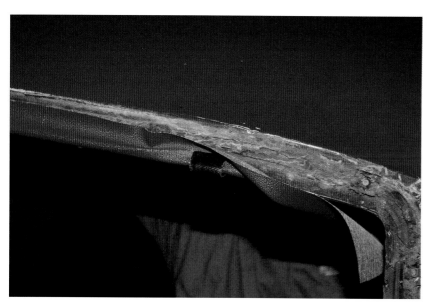

Adjust the headliner until it is taut and even. This takes some time. Once in position, the glue is applied and the edges are clamped in place using pinch welt. This plastic welting has a metal insert that holds pressure on the inner channel. It can be found at most any upholstery shop.

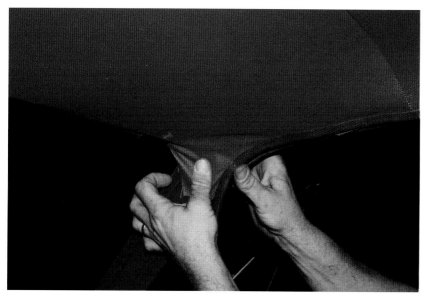

Once the adhesive is dry, the rest of the interior can be reinstalled. Now you can trim the excess material.

MODIFYING DOOR PANELS

Modifying door panels requires forethought. A proper plan is important here, otherwise the panel will not come out like you want it. There are quite a few different materials you can use with door panels, and a million and one designs. The more advanced the design, the more difficult the task. Modifying an existing panel can be as simple as adding a section for a door speaker or reworking the shapes. Most pre-1980s cars have speakers in the dash, and not in the doors. Moving the speakers to the doors brings the sound stage down to where it should be and yields a better stereo image, though moving the speakers to the kick panels is the best option. Kick panel speakers are not always possible, especially with a manual-shift transmission, as the clutch pedal takes up valuable space.

CUSTOM PANELS

Building simple custom panels from scratch is not difficult; it just requires some patience and planning. The key to building a good-looking panel that fits well is to use the original as a template. If the original panel is still available and not in pieces, the basic shape is there. For many muscle car–era vehicles, the door panels were made from fiberboard, a thick cardboard material that does not survive against the elements very well, with a stamped steel upper shell that hooks over the top of the door. This steel piece is the most important, as it is difficult to re-create. Using the stamped steel top piece and the fiberboard as a guide, creating the base for the custom panel is easy.

145

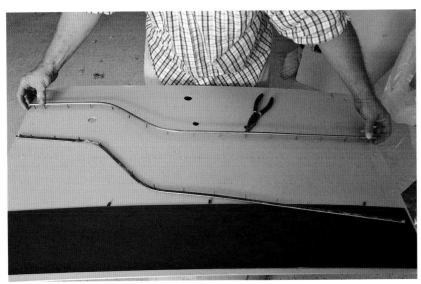

Custom door panels take a lot of forethought. Using a series of fiberboard panels and some chrome trim, the design was laid out and set up on the work table. While this design is actually a restoration effort, the work process is the same.

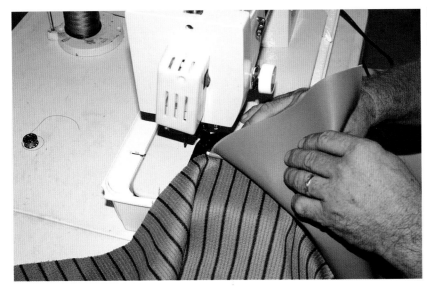

With the material cut and ready, each section was sewn together on the Mini-Brute. Because the seam on this panel will be hidden, a simple stitch was used.

The vinyl and door panel were sprayed with adhesive and applied to each other. The trim tools help get the vinyl to crease left by the raised sections of board. The result is a smooth, flat panel, as the crease allows room for the seam to rest without bulging the material.

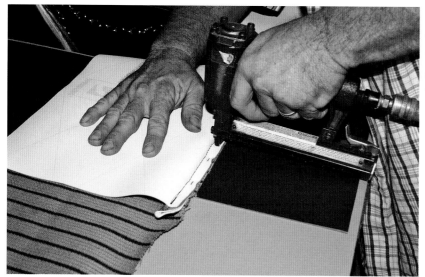

Some areas are simply stapled in place. When stapling to fiberboard, short staples must be used, and the edges that poke through the other side should be flattened with a tack hammer or the butt of a screwdriver handle. If you use ABS plastic panels, staples won't work; the plastic is too heavy and you run the risk of shattering, so the glue is the only binder.

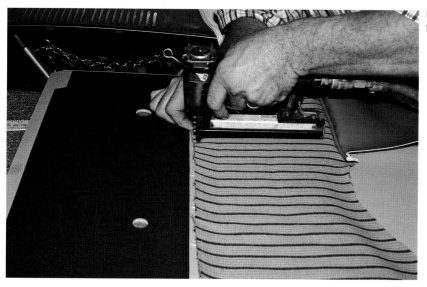

Precision is the key for this area. The chrome trim will hide the edge, but one misplaced staple can ruin the whole job.

The chrome trim was pressed in place. The panels were drilled out in the correct areas before the material was applied. You can't just push the brads on the back side of the strip through the panel.

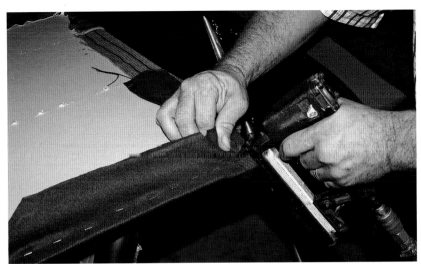

More staples were used to secure the excess material on the back side. Short staples are absolutely crucial here; we don't want any staples poking through the other side.

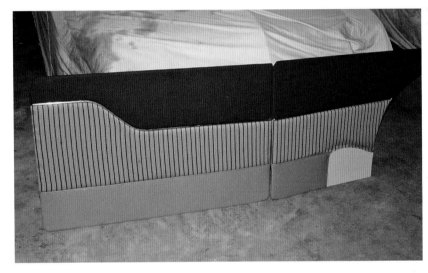

The finished panels look great. These restored panels finished with original materials are going into a 1951 Ford Shoebox street machine.

Choosing a different material for the actual panel is a good idea. Fiberboard is cheap and easy to cut, but it lacks durability. Fiberboard is also a little on the flimsy side; it flexes a good deal and is easy to crease. A better choice would be ABS plastic. ABS plastic is easy to cut, easy tofind, and lightweight, just like fiberboard. Because it is plastic, the elements have no effect, so the panel will last much longer.

Using plastic for the panel allows you to use heavy staples or rivets, rivets being the preferred method. Don't worry about the bumps created by the staples or rivets; they will not be seen. Depending on the design, the outer fabric or vinyl is either glued or sewn to a foam backing that covers the slight bumps and edges from the transition of plastic to steel and the rivets.

WIRING

Every street machine needs wiring. While the original wiring is sufficient for the basics, too many times the factory wiring has been fixed, spliced, and taped and all other manner of things you can do to wiring, none of which are good things. Forty-year-old wiring also adds more resistance to any circuit. Over time as current flows through the wire, it heats and cools. Eventually the wire oxidizes, and resistance builds in the wire. This makes it harder for the electricity to flow through the wire, generating more heat. This is not good, as the wire can catch fire, burning down the entire car. It happens more often than you may think.

When building a street machine from scratch, it is always a good idea to replace the existing wiring. Complete vehicle wiring harnesses are not that expensive. You can get a simple 12-circuit wiring harness from Rebel Wire for under $200. These are simplistic harnesses, but they are made with quality wire and components. You can find more complex wiring harnesses from Painless Wiring for under $500. The point is that you need to ensure that the car will run and that the electrical circuits are in good shape.

WIRING A STREET MACHINE

Spaghetti, rats nest, fire hazard. These are terms that describe the bound-up, tangled mess of wires under the dash called a wiring harness. After 30-plus years, any factory wiring is liable to have been hacked up and modified. This was certainly the case with my 1971 Buick GS convertible. The engine harness had more cracks and breaks than a relay race in a nursing home. The wiring under the dash had been sliced and spliced more times than I care to remember, leaving a jumbled mess.

There really was only one solution, which was to replace the wiring. A daunting task for anyone. Rewiring a car can be intimidating. You could try to make your own harness, buying miles of wire and trying to sort out the plugs and connections, or you could buy a kit.

Painless Wiring offers many kits for various makes. Most kits come complete with factory plugs, terminals, and circuits. As an added benefit, the kits replace the stock glass-style fusebox with new blade-style fuses, which are more reliable and easier to find in an emergency, while maintaining the OEM fuse panel shape in vehicle-specific kits.

While a Painless Wiring kit might not be the choice for a concours restoration, for anything else it's the best choice. You can choose a 12- or 18-circuit, a complete chassis kit, or an engine harness. The wire used in Painless kits is rated for more than 600 volts at 275 degrees— twice the rating of standard GPT wiring (which is the term for automotive primary wiring and uses an 80-degree Celsius PVC jacket), meaning a Painless kit will provide durable, reliable power to feed your muscle car. Each wire is preprinted with its function and bundled with other corresponding wires to further simplify the process.

Painless offers additional accessories such as H4 halogen headlight kits and electric fan and fuel pump wiring kits to fully modernize your ride without complicating the wiring.

Painless Wiring sent out their 20102 1969–1974 GM Muscle Car 18-circuit wiring kit to replace the wiring in my 1971 Buick GS convertible. The process takes upward of two to three days, depending on how assembled the vehicle is. The GS was sans engine and interior for this build, so that made things go a little faster. Follow along and see how easy it is to straighten out the spaghetti.

The under-dash wiring has become a horrible rat's nest after more than 35 years on the road. There are several shorts and open circuits in this jumbled mess of wire, which not only make it an eyesore but a serious hazard as well.

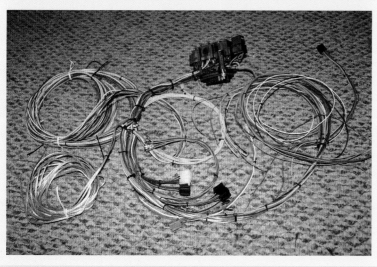

The Painless Wiring kit comes with everything needed to rewire the car, except for ground wires. Each group of circuits is bundled together. Most of the bundles are correct, but there are the few errant wires that require rerouting.

In order to mount the fusebox, the original screw holes need to be opened up using a 1/4-inch drill bit. The original hole in the firewall is perfect for the new box and does not need modification. Using a 7/16-inch backup wrench and a buddy, the fusebox is mounted with a flat-blade screwdriver.

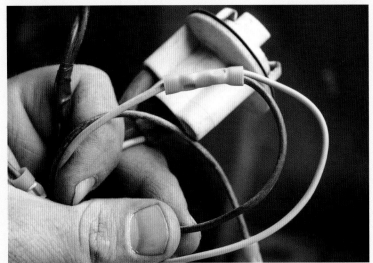

While the kit has most of the plugs needed, there are a few pieces that must be cut off the old harness. The turn signals and parking light plugs are two of them. The kit supplies one wire for each side for parking lights and one for turn signals. The parking light and turn signal wires need to be connected to both the bumper plug and the side marker plug.

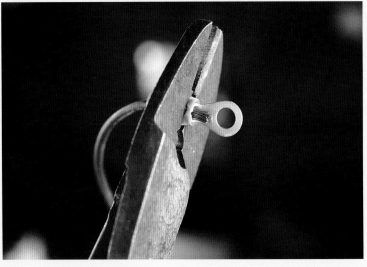

The only ground wires supplied in the kit are for the headlights. This wire gets a ring terminal so it can be screwed to the core support, as was the original. All the rest of the grounds must be supplied by the builder, though Painless does offer a ground wire kit.

Even though the car is a floorshift, GM put the neutral safety switch on the column, as if it were column-shifted. This is important to know when ordering a kit, or the wrong length of wire will be sent and you'll have to cut or lengthen the wires. The neutral safety switch has two plugs: one for the back-up lights and one for the starter switch. Solder the starter wires, as this is an important connection. The kit also includes a Maxi Fuse for the starter wire for safety.

The gauge wiring plugs vary from model to model, so the kit supplies preterminated wires to be installed in the old plugs. Here the old wires are removed from the plug using a small screwdriver or pick. Once the terminal clicks, the wire slides right out.

Remove and reinstall the color-coded wires one at a time so the positions are correct. Each wire has matching color, with each plug requiring a lighting wire. The kit only supplies one lighting wire so it is spliced into the other wire.

You do not have to replace the entire harness. If the wire under the dash is in good shape, free of multiple splices and so on, then you can keep it, as long as the wire is good. Using a multimeter, you can test the resistance level of the wire. Set the meter to ohms (the little horseshoe or omega symbol Ω) and touch one probe to the wire's end and the other to the opposite side of the wire, that is, the fuse block to the end terminal. In automotive applications you need to see less than 0.6 ohms. This is a function of Ohm's law. Most 12-volt (which is what most cars run on) components require 11 volts to function; some will operate on less, but at 10 volts, most do not. Considering that Ohm's law states that

$$\text{Resistance} = \frac{E \text{ (voltage)}}{I \text{ (amperage)}}$$

take a 20-amp, 12-volt circuit (which would use an 11-volt working voltage; therefore, we calculate the amount of useable voltage drop, here being 1 volt), R = 1/20 works out to R = 0.05 ohms. This means that a 20-amp, 12-volt circuit being fed by a wire with only 0.05 ohms resistance will have a voltage drop of 1 volt. While the alternator may maintain 13.4 volts, when the engine is off, that circuit and component may have issues operating. Looking at an operating voltage or 13.4 volts, apply the same formula; R = 2.4/20 equals R = .012 ohms of resistance. This is only better since the alternator is feeding a higher working voltage. Modern electrical components use microchips and processors and not solid-state components such as diodes and resistors, which means that they must have more reliable voltage. If the above circuit was powering an EFI computer or distributor, the engine would have trouble starting because of the high resistance in the wire. It is common to have 0.05 ohms and higher in 30-plus-year-old wiring.

Another critical component of the overall interior design is the gauges. With a high-performance engine, the need to carefully monitor the vitals becomes even more important, especially on a boosted motor, where things can go from blown to blown-up in a hurry. Stock gauges are simply too unreliable to be trusted. Aftermarket gauges are the only way to go. That said, you don't have to screw a little set of cheap triple gauges under the dash to monitor your engine; those tiny gauges are not as reliable as the 30-year-old stockers anyhow. There are some options for retrofitting aftermarket gauges to your dash without hacking it up. Of course, you can always go full-custom too.

Besides the basic speedometer and tachometer, you need the four basics: fuel, oil pressure, water temperature, and voltage. These will get you the basic information you need to operate your street machine. As you start adding stuff like nitrous, turbos, or superchargers, you need to have more. If you are running an aftermarket fuel-injection system like the FAST XFI, you can simplify all of these things into one compact data logger unit. These devices not only perform data logging of all the temps, pressure, spark, and so on, but they can also display these items on a video screen. If you go the full-custom route, you can eliminate the need for a bunch of individual gauges and install a single screen that tells you everything all at once.

If you prefer the old-school approach, individual gauges are the ticket. Most of the gauges you install in the dash or console (anywhere inside the car) should be electronic. There is no real need to pump hot oil to the dash, or install a mercury-filled tube somewhere. Electronic sending units are compact, easy to route and hide the wires, and are reliable. Fuel pressure and nitrous pressure should *always* be sent electronically, as you don't want fuel or nitrous leaking inside the car.

For the most popular muscle cars, there are bolt-in options that replace the factory cluster. These packages typically include speedometer, tachometer, oil pressure, water temp, voltage, and fuel level. The rest of us have to find ways to make the available standard-size gauges fit our cars. Auto Meter certainly tries to help out along the way, with standard gauge sizing and unique concepts that can really add some dimension to your interior design.

One of those unique concepts is the quad gauge. These gauges, typically found in hot rods and customs, feature four individual gauges in a single body. Previously only available in the large 5-inch platform (which fits nicely in a 1950 Ford but not so much in a 1972 El Camino), Auto Meter recently introduced the quad system in the more popular 3 3/8-inch size. This size fits quite well in early 1970s gauge clusters without much work. You can even adjust for gearing and tire size changes with the included electronic programmable speedometer. For those who need more detailed monitoring, the classic 2 1/16-inch size allows for a larger sweep, which translates into easier reading at a glance. All the basics are available, as are the more specialized gauges such as wide-band O_2, boost, pyrometers, nitrous pressure, and so on.

The new DPSS digital shift light reminds you to shift with a set of ultra-bright LEDs. The single stage is nice, but for us, the four-stage with its progressive color scheme is the way to go. In addition, the four-stage unit has peak recall, a launch light, and seven-color lighting. If the nearest drag strip is a little too far away, you could always install a D-PIC performance meter. This easy-to-use gauge measures quarter-mile times, 0 to 60, 60 to 0 braking, g's, reaction time, and it calculates horsepower, all in a compact 2 1/16-inch gauge.

Sometimes installing all the gauges you want is not so easy in a compact space. Drastic changes are sometimes in order and, in a street machine, almost expected. There are a hundred ways to install custom gauges, from the most basic to radical fabrication.

Gauges are critical for any high-performance machine. Most factory gauge clusters are not conducive to retrofitting aftermarket gauges, so custom work must be done. Here an Auto Meter gauge is test fit in a Buick GS gauge cluster.

For a simple solution, three 5-inch gauges were mounted in the stock cluster using ABS panels bolted in from behind like the factory pods. Here we have a speedometer, tachometer, and quad gauge. The quad gauge features a voltmeter, fuel level, oil pressure, and water temperature gauges all in one housing. It's perfect for situations like these.

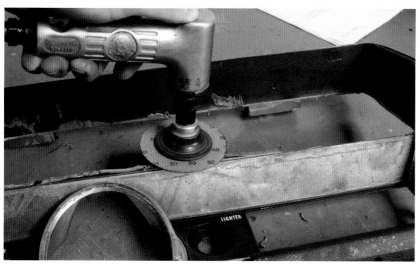

For the more adventurous, you can build a full-on custom cluster. Using the same stock panel for the Buick GS, the gauge cluster section was cut away and ground level with a die grinder.

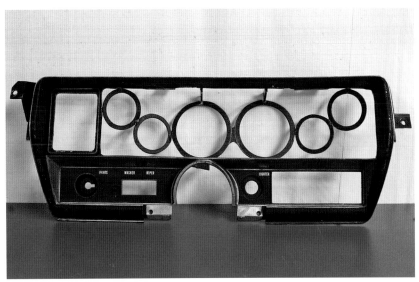

Using ABS plastic, a series of rings were cut to fit the new gauges. The rings were glued to the cluster housing with CA glue (otherwise known as super glue, available at any hobby shop) with small stand-offs.

A mixture of plastic filler and Duraglas (fiberglass-reinforced body filler) was used to complete the build. Mixing the two gives you the strength of Duraglas with the smooth characteristics of the regular filler.

The front side of the cluster was taped up with 3M tape to keep the filler where we wanted it. Then the filler was applied, and care was taken to get it in all the crevices and build it thick so the panel would be strong.

Once the filler had cured, the tape was removed. The result was a clean look that needed a lot more work! A couple of hours worth of sanding, shaping, and more filler got the gauge cluster just how we wanted it.

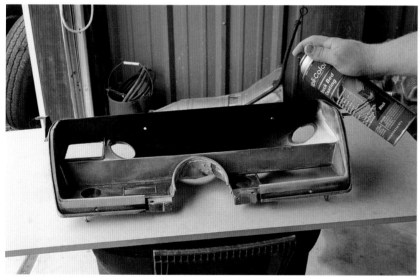

Once it was smooth and ready, the cluster was sprayed with some Duplicolor bed liner. It may sound strange, but this car is restomod, and everything needed to look like it was a factory option. The factory used lots of grain textures and the bed liner, when sprayed from a distance of about 12 to 18 inches, provided the perfect texture.

With the gauges installed, the dash looks perfect. A factory vent will go into the open space to the left of the gauges. The rest of the factory switches and controls that were originally found in the cluster will be reinstalled.

ROLL BARS AND CAGES

As far as safety goes, a roll bar and cage are a good thing. For certain quarter-mile times and classes, they are mandatory. Specifically, the *NHRA Rulebook* specifies that any car running faster than 11.49 quarter-mile elapsed time (ET) requires a roll bar, while 9.99 requires a cage. Things slow down a bit for convertibles, as any convertible running faster than 13.49 requires a roll bar, 9.99 for a cage. If the floor or firewall has been modified, then the roll cage ET cutoff is 10.99. Any car running faster than 135 miles per hour, regardless of ET, requires a full cage.

The construction of the roll bar and roll cage is determined by the sanctioning body, but for NHRA rules, a roll bar must be a minimum of 1¾ inches by .118 mild steel or 1¾ by .083 chrome moly tubing, and cages must be a minimum 1⅝ by .118 mild steel or 1⅝ by .083 chrome moly tubing. Specific diagrams for the dimensioning are shown in the captions.

While a roll bar or roll cage looks great, and certainly screams *street machine*, they can be a bit of a hindrance on the street. Not only do they make getting in and out of the car more difficult, but smacking your head on a roll bar leaves quite a lump on your head and can actually turn a minor accident into a serious trauma. Do not make the decision to add a bar or cage to your street machine lightly. Roll cages and bars are designed to be used with a helmet on. If the car is a street vehicle, as most street machines are, at least try to install the bar where your head will clear it. Adding a bar for appearance only is just not a good idea. Keep in mind, at the

Not all roll cages and bars are welded together. For street machines, Air Ride Technologies created its new TigerCage bolt-in roll bar system. This is a modular kit that simply bolts together using a tubular clamping system. This greatly increases the speed of the installation, while reducing the skill level required as well.

cruise nights, hangouts, drag strips, and car shows, you'll have to back up the need for the cage.

If you need a bar or cage, there are quite a few options. S&W Race Cars offers pre-bent bars and cages for just about any vehicle you may have. These units have enough material to fit in the vehicle, but you will still have to cut, notch, and weld it together. Most roll bars and cages are weld-in style. Air Ride Technologies offers a product to make it easier to install a quality roll bar into the most popular muscle cars. Their TigerCage line is pre-engineered to fit inside the car, stiffen the chassis, and protect the occupants without welding using patented collar clamps. Each kit can be installed in about six hours, all without a welder.

You can always go the custom route and build your own roll cage. It may take some trial and error, but for custom applications, once you get the hang of it, bending and fitting the tubing is rewarding. Most pre-fit kits do not fit tight to the lines of the interior. With a custom-built cage, you can pull the tubing closer to the wall of the interior, making for a much tighter fit, and in some cases, you can just about hide the entire thing. The most important aspect of a roll bar and cage is the attachment points. In order to stiffen the chassis, the cage needs to mount to the chassis. For unibody cars, the roll bar should connect to the front and rear suspension mounts at the main hoop if at all possible, otherwise the following statement applies. The front and rear down bars connect to the body using 6-inch square plates above and below the body sheet metal, bolted together with at least four ⅜-inch bolts *or* with the top plate welded to the body. For full-frame cars, the bars are welded directly to the frame. A cage not only makes the car safer in the event of a crash but also adds significant strength to the chassis, particularly in unibody cars.

To build your own chassis or cages, you need a good tubing bender. For more than 25 years, JD Squared has been building these affordable tubing benders for the professional and the hobbyist alike. For less than $400 (not including the necessary dies), this bender can handle just about any tubing job, even square tubing. This bender is much better than the cheap bargain tool house benders that are good for nothing but ruining a lot of tubing (the cheap ones are meant for thick-walled pipe, not thin-wall tubing).

Chapter 10
Wheels and Tires

Nothing changes the look of a car faster than a wheel change. The wheels and tires can make or break the look of an entire project. As a rule, it is a good idea to pick out the wheels and tires before you do anything else. Even a crusty beater can look righteous with the right set of rollers.

Before you go off and make a purchase, there are some things to consider. The overall plan will have a big effect on the wheel sizing. Chassis modifications, brake sizing, and suspension settings will alter the available room in the wheelwells. First things first: you need to measure the stock wheels.

Measuring wheels is fairly simple, but too often builders make simple mistakes that can end up costing quite a bit. Once you buy wheels and have tires mounted, they are yours, no returns, so you had better make sure they fit. To measure a wheel, you need a long straightedge and a measuring tape. Place the straightedge along the back lip of the wheel, preferably without a tire. If you can't take the tire off, air it down and press the straightedge to the metal. Using the measuring tape, measure the distance from your straightedge to the wheel-mounting flange. You want to measure where the wheel contacts the rotor or hub. This measurement

The right wheels are critical for any street machine build. Too big, too small, or the wrong offset can make or break the looks of the car.

Classic looks combined with modern wheel technology put a new spin on old designs. These wheels from Oasis are patterned after a Hurst design from the late 1960s. In 18- and 17-inch versions, the wheels look old school but have a modern application.

is the backspacing. If the tire is off the wheel, measure the overall width of the inside of the wheel hoop, bead to bead (where the tire sits). Otherwise, measure the front side of the wheel as you did the rear side to find the front spacing. Wheels are typically only made in 0.5-inch increments: 6, 6.5, 7, and so on. Add these two together and you have your wheel width. The wheel diameter will be fairly obvious if you have a tire mounted and can reference its sidewall markings. If not, measure the outer diameter of the wheel hoop at its widest point.

The wheel offset is another key element. The wheel offset is the distance from the hub-mounting surface to the centerline of the wheel. Matching the stock backspacing and offset will ensure that your new hoops have no effect on the car's handling or, in the front, scrub radius, which is the distance between the center of the tire contact patch and the point where the steering axis intersects with the ground.

Measuring the offset will help to ensure that the wheels fit and clear all of the components and the inner wheelwell.

There are three types of offset: zero, positive, and negative. To measure offset, you need to know the backspacing, wheel width, and wheel centerline. To determine the centerline, simply divide the wheel width by two. In order to determine the wheel offset, you simply subtract the wheel centerline measurement from the backspacing measurement. If the backspacing is less than the centerline, the offset is negative; if the backspacing is greater than the centerline, the offset is positive.

Changing the offset will have mixed results. Running a smaller offset pushes the wheel outward, which widens the track width. The wider the track width, the more stable the car becomes, to a point. Eventually the tire gets too close to the fender, and scrubs the fender in turns and at some point during suspension articulation. A smaller offset allows for an overall wider wheel, which increases drag, but the benefits of a more stable front end outweigh the drag increase. For show-oriented cars, filling the wheelwell is important. A small offset does that, as it pushes the tire and wheel outward.

Measuring backspacing is easy. Lay a straight edge across the center of the hoop (preferably without a tire), and measure to the wheel mounting pad.

Offset is a function of the wheels' front and rear backspacing, in relation to the wheel center. Divide the actual wheel centerline width by 2, then subtract the backspacing from the centerline. Most wheel companies use millimeters instead of inches, so convert inches to millimeters by multiplying the inch figure by 25.4. A positive number, + 41 millimeters would represent a positive offset, while a -15 millimeters would demonstrate a negative offset.

Pulling the wheel inward by running a larger offset creates other issues, such as suspension clearance. Rubbing a tire against suspension components is really not a good idea. You have to be careful when selecting the wheel sizing. When increasing the wheel width, it is a good idea to add half of the extra width to the backspacing. This should maintain the original offset. Going from a 15 × 7 with 4.5-inch backspacing to a 15 × 8 with 5-inch backspacing maintains the offset, as long as that extra inch still clears everything.

Measuring the bolt circle is probably the most confusing, even though it is fairly easy. For five-lug wheels, always measure from the outer edge of one bolt hole to the center of the opposing bolt hole (skip from the first bolt hole to the third, for example). For even-numbered patterns, you measure center to center, directly across from each other. The same goes for the wheel studs on the rotor or drum.

Determining what wheels will fit the car takes a little more measuring. While it was stated that picking out the wheels should be the first thing you do, that does not necessarily mean you need to buy them yet. If you plan on making significant changes to the suspension, front or rear,

then those changes need to be made and new measurements need to be taken before you buy the wheels. Suspension components that can get in the way include tie rod ends, A-arms, brake calipers, shocks and mounts, and the inner and outer fenders.

The first dimension to check is the caliper overhang, assuming you are running disc brakes. Caliper overhang is the outer side of the caliper and the inner side of the wheel face. Wheel drop, the center section of the wheel where the hoop steps in to meet the center section, affects caliper clearance as well. You also need to know the caliper radial clearance, which is the height of the caliper to the centerline of the hub. As a general rule, there should be a minimum of ¼inch clearance for any brake or suspension component. Aftermarket brake manufacturers list the smallest wheel diameter that will fit with their rotors and calipers. This is just a minimum; some wheels will fit and others won't. You have to measure everything, and in the end, sometimes the only way to know is to bolt on a wheel. Consult your wheel and brake manufacturers for details on those specific components.

Measuring bolt circles, particularly five-lug, is a source of confusion. The trick is to measure from the center of one bolt hole to the outside edge of a hole across from it, like this (4.5 inches).

(Information provided by Vintage Wheel Works)

Axle pad or **hub flange:** The area of a wheel where it contacts the car.

Bolt pattern, lug pattern, or **bolt circle:** These refer to the number of fasteners (lug studs) and diameter of the circle on which they are positioned. (5 × 4.5 inches would be "five by four and one-half.")

Barrel: The outermost part of a wheel. It is the area where a tire is mounted.

Center cap: The wheel part that covers the center bore of the wheel on the outer face of the wheel.

Center disc: The portion of a wheel that consists of the axle mounting pad and the spokes.

Drop center: The smallest inside diameter area of the outer barrel of a wheel. It is used to facilitate the installation of a tire onto a wheel. Additionally, it is used as an area for placing a center disc for some two-piece wheels during the manufacturing process.

Back space or **rear space:** The distance from the axle pad to the inner edge plane (inboard flange).

Front space: The distance from the axle pad to the outer edge plane (outboard flange).

Hub diameter or **center bore:** This is the size of the hole in the center of a wheel.

Offset: The distance +/- from wheel centerline, indicated in millimeters.

Negative offset: When the axle pad of the wheel is closer to the inner (car underside) edge plane.

Positive offset: When the axle pad of the wheel is closer to the outer (street side) edge plane.

Zero offset: A situation when both the back spacing and front spacing are equal. The axle flange is centered between the outer-edge plane and inner-edge plane.

Wheel stud, lug stud, or **axle bolt:** The "BOLT" portion of the wheel-fastening device. It is what the "lug nut" threads onto.

Lug nut or **wheel nut:** The "NUT" portion of the wheel-fastening device. It threads onto a lug stud.

Tire mounting size: The portion of the wheel that reflects what size tire it can accommodate. Not the overall size of the wheel. Usually used when talking about a wheel size (15 × 7 inches, 16 × 8 inches, 17 × 7inches, and so on).

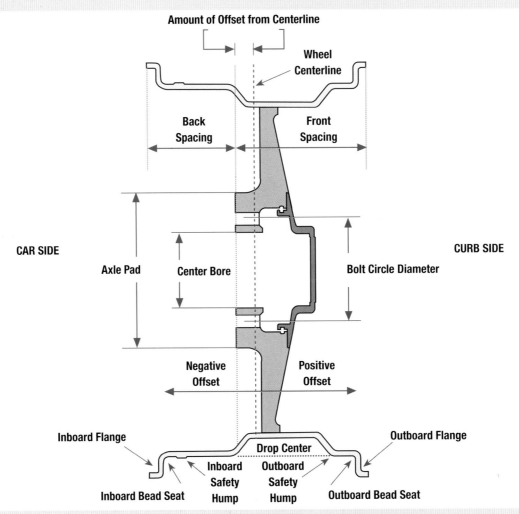

This diagram depicts the terminology of a wheel. Use this guide along with the definitions and formulas to determine wheel fit. *Vintage Wheel Works*

WHEELS AND TIRES

While you can buy special tools to check tire and wheel fit, you can easily build one yourself using simple parts you probably already have on hand. Use a long piece of aluminum angle, long enough to extend out to the full radius of the tire and wheel combo you are considering. If you are considering a 17-inch wheel with a 27-inch-tall tire, your aluminum (or steel) angle needs to reach at least 30 inches. You must consider the bolt circle diameter into the length, as the angle will attach to two wheel studs. Drill one end with holes to fit across two lugs (not as you would measure the bolt pattern, but to clear the hub), and slot the opposite end. Using a

piece of all-thread and a couple of washers and nuts, fasten the all-thread through the slotted end and adjust the rod to simulate the tire diameter. Using this tool, you can rotate the rotor and find out where the rod hits something. Continue pulling the all-thread out until it clears everything, inside and outside. Measure the length inward and outward, and you will have the parameters for your tire and wheel fit. The front suspension is a little tricky, as the front suspension moves throughout its travel in an arc, so you have to make some concessions. All measurements need to be made with the suspension at ride height.

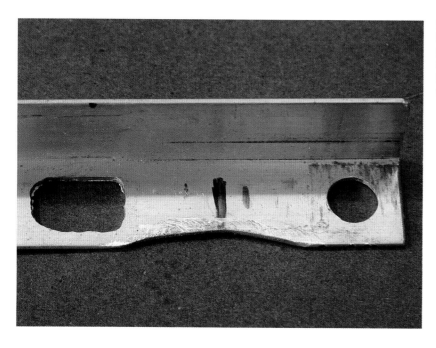

Determining wheel fit requires a lot of careful measuring. Making a tool to do this simplifies the process. Using a piece of L-channel, aluminum in this case, two holes were drilled to match the bolt pattern so it could be bolted to the rotor. This is two-piece tool, so it is adjustable. We cut a second piece of L-channel and drilled it on each end.

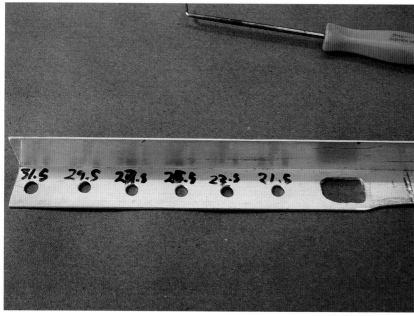

On the piece that bolts to the rotor, a series of holes were drilled to mount the outer section we will use for the measuring. You can do this with a slot instead of the holes.

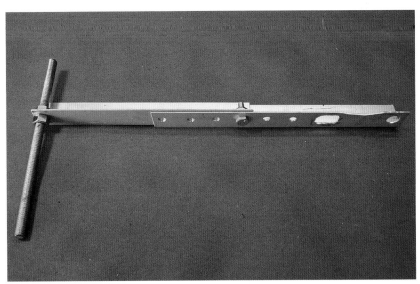

A piece of all-thread was cut to size. You can cut this to tho oxact width of wheel and tire you are using or you can make it larger. This will allow you to determine the maximum fit.

With the car supported by jack stands, the tool bolts to the rotor and is rotated through the arc to find the maximum inner and outer clearance.

Because this muscle truck is lowered with air bags, we also used the same tool to determine the clearance of the tires when the truck is fully lowered. It was obvious that the inner fender wells needed to be modified to get the necessary clearance.

Choosing the right wheels all depends on your style, so to each his or her own, but there are a few other things to consider. Wheel construction is just as important as the design. Steel wheels, aftermarket or factory, are fairly heavy. The rotational forces compound the weight of the wheels. Throw in a large-diameter tire, and you have a lot of inertia added to the rest of the car. This is important, as upgrading the wheels and tires from stock changes the dynamics a little. Aluminum is lighter than steel; cast aluminum is about a third lighter, while forged aluminum is a little lighter still.

Stock steel wheels look great, especially on a sleeper-style street machine or mild restomod. Companies such as Wheel Vintiques even sell widened stock steel wheels and a few larger-diameter stock-style wheels, such as the ever-popular Chevy Rallye, in 16- and 17-inch versions. These wheels look great and perform just like the stock wheels, only with more options for wider tires.

Stock upgrade wheels like these Buick Rallye wheels certainly have their place. For a restomod, these are perfect. There are several companies in the marketplace that can widen stock wheels, so you can look stock, but have an 8-, 10-, or even 12-inch-wide rear wheel.

This Buick takes on an entirely new look with this set of Centerline Retro 17-inchers. Wrapped in Kumho ultra-high-performance rubber, the GS sports a classic look.

On the larger side of things is the Buick GS sporting a set of Foose Knights in 20s and 18s. These wheels are patterned after GM factory Rallye wheels, but with Chip Foose's stylistic additions. There is a trick to choosing big wheels, which is staggered sizing. By putting 20 × 10s out back and 18 × 7s up front, we emulate the look of "big 'n littles" without the risks. Matching sizes between the front and rear tends to make the rear wheels look smaller. Because the rear wheelwells wrap closer around the wheels, it is an optical illusion. Twenty-inch wheels all the way around take a lot of muscle car feel away from the car.

Stepping into the aftermarket designs, there are two trains of thought when it comes to street machines: slightly larger wheels—up to 17-inch diameter for the classic look—or the pro-touring look with up to 20-inch wheels. While some may balk at a 20-inch wheel on a street machine, the masses tend to love them, especially when done tastefully and the car is built to handle the larger rims. The traditional street machine approach used to be "big 'n littles," where the rear tires were very wide and tall, while the front tires were much narrower. This emulates the drag slicks and front runners of a drag car. While some pro-street style cars did this for actual straight-line performance (the narrow front tires reduce drag, hence a faster speed, while the wider rear tires add traction), most used this style for looks. The biggest problem with running a big 'n little combo is safety. The majority of the braking force on any vehicle is on the front tires. By reducing the contact patch of the tire, the front end has less grip on the road. This is not a huge deal for the drag strip, but on the street this is plain insanity. One hard stop and you go sliding into a

For serious racing, you need race wheels. These Centerline forged "Fuel" drag wheels are very lightweight. They feature ribs in the center of the hoop for lateral strength. Some drag race–designed wheels are safe for street use, like the Fuel wheel, but others are not. Lightweight drag wheels are typically not designed to handle heavy cornering loads, posing a risk to the driver.

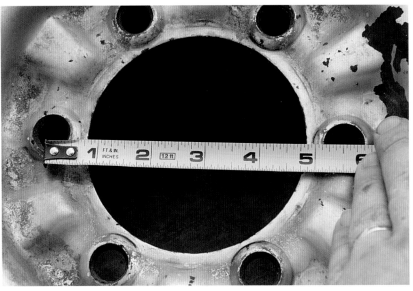

Even-numbered lug patterns are much easier. Simply measure center to center, directly across (5.5 inches here).

ditch or worse. A 6-inch-wide wheel is the minimum you should run on front of any street car; 4-inch-wide wheels are for the drag strip only.

A lowered suspension, tucking the top edge of the rim, is a good look. Low-profile tires complete the set. When you choose to run large-diameter wheels, it is a good idea to run a slightly smaller wheel up front. The 17-inchers work great all the way around (provided the rear tires are a little larger), but 20s and 20s tends to take the street machine look away in favor of more of a low-rider look. Also, a drum brake behind a 20-inch wheel really looks a little silly. Replace that with a clean 11- to 13-inch disc brake, and all is better. The wheel design and size have a lot to do with the overall look of the car.

FORD

1965–1966 Mustangs
It is recommended that you lower the upper control arms per Shelby. Aftermarket kits that incorporate or improve upon the
 "Shelby Modification" are okay.
15 × 4 No specific tire recommendations
15 × 7 195 or 205 or 225/60/15 front and rear
15 × 7 245/60/15 rear only
16 × 7 195 or 205 or 225/50/16 front and rear
16 × 8 205 or 225/50/16 front and rear
 (lowered control arms required with the 225)
16 × 8 245/50/16 rear only
17 × 7 195 or 205 or 225/40/17 front and rear
17 × 8 205 or 225/40/17 front and rear
 (lowered control arms required with 225)
17 × 8 245/40/17 rear only

1967–1973 Mustangs
15 × 4 No specific tire recommendations
15 × 7 195 or 205 or 225/60/15 front and rear
15 × 8 245/60/15 rear only
16 × 7 195 or 205 or 225/50/16 front and rear
16 × 8 225 or 245/50/16 front and rear
16 × 8 255/50/16 rear only
17 × 7 195 or 205 or 225/40/17 front and rear
17 × 8 205 or 225or 245/40/17 front and rear
17 × 8 255/40/17 rear only

1963–1967 Falcons/Rancheros
15 × 4 No specific tire recommendations
15 × 7 195 or 205 or 225/60/15 front and rear
16 × 7 195 or 205 or 225/50/16 front and rear
16 × 8 205 or 225/50/16 front and rear
 (lowered control arms required with 225)
17 × 7 195 or 205 or 225/40/17 front and rear
17 × 8 205 or 225/40/17 front and rear
 (lowered control arms required with 225)

Courtesy Vintage Wheel Works

GM

1967–1968 Camaro
15 × 4 No specific tire recommendations
15 × 7 195 or 205 or 225/60/15 front and rear
16 × 7 195 or 205 or 225/50/16 front and rear
16 × 8 205 or 225/50/16 front and rear
16 × 8 245/50/16 rear only
17 × 7 195 or 205 or 225/40/17 front and rear
17 × 8 205 or 225/40/17 front and rear
17 × 8 245/40/17 rear only

1969 Camaro
15 × 4 No specific tire recommendations
15 × 7 195 or 205 or 225/60/15 front and rear
15 × 8 245 or 255/60/15 rear only
16 × 7 195 or 205 or 225/50/16 front and rear
16 × 8 205 or 225 245 or 255/50/16 front and rear
17 × 7 195 or 205 or 225/40/17 front and rear
17 × 8 205 or 225 245 or 255/40/17 front and rear

1970–1982 Camaro
15 × 4 No specific tire recommendations
15 × 7 195 or 205 or 225/60/15 front and rear
16 × 7 195 or 205 or 225/50/16 front and rear
16 × 8 205 or 225/50/16 front and rear
16 × 8 245/50/16 rear only
17 × 7 195 or 205 or 225/40/17 front and rear
17 × 8 205 or 225/40/17 front and rear
17 × 8 245/40/17 rear only

1963–1967 Corvettes
15 × 4 No specific tire recommendations
15 × 7 195 or 205 or 225/60/15 front and rear
16 × 7 195 or 205 or 225/50/16 front and rear
16 × 8 205 or 225/50/16 front and rear
17 × 7 195 or 205 or 225/40/17 front and rear
17 × 8 205 or 225/40/17 front and rear

1968–1982 Corvettes
15 × 4 No specific tire recommendations
15 × 7 195 or 205 or 225/60/15 front and rear
15 × 8 245/60/15 rear only
16 × 7 195 or 205 or 225/50/16 front and rear
16 × 8 225 or 245/50/16 front and rear
16 × 8 255/50/16 rear only
17 × 7 195 or 205 or 225/40/17 front and rear
17 × 8 205 or 225 or 245/40/17 front and rear
17 × 8 255/40/17 rear only

1964–1966 GTO
15 × 4 No specific tire recommendations
15 × 7 195 or 205 or 225/60/15 front and rear
15 × 8 245/60/15 rear only
16 × 7 195 or 205 or 225/50/16 front and rear
16 × 8 205 or 225 or 245/50/16 front and rear
17 × 7 195 or 205 or 225/40/17 front and rear
17 × 8 205 or 225 or 245/40/17 front and rear

Courtesy Vintage Wheel Works

1969–1970 AMX
15 × 4 No specific tire recommendations
15 × 7 195 or 205 or 225/60/15 front and rear
15 × 8 245/60/15 rear only
16 × 7 195 or 205 or 225/50/16 front and rear
16 × 8 205 or 225 or 245/50/16 front and rear
17 × 7 195 or 205 or 225/40/17 front and rear
17 × 8 205 or 225 or 245/40/17 front and rear

1970–1974 "E" Body
Challenger and Barracuda
15 × 4 No specific tire recommendations
15 × 7 195 or 205 or 225/60/15 front and rear
16 × 7 195 or 205 or 225/50/16 front and rear
16 × 8 205 or 225/50/16 front and rear
16 × 8 245/50/16 rear only
17 × 7 195 or 205 or 225/40/17 front and rear
17 × 8 205 or 225/40/17 front and rear
17 × 8 245/40/17 rear only

1968–1972 "B" Body
Satellite, GTX, Road Runner, and so on
15 × 4 No specific tire recommendations
15 × 7 195 or 205 or 225 or 245/60/15 front and rear
15 × 8 245 or 255/60/15 rear only
16 × 7 195 or 205 or 225 or 245/50/16 front and rear
16 × 8 205 or 225 or 245 or 255/50/16 front and rear
17 × 7 195 or 205 or 225 or 245/40/17 front and rear
17 × 8 205 or 225 or 245 or 255/40/17 front and rear

Courtesy Vintage Wheel Works

As the wheels get larger, the rotational mass and inertia change. Because aluminum wheels are lighter, you can typically run a larger wheel with a similarly sized low-profile tire as a steel wheel without having any braking issues. The rotating force is similar because the tire diameter remains the same and the alloy wheel weighs less. Once you go beyond those specs, your wheels put an extra burden on the braking system. A 22-inch wheel with a 40-series tire will be much more difficult to stop than a 15-inch wheel and a 60-series tire. When running a large-diameter wheel (18 inches or larger), it is highly suggested to use a larger front rotor and caliper at the least. If not, add rear discs as well.

TIRE FIT

The following tire suggestions come from Vintage Wheel Works and are based on factory ride height, suspension brakes, and sheet metal. These tire sizes are known to fit the vehicles listed properly with no clearance issues.

Tire sizing codes have long been a sticking point. The codes seem confusing, but in reality they are easy to figure if you know code. Using the sample tire size 245/40R17 96Z as an example, the breakdown is as follows:

245: Cross-section width in millimeters
40: Aspect ratio in percent
R: Construction, radial

These are the Uniform Tire Quality Grading (UTQG) tire markings you need to be concerned about. The tire manufacturer's website should list all of the pertinent details for the tire you are considering.

17: Rim diameter, 17 inches
96: Load index, 1,565 pounds
Z: Speed rating, Z = 149-plus miles per hour

Dissecting the tire sizing codes is simple. Multiply the width by the aspect ratio (245 × 0.40 – 98). Then divide the result, 98, by 25.4 to convert this spec to inches: 3.86 inches. Multiply 3.86 inches by 2 (upper and lower sidewalls), which equals 7.72 inches. Add the sidewall height to the rim diameter, 7.72 inches + 17 inches = 24.72 inches. This is the overall tire height, to a point. Each tire will have variations due to the manufacturer's tolerance and design.

The last two specs are part of a large group of specs. Beginning with 71, the load index lists the overall load capacity of the tire.

Last, the speed rating is an important one for street machines. This spec notes the maximum sustainable speed for a 10-minute period without issue.

The Uniform Tire Quality Grading (UTQG) ratings list three components: treadwear, traction, and temperature.

Treadwear

The treadwear grade details how the tire wears according to how other tires wear when tested on a government track under specific controlled conditions. A tire graded at 400 lasts twice as long as a tire graded at 200. High-performance tires are typically in the low 300s to high 200s, whereas ultra-high-performance tires run in the low 200s. This means that the tires will not last as long as a 400-rated tire under normal conditions. Doing smoky burn-outs every time you leave a stoplight on 400-rated tires is going to seriously reduce the life of the tire.

Traction

The traction grades are rated from C, being the lowest, to B, A, and AA, which is the highest. The ratings refer to the tire's ability to stop on wet pavement under controlled test conditions.

Load Index	Pounds	Kilograms	Load Index	Pounds	Killograms
71	761	345	91	1,356	615
72	783	355	92	1,389	630
73	805	365	93	1,433	650
74	827	375	94	1,477	670
75	853	387	95	1,521	690
76	882	400	96	1,565	710
77	908	412	97	1,609	730
78	937	425	98	1,633	750
79	963	437	99	1,709	775
80	992	450	100	1,764	800
81	1,019	462	101	1,819	825
82	1,047	475	102	1,874	850
83	1,074	487	103	1,929	875
84	1,102	500	104	1,984	900
85	1,135	515	105	2,039	925
86	1,168	530	106	2,094	950
87	1,201	545	107	2,149	975
88	1,235	560	108	2,205	1000
89	1,279	580	109	2,271	1030
90	1,323	600	110	2,337	1060

Speed Rating

Code	MPH	KM/H	Code	MPH	KM/H
A1	3	4	L	75	120
A2	6	10	M	81	130
A3	9	15	N	87	140
A4	12	20	P	94	150
A5	16	25	Q	100	160
A6	19	30	R	106	170
A7	22	35	S	112	180
A8	25	40	T	118	190
B	31	50	U	124	200
C	37	60	H	130	210
D	40	65	V	149	240
E	43	70	Z	over 149	over 240
F	50	80	W	168	270
G	56	90	(W)	over 168	over 270
J	62	100	Y	186	300
K	69	110	(Y)	over 186	over 300

Drag slicks provide the necessary traction on the drag strip. They should never be used on the street. Sure, they look cool, but hit a small puddle or even a little oil, and you will quickly learn how little traction they offer when wet. Using front runners isn't any safer. The Toyo 4-inch-wide front runners offer minimal rolling resistance, which allows the car to travel down the strip quicker. Put these on the front of a street car and make a panic stop, and that minimal resistance will come into play and provide little stopping force.

Temperature

The temperature grades are A, B, and C, A being the highest. This spec regards the tire's resistance to the generation of heat.

CHOOSING TIRES

Choosing the right tire for your application is determined by how you intend to use the car. A drag car needs sticky rear tires for traction with narrow front tires to reduce drag; a road course car needs sticky, wide tires at each corner for better handling; and a street machine needs a little of both. How you drive, where you live, and when you use your street machine all have an effect on what tires you need. DOT-legal street slicks are great for the occasional cruise on warm summer nights, but toss in some rain, and things can get intense quickly. Evaluate how you will use your street machine before buying your tires.

Most builders will look at two main categories: high performance and ultra-high performance. Ultra-high-performance tires have lower UTGC treadwear ratings, so they wear out faster, but they handle much better. Less sidewall deflection, better grip, and aggressive tread are perfect for a high-powered street machine with the ability to corner well. Ultra–high-performance tires, almost as a rule, are not designed for snow. Not many street machines get driven in the snow, but if you get caught in a snowstorm in your street machine, you might as well be driving with slicks at each corner. A high-performance tire has slightly less grip, but the tread wears better, and most are all-season tires, so they handle well in the wet and the dry.

If you live in a rural area, or the roads are marked with potholes and in general are not good, the really low-profile tire might not be a good choice, at least not with aluminum wheels. Aluminum wheels bend fairly easily; cast wheels can even break. One of the benefits of a taller sidewall is more give for potholes and road debris. Of course, increased sidewall deflection is one of the biggest drawbacks, so a 50-series tire (50 percent shorter than the overall width) is a good place to start. The 35-series tires look great, but the ride is a little harsh.

There are a ton of different grades of tires, each with its own characteristics, but street machines mean performance. These Kumho Ecsta-series tires are an ultra-high-performance design. They are summer tires, meaning no snow or ice. Not that you are going to cruise your 600-horsepower street machine in the snow—right?

For more utilitarian vehicles, such as muscle trucks, you might want to consider an all-season tire, like the classic BF Goodrich Radial TA shown on this 1967 C10. They look great with the classic raised white lettering and will last, according to their high treadwear ratings. Unless you have a heavy foot, that is.

Here's a gratuitous burn-out shot. Once you have the wheels and tires you want, you don't need the old ones right?

Chapter 11
Power-Adders

Building a street machine is all about high-performance. Building a radical engine to pump out massive amounts of horsepower can be quite expensive, and pushing the engine to its limits is not always a good idea, especially for the budget-conscious. There are less expensive ways to add some extra punch to an otherwise healthy stock or rebuilt motor.

NITROUS

When it comes to horsepower per dollar, nothing beats nitrous. Nitrous oxide, also known as laughing gas, is a combination of two nitrogen molecules and one oxygen molecule. This nonflammable gas has been used in dentistry for many years. Once its properties as an oxidizer were discovered, nitrous oxide use was forever changed. Nitrous oxide is a popular oxidizer for rocket motors, because it is nontoxic, stable at room temperature, easy to store, and safer than other oxidizers for flight. Nitrous oxide was recently used in the fuel combination that powered SpaceShipOne (the spaceplane that completed the first privately funded "Human spaceflight" human spaceflight in 2004).

In an internal-combustion engine, nitrous oxide increases the amount of air and fuel the engine can burn, the end result of which is more power. Nitrous is stored as a compressed liquid. As the liquid hits the intake manifold, it expands and cools the air and fuel in the intake, which means the air charge is more dense. This further allows more air and fuel to enter the combustion chamber. There are two main styles of nitrous injection: plate style, which injects the nitrous into the intake, and direct-port injection, which pumps the nitrous directly into the intake port just ahead of the cylinder head. For modern nitrous oxide systems, the bottles are marked "Nytrous +." This means that the bottle can only be filled with a special nitrous oxide/sulfur dioxide mix that makes the nitrous unbreathable to prevent its use as a drug. The sulfur also adds a smell to let you know if it is leaking.

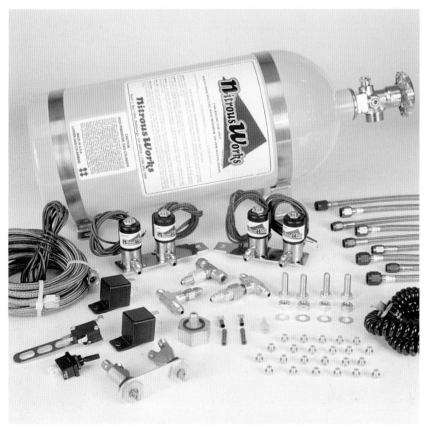

Nitrous is the great equalizer. In terms of instant horsepower, nitrous gives the best bang for the buck. Making big horsepower is expensive, and the ability to use 500 horsepower to its fullest on a street car is limited. When you need it, nitrous can add that extra power at a fraction of the cost of other power-adders.

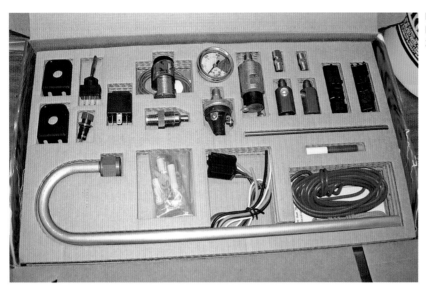

Installing a nitrous system is fairly simple. This Nitrous Express kit has everything needed to install the 200-horsepower system on a 1998 Mustang GT.

There are two solenoids for all "wet" nitrous kits. This is the nitrous solenoid. A purge valve (the black valve on the back of the blue T-fitting) is used to purge nitrous vapor from the system so that there is no delay in liquid nitrous reaching the engine. Never put thread lock on AN fittings, but you do want thread sealant on the pipe fittings.

The fuel solenoid is the second part of the equation. The pressure fitting on the fuel solenoid is used to kill the power to both solenoids should there be an unsafe drop in fuel pressure, which would result in engine damage.

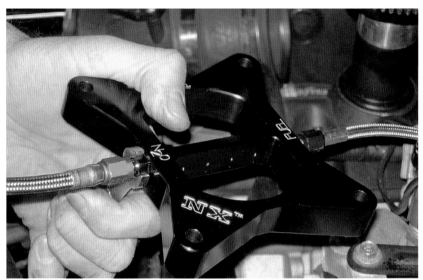

This is a plate system, meaning that the nitrous is injected into the intake with a plate that fits under the throttle body (or carburetor). The jets are in the ends of plate, where the braided lines connect.

Using an adjustable AN-wrench (this special anodized wrench protects the anodized coating on the AN fittings), the line was torqued handtight. AN fittings do not require much torque, just beyond handtight.

The purge lines were routed to the windshield cowl to produce that ever-cool white fog.

The completed plate system was bolted under the throttle body elbow on the 4.6-liter mod motor. This system was jetted for 100 horsepower.

You need at least two switches for any nitrous system. This one used four: bottle heater, arm, trigger (not shown), and purge. The safety covers not only look killer but keep the system from being accidentally armed and triggered. The bottom switch in this photo activates the car's line lock system.

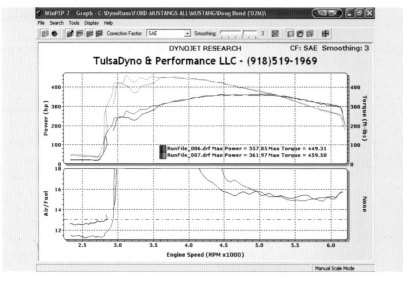

Here are the results of the dyno runs. The nitrous added a little more than 102 horsepower and an unexpected 157 foot-pounds of torque.

The biggest issue with nitrous is also its benefit—that it is an oxidizer. If you spray too much nitrous and don't add enough extra fuel, the engine will get very lean, which will cause engine damage. A nitrous knock or detonation can literally punch a hole right into the top of the piston, wrecking the motor. You must add an appropriate amount of fuel to the engine in accordance to the amount of nitrous you are spraying. Most nitrous kits come with a fuel solenoid and proper jets to make this happen. The proper ratio of nitrous to fuel is 9.5:1; that means that for every 9.5 parts of nitrous, you must inject 1 part fuel.

There is a fair amount of debate over wet versus dry nitrous systems. A wet nitrous system injects additional fuel to the engine; a dry system provides nitrous only. There are a few instances where a dry system is actually acceptable, such as fuel-injected and diesel motors where the injectors are set up to pump more fuel. Diesel engines actually require dry nitrous, as you can't just simply add a diesel solenoid to inject diesel fuel to the engine.

If the motor is healthy, you can safely run up to a 125-horsepower shot of nitrous oxide into a motor with cast pistons without worrying too much about tweaking the timing or burning down the motor. That is not to say that you can't ruin a motor spraying a 125-horsepower shot, but cast pistons can handle up to a 125-horsepower shot. If you want to spray more, you need forged pistons.

When adding more nitrous, you need to ensure the rest of the system can handle the sudden burst of power. The fuel system, ignition system, and driveline must all be capable of handling the power. If any of these systems are weak, the hard hit from the nitrous could frag the transmission, or the sudden extra draw on the fuel system could cause a lean running condition.

IGNITION

Nitrous-fed motors require a more powerful spark. Because the nitrous oxide increases combustion pressure, the ignition system actually sees the increased pressure as if the spark plug gap has increased, making it more difficult for the spark to jump the gap. A weaker spark due to increased pressure will actually decrease overall power, and as the resulting mixture of unburned air and fuel enters the exhaust, a backfire could destroy mufflers and catalytic converters. Later-model stock ignition systems with EFI are only set up to handle stock situations, not serious nitrous injection. The stock ignition system needs to be bolstered with an ignition box, or the stock system needs to be tuned to be able to compensate for the increased ignition demands.

Another ignition-related issue is timing. The timing for a nitrous motor must be retarded in order to decrease the possibility of detonation. The following is a general guideline for nitrous timing:

Up to 100 horsepower: use normal timing
100 to 150 horsepower: retard 2 degrees
150 to 200 horsepower: retard 4 degrees
200 to 325 horsepower: retard 6 degrees
325 horsepower and up: retard 8 degrees

These basic guidelines will help keep your motor together when you hit the spray. Because we are talking about street machines, these are mostly street-driven cars. Driving around with the ignition retarded 4 degrees might not give you the best performance around town. Use the recommended figures to pull back the timing at the strip and then bump the timing back up for the trip home. Or use an ignition box with a nitrous function. This will automatically retard the timing by a specific amount (you select the amount) when the nitrous system is armed, allowing for quick, easy, and safe nitrous play.

FUEL

The fuel system absolutely has to be up to the task of supplying both the engine and the nitrous system with plenty of fuel. A stock fuel system can typically handle the demands of a stock motor and up to 100-horsepower shots of nitrous. If the motor has been modified and requires more fuel, adding a nitrous system will tax it even more, possibly to the point of failure. With even the slightest hint that the fuel system is not up to the task, do not take the risk. There are two methods of bolstering the fuel system for nitrous: increase the capacity of the main system, or add an additional fuel pump for the nitrous. Adding a bigger fuel pump will help provide the engine with the necessary fuel to make it run. A slightly modified engine with a high-flow fuel pump should handle moderate amounts of nitrous. If you are planning on spraying a significant amount, 200 horsepower or more, then you really should consider a secondary nitrous fuel pump. Along with adding extra fuel, it is crucial to add a throttle switch, so that the system is only capable of spraying while the engine is at wide-open throttle. Otherwise, an accidental triggering of the nitrous could destroy the motor.

DRIVELINE

Sudden bursts of power induce shock to the driveline. A weak 40-year old automatic transmission might just blow apart or at least start slipping when hit by a big shock. Ensuring that all of the components are in good health and can handle the increased horsepower and torque from the nitrous is the key. While most nitrous systems certainly increase the horsepower by the advertised number at the rear wheels, what many builders do not consider is that the nitrous will also boost the torque figures by the same margin. A 100-horsepower shot will typically boost the torque output by about 100 foot-pounds as well.

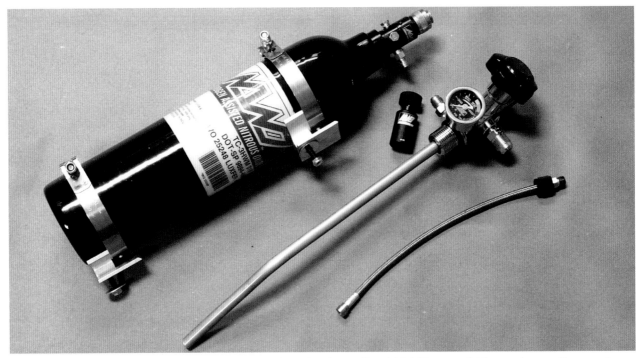

One of the biggest problems with nitrous is bottle pressure. Things like tank heaters have been used to maintain bottle pressure, but these are dangerous. Over-pressurize a nitrous bottle, which you can do by accidentally leaving the heater on, and the resulting explosion can destroy an entire house. This system, from NANO Nitrous, uses inert nitrogen to reduce the effective bottle size as the nitrous is used from the main bottle, allowing the nitrous to react to an ever-smaller environment, thus yielding consistent bottle pressure. This is not a push system and is legal in most nitrous racing classes.

One of the biggest advances in nitrous technology is nitrogen. Nitrogen-assisted nitrous oxide (NANO) technology maintains bottle pressure without expensive and dangerous bottle heaters. As you spray the nitrous down the track, the bottle pressure decreases, because the bottle is becoming less full. This, in turn, reduces the pressure to the solenoids, and the result is less nitrous flow into the engine, reducing its effect. With NANO technology, the bottle pressure is maintained by injecting inert nitrogen into the bottle from a separate piggyback bottle. This does not push nitrous out; instead it simply takes up the additional space in the tank, allowing the nitrous to simply react to the bottle as it if were becoming smaller, maintaining consistent nitrous density. This maintains full pressure without a bottle heater.

SUPERCHARGERS

For more consistent power, a bolt-on supercharger delivers. Unlike nitrous, a supercharger is always there, forcing air into the motor. There are two main styles of superchargers: Roots and centrifugal. They both perform the same function, but with different mounting options. A supercharger uses rotors, impellers, or screws to force outside air into the motor. One of the greatest things about a blower is that the intake design becomes moot. It really doesn't matter if the intake does not flow well. A stock, chunky cast-iron intake can make great power when the air is being forced inside. Supercharging is

a great option for otherwise healthy low-compression stock motors. You can realize a 40 percent increase in horsepower from a simple Roots supercharger install on a stock motor.

Roots

There are two styles of Roots-based blower: the true Roots design and the screw design. The Roots blower gets its name from the inventors, the Roots brothers, who used the mechanism to pump air into mineshafts. Most Roots blowers run two- or three-lobe rotors. As the engine spins, the rotors compress and pump air into the engine. Roots-style blowers are draw-through, meaning they draw air through the carburetor or throttle body. Installing a Roots blower requires an engine-specific intake manifold or a custom sheetmetal intake. Roots blowers make power from just above idle to wide open throttle (WOT), though the boost level tapers off at high rpm. Additionally, nothing looks more aggressive than a Roots blower hanging out of the hood.

Screw-style superchargers are based on the Roots design but are a little different. These blowers are more efficient than the Roots design and therefore can pump more air into the engine. Whipple superchargers use the screw design with great success. They make great power at low rpm, are reliable, and do not generate as much heat as a Roots blower. The overall level of boost is not as high as the other design, and they have a flat power curve.

Whipple superchargers are based on the screw design. Just like the screw air compressor, the Whipple charger compresses the air as it comes into the unit. This yields a consistent level of boost throughout the rpm range and with very high efficiency.

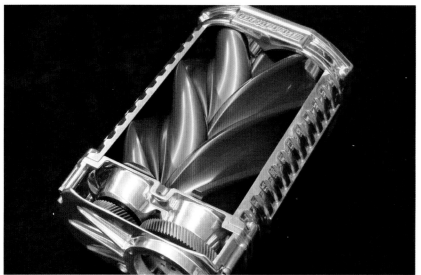

The screws themselves are the key to the Whipple charger. One male rotor and one female rotor rotate together to compress the air that gets trapped between the screws. This is what generates the boost.

The traditional Roots supercharger is not as efficient as the screw type, but it offers things the Whipple does not, like the classic gear whine, the appearance of a big, obnoxious blower hanging out of the hood—all the cool stuff. This Roots unit from Magnuson is compact and fits under the hood for many applications.

Where other Roots blowers have a mostly flat rotor, the Magnacharger uses a 72-degree twist on the lobes of the rotors. This creates a high helix, which makes the blower much more efficient and produces less noise. This design makes a real difference. Most builders who use a Magnacharger see a real power increase of 40 percent in the midrange, not in the upper end, as with the centrifugal supercharger.

The centrifugal supercharger is the most flexible in terms of installation. Where screw and Roots units require engine-specific intake manifolds, the centrifugal unit simply mounts to the front of the engine and is powered off the main belts. If there is not a bracket for your engine, you can make one a lot easier than you can fabricate an intake.

Vortech uses this carburetor enclosure to force the boosted air into the engine, which allows the entire carb to work within the pressurized environment created by the supercharger. For more custom applications, a simple carburetor hat will do the trick.

CENTRIFUGAL

What has become the standard for aftermarket superchargers, the centrifugal supercharger is the most versatile. Because most centrifugal blowers are of the blow-through design, the centrifugal unit mounts to the front of the motor, allowing nearly any engine to be supercharged. There are some custom-designed draw-through centrifugal setups, but most simply use a blower hat that installs over the carburetor or throttle body like an air cleaner. Centrifugal superchargers use an impeller, much like a turbocharger, which pulls air into the inlet and forces it out to the motor. Being belt-driven, there is not as much lag as you have with a turbo setup; however, this means that there is some extra drag on the engine, which means that the horsepower increase costs a little more in terms of power consumption. Centrifugal superchargers run cooler, so the air charge is cooler, and they are incredibly reliable. The major drawback for these superchargers is that they make most of their power on the top end, rather in than in the lower rpm range. For a stoplight-to-stoplight car, a Roots blower will have more impressive boost, but on the highway, the centrifugal blower will have more punch, as the motor spins faster.

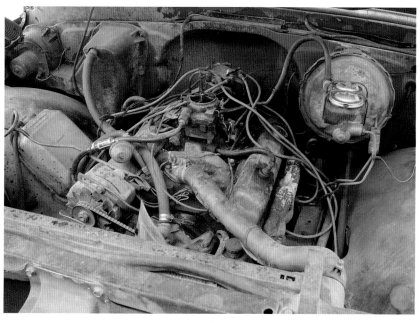

Installing a Roots supercharger is only slightly more complicated than installing a new intake. This otherwise stock 327 in a 1967 Chevy C10 makes just over 250 horsepower with its puny two-barrel carburetor and weak intake design.

To boost the output, a Magnacharger MP112 unit will be bolted on the 327. The entire process should take less than six hours.

The lower crank pulley piggybacks the V-belt crank pulley. Longer bolts are included with the kit. We could have gone with a serpentine setup, but the goal of this project was to show what a stock motor could do with a Magnacharger.

The lower intake tube replaces the stock intake. All of the bolts for the intake are inside the tub, for a clean look. A liberal amount of anti-seize was applied to each bolt.

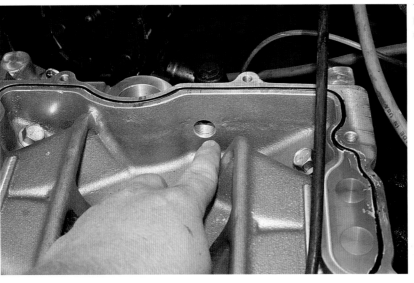

There is a boost reference port on the back of the tub. If you are using a boost gauge, this is where the sending unit goes. If not, plug the hole.

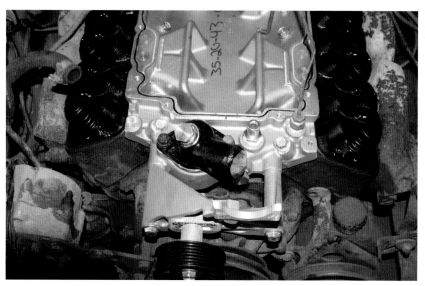

The rest of the intake components bolt on, like the water neck, water temp sender, and heater hose return. The engine will get some dress-up stuff later, but for a retro shop truck, this is perfect.

The intake comes with a strip of O-ring material that rides in a groove on the lower tub. A dab of silicone was applied at the gap so that there would be no leaks.

The final installation looks great. Sure the engine bay is faded and the motor is not bright and shiny, but that is kind of the point for this build. The truck was pulled from a junkyard, got up and running, bagged, and then the supercharger was bolted on. All told, the 327 made 371 horsepower on the dyno. That is a total improvement of 113 horsepower, which is an increase of 43 percent. Not bad for just one day of work.

Regardless of the type of supercharger, there are a few things to consider on the engine itself. Boost means higher cylinder pressures. As the compression ratio increases, the engine's ability to stave off detonation decreases. Boosting an 8.5:1 compression motor with 10 psi is no big deal; it will run great on pump gas. Add the same boost to a 10:1 motor and detonation will become a serious problem. There are some fixes for that, such as high-octane fuel and water injection. For a regularly driven street car, boosting a 10:1 or higher motor with 10 psi is probably not a great idea, and finding the necessary fuel can be tough. If the car is only driven occasionally on the street and sees more track time, then it would not be as big of a deal.

TURBOCHARGERS

The basic structure of a turbocharger is similar to a centrifugal supercharger, as it uses an impeller to produce boost. The biggest difference is that turbos use exhaust pressure and heat to spin the impeller. The basic turbo setup uses a turbine, which is an impeller in reverse, to catch the exhaust gasses on their way out of the motor. This is typically done as close to the engine as possible to maximize power and minimize lag time. The turbine is connected via a bearing-supported shaft to the turbo impeller. From here, the impeller acts just like a supercharger (which it is, but it uses an exhaust drive instead of belt drive) to force air into the engine. There are both blow-through and draw-through turbo systems. Many OEM turbos for carbureted engines are draw-through designs, such as the 1978–1983 Buick V-6 hot-air (non-intercooled) turbo engines, while most aftermarket units are blow-through for ease of installation and versatility. The biggest drawback of a draw-through design is the fact that you can't run an intercooler (atomized fuel may drop out, which pools and is an explosion waiting to happen), as the carburetor is mounted in front of the turbo. Fuel-injected engines are all blow-through designs, and most late-model turbo engines uses intercoolers.

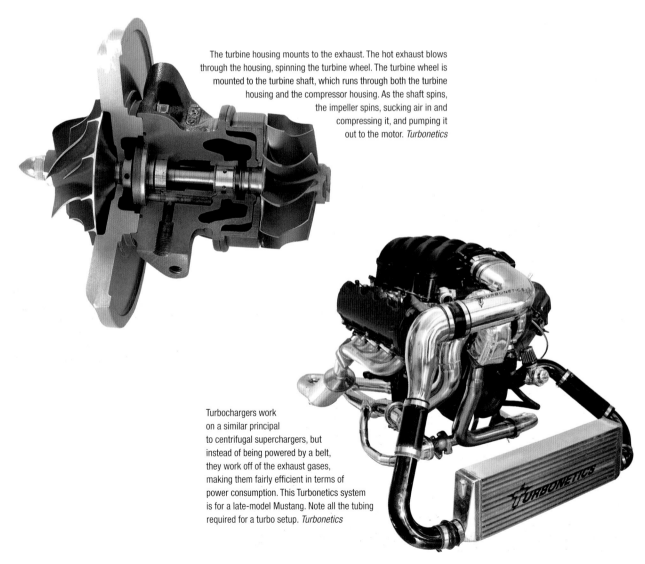

The turbine housing mounts to the exhaust. The hot exhaust blows through the housing, spinning the turbine wheel. The turbine wheel is mounted to the turbine shaft, which runs through both the turbine housing and the compressor housing. As the shaft spins, the impeller spins, sucking air in and compressing it, and pumping it out to the motor. *Turbonetics*

Turbochargers work on a similar principal to centrifugal superchargers, but instead of being powered by a belt, they work off of the exhaust gases, making them fairly efficient in terms of power consumption. This Turbonetics system is for a late-model Mustang. Note all the tubing required for a turbo setup. *Turbonetics*

This twin-turbo setup is on a different type of street machine, a Volvo wagon. While the exterior says "grocery getter," the turbo'd LS1 says "street machine." The engineering on this car is incredible.

The turbo headers are incredibly complicated. This design was all built by the owner, Doug Strickler. These headers are works of art, but they are quite functional.

The blow-off valve, or BOV, is what gives the turbo car its distinctive "whoosh" sound. When you let off the gas, the boost needs to go somewhere. Rather than bouncing back to the compressor and stalling out its blades, which can cause damage, this valve vents off the extra pressure. These can be quiet or very loud, it all depends on how much attention you want. The volume of the BOV does not have much effect on the performance.

Buick made the turbo wildly famous with its Grand National and T-Type Regals in the late 1970s through the mid-1980s. These six-cylinder Buicks made monster power stock and with just minor tuning changes were easily capable of 12-second quarter-mile times without ever popping a seal on the motor.

Heat is a big factor with turbos. The turbine is run off the exhaust gases, so the impeller side is subjected to some intense heat. While running, it is not uncommon for the turbine to literally glow red with heat. This heat is added to an already-hot engine compartment.

On the intake side, the main source of heat is a result of thermodynamic law that states that as air is compressed, its temperature increases. Older OEM designs simply dumped the high-pressure heated air into the engine, which can work just fine, but things could be better. Using an intercooler, the boosted air is cooled down, resulting in considerably more power. There are two main types of intercoolers: air-to-air and liquid-to-air. An air-to-air intercooler passes the intake air through a large radiator with fins, typically mounted in the front of the car just like the coolant radiator. As the ambient air hits the fins, it cools

Intercoolers dramatically increase the ability of a turbo system to produce power. Heat kills power, and a turbo works off heat, so there is a lot of heat that goes back into the combustion chamber. By adding an intercooler, much of that heat can be radiated out. This intercooler kit from TurboXS will make a big difference.

Adding a cooling ring to the intercooler helps cool things down even more. This intercooler ring kit from Nitrous Express sprays either nitrous or nitrogen.

down the boosted air inside, which then goes on to the motor. For street cars, these are great, although they take up a significant amount of space. Liquid-to-air intercoolers are just like the engine coolant radiator, in reverse. The boosted air flows through radiator tubes inside a coolant box that circulates water. The boosted air transfers the heat to the water, cooling the boosted air on its way to the engine. These systems can take up less space (they can also be made really big, taking up the entire passenger seat for race cars) and be mounted just about anywhere, so they are space-efficient. On the street, a liquid cooler is less important. They require more upkeep with changing water, and eventually, the water becomes heat soaked on longer drives. But for drag racing, they are the best bet. You can fill a liquid cooler with ice water for a really cold intake charge.

Another trick for air-to-air intercoolers is the spray bar. Using compressed gas like nitrogen or nitrous oxide, the intercooler is sprayed as you race, significantly dropping the boosted air temperature, which makes for a dense air charge of pressurized air. These systems work just like nitrous oxide, but only for cooling the air charge.

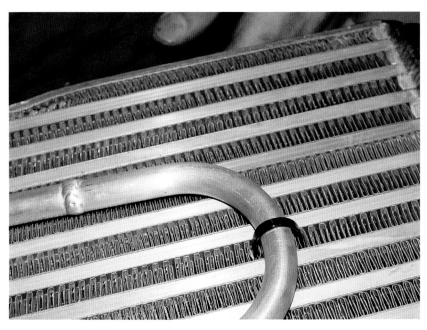

As the compressed gas exits the ring rapidly, it cools the intercooler. It simply mounts with a few zip ties through the fins of the intercooler.

Front-mounting an intercooler is the best option. You want to get as much air to run through the fins as possible. This may require some grille modifications, though. You can remote mount it and use electric fans, but that does not look nearly as cool.

Most intercoolers use a combination of hard tubing and silicone sleeves to make all the connections.

The routing of air in a turbo system is important. You want the boosted air to get to the motor as quickly as possible and with the least amount of restrictions.

SUMMARY

As you can see, designing and building a street machine is not easy. Simply picking a few parts out of a catalog and bolting them on makes for a slightly modified car, not a street machine. A true street machine build has to be planned out and built with care and purpose. If you do not plan it out and build the car toward a specific end, it will never come out right. That said, if you choose to build the car as a street-legal drag car and really enjoy driving it on the street, it may be a little miserable in the long run, so choose wisely.

I hope this book will help you build your street machine. A little caution and patience goes a long way when it comes to a full vehicle build. While some builders can manage to put together world-class cars in a few weeks, the average builder requires years of weekends, vacation time, and late nights bringing the street machine of their dreams to fruition. The Buick GS featured throughout this book took more than four years to complete. Have fun, be safe, and enjoy it. After all, if you don't have fun building it, what is the point?

Index

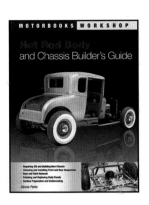
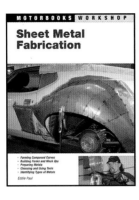

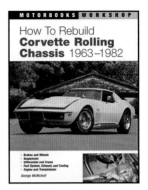

Seventh Edition

MULTICULTURAL LAW ENFORCEMENT

STRATEGIES FOR PEACEKEEPING IN A DIVERSE SOCIETY

Robert M. Shusta
Deena R. Levine
Aaron T. Olson

 Pearson

330 Hudson Street, NY NY 10013

Vice President, Portfolio Management: Andrew Gilfillan
Portfolio Manager: Gary Bauer
Editorial Assistant: Lynda Cramer
Field Marketing Manager: Bob Nisbet
Product Marketing Manager: Heather Taylor
Director, Digital Studio and Content Production: Brian Hyland
Managing Producer: Jennifer Sargunar
Content Producer: Rinki Kaur
Manager, Rights Management: Johanna Burke
Operations Specialist: Deidra Smith

Creative Digital Lead: Mary Siener
Managing Producer, Digital Studio: Autumn Benson
Content Producer, Digital Studio: Maura Barclay
Full-Service Project Manager: Ranjith Rajaram
Full-Service Project Management and Composition: Integra Software Services Pvt. Ltd.
Cover Designer: Studio Montage
Cover Art (or Cover Photo): Alexander Kirch/Shutterstock
Printer/Binder: LSC Communications, Inc.
Cover Printer: LSC Communications, Inc.
Text Font: Palatino LT Pro 10/12

Library of Congress Cataloging-in-Publication Data

Names: Shusta, Robert M., author. | Levine, Deena R., author. | Olson, Aaron T., author.
Title: Multicultural law enforcement: strategies for peacekeeping in a diverse society / Robert M. Shusta, Deena R. Levine, Aaron T. Olson.
Description: Seventh Edition. | Hoboken: Pearson, [2017] | Revised edition of the authors' Multicultural law enforcement, [2015]
Identifiers: LCCN 2017037642 | ISBN 9780134849188 | ISBN 0134849183
Subjects: LCSH: Police-community relations—United States. | Discrimination in law enforcement—United States. | Multiculturalism—United States. | Intercultural communication—United States.
Classification: LCC HV7936.P8 M85 2017 | DDC 363.2/3—dc23
    LC record available at https://lccn.loc.gov/

                                    2017037642

1 18

ISBN 13: 978-0-13-484918-8
ISBN 10:   0-13-484918-3

Dedication

This book is dedicated to police officers and other law enforcement professionals who are building collaborative partnerships, based on trust and mutual respect, with the communities they serve.

CONTENTS

FOREWORD

One of the most profound social changes to impact American law enforcement is the changing nature of our country's diversity. Police agencies across America have struggled for many years with issues of race and ethnicity. Over the last 50 years, these struggles have become even more complex and challenging as large numbers of non-English-speaking immigrants, both documented and undocumented, have come to America seeking economic, religious, or political freedom. The barriers of language, culture, ethnicity, and social expectations have added significantly to the challenges of policing a heterogeneous society. Law enforcement professionals frequently encounter cultural and racial tensions, as well as strongly held suspicion and fear of the police that immigrants bring with them from their countries of origin. Clearly, effective policing of multicultural communities remains an enormous challenge.

As an Arab-American Police Chief in Dearborn, Michigan, a highly diverse city, I am acutely aware of the need to emphasize cultural awareness, including bias-free training and education in law enforcement. Having served on several committees for the U.S. Department of Homeland Security, I can attest to the need for community understanding, accompanied by effective communication and rapport building with people of all backgrounds. Much of the text's message reflects what I have strived to convey in educational projects with local, national, and global law enforcement professionals—the more people trust us in law enforcement, the safer it is for those of us who have chosen to serve.

By embracing the philosophy of community partnerships and community policing strategies, law enforcement agencies, together with citizens, have created some safer towns and cities. To be effective, police officers cannot operate alone; they require the active support and assistance of citizens in their jurisdictions. Central to maintaining that support is the recognition that law enforcement agencies must reflect the diversity of the communities they serve. Every day, officers encounter individuals from different cultural backgrounds, socioeconomic classes, religions, sexual orientations, as well as differing physical and mental abilities. Each of these groups brings a different perspective to police community relations and, as a result, our officers must be prepared to respond appropriately to each group. Failure to recognize and adjust to community diversity can foster confusion and resentment among citizens, quickly leading to a breakdown in the critical bond of trust between a law enforcement agency and its community.

Policing has changed dramatically since the publication of the first edition of this book. There has been a generational shift within the law enforcement community, both in terms of age and diversity. Nevertheless, the challenge of policing an increasingly complex society remains. The need to find ways to address this challenge helps explain the continued interest in this work.

Thus, readers are fortunate now to have access to this seventh edition. Since its first publication in 1995, this work has established itself as a classic in the criminal justice field. The fact that the text has been adopted by and used in police and corrections academies, advanced officer courses, and criminal justice courses is testimony to its far-reaching acceptance.

Multicultural Law Enforcement's major sections effectively address the key cultural needs of law enforcement as practitioners, in increasing numbers have discovered for themselves. The practical contents of the book provide critical information and insight that will improve police performance and professionalism. The subject matter herein, especially the cultural-specific information, continues to be on the leading edge. This edition of *Multicultural Law Enforcement* enables agencies and departments to prepare officers to form partnerships for successful community policing practices within our multicultural communities. It delves into other related topics too, such as gangs, victims of human trafficking, the homeless, the mentally ill as well as international events and their impact on policing in America.

The authors' diversity and collective competence are quite impressive. The three coauthors, collectively, have many years of professional work, including active state and local law enforcement experience and years of conducting training, teaching criminal justice college classes, and consulting. Each author has sought additional cultural information and input from criminal justice professionals and cross-cultural experts from the diverse backgrounds about which they write. I feel confident in recommending this text, and I encourage all who use it to put into action the strategies and tools of this exceptional work for the betterment of your agencies, communities, and the larger society.

Chief Ronald Haddad
Chief of Police, Dearborn, Michigan
Retired Deputy Police Chief, Detroit Police Department
Former Deputy Chief of Homeland Security (Detroit)

PREFACE

This seventh edition of *Multicultural Law Enforcement: Strategies for Peacekeeping in a Diverse Society* is a continuing tribute to all our readers who enthusiastically received the first six editions. It is a textbook designed for use in police departments and academies as well as college and university criminal justice programs; it is used in a wide range of agencies for in-service training programs and advanced officer courses. While the text's focus has primarily been on police officers, in addition to law enforcement, the content applies to other criminal justice professionals, emergency service personnel, correctional officers, border patrol agents, marshals, federal agents, and campus and military police.

Multicultural Law Enforcement, with accompanying instructional tools, is a complete learning package designed to assist users in understanding the pervasive influences of culture, race, ethnicity, gender, and sexual orientation in the workplace and in multicultural communities.

The seventh edition contains updated and expanded information for leaders, officers, managers, supervisors, new recruits, and instructors. It is based on research of current issues facing law enforcement professionals and the communities they serve. For some new sections, authors have conducted interviews with criminal justice professionals and cross-cultural experts from diverse backgrounds. The content revision includes:

- Updated demographics from the latest census, FBI and DOJ statistics
- New section on police–community mutual stereotypes
- Updated examples of police–community outreach programs
- Expanded information on the type of refugees and immigrants police encounter
- Key research findings on implicit bias and its relationship to law enforcement
- New section on the importance of verbal de-escalation
- Updated examples of law enforcement workforce diversity and workplace inclusion
- New content on LGBTQ issues in law enforcement
- Updated national issues affecting cultural, ethnic, racial and community groups
- Expanded information on gangs, the homeless and persons with mental illness
- New chapter section on law enforcement contact with victims of human trafficking
- Consolidated Hate Crimes chapter
- Expanded sections on hate crimes, including additional information on anti-Muslim hate crimes
- New and updated coverage of federal laws pertaining to crimes motivated by hate/bias and information on racial profiling
- New appendices

Throughout the text, we stress the need for understanding of cultural differences and respect toward those of different backgrounds. We encourage readers to examine preconceived notions they may hold of specific groups. We outline why agency executives and managers should build awareness and promote cultural understanding and tolerance within their agencies.

An increasing number of leaders in law enforcement and criminal justice agencies and their employees have accepted the premise that greater cross-cultural competency and improved cross-racial and interethnic relations must be a key objective of all management and professional development. Demographic changes have had a tremendous impact not only on the types of crimes committed, but also on the composition of the workforce and the people with whom officers make contact. To be effective, executives must understand and be responsive to the diversity in their workforces and in their changing communities. Professionalism today includes the need for greater consideration across cultures and improved communication with members of diverse groups.

In an era when news is accessed and streamed instantaneously, the public can witness cross-cultural and interracial contact between law enforcement agents and citizens, as events are occurring or seconds after interactions occur. Community members have become increasingly sophisticated and critical regarding the treatment of members of diverse cultural and racial groups. Police departments, criminal justice and emergency services agencies are now serving communities whose members carefully observe them and hold them accountable for their actions.

With cross-cultural knowledge and sensitivity, those who are charged with the responsibility of peacekeeping and public safety will improve their image while demonstrating greater professionalism within the changing multicultural workforce and community.

We offer instructors and trainers using *Multicultural Law Enforcement: Strategies for Peacekeeping in a Diverse Society* a complete learning package, including an Instructor's Manual, PowerPoint slides, and chapter quizzes. We hope our readers will find our revised and updated text an enhancement to their law enforcement, criminal justice, and public safety programs.

INSTRUCTOR SUPPLEMENTS

Instructor's Manual with Test Bank. Includes content outlines for classroom discussion, teaching suggestions, and answers to selected end-of-chapter questions from the text. This also contains a Word document version of the test bank.

TestGen. This computerized test generation system gives you maximum flexibility in creating and administering tests on paper, electronically, or online. It provides state-ofthe-art features for viewing and editing test bank questions, dragging a selected question into a test you are creating, and printing sleek, formatted tests in a variety of layouts. Select test items from test banks included with TestGen for quick test creation, or write your own questions from scratch. TestGen's random generator provides the option to display different text or calculated number values each time questions are used.

PowerPoint Presentations. Our presentations offer clear, straightforward outlines and notes to use for class lectures or study materials. Photos, illustrations, charts, and tables from the book are included in the presentations when applicable.

To access supplementary materials online, instructors need to request an instructor access code. Go to **www.pearsonhighered.com/irc,** where you can register for an instructor access code. Within 48 hours after registering, you will receive a confirming e-mail, including an instructor access code. Once you have received your code, go to the site and log on for full instructions on downloading the materials you wish to use.

ALTERNATE VERSIONS

eBooks. This text is also available in multiple eBook formats. These are an exciting new choice for students looking to save money. As an alternative to purchasing the printed textbook, students can purchase an electronic version of the same content. With an eTextbook, students can search the text, make notes online, print out reading assignments that incorporate lecture notes, and bookmark important passages for later review. For more information, visit your favorite online eBook reseller or visit **www.mypearsonstore.com.**

ACKNOWLEDGMENTS

We sincerely thank our spouses, Midge Shusta, Michael Lipsett, and Susan Olson, for their unending patience and support during the revision and update of this seventh edition. We are grateful for their understanding of our need to spend innumerable hours at the computer over many months.

We also thank the many experts and reviewers who contributed to this edition. Cultural resources and specialists read and checked our chapters for accuracy. Other contributors provided us with written, up-to-date material that we incorporated in our revisions. Still others provided invaluable editorial and research assistance, enhancing the overall quality of this edition. For this seventh edition, we express our thanks, in particular, to the following individuals, some of whom have also contributed to previous editions:

- Nicole Doctor, Ivy Tech Community College
- Hilda Kogut, Dominican College - Grangeburg, NY
- Rex Scism, Columbia College
- Ken Carlson, Sergeant, Concord (California) Police Department
- Teresa Ewins, Captain, San Francisco (California) Police Department
- Lorie Fridell, PhD., National Expert on Biased Policing; former Director of Research at the Police Executive Research Program (PERF);
- Ronald Haddad, Chief of Police, Dearborn (Michigan) Police Department;
- Ron Hampton, retired Police Officer, DC Metropolitan Police Department; former Executive Director of National Black Police Association; and former Adjunct Criminal Justice Professor, University of the District of Columbia;
- Megan Hustings, Director of National Coalition for the Homeless, Washington D.C.;
- Karina Ioffee, Editor and research assistant;
- Lubna Ismail, President, Connecting Cultures, Washington, D.C.;
- Kay Jones, Intercultural Specialist, Editor and research assistant;
- Howard Jordon, retired Chief of Police, Oakland (California) Police Department;
- Shira Levine, Immigration Attorney, Centro Legal De La Raza, Oakland, California;
- Ilana Lipsett, Director of Social Impact for Tidewater Capital and Community Manager at the Hall;
- Susan Olson, Editor and research assistant;
- Skipper Osborne, former President, Portland Branch NAAC, Civil Rights Advocate;
- Katherine Spillar, Co-founder of the National Center for Women and Policing and Executive Director, Feminist Majority Foundation;
- Glen Ujifusa, Deputy District Attorney, Multnomah County District Attorney's Office, Portland, Oregon.

We continue to be grateful to contributors to **previous editions** for valuable input upon which we have developed further material. We owe appreciation to the following people for their helpful cross-cultural wisdom and its application to law enforcement and criminal justice as well as to those who assisted with our chapter development: Judi Lipsett, editorial assistant; Humera Khan, Executive Director at Muflehun, Washington, D.C.; Christopher Martinez, former Program Director—Refugee and Immigrant Services of the Catholic Charities of San Francisco; Mitchell Grobeson, Sergeant (retired), Los Angeles Police Department; Anthony Pan, Asia Cross-Cultural Consultant; James Johnson, PhD, Social Science Analyst, Administrative Office of the U.S. Courts; Thomas Kochman, Founder and COO of KMA Associates, internationally known diversity specialist; Lieutenant Matt Nemeth, Executive Director of PAL in Jacksonville, Florida; Larry Becker, Deputy Chief of S'Klallam Tribes in Kingston, Sequim, and Port Angeles, Washington; Betsy Brantner-Smith, Sergeant (retired), Naperville Police Department, Illinois; Kathy Bierstedt, Sergeant (retired), Metro Dade, Florida Police Department; and Steven P. Wallace, PhD, UCLA Chair and professor, Department of Community Health Sciences, Los Angeles, California; Kim Ah-Low, Georgia; Chung H. Chuong, California; Ondra Berry, retired Assistant Police Chief, Reno, Nevada Police Department; Jim Cox, retired Police Chief, Midwest City Police

Department, Oklahoma; Captain S. Rob Hardman, USCG (retired), Virginia; Wilbur Herrington, Massachusetts; Jim Kahue, Hawaii; Chief Susan Jones (retired), Healdsburg, California Police Department; Charles Marquez, Colorado; Mohammed Berro, (retired) Corporal, Dearborn Police Department, Michigan; Sarah Miyahira, PhD, Hawaii; Margaret Moore, Washington, D.C.; Jason O'Neal, Police Chief Chickasaw Nation Lighthorse Police, Ada, Oklahoma; Jim Parks, J.D., Criminal Justice Department Chair, Portland Community College, Portland, Oregon; JoAnne Pina, PhD, Washington, D.C.; Eduardo Rodela, PhD, Washington, D.C.; Darryl McAllister, Chief, Union City (California) Police Department, Hayward, California; (late) George Thompson, Founder of Verbal Judo Institute, Inc.

The following additional individuals provided important input to past editions: David Barlow, PhD, Professor and Interim Dean, Fayetteville State University, North Carolina; Danilo Begonia, JD, Professor, Asian American Studies, San Francisco State University, San Francisco, California; Peggy Bowen-Hartung, PhD, Assistant Professor of Criminal Justice, Alvernia College, Reading, Pennsylvania; John Brothers, Executive Director, Quincy Asian Resources, Inc., Quincy, Massachusetts; Patricia DeRosa, President, ChangeWorks Consulting, Randolph, Massachusetts; Ronald Griffin, Pastor and Community Leader, Detroit, Michigan; Sari Karet, Executive Director, Cambodian American Foundation, San Francisco, California; Marilyn Loden, Organizational Diversity Consultant with Loden Associates, Inc., Tiburon, California; Paula Parnagian, World View Services, Revere, Massachusetts; Oscar Ramirez, PhD, Police and Court Expert Consultant, San Antonio, Texas; Jose Rivera, retired Peace Officer, Education Director—Native American Museum, Sausalito, California; Greg Patton, Criminal Justice Cultural Diversity Instructor at Portland Community College; Lourdes Rodriguez-Nogues, EdD, President, Rasi Associates, Boston, Massachusetts; Helen Samhan, Executive Director, Arab American Institute Foundation, Washington, D.C.; Margaret D. Shorter, Sergeant, Royal Canadian Mounted Police and officer of the International Association of Women and Policing; Victoria Santos, President, Santos & Associates, Newark, California; Michael Stoops, Executive Director of the National Coalition for the Homeless, Washington D.C.; Reverend Onasai Veevau, Pastor and Pacific Islander Community Leader, San Mateo, California; Norita Jones Vlach, PhD, Professor, School of Social Work, San Jose State University, San Jose, California; James Zogby, PhD, Director, Arab American Institute Foundation, Washington, D.C.; John Zogby, PhD, President, Zogby International, New York, New York; Brian Withrow, Professor, School of Community Affairs, Wichita, Kansas.

ABOUT THE AUTHORS

Robert M. Shusta, Captain (retired), MPA, served over 27 years in law enforcement, and retired as Captain at the Concord (California) Police Department. He has been a part-time instructor at numerous colleges and universities in northern California and at police academies. He is a graduate of the 158th FBI National Academy and the fourth California Command College conducted by POST. He has served on state commissions responsible for developing POST guidelines and state policy recommendations. (Retired) Captain Shusta has conducted extensive training on cultural awareness and hate crimes as well as Train the Trainer programs on combatting domestic violence. His interest in increasing officers' familiarity with the challenges of policing a multicultural society began with his Command College thesis, introducing a model development plan for law enforcement agencies experiencing demographic changes dues to immigration. (Retired) Captain Shusta is one of the early pioneers to bring attention to the need for cross-cultural awareness in law enforcement.

Deena R. Levine, MA, has been providing consulting and training to organizations in both the public and the private sectors for nearly 30 years. She is the principal of Deena Levine & Associates, LLC, a firm specializing in multicultural workplace training as well as global cross-cultural business consulting. She and her associates, together with representatives from community organizations, have provided programs to law enforcement agencies, focusing on cross-cultural and human relations. Ms. Levine has also consulted with and provided training to social service agencies, educational institutions and corporations. She began her career in cross-cultural training at the Intercultural Relations Institute, formerly at Stanford University, developing multicultural workforce understanding for managers and supervisors. She has published additional texts on the cultural aspects of communication, including *Beyond Language: Cross-Cultural Communication* (Regents/Prentice Hall).

Aaron T. Olson, M.Ed., is an adjunct professor at Portland Community College (PCC), Portland, Oregon, and Eastern Oregon University (EOU), La Grande, Oregon, where he teaches courses on multicultural diversity. He designed the first cultural diversity courses and curricula for PCC's criminal justice program in 2001, fire protection program in 2009, and EOU's fire service administration program in 2011. Outside of academia, he is an independent consultant, specializing in staff development, training, and problem-solving for businesses and government agencies. Since 2003, he has provided multicultural training for fire, police and 9-1-1 public safety personnel. He is a U.S. Army Veteran, retired Oregon State Police patrol sergeant and shift supervisor with 26 years of police experience in communications, recruiting, and patrol assignments. He is a former investigator with Local Government Personnel Institute with an expertise in investigating elected city and county officials, police chiefs, and other government employees for workforce misconduct, sexual harassment, sexual discrimination, retaliation, and gender bias. In 2002, he established public safety workshops for immigrants and refugees at the Immigrant Refugee Community Organization, Portland, Oregon, which ended in 2015.

Impact of Cultural Diversity on Law Enforcement

Part One of *Multicultural Law Enforcement: Strategies for Peacekeeping in a Diverse Society* introduces readers to the wide-ranging implications of our multicultural society for law enforcement, both within and outside the police agency.

Chapter 1 provides in-depth foundational concepts and a framework for discussion of material presented in subsequent chapters. It presents historical and current perspectives of the U.S. multicultural society and demographic changes that have taken place, including the global phenomenon of refugees and immigrants and its impact on law enforcement. Multiple aspects of diversity are introduced, spanning race, ethnicity, culture, and immigrant generations. The subjects of bias and prejudice and their effects on law enforcement are emphasized. The chapter ends with a brief description of effective police management and leadership in a multicultural society.

Chapter 2 presents demographic changes taking place within law enforcement agencies, as well as reactions and responses to diversity within police departments. In addition to content on ethnic and racial groups, this chapter provides information on issues facing women and LGBTQ officers. The chapter also presents the need for proactive work focusing on conflict resolution and on the elimination of discrimination and racism between law enforcement agencies and vulnerable communities. Realities of the changing police workforce are emphasized along with the corresponding need for leaders to bridge cultural and racial gaps within the department.

Chapter 3 discusses challenges in recruitment, retention, and promotion of police personnel, focusing on issues related to gender, race, ethnicity, and sexual orientation. The pool of qualified applicants for law enforcement is significantly smaller than in the past, not only because of the unflattering media images and well-known dangers of law enforcement but also because of societal changes and trends. Strategies for recruitment are presented, including the need for the police chief's commitment to assess and address all employees' levels of comfort and inclusion in their agencies. The chapter describes the pressing need facing departments to build a diverse workforce of highly qualified individuals in which everyone has equal opportunities in the hiring, retention, and promotion processes. It also presents a creative model for recruitment using community policing.

Chapter 4 provides practical information highlighting the dynamics of cross-cultural communication in law enforcement, including specific problems officers face when communicating with speakers of other languages. Communication and responses to cross-cultural contact are discussed along with the importance of verbal de-escalation. In addition, the chapter covers differences in nonverbal communication across cultures and addresses some of the gender-related communication issues in law enforcement agencies. Finally, skills and techniques for officers to use in situations involving cross-cultural contact are outlined.

Each chapter ends with summary points, discussion questions, and a list of references.

- Appendix A, *General Distinctions among Generations of Immigrants*, corresponds to content in Chapter 1.
- Appendix B, *Cross-Cultural Communication Skills Assessment for Law Enforcement Professionals*, corresponds to content in Chapter 4.

1

Multicultural Communities
Challenges for Law Enforcement

LEARNING OBJECTIVES

After reading this chapter, you should be able to:

- Discuss the impact of diversity on law enforcement and the corresponding need for community policing outreach programs.
- Understand past and current reactions to the U.S. multicultural society.
- Summarize key demographic trends related to minority and foreign-born populations in the United States and globally.
- Provide an understanding of aspects of immigration to the United States.
- Define "culture" and "ethnocentrism" and discuss their relevance to law enforcement.
- List the primary and secondary dimensions of diversity as well as generational differences among immigrant and ethnic groups.
- Apply the concepts of stereotyping, prejudice and implicit bias to police work.
- Describe ways that law enforcement leaders and managers can promote bias-free policing in a multicultural society.

OUTLINE

- Introduction
- The Interface of Law Enforcement and Diverse Communities
- Attitudes about the Multicultural Society: Past and Present
- Global Migration, Refugees and Immigrants in the United States
- Culture and Its Relevance to Law Enforcement
- Dimensions of Diversity
- Prejudice and Bias in Law Enforcement
- Police Leadership in a Multicultural Society
- Summary
- Discussion Questions and Issues
- References

INTRODUCTION

> Multiculturalism in the United States has a long silent history. The United States has, from its founding, taken in immigrants from different cultural backgrounds, many of whom were, at the time, controversial. First, it was the Germans, about whom questions were raised as to whether they could or would become "real Americans." Then questions were raised about the Chinese and after them Irish and the Eastern European immigrants. Now it is Hispanic-Americans and Muslim-Americans, of whom we ask those questions. New waves of immigrants have always produced worries about assimilation, but over time, the country's experience is that they have almost all become Americans.
>
> —*Multiculturalism in the U.S.: Cultural Narcissism and the Politics of Recognition Renshon, Stanley. (2017). Professor of Political Science, CUNY Graduate Center, personal communication, January 3*

Multiculturalism and diversity are at America's very core, describing the ever-changing face of the nation. The word *multiculturalism* in this textbook is a descriptive term, and does not refer to a movement or political force, nor is it an anti-American term. The United States is an amalgam of races, cultures, and ethnic groups, evolving from its history of slavery as well as successive waves of immigration. The United States, compared to virtually all other nations, has experienced unparalleled growth in its multicultural population. Reactions to these changes range from appreciation and even celebration of diversity to an absolute intolerance of differences. In its extreme form, intolerance resulting in hate crimes is a major law enforcement and criminal justice concern. Immigration and diversity both unite and divide Americans, but there is no question that they also define who Americans are as a people.

The United States has always been a magnet for people from all over the globe; consequently, demographics continue to undergo constant change. Through increased awareness, cultural knowledge, and communication skills, law enforcement personnel can enhance their relationships, cultural competence, and professional effectiveness with people from all backgrounds. This involves:

- Knowledge of and sensitivity to cultural, national, racial, and social backgrounds (e.g., language and communication issues, minority group history with police, inter-ethnic rivalries, and global events affecting local populations);
- Communication skills for approaching, building rapport, and de-escalating conflict;
- Recognition that biases exist in all human beings, and therefore in all officers; thus, its impact on perceptions, decisions, and actions must be explored;
- Shared understanding, within the law enforcement agency of principles, attitudes, and policies enabling all individuals to work effectively and equitably across and despite racial, ethnic, and cultural differences, with a commitment of equal justice for all.

Individuals must seek a balance between downplaying and even denying the differences of others and, on the other hand, distorting the role of culture, race, ethnicity, and all other forms of diversity. In an effort to "respect all humans equally," we may inadvertently diminish the influence of culture, race, or ethnicity, including the role they have played historically in our society.

In a speech entitled, "Hard Truths: Law Enforcement and Race," former FBI director James Comey said:

> …all of us in law enforcement must be honest enough to acknowledge that much of our history is not pretty. At many points in American history, law enforcement enforced the status quo, a status quo that was often brutally unfair to disfavored groups…The Irish had tough times, but little compares to the experience on our soil of black Americans. That experience should be part of every American's consciousness, and law enforcement's role in that experience—including in recent times—must be remembered. It is our cultural inheritance…One reason we cannot forget our law enforcement legacy is that the people we serve and protect cannot forget it, either. So we must talk about our history. It is a hard truth that lives on. (Comey, 2015)

Diversity has enriched our nation, but has also made many police procedures and interactions with individuals more complex. Racial tensions and communication challenges with immigrants, for example, are bound to complicate some police encounters. Day-to-day activities can be far more challenging when police interact with citizens and non-citizens whose backgrounds are unfamiliar. Regardless of an officer's personal views about the rapidly changing demographic changes in U.S. society, it is essential to work toward effective interpersonal relations and contact across cultural, ethnic, and racial lines.

THE INTERFACE OF LAW ENFORCEMENT AND DIVERSE COMMUNITIES

Those whose professional ideal is to protect and serve people equally from all backgrounds must face the challenges and complexities of a diverse society. A lack of communication effectiveness, coupled with minimal understanding of cultural, racial, and ethnic backgrounds, can result in officer safety issues as well as violations of individuals' rights. Officers, even more than average citizens, must ensure that they refrain from acting on their biases. Officers are held to a higher standard than most others in their contacts and relationships with individuals. Technology and social media have dramatically magnified public scrutiny of police interactions and behaviors.

Ondra Berry, Retired Deputy Police Chief, Reno, Nevada, stated:

> Law enforcement is under a powerful microscope in terms of how citizens are treated. In an age when information about what happens in a police department on the East Coast speeds across to the West Coast with lightning speed, law enforcement officials must be aware. They must be vigilant. They must do the right thing. (Berry, 2017)

A 2016 Gallup poll of a random sample of more than 1,000 people across the country, included the question: "How much respect do you have for the police in your area—a great deal, some or hardly any?" A majority of all Americans expressed "a great deal of respect," although a higher percentage of whites indicated respect for police in comparison to nonwhites. For both whites and blacks, there was a significant increase from 2015 to 2016 (McCarthy, 2016).

This question has been asked in Gallup polls nine times since 1965. Respect for police had fallen to an all-time low in 2015, when racial tensions flared after multiple shootings of unarmed African American men (ibid.). Research published by the National Institute of Justice Journal and the Police Quarterly, to name only a couple of sources, corroborated that the public's trust in law enforcement tends to decline significantly with publicity around such high-profile incidents (Skogan, 2005).

The significantly higher Gallup poll figures from October 2016 followed the tragic murders of several police officers, which had taken place three months earlier. Along with media publicity of overt anti-police sentiments and attitudes in 2016, poll data showed a strong balancing sentiment of respect for and confidence in law enforcement.

Stereotypes about groups, such as communities of color *as well as* the police, are related to the human tendency to overgeneralize, and to base perceptions and conclusions on insufficient contact with other group members as well as inadequate information. In a 2017 survey of almost 8,000 police officers, respondents were nearly unanimous in their belief that the public does not truly understand the challenges and risks of police work (Gramlich, 2017). Lack of information and misinformation contribute greatly to the public's misperception and judgments about police. The media (including social media) from the entire political spectrum play a huge role in how events are reported and how whole groups of people are perceived. Just as minority, racial and cultural groups are subject to stereotyping, the police—as a professional group—are also subject to similar harmful overgeneralizations. People who are prone to stereotyping, including those who stereotype police officers, often categorize the behavior of an entire group based on limited knowledge of a very small number of people in that group. Stereotyping or describing behavior and characteristics based on a small "sample size" is one aspect of how our brains organize observations into categories, but it is a dangerous and inaccurate way of understanding group and individual complexities. (Stereotyping is discussed further on p. 33.)

Community Policing Outreach: Breaking Down Mutual Stereotypes

In urging closer ties between police and communities, former FBI director James Comey said, "We simply must see the people we serve. But the 'seeing' needs to flow in both directions. Citizens also need to see the men and women of law enforcement…They need to see the risks and dangers law enforcement encounter on a typical late-night shift [and the]…difficult and frightening work [officers] do to keep us safe" (Comey, 2015).

A key strategy for peacekeeping in a diverse society involves breaking down barriers and stereotypes that exist for both citizens and law enforcement personnel. This means building mutual understanding in explicit and deliberate ways. Community policing models have always emphasized direct involvement and partnership with civic organizations, citizens and residents, with the ultimate goals of improving trust and safety. Frequent, planned contact between citizens and officers form a basis for improving relationships between officers and community members, one individual at a time. The organizational culture of a police department plays a key role in the success or failure of any specific model of community policing. (Such models have taken different forms, and are referred to in multiple ways, including community-oriented policing, service-oriented policing, and problem-oriented policing.)

Leaders from both law enforcement agencies and the community realize that everyone benefits when each group seeks mutual assistance and understanding. In efforts to be both proactive and responsive to diverse communities, police organizations throughout the United States have been working to develop direct relationships promoted in community-based policing models. Both community groups and the police commit to the notion of shared responsibility for problem solving so that dialogue and communication on public safety issues can take place. This is not a simple proposition; dialogue, relationship-building, and collaboration with community must be an explicit departmental priority, requiring rank and file as well as leadership to embrace a broader beyond criminal justice enforcement.

Many police departments have already adopted community policing as a strategy to meet the challenges of a pluralistic society. The establishment of community partnerships is becoming an increasingly important aspect of facing today's challenges. Human relations training within the agency, whether it focuses on cross-cultural awareness or race relations, for example, will likely be more effective if police–community relationships are developed, utilized, and maintained. The police chief plays an important role in creating and sustaining ongoing communication with all segments of the community. By partnering with diverse community organizations, police have a better chance to

- build relationships with community-based partners and effective collaboration, and often, *before* conflicts arise
- improve understanding of and insight into the needs of specific diverse communities
- reach and establish trust with the most vulnerable groups in the community.

An in-depth discussion of community policing is beyond the scope of this text; however, there are many resources and publications on this topic. Below we present three innovative examples of community policing outreach programs, in which officers have had opportunities for contact and relationship-building with members of diverse communities. Each program example demonstrates a willingness to have officers play nontraditional roles to create structures that can foster positive interactions and trust between police and community members.

Many law enforcement agencies have experimented with a wide variety of programs within their particular community policing model. The New York Police Department (NYPD), for example, under the umbrella of Community Affairs, has created a "Clergy Liaison Program." The NYPD connection with clergy is a dedicated vehicle for communication with thousands of New York residents from many diverse communities. Members of the clergy are usually trusted leaders in a wide variety of communities, including those of color and immigrant communities, and, thus, are in positions to help facilitate dialogue with law enforcement. This community outreach program is described on the NYPD Web site as follows:

The Clergy Liaison Program formalizes the important relationship between members of the clergy, their congregations and the police department, especially during times of community crisis or unrest. Each precinct commander may nominate up to five clergy from across denominations to serve as a link between the Department and the various congregations and faith groups in that community. Clergy receive specialized training from the Department on topics, including bias crime prevention, domestic violence…The Department currently has over 500 clergy in the program. (NYPD, 2016)

The second example involves police–community collaborations in 2016, culminating in job fairs targeted largely to individuals involved in drug activity in the Tenderloin District in San Francisco. Then Captain Teresa Ewins (now Commander) of the San Francisco Police Department always had a strong interest in promoting economic opportunities for young people, especially those in her district who wanted to "get off the streets" (Ewins, 2017). She enthusiastically agreed to partner with multiple local organizations to make the job fairs possible. Her community partners included San Francisco's Office of Economic and Workforce Development, Code Tenderloin (a workforce development nonprofit), The Hall (a temporary upscale food court that also served as a community gathering space bordering the Tenderloin), and several others. In discussion with the Hall's Community Manager, Ewins committed her officers to distribute job fair announcements to people in the Tenderloin, and especially to those on the street known by officers to be unemployed, and in some cases engaged in the drug trade. The job fairs not only resulted in work for some of the job seekers, but also in opportunities for positive contact between African Americans, Latino/Hispanic, Middle Eastern, Pacific Islander, Cambodian, Vietnamese, and SFPD officers (Lipsett, 2017). As district Captain, Ewins encouraged her officers to engage regularly with people on the street to learn about their needs, and to connect them with appropriate organizations (e.g., to help transition homeless people into housing). These types of interactions, including initiatives such as job fairs, are especially valuable in communities where minority group members can see police not only as authority figures who make arrests, but also as concerned law enforcement representatives, actively responding to social issues.

The third example of a community policing program involves outreach to immigrants and refugees in the Portland, Oregon, area. Over a period of 13 years and until 2015, thousands of immigrants and refugees participated in a police outreach collaboration with immigrants and refugees. As part of his community outreach, one of the coauthors of this textbook, established ongoing outreach to new Americans through the Immigrant and Refugee Community Organization (IRCO) (Olson, 2017). Police and community educators oriented new immigrants and refugees about American police and basic U.S. law enforcement expectations of immigrants and refugees.

The police instructors shared with their departments what they learned from immigrants about their countries of origin (see pp. 25–26 for examples). Law enforcement representatives learned that due to major social and cultural differences in other countries regarding law enforcement, many newcomers need basic education about U.S. laws and police-related expectations. The education programs served as a bridge between immigrants and law enforcement. Community policing programs invite mutual education, whether formally or informally, with the ultimate goal of officers' serving the community effectively, and community members' learning to respect the role of the officers' roles and U.S. laws. Community outreach educational programs, codesigned and co-taught by police officers, contribute greatly to relationship building and trust with new community members (Olson, 2017).

The barriers immigrants bring to the relationship with police suggest that officers have to make greater efforts to create opportunities for direct contact in order to be able to communicate effectively and to educate. A further challenge for law enforcement is that new immigrants often become victims of violent crimes. In part, the acculturation and success of immigrants in this society depend, in part, on how they are treated while they are still ignorant of the social customs and laws. The experience in the Portland area demonstrates that community policing outreach, including one-on-one and group contact with newcomers, can set the stage for improved police–community relationships and open communication when it is needed. Further examples of excellent outreach programs in nine different police departments are provided in *Engaging Police in Immigrant Communities,* published by COPS and Vera Institute of Justice (Saint-Fort, Yasso, & Shah, 2012).

ATTITUDES ABOUT THE MULTICULTURAL SOCIETY: PAST AND PRESENT

> I am descended from Irish immigrants. A century ago, the Irish knew well how American society—and law enforcement—viewed them: as drunks, ruffians, and criminals. Law enforcement's biased view of the Irish lives on in the nickname we still use for the vehicles we use to transport groups of prisoners. It is, after all, the "paddy wagon." (Comey, 2015)

In recent years, there has been a growing and bitter divisiveness in U.S. society with respect to attitudes about multiculturalism. On the one hand, some fear that "American values" are being threatened by foreign influences (i.e., with the arrival of refugees and immigrants). On the other hand, others feel that a mosaic of cultures strengthens America, with many immigrant groups' bringing innovative ideas and an entrepreneurial spirit. This divide was particularly evident in the 2016 presidential campaign and in the following months, with the two major political parties' being as far apart on the issue of immigration as ever before.

Accepting multiculturalism and diversity has always been a difficult proposition for many Americans (Miller, 2017), but most police officers go into the profession to serve all people effectively and justly. However, when anti-immigrant or multicultural animosity exists, in the larger society, then any individual or institution can harbor "implicit bias" (see pp. 33–34). Psychological research has shown that all people have implicit bias; this does not necessarily mean that they are explicitly racist or bigoted (Project Implicit, 2011). Rather, it means that people do pay attention to the society around them and to commonly held beliefs and stereotypes.

Typical reactions to immigrants, now and historically, have always included such sentiments as: "They don't contribute to society," "They hold on to their cultures," "They don't learn our language," "Their customs and behavior are strange," "They form cliques," "They take our jobs," and "The economy is suffering because of them."

Are reactions to newcomers today so different from those directed at earlier waves of immigrants? For example, there was extreme hostility toward Irish immigrants who, by the middle of the nineteenth century, constituted almost 45 percent of the foreign-born population. Approximately, 4.25 million people left Ireland, fleeing famine, and seeking economic opportunity. Many had come from rural areas, but ended up in cities on the East Coast. Most were illiterate; some spoke only Gaelic (Kennedy, 1986). Their reception in America was anything but welcoming, exemplified by the plethora of signs saying, "Jobs available, no Irish need apply." Many newcomers, in fact, have congregated in ethnic enclaves; this is particularly true for the first generation of immigrants who, as a rule, have not been accepted by mainstream society.

> The Irish…endure[d] the scorn and discrimination later to be inflicted, to some degree at least, on each successive wave of immigrants by already settled "Americans." In speech and in dress, they seemed foreign; they were poor and unskilled and they were arriving in overwhelming numbers…The Irish found many doors closed to them, both socially and economically. When their earnings were not enough…their wives and daughters obtained employment as servants. (Kennedy, 1986)

If this account were written without specific references to time and cultural group, it could easily describe contemporary reactions to newcomers. We could have taken this passage and substituted Jewish, Italian, or Polish at various points in history. Today, it could be used to refer to Syrians, Iraqis, Afghans, Central Americans, Sudanese, Central Africans, Chinese, Koreans, or Indians. If we compare overall migration patterns, including voluntary immigration in the past few decades with those during earlier periods in U.S. history, we find similarities as well as significant differences. The cultures of more recent immigrants have been obviously different from mainstream society. For example, many "new Americans" from parts of Asia, Africa, and the Middle East bring values, customs unknown to many mainstream American values and language. Middle Easterners bring customs unknown to many U.S.-born Americans. (For cultural specifics, see Chapters 5 to 9.) Many refugees bring scars of political persecution or war trauma, the nature of which the majority of Americans cannot even fathom. The *relatively* mild challenges of those who came to the United States as voluntary migrants do not compare with the tragedies and horrific experiences of many of the more recent refugees. Desperate economic conditions compelled many early European immigrants to leave their countries; thus, their leaving was not entirely voluntary. However, their experiences do not parallel the stories of people who have arrived in the United States, for example, from war-torn Eastern Europe in the 1990s, from Afghanistan and Iraq after 2000, from gang violence in Central and South America, from state violence and religious persecution in African countries, and from the destruction of and terrorism in Syria.

Disparaging comments were once made toward the very people whose descendants would, in later years, constitute much of mainstream America. Many fourth- and fifth-generation immigrants have forgotten their history (Miller, 2017) and are intolerant of the "foreign ways" of emerging new immigrant groups. Every new group seems to be met with some suspicion and, often, hostility. Adjustment to a new society has always been a long and difficult process, and the first-generation immigrant group suffers, whether Irish, Polish, Afghani, Filipino, Central American, African, or Syrian. Also, many recent groups did not come to the United States of their own free will, but are refugees who have been victims of corrupt and violent governments or war, and thus forced to abruptly cut their roots and escape their homelands. Although grateful for their welcome to this country, such newcomers did not want to be uprooted. Most new Americans had no part in the creation of the violent events that led to their flight from their countries.

The Melting Pot and the Mosaic

Was the "melting pot" ever an accurate description of U.S. society? The metaphor depicts an image of people coming together and forming a unified culture. History reminds us that it is a romantic myth about the "good old days." From the time the United States was founded, Americans were never a homogeneous people. The indigenous peoples of America, the ancestors of the American Indians, were here long before Christopher Columbus "discovered" them. There is even strong evidence that the first Africans who set foot in this country came as free people, 200 years before the slave trade from Africa began (Rawlins, 1992). Furthermore, most people in America can claim to be the children, grandchildren, or great-grandchildren of people who have migrated here. Americans did not originate from a common stock. One of the earliest uses of the term was in the early 1900s, when a famous American playwright, Israel Zangwill, referring to the mass migration from Europe said, "America is God's crucible, the great Melting-Pot where all the races of Europe are melting and re-forming…Germans and Frenchmen, Irishmen and Englishmen, Jews and Russians—into the Crucible with you all! God is making the American!" (Zangwill, 1908).

Here "melting pot" was intended to incorporate only Europeans including Eastern Europeans. African Americans, brought forcibly to this country between 1619 and 1850, were never part of the early descriptions of the melting pot. Likewise, Native American peoples were not considered for the melting pot. It is not coincidental that these groups were non-white and therefore could not "melt" easily into the mainstream. Furthermore, throughout our past, great efforts have been made to thwart any additional diversity. Most notable in this regard was the Chinese Exclusion Act in 1882, which denied Chinese laborers the right to enter America. In the early twentieth century, organized labor formed the Japanese and Korean Exclusion League "to protest the influx of 'Coolie' labor, fearing a perceived threat to the living standards of American workingmen" (Kennedy, 1986). Immigration was discouraged or prevented if it did not add strength to what already existed as the European-descended majority of the population (Handlin, 1975).

Even at the peak of immigration in the late 1800s, New York City exemplified how different immigrant groups stayed separate from each other, with little of the "blending" that people often imagine taking place (Miller, 2017). Three-fourths of New York City's population consisted of first- or second-generation immigrants, including Europeans and Asians. Eighty percent did not speak English, and there were 100 foreign-language newspapers in circulation. The new arrivals had not been accepted by those who had already settled, and newcomers found comfort in an alien society by choosing to remain in ethnic enclaves with people who shared their culture and life experiences.

The first generation of every immigrant and refugee group, who saw the United States as the land of hope and opportunity, had always experienced obstacles in acculturation and integration into the new society. In many cases, people resisted Americanization and kept to themselves. Italians, Irish, Eastern European Jews, Portuguese, Germans, and virtually all other groups tended to remain apart when they first came. Most previously settled immigrants were distrustful and disdainful of each new group. "Mainstreaming" began to occur only with children of the immigrants, although some people within certain groups tried to assimilate more quickly.

For the most part, however, society did not permit a quick shedding of previous cultural identity. History has never supported the metaphor of the melting pot, especially regarding the first and second generations of most immigrant groups. Despite the reality of past multicultural disharmony and tension in the United States, however, the notion of the melting pot endured as a component of America's national mythology. Some believe that the terms *mosaic* and *tapestry* more accurately portray diversity in America. These terms are intended to describe a society in which all backgrounds contribute their parts to form society as a whole, but one in which groups do not lose their characteristics in order to "melt" together.

Some want a return to a time when there was much less racial and ethnic diversity in the United States, a return to a more homogeneous population. Leaders and representatives of law enforcement are called upon to call out hate speech and prosecute crimes that marginalize and victimize immigrant and refugee groups that can be vulnerable. In February 2017, two Indian engineers were targeted in a bar in a Kansas because of their foreign-born status. The shooter, another patron in the bar, was reported to have said, "Go back to your country," before shooting. One of the Indian men was injured; the other, killed. In response, a spokesperson from the U.S. Embassy in New Delhi said, "The U.S. is a nation of immigrants, and welcomes people from across the world to visit, work, study and live" (The Guardian, 2017). Law enforcement needs to be ever vigilant about rising anti-immigrant and anti-foreigner sentiment, and must reinforce messages of tolerance.

Changing Population

Record numbers of foreign-born individuals came to the United States at the end of the twentieth century (see Exhibits 1.1 and 1.2) adding greatly to the U.S. multicultural society. In the culture-specific chapters of this book, we discuss Asian and Pacific Americans, African Americans, Latino and Hispanic Americans, Arab Americans and other Middle Eastern groups, and Native Americans. Some individuals may belong to two or more groups; race and ethnic background are not mutually exclusive. For example, black Latinos, such

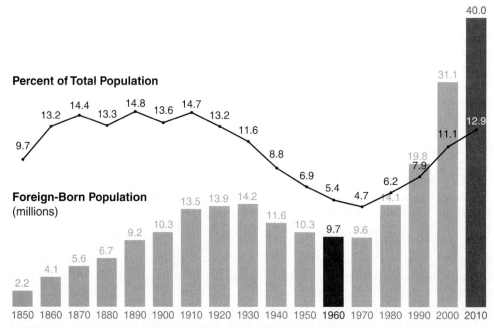

EXHIBIT 1.1   Foreign-Born Population and as Percentage of Total Population

Source: U.S. Census Bureau, 1850–2000 Decennial Census; 2010 American Community Survey. Reprinted with permission.

U.S. Foreign-Born Population Reaches New High

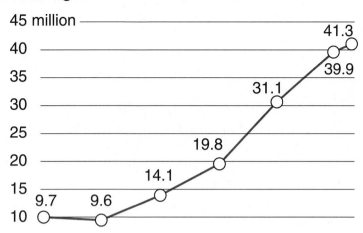

EXHIBIT 1.2   Foreign-Born Population between 1960 and 2013

Source: Pew Research Center, Hispanic Trends, 2015.

as people from the Dominican Republic or Brazil, may identify themselves as both black and Latino. "Hispanic" is considered a category of ethnicity, not a race. Therefore, people of Latino descent can count themselves as part of several races. Selecting a clear-cut category is not as simple as it may appear. In the 2010 census, "Hispanics" primarily identified themselves as either white or "some other race" (U.S. Census Bureau, 2011).

> **Heterogeneous**   Dissimilar, or composed of unrelated or unlike elements. A **heterogeneous society** is one that is diverse, and frequently refers to racial, ethnic, religious, and linguistic composition.

Beginning with the 2000 census, biracial individuals could report being a multi-race combination. U.S. Census information released in 2008 projected that, by 2050, the number of people who identify belonging to two or more races will more than triple, from 5.2 to 16.2 million (U.S. Census Bureau, 2012b). The numbers are probably underestimates. According to the Pew Research Center, the percentage of mixed-race adults may be triple those reported by the U.S. Census (Pew Research Center, 2015). The face of America has been changing for some time. In 1790, the first census had three demographic classifications: free whites, all other free persons and slaves. In 1860, there were still only three but different census categories: black, white, and "quadroon" (i.e., a person who has one black grandparent or the child of a mulatto and a white). Beginning with the 2000 census, there were 63 possible options for marking racial identity, or 126, including Hispanic ethnicity plus race, if people responded in the affirmative to whether or not they were of Hispanic ethnicity. As of 2012, the U.S. Census Bureau established a National Advisory Committee on Racial, Ethnic, and Other Populations to "help us meet emerging challenges the Census Bureau faces in producing statistics about our diverse nation," according to then acting director Thomas L. Mesenbourg (U.S. Census Bureau Reports, 2012a).

Minority Populations

Documented changes in population characteristics between 2000 and 2010 have been dramatic, and patterns are projected to continue through the next decade and beyond. The 2010 census projections show that "The next half century marks key points in continuing trends—the U.S. will become a plurality nation, where the non-Hispanic white population remains the largest single group, but no group is in the majority," according to Mesenbourg (U.S. Census Bureau Reports, 2012a).

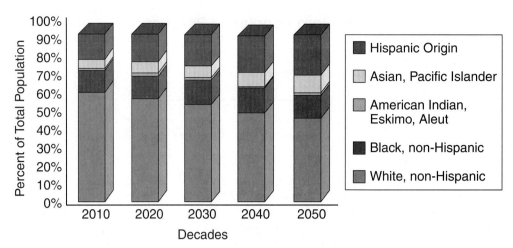

EXHIBIT 1.3   Resident Population by Race and Hispanic Origin Status—Projections: 2010–2050
Source: U.S. Census Bureau, Statistical Abstract of the United States, 2002.

Minority group   Refers to a category of people differentiated from the social majority; part of the population that differs in certain ways from the majority population and is sometimes subjected to differential treatment; a demographic group that is smaller in number than the majority cultural group.

Consider the following report released in 2015

- Around the time the 2020 Census is conducted, more than half of the nation's children are expected to be part of a minority race or ethnic group.
- This proportion is expected to continue to grow, so that by 2060, just 36 percent of all children (people under age 18) will be single-race non-Hispanic white, compared with 52 percent today.
- The U.S. population as a whole is expected to follow a similar trend, becoming majority-minority in 2044. Today's combined minority populations are projected to rise to 56 percent of the total population in 2060, compared with 38 percent in 2014. (U.S. Census Bureau, 2015)

Exhibit 1.3 shows projected rates of growth on nonwhite groups through 2050 and the corresponding decline in the white (non-Hispanic ethnicity) population.

Some of these population shifts give rise to nuances and controversies associated with the word "minority." U.S. Census information released in 2013 indicated that approximately 11 percent of counties (353 of over 3,000 counties) are "majority-minority." Four states— California (60.6 percent minority), Hawaii (77.2 percent), New Mexico (60.2 percent), and Texas (55.5 percent)—and the District of Columbia (64.5 percent) are majority-minority states; this means that the percentage of minority residents in these counties and states has exceeded 50 percent (U.S. Census Bureau, 2013). Majority-minority counties are growing in rural and urban areas alike. This change has had a huge impact on many institutions in society, including the law enforcement workforce. (See Chapter 2.)

GLOBAL MIGRATION, REFUGEES AND IMMIGRANTS IN THE UNITED STATES

To provide a global perspective on refugees in 2016, one out of every 113 people in the world had been displaced by war, persecution, or threat of death from or within his or her country of origin. The United Nations High Commissioner for Refugees (UNHCR) reported that, at the end of 2016, there were 65.6 million displaced people, a record number, and greater than after World War II (UNHCR, 2017).

The majority of the 70,000 refugees who came to the United States that year were from Somalia, Myanmar, and Iraq. In 2015, Syrian refugees represented only 2 percent of the overall refugee population to the United States (UNHCR, 2016b). The vast majority of refugees from Syria have gone to neighboring countries, Turkey, Lebanon, and Jordan, the next largest number to Europe, and a relatively small number to the United States (approximately 12,500 as of December 2016 [ibid.]). In 2015 and 2016, as Americans increasingly learned of the migration of Syrian refugees through Europe's open borders, strong reactions from all political points of view followed. The rigorous vetting process for U.S. refugees, *prior* to their arrival in the United States, is not at all similar to the manner in which asylum seekers have entered Europe, where there has been no vetting at all. The phenomenon of legal refugees from Syria has sparked a fierce backlash from some Americans, even though Syrian refugees have entered the United States, legally. At the same time, many volunteers have stepped forward through resettlement agencies and faith organizations to contribute compassionately to refugee resettlement. Presented with a choice to return to their homelands if there were no threat of persecution or death, many refugees would likely choose to return home. Newspaper articles reporting, on Syrian refugees for example, alluded to the dream that many have to return to Syria when the country is no longer torn apart by civil war and terrorism (Based on Tharoor, 2016; Miles, 2016).

> **Refugee**   "Any person who is outside his or her country of nationality who is unable or unwilling to return to that country because of persecution or a well-founded fear of persecution. Persecution or the fear thereof must be based on…race, religion, nationality, membership in a particular social group, or political opinion. People with no nationality must generally be outside their country of last habitual residence to qualify as a refugee." (Department of Homeland Security, 2013a)

Global migration and displacement affect the U.S. population in a direct way. According to treaties signed at the "Convention Relating to the Status of Refugees," also known as the 1951 Refugee Convention, individuals defined as refugees have a legal right NOT to be sent back home, where their lives are in danger. "Since by definition, refugees are not protected by their own governments, the international community steps in to ensure that they are safe and protected" (UNHCR, "Convention and Protocol Relating to the Status of Refugees,"). This treaty was created after hundreds of thousands of people had been displaced throughout Europe following WWII. The 1951 Treaty was later expanded to include refugees from countries outside Europe (ibid.).

> The core principle [of the Convention and Protocol Relating to the Status of Refugees]
>
> …asserts that a refugee[s] should not be returned to a country where they face serious threats to their life or freedom. This is considered a rule of customary international law. (UNHCR, 1951 Refugee Convention)

Treaties giving rights to refugees mandate that the signatory countries have a legal obligation to protect those whose lives are endangered, and who cannot go home. Over the past several decades, 145 countries, including the United States, have signed on to both the 1951 Refugee Convention and the 1967 amended treaty (ibid.).

Refugees who enter into the United States are rigorously vetted (see Exhibit 1.4); the process takes from 18 to 24 months. In the case of Syrian refugees, the process has been even more rigorous, and includes extra security checks (U.S. Department of State, 2015a). This is in stark contrast to migrant entry in Europe, where people do not have refugee status before they arrive. At the time of this writing, the refugee vetting process involved multiple agencies, in the following order (Whitehouse.gov, 2015):

The Foreign-Born Population in the United States

"Foreign born" are considered to be individuals who were not U.S. citizens at birth, and include the following:

- Naturalized U.S. citizens (i.e., immigrants who have been granted U.S. citizenship)
- Legal (or lawful) permanent residents (i.e., non-citizens who are authorized to live and work in the United States on a permanent basis)

- United Nations High Commissioner for Refugees (UNHCR)
- Resettlement Support Centers
- National Counterterrorism Center/Intelligence Community
- Federal Bureau of Investigation
- Department of Homeland Security
- U.S. Department of State
- U.S. Customs and Immigration Service
- U.S. Department of Defense

EXHIBIT 1.4   The Screening Process for Refugee Entry into the
United States (18–24 Month Process)
Source: Whitehouse.gov, 2015.

- Legal (or lawful) Temporary migrants (i.e., non-citizens who have been granted the right to live and work temporarily in the United States)
- Humanitarian migrants (i.e., refugees and "asylees" [individuals seeking asylum])
- Unauthorized immigrants or migrants (i.e., individuals in the United States without documentation, primarily from poor countries) (U.S. Census Bureau, American Community Survey, 2010).

Immigrant or **"Permanent Resident Alien"**   "An [individual] admitted to the United States as a lawful permanent resident. Permanent residents are also commonly referred to as immigrants; however, the Immigration and Nationality Act (INA) broadly defines an immigrant as any alien in the United States, except one legally admitted under specific nonimmigrant categories (e.g., temporary workers) ... Lawful permanent residents are legally accorded the privilege of residing permanently in the United States. They may be issued immigrant visas by the Department of State overseas or adjusted to permanent resident status by the Department of Homeland Security (DHS) in the United States." (Department of Homeland Security, 2013b)

Immigration, from the beginning, has been fundamental to the creation and growth of the United States. Virtually every citizen, except for the indigenous peoples of America, is either an immigrant or can claim to be a descendent of someone who emigrated, whether voluntarily or not, from another country. Immigration levels per decade reached their highest absolute numbers ever, from 1991 to 2000, when the number of immigrants surpassed 9 million not including the estimated 11 million undocumented immigrants living in the United States at that time. The U.S. Census Bureau American Community Survey (ACS) reported that in 2013 there were 41.3 million foreign-born individuals living in the United States, approximately 13 percent of the population. Exhibit 1.7 shows the countries of birth of the top five foreign born populations in the U.S; those born in Mexico comprise almost 30% of the U.S. foreign born population. Exhibit 1.8. shows the top ten U.S. states with the highest percentages of foreign born (the District of Columbia with nearly 14% is also included).

At one time, European immigration represented the bulk of American newcomers. In 1960, almost 75 percent of the U.S. foreign-born population were immigrants from Europe (Census Bureau Reports, 2010). However, by 2014, European immigrants totaled 4.8 million out of a total immigrant population of 42.4 million (Migration Policy Institute, 2015).

European Immigration

As shown in Exhibit 1.5, by 2013 approximately 80 percent of immigrants in the United States were from Mexico, Latin America, and Asia combined; 14 percent were from Europe and Canada with 11 percent immigration from Europe (U.S. Census American Community Surveys 2011, 2013 and 1960 U.S. Census data). Although the majority of people in the United States are of European descent, by July 2011, for the first time in history, children born to non-white parents outnumbered those born to whites of European ancestry.

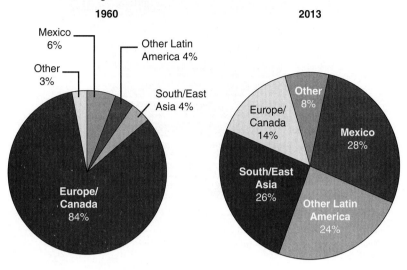

From Europe and Canada to Latin America and Asia: A Dramatic Shift in Immigrant Origins

% of U.S. immigrants born in ...

EXHIBIT 1.5 Immigrant Origins

Source: Pew Research Center, 1960; U.S. Census Data and American Community Survey, 2013.

Multiculturalism in U.S. society often focuses on diversity among immigrants and foreign-born from cultures very different from "mainstream" U.S. culture. However, among immigrants of European descent, themselves, there is considerable diversity.

Europe is not homogeneous, and most Europeans are not of the same ethnicity. Europe can be divided into four regions—east, west, north, and south—and has a population of 740 million people (Population Reference Bureau, 2013). Europe has 45 different countries, each with a unique national character, government and, for the most part, language. To illustrate European heterogeneity, there are 23 different official languages spoken in the Parliament of the European Union (compared to only six official languages in the United Nations. The countries listed in Exhibit 1.6 represent the continent of Europe, divided by regions.

During the decades that Eastern Europe was ruled by communist regimes, there was little immigration from these countries. However, since the democratization of many of these

---

Northern Europe: Denmark, Finland, Iceland, Ireland, Norway, Sweden, and the United Kingdom

Western Europe: Austria, Belgium, France, Germany, Liechtenstein, Luxembourg, Monaco, the Netherlands, and Switzerland

Southern Europe: Andorra, Greece, Italy, San Marino, Malta, Portugal, and Spain

Eastern Europe: Albania, Belarus, Bosnia and Herzegovina, Bulgaria, Croatia, Czech Republic, Estonia, Hungary, Kosovo, Latvia, Lithuania, Macedonia, Moldova, Montenegro, Poland, Romania, Russia, Serbia, Slovakia, Slovenia, Ukraine, and Yugoslavia

---

EXHIBIT 1.6 European Regions and Countries

Mexico – 11.7 million or 28%

China – 2.2 million or 5%

India – 1.8 million or 4%

Philippines – 1.8 million or 4%

Vietnam – 1.2 million or 3%

EXHIBIT 1.7 Top Five Foreign-Born Populations by Countries of Birth of Immigrants in the United States in 2010; Percentage of Total Foreign-Born Population

Source: U.S. Census Bureau, American Community Survey, 2010.

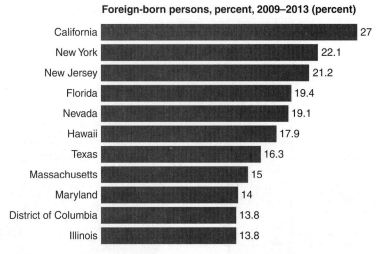

EXHIBIT 1.8   Percentage of Population per State in the Top Ten States with the Highest Percentages of Foreign Born

Source: U.S. Census Bureau, American Community Survey, Five-Year Estimates; 2009–2013.

countries began in the late 1980s and early 1990s, the United States has seen an enormous increase in immigration numbers from Eastern Europe. In 2014, an estimated 44 percent of European immigrants, or 2.1 million people, were born in Eastern Europe, with the most coming from Poland, Romania, Russia, Ukraine, and Bosnia and Herzegovina (Migration Policy Institute, 2015).

Many Eastern European immigrants to the United States came to reunite with family or escape ethnic violence and wars that followed the dissolution of the Soviet Union. This has resulted in large populations of Eastern European refugee communities concentrated in U.S. cities with small non-refugee/immigrant populations. St. Louis, Missouri, for example, is home to the largest Bosnian community outside of Bosnia, many of whom arrived prior to 2001, but now make up a thriving Bosnian community (Gilsinan, 2013).

Distinction between Immigrants and Refugees

Many individuals whom law enforcement officers encounter are born outside the United States; therefore, it is important to understand some key aspects related to immigration status.

Refugees are sponsored under the authority of the U.S. government (see the definition of "refugee" in Exhibit 1.11). Although many ethnic groups have come in under the sponsorship of the federal government with refugee or immigrant status, the largest numbers came from Southeast Asia as a result of the upheaval brought on by the Vietnam War. Refugees, sponsored by the government, are expected to receive public support services such as welfare, tuition reimbursement, job training programs, and "English as a second language" programs for approximately one year. Case managers are often assigned to refugee families to ensure that family members can utilize all of the available services. Some critics of immigration policy believe that such participation in public programs creates dependency and learned helplessness; others feel that this initial support is justified during a brief transitional period.

Immigrants, on the other hand, enter the country under the direct sponsorship of their families already residing in the United States. The federal government mandates that immigrants be allowed entry only if their families can support or provide work for them. In fact, one criterion for being able to attain permanent residence status (a "green card") is that the immigrant will not become a burden to the government; this means that participation in any public-funded program may jeopardize that individual's chances for attaining permanent residence status.

Immigrants generally come to the United States for two reasons:

- they are joining family members who already live in this country;
- they are "economic migrants" seeking work and a better life for themselves (and their families).

Economic migrant or refugee   this term generally refers to people fleeing devastating poverty from third world countries, who are not able to survive in their own countries (The Rockridge Institute, 2003).

Though the term "economic migrant" is sometimes referred to as "economic refugee," and can be distinguished from "political refugee," the distinctions can be complex. For example, the U.S. government classifies refugees from Haiti as "economic refugees," though Haitians have come to the United States in huge numbers for *both* political and economic reasons. When undocumented arrivals are designated as economic immigrants, they may be deported, whereas political refugees cannot. This type of undocumented immigrant generally has few occupational skills and is willing to accept menial jobs that many native-born citizens will not take; thus, certain industries dependent on low-wage labor rely heavily on this labor pool (e.g., restaurants and hotels).

An immigrant's appearance is not an accurate guide as to who has legal status and who does not. Both undocumented and legal immigrants may live in the same neighborhoods. In addition, the U.S. government has occasionally legalized significant numbers of some populations of formerly undocumented immigrants, usually in recognition of special circumstances in those persons' home countries, such as large-scale natural disasters or serious political instability.

Unauthorized Immigrants and Related Terminology

The terms *illegal immigrant, illegal alien, undocumented immigrant*, and *unauthorized immigrant* or *migrant* are sometimes used interchangeably, but the use of these labels often reflects individual political views on immigration. (Discussion of this controversy is beyond the scope of this chapter.) In this text, we use two common terms—*undocumented immigrant* and *unauthorized immigrant or migrant*. There are two major groups of undocumented or unauthorized immigrants: those who cross into the United States without having been "inspected" and those who enter the country with legal documents as temporary residents, but have overstayed and therefore violated their legal admission. Exhibits 1.9 and 1.10 show the concentration of unauthorized immigrants in the U.S. by state.

Unauthorized immigrants % of total state population

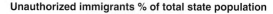
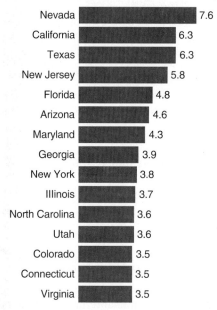

State	%
Nevada	7.6
California	6.3
Texas	6.3
New Jersey	5.8
Florida	4.8
Arizona	4.6
Maryland	4.3
Georgia	3.9
New York	3.8
Illinois	3.7
North Carolina	3.6
Utah	3.6
Colorado	3.5
Connecticut	3.5
Virginia	3.5

EXHIBIT 1.9   States with Largest Shares of Unauthorized Immigrants in the Population, 2012

Source: Pew Research Center, 2014, http://www.pewhispanic.org /2014/11/18/chapter-1-state-unauthorized-immigrant-populations/

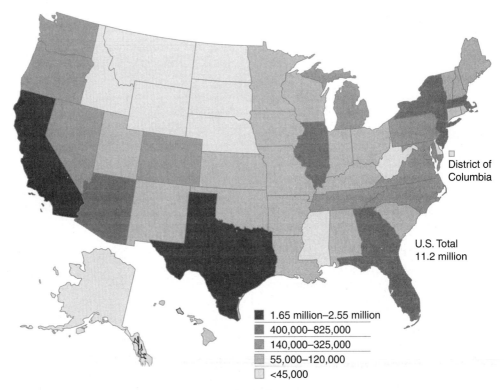

District of
Columbia

U.S. Total
11.2 million

- 1.65 million–2.55 million
- 400,000–825,000
- 140,000–325,000
- 55,000–120,000
- <45,000

EXHIBIT 1.10   Unauthorized Immigrant Population by State

Source: Passel and Cohen, Pew Research Center, 2011. Used with permission.

Refugees—People who fear persecution and/or death in their countries of origin because of war or violence; persecution can be based on race, religion, nationality, membership in a particular social group, or political opinion. Refugees are heavily vetted, and are granted legal status to be in the United States *before* they arrive.

Immigrants—Generally speaking, people who have voluntarily left their countries of origin in order to join family members and/or make better lives for themselves in the United States. Authorized or documented immigrants are legally admitted into the United States. Unauthorized or undocumented immigrants enter the United States without legal documentation.

Asylum seekers—People who have escaped their countries of origin because of well-founded fears of persecution. After entering the United States without papers, they apply for protection to remain legally in the United States. They are considered "asylum seekers" while their applications for legal protection are being processed.

EXHIBIT 1.11   Selected Distinctions: Refugees, Immigrants, and Asylum Seekers

The terms above are sometimes used inconsistently within countries and across continents. These distinctions generally apply to the way the terms are used in the United States.

The Pew Hispanic Research Center estimated the number of unauthorized immigrants by state in 2011. While California has the largest number of unauthorized immigrants, Nevada has the largest proportion of unauthorized immigrants, i.e., 7.2 percent of the total population (The Rockridge Institute, 2003).

Asylum Seekers

Asylum Seeker is defined by the U.S. Citizenship and Immigration Services as,

> A foreign-born individual in the United States or at a port of entry who is found to be unable or unwilling to return to his or her country of nationality, or to seek the protection of that country, because of persecution or a well-founded fear of persecution. Persecution or the fear thereof must be based on the individual's race, religion, nationality, membership in a particular social group, or political opinion. (U.S. Citizenship and Immigration Services [USCIS], 2013)

Among industrialized countries in 2015, there were 2 million requests worldwide for asylum. After Germany, the United States had the highest number of asylum claims (172,700). Many asylum seekers in the United States had fled Central America, escaping gang-related violence (UNHCR, 2016a). The violence in both Mexico and Central America propelling people to flee is described in greater detail below.

How are asylum seekers different from refugees? Individuals who fear harm or persecution in their home country may request legal protection known as "asylum" *after* arriving in the United States. They enter the United States without documentation, with the hope that they can remain by requesting legal assistance to become asylees. Those who seek asylum need to make the legal case that they would face persecution, and possibly death, if they were to return to their native countries.

In contrast, individuals with *refugee* status, as opposed to asylum seekers, are individuals have received *prior* approval by a U.S. Refugee Admission Program to be admitted as "refugees." Once individual refugees or refugee families receive approval, they are eligible for assistance through refugee resettlement programs, designed to facilitate aspects of their transition to the United States. The monetary assistance is minimal, and the services they receive from such programs are generally short-term; refugees are expected to become self-sufficient within a year of arriving to the United States.

People applying for asylum must prove that they have a "credible fear" of persecution in their country of origin based on their race, religion, nationality, social group or political opinion. To be considered for asylum, individuals must apply within one year of arriving in the United States (U.S. Citizenship and Immigration Services, 2015).

Unlike refugees, asylum seekers are not entitled to government benefits after they have entered the United States, and must largely depend on family members (if they are fortunate enough) or other personal connections, churches or interfaith efforts for basic support. The process of applying for and being granted asylum can take years, and there is an enormous backlog of asylum cases. There were more than 620,000 cases in 2016 pending in the U.S. immigration court and asylum systems (American Immigration Council, 2016b). Although asylum seekers may apply to work legally in the United States 150 days after applying for asylum, they still face major uncertainties about health care, education, employment and other dimensions of life, including coping with anxiety, fear, and other psychological trauma resulting from their experiences before coming to the United States. "Asylum seekers include some of the most vulnerable members of society—children, single mothers, victims of domestic violence or torture, and other individuals who have suffered persecution and trauma" (ibid.).

Examples from Mexico and Parts of Central America*—Reasons for Seeking Asylum

In recent years, tens of thousands of people, including unaccompanied children, have fled from Honduras, Guatemala, and El Salvador, a region known as "The Northern Triangle." Almost 10 percent of the population of these three countries has come to the United States. Between October 2013 and July 2015, the number of unaccompanied minors arriving in the United States from these three countries totaled nearly 100,000. In 2013 and 2014, there was a 90 percent increase in the number of these minors crossing the U.S.-Mexico border (Center for American Progress, 2014).

Why are there such large numbers of asylum seekers from Central America? According to the Council on Foreign Relations, the principal reason is the growth of organized criminal violence, a legacy of many decades of war (CFR, 2016). Violent gangs (e.g., "MS-13" and "M-18") control large areas of land, participate in drug trafficking, and perpetrate gang violence and extortion (ibid.). It is beyond the scope of this chapter to present the history of these violent criminal organizations; however, the flourishing of these groups in an environment of weak and corrupt governments has pushed many people to apply for legal protection (asylum). These asylum seekers' experiences (as well as those of immigrants from other world regions) affect their attitudes toward and interactions with police in the United States.

People applying for asylum must prove that they have a "credible fear" of persecution in their country of origin based on their race, religion, nationality, social group, or political opinion. To be considered for asylum, individuals must apply within one year of arriving in the United States (U.S. Citizen and Immigration Services, 2015).

Women and Children Seeking Asylum

Many asylum cases of Immigration Attorney Shira Levine involve children and women with children who have fled Central America to escape domestic abuse, gang violence, persecution of indigenous people, and forced, often violent recruitment of teenaged girls and boys into gangs. Often, these asylum

(continued)

seekers have suffered sexual violence, beatings, and other physical abuse (Levine, 2017). In El Salvador, refusing to become a gang member's girlfriend can be fatal. In some cases, girls are taken from their families, then raped for days by gang members before being returned home. In other cases, gangs demand a weekly fee from families in exchange for not raping the daughters (American Immigration Council, 2016a).

"Machismo" attitudes—characterized by a strong and sometimes aggressive sense of male pride—along with governmental impunity for crimes against women—explain, in part why so many women end up fleeing domestic violence and risk a perilous journey to reach the United States (Levine, 2017). Abused women are often viewed as property of their boyfriends and husbands, and children as property of their parents. Perpetrators of domestic violence, rape, or other violent crimes are rarely prosecuted, fostering an atmosphere of widespread lawlessness. It is not uncommon for asylum seekers to come to the United States with copies of police department records, documenting that nothing was done to help them when they reported violence in their own homes (ibid.).

Attitudes toward Police in the Home Country

Sexual violence and abuse, murder, extortion, kidnapping, torture, and human trafficking are well documented in Mexico and Central America (U.S. Department of State, 2015b). Asylum seekers from this region harbor a great deal of fear with respect to police and legal authorities. Asylum seekers questioned by immigration attorneys often explain that they could not report crimes to the police, who were known to be "comprados" (i.e., bought) by gangs and corrupt officials (Levine, 2017). Gang members and sympathizers are also embedded in the ranks of police, and are known to extort families with demands for money in exchange for not killing or raping the children (ibid.). Victims of rape or extortion who report the crime are likely to be killed by gang members. Family members frequently face violent retribution if they report crimes.

Tips for Police Interaction with Asylum Seekers

It would seem obvious that in jurisdictions where immigrants and asylum seekers reside, police department budgets should provide funding for language translation services; however, this is not always the case. What is not obvious is that sometimes the language of a victimized individual or one seeking

protection may differ from the official language(s) of their country of origin. For example, non-Spanish indigenous languages are spoken in Central America and Mexico. Some asylum seekers may not speak any Spanish at all.

Where law enforcement agencies do not have partnership agreements with ICE (see p. 23), and where there is a need to obtain information from asylum seekers (e.g., if they are crime victims), officers can explicitly say, "We are not from immigration. We will not contact immigration authorities." Furthermore, when officers show sensitivity and assure asylum seekers that they (officers) understand their fears, crime victims will likely be more willing to disclose information than they would otherwise.

In communicating with asylum seekers and other unauthorized immigrants, police officers need patience. Individuals may not be forthcoming with information all at once (e.g., if they are witness to or have been victims of a crime). Their stories may take time to unfold, especially if they have experienced trauma, which virtually all have (Levine, 2017). In Levine's experience, when individuals relay information, their accounts may be abbreviated at first because of shame and fear associated with reporting violence. Ms. Levine noted that in preparing asylum documents, she often needs to meet with clients three to four times as their stories begin to evolve. While police officers usually do not have the luxury of meeting several times in order to hear a full story, this information serves as a reminder that when people feel safe, their willingness to open up increases.

"Asylum applicants who have filed asylum claims and have passed credible fear interviews are highly motivated to present their cases to court and are committed to remaining with their families in the communities in which they live" (ibid.). The process of waiting to find out if one's asylum request is granted can take many months to years. Asylum seekers are often placed in detention centers until their claims have been adjudicated. Levine added that law enforcement representatives should be aware that women who have been released from detention centers while their claims are pending are often required to wear GPS tracking devices as a condition of their release and not because of any criminal activity on their part (ibid.).

---

*Between 2010 and 2014, the U.S. granted asylum to individuals from a number of countries, including China, Egypt, Mexico, Honduras, Guatemala, El Salvador, Venezuela, Syria, Iran, Iraq, Ethiopia, Haiti, and Eritrea (Department of Homeland Security, 2014).

Battered Immigrant Women

Even though the frequency of domestic violence is consistent across socioeconomic classes, racial groups, and geographic areas, immigrant women still face additional challenges in seeking help from their communities.

> The Violence Against Women Act (VAWA), passed by Congress in 1994 and improved in 2000 [then reauthorized in 2005 and 2013], set out to reform the manner in which officers responded to domestic violence calls for help…The lack of appropriate response to domestic violence from the police is further compounded when the battered woman is an immigrant. The police often do not have the capacity to communicate effectively with the immigrant victim in her own language. The police may use her abuser or her children to translate for her, and/or police may credit the statements of her citizen spouse or boyfriend over her statements to the police due to gender, race or cultural bias. (Orloff, 2003)

The most recent reauthorization (2013) expands protections for immigrants, including the addition of stalking to the list of serious crimes covered by the U visa, a little-known law created by Congress and a path to citizenship (see pp. 24–25 for further explanation). It also added an "age-out" provision to protect children of immigrants who filed for the U visa. Previously, children who turned 21 before a U visa application was approved were not protected, but the 2013 VAWA reauthorization extended the reach of the protections to include children who were younger than 21 at the time of the U visa filing.

Women subjected to domestic violence in their home countries confront societal, familial, and legal systems that fail to acknowledge the seriousness of the problem or to protect victims. In many countries, the voices of the victims go unheard, due to cultural traditions of female subjugation: women are supposed to serve their husbands no matter how badly they are treated. Often families do nothing to help the victim of spousal abuse, instead "forcing" her to "endure"—as generations of women have done. Outside the family network, women find little assistance in the legal system. Many countries do not codify domestic violence as a separate crime, and some countries treat domestic violence strictly as a family issue to be dealt with in a private manner. Few countries have enacted protections for domestic violence victims. Moreover, measures that have been enacted often fall short because they are not enforced. While a growing number of countries have laws on domestic violence, more than 100 countries still have no specific legal provisions: spousal rape is not considered a prosecutable offence in over 53 nations (UNIFEM, 2013).

While all battered women have been traumatized, both physically and psychologically, battered immigrant women face many additional hardships in seeking protection or reporting the crimes against them:

- Some battered immigrant women are completely isolated in the United States. They may have never established a legal identity in the United States, and thus may be staying away from public places.
- Batterers compound to victims' fears by threatening to contact Immigration and Customs Enforcement (ICE) about deportation.
- Women fear losing their families and being deported to the hostile society that they had fled. (In Latin America, for example, a woman returning to her own village without her husband and children is often ostracized.)
- Victims are often not aware that protection is available, nor do they know how to find it.
- Many victims do not speak English and have no understanding of U.S. criminal and immigration laws and systems (Tiede, 2001).

In addition, a battered immigrant woman may not understand that she can personally tell her story in court, or that a judge will believe her. Based on her experience in her native country, she may believe that only those who are wealthy or have ties to the government will prevail in court. Batterers manipulate these beliefs by convincing the victim that he will prevail in court because he is a male, is a U.S. citizen, or has more money (Orloff, 2003).

Additional hardships of unauthorized immigrant women have been documented regarding domestic violence. Sister Rosemary Welsh, Executive Director of Casa de Misericordia ("House of Mercy") a shelter for battered women in Laredo, Texas, explains:

> One of the ways men would keep [undocumented immigrant women] in a domestic violence situation [is] saying that "I am a U.S. citizen," or "I am a legal permanent resident, and you call the police, and they will deport you and I will stay with the kids." It [is] a way of terrorizing the women and, also, keeping them in bondage and keeping them in a violent situation. (PRI, 2013)

Officers need to be aware of community assistance programs specifically created to address the needs of battered immigrant women. In some jurisdictions, law enforcement management may even encourage or mandate that officers make initial calls to local nonprofits or other organizations while still with the victim. The Women's Justice Center in Santa Rosa, California, is an example of such a community resource. Exhibit 1.12 lists advice from this Center to immigrant women, victims of domestic violence.

Fear of Deportation, Law Enforcement and ICE

Social Worker and Mental Health professional, Vanessa Castillo, with La Clinica de la Raza in Northern California leads support groups for and provides counseling to Latino community members who experience depression and anxiety. She has observed a marked increase

Women's Justice Center HELP Special for Immigrant Women

1. You deserve help, and as a crime victim, you have a right to all the same crime victim services as any crime victim born in the United States.

   —Do not be shy about calling police, using women's shelters, calling rape crisis centers…or going to restraining order clinics.

2. What if the person abusing you says that he will call ICE and get you deported if you call the police or try to get help?

   —It is very, very common for violent men to make this threat to immigrant women who are their victims. But it is virtually impossible for these men to carry out the threat.

3. If you are still afraid to seek help, ask someone to make the phone calls for you, and to be with you when you deal with police and other crisis workers.

   —It's a very good idea when you get help for domestic violence and rape to have someone at your side.

4. What if you can't find anyone who can go with you?

   It's very common for abusers and men who rape to isolate you from human contact, especially if you have just arrived to the United States. You can ask others for help even if you don't tell them everything. For example, you can say, *"Will you call this number for me and ask if they have someone who speaks Spanish?"* Or, you can say, "I have been a victim of a crime and I need to go to court. Will you watch my children for the afternoon?" Or, you can say, *"My husband is abusive and I need a ride to the police."*

5. Insist on good translations.

   —The U.S. Constitution says that all persons must be given equal protection of the laws. The courts have repeatedly ruled that this means everyone from native-born citizens to newly arrived immigrants, whether or not they have the proper documentation. Every human being has a right to equal protection under the laws.

EXHIBIT 1.12   Advice to Immigrant Women from the Women's Justice Center
Source: De Santis, Women's Justice Center, 2013, www.justicewomen.com. Used with permission.

in the following tendencies of some of her Latino clients since late 2016, noting that "families are on high alert, and feeling more acutely than before, the need to remain in the shadows" (Castillo, 2017):

- Refraining from attending schools, and places of worship for fear of being picked up by ICE; avoiding places where ICE alerts have been seen;
- Missing doctors' and other appointments for fear of being reported to and then deported by ICE;
- Being unwilling to report unsafe working conditions on-the-job;
- Fearing going to the emergency room or having to register for anything "official," including needed mental health services;
- Refusing to report crimes, including rape, domestic and community violence. (Ibid.)

The principal barrier to establishing trust with undocumented immigrants is their fear of being reported to ICE, the largest investigative arm of the Department of Homeland Security. Entire communities may resist reporting crimes because of the fear of deportation. These immigrants are often already located in high-crime areas, and become even more vulnerable because of their fears of deportation.

Law enforcement's involvement with undocumented immigrants has been the subject of controversy for decades, even prior to the 1995 publication of the first edition of this text; as of the writing of this seventh edition, the controversy continues unabated. Since 1990, there has been a marked increase in the deportation of undocumented immigrants, from 30,000 a year to almost 400,000 annually (Migration Policy Institute, 2017).

Americans have always been deeply divided on immigration issues, in general, including the role of local police forces in immigration enforcement and deportations. The intensity of these divisions as well as heightened anxiety in communities of undocumented individuals increased in the 2016 presidential campaign, and thereafter. With an increased administration emphasis on detention and deportation of undocumented immigrants, fear has been increasing in immigrant communities (Lewis, 2017; Mejia, 2017; Richards, 2017).

Comparing January 2016 with January 2017, three times as many family units (approximately 3,000 vs. 9,000) were apprehended at the U.S. Mexico border though deportations. As of June 2017, the number fell from the previous year as fewer people tried to cross the border. (Migration Policy Institute, Fact Sheet, 2017; Taxin, 2017). According to the Associated Press, as of June 2017, ICE tracked, with deportation orders, 970,000 immigrants of which 82 percent had no criminal record (Taxin, 2017).

The Illegal Immigration Reform and Immigrant Responsibility Act of 1996 added a provision, Section 287(g), authorizing the director of ICE to enter into agreements with state and local law enforcement agencies, under which officers perform immigration law enforcement functions. Under Homeland Security, in 2006, this ICE law enforcement partnership actively began with 29 participating law enforcement agencies. Under 287(g) agreements, ICE provides state and local law enforcement with the training and delegated authority to enforce immigration law within their jurisdictions (U.S. Immigration and Customs Enforcement, 2017).

As of June 2017, ICE had 287(g) agreements with 42 law enforcement agencies in 17 states, mandating that these police jurisdictions assist federal authorities enforce immigration laws (U.S. Immigration and Customs Enforcement, 2017). Law enforcement views differ with respect to undocumented immigrants. These include leaving them alone unless they have committed a criminal act or are creating a disturbance. This is based on the perspective that tracking down and deporting immigrants has technically been the job of ICE and not that of the state or local police. While some people believe that these partnerships are beneficial, officials in many other parts of the country remain reluctant about police officers' having any role in immigration enforcement, because they fear losing the trust of the immigrant communities and worry about accusations of racial profiling. Police Chief Harry Dolan of Raleigh, North Carolina agrees that undocumented immigrants are reluctant to report crimes, particularly when they have been the victim. "The challenge today that we're finding is that the trust is diminishing because they're concerned what would happen to a family member if they called the police" (Pardo, 2010). In contrast, the National Sherriff's Association, in a position paper on Comprehensive Immigration Reform, strongly supported 287(g) programs: "It is critical that law enforcement maintain and build upon the partnerships with federal law enforcement to ensure that collectively we can promote, protect and preserve the public safety and homeland security" (National Sherriff's Association, 2011).

The Department of Justice as well as the ACLU conducted investigations concluding that 287(g) agreements have resulted in widespread racial profiling (American Immigration Council, 2016c). Other studies of the 287(g) programs show that they have interfered with the effectiveness of community policing. The International Association of Chiefs of Police (IACP) stated,

> ...local police agencies depend on the cooperation of immigrants, legal and illegal, in solving all sorts of crimes and in the maintenance of public order. Without assurances that they will not be subject to an immigration investigation and possible deportation, many immigrants with critical information would not come forward, even when heinous crimes are committed against them or their families. (IACP, 2015)

Echoing the sentiments above, law enforcement officials in Los Angeles, Houston, and Denver in 2017, stated that the changes in policy and the administration's public statements about immigration resulted in fewer immigrants' reporting crimes. For example, the chief of the Houston Police Department announced that, in the first three months of 2017, the reporting of rapes had dropped by 42.8 percent compared to the same period the previous year, adding his concern that this was a significant drop (Lewis, 2017; Medina, 2017).

The "Secure Communities" program, which has been replaced by Priority Enforcement Program (PEP), led to fears of deportation as well. Under Secure Communities, local law enforcement agents sent fingerprints collected during the booking process to the FBI, which then checked them against the DHS immigration database. While local law enforcement was involved in the collection process, federal ICE agents determined the course of action to take to enforce applicable immigration laws. Under Secure Communities, law enforcement agencies had a great deal of discretion as to who could be arrested; officers could arrest individuals solely on the basis of "reason to believe" that an individual was undocumented, resulting in racial profiling of individuals, and especially those of Hispanic/Latino backgrounds (Chief Justice Warren Institute on Law and Social Policy, 2011).

Since 2013, the Major Cities Chiefs Association, an organization made up of dozens of senior law enforcement executives from the nation's largest cities, has publicly rejected efforts to enlist state and local law enforcement as ad hoc immigration officers and has opposed measures that would punish cities financially if they fail to cooperate with such initiatives. The following is a summary of their major concerns:

1. [A law enforcement-ICE partnership] undermines the trust and cooperation with immigrant communities which are essential elements of community-oriented policing.
2. Local agencies do not possess adequate resources to enforce these laws in addition to the added responsibility of homeland security.
3. Immigration laws are very complex and the training required to understand them significantly detracts from the core mission of local police to create safe communities.
4. Local police do not possess clear authority to enforce the civil aspects of these laws. If given the authority, the federal government does not have the capacity to handle the volume of immigration violations that currently exist.
5. The lack of clear authority increases the risk of civil liability for local police and government. (Major Cities Chiefs Association, 2013)

The Secure Communities program was discontinued when PEP was established in November 2014. Certain procedures under the PEP program, such as the use of fingerprint biometric data submitted to the FBI during the booking process have not changed.

One significant difference between the Secure Communities Program and PEP concerns the threshold of criminal activity required to subject an individual to arrest (U.S. Immigration and Customs Enforcement, 2014). Under the Secure Communities Program, low-level offenders and people without criminal records could be arrested along with those who committed heinous crimes. In contrast, PEP's focus is on people who:

- have been convicted of an offense listed under the DHS Civil Immigration Enforcement priorities;
- have intentionally participated in organized criminal gangs to further the illegal activity of the gangs;
- pose a danger to national security. (ibid.)

Undocumented Immigrants: The "U" Visa and the Safe Reporting of Crimes

With the passage of the Victims of Trafficking and Violence Protection Act of 2000 (including the Violence Against Women Act (VAWA), and the Battered Immigrant Women's Protection Act), Congress also created the "U" visa, which can affect community members and law enforcement.

> Victims of certain criminal activities that either occurred in the United States or violated U.S. laws may be eligible to petition for "U" (nonimmigrant status) visa to USCIS. Victims must have suffered substantial mental or physical abuse due to the criminal activity and possess information concerning that criminal activity. Law enforcement authorities must also certify that the victim has been, is being, or is likely to be helpful in the investigation or prosecution of the criminal activity. (U.S. Department of State, Bureau of Consular Affairs: Visas for Victims of Criminal Activity)

Thus, the U visa is a path to citizenship. Often, when undocumented immigrants call the police, they are likely to have been victims of or witnesses to a crime. If they actively cooperate with law enforcement and provide information about the crime, they are entitled to a U visa or a nonimmigrant visa, which can later be used in applying for a legal work permit and a social security number. The U visa is distinct from the "T" visa, another protective measure designed specifically for victims of human trafficking, including sex and labor trafficking. U visas are difficult to obtain, but undocumented immigrants who receive them may eventually apply for residency. Application for the U visa needs to include a "Certification of Helpfulness" from a certifying agency. This means that the individual petitioning for the

U visa must "provide a Nonimmigrant Status Certification from a federal, state or local law enforcement official that demonstrates the petitioner 'has been helpful, is being helpful or is likely to be helpful' in the investigation or prosecution of the criminal activity." The USCIS began issuing U visas in 2008. At least through 2015, the U. S. Citizenship and Immigration Services continued to approve the statutory maximum of 10,000 U visas per fiscal year (U.S. Citizen and Immigration Services, 2015).

In the experience of Christopher Martinez, Chief Program Officer for refugee and immigrant services of Catholic Charities of the East Bay (California), U visa applicants must have the support of the police department and/or the district attorney's office for the processing of U visa applications (Martinez, 2017). It is important, for the safety of *all* members of the community, that immigrants feel safe and protected in reporting crimes to local law enforcement (ibid.).

> A woman and her child living on the East Coast witnessed a heinous crime involving the murder of her husband. While at the time of the crime, the U-Visa law did not exist, this woman came forward, cooperating fully with the authorities. Ultimately, the perpetrator was caught and convicted. The woman later became eligible for a U-Visa, and had the full backing of the District Attorney's office in the city in which she and her child lived. (ibid.)

CULTURE AND ITS RELEVANCE TO LAW ENFORCEMENT

An understanding of accepted social practices and cultural traditions in individuals' countries of origin can provide officers with insight into predicting some of the reactions and difficulties of new immigrants and refugees, particularly those who have been in the United States for five years or fewer. Below are a few examples of practices, expectations and laws in the United States contrasted with those in other countries. These were compiled from courses provided to newcomers as part of a community policing outreach educational program; a general course outline is shown in Exhibit 1.13 (Olson 2017):

- In a U.S. traffic stop, law enforcement personnel do not allow the driver or passengers to exit their car and walk back to the police car. (*In some countries, e.g., Cuba, Japan, Mexico, and Russia), motorists generally get out of their car and walk back to the police officer. Getting out of the car can even be a sign of courtesy toward officers.*)
- It is illegal for police in the United States to accept bribes of any kind. (*Many police officers in regions such as Eastern Europe and South America expect to receive bribes when they stop a motorist.*)
- There are specific sexual misconduct laws in the United States and prostitution is illegal in the United States except in parts of Nevada. (*Many newcomers don't understand how a man can be arrested for sexual contact with a woman.*)

To better serve new immigrants and refugees coming to the United States from around the world, some nonprofit organizations, in collaboration with local police trainers, offer public safety and basic law workshops. Immigrants and refugees attending these workshops typically have only been in the United States for several weeks, and have had no previous exposure to information about American police, laws, or emergency services. These sessions, with interpreters, can include such basic topics as:

- The roles of the police officer in the United States
  Traffic and criminal laws
- U.S. laws pertaining to domestic violence
- What to do if stopped by a police officer
- How to use 911 for emergencies
  Reporting a crime
  Calling the police for nonemergencies
- FBI and ICE
- State Police, sheriff's departments and city police departments

---

EXHIBIT 1.13   IRCO Workshops for Immigrants and Refugees on U.S. Police, Laws and Emergency Services
Source: Olson, Aaron T., 2017. Used with permission.

- Domestic violence is a crime in the United States and the laws are very specific. (*Domestic violence laws are nonexistent or not enforced in many countries; family matters may be viewed as personal and private. Therefore, some immigrants and refugees do not understand that abuse by their partners is illegal.*)

Some traditional practices in other countries are illegal in the United States. Cultural differences or ignorance of U.S. law is not an acceptable defense for committing a crime. Nevertheless, officers and others in the criminal justice system should be aware of these cultural differences and how these may have affected the mindset of the perpetrator. For example, female circumcision is illegal in the United States, but is still practiced in certain African countries. The Hmong, mountain people of Southeast Asia and Laos have a tradition considered to be an acceptable form of eloping. This Hmong tradition allows a male to abduct a woman for marriage; even if she resists, he may take her home, and consummate the union. However, "marriage by capture" would constitute kidnap and rape in the United States.

In interviews with a deputy public defender and a deputy district attorney, a legal journal posed the following question: Should our legal system recognize a "cultural" defense in criminal cases? The deputy district attorney's response was, "No. You're treading on shaky ground when you decide something based on culture, because our society is made up of so many different cultures. It is very hard to draw the line somewhere, but [diverse cultural groups] are living in our country, and people have to abide by [one set of] laws or else you have anarchy." The deputy public defender's response to the question was: "Yes. I'm not asking that the [various cultural groups] be judged differently, just that their actions be understood according to their own history and culture" (Sherman, 1986). This advice continues to reflect current legal decisions about culturally influenced criminal actions today.

If law enforcement's function is to protect and serve individuals from all cultural backgrounds, it is helpful to understand the cultural dimensions of crimes. Obviously, actions that may be excused in another culture must not go unpunished if they are considered crimes in this country (e.g., spousal abuse). Nevertheless, there are circumstances in which law enforcement officials at all levels of the criminal justice system would benefit by understanding the cultural context in which a crime occurred. Law enforcement professionals must use standard operating procedures in response to specific situation; these procedures cannot be altered for different groups based on their ethnicity or national origin.

In a multicultural society, however, an officer can modify the way he or she treats a suspect, witness, or victim, based on knowledge of what is considered "normal" in that person's culture. When officers suspect that cultural background is a factor in a particular incident and are willing to evaluate arrests in lesser crimes, they may earn the respect of—and therefore cooperation from—ethnic community members. For example, certain aspects of what is considered "normal" in the Sikh culture and religion can cause confusion for officers who have not been exposed to Sikh traditions and practices (Sikhism is a religion followed by a minority of people who are mainly from northern India). Sikh men wear turbans because they are required to cover their hair in public. For a Sikh man, removing his turban in public can be likened to a strip search and would need to be done in a culturally sensitive manner. Sikh men carry a *kirpan* (sheathed knife); a *kirpan* is not a concealed weapon.

All people, except for very young children, adhere to cultural dos and don'ts, and identify with their group, both consciously and unconsciously; individuals have varying degrees of attachment to their cultural group's traditional values. A person's identity is sanctioned and reinforced by the society in which he or she has been raised. Culture has a significant influence on people's behavior and interacts with other variable such as age, gender, race, and socioeconomic status. Culture's influence is largely unconscious, and it is virtually impossible to lose one's culture completely when in a new environment.

The Definition of Culture

Although there are many definitions of culture, we are using the term to mean beliefs, habits, attitudes, values, patterns of thinking, behavior, and everyday customs that have been passed on from generation to generation. Culture is learned rather than inherited and is manifested largely in unconscious and subtle behaviors. With this definition in mind, consider that most children have acquired a general cultural orientation by the time they are five or six years old. Because culture is so deeply embedded in individuals, it is difficult for adults to quickly change their cultural behavior and attitudes when they are first immersed in a new culture. Many layers of cultural behavior and beliefs are subconscious. In addition, many people assume that what they take for granted is taken for granted by all people ("all human beings are the same"), and they do not even recognize their own culturally influenced behavior. Anthropologist Edward T. Hall (1959) said, "Culture hides much more than it reveals and, strangely enough, what it hides, it hides most effectively from its own participants." In other words, people are blind to their own deeply embedded cultural behavior.

> **Ethnocentrism** is an attitude of seeing and judging other cultures from the perspective of one's own cultural group; using the latter as a standard for judging others, or thinking of it as superior to other cultures that are merely different. An ethnocentric person would say there is only one way of being "normal" and that is the way of his or her own culture.

Ethnocentrism is a barrier to acknowledging that there are other valid beliefs, communication styles, customs, or values that can lead to culturally different behavior. Ethnocentrism often causes a person to assign a potentially incorrect meaning or attribute an incorrect motivation to a given act.

To further understand the hidden nature of culture, picture an iceberg. The only visible part of the iceberg is the tip, which typically constitutes about 10 percent of its mass. Like most of culture's influences, the remainder of the iceberg is submerged beneath the surface. What this means for law enforcement is that there is a natural tendency to interpret behavior, motivations, and criminal activity from the officer's cultural point of view. This tendency is due largely to an inability to understand behavior from alternative perspectives and because of the natural human inclination toward ethnocentrism. The following case studies illustrate that culture can affect interpretations, meaning, and intentions.

Mini Case Studies and Cultural Practices: Does Culture Matter?

The following descriptions of cultural practices or mini case studies involve crimes or offenses with a cultural component. If the crime is a murder or something similarly heinous, most people will not be particularly sympathetic to a "cultural defense" argument. However, consider that understanding other cultural patterns gives one the ability to see and react in a different way. The ability to withhold judgment and to interpret a person's intention from a different cultural perspective is a skill that can enable someone to identify his or her own cultural blinders.

The examples describe "crimes" of varying severity. The corresponding questions at the end of the chapter (p. 38) will allow you the opportunity to discuss the degree to which culture matters, or does not matter, in each of the following cases:

1. Culture Matters? The Sword in a Public Park

A City University of New York study entitled, "Police Narratives about Racial and Ethnic Identity" illustrates culture and "crime" involving a cultural practice in parts of Asia, associated with the martial art of Tai Chi. Tai Chi practitioners carry a sword with them to public parks, and then perform Tai Chi movements, using the sword. For an immigrant who does this, there is clearly no criminal intent since the practice is accepted as "normal" in the person's country of origin. Yet, in the United States, this would potentially be considered a crime.

2. Culture Matters? The Turban and the *Kirpan*

In a previous section entitled, "Culture and Its Relevance to Law Enforcement," you learned that removing a Sikh's turban in public would be, for him, like doing a strip search. Sikh men are required by their religion to carry a *kirpan* (sheathed knife) at all times, and for some, this extends to when they are asleep. A police officer arrives at the home of a Sikh couple after a neighbor calls the police, saying that she heard specific verbal threats (with intimations of violence) toward the wife. The officer arrests the husband, pats him down and searches him, and finds, incidental to the arrest, the husband's *kirpan*. The Sikh is now additionally charged with "possession of a concealed weapon."

3. Culture Matters? A Tragic Case of Cross-Cultural Misinterpretation

In parts of Asia, there are medical practices unfamiliar to many law enforcement officials (as well as medical practitioners) in the West. A number of these practices result in marks on the skin that can easily be misinterpreted as abuse by people who have no knowledge of these culturally based medical treatments. The practices include rubbing the skin with a coin ("coining," "coin rubbing," or "wind rubbing"), pinching the skin, touching the skin with burning incense, or applying a heated cup to the skin ("cupping"). Each practice

(continued)

leaves highly visible marks, such as bruises and even burns. The following is an account of a serious misreading of some very common Southeast Asian methods of traditional folk healing by American school authorities and law enforcement officials.

A young Vietnamese boy had been absent from school for a few days with a serious respiratory infection. His father, believing that coining would help cure him, rubbed heated coins on his back and neck. The boy's condition seemed to improve and he was able to return to school. Upon noticing heavy bruising on the boy's neck, the teacher immediately informed the school principal, who promptly reported the "abuse" to the police (who then notified Child Protective Services). When the police were notified, they went to the child's home to investigate. The father was very cooperative when questioned by the police and admitted, in broken English, that he had caused the bruising on his son's neck. The man was arrested and incarcerated. While the father was in jail, his son, who was under someone else's custody, apparently relapsed and died of his original illness. On hearing the news, the father committed suicide in his jail cell. The tragic misinterpretation on the part of the authorities involved, including the teacher, the principal, and the arresting police officers, provides an extreme case of what can happen when people attribute meaning solely from their own cultural perspective.

Cultural understanding would not have cured the boy, but informed interaction with the father could have prevented the second tragedy. All of the authorities were interpreting what they saw with "cultural filters" based on their own belief systems. Ironically, the interpretation of the bruises (i.e., child abuse) was almost the opposite of the father's intention (i.e., healing). Even after some of the parties involved learned about this very common Southeast Asian practice, they still did not accept that it existed as an established practice, and they could not fathom how others could believe that coining might actually cure illness. Their own conception of medical treatment did not encompass what they perceived as "primitive."

4. Culture Matters? Latino Values as a Factor in Sentencing

In a court of law, a cultural explanation or rationalization (i.e., a cultural defense) rarely affects a guilty or not-guilty verdict. Nevertheless, culture may affect sentencing. Consider the following case, in which, according to retired Judge Lawrence Katz, cultural considerations lessened the severity of the sentence:

A Mexican woman living in the United States became involved in an extramarital affair. Her husband became outraged when the wife bragged about her extramarital activities at a picnic at which many extended family members were present. At the same time, the wife also made comments about her husband's lack of ability to satisfy her and how, in comparison, her lover was far superior. On hearing his wife gloat about her affair, the husband left the picnic and drove five miles to purchase a gun. Two hours later, he shot and killed her. In a case such as this, the minimum charge required in California would be second-degree murder. However, because the jury took into consideration the cultural background of this couple, the husband received a mitigated sentence and was found guilty of manslaughter. It was argued that his wife's boasting about her lover and her explicit demeaning comments completely undermined his machismo, masculine pride and honor. To grasp the emotional severity of the wife's behavior, the officer and the prosecutor had to understand what it means to be humiliated in such a manner in front of one's family, in the context of Latino culture. (Katz, 2017)

The purpose of these "Culture Matters" descriptions or mini-case studies is not to judge whether others' values, customs, or beliefs are right or wrong; rather, that officers should be encouraged to consider potential cultural influences when investigating and presenting evidence regarding an alleged crime or incident involving people from diverse backgrounds. This does not mean that standard operating procedures should be changed or that felonies such as murder or rape should be excused on cultural grounds. However, as a matter of course, officers can develop cultural competence to help understand, assess, and report certain kinds of incidents and crimes.

Law enforcement representatives have discretion whether to arrest or admonish someone suspected of a crime. According to retired Judge Katz, "Discretion based on cultural competence at the police level is much more significant than what happens at the next level in the criminal justice system (i.e., the courts)" (Katz, 2017). Police officers have opportunities to develop positive relationships with members of an ethnic community when they demonstrate cultural sensitivity and respect. Katz cited an example of police contact with San Francisco Bay Area Samoan community members, whose barbecues and parties may include drinking, resulting in loud sustained noise in neighborhoods or even fights (ibid.). Police, responding to neighbors' complaints, could come in aggressively and use a threatening stance. However, word would spread that the police officers had no respect for the people involved. This would widen the gap that already exists between police and many Pacific Islander and other Asian groups and would not be a way to foster trust in the Samoan community. Alternatively, the police could locate the leader, or the "chief," of this group and work with that person to deal with the problem in the way that he would have handled the out-of-control gathering and conflict in Samoa. There is no question about the chief's ability to handle the problem. The chief can serve as a bridge and help foster trust between the police and the community (ibid.). The *matai* is also a resource; he is an elder who has earned the respect of the community.

The heads of Samoan communities are traditionally in full control of members' behavior, although this is changing somewhat in the United States. Given the power entrusted to the chiefs, it is reasonable to encourage officers first to work with them and elicit their assistance. This recommendation does not imply, in any way, that specific ethnic communities should be left to police themselves; instead, understanding and working with the leadership of a community represents an opportunity to create a productive partnership.

Awareness of and sensitivity to cross-cultural issues can have an impact on the criminal justice system, in which police have the power to either inflame or calm the people involved in a particular incident. According to Katz, "Many cases, especially those involving lesser offenses, can stay out of court." He asks, "Do you always need a show of force? Or can you counsel and admonish instead?" In certain situations, such as the one described earlier, officers can rethink traditional police methods in order to be as effective as possible. Doing so requires learning about ethnic communities and desiring to establish a positive and trustworthy image in those communities (ibid.).

DIMENSIONS OF DIVERSITY

To develop a deeper understanding of groups in society, and in the workplace, it is useful to examine multiple dimensions and layers of diversity. These dimensions can help deepen understanding of broad cultural groups, and discourage overgeneralizations and stereotyping. Dimensions of diversity should not be understood as finite and definitive labels; they should be seen as overlapping in dynamic ways that shape individuals.

Primary Dimensions of Diversity

A primary dimension is a core characteristic that accompanies a person from birth to death. According to one diversity scholar, people have a minimum of six primary dimensions as follows (Loden, 2013), but there are other dimensions as well (e.g., social class and spiritual orientation, see Exhibit 1.14):

1. Age
2. Ethnicity
3. Gender
4. Mental/physical abilities and characteristics
5. Race
6. Sexual orientation. (Ibid.)

Most people are aware of the meanings of these categories. For the sake of clarity, the following terms are included in the category "sexual orientation": heterosexual, homosexual, lesbian, gay, bisexual, transgender, asexual, and queer. All of the six primary dimensions are major characteristics that contribute to being advantaged or disadvantaged in the workforce and in society. Victims of hate bias crimes are targeted because of these dimensions of diversity—age, ethnicity, gender, disability status, race, and sexual orientation, as well as religion. (See Chapter 11 for detailed information on Hate Crimes.) The primary dimension associated with age also includes generational differences. In the law enforcement workforce, values may collide among the generations; leaders and managers need to be cognizant of this dimension of diversity. For example, millennials (young adults between the ages of 18 and approximately 30) are the most tolerant of the generations on issues connected to immigration, race, and sexual preference (Pew Research Center, 2010).

Secondary Dimensions of Diversity

A secondary dimension is a characteristic a person acquires, including:

1. Communication style
2. Education
3. Family status

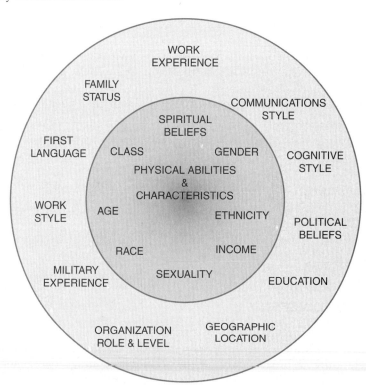

EXHIBIT 1.14   Dimensions of Diversity
Models such as the diversity wheel, designed by Loden Associates,
facilitate understanding of a broad range of primary and secondary
dimensions of diversity.
Source: Loden Associates Inc., 2013. Reprinted with permission of Marilyn Loden.
http://www.loden.com

4. Military experience
5. Organizational role and level
6. Religion
7. First language
8. Geographic location
9. Income
10. Work experience
11. Work style
12. Others. (Loden, 2013)

Both primary and secondary dimensions of diversity influence the personal and professional lives of law enforcement personnel. Tensions with supervisors and coworkers are often caused by the differences in these secondary dimensions. Similarly, a police officer's ability to establish rapport with individuals can also be related to either the actual or the perceived degree to which dimensions are shared.

Exhibit 1.14 presents a schematic of primary and secondary dimensions of diversity influencing people. "While each dimension adds a layer of complexity, it is the dynamic interaction among all the dimensions of diversity that influences one's self-image, values, opportunities, and expectations. Together, the primary and secondary dimensions give definition and meaning to our lives by contributing to a synergistic, integrated whole—the diverse person" (ibid.).

Further Diversity within and among Ethnic Groups in the United States

As much as we may try to categorize people into distinct ethnic categories, there are additional factors that can increase understanding and improve communications between law enforcement and the members of minority communities. Take, for example, "age" as a primary dimension of diversity. Some people, especially immigrants from Asia, may self-report a different age than what is shown on their official identification documents. In some cultures, children are considered to be one year old when they are born; in others, birthdays are based on the lunar calendar and thus at certain times of the year, reported ages don't match "official" ages. Among immigrants, entry papers may occasionally be falsified, leading to discrepancies. Thus, there are nuances even with this primary dimension of culture.

Other diversity factors include:

- Comfort with and competence in English;
- Generational status in the United States (refer to Exhibit 1.15 as well as Appendix A for more detail); first-generation refugees or immigrants are likely to deviate from traditional cultural norms more than their second- or third-generation offspring);
- Degree of identification with one's country and/or region of origin;
- Family structure and the extent of family dispersion in the United States and globally;
- Degree to which individuals are embedded in their ethnic community network;
- Cultural values and norms;
- Extent to which individuals relate to issues, concerns, and problems shared by other ethnic/racial groups.

General Distinctions among Generations of Immigrants

The dimension of diversity associated with generational status is significant. Following are some distinctions to help explain differences between generations Appendix A (pp. 365–366) provides general descriptions of each type listed in Exhibit 1.15. These serve as a reminder to distinguish between newcomers and those who have been in the United States for several generations.

Type	Description	Behavioral Differences
Type I	Recently arrived adult immigrant or refugee (fewer than five years in the United States)	Survival needs; often living within ethnic enclaves
Type II	Recently arrived adolescent teen or immigrant refugee (fewer than five years in the United States)	Adjustment and "fitting in"; identity is a combination of new and former cultures
Type III	Adult immigrant or refugee (five or more years in the United States)	Preserving culture of origin or aspects thereof, while still striving to adapt
Type IV	Second-generation individual (U.S.-born offspring of immigrants or refugees)	Straddling two cultures; significantly more assimilated than parents;
Type V	Third-generation (and beyond)	Fully or nearly fully assimilated; may choose to identify bi-culturally

EXHIBIT 1.15 General Distinctions among Generations of Immigrants
Please see Appendix A, p. 365–366, for general descriptions of each type.

Intersection of Diversity Factors

Millennials are the most diverse generation in history: almost 40 percent self-identified as nonwhite or as belonging to an ethnic group (Pew Research Center, 2010). At the same time, poll results showed Millennials to be less likely to label themselves using traditional diversity categories (ibid.). Individuals are not merely defined by one thread of diversity, but rather by overlapping characteristics of their identity. "She is black," or "He is gay," are unidimensional statements. The diversity wheel above (Exhibit 1.14) illustrates how many layers make up individuals' social identities. When it comes to hate, prejudiced people might focus on one or more primary dimensions of diversity such as race, or sexual orientation, and this is all they see. More often than not, prejudiced individuals harbor multiple biases, spanning most of the primary dimensions, and religion, one of the secondary dimensions.

PREJUDICE AND BIAS IN LAW ENFORCEMENT

Police officers participating in a human relations program were asked to do the following:

"Raise your hand if you are a racist." Not a single officer raised a hand.

"Raise your hand if you think that prejudice and racism exist outside this agency." Most officers raised their hands.

The instructor then asked with humor: "Where were you recruited from?". (Berry, 2017)

When discussing the implications of multicultural diversity for police officers, it is not enough simply to present the need to understand cultural background and race relations. Whenever two groups are from different ethnic or racial backgrounds, prejudice may exist because of fear, lack of contact, ignorance, and stereotypes. To deny the existence of bias, prejudice or racism in any given law enforcement agency is to deny that it exists outside the agency.

To stereotype To believe that people conform to a pattern or manner with all other individual members of a specific group. People who are prone to stereotyping often categorize the behavior of an entire group based on limited or no experience with people in that group. The characteristics ascribed to others are mostly negative; this negative stereotyping classifies people in the targeted group by the use of slurs, innuendoes, names, or slang expressions, depreciating the group as a whole as well as individuals in it.

Prejudice A judgment or opinion formed before facts are known, usually involving negative or unfavorable thoughts about groups of people.

To scapegoat To falsely blame the failures and shortcomings of an individual, organization, cultural/racial group, etc., on other often innocent people.

Discrimination Action based on prejudiced thought and biases; the denial of equal treatment to individuals or groups because of their age, disability, employment, language, nationality, race, ethnicity, sex, gender and gender identity, sexual orientation, religion, or other form of cultural identity.

Bias A preformed negative opinion or attitude toward a group of persons based on their race, religion, disability, sexual orientation, ethnicity, gender, or gender identity.

Explicit bias Conscious negative feelings toward a particular group.

Implicit bias Unconscious biases, held by all people, that can potentially influence judgments and actions; implicit bias results in an automatic association between groups of people and stereotypes about those groups.

Bias-based policing Intentional and unintentional acts of applying or incorporating personal, societal, or organizational biases and/or stereotypes in decision-making, police actions, or the administration of justice; the inappropriate consideration of specified characteristics (i.e., race, ethnicity, national origin, gender, gender identity, sexual orientation, socio-economic status, religion, disability, and/or age) in carrying out duties when making law enforcement decisions.

Prejudice and Bias

Prejudice is a judgment or opinion formed, usually involving negative or unfavorable thoughts about groups of people. Bias, which can be conscious or unconscious and may be "explicit" or "implicit," influences behavior, decision-making or action, reflecting a tendency to make certain choices based on one's inclination. Discrimination is action or policy based on prejudiced thought and biases.*

Increasingly, researchers in the social sciences contend that all people have biases, which are largely out of conscious awareness. Every individual has "implicit biases"; this is part of being human. Even people who are not prejudiced against other groups have implicit biases, which do not necessarily make them bigots or racists.

*The Community Relations Service Department of the DOJ has produced an excellent "toolkit" for policing entitled, *Understanding Bias: A Resource Guide (USDOJ/CRS).*

How Prejudice Influences People

We discussed stereotyping at the beginning of this chapter, pointing out that many people hold stereotypes about police officers. Prejudice is encouraged by stereotyping, which is a shorthand way of thinking about people who are different. Officers need to become increasingly aware of their own biases—conscious and unconscious—and, to the greatest extent possible, avoid allowing those biases to interfere with their decisions-making. Police actions that rely on stereotypes do not serve officers or members of the public as these actions can be unsafe, and are ineffective as well as unjust. The stereotypes underlying people's prejudice can be so deeply embedded psychologically that they can easily rationalize their racism, sexism, or other bias on this basis. Such individuals may even believe that they are tolerant and unprejudiced, but may still make statements such as, "I'm not prejudiced, but let me tell you about those—I had to deal with today." Coffey, Eldefonson, and Hartinger (1982) discuss the relationship between selective memory and prejudice:

> A prejudiced person will almost certainly claim to have sufficient cause for his or her views, telling of bitter experiences with refugees, Koreans, Catholics, Jews, Blacks, Mexicans and Puerto Ricans, or Indians. But in most cases, it is evident that these "facts" are both scanty and strained. Such a person typically resorts to a selective sorting of his or her own memories, mixes them up with hearsay, and then overgeneralizes. No one can possibly know all refugees, Koreans, Catholics, and so on. (ibid.)

One of the most dangerous types of prejudice is sometimes referred to "character-conditioned prejudice;" someone with this condition may hold hostile attitudes toward many ethnic groups, not just one or two. People who tend to mistreat or oppress others because of their prejudices were often mistreated themselves during childhood and adolescence, and this experience can leave them extremely angry and distrustful of others. In addition, people who have strong prejudices can be insecure and frustrated because of their own failures. Consequently, they blame or scapegoat others. Frequently, members of racial supremacist organizations fit the description of having character-conditioned prejudice; for these people, mistrust and hate of all others is a way of life.

Another type of prejudice is acquired during "normal" socialization. This type of prejudice results when a person belongs to an ethnic or racial group, and many people in the group hold negative views of other specific groups (e.g., Palestinians and Israelis). When there is a pattern of prejudice within a particular racial or national group, for example, the "normal" person is the one who adopts the group's prejudice. From childhood, parents pass on stereotypes of the out-group into the child's mind because of their "normal" prejudices. By adulthood, the person who has learned prejudice against a particular group can easily justify the prejudice (ibid.).

> If you are normal, you have blind spots that will give you an unbalanced view of people who are different from you. Officers must look at themselves and understand their own biases first before getting into situations in which they may act upon them. (Berry, 2017)

Implicit Bias

Many biases are powerful, and often hidden. "Project Implicit," founded in 1998 resulted from the collaboration of scientists from three universities who developed tools, and laboratory methods to assess individuals' biases (Project Implicit, 2011). Professionals in law enforcement have applied research findings around biases to police training, raising awareness that, like everyone else, police have implicit biases that can interfere with or influence decision-making. (Chapter 6 presents specific research related to police decision-making in the context of bias against African Americans.)

The following is an example of implicit bias, in this case on the part of a flight attendant. This example shows how societal bias can manifest as implicit bias within an individual:

> In late 2016, a young, African American, female physician responded to an emergency situation during a flight by offering her medical services when another passenger screamed for help because the passenger's husband was unresponsive. Dr. Tamika Cross unbuckled her seat belt and was about to stand up when the flight attendant told everyone to remain seated and stay calm, saying that the passenger was only experiencing a "night terror." The flight attendant dismissed Dr. Cross's offers

to help, refusing to believe that Dr. Cross was a real doctor, and spoke to her in a highly condescending way. Dr. Cross had not yet been asked to show identification of her medical professional status. Next, an overhead page came on, asking whether there was a physician on board. Dr. Cross raised hand only to hear, "Oh no, sweetie. Put your hand down. We are looking for actual physicians or nurses or some type of medical personnel …" At that point, a white, male physician offered to help, prompting the attendant to tell Dr. Cross, "Thanks for your help, but he can help us, and he has his credentials." Dr. Cross, furious, remained seated. Ten minutes later, and after realizing that Dr. Cross could be of help (finally understanding and saying, "Oh, wow. You're an actual physician?"), the flight attendant asked Dr. Cross for her input on what next medical steps should be taken, and Dr. Cross provided her with medical advice.

Source: Based on Hauser and Wible, 2016.

The incident ended with a full investigation of the incident by Delta Airlines, a formal apology to Dr. Cross as well as changes related to the airline's policies and training (Delta News Hub, 2016). This flight attendant was likely unaware of her biases—the deeply embedded messages within her brain that influenced her perceptions and actions.

Dr. Lorie Fridell, professor of criminology at the University of South Florida, a former director of research at PERF (Police Executive Research Program), and expert on biased policing, together with law enforcement curriculum specialist Ms. Anna Laszlo, outline the following basic concepts related to bias in widely used training programs for police recruits, officers, supervisors, and trainers (FIP Web Site, 2017; Fridell, 2017a).

Fundamental Concepts of Human Bias

- Biases are often unconscious or implicit.
- Implicit biases manifest even in individuals who, at the conscious level, reject prejudices and stereotyping.
- Understanding how implicit biases can affect our perceptions and behavior is the first step in "overriding" implicit bias.

One of the most important aspects of the Fair and Impartial Policing (FIP) training is the understanding that even when officers feel that they do not have biases, their decision-making may, nevertheless, be unconsciously influenced by biases. The FIP training curricula convey how biased policing impacts community members and departments, and how supervisors can help to promote fair and impartial policing (ibid.). Additionally, the FIP command-level training provides guidance to police leaders on topics related to bias-free policing including recruitment, hiring, outreach to diverse commu nities, and accountability (Fridell, 2017b). The command-level training is summarized in *Producing Bias-Free Policing: A Science Based Approach* (ibid.). The FIP Web site also includes resources for police chiefs, spanning policy, federal guidelines on discrimination, and organizational mandates for bias-free policing (FIP Web site, 2017).

POLICE LEADERSHIP IN A MULTICULTURAL SOCIETY

Police management can help officers understand the nature of prejudice and unconscious bias, and how decision-making can, in a split second, reflect such bias. While police officers are entitled to their own beliefs, police chiefs must try to ensure that that officers will not act on their prejudices or be so unaware of unconscious biases that they do not realize the connections between their actions and their biases. All officers must understand where the line is between prejudice and acts of discrimination, whether within the law enforcement agency or with the public. Prejudice and bias in the law enforcement agency must be addressed so that they do not result in differential treatment.

Police prejudice has received a great deal of attention at least since the late 1990s when it was addressed as a topic of concern in the President's Initiative on Race ("One America," 1998).

> Racial disparities and prejudices affect the way in which minorities are treated by the criminal system. Examples of this phenomenon can be found in the use of racial profiling in law enforcement and in the differences in the rates of arrest, conviction, and sentencing between whites and minorities and people of color. Law enforcement professionals have recognized, especially as they enter the twenty-first century, that prejudices unchecked can result in not only citizen humiliation, lawsuits, loss of jobs, and long-term damage to police—community relations but in personal tragedy as well.

Sometimes, training changes behavior and, possibly, attitudes. Consider the example of firing warning shots. Most officers refrain from this action because they have been mandated to do so. They have gone through a process of "unfreezing" normative behavior (i.e., what has previously been customary) and have adopted a new desired behavior. Explicit directives from the top can result in profound changes in officers' decision-making and actions. Clear policies that, in no uncertain terms, condemn racist acts or forms of speech will prevent most outward demonstrations of prejudice. It is not acceptable to ask a citizen, "What are you doing here?" just because he or she is of a different background than the majority residing in a particular neighborhood. Officers pay attention to these specific and unequivocal directives coming from their chief of police. It may be difficult to eliminate some officers' stereotypes, but eliminating acts of prejudice becomes the mandate of the department.

Challenging Others' Expressions of Prejudice

Expressions of prejudice in police departments may go unchallenged because of officers' needs to conform or to fit into the group. It is not easy for police officers to question peers or challenge their attitudes. Peer behavior in groups can reinforce acts or expressions of racial bias. For example, when someone in a group makes an ethnic slur, others may begin to express the same hostile attitudes more freely. This behavior is particularly relevant in law enforcement agencies, given the nature of the police subculture and the strong influence of peer pressure. Thus, law enforcement leaders must unambiguously direct their subordinates to avoid any expressions of prejudice, even among peers, and to encourage them to speak out against when any officer verbalizes prejudiced or racist thoughts.

When it comes to expressions of prejudice, no one has to accept sweeping and demeaning stereotypes. An effective way to counter manifestations of prejudice is to interrupt biased speech and discriminatory behavior at all levels. Officers have to be willing to remind their peers that ethnic slurs and offensive language, as well as differential treatment of certain groups of people, are neither ethical nor professional. An officer or a civilian employee who does nothing in the presence of biased, racist, or other discriminatory behavior by his or her peers becomes a silent accomplice.

Mandating Change

When top management has mandated change, officers have no choice but to adopt a new standard of behavior. If discrimination occurs, police departments will be subjected to adverse media attention, lawsuits, citizen complaints, human relations commission involvement, or dismissal of the chief or other management. What may have been acceptable in the past may result in discipline, monetary sanctions, or worse. When police officers fail to control their biases, either in either speech or behavior, the resulting publicity can affect the reputations of all police officers reinforcing the popular stereotype that police are racists or bigots.

One example of this involved a suburban police department that was besieged by the press and outraged citizens for over two years after several police officers were found to have exchanged racist messages on their mobile computers, making references to "Nigger" and to the Ku Klux Klan. This resulted in a citizens' investigation of the department to assess the extent of the institutionalized racism. In their report, the committee members wrote that the disclosure of the racial slurs was "an embarrassment and a crushing blow" to the image and credibility of the city and the police department. In addition, they demanded that the chief resign. In subsequent, mandated cultural diversity workshops, officers said they believed that the entire incident had been overblown since there had been no "victim." These individuals failed to understand that officers' use of derogatory terms alone was inappropriate and offensive. Individuals feel insecure for their safety and mistrustful when officers who are sworn to protect the public harbor hateful beliefs and attitudes. Such incidents are extremely costly from all points of view.

Beyond eliminating prejudice manifested in speech, police management can teach officers how to reduce or eliminate acts of bias and discrimination. A large metropolitan police department hired several human relations consultants to help assess community–police problems. The chief insisted that they ride in a police car for four weekends so that they would "appreciate the problems of law officers working in the black ghetto." Every Friday through Sunday night, the consultants rode along with a unit that other officers had designated as the "Gestapo police." When the month ended and the chief asked what the consultants had learned, they replied, "If we were black, we would hate the police." The chief, somewhat bewildered, asked why. "Because we have personally witnessed black citizens experiencing a series of unjust, unwarranted intimidations, searches, and series of harassments by unprofessional police." Fortunately, that chief, to his credit, accepted the feedback and introduced a well-received course in human relations skills. After this training, the officers demonstrated greater professionalism in their interactions with members of the black community.

Image and Professionalism with Diverse Communities

Law enforcement and criminal justice professionals need to act proactively and knowledgeably as they face the myriad challenges of neighborhood transition, race relations, integration of immigrants and refugees, economic constraints, and the complexity of crimes. They have to be vigilant about avoiding racist, sexist, and homophobic behavior that can trigger violent social protest. Representatives of the law enforcement profession, together with local, state and national leaders, must track and prosecute hate crimes as well as continually communicate to the public the dangers of hate speech. Leaders are the role models who must exhibit ethical and just behavior, ensuring that other department members do the same.

How the public views law enforcement depends largely on the professionalism that officers display with regard to bias-free policing, cultural competence, knowledge of police procedures, and communication. The images of law enforcement projected by police officers, their organizations, and the media are especially important in multicultural contexts. Lack of professionalism and inadequate staff training can cause significant harm to any organization. In the public sector, such problems can damage the individuals' careers as well as their agencies and society as a whole.

Current demographic trends indicate that multiculturalism will continue to increase in the general population and in the workforce. In recognition of this phenomenon, dedicated law enforcement professionals need to support policies that promote collaboration among people of diverse backgrounds, and work with the public to counteract hate speech, hate crimes and intolerance, a key strategy for peacekeeping in a diverse society.

Seven Tips for Improving Law Enforcement in Multicultural Communities*

- Engage with community members from diverse backgrounds—make positive contact with community group members. Don't let them see you only when something negative has happened. Allow the public to see you as much as possible in a nonenforcement role.
- Make a conscious effort in your mind, en route to every situation, to treat all people objectively and fairly.
- Remember that all groups have some bad, some average, and some good people within them.
- Don't appear uncomfortable with or avoid discussing racial and ethnic issues with other officers and members of the public.
- Take responsibility for patiently educating citizens and the public about the role of the officer and about standard operating procedures in law enforcement. Remember that citizens often do not understand "police culture."
- Don't be afraid to be a change agent in your organization when it comes to improving cross-cultural and interracial relations within your department as well as between police and community. It may not be a popular thing to do, but it is the right thing to do.
- Remember the history of law enforcement with all groups and ask yourself the question, "Am I part of the past, or a part of the future?"

*Tips and quotes are from Ondra Berry, retired deputy chief of Reno Police Department, 2017.

Summary

- A diverse society contributes to the challenges of a law enforcement officer's job. Diversity enriches our society, but increases the complexity of many police procedures and interactions with the public. A key strategy for peacekeeping in a diverse society involves breaking down the respective barriers and stereotypes that exist between law enforcement personnel and members of the public. Community policing, whatever the particular model, has always emphasized direct involvement with civic organizations, citizens and residents with the ultimate goals of improving trust and safety.

- Multiculturalism has been present in this country since its founding. America has often been referred to as a melting pot, a term depicting an image of people coming together and forming a unified culture. However, the melting pot did not really ever exist. The first generation of every immigrant and refugee group in the United States has always experienced obstacles to acculturation into the new society. History does not support the metaphor of the melting pot, especially with regard to the first and second generations of most immigrant groups. The terms *mosaic* and *tapestry* more accurately portray American diversity. The terms describe a society in which people of all colors and backgrounds contribute to form society as a whole—and one in which groups are not required to lose their characteristics in order to "melt" together. The idea of a mosaic portrays a society, in which groups are seen as separate and distinct, contributing their own colors, shapes, and designs to the whole.

- Global migration and displacement affect the U.S. population directly. After World War II, the United States signed treaties related to the status of refugees, granting them the legal right not to be sent back home, where they would be at risk of persecution, torture, and/or death. The core principle of these treaties asserts that refugees should not be returned to countries where they face serious threats to their lives or freedom. Refugees and immigrants in the United States represent a significant percentage of the population, especially in certain cities and states. Key issues for law enforcement related to immigrant and refugee populations include reluctance to report crimes, fear of deportation, and hate crimes and hate speech.

- "Culture" is defined as beliefs, values, patterns of thinking, behavior, and everyday customs that have been passed on from generation to generation. Culture is learned rather than inherited, and is typically manifested in unconscious and subtle behavior. If law enforcement's function is to protect and serve citizens from all cultural backgrounds, it becomes vital to understand the cultural dimensions of crimes. Obviously, behaviors or actions that may be acceptable in another culture must not go unpunished if they are considered crimes in this country. Nevertheless, there are some circumstances in which law enforcement officials at all levels of the criminal justice system would benefit by understanding the cultural context in which a crime or other incident occurred. When officers suspect that an aspect of cultural background is a factor in a particular incident, they may earn the respect of—and therefore cooperation from—ethnic communities if they are willing to evaluate their arrests in lesser crimes.

- A "primary dimension of diversity" is a core characteristic with which a person is born and which remains with the individual in all stages of his or her life. A "secondary dimension of diversity" is a characteristic that a person acquires by choice, usually made by that person or his or her family. Among various ethnic groups, there are nuanced diversity factors that should be further considered, including how age is seen in different cultures, competence in English, generational status, and family composition among others. Understanding such differences helps to counter the tendency to overgeneralize about groups.

- Increasingly, researchers in the social sciences contend that all people have biases, and that such biases are largely out of conscious awareness. Every individual, regardless of his or her line of work or background, has "implicit biases"; this is part of being human. Even non-prejudiced people have implicit biases, which do not make them racists, however. Law enforcement personnel have their own biases—implicit and sometimes explicit. To deny the existence of bias, prejudice or racism in any given law enforcement agency would be to deny that it exists outside the agency. Members of the law enforcement profession have to examine their words, behaviors, and actions to evaluate whether they are conveying professionalism and respect to all people within the workplace and on the streets, regardless of race, culture, religion, or ethnic background. To function effectively in a multicultural society, officers and civilian employees have a responsibility to refrain from expressions of prejudice, recognizing when bias and stereotypes are contributing to biased judgments and potentially differential treatment of members of the public.

- Within diverse communities, effective law enforcement and criminal justice professionals need to act proactively and knowledgeably as they face the myriad challenges of neighborhood transition, race relations, integration of immigrants and refugees, economic constraints, and the complexity of crimes. They have to be vigilant about avoiding racist, sexist, and homophobic behavior that can trigger violent social protest. Representatives of the law enforcement profession, together with local, state and national leaders, must track and prosecute hate crimes as well as continually communicate to the public the dangers of hate speech. Leaders are the role models who must exhibit ethical and just behavior, ensuring that other department members do the same.

Discussion Questions and Issues

1. *Importance of History in Policing:* Discuss the following quote from a speech on Race and Law Enforcement by former FBI director, James Comey.

   One reason we cannot forget our law enforcement legacy is that the people we serve and protect cannot forget it, either. So we must talk about our history. It is a hard truth that lives on. (Comey, 2015)

2. *Views on the Multicultural Society.* The following viewpoints regarding our increasingly multicultural population reflect varying levels of tolerance, understanding, and acceptance. Discuss the following points of view and their implications for law enforcement:
   • Diversity is acceptable if there is not too much of it, but the way things are going today, it is hard to absorb and it just may result in our destruction.
   • They are here now, and they need to do things our way.
   • To advance in our diverse society, we need to accept and respect our differences rather than maintain the myth of the melting pot.

3. *Global Migration and U.S. Refugees and Immigrants.* Discuss how global migration and displacement affect the United States in a direct way. Include in your response the impact of the 1951 Treaty regarding refugees.

4. *Interacting with Undocumented Immigrants.* Does the police department in which you work (or in the city in which you reside) have an agreement with ICE regarding unauthorized immigrants? Are officers instructed not to inquire into their status unless a crime has been committed? How do people within your department (if applicable) feel about cooperation with ICE with respect to undocumented immigrants with no record or with only misdemeanors.

5. *Mini Case Studies and Cultural Practices: Does Culture Matter?—Discussion Questions*
   5. A. *Culture Matters?* Reread, then discuss.

      The Sword in a Public Park
      • What are the laws pertaining to knives or swords in public places in the jurisdiction where you live or work?
      • What would you do if you were a police officer encountering an individual practicing Tai Chi with a sword in a public park?
      • What would you say and what would your approach be?

   5. B. *Culture Matters?* Reread, then discuss.

      The Turban and the *Kirpan*
      • What laws pertain to carrying a *kirpan* (sheathed knife) in your city, county, or state?
      • Find out and discuss how Sikh *kirpans* are handled within the school district in which you live or work? How about within public buildings in your jurisdiction?
      • Regardless of the guilt or innocence of the Sikh individual who is arrested, the surrounding close-knit Sikh community will likely judge the manner in which a Sikh is treated. If you were a police officer in a situation such as the one described, what would you want the community to say about the way you confiscated the *kirpan* and removed the turban (i.e., assuming you also had reason to do the latter)?

   5. C. *Culture Matters?* Reread, then discuss.

      A Tragic Case of Cross-Cultural Misinterpretation
      • Do you think this case would have proceeded differently if all the authorities involved understood the cultural tradition of the medical practice ("coin rubbing") that caused the bruising? Explain your answer.
      • Discuss whether you think Southeast Asian refugees should give up this medical practice because it can be misinterpreted.

   5. D. *Culture Matters?* Reread, then discuss.

      Latino Values as a Factor in Sentencing
      • Discuss whether culture should play any part in influencing the sentencing of a criminal convicted of violent crimes such as murder and rape. Was the lighter verdict in this case justified? Explain your answer.
      • According to retired Superior Court Judge Katz, culture influenced the sentencing in this case. In your opinion, if the husband involved were not Latino, would the sentence have been the same?

6. *Bias, Prejudice, and Discrimination in Police Work.* In your own words, define implicit and explicit bias, prejudice and discrimination. Give examples of: (a) discrimination in society in general, (b) prejudice and bias against police officers, and (c) discrimination toward minorities by police officers. Discuss what law enforcement managers and leaders can do to control the expressions of prejudice in their departments. How can police officers be role models in this regard?

References

American Immigration Council. (2016a). "El Salvador's Gang Violence is Forcing Thousands to Flee," by Walter Ewing. http://immigrationimpact.com/2016/10/21/el-salvadors-gang-violence-forcing-thousands-flee/ (accessed November 3, 2016).

American Immigration Council. (2016b). Fact Sheet: Asylum in the United States. www.americanimmigrationcouncil.org/research/asylum-united-states (accessed November 13, 2016).

American Immigration Council. (2016c). Fact Sheet: The 287(g) Program: A Flawed and Obsolete Method of Immigration Enforcement. www.americanimmigrationcouncil.org/research/287g-program-flawed-and-obsolete-method-immigration-enforcement (accessed November 15, 2016).

Berry, Ondra. (2017). Retired Deputy Police Chief, Reno, Nevada Police Department, personal communication, March 15.

CFR. (2016). Central America's Violent Northern Triangle by Danielle Renwick, January 19. Council on Foreign Relations. www.cfr.org/backgrounder/central-americas-violent-northern-triangle (accessed August 29, 2017).

Castillo, Vanessa, LCSW. (2017). Social Worker/Integrated Behavioral Clinician III-Lead, personal communication, June 28.

Center for American Progress. (2014). "5 Things You Need to Know about Unaccompanied Children," by Wogin and Kelley. www.americanprogress.org/issues/immigration/news/2014/06/18/92056/5-things-you-need-to-know-about-the-unaccompanied-minors-crisis/ (accessed November 16, 2016).

The Chief Justice Earl Warren Institute on Law and Social Policy. (2011). University of California Berkeley Law School. "Secure Communities by the Numbers: An Analysis of Demographics and Due Process" by Kohli, Markowitz, and Chavez. www.law.berkeley.edu/files/Secure_Communities_by_the_Numbers.pdf (accessed November 12, 2016).

Coffey, Alan, Edward Eldefonson, and Walter Hartinger. (1982). *Human Relations: Law Enforcement in a Changing Community*, 3rd ed. Englewood Cliffs, NJ: Prentice-Hall.

Comey, James B. (2015). "Hard Truths: Law Enforcement and Race." Former FBI Director's speech at Georgetown University, Washington, D.C. February 12. www.fbi.gov/news/speeches/hard-truths-law-enforcement-and-race (accessed December 1, 2016).

De Santis, Marie. (2013). "Help: Special for Immigrant Women." Women's Justice Center. www.justicewomen.com (accessed April 15, 2013).

Delta News Hub. (2016). "Delta Uses Social Feedback as Opportunity to Improve." December 19. http://news.delta.com/delta-uses-social-feedback-opportunity-improve (accessed April 2, 2017).

Ewins, Teresa. (2017). Captain, San Francisco Police Department, personal communication, May 24.

FIP Web Site. (2017). "Fair and Impartial Policing," USDOJ COPS supported training programs for Law Enforcement (*Command Level, Supervisor, Patrol and Train the Trainer* developed between 2008 and 2014; 2017 update FIP, LLC). www.fairimpartialpolicing.com/ (accessed December 15, 2016).

Fridell, Lorie. Ph.D. (2017a). Former Director of Research at the Police Executive Research Program (PERF); National Expert on Biased Policing, personal communication, January 31.

Fridell, Lorie. Ph.D. (2017b). *Producing Bias-Free Policing: A Science Based Approach*. New York, NY: Springer Publishers.

Gilsinan, Kathy. (2013). "Why Are There So Many Bosnians in St. Louis?" *The Atlantic Cities*. www.theatlanticcities.com/politics/2013/02/why-are-there-so-many-bosnians-st-louis/4668/ (accessed August 4, 2013).

Gramlich, John. (2017). "Black and White Officers See Many Aspects of Policing Differently." January 12. Pew Research Center. www.pewresearch.org/fact-tank/2017/01/12/black-and-white-officers-see-many-key-aspects-of-policing-differently/ (accessed January 18, 2017).

The Guardian. (2017). "Man Charged with Killing Indian Said to Have Shouted 'Go Back to Your Country'." February 24. https://www.theguardian.com/us-news/2017/feb/24/killing-of-indian-man-in-kansas-bar-investigated-possible-hate-crime (accessed March 1, 2017).

Hall, Edward T. (1959). *The Silent Language*. Greenwich, CT: Fawcett.

Handlin, Oscar. (1975). *Out of Many: A Study Guide to Cultural Pluralism in the United States*. Anti-Defamation League of B'nai B'rith. Louisville, KY: Brown & Williamson Tobacco Corporation.

Hauser, Christine. (2016). "Black Doctor Says Delta Flight Attendant Rejected Her; Sought 'Actual Physician'." October 14. *The New York Times*. www.nytimes.com/2016/10/15/us/black-doctor-says-delta-flight-attendant-brushed-her-aside-in-search-of-an-actual-physician.html?_r=0 (accessed December 27, 2016).

IACP. (2015). "IACP National Policy Summit on Community-Police Relations: Advancing a Culture of Cohesion and Community Trust." January. International Association of Chiefs of Police. http://www.iacp.org/Portals/0/documents/pdfs/CommunityPoliceRelationsSummitReport_web.pdf (accessed February 15, 2017).

Katz, Lawrence. (2017). Retired Presiding Judge, Juvenile Court of Contra Costa (California) County, personal communication, April 26.

Kennedy, John F. (1986). *A Nation of Immigrants*. New York, NY: Harper & Row, p. 14.

Levine, Shira. (2017). Immigration Attorney at Centro Legal De La Raza, Oakland, CA, personal communication, November 15, 2016.

Lewis, Brooke. (2017). "HPD Chief Announces Decrease in Hispanics Reporting Rape and Violent Crimes Compared to Last Year." April 6. www.chron.com/news/houston-texas/houston/article/HPD-chief-announces-decrease-in-Hispanics-11053829.php (accessed May 23, 2017).

Lipsett, Ilana. (2017). Director of Social Impact for Tidewater Capital and Community Manager at the Hall, San Francisco, CA, personal communication, May 1.

Loden Associates Inc. (2013). Primary and Secondary Dimensions of Diversity. www.loden.com/Web_Stuff/Dimensions.html (accessed July 24, 2013).

Loden, Marilyn. (2013). Organizational Diversity Consultant, Loden Associates Inc., personal communication, June 13, 2016.

Major Cities Chiefs Association. (2013). Immigration Policy. Major Cities Chiefs. https://www.majorcitieschiefs .com/pdf/news/2013_immigration_policy.pdf (accessed August 25, 2017).

Martinez, Christopher. (2017). Chief Program Officer, Catholic Charities of the East Bay (California), personal communication, June 23.

McCarthy, Justin. (2016). "Americans' Respect for Police Surges," Gallup Poll, October 24. www.gallup.com /poll/196610/americans-respect-police-surges.aspx (accessed November 1, 2016).

Medina, Jennifer. (2017). "Too Scared to Report Sexual Abuse. The Fear: Deportation." April 30. https://www.nytimes .com/2017/04/30/us/immigrants-deportation-sexual -abuse.html?_r=0 (accessed May 23, 2017).

Mejia, Brittny. (2017). "Gripped by Fear of ICE Raids and Deportations, One Town Tries to Separate Fact from Rumor." February 24. www.latimes.com/local/california/la-me-ln -santa-paula-20170224-story.html (accessed April 1, 2017).

Migration Policy Institute. (2015). "European Immigrants in the United States." Table I. Distribution of European Immigrants by Region and Top Country of Origin, 2014. www.migrationpolicy.org/article/european-immigrants -united-states (accessed September 1, 2016). http://www .migrationpolicy.org/topics/deportationsremovals (accessed May 23, 2017).

Migration Policy Institute. (2017). "Deportations/Removals." www.migrationpolicy.org/topics/deportationsremovals (accessed May 22, 2017).

Miles, Tom. (2016). "Syrian Opposition Says Refugees will Return Home as Soon as it is Safe." March 18. *Reuters*. www .reuters.com/article/us-mideast-crisis-syria-muslat -idUSKCN0WK1LL (accessed October 30, 2016).

Miller, Char. (2017). (Former) Professor of History, Trinity College, San Antonio, TX, personal communication, February 15.

National Sherriff's Association. (2011). National Sherriff's Association Position Paper on Comprehensive Immigration Reform. http://cis.org/sites/cis.org/files/articles/2012 /nsa-position-paper-on-immigration-and-border-security .pdf (accessed November 15, 2016).

NYPD. (2016). New York Police Department, Community Affairs: Special Outreach Programs and Services. www .nyc.gov/html/nypd/html/community_affairs/special _outreach_programs.shtml#CommunityPartnership (accessed November 30, 2016).

Olson, Aaron T. (2017). Former Instructor at IRCO sponsored sessions "Helping Immigrants and Refugees: Police and Emergency Training," Portland, OR, personal communication, January 16.

"One America in the 21st Century: Forging a New Future," Executive Summary, Advisory Board to the President's Initiative on Race, September 1998.

Orloff, Leslye. (2003, February 27). Testifying as the director of the Immigrant Women Program, NOW Legal Defense and Education Fund, before the Subcommittee on Immigration, Border Security, and Claims House Judiciary Committee.

Pardo, Charles C. (2010, January 14). "Crimes Go Unreported by Undocumented Immigrants, RPD Chief Says." *Raleigh Public Record*. http://raleighpublicrecord.org/news /2010/01/14/crimes-go-unreported-by-undocumented -immigrants-rpd-chief-says/ (accessed July 29, 2013).

Passel, Jeffrey and D'Vera Cohn. (2011). "Unauthorized Immigrant Population: National and State Trends, 2010." February 1. Pew Research Hispanic Trends Project. www .pewhispanic.org/2011/02/01/appendix-c-maps / (accessed August 25, 2013).

Passel, Jeffrey and D'Vera Cohn. (2014). "Chapter 1: State Unauthorized Immigrant Populations." November 18. Pew Research Hispanic Trends. www.pewhispanic.org /2014/11/18/chapter-1-state-unauthorized-immigrant -populations/ (accessed June 14, 2017).

Pew Research Center. (2010). "Millennials: A Portrait of Generation Next." www.pewsocialtrends.org/files/2010/10 /millennials-confident-connected-open-to-change.pdf (accessed September 1, 2016).

Pew Research Center. (2015). Multiracial in America. June 11. www.pewsocialtrends.org/2015/06/11/chapter-2-counting -multiracial-americans/ (accessed October 1, 2016).

Pew Research Center Hispanic Trends Project. (2015). "U.S. Foreign-Born Population Reaches New High." September 23. www.pewhispanic.org/2015/09/28/modern-immigration -wave-brings-59-million-to-u-s-driving-population -growth-and-change-through-2065/ph_2015-09-28 _immigration-through-2065-52/ (accessed January 17, 2017).

Population Reference Bureau. (2013). 2012 World Population Data Sheet. www.prb.org/Publications/Datasheets /2012/2012-world-population-data-sheet.aspx (accessed May 19, 2013).

PRI, 2013. "Some Immigrant Women, Victims of Domestic Violence, Afraid to Seek Help," March 21, 2013. PRI's The World. https://www.pri.org/stories/2013-03-21/some -immigrant-women-victims-domestic-violence-afraid-seek -help (accessed August 229, 2017).

Project Implicit. (2011). Project Implicit. https://implicit .harvard.edu/implicit/ (accessed June 29, 2013).

Rawlins, Gary H. (1992, October 8). "Africans Came 200 Years Earlier." *USA Today*, p. 2a.

Renshon, Stanley. (2017). Professor of Political Science, CUNY Graduate Center, personal communication, January 3.

Richards, Sarah E. (2017). "How Fear of Deportation Puts Stress on Families." March 22. www.theatlantic.com/ health/archive/2017/03/deportation-stress/520008/ (accessed April 1, 2017).

The Rockridge Institute. (2003). Project Economic Refugee. What are Economic Refugees? www.economicrefugee.net /what-does-economic-refugee-mean/ (accessed November 13, 2016).

Saint-Fort, Pradine, Noelle Yasso, and Susan Shah. (2012). "Engaging Police in Immigrant Communities: Promising Practices from the Field." October. Community Oriented Policing Services (COPS/DOJ) and Vera Institute of Justice. http://archive.vera.org/sites/default/files/resources /downloads/engaging-police-in-immigrant-communities .pdf (accessed January 15, 2017).

Sherman, Spencer. (1986). "When Cultures Collide." *California Lawyer*, 6(1), 33.

Skogan, Wesley G. (2005). "Citizen Satisfaction with Police Encounters," *Police Quarterly*, September 1, 2005. Vol. 8, Issue 3. http://journals.sagepub.com/doi/abs/10.1177 /1098611104271086 (accessed November 30, 2016).

Taxin, Amy. (2017). "Immigrants with Old Deportation Orders Arrested at Check-Ins, June 8, 2017." *The Washington Post*

(Associated Press). https://www.washingtonpost.com /national/under-t (accessed June 11, 2017).

Tharoor, Ishaan. (2016, January 26). Based on "Some Syrian Refugees in Canada Already Want to Return to the Middle East." *The Washington Post.* Washingtonpost.com/news /worldviews/wp/2016/01/26/some-syrian-refugees-in -canada-already-want-to-return-to-the-middle-east/?utm _term=.70a297465e22 (accessed December 27, 2016).

Tiede, Lydia B. (2001). "Battered Immigrant Women and Immigration Remedies: Are the Standards Too High?" *Human Rights Magazine.* Section Individual Rights and Responsibilities, American Bar Association, Winter 2001; Vol. 28, No. 1. (Excerpted with permission June, 2009).

UNHCR. (2016a). "With 1 Human in Every 113 Affected, Forced Displacement Hits Record High." www.unhcr .org/en-us/news/press/2016/6/5763ace54/1-human-113 -affected-forced-displacement-hits-record-high.html (accessed November 5, 2016).

UNHCR. (2016b). Syrian Regional Refugee Response. http:// data.unhcr.org/syrianrefugees/regional.php (accessed December 15, 2016).

UNHCR. (2017a) "Convention and Protocol Related to the Status of Refugees." Text of the 1951 Convention Relating to the Status of Refugees. Text of the 1967 Protocol Relating to the Status of Refugees. UNHCR home page www.unhcr .org/en-us/about-us.html [under UNHCR Convention and Protocol] (accessed November 1, 2016).

UNHCR. (2017b) The UN Refugee Agency. "The 1951 Refugee Convention." www.unhcr.org/en-us/about-us.html (accessed December 18, 2016).

UNHCR. (2017c). Figures at a Glance. http://www.unhcr .org/figures-at-a-glance.html (accessed August 25, 2017).

UNIFEM. (2013). UN Women: Violence Against Women. www .unifem.org/gender_issues/violence_against_women/ (accessed 24, 2013).

U.S. Census Bureau. American Community Survey. (2010). "The Foreign-Born Population in the U.S." https://www .census.gov/newsroom/pdf/cspan_fb_slides.pdf (accessed September 1, 2016).

U.S. Census Bureau. (2010). State and Country Quick Facts: Foreign-Born Persons. http://quickfacts.census.gov/qfd / (accessed May 27, 2013).

U.S. Census Bureau. (2011). Overview of Race and Hispanic Origin: 2010. www.census.gov/prod/cen2010/briefs /c2010br-02.pdf (accessed June 26, 2013).

U.S. Census Bureau. (2012a). "Census Bureau Establishes National Advisory Committee on Race, Ethnic and Other Populations." October 12. www.census.gov/newsroom /releases/archives/miscellaneous/cb12-195.html (accessed June 27, 2013).

U.S. Census Bureau. (2012b). The Two or More Races Population: 2010. www.census.gov/prod/cen2010/briefs /c2010br-13.pdf (accessed May 27, 2013).

U.S. Census Bureau. (2013). How Do We Know? www.census .gov/how/infographics/foreign_born.html (accessed June 27, 2013).

U.S. Census Bureau. (2014). American Community Survey 5-Year Estimates, 2009–2013. "United States Foreign-Born Population Percentage by State." www.indexmundi.com /facts/united-states/quick-facts/all-states/foreign-born -population-percent#chart; http://factfinder2.census.gov (accessed September 30, 2016).

U.S. Census Bureau. (2015). "Projections of the Size and Composition of the U.S. Population: 2014–2060." March 3. http://www.census.gov/newsroom/press-releases /2015/cb15-tps16.html (accessed October 15, 2016).

U.S. Citizenship and Immigration Services. (2013). Department of Homeland Security. Information Resources and Immigration Services, Data Integration Division, U.S. Census Bureau. www.uscis.gov/portal/site/uscis (accessed June 29, 2013).

U.S. Citizenship and Immigration Services. (2015). Department of Homeland Security. The Affirmative Asylum Process. www.uscis.gov/humanitarian/refugees-asylum /asylum (accessed November 2016).

U.S. Department of Homeland Security. (2013a). Definition of Terms. www.dhs.gov/definition-terms (accessed May 18, 2013).

U.S. Department of Homeland Security. (2013b). FY 2013 Budget in Brief. www.dhs.gov/xlibrary/assets/mgmt/dhs -budget-in-brief-fy2013.pdf (accessed June 5, 2013).

U.S. Department of Homeland Security. (2014). "Refugees and Asylees: 2014." www.dhs.gov/sites/default/files /publications/Refugees%20%26%20Asylees%20Flow%20 Report%202014_508.pdf." (accessed November 3, 2016).

U.S. Department of State. Bureau of Consular Affairs. Visas for Victims of Criminal Activity. https://travel.state.gov /content/visas/en/other/visas-for-victims-of-criminal -activity.html (accessed December 14, 2016).

U.S. Department of Justice. (2013). Tribal Law and Order Act. www.justice.gov/tribal/tloa.html (accessed July 5, 2013).

U.S. Department of State. (2015a). Background Briefing on the United States Refugee Admission Program. www.state .gov/r/pa/prs/ps/2015/09/246742.htm (accessed December 21, 2016).

U.S. Department of State. (2015b). Honduras 2015 Human Rights Report: Executive Summary. www.state.gov/documents /organization/253235.pdf (accessed December 16, 2016).

U.S. Immigration and Customs Enforcement. (2014). Department of Homeland Security. Priority Enforcement Program. www.ice.gov/pep (accessed December 20, 2016).

U.S. Immigration and Customs Enforcement. (2017). Department of Homeland Security. U.S. Immigration and Customs Enforcement: Fact Sheets 287g. www.ice.gov /factsheets/287g (accessed May 23, 2017).

Whitehouse.gov. (2015). Infographic: The Screening Process for Refugee Entry into the United States. The White House. www.whitehouse.gov/blog/2015/11/20/infographic- screening-process-refugee-entry-united-states (accessed September 30, 2016).

Wible, Pamela. (2016). "Her Story Went Viral. But She Is Not the Only Black Doctor Ignored in an Emergency." October 20. *The Washington Post.* www.washingtonpost.com/national /health-science/tamika-cross-is-not-the-only-black-doctor -ignored-in-an-airplane-emergency/2016/10/20/3f59ac08 -9544-11e6-bc79-af1cd3d2984b_story.html?utm _term=.6d7235d0957b (accessed December 27, 2016).

Zangwill, Israel. (1908). *The Melting Pot: Drama in Four Acts.* New York, NY: Macmillan.

2

The Changing Law Enforcement Agency
A Microcosm of Society

LEARNING OBJECTIVES

After reading this chapter, you should be able to:

- Identify how the ethnic, racial, and gender composition of law enforcement agencies is changing in the United States.
- Define racism and understand the steps managers and supervisors can take to identify and control prejudicial conduct by employees.
- Describe methods for defusing conflicts within the organization and community related to issues of gender, sexual orientation, race, and ethnicity.
- Explain the history of women in law enforcement and the issues confronting them.
- Define LGBTQ and gender identity.
- Explain how law enforcement chief executives must convey zero tolerance for discrimination based on sexual orientation.
- Explain the role of police department leadership in providing a workplace environment that is inclusive of all employees.

OUTLINE

- Introduction
- Changing Workforce
- Racism within the Law Enforcement Workforce
- Women in Law Enforcement
- LGBTQ Employees in Law Enforcement
- Commitment, Leadership, and Management in the Diverse Workforce
- Summary
- Discussion Questions and Issues
- References

INTRODUCTION

In Chapter 1, we reviewed the evolution of multicultural communities and the demographic changes that the United States has experienced in recent decades. The most notable demographic changes mentioned involve the increases in racial, ethnic, and immigrant populations in our country. Even the connotations of the words *majority group* and *minority group* have changed since, in some cities and counties around the country, the demographic majority is comprised of people of color. Some react negatively to the term *minority*, which can carry, in some contexts, overtones of inferiority and inequity. The word, technically, is used to describe numerical designations, but over the years it has come to have much larger implications. While in this book we continue to use the term, we also want to remind the reader of the controversy around the term.

The range of reactions to demographic changes in society as a whole is no different from the reactions within law enforcement agencies. Members of police communities across the country have demonstrated both tolerance of and resistance to the changing society and workforce. While it is a fact of U.S. life, some officers resent the multicultural workforce and the involvement of women in policing, although the latter is becoming a nonissue. In the case of these officers, their own prejudices or biases inform their lack of acceptance of diversity.

> Today productivity must come from the collaboration of culturally diverse women and men. It insists that leaders change organizational culture to empower and develop people. This demands that employees be selected, evaluated, and promoted based on *performance and competency*, regardless of sex, race, religion, or place of origin. Beyond that, leaders must learn skills to enable men and women of all backgrounds to work together effectively. (Simons, Vazquez, & Harris, 2011)

Leading positively within a diverse agency are the keys to meeting the challenge of policing multicultural communities. As discussed in Chapters 1 and 6, serious racial and ethnic tensions exist between minority communities and law enforcement, especially since the multiple fatal shootings of African American men and resulting violence between 2014 and 2016. In 2015, the President's Task Force on 21st Century Policing report provided many recommendations related to the need for more diversity in law enforcement agencies. Agency personnel must address the conflicts in their own organizations before dealing with racial, ethnic, or sexual orientation issues in the community. For example, if there are allegations of harassment, a hostile work environment, or differential treatment within the agency, these allegations must be addressed on a timely basis, or they fester and result in lawsuits, court injunctions, and unhappy employees who do not remain with the organization.

Law enforcement agencies themselves determine, by their action or inaction, whether social problems that manifest within the agencies are resolved. Across the United States, the national press has reported numerous cases in which law enforcement agencies did nothing or took the wrong action. In some cases, such as with the Los Angeles Police Department, federal consent decrees with the Department of Justice have mandated changes in organizational culture and practices (see Chapter 6). Whether they like it or not, police officers are primary role models for citizens and are judged by a higher standard of behavior. While supervision of police officers is important to ensure that this higher standard of behavior is maintained, no amount of supervision of officers working with the public, no matter how thorough and conscientious, will prevent some officers from violating policies; there simply are too many police officers and too few supervisors. Thus, it is important that police officers demonstrate integrity and a stable set of core virtues. These virtues must include the ability to remain professional in protecting and serving a diverse public.

As stated in Chapter 1, those concerned with peacekeeping and enforcement must accept the realities of a multicultural society as well as the diversity within their workforce. The irony is that the law enforcement representatives sworn to uphold laws pertaining to acts of bias sometimes themselves become perpetrators, even against their peers. If police departments are to be representative of the populations served, police executives must effect changes. These changes have to do with the treatment of peers as well as recruitment, selection, and promotion of employees who have traditionally been under-represented in law enforcement. The argument (Chapter 1) that the United States has never really been a melting pot also applies to the law enforcement community. In some cases, relationships are characterized by disrespect and tension, within the law enforcement workplace, especially as diversity increases. Although many in the police subculture would argue that membership implies "brotherhood" (inclusion) or familial relationship and therefore belonging, this membership has traditionally excluded certain groups in both subtle and obvious ways.

CHANGING WORKFORCE

Historically, American policing has involved predominantly white males. However, as microcosms of their communities, law enforcement agencies increasingly include women, members of LGBTQ, and ethnic and racial minority communities among their personnel. Although such groups are far from achieving parity in most law enforcement agencies in the United States, advances have been made. The U.S. Bureau of Labor Statistics reports analyzing workforce participation show that rates for men and women in the workforce have been converging over the last several decades (see Exhibits 2.1, 2.2, and 2.3).

This profound shift in demographics has resulted in significant changes in law enforcement. In many regions of the country, today's law enforcement workforce differs greatly from

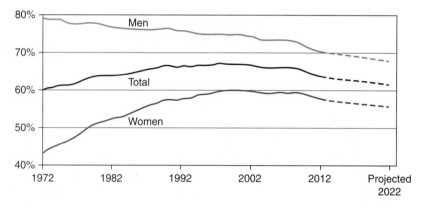

EXHIBIT 2.1   Labor Force Participation Rates for Men and Women, 1972–2012 and Projected 2022, in Percent
Source: Occupational Outlook Quarterly, Winter 2013–2014. U.S. Bureau of Labor Statistics.

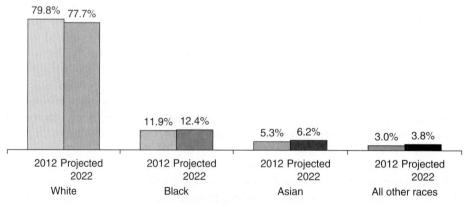

EXHIBIT 2.2   Percent Distribution of Labor Force by Race, 2012 and Projected 2022
Source: Occupational Outlook Quarterly, Winter 2013–2014. U.S. Bureau of Labor Statistics.

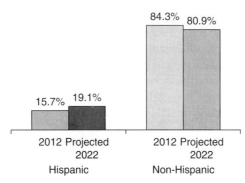

EXHIBIT 2.3   Percent Distribution of Labor Force by Ethnic Origin, 2012 and Projected 2022

Source: Occupational Outlook Quarterly, Winter 2013–2014. U.S. Bureau of Labor Statistics.

the workforce of the past. For example, the Hispanic population is growing at such a rate that it is difficult for public sector agencies, especially law enforcement, to have proportionate representation in the workforce. It is also difficult to keep up with the organizational changes required not only to provide police services, but also to recruit and retain personnel from the Hispanic/Latino population. For a law enforcement agency to maintain the support and trust of any community, it is essential that the organization reflect the diversity of the area it serves. In communities across the nation, officers come into contact with people from all different backgrounds on a daily basis. Each of these groups brings a different perspective to police–community relations. Frustration and resentment often result among citizens when their law enforcement agency fails to recognize and adjust to the diversity in the community. Such a failure can lead to the breakdown of the important, and often critical, bond of trust between community members and police.

Law Enforcement Diversity: A Microcosm of Society

According to Mike Maciag, data editor for the Governing magazine, minority groups remain underrepresented in local law enforcement agencies serving at least 100,000 residents.

> Racial and ethnic minorities are underrepresented by a combined 24 percentage points on average when each police department's sworn officer demographics are compared with census estimates for the general public. In 35 of the 85 jurisdictions where either blacks, Asians or Hispanics make up the single largest racial or ethnic group, their presence in the police department is less than half their share of the population. (Maciag, 2015)

A nationally representative census of law enforcement agencies, including organizations at the city, county, state, and federal levels, is conducted every four years by the Bureau of Justice Statistics (BJS). This is accomplished using a Law Enforcement Management and Administrative Statistics (LEMAS) data collection survey. There are approximately 18,000 federal, state, county, and local law enforcement agencies in the United States. Data collected from the BJS 2013 LEMAS survey provided the following demographics:

Local Police Departments

Of the estimated 12,000 local police departments in 2013 which employed about 477,000 sworn officers:

- 48 percent of the departments employed fewer than 10 officers
- 54 percent of the officers were employed by jurisdictions with 100,000 or more residents
- 12 percent of the officers were female
- 10 percent of the female officers were first-line supervisors
- 27 percent of the officers were members of a racial or ethnic minority.

Significantly, the number of minority officers increased by 78,000 officers or 150 percent between 1987 and 2013. During that same time frame, the number of Hispanic or Latino officers increased by 16 percent while the percentage of African American officers remained steady (Exhibit 2.4) (Reaves, 2015).

The percentage increase in local police departments of full-time sworn officers who are also people of color between 1987 and 2013 is shown in Exhibit 2.5.

Sheriffs' Offices

Of the estimated 3,012 sheriffs' offices in the nation in 2013, which employed approximately 189,000 full-time sworn officers:

- 14 percent were women
- 12 percent of the women were first-line supervisors
- 22 percent were racial or ethnic minorities with Latino officers making up the largest share (11 percent), closely followed by African American officers (9 percent) shown in Exhibit 2.6.

Some major law enforcement agencies have already achieved parity with respect to the percentage of minority employees as compared to demographics in the population of their communities, but most have not.

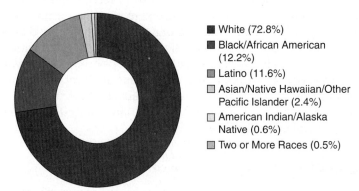

■ White (72.8%)
■ Black/African American (12.2%)
■ Latino (11.6%)
□ Asian/Native Hawaiian/Other Pacific Islander (2.4%)
□ American Indian/Alaska Native (0.6%)
■ Two or More Races (0.5%)

EXHIBIT 2.4   Local Police Departments by Race (2013)
Source: Adapted from Reaves, Brian. (2015). "Local Police Departments, 2013: Personnel, Policies, and Practices. U.S. Department of Justice, Bureau of Justice Statistics. www.bjs.gov/content/pub/pdf/lpd13ppp.pdf (accessed January 6, 2017).

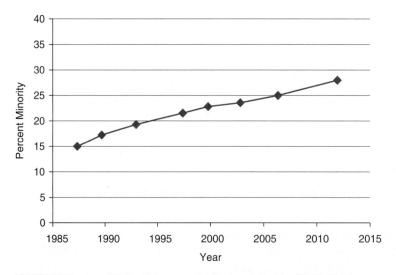

EXHIBIT 2.5   Local Police Departments: Percent Minority (1987–2013)
Source: Adapted from Reaves, Brian. (2015). "Local Police Departments, 2013: Personnel, Policies, and Practices. U.S. Department of Justice, Bureau of Justice Statistics. www.bjs.gov/content/pub/pdf/lpd13ppp.pdf (accessed January 6, 2017) .

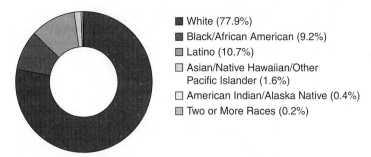

White (77.9%)
Black/African American (9.2%)
Latino (10.7%)
Asian/Native Hawaiian/Other Pacific Islander (1.6%)
American Indian/Alaska Native (0.4%)
Two or More Races (0.2%)

EXHIBIT 2.6   Sheriffs' Offices Breakdown by Race (2013)

Source: Sheriffs' Offices Breakdown by Race (2013). Retrived from https://www
.eeoc.gov/eeoc/interagency/police-diversity-report.cfm - _ftn46

RACISM WITHIN THE LAW ENFORCEMENT WORKFORCE

Workplace racism deeply disrupts relationships and morale within a police department, and once the public hears of it, erodes the trust and confidence of the community. Officers who apply unequal justice under the law break the oath they took at the department and subject their employer to lawsuits, which drain departmental resources.

There are different types of racism as well as biases, and they have been characterized in multiple ways. On the racism spectrum, there is "personally mediated," "institutional," and "internalized" racism. *Personally mediated* racism is what most people think of when they hear the word *racism* (Feagin, 2006). It includes specific attitudes based on stereotypes, biases, beliefs, practices, and behaviors leading to acts of prejudice, and discrimination directed toward others. It is explicit and overt.

Institutional racism is the failure of an organization, public or private, to provide goods, services, or opportunities to people because of their color, culture, or ethnic origin. This could be a failure of lenders to give home loans to people of certain races, a practice known as redlining, or when teachers and school administrators administer stricter punishment, such as detention or suspensions, to students of color.

Internalized racism is, in general terms, the personal conscious or sub-conscious acceptance of the dominant society's views, stereotypes, and biases of ethnic, racial, and other protected classes of people. In chapters 1 and 6 of this textbook, we focus on "implicit bias," and its direct implications for law enforcement.

Racism   Total rejection and discrimination of others for reasons of race, color, and sometimes cultural background.

Discrimination   Action based on prejudiced thought and biases; the denial of equal treatment to individuals or groups because of their age, disability, employment, language, nationality, race, ethnicity, sex, gender and gender identity, sexual orientation, religion, or other form of cultural identity. The terms "racial" and "ethnic" discrimination are sometimes used interchangeably.

Prejudice   A judgment or opinion formed before facts are known, usually involving negative or unfavorable thoughts about groups of people.

Bias   A preformed negative opinion or attitude toward a group of people based on their race, religion, disability, sexual orientation, ethnicity, gender, or gender identity.

Protected Classes   Groups of people who the law protects against illegal discrimination including the disabled, members of religious groups, pregnant women, people over 40, members of ethnic groups, LGBTQ people, and veterans. The law also protects people from "retaliation," who assert "their rights to be free from employment discrimination including harassment." (U.S. Equal Employment Opportunity Commission)

Racism has existed throughout human history as groups of individuals have always demonized the "other." Racism involves the underlying assumption that one race, almost always the white race, is superior to all others. *Racist* is the term applied to those who subscribe to this belief. Examples of racism are found not only in the words and actions of white supremacist groups, however, but also, unfortunately, in the words and actions of members of society who are not part of hate groups. Racism takes many forms, is often unconscious, and affects all kinds of people.

Institutional racism, or the appearance of the same, is devastating to those impacted by the practice, whether it is intentional, unintentional, or covert. One example of institutional racism is the use of pre-employment standardized tests as this kind of assessment is often significantly biased toward people of a certain cultural and social background, resulting in lower scores on the part of racial minorities. Unpaved roads in predominantly black neighborhoods can be viewed another example of institutionalized racism, as could the presence of older-edition, used textbooks in schools that are predominantly black.

Personally mediated or institutionalized racism within law enforcement agencies has been documented for decades. An African American history display at the New York Police Academy contains the following written account of the experiences of one of the first black officers in the New York Police Department:

> Seven years before the adoption of the charter creating New York City, Brooklyn, then an independent city, hired the first black policeman. Wiley G. Overton was sworn in on March 6, 1891… His first tour of duty was spent in civilian clothing because fellow officers breaking with tradition refused to furnish him with a temporary uniform…Officers in his section refused to sleep in the same room with him…The officers in the precinct ignored him and spoke only if it was necessary in the line of duty.

The New York Police Department is not alone. Racism can occur in police departments regardless of size or region. Unfortunately, racism has been an issue for decades. In an article published in 2014 for *The Western Journal of Black Studies*, Charles Wilson, the first African American chief of police of Woodmere Village (Ohio) Police Department and Shirley Wilson, a professor specializing in instruction on organizational behavior and global diversity at Bryant University, used surveys of African American police officers to determine their perceptions of the positive or negative effects of their presence in local police agencies. Their findings indicate that African-American police officers:

- continue to find themselves victims of racial indifference and seemingly hostile work environments;
- believe that racial profiling is both practiced and condoned by their agencies; that agencies do little to improve diversity and provide little support for their efforts;
- strongly perceive their presence in these smaller agencies to have a positive impact on police interactions in the minority community. (Wilson & Wilson, 2014)

Throughout the seven editions of this textbook, the authors have interviewed officers from different jurisdictions around the country about racism in their departments. These interviewees, for the most part, have requested that their names be omitted, because they were worried about repercussions. One African American officer recalled almost coming to blows with a white officer who used a racial slur against him; the use of such slurs was commonplace for the white officer and his friends. A Cuban American officer recounted the story of a nonresistant Latino suspect who was caught in the commission of a minor crime and beaten by the white arresting officers, who used racial epithets. One major city in Massachusetts suspended a deputy superintendent of police for using the word "nigger" directed toward one of his own officers. An African American officer in a large city in Florida was fired after using racial epithets against other blacks in violation of a strict citywide policy. In this particular case, the African American officer's conduct was reported by another officer at the scene. In yet another city, an African American officer was overheard telling a white prisoner, "Wait until you get to central booking and the niggers get hold of you."

In 2016, three police officers at San Francisco Police Department officers were investigated for sending text messages in which they referred to Latinos as "beaners," and Muslims as "rag heads." The allegations resulted in a federal review of the department amid a national debate about policing in minority communities. All officers were ordered to take an antiharassment class. Similar scandals occurred in two Florida police departments.

Institutional or personally mediated racism and discrimination is combated by using federal law. Under Title VII of the Civil Rights Act of 1964, the Americans with Disabilities Act, and the Age Discrimination in Employment Act, it is illegal to discriminate in any aspect of the hiring process or in employment. All workers in the United States are protected from harassment, discrimination, and employment decisions based on certain criteria. Complaints and allegations of discrimination in both the public and private sector are investigated, litigated, and resolved by the Equal Employment Opportunity Commission (EEOC), a federal agency. To be protected, individuals must be part of a "protected class" as described by federal or state law, policy, or similar authority; however, they must still exhibit necessary qualifications for the job, follow all company guidelines, and conduct themselves in a manner expected and required of all employees. The "protected class" designation means that workers are protected from employment discrimination on the basis of sex, race, religion, color, national origin, age (over 40), physical or mental disability, and retribution. In addition, Title II of the Genetic Information Nondiscrimination Act of 2008 (GINA) prohibits genetic information discrimination in employment. The Pregnancy Discrimination Act (PDA) forbids discrimination based on pregnancy when it comes to any aspect of employment, layoff, training, fringe benefits, such as leave and health insurance, and any other term or condition of employment (U.S. Equal Employment Opportunity Commission). It is also illegal for employers to retaliate against any employee or applicant who has filed a complaint about discrimination. In 2009, the U.S. Supreme Court ruled that workers who cooperate with their employers' internal investigations of discrimination may not be fired in retaliation for implicating colleagues or superiors (Crawford v. Metropolitan Gov't of Nashville and Davidson County, No. 06-1595, 2009).

On January 17, 2017, it was reported that the Secret Service had settled a two-decade-old case involving more than 100 black agents. In the suit, agents had alleged that the agency allowed a racist culture and repeatedly promoted white agents over more qualified African Americans. The Secret Service, even though settling, admitted no wrongdoing or institutional bias (Leonnig, 2017). Discrimination can also involve white employees. In 2012, a white police officer in Ithaca, New York, was awarded $2 million dollars in a federal lawsuit for what he alleged was race discrimination and retaliation. His claim asserted that he was denied a promotion due to being white, and that following the lawsuit, management changed his work assignment in retaliation. Ultimately, an all-white jury voted that his claims were legitimate, awarding him $2 million dollars (Hsieh, 2012).

For the fiscal year 2016, the EEOC investigated 42,018 charges of retaliation, making up 45 percent of all complaints filed, and the most frequent complaint (U.S. Equal Employment Opportunity Commission, 2016). Retaliation charges have increased each year and is attributed to employees becoming more aware or educated of their rights and willing to exercise them (Baumann, 2016; Trank, 2014).

Title VII of the Civil Rights Act of 1964 prohibits employment decisions based on stereotypes and assumptions about the abilities, traits, or performance of individuals of certain racial and ethnic groups. Additionally, both intentional discrimination and neutral job policies that disproportionately exclude minorities and that are not job-related are included in Title VII of the Civil Rights Act. For fiscal year 2016, the EEOC resolved nearly 97,500 charges of employment discrimination and obtained $482 million for victims of discrimination in the private sector and state and local government workplaces through voluntary resolutions and litigation.

The following shows the number of charges by category and percent of the total:

- *Race discrimination:* 32,309 (35.3 percent)
- *Religion-based discrimination:* 3,825 (4.2 percent)
- *National origin-based discrimination:* 9,840 (10.8 percent)
- *Color discrimination:* 3,102 (3.4 percent)

The numbers in all categories represent an increase over previous years. The year 2016 marks the first time that EEOC has included LGBTQ charges in its year-end summary. EEOC resolved 1,650 of these charges, and recovered $4.4 million for LGBTQ individuals who filed sex discrimination charges that fiscal year (EEOC, 2017). Chief executives, managers, supervisors, and employees should recognize from these figures the importance of defusing and controlling institutional or personally mediated racism and discrimination in the workplace.

Defusing Racially and Culturally Rooted Conflicts in the Workplace

To defuse racist attitudes, behaviors, and/or practices in all institutions, organization must be transparent about the racism that exists, and proactive about strategies to respond to and prevent racist acts. A good place to start is to recognize that people from all cultures, races, ethnic groups, and nations are equally susceptible to racist and exclusionary attitudes, practices, and behaviors. Whites are often on the defensive; any educational or training effort should not single out white employees (or students). If this happens, then there is very little chance of useful or productive dialogue, or appreciation for other racial experiences and perceptions.

One of the greatest challenges for police officers is dealing with their own conscious or unconscious negative bias, stereotypes, and prejudices. No one is able, nor can be forced, to abandon long-held prejudices easily. However, with the knowledge that racist acts can end in loss of life for both citizens and officers, and lawsuits can seriously ruin relations with the community, officers have no choice but to act professionally, treating all individuals with equal justice.

The first step in addressing racism is for police department personnel, on all levels, to admit, rather than deny, that racism exists. Police department command must encourage the use of conflict resolution techniques by officers of all backgrounds as a way of handling issues *prior* to their becoming flash points. Police command must also be trained to mitigate racial tensions or conflicts in the workplace with established techniques. With a high degree of professionalism and patience, conflict resolution techniques will, in most cases, reduce racial and ethnic problems within both the workforce and the neighborhoods. (In addition to the following, Chapter 4 includes a section on de-escalating conflict.)

Conflict Resolution Tips

The National Crime Prevention Council (NCPC) has developed the following list of things to remember when managing conflict:

1. Note that anger is a normal feeling.
2. How we handle our anger and how we deal with other people who are angry can make the difference between managing conflict effectively and having conflict end in violence.
3. Be aware of triggers, which are any verbal or nonverbal behaviors that result in anger or other negative emotional reactions that can get in the way of resolving conflicts.
4. Triggers are like lightning bolts. When they strike, they can interfere with communication.
5. To avoid pulling others' triggers, pay particular attention to your own behavior, even your body language.
6. Note that people already use strategies to control their anger (e.g., walking away from a dangerous situation), and need to continue to build on that foundation.
7. Continually work on staying calm and being an effective and respectful listener.
8. The less "hot" the anger, the more you can control it.
9. Even though your anger may be legitimate, it usually doesn't help to show your anger to the other person. Sometimes the other person will take you more seriously if you remain calm and courteous.
10. Remember that your goal is to be able to get angry without becoming abusive or violent, and to communicate your wants and needs effectively without threatening others. It may be necessary to define acceptable behavior. (National Crime Prevention Council)

It is important that law enforcement leaders acquire the skill sets required to resolve conflict among employees. A leadership advisor to Fortune 500 CEOs advises:

> Perhaps most importantly for leaders, good conflict resolution ability equals good employee retention. Leaders who don't deal with conflict will eventually watch their good talent walk out the door in search of a healthier and safer work environment. (Myatt, 2012)

Most law enforcement agencies across the nation have department codes of conduct and ethics that mandate appropriate behavior in the work place; nevertheless, harassment, discrimination, and conflict occur on a regular basis. Beyond the codes of behavior and contractual obligations of officers exist racially and culturally rooted conflicts requiring attention involving human relations skills, such as conflict resolution on the part of management.

Departmental General Orders for Control of Prejudicial Conduct

As we have mentioned previously, it is impossible to control or stop racist and prejudicial thinking. However, mandates can stop or control behavior. We include as an example the Lakeland (Florida) Police Department's Codes of Conduct, established in 2012. The following are the department's general orders whose objective is to prevent and control behavioral manifestations of prejudice:

3-1.7 Harassment in the Workplace
Members shall not engage in any conduct that constitutes racial, ethnic, gender or sexual harassment or abuse of authority as defined in the Department's general orders and procedures, or City of Lakeland Personnel Policy and Procedure Manual.

3-1.8 Bias-Based Policing
It is strictly prohibited for members to engage in the practice of bias-based profiling. Sworn members shall not take any police action that is based solely upon personal traits that include, but are not limited to race, ethnic background, gender, sexual orientation, religion, economic status, age and cultural group.

3-1.9 Member's Duty to Report Misconduct
Members shall promptly report any knowledge of another member's non-compliance with any federal, state or local law, City of Lakeland ordinance, Code of Ethics, Department directive, general or special order, policy or procedure, to their supervisor or personnel assigned to the Office of Professional Standards.

3-1.10 Courtesy, Responsiveness, and Impartiality
Members will exercise reasonable courtesy in all interaction with the public. Members will not use rude, cruel or profane language toward any citizen. Members will remain professional toward all individuals during the performance of their duties and while in the presence of the public. Members shall not express, whether by act, omission or statement, any prejudice concerning race, creed, gender, disability, ethnic background, sexual orientation, religion, economic or marital status, political or cultural group, national origin or other similar personal characteristics.

Members will provide all citizens with professional, effective and efficient police service.

Members shall not allow their decisions to be influenced by race, creed, gender, disability, ethnic background, sexual orientation, religion, economic or marital status, political or cultural group, national origin or other similar personal characteristics.

Members will not permit their personal opinions, associations or friendships to influence their decisions and shall remain impartial in the performance of their duties. (Lakeland Police Department Codes of Conduct, 2012)

The San Francisco Police Department in 2015 adopted a pledge used to guard against biases, intolerance, and bigotry:

San Francisco Police Department Not On My Watch Pledge

- I pledge to serve the people of San Francisco faithfully and honestly without prejudice.
- I will not tolerate hate or bigotry in our community or from my fellow officers.
- I will confront intolerance and report any such conduct without question or pause.
- I will maintain the integrity of the San Francisco Police Department and safeguard the trust of the people of San Francisco.
- I will treat members of the community as I would hope to be treated myself.
- I will pursue justice with compassion and respect the dignity of others.
- For those who would suggest there is any place for the stain of intolerance

I pledge, Not On My Watch.

(SFPD, 2017)

When police departments exhibit a pattern of violating their own codes of ethics and conduct with harassment and discrimination within the agency and/or patterns of racist behavior toward citizens, they may be subject to federal consent decrees. A consent decree is an agreement between the Department of Justice and a law enforcement agency and implemented by a court-appointed monitor to make sure that a department is fully accountable for changes that need to be made. Consent decrees are discussed in Chapter 6.

Police Organizations

Police fraternal, religious, racial, and ethnic organizations offer their members social activities, fellowship, counseling, career development, resources, and networking opportunities with persons of common heritage, background, or experience. The New York Police Department, for example, has many clubs, societies, and associations to address some of the needs of its diverse organization. For example, at the New York Police Department, the Irish are represented by the Emerald Society, African Americans by the Guardians Association, Christian officers by Police Officers for Christ, those of Asian or Pacific Islander heritage (which includes Chinese, Japanese, Korean, Filipino, and East Indian officers) by the Asian Jade Society, Muslims by the Muslim Officers Society, and the Italian officers by the Columbia Association.

Police work is stressful, so it's natural that people from different backgrounds seek comfort by socializing with those of a similar background. Membership in these groups can often mean a break from the stereotyping, hostility, indifference, ignorance, or naïveté that members encounter when interacting with residents in the greater community or even other police officers.

Occasionally we hear of criticism within a department or by the public that such organizations highlight the differences between groups of people. At a National Organization of Black Law Enforcement Executives (NOBLE) conference, a white female (non-member attendee) asked the meaning of the acronym NOBLE. When given the answer, she asked: "Is it ethical for blacks to have their own organization? Could whites have an organization called the 'National Organization of White Law Enforcement Executives' without being referred to as racists? Why can't the multicultural, social, and professional organizations that already exist satisfy the needs of everyone?"

The woman's concern was brought up directly with one of the African American speakers, who, at the time, was a state trooper. The speaker said that African American officers needed their own groups because they could not assimilate into the greater society nor express themselves freely in a white-dominant society or organization. Race- or ethnicity-based organizations served as a place where officers could feel comfortable, foster cultural pride and be around people who shared the same background and, often, frustrations.

Thus, African American law enforcement organizations and other associations for diverse groups provide a network of people with similar interests, concerns, and backgrounds. It is because of the stresses associated with minority status, prejudice and discrimination that many police associations were created.

Another nonprofit organization is the Hispanic National Law Enforcement Association (HNLEA), formed in 1988. HNLEA is involved in the "administration of justice and dedicated to the advancement of Hispanic (Latino) and minority interests within the law enforcement profession" (HNLEA.org). The organization focuses on increasing the representation of Hispanics and other minorities in the law enforcement field, and acts as a liaison to various communities, minority officers, and law enforcement agencies.

The racial, ethnic, religious, and sexual orientation organizations within law enforcement are not meant to divide, but rather give support to groups that traditionally have not been fully accepted in law enforcement and had no power within the organization. Yet the sentiment expressed by the woman who inquired into the meaning of NOBLE is not uncommon among police officers. Police command officers and supervisors must not ignore this debate (whether expressed or not), and should address the issues *underlying the need* for the support groups within the department. They must also foster dialogue and shared activities between all formalized groups within the organization. Officers will benefit by learning about why their fellow officers join these associations. Having open and carefully facilitated dialogue about the need for such organizations will help guard against divisiveness, either real or perceived, within law enforcement agencies.

Assignments Based on Diversity

Although citizens may appreciate having officers from their own backgrounds work in their neighborhoods and jurisdictions, this deployment strategy may have the unintended and potentially unfair consequence of very different career paths for minority officers compared to those of white officers. Not all racially or ethnically diverse officers have the skills or desire to work with their own cultural or racial group. Assignments based on diversity alone, therefore, are generally unfair and may be a disservice to both the officer and the neighborhood. Officers should not be restricted to working in specific areas based on the notion that police–community relations will automatically improve. Furthermore, officers who are the same ethnicity or race as residents in a neighborhood may not necessarily make the best crime fighters or problem solvers in that locale. In addition, it is not a given that an officer who is of the same background as citizens will always show sensitivity to his or her community's particular needs.

Ronald Hampton, a retired Washington, D.C., Metropolitan police officer who was on the force for 23 years and was the executive director of the National Black Police Officers Association, illustrated this point at a conference when he discussed the reasons for a new African American recruit's wanting to work the black areas of Washington, D.C. The recruit felt that he could tell other African Americans what to do, but did not always have the same level of comfort in doing so in predominantly white neighborhoods. Hampton noted, however, that the young recruit referred to people from his neighborhood as "maggots." Hampton made the point that this hate speech was completely inexcusable and that supervisors will hold all subordinates accountable for their conduct and will apply discipline regardless of who is saying what about whom (Hampton, 2017). We present this example also to illustrate that it happens that officers can internalize the hatred society has directed toward them and, consequently, are not automatically fit to provide service in certain neighborhoods.

When Chief Robert Burgreen, 1988–1993, was the top executive of the San Diego Police Department, he, like many other law enforcement managers, did not deploy officers according to race, sexual orientation, or ethnicity. Deployment was based on the best fit for the neighborhood and was related to an officer's competence and capabilities. Chief Burgreen had four community relations sergeants, each acting as a liaison for one major group in the city: Hispanic, African American, Asian, and gays and lesbians. He described these sergeants as his "eyes and ears" for what was going on in various communities. Some cities use cultural affairs committees to perform a similar function, made up of people from diverse community groups as well as the officers from different backgrounds.

WOMEN IN LAW ENFORCEMENT

Women in the Workforce

Women have long been part of the general workforce in American society, albeit for many years in primarily traditional female employment roles, such as nurses, secretaries, schoolteachers, waitresses, and flight attendants. The first major movement of women into the general workforce occurred during World War II, although some say it was as early as the Civil War. With men at the front, women entered the workforce in large numbers and successfully occupied many nontraditional employment roles. A nontraditional occupation for women is defined as one in which women comprise 25 percent or less of total employment. After World War II, 30 percent of all women continued working outside the home ("History of Women in the Workforce," 1991).

According to the United States Bureau of Labor Statistics, the number of women in the labor force increased at an extremely rapid pace between 1950 (18 million, or 34 percent) and 1999 when numbers reached a peak (66 million, or 60 percent), which was an annual growth rate of 2.6 percent. Since then, and as of 2014, the labor force participation among women declined to 57 percent of the civilian U.S. workforce, down 0.2 percentage point from the year before (see Exhibit 2. 7).

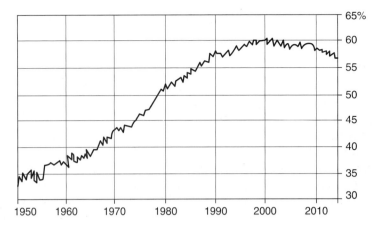

EXHIBIT 2.7   Women at Work—Female Market Participation Has Been Declining since 2000

Studies have projected that the participation of women in the labor force will significantly slow down over the next 50 years, with 92 million women projected to be in the formal workplace by 2050 (U.S. Department of Labor, 2015).

Women hired as police officers during the early years were given duties that did not allow them to work street patrol. Assignments and roles were limited to positions such as juvenile delinquency and truancy prevention, child abuse, crimes against women, and custodial functions (Bell, 1982). In 1845, New York City hired its first police "matron," and in 1888, Massachusetts and New York passed legislation requiring communities with a population over 20,000 to hire police matrons to care for female prisoners. According to More (1992), during the first half of the nineteenth century, a number of police practices were challenged, thus allowing for the initial entry of women into the police field. In 1905, the Portland (Oregon) Police Department boasted of its first woman in the department sworn to uphold duties of a police officer; however, she did not work patrol. In 1922, the International Association of Chiefs of Police passed a resolution supporting the use of policewomen; no women worked patrol or as detectives at the time. Historically, there has been a predominant belief that women are not capable of performing the law enforcement functions of exercising authority and using force.

It was not until 1968 that the Indianapolis Police Department made history by assigning the first two female officers to patrol on an equal basis with their male colleagues (Schulz, 1995). Other landmarks for women in law enforcement occurred in 1985, with the appointment of the nation's first woman chief of police, Penny Harrington, in Portland, Oregon, and in 1994, with the appointment of the first African American woman chief of police, Beverly Harvard, in Atlanta, Georgia.

Title VII of the Civil Rights Act of 1964, referred to earlier, played an important role in opening police departments to women. Adoption of affirmative action policies, now illegal in many states, along with court orders and injunctions, also played a role in bringing more women into law enforcement. Although more women were entering law enforcement, they still encountered blatant and open skepticism, resentment, and hostility from male officers.

Historically, law enforcement agencies' requirements or standards pertaining to minimum height and weight, strength, and agility posed one of the many barriers to female entry into the police field (Polisar & Milgram, 1998). Most civil service tests modified these requirements in order to comply with court-ordered legal mandates and injunctions by the early 1980s (Balkin, 1988). However, a study published by the National Center for Women and Policing (NCWP) in 2003 concluded that there is still an adverse impact on women due to entry-level physical agility testing standards that eliminates a large number of women (National Center for Women and Policing, 2003). NCWP suggests that there are other options that will yield the benefits of qualified women entering the profession and eliminate this obstacle to their being hired (Lonsway, Wood, Fickling, De Leon, Moore, Harrington, Smeal, & Spillar, 2002). This study is discussed more fully in Chapter 3.

Number of Women in Law Enforcement

Between 2007 and 2013, female representation of sworn personnel remained consistent. In 2013, statistics showed that about 58,000 or 12 percent of full-time sworn personnel in local police departments and about 26,100 or 14 percent in sheriffs' offices were women. The percentage increase in local police departments of full time, sworn women police officers between 1987 and 2013 is shown in Exhibit 2.8 and the percentage increase in sheriffs' offices is shown in Exhibit 2.9 (Reaves, 2015).

Women are underrepresented in law enforcement, with the percentage of women still small. The numbers are increasing slowly; mostly at large urban police departments. It is not uncommon for smaller police departments to have either no women to just a small percentage of women on the force. Approximately 5 percent of African American women make up law enforcement (ibid.).

Workplace Issues

The integration of women into policing as well as retention problems have led many law enforcement chief executives, managers, and supervisors to grapple with workplace issues within their departments. Women still face some unique obstacles, including overcoming the attitudes of society and of some of their male coworkers and bosses. One such attitude is the stereotype held by civilians and male police officers that women don't truly have the strength to do the physical part of the job. There is also an associated belief that women are given an entry break into law enforcement due to their gender. However, women must meet the same physical and emotional requirements as men. Studies have shown that the single largest issue facing the recruitment and retention of women is "cultural barriers" in law enforcement (Matthies, Keller, & Lim, 2012). Workplace issues confronting law enforcement agencies, and especially women in law enforcement, involve sexual harassment, gender discrimination, role barriers, the "brotherhood," a double standard, differential treatment, and career-versus-family issues. Though gains have been made, many women officers assert that being accepted in a largely male-dominated work culture continues to be a challenge. According to Commander Teresa Ewins of the San Francisco Police Department (SFPD), and one of two female district captains to head the Tenderloin police station in the city, "Women can be eventually accepted by their departments, but they have to work hard to prove themselves. They have to show their competence and that they are able to care of themselves" (Ewins, 2017).

SEXUAL HARASSMENT   Sexual harassment has a significant impact on the health of an organization, on the victims and on the perpetrators. In law enforcement, where people work long

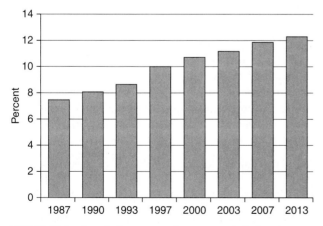

EXHIBIT 2.8   Female Representation among Full-Time Sworn Personnel in Local Police Departments, 1987–2013

Note: Figure includes all years for which data were collected.

Source: Bureau of Justice Statistics, Law Enforcement Management and Administrative Statistics (LEMAS) Survey, 1987–2013.

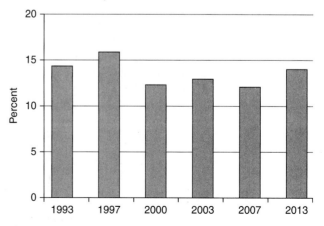

EXHIBIT 2.9   Percent of Full-Time Sworn Female Personnel in Sheriffs' Offices, Selected Years 1993–2013

Source: Bureau of Justice Statistics, Law Enforcement Management and Administrative Statistics (LEMAS) Survey, 1993, 1997, 2000, 2003, 2007, and 2013.

hours and respond to dangerous calls, an environment where sexual harassment exists is detrimental to officers' missions, and to safety. Sexual harassment is any unwelcome behavior characterized by the abuse of one's power over another and comes in different forms:

- *Hostile environment,* which consists of unwelcome sexual behavior, such as "jokes," cartoons, posters, banter, repeated requests for dates, requests for sexual favors, references to body parts, or physical touching, are all forms of sexual harassment have the intentional or unintentional purpose or effect of unreasonably interfering with an individual's work performance and/or creating an intimidating, hostile, or offensive working environment.
- *Quid pro quo sexual harassment,* which means one is asked to perform sexual acts in return for a job benefit. For example, individuals are told that they will pass probation, get a promotion or performance evaluation, or that they will not be written up for doing something wrong if they engage in some type of sexual behavior.
- *Gender harassment,* which is behavior that is not based on sexual behavior, but is based on gender. It is also known as sex-based harassment. Examples include comments such as "Women don't have it in them to be police officers," or "Women should stay where they are needed—at home—and leave policing to us men," or "She will never be able to handle the streets…"

Sexual harassment can occur in a variety of circumstances including, but not limited to, the following:

1. Victims, as well as the harassers, may be women, men or any individuals who see themselves on the gender spectrum (defined later in the chapter). Victims can be the same gender, the opposite gender or anywhere on the gender spectrum.
2. The harasser can be the victim's supervisor, an agent of the employer, a supervisor in another area, a coworker, or a nonemployee.
3. The victim need not only be the person harassed, but could be anyone affected by the offensive conduct.
4. Unlawful sexual harassment may occur without economic injury to or discharge of the victim.
5. The harasser's conduct must be unwelcome.

Employers are encouraged to take steps necessary to prevent sexual harassment from occurring; prevention, which includes education, is the best tool to eliminate it in the workplace. Employers should clearly communicate to employees that sexual harassment will not be tolerated. They can do so only by establishing an effective complaint or grievance process and take immediate and appropriate action when an employee complains (U.S. Equal Employment Opportunity Commission, 2010). Although sexual harassment exists in both private and public sectors, we believe it is particularly problematic in law enforcement—an occupation that is still mostly male-dominated.

The majority of women officers interviewed for each edition of this book (and who requested that their names not be used) said they had been sexually harassed in the workplace. Most of them indicated that when male officers were offensive, they remained quiet, and did not report misconduct for fear of retaliation by those officers. Katherine Spillar, executive director of the Feminist Majority Foundation, who oversees the National Center for Women and Policing, a division of the Feminist Majority Foundation, relayed the following extreme example of retaliation:

> Women officers have told us [i.e., in the Feminist Majority Foundation] that their male counterparts threaten not to answer backup calls. One told us about how male officers stood by while a woman officer was brutally beaten by the suspect at the scene of a felony domestic violence call. (Spillar, 2017)

This lack of reporting can also be directly attributed to the code of silence in law enforcement agencies and the severe retaliation that occurs when women report misconduct. Even outside of law enforcement, however, women are reluctant to report harassment. Estimates indicate that "only 5 to 15 percent of harassed women formally report problems of harassment to their employers or employment agencies such as the EEOC" (U.S. Equal Employment Opportunity Commission, 2010). Those interviewed revealed that sexual harassment occurs at all levels of an organization and is not limited to male harassment of women.

Department executives must institute a zero-tolerance sexual harassment policy and send that message throughout the department. Policy-specific training must also be provided on sexual harassment and its prevention. Some departments have revised their promotional exam to include questions on the department's sexual harassment policies and procedures. The Albuquerque (New Mexico) Police Department went so far as to move the investigation of sexual harassment complaints from within the department to an external city agency with expert Equal Employment Opportunity investigators on staff. Per the Albuquerque Police Department, this approach tends to speed up the process, ensure impartiality, and increase confidence in the procedures. Officers who make a complaint do not have to go through the chain of command. An eight-hour police-specific training course for sworn supervisors on preventing sexual harassment, developed by the Institute for Women in Trades, Technology and Science (IWITTS), is also of value. It is presented in a case-study format that analyzes police legal cases, and it has been highly rated by those who have attended. The IWITTS course provides those who attend with a "Law Enforcement Assessment Tools" kit, which enables agencies to conduct an organizational self-assessment and develop a strategic plan to recruit women, prevent sexual harassment, and ensure fair promotion.

When harassment takes place, the results are often devastating to employees' careers, the internal environment of the organization, and the department's public image. Training all law enforcement employees, both sworn and nonsworn, on the issues of sexual harassment is mandatory, and should not be a one-time event. It should deal not only with legal and liability issues, but also with deep-seated attitudes and unconscious attitudes about power.

GENDER DISCRIMINATION Gender discrimination occurs when a person is subjected to unequal treatment in the workplace based on one's gender. A few examples of workplace gender discrimination are:

- Assigning women to jobs or programs that are considered "traditionally women's" instead of the nontraditional positions such as SWAT teams, K9, gang units, and narcotics
- Using tests for promotions or other job opportunities that are not job-related or represent a small part of the job duties, which result in women not getting promoted at the same rate that men are promoted
- Holding women to a higher or different level on performance evaluations
- Not giving women equal consideration for specialized training, conferences, and specialty job assignments
- Not giving pregnant women light duty, but giving such assignments to men who are injured off-duty (National Center for Women and Policing, 2005).

The federal Pregnancy Discrimination Act (PDA) requires employers to treat "women affected by pregnancy, childbirth or related conditions" the same "as other persons not so affected but similar in their ability or inability to work" (U.S. Equal Employment Opportunity Commission). One of the biggest complaints from pregnant sworn officers is that when they notify their department they are pregnant, they are removed from their position, and there is little or no effort to find a light-duty position. Discrimination based on pregnancy, childbirth, or a related medical condition is discrimination on the basis of gender. Nor may a law enforcement agency refuse to preserve a job for an employee on maternity leave when it protects the jobs of others temporarily disabled; deny seniority status upon return from maternity leave; or refuse to grant pension service time for the period of leave unless other disabled employees are similarly disadvantaged. City, county, state, and federal employers must know the laws pertaining to such workplace issues and train their employees accordingly to avoid costly lawsuits.

ROLE BARRIERS Barriers for and hostility toward women in the workplace have no doubt diminished, both in the general population and within law enforcement. For example, traditional ideas about protection differ by gender, with women historically considered the protectors of children and men the protectors of women. In the act of protecting, the protectors become dominant and the protected become subordinate. Although this assumed gender-role division still exists, and especially in the law enforcement and corrections workforce, it is beginning to shift due to the (slowly) increasing number of women as well as the younger male officers who are entering these professions today. Many veteran police and correctional officers initially grappled to adapt to women in the industry, which they felt required "male" strength and abilities. The result has been described as a clash of cultures—the once male-dominated workforce versus the new one in which women are an integral part of the organization.

These feelings, attitudes, and perceptions can make men and women in law enforcement positions uncomfortable with each other. Women sometimes feel patronized, overprotected, or merely tolerated rather than appreciated and respected for their work. Many in the new generation of male officers are more willing to accept women in law enforcement. In our numerous interviews with veteran officers, we found that, with few exceptions, women were generally accepted by men, but the acceptance was related to how well a specific woman performed her duties.

According to retired sergeant Betsy Brantner Smith, "there are fewer role barriers to women in law enforcement than in the past. Although still not a perfect world, there are more opportunities for women in special assignments and promotions if they prepare themselves to meet the standards and requirements" (Smith, 2017). She says that women must try to be "marketable" for the position they want, whether it be a promotion or special assignment, and that they need to raise their competency level and acquire the skill sets, knowledge, and abilities required for the position. Smith further adds that, paradoxically, if we strive to treat everyone equally, we, in fact, may run the risk of ignoring gender differences, and this may end up being the *wrong* thing to do. Smith believes that we should admit that we are not all equal, pointing out that the word, diversity does not mean equality, but rather the state of being different (ibid.).

Many leaders and managers attempt to treat everyone equally by ignoring gender differences or by going to the opposite extreme and overcompensating. An example of overcompensation would be retaining and promoting women based on gender and not on competence. Most women officers would much rather work for a male boss who knows how to lead and treats people fairly, rather than for an incompetent female boss. Making a department look more diverse should never be the sole objective (ibid.). Men and women are not equal in their abilities in the law enforcement workforce and there is much evidence that women *tend to* have superior communication skills, enabling them to deflect aggressive communication, resulting in less violent reactions on the part of people they encounter on the street. (Discussed further in the chapter and in Chapter 4.)

THE BROTHERHOOD   (Also referred to as the Old Boys' Network) Women who are accepted into this "network" or "brotherhood" of police or correctional officers have generally had to become "one of the guys." (Refer to Chapter 4 for more information on how language used in the brotherhood excludes women.) Women police officers who wish to be part of the brotherhood believe that:

> Peer acceptance is one of the greatest pressures operating within police organizations. The desire to be known as a "good officer" is a strong motivating factor, and failure to achieve that status can be very demoralizing and devastating. Unlike their male counterparts, women must overcome the societal prejudice of being known as the "weaker sex". Many female officers also report feeling they have to work twice as hard to prove themselves and to be accepted, whereas male officers can just show up and gain acceptance. (Woolsey, 2010)

According to Susan Jones, former chief of police of the Healdsburg (California) Police Department, the term *brotherhood* still exists today, along with associated behavior. Jones hopes that one day there will be just the "family of law enforcement" (Jones, 2017). The term *brotherhood* is outdated in today's coed law enforcement environment, and those who still use it demonstrate a lack of cultural competency. Sergeant Betsy Brantner Smith (2017) said that while she agrees that "the family of law enforcement" sends the right message, she doesn't see *brotherhood* as a negative term, as it describes what it is. Katherine Spillar, however, disagrees. "I would argue language matters, and we should insist on calling police officers 'officers,' not 'policemen or policewomen'" (Spiller, 2017). The Brotherhood and Old Boys' Network are largely synonymous terms with usage variation across the country. Another example of outdated language is "The Fraternal Order of Police," historically given to any police union.

Often a woman who tries to act like "one of the guys" (i.e., be part of the brotherhood) on the street or in a jail or prison is considered hard, coldhearted, or unemotional and may be criticized for these traditionally "unfeminine" behaviors by peers and supervisors. Although perhaps this is exaggerated, some women have been described as "Jane Waynes" because they swagger, swear, spit, and are highly aggressive. Yet when a female officer is "too feminine" or not sufficiently aggressive, men have not taken her seriously, and, consequentially, this can impact the quality of her work in both police or in correctional work. Women traditionally have been confronted with a dilemma: They must be aggressive enough to do the job but feminine enough to be acceptable to male peers, and they must also be able to take different approaches to problems.

When women feel compelled to behave like men in the workplace, the results can be counterproductive and can even result in disciplinary action. This phenomenon is not unique to law enforcement, as women in construction trades, historically male-dominated turf, have asserted. Women may feel that to succeed they have to stay within the narrow bands of acceptable behavior and exhibit only certain traditionally masculine or feminine qualities. Walking this fine line is difficult.

Studies have found that most women police officers have a different style of policing, a "service-oriented style," and they see their roles as peace restorers while male officers typically view their roles as crime fighters and use physical force more often than their women counterparts. According to a 2010 study by the National Center for Women and Policing, involving seven major U.S. police agencies:

Women officers are substantially less likely than their male counterparts to be involved in problems of excessive force…Given that women currently comprise 12.7 percent of sworn personnel in big city police agencies, we would expect that female officers in these agencies should be involved in approximately 12.7 percent of the citizen complaints, sustained allegations, or payouts for excessive force. Yet the data indicate that only 5 percent of the citizen complaints for excessive force and 2 percent of the sustained allegations of excessive force in large agencies involve female officers. The average male officer is two to three times more likely than the average female officer to have a citizen name him in a complaint of excessive force (Lonsway et. al., 2002).

> Officers' willingness to use force to resolve conflict can be explained, in part, because men are inherently stronger than women. That said, women now comprise tactical and SWAT teams, and have proven that they are capable and strong in fights. Women have shown that they can take care of themselves on the streets, but there is generally a different mentality operating with women than with men. Because of a greater tendency toward "machismo" in many men, there is more of a readiness to confront physically, especially when facing another male. A dynamic ensues with men in some particularly macho cultures (e.g., Latino and African American) where men may be reluctant to back down because that makes them "less of a man." This attitude, on the part of the citizen, can then trigger a more aggressive response in a male officer. As a general rule, women officers are more likely to use the tools of negotiation, persuasion and communication skills in attempts to diffuse potential physical confrontations. Ironically, the president's 21st century policing guidelines ask law enforcement officers to be just that…communicators, negotiators, and persuaders. This communication skill focus is also supported in guidelines and recommendations by DOJ Guidelines, resulting from its review of SFPD. (Ewins, 2017)

Sergeant Kathy Bierstedt, who retired from a large police department in Florida, said that "Men are usually physically stronger than women. But even so, women can use this to their advantage when arresting a male subject. Because it's a given that a male is stronger, he usually does not feel the need to prove his masculinity by fighting with a female officer. However, in a confrontation with a male officer, the male subject might feel the need to prove 'he's a man,' and fight back with the male officer" (Bierstedt, 2017). Sergeant Bierstedt added further that, on many occasions, she had told an aggressive male that he was stronger and would probably win if he resisted arrest, but that he could let her handcuff him and go quietly with dignity. If not, she could have other officers respond to subdue him, at which time he would likely receive injuries as well as additional charges for resisting arrest and the battery of the officers. That seldom failed to ensure compliance. Verbal skills are a must not only for the female officers, but for all officers. Sergeant Bierstedt explained that "gender intelligence is important to understand. Most women officers instinctively will utilize verbal skills to handle situations wherein a male officer may resort to force more quickly." However, she questioned whether trainers in law enforcement and corrections have the right training to teach these verbal skills to officers. If not, she suggested, this should be made a priority (ibid.).

Retired South San Francisco officer, Joni Lee's approach dealing with gender discrimination was to work every job in the department, including gangs, narcotics, sex crimes, and street patrol. She was one of the first women hired by the West Coast police department in 1980 and summed up her philosophy this way: "Women can do police work, we just don't get in as many fights" (Lee, 2017).

> When I was hired, I had to prove that I could do the job twice as hard as a male recruit. I made more arrests, wrote more citations, initiated more contacts, etc. I would arrest the largest guy so people wouldn't think I couldn't handle myself. In retrospect, that was pretty Jane Wayne of me. I wouldn't recommend new female officers do what I did. I also encountered male officers telling me that women could not do the job, and if my reason for becoming an officer was to sleep around with the male officers, then I should just leave now. The wives of the officers also had issues with my being hired and the Chief had meetings with the wives prior to my on-the-job start date. (Ibid.)

Additionally, women officers, and especially those who are members of minority groups, often feel that they have to go way out of their way to prove themselves, including putting on a brave face. Bisa French, in 2016, was promoted to deputy chief of the Richmond (California) Police Department. During an interview, she said that she had to learn fast when she first became an officer:

> We are a really progressive agency now, but back then, it was your typical older, policing-as-usual environment…It was a male-dominated field, and I had to put a brave face on and prove myself… It was more of a one-way communication model back then…And that included me, because my biggest mistakes as a young officer were not listening enough, not engaging enough. Now, collaboration and relationship-building is a top priority in this department. (French, 2017)

A DOUBLE STANDARD Interviews with women officers showed that the majority felt they had to perform better than male officers just to be considered equal—a double standard. These women spoke of how they put pressure on themselves to perform up to or exceed the expectations of their male peers. (LGBTQ employees often express the same sentiment.) One female officer explained that many women were using a community policing philosophy long before it became the practice of their agency. She mentioned that when she tried to do problem solving, she was criticized in her evaluations. Her supervisor rated her negatively for "trying too hard to find solutions to complainants' problems," saying that she "spends too much time on calls explaining procedures" and "gets too involved" (Jones, 2017). Today, however, women police officers report that the double standard is less common because of the emphasis that law enforcement places on community policing. Now this approach is seen as the norm and is expected of all officers (Jones, 2017).

DIFFERENTIAL TREATMENT In the past, many women in law enforcement indicated that staff members treated them differently from men, and that they were frequently held back from promotions or special assignments in areas like special weapons and tactics, homicide investigations, and motorcycle units because of the perception that these are "male" jobs. They reported feeling that they were also held back from training for these assignments and were not promoted at the same rate as men. Over the years, some change has occurred: More women officers are now serving in special assignment and showing no special problems with performance. However, a study regarding women participating on special weapons and tactical (SWAT) teams concluded that "although the research is exploratory and the findings are difficult to generalize, the results suggest that law enforcement's militaristic nature and role specialization continue to impede integrating female officers into SWAT subcultures." The study indicated that although male SWAT members surveyed were somewhat receptive to women on the team, they generally felt that women lacked the needed strength and skills (Dodge, Valcore, & Gomez, 2010).

Police executives must determine if their female officers are receiving equal opportunities for assignments and training that will provide the groundwork and preparation for their eventual promotion. They need to determine if female officers are applying for promotions in numbers proportionate to their representation in the department. If not, supervisors, mentors, and informal network associates need to encourage them. It is also possible that the promotion process disproportionately screens out female officers. Research shows that the more subjective the process is, the less likely women are to be promoted. The use of assessment center and "hands-on" testing is said to offer some safeguards against the potential for the perception of bias against women. Utilizing structured interviews and selecting interview board members who represent different races and genders can also minimize this risk. Many departments are now training interview board members on interviewing techniques. The IWITTS has developed a well-received half-day training session for supervisors, "Creating a Supportive Work Environment," to address issues of integration and retention of women.

CAREER VERSUS FAMILY Women in law enforcement are faced with another dilemma—trying to raise a family and have a successful career, two goals that are often difficult to combine. Women, especially single mothers, who had children when they entered law enforcement, frequently find that they have difficulty balancing their commitments to family and work. If they had children after entering the occupation, they may be confronted with inadequate pregnancy policies and maternity-leave policies (see earlier discussion). In both cases, women often feel a sense of guilt, stress, and frustration in trying to both do well in a job and maintain a family. Up-to-date law enforcement organizations offer innovative work schedules, modified duty assignments during pregnancy, child care programs, mentoring and support groups, and a positive work atmosphere for women. Such programs benefit all employees within the organization and help retain employees. In addition, since men are increasingly taking a more active role in parenting, creative work schedules, and even maternity or parental leave are important to them as well.

Sergeant Kathy Bierstedt said that during the hiring process, officers sign a document that informs them that they are required to work various shifts and sites, including graveyard. The form also notifies them that assignments are based upon seniority. However, if there are extenuating circumstances, such as a severely ill family member, they can submit a "hardship" request. If granted, it is a one-time exception and only for a period of one shift change, approximately four months. This is to allow time to make arrangements as necessary. This "hardship" is usually requested for officers in uniform patrol, as specialized units make adjustments as their staffing needs allow. Having children does not constitute a "hardship," according to Bierstedt, who says that women in a two-parent home are reminded that their spouse should also care for their child or children whenever needed (Bierstedt, 2017).

Mentor and Informal Networking Programs for Women

Women's performance and attitudes can be enhanced if they have access to a **mentor** and to **informal network** programs. The mentor provides information, advice, support, and encouragement to someone who is less experienced. Mentoring involves leading, developing, and guiding by example to facilitate the protégé's personal development, for the benefit of both the individual and the organization. There is a great deal of research on the topic of mentoring and networking for women as well as for minorities. Law enforcement management is well advised to consult these studies, the information from which will contribute to the successful creation of such programs.

Mentor A trusted counselor or guide.

Informal networks A system of influential colleagues who can, because of their position or power within an organization, connect the employee with information, resources, or other contacts helpful to the employee's promotion or special-assignment prospects.

Usually mentoring occurs in a one-on-one coaching context over a period of time through suggestions, advice, and support on the job. There are many reasons for law enforcement agencies to provide for or encourage the use of mentor and support programs. Studies over the years have found that women who have had one or more mentors reported greater job success and job satisfaction than women who did not have a mentor. Lack of access to such networks can be a key barrier to promotions and special assignments. Sergeant Smith firmly believes in mentoring as a tool to improve and build the person mentored, either male or female, to make them more successful (Smith, 2017). In an article, she wrote for *PoliceOne*, she said, "Find a mentor, preferably several, but choose wisely. Look for not only supervisors and field training officers, but informal leaders in the organization as well as other personnel from other agencies. Make sure they have good reputations and good attitudes, and that you adhere to the chain of command. Surround yourself with positive people in general; it makes life easier" (Smith, 2017).

Pervasive stereotypes of Latina and Asian American women may make it easier to overlook them in the workplace, resulting in being passed up for promotions or special assignments where they have a chance to demonstrate their skills. Managers should encourage experienced Asian American women and Latinas to serve as mentors for younger women, although they should not be limited to working only with women of the same race/ethnicity.

Several associations provide an organized voice for the interests of women in policing: The International Association of Women Police (IAWP), the National Association of Women Law Enforcement Executives (NAWLEE), and the National Center for Women and Policing (NCWP). The NAWLEE focuses on helping women strengthen their leadership roles in policing, while the NCWP focuses on research and policy. However, while these organizations provide excellent resources, they cannot take the place of departmental, in-house mentoring programs or informal networks for women.

The Transition of Women into Law Enforcement

Women remain a minority in law enforcement, but increasingly have proven that they are as competent as men in their role as officers equal to their male peers. While there is still progress to be made, women perceive that their working conditions have improved and that there is less harassment than in the past. Now a woman's ability to perform the job is increasingly less likely to be measured by traditional standards. For example, verbal communication skills are equally and potentially more important than physical strength (i.e., an officer's non-defensive communication can help to defuse many situations where aggressive behavior may otherwise occur).

> The benefits of increasing women's numbers and influence in policing go far beyond improving police responses to violence against women, though that improvement alone would more than justify the cause. Every progressive goal for improving police services, whether ending police brutality, promoting community policing, reducing community complaints, or reducing lawsuits, is well proven to be enhanced by increasing women's presence in policing. (Women's Justice Center, 2010)

The progress of women in law enforcement can also be seen in leadership. There have been many women who have worked their way up the ranks and serve as chiefs of police or sheriffs in small and large agencies across the country.

LGBTQ EMPLOYEES IN LAW ENFORCEMENT

> *Many of the terms that we use in this chapter section are defined in an FBI-collated glossary in the Hate Crimes chapter on pp. 302–303. We have also included in this chapter section definitions of additional terms related to LGBTQ.*

Commander Teresa Ewins heads the San Francisco Police Department's Pride Alliance organization, and reports that it is generally "safer" to be an LGBTQ officer in today's world of policing than it once was (Ewins, 2017). Despite this, harassment and discrimination against LGBTQ employees in law enforcement agencies have come to light, and have been characterized as an "ongoing and pervasive" problem (Mallory, Hasenbush, & Sears, 2013). The acts of hate toward LGBTQ officers have ranged from homophobic comments to general exclusion to limits on promotion by management (ibid.). Author Greg Miraglia wrote, *Coming Out from behind the Badge*, to let other officers know the pain of being a "closeted" officer for about 25 years, but who had the courage to "come out" to his fellow officers (Miraglia, 2016). Miraglia says that law enforcement officers are role models to others, but that officers, themselves, need to look up to and learn from other officers who can serve as role models to them. He demonstrates in his book that gay officers perform their duties as sworn professionals, and that they perform with the same pride as officers who are not gay.

Attitudes toward LGBTQ employees in law enforcement, particularly on the East and West Coast and in larger metropolitan departments, have advanced significantly in recent years. With the legalization of gay marriage, mainstream attitudes have shifted towards far more acceptance than during the writing of all previous editions of this textbook Additionally, the vocabulary and awareness associated with gender identity and sexual orientation has expanded rapidly, especially in the last few years. The abbreviation, "LGBTQ," has, in some areas and institutions, replaced "LGBT," i.e., standing for: lesbian, gay, bisexual and transgender (see Chapter 10, pp. 302–303 for the definitions of these terms). There is not across the board agreement as to what the "Q" stands for in LGBTQ. In doing an informal interview of a dozen people both in law enforcement and outside the profession, the authors found that there was not agreement on the "Q." One meaning is "questioning," which implies that individuals are unsure of their orientation, and are not comfortable with the existing, established categories (i.e., LGBT). Most millennials define the "Q" as, "Queer," which at one time was a highly derogatory word, signifying homosexual. "Queer" for many younger people has lost the derogatory connotations it once had. Universities have "queer" studies programs in many college curricula that run the gamut on a variety of topics related to sexual orientation and gender identity. "Queer" (also referred to as gender queer or gender nonconforming) has come to be an umbrella term for individuals who do not see themselves in fixed binary categories, such as male or female, or gay or lesbian. It is a term that is often used to encompass all people with non-heterosexual orientation, and one that focuses on fluidity with respect to gender. Genderqueer and other gender nonconforming (also referred to as gender questioning) individuals continue to be largely misunderstood in society. When people speak about *gender identity*, this refers to a sense of who people are in terms of gender (i.e., the sex they were born with). Gender identity is viewed as a broad spectrum.

Policy versus Practice

According to Sergeant Ken Carlson of the Concord (California) Police Department, who is gay, there are no longer bans on hiring LGBTQ people by law enforcement agencies. Sergeant Carlson has been with the Concord Police Department for almost 28 years and "came out" in 2002. Since coming out, he has been openly accepted by his colleagues. He is active with the Rainbow Community Center, under the umbrella of Family Justice Alliance and a member of the Pleasant Hill City Council, the community in which he resides. Sergeant Carlson feels that discrimination against LGBTQ employees is generally not open and explicit any longer, but that exists in much more subtle ways (Carlson, 2017). Commander Ewins agrees with this, stating that explicit bias against gays and other sexual minorities is far less common than it used to be, but has not disappeared. She feels that bias against LGBTQ officers is "expressed more behind closed doors. Additionally, LGBTQ individuals are scrutinized daily (i.e., more often than others are) as well as judged on the actions of other LGBTQ officers, and less on their own capabilities" (Ewins, 2017).

Recruitment

Frequently, recruiters from large law enforcement agencies with LGBTQ communities attend Gay Pride marches and other events organized by LGBTQ communities. (Small and medium-sized departments, for budgetary reasons, often do not have the capacity to send recruiters to LGBTQ events to seek applicants.) To ensure equal opportunity, it is critical to go beyond event attendance. Departments must conduct applicant tracking, in which, for example: (a) applicant information is taken at an event, (b) contact with the applicant is maintained, and (c) document is available to show whether the applicant has been hired or at which point in the process he or she has become disqualified. If a disproportionate number of these applicants fail during a specific part of the hiring process, such as interviews, background investigations, or polygraph exams, then administrators must be able to capture this information starting from the original point of contact. Further, this approach can help determine if committing resources for LGBTQ events or advertisements is an effective use of public funds.

According to Commander Ewins, bias, both, explicit or implicit, may be responsible for the lack in hiring of LGBTQ employees:

- Older officers, if part of the recruitment and hiring process, are more likely to have bias against LGBTQ individuals.
- Bias or prejudice on the part of the psychologist or polygraph operator may also be at play.
- Bias or prejudice may exist on the part of a person(s) on the candidate interview or screening process. (Ewins, 2017)

Additionally, Commander Ewins believes that hiring authorities at police agencies tend to lump LGBTQ people together in one category. "A lot of departments are not open to gay and transgender recruiting. If they have a lesbian, they can check off the box for diversity and that is it. The hiring of one or two lesbians does not represent all of LGBTQ" (ibid.).

Changing Attitudes

Concerns about homosexuals in the military or in law enforcement used to include beliefs that gay soldiers or police officers would walk hand in hand, dance together at clubs, make passes at non-gay colleagues, or display other socially unacceptable aspects of their private lives. Just as most professional heterosexual's officers do not draw attention to their sexual orientation on the job, neither do most LGBTQ officers flaunt their sexual orientation. Like other employees, many LGBTQ employees would like to feel free to display framed photographs of their significant others on their desks or in their lockers.

Sergeant Carlson explained that even though he knows he can be openly affectionate with his husband around heterosexual officers or around community members, he is reluctant to do so because this behavior might make *them* uncomfortable. He calls this, "… feelings of exclusion, but it results from a self-imposed withdrawal" (Carlson, 2017). Since he came out in his department, his experiences have been positive. "I hid my homosexuality for 15 years. Coming out to my colleagues has not been an issue; the more you work together, the more the stereotypes break down. This also has to do with your own comfort, just being able to be who you are" (ibid.).

Commander Ewins shared that LGBTQ police officers feel that it's "safer" to display affection toward their significant others, even though there are still officers who are uncomfortable around gay people. Many of her colleagues can't understand why she is gay and are curious. The discomfort comes from not understanding. She said that she can be very open within her department and that people feel free to ask her any questions about being gay. She explains to other officers that LGBTQ officers, like all officers, only want to be judged on their work and capabilities, and not on their private lives (Ewins, 2017).

Differences in Treatment of LGBTQ Officers

Historically, many law enforcement officers have thought that because of the "macho" requirements of police work, a double standard exists with respect to the way LGBTQ officers are viewed. The traditional male dominance of the profession has made it difficult for many male officers to accept that women or LGBTQ employees are equally able to perform the same tasks they do. They view their work as an occupation for only the "strongest and the toughest." Sergeant Carlson indicates there are "macho" women in law enforcement who are not gay, but that stereotypes and a degree of discrimination against them exists. "She looks and acts 'butch,' she has to be gay" (Carlson, 2017). Many officers still assume that "macho" women are lesbians and that stereotypically "feminine" women are heterosexual, although such mapping of gender roles onto sexual orientation is frequently wrong.

Commander Ewins believes that police officers are generally more accepting today of lesbian officers than of gay and transgender officers. "The bottom line is that if you (i.e., patrol officers) cannot physically take care of yourselves on the street, then people will judge you regardless of gender or sexual orientation. Officers have to be able to handle themselves when being physical; if they cannot, and if they happen to be gay or LGBTQ, then others blame that fact on their sexual orientation and this reflects poorly on the rest of us" (Ewins, 2017). Drawing generalizations and coming to conclusions about others in the same grouping on the basis of one person is stereotyping; this is the nature of prejudice.

Many male officers' self-esteem can be threatened by the ability of women and LGBTQ officers to do their job. (This issue has already been discussed in the section entitled, "Women in Law Enforcement"). For example, allowing openly gay men to serve as officers is perceived by many as threatening to the macho image of police work: If a gay man can successfully complete the necessary tasks, then their job is less macho. Further, those officers whose self-image is based on their job, perceiving themselves as "John Wayne," are generally the most uncomfortable with the concept of working with gay officers. The pervasive stereotype of gay men as effeminate remains a factor in some officers' bias against their fellow officers. But these stereotypes are changing.

> We have reached a time when sexual orientation is not the primary focus and that, today, officers usually don't drag their orientation to work so it is not as much an issue. In many cases, it just doesn't matter; we have gotten to the point when you don't necessarily think *gay* when you look at gay and lesbian officers. However, this is not true of police officers' view of transgender officers who face huge challenges in the police department. It will take time for attitudes about transgender officers to shift, and training is necessary. (Carlson, 2017)

The Transition of LGBTQ Individuals into Law Enforcement

Problems still surface within law enforcement agencies as LGBTQ officers "come out of the closet." In many agencies, officers thought to be or who are openly LGBTQ have encountered discriminatory treatment and/or hostility because of other employees' negative stereotypes and attitudes. The more that officers who are openly LGBTQ are recruited and hired, the more law enforcement organizational culture will treat them as "normal." Law enforcement agencies should have written policies to assist LGBTQ officers' transition into the department as well as operational plans to promote employee acceptance of these officers.

It is vital that agency officials establish openly LGBTQ officers as liaisons to the LGBTQ community. This type of placement has the added advantage of providing role models for people living in the community who may be interested in a career in law enforcement. With the prevalence of hate crimes against LGBTQ community members, LGBTQ police officers may have a unique understanding and compassion to dealing with these crimes that is likely to elicit more cooperation and information, increasing the chances that these crimes get solved (Ewins, 2017). Police officials realized years ago, that it is an invaluable service to provide women rape victims the comfort of being interviewed by female officers. That need is duplicated when it comes to LGBTQ hate crime victims (see Chapter 11). Moreover, given the reticence of LGBTQ crime victims to come forward due to the real or perceived bias of law enforcement personnel, the availability of an LGBTQ officer helps negate the fear of "double victimization."

Discrimination and Harassment against LGBTQ Law Enforcement Officers

LGBTQ law enforcement officers, themselves, often become victims of discrimination and harassment within their workplace. (Statutes and policies to stop discrimination and harassment of LGBT persons in the workplace are discussed later in this chapter.) While LBGTQ officer treatment in some police departments around the country have improved, studies reveal that LGBTQ officers still face "pervasive discrimination" (Mallory et al., 2013).

Key findings from a comprehensive report titled, "Discrimination against Law Enforcement Officers on the Basis of Sexual Orientation and Gender Identity" (ibid.) indicate that:

- The discrimination [against LGBTQ] encountered often went beyond firing or demotion and included severe verbal harassment and sexual harassment, including a death threat, discriminatory slurs, indecent exposure and inappropriate touching.
- Many of the reports revealed physical harassment or violence towards the officers. These included reports of being slammed into a concrete wall, attacked with a chair, and repeated reports of officers being refused back-up, placing their personal safety in danger.

- A survey of 60 members of TCOPS, an organization for transgender law enforcement officers, found that over 90 percent reported negative experiences with their departments.
- Over two-thirds of LGBT law enforcement officers reported hearing homophobic comments on the job and over half reported being treated like an outsider by their colleagues. (Ibid.)

Officers today are much more sensitive to LGBTQ employees. However, my own fear of the *potential* for harassment led me to avoid others and stay to myself. Prior to coming out in 2002, I had received every transfer assignment that I requested. I noticed, however, there was a change in how management viewed my work. Between 2005 and 2009, and after coming out, I applied 13 times to the K9 or motorcycle unit and was not transferred. Before that, I got to do anything I wanted. Ultimately, after raising the issue with the Chief, I was placed in the motor unit. The supervisor of the motor unit had simply said that I wasn't what he was looking for. In another domain, a religious Christian officer once left me "reprogramming" literature so that I could be converted from homosexual to heterosexual. I did not consider this attempt to be malicious, discriminatory or hostile because he truly believed I needed to do this to be saved. (Carlson, 2017)

Potential Consequences of Discrimination and Harassment in the Workplace

Even though there has been a reduction of discrimination and harassment of LGBTQ employees after decades of complaints and lawsuits, these acts of hate still take place. Some of the high-profile cases have resulted in millions of dollars of jury awards and settlements by city, county, and state employers nationwide. A few of these include:

- Nevada: Transgender Police Officer Wins Title VII Claim against School District. (McGinnis, 2016)
- Alaska: Jury Awards Former Anchorage Police Officers nearly $1 Million each in Racial Discrimination Suit. (Andrews, 2017).
- California: The Los Angeles City Council approved a $1.5 million settlement in a case involving a gay police officer who alleged he was the victim of harassment and retaliation by a supervisor. (Based on Orlov, 2013; Ocamb, 2013)

Statutes and Company Policy Pertaining to Discrimination Based on Sexual Orientation

Discrimination based on an individual's gender identity and sexual orientation occurs in both private and government workplaces. An employee of the federal government is protected from sexual orientation discrimination in the workplace. However, unlike race, gender, and other types of discrimination covered by EEOC laws, no single law applies to ban the discrimination of people based on their sexual orientation. However, the growing awareness of the issue has prompted more employers to take steps to prevent and punish instances of discrimination based on sexual orientation or gender identity. Almost half of all states, including the District of Columbia, have laws that prohibit discrimination based on sexual orientation or gender identity in both private and public workplaces (ACLU, 2016).

As of February 2017, these states include:

California	Colorado	Connecticut	Hawaii	Illinois
Iowa	Maine	Maryland	Massachusetts	Minnesota
Nevada	*New Hampshire	New Jersey	New Mexico	*New York
Oregon	Rhode Island	Vermont	Washington	*Wisconsin

*State laws protecting sexual orientation only, not gender identity

If a state, city or county does not have such laws or ordinances, the city, county, or law enforcement agency needs to adopt such policies. There are a few states that prohibit sexual orientation discrimination only in public workplaces, such as for state employees: Delaware, Indiana, Michigan, Montana, and Pennsylvania. In some states, city and county governments have established policies against sexual orientation workplace discrimination in the form of city ordinances.

Some court cases that seek to protect LGBTQ personnel are filed as class action lawsuits because state and local ordinances prohibiting harassment and discrimination are seldom used. Even where there are policies in place, often there is neither enforcement nor means of forcing compliance by the law enforcement agency. Municipalities often choose to settle lawsuits rather than risk a court trial. The elimination of discrimination and harassment of LGBTQ employees should remain an area of concern to agency leadership, who will benefit through a more accepting and welcoming workplace environment and fewer lawsuits.

The chief executive must establish departmental policies and regulations regarding LGBTQ officers. These policies must clearly state that discrimination, harassment, and failure to assist fellow LGBTQ officers are unacceptable and will result in severe disciplinary action. The chief executive must obtain the support of his or her supervisors and managers to ensure that the intent of these rules, policies, and procedures is clear and that all employees adhere to these regulations. All employees must be held accountable, and those who do not support these antidiscrimination policies should not be promoted or awarded special assignments. Department executives must be aware that gay and lesbian officers might not report victimization by other employees.

City or county officials must support and possibly even champion legislation. Any proposed or enacted policy should establish that

- Sexual orientation is not a hindrance in hiring, retention, or promotion.
- Hiring is based solely on merit and all individuals meet objective standards of employment.
- Hiring is done on the basis of identical job-related standards and criteria for all individuals.

Law enforcement managers and supervisors must routinely check to ensure that the policy is being carried out as intended.

Training on LGBTQ Issues

Multicultural awareness and diversity programs now, very often, include components on LGBTQ populations. Effective training will challenge stereotypes and myths, and ensure that people understand that there are huge differences among LGBTQ individuals as there are among all other groups. Training must also cover legal rights, including a discussion of statutes and departmental policies on nondiscrimination and the penalties for violating them. Often, involving in these training programs openly LGBTQ officers, including from other agencies, provides the best outcome. Since police officers are often less receptive to outside trainers, especially those who are not from the law enforcement field, it is best to train using the department's own personnel. Once training is completed, officers may be more receptive to "cultural awareness or understanding" training from trainers outside the agency (and it is generally preferable not to call it "cultural sensitivity" training) (Carlson, 2017). Ideally, this training enables employees to treat LGBTQ officers they work with as human beings, reduce prejudices and dispel false assumptions, and begin to change their behavior. This type of training furthers the ideal of respect for all people. A secondary benefit of this training is the decreased likelihood of personnel complaints and lawsuits by gay or lesbian employees or community members against a city, county, or individual officer.

Commander Ewins, in addition to having been a district station captain, also teaches at the San Francisco Police Academy, where she brings LGBTQ speakers from the community who not only raise awareness of the topic, but also provide a historical view of the community in San Francisco. She often begins her training with the following question:

How many of you have someone in your family who identifies as LGBTQ? (Ewins, 2017)

Indeed, most people raise their hands and, thus, Commander Ewins has established that the topic touches almost everyone on a personal level. Both class members and instructors are given ground rules before the training starts. They are asked to be respectful of each other, but are encouraged not to hold any questions back. "Once students are given permission to ask questions, the questions keep on coming" (ibid.). The training begins with initial awareness, including some foundational information about proper terms and pronouns. For example, with transgender individuals, the most respectful way to determine how a person wants to be referred to is to ask, "Would you like to be called, Sir or Ma'am?" (U.S. Department of Justice, 2016).* Then the officer will know which pronoun to use, i.e., either "he" or "she." Officers should also be aware that there are some people on the gender identity spectrum, who consider themselves neither "she" nor "he," and have begun to use gender neutral pronouns, including, "they." This may be difficult or awkward at first for officers, and it is possible that pronoun usage will change over time. To people who consider themselves "gender nonconforming" or "queer nonconforming," it is acceptable to ask, "What pronoun do you prefer to use?" (ibid.)

When communicating with children of LGBTQ parents, officers can ask "Is your parent or guardian at home?" This helps the parties—especially juveniles—feel more comfortable; at the same time law enforcement professionals are exhibiting professionalism and sensitivity to all types of families.

LGBTQ training needs to include discretion and careful communication, especially when investigating domestic violence cases as people may not be "out." Officers need to be sensitive in talking to gay men who are reporting being violated in order to determine what happened, possibly arresting the responsible party and providing referral services to the victim (Ewins, 2017). Domestic violence is a key training topic.

DOMESTIC VIOLENCE IN LGBTQ RELATIONSHIPS Since June 2015, same-sex marriage has been legal in all states, Washington, D.C., and all U.S. territories except American Samoa and Indian lands. A U.S. Supreme Court, landmark ruling struck down the federal Defense of Marriage Act (DOMA), which had allowed states to refuse to recognize same-sex marriage laws of other states; on the same day, the court also ruled against California's Proposition 8, which had made same-gender marriage illegal in that state. The Court held in a 5-4 decision that the fundamental right to marry is guaranteed to same-sex couples by both Due Process Clause and the Equal Protection Clause of the Fourteenth Amendment to the United States Constitution (*Obergefell v. Hodges*, 2015).

Thus, another new critical area for law enforcement training pertaining to the LGBTQ community involves the issue of domestic violence also known as "Intimate Partner Violence." No different than in heterosexual relationships, domestic violence occurs among LGBTQ individuals, and it is an important social problem. "Lesbians who abuse another woman may do so for reasons similar to those that motivate heterosexual male batterers" (Rose, 2000). According to a National Violence Against Women survey, 21.5 percent of men and 35.4 percent of women living in same-sex partner relationships experienced intimate partner violence in their lifetimes, compared with 7.1 percent and 20.4 percent for men and women, respectively, with a history of only opposite sex cohabitation. Transgender respondents had an incidence of 34.6 percent over a lifetime (Glass, 2014). Commander Ewins provides several reasons for which men and women in a same-sex relationship are hesitant to report domestic violence. For example, they may be embarrassed because they have not "come out" or the batterer uses threats and may be skilled at lying to the police. If victims of domestic violence are undocumented immigrants, perpetrators threaten to tell the police, playing on victims' fear of being deported. If battered partners' friends or relatives don't know that they are in a same-sex relationship, the batterer threatens to "out" the victim. (Ewins, 2017).

For police officers, domestic violence calls are often the most difficult and the most dangerous part of their job. Officers responding to any domestic violence call first need to stabilize the situation, and then move to the next level, which may involve an arrest and providing advice and referrals to the person determined to be the victim (ibid.).

When responding to domestic disputes between same-gender married couples, it is not always simple to determine who the primary aggressor is. This situation, especially where there is

---

* The DOJ 2016 video, entitled, "Law Enforcement and the Transgender Community—CRS Roll Call Training Video" is a valuable resource (U.S. Department of Justice, 2016).

evidence of physical violence, may result in the need to book both people. Officers may not always know the right questions to ask in LGBTQ domestic violence situations. It can be similar working with people from different cultures. Another consideration for which officers need to be prepared is when the domestic violence involves two men. Due to strength, it can be extensive. (Ibid.)

TRANSGENDER POLICIES, PROTOCOL, AND TRAINING "Transgender identifies people whose gender identity, gender expression, or behavior does not conform to that typically associated with traditional notions of male and female or which mixes different aspects of traditional female and male gender roles." Most law enforcement personnel are unlikely to have had any significant contact with members of the transgender community prior to or even during their careers, depending upon where they work. Most problems for police officers in their encounters with transgender individuals, who don't consider themselves gay, involve a lack of experience, training or department policy. Therefore, it is important that officers receive training on transgender issues to not only make the officer feel more comfortable when dealing with LGBTQ people, but also the community.

According to the findings of a 2015 survey of transgender people by the National Center for Transgender Equality (National Center for Transgender Equality, 2016):

- **Respondents experienced high levels of mistreatment and harassment by police.** In the past year, 58 percent of respondents who interacted with police or law enforcement officers who thought or knew they were transgender said that they experienced some form of mistreatment. This included being verbally harassed, repeatedly referred to as the wrong gender, physically assaulted, or sexually assaulted, including being forced by officers to engage in sexual activity to avoid arrest.
- **Police frequently assumed that respondents—particularly transgender women of color—were sex workers.** In the past year, of those who interacted with law enforcement officers who thought or knew they were transgender, one-third (33 percent) of Black transgender women and 30 percent of multiracial women said that an officer assumed they were sex workers.
- More than half (57 percent) of respondents said they would feel uncomfortable asking the police for help if they needed it.
- Of those who were arrested in the past year (2 percent of the total population?), nearly one-quarter (22 percent) believed they were arrested because they were transgender.

Police officers take an oath to protect all individuals in a diverse society. If officers have a bias against LGBTQ individuals, they cannot engage in biased behavior or discriminatory actions because of their personal beliefs. Police officers uphold the rights of all individuals, and especially those in vulnerable populations. Additionally, officers cannot remain silent if they witness harassment or a discriminatory act or crime of any kind committed by fellow employees. Officers, despite their personal beliefs, must maintain good working relationships with peers who may be different from themselves. Police officers represent the entire community, and any discriminatory act they commit while on (or off) duty can dishonor them and their agency, the community they serve, and the entire profession of law enforcement.

Law enforcement agencies should have guidelines and protocols as well as provide training to sworn and nonsworn employees on the arrest and search of transgender individuals. The following (selected) guidelines were developed collaboratively with the LAPD, members of the LGBTQ community and the Los Angeles County's Human Relations Commission's Transgender Working Group (LAPD, 2012).

A. Guidelines to Ensure Professional, Respectful, and Courteous Police Contact
- Refrain from using language that would be considered demeaning or disrespectful to a person's gender identity or expression
- Using a person's preferred name, title ("Sir/Miss"), and gender appropriate pronouns
- Understanding that non-traditional gender identity/expression is not a reasonable suspicion of a person's engagement in prostitution or other crime

B. **Determining How to Address a Transgender Individual or a Person Whose Gender Identity/Expression May Be Unclear**
- Respecting and not questioning a person's gender identity/expression
- Using a person's gender presentation as a basis for gender determination
- Inquiring how a person wishes to be addressed
- Using government issued identification as evidence of gender identity in the absence of a person's self-identification or other clear expression/presentation of gender identity
- Documentation of transgender status to ensure continuity of appropriate treatment
- Non-disclosure of transgender status to non-involved persons

C. **Procedures during Field Searches Involving Transgender Individuals**
- Not performing a search or frisk for the purpose of determining anatomical gender
- Not subjecting transgender people to more invasive search procedures than non-transgender people
- Not questioning the gender identification of a person who is identified as transgender
- Not inquiring about intimate details of a person's anatomy or surgical status as a basis of determining gender—"No proof of an individual's gender is required."
- Not removing appearance-related items (prosthetics, gender-coded clothing, wigs, cosmetics) in a manner similar to non-transgender people.
- Not using anatomical gender as the basis of deciding by whom a transgender person will be searched. Instead inquiring of the transgender person whether there is a preference to be searched by a male or female officer and granting the request if such a request can be reasonably accommodated without risk to officer safety.
- Not refusing to search a transgender person based upon a person's identification as transgender (LAPD, 2012; Vasquez, 2012).

Departments should also have programs or designated liaison officers to work with transgender organizations or transgender individuals in the community. Departments that have policies, liaison, and employee training improve rapport and relations with the transgender community, which also reduces exposure to complaints and lawsuits.

COMMITMENT, LEADERSHIP, AND MANAGEMENT IN THE DIVERSE WORKFORCE

In today's changing workforce, law enforcement leadership goals need to encompass the bridging of cultural and racial gaps within police department and the acceptance of officer diversity. Professional law enforcement leaders take the initiative in guiding their departments to cultural competence in a proactive manner. The specific challenges for law enforcement include recognizing and appreciating diversity within both the community and the workforce, while using such insights advantageously. Human diversity must become a source of renewal rather than be simply tolerated legislated requirements within the agency and community.

The Role of the Chief Executive

Organizations in a diverse community that adopt and implement fair and just policies signal to the public that they are explicitly committed to policing a heterogeneous society. The chief executive sends messages—via mission and values statements, policies and procedures—that the agency does not tolerate discrimination, abuse, or crimes motivated by hate against protected classes within the community or within the agency itself. The agency takes a proactive stance by conducting training on and informing employees about federal EEOC regulations as well as state, local, or agency laws and regulations pertaining to discrimination, and associated consequences for violating them. Chief executives who continually send the message about treating all persons with respect and equal justice will, in turn, win back respect from the community.

Community Relations and Support

Police chiefs, sheriffs, and directors of state law enforcement and their executive management should meet with community leaders and officers from diverse backgrounds to learn what institutional barriers exist within the department that would discourage minority hiring. The executives then institute policies that develop positive attitudes toward a diverse workplace and community, starting with the selection process (see discussion in Chapter 3).

Leadership and team building are crucial to managing a diverse workforce and establishing excellent relations with community groups. The supervisory and management team must take the lead in this endeavor by:

- Demonstrating commitment and providing new leadership models, and communicating these to the community
- Developing police–community partnerships (community-based policing) and convening frequent meetings with community partners

Managing Change Processes during Transitions

The department leadership is responsible for managing change processes and action plans as an integral part of implementation and transition management when the organizational culture is actively making changes. Management staff continually monitor progress on all programs and strategies to improve police–community relations. Managers and supervisors lead by example. When intentional deviation from the system is discovered, retraining and discipline should be quick and effective. It is highly recommended that employees, and especially patrol officers, be rewarded and recognized for their ability to work with and within a diverse community. The reward systems for employees, especially first- and second-line supervisors, ideally, recognizes those who foster positive relations with individuals of different gender, ethnicity, race, or sexual orientations, in the workplace and the community.

Summary

- There continues to be profound shifts in U.S. demographics, resulting in significant changes in the make-up of the law enforcement workforce, including increased numbers of women, racial and ethnic minorities, and individuals who identify as LGBTQ.
- Racism exists within law enforcement organizations because it exists in the greater society. Racism takes many forms, is often unconscious, and affects all kinds of people.
- Despite that, racism in the workplace deeply disrupts relationships and morale within a police department, and erodes trust and confidence in the surrounding community. Officers who do not apply equal justice under the law are breaking the oaths of honor they took upon joining their agencies.
- Equal Employment Opportunity laws were passed to correct a history of unfavorable treatment of women and members of groups deemed at risk of discrimination based on their ethnicity, religion, color, or national origin, age or physical or mental handicaps. The U.S. Supreme Court in 2009 ruled that workers who cooperate with their employers' internal investigations of discrimination may not be fired in retaliation for implicating colleagues or superiors.
- The past two decades have seen the removal of the explicit ban against employing LGBTQ individuals by most law enforcement agencies. The rejection of LGBTQ in law enforcement by some agencies continues despite studies that show that the presence of openly LGBTQ personnel improve service and do not negatively impact morale or unit cohesion. However, it is imperative that the chief executive establish departmental policies and regulations regarding LGBTQ officers, clearly stating that discrimination, harassment, and failure to assist fellow LGBT officers will result in disciplinary action.
- Law enforcement leaders must be committed to setting an organizational tone that does not permit racism or discriminatory acts and must act swiftly against those who violate these policies. They must monitor and quickly deal with complaints both from within their workforce and from the public they serve.
- Professional law enforcement leaders must take the initiative to guide their departments to cultural competence, seeking to develop human potential for the betterment for, both, the law enforcement workforce and the community.

Discussion Questions and Issues

1. *Measuring Responsiveness to Diversity.* Using the check-off and scoring sheet (Exhibit 2.10), determine how responsive your police department has been to the diversity of the jurisdiction it serves. If you are not affiliated with an agency, choose a city or county police department and interview a command officer to determine the answers and arrive at a score. Discuss with the command officer what initiatives his or her department intends to undertake to address the issues of community? Department? Diversity?

2. *Institutional Racism in Law Enforcement.* Law enforcement agencies typically operate under the pretense that all their members are one color, and that the uniform or job makes everyone brothers or sisters. Many members of diverse ethnic and racial groups, particularly African Americans, do not agree that they are consistently treated with respect, and believe that there is institutional racism in law enforcement. European Americans clearly dominate the command ranks of law enforcement agencies. Discuss with other students in your class whether you believe this disparity is the result of subtle forms of institutional racism, or actual conscious efforts on the part of the persons empowered to make decisions. Consider whether tests and promotional processes give unfair advantage to white applicants, and whether they discriminate against department employees of other races and ethnicities. Do officers from diverse groups discriminate against members of other cultures?

3. *Defusing Racially and Culturally Rooted Conflicts.* What training does the police academy in your region provide on defusing racially and culturally rooted conflicts? What training of this type does your local city or county law enforcement agency provide to officers? What community (public and private) agencies are available as referrals or for mediation of such conflicts? Discuss what training should be provided to police officers to defuse, mediate, and resolve racially and culturally rooted conflicts. Discuss what approaches a law enforcement agency should utilize.

4. *Women in Law Enforcement.* How many women officers are there in your local city or county law enforcement agency? How many of those women are in supervisory or management positions? Are any of the women assigned to nontraditional roles such as special weapons and tactics teams, motorcycle enforcement, bomb units, hostage negotiations, or community relations? Have there been incidents of sexual harassment or gender discrimination against women employees? If so, how were the cases resolved? Has the agency you are examining implemented any programs to increase the employment of women, such as flextime, child care, mentoring, awareness training, or career development? Has the agency

---

Use the following simple assessment to analyze your organization's diversity and multicultural profile. If the majority of the responses are below 3, your management and leadership should consider taking actions to alter both the organizational practices as well as its image.

1......2......3......4......5
(1 = minimally; 5 = to a great extent)

A. To what extent does your organization integrate policies related to various workforce/community demographics, including religion, race, ethnicity, sexual orientation, and multicultural relations into its overall mission and vision statements?

B. To what extent does your organization integrate policies related to religion, race, ethnicity, sexual orientation, and multicultural relations into its strategic plan (i.e., to what extent do leaders prepare officers to "walk the talk")?

C. To what extent does your organization's hiring practices, assignments, and promotions consider officers' knowledge related to community policing within diverse communities?

D. To what extent does your organization recruit culturally diverse and minority candidates in an attempt to achieve parity?

E. To what extent do ethnically and culturally diverse community groups provide input into your organization's educational programs focusing on crime prevention and/or cultural awareness?

F. To what extent has your organization provided cross-cultural awareness training focusing on specific immigrant and refugee populations in your city?

G. To what extent has your organization provided diversity education, focusing on workforce issues such as respect for differences (including sexual orientation, religious background, etc.)?

H. To what extent does your organization use interpreters to assist with non-English or English as a Second Language speakers?

I. To what extent is your organization's Web site or other publicity bilingual or multilingual (i.e., in multicultural communities)?

J. To what extent does your organization's Web site and other publicity portray a multicultural and/or multiracial community?

EXHIBIT 2.10   Analyzing Your Organization's Diversity and Multicultural Awareness Profile

been innovative in the recruitment efforts for women applicants? Discuss your findings in a group setting.

5. ***Diversity in Law Enforcement.*** What is the racial breakdown in your agency and how are these positions distributed? Who holds supervisory or management positions?

Have there been reported acts of discrimination against people of diverse backgrounds? Has the agency you are examining implemented any programs to increase the employment of minorities? Discuss your findings in a group setting.

References

ACLU. (2016). "Past LGBT Nondiscrimination and Anti-LGBT Bills across the Country," American Civil Liberties Union. www.aclu.org/map/non-discrimination-laws-state-state-information-map (accessed May 17, 2017).

Andrews, Laurel. (2017). "Jury Awards Former Anchorage Police Officers Nearly $1 Million Each in Racial Discrimination Suit." *Alaska Dispatch Publishing*. www.adn.com/alaska-news/crime-courts/2017/03/07/jury-awards-former-anchorage-police-officers-nearly-1-million-each-in-racial-discrimination-lawsuit/#6223 (accessed August 30, 2017).

Balkin, J. (1988). "Why Policemen Don't Like Policewomen." *Journal of Police Science and Administration, 16*(1), 29–38.

Baumann, Bill. (2016). "2015 EEOC Statistics and EPLI: Why Are Retaliation Claims Increasing?" www.genre.com/knowledge/blog/eeoc-statistics-and-epli-en.html (accessed February 17, 2017).

Bell, Daniel. (1982). "Policewomen: Myths and Reality." *Journal of Police Science and Administration, 10*(1), 112.

Bierstedt, Kathy. (2017). Retired Sergeant, Florida Police Department, personal communication, January 5.

Carlson, Ken. (2017). Sergeant, Concord California Police Department, personal communication, January 30.

Crawford v. Metropolitan Gov't of Nashville and Davidson County, No. 06-1595. (2009). Supreme Court of the United States October 2008 Term. January 26. www.supremecourt.gov/opinions/08pdf/06-1595.pdf (accessed May 9, 2017).

Dodge, Mary, Laura Valcore, and Frances Gomez. (2010). "Women on SWAT Teams: Separate but Equal?" *Policing: An International Journal of Police Strategies and Management, 34*(4): 699–712, November 2011.

Ewins, Teresa. (2017). Commander, San Francisco Police Department; President of SFPD Pride Alliance. San Francisco, CA, personal communication, January 24.

Feagin, Joe R. (2006). *Systemic Racism: A Theory of Oppression.* New York, NY: Routledge.

French, Bisa. (2017). Deputy Chief of Police, Richmond, California Police Department personal communication, May 5.

Glass, J.D. (2014). "2 Studies That Prove Domestic Violence Is an LGBT Issue." *Advocate.* www.advocate.com/crime/2014/09/04/2-studies-prove-domestic-violence-lgbt-issue (accessed February 8, 2017).

Hampton, Ronald E. (2017). Retired Police Officer, DC Metropolitan Police Department. Former Executive Director of National Black Police Association. Former Adjunct Criminal Justice Professor, University of the District of Columbia, personal communication, February 2.

Hispanic National Law Enforcement Association (HNLEA). www.hnlea.com/#Home Page (accessed February 17, 2017).

"History of Women in the Workforce." (1991, September 19). *Business Week*, p. 112.

Hsieh, Sylvia. (2012). "White Police Officer Wins $2 Million in Discrimination Suit." November. *Lawyers.com.* www.blogs.lawyers.com/2012/11/white-police-officer-wins-2-million-in-discrimination-suit/ (accessed December 1, 2016).

IACP. (International Association of Chief's of Police). "Police Leadership in the 21st Century: Achieving and Sustaining Executive Success." www.theiacp.org/Portals/0/pdfs/Publications/policeleadership.pdf (accessed December 1, 2016).

Jones, Susan. (2017). Former Chief of Police, Healdsburg, California Police Department, personal communication, January 17.

Lakeland Police Department Codes of Conduct. (2012, August 8). Lakeland Police Department, Florida. www.lakelandgov.net/lpd/ (accessed January 26, 2017).

LAPD. (2012). "LAPD Develops Guidelines to Improve Interactions with Transgender Individuals New Procedures to Be Discussed at Special Community Forum NR12169rf." Los Angeles Police Department Official Site. www.lapdonline.org/april_2012/news_view/50748 (accessed May 22, 2017).

Lee, Joni. (2017). Retired Police Officer, South San Francisco, personal communication, January 17.

Leonnig, Carol. (2017). "Secret Service agrees to pay $24 million to settle decades-old race-bias case brought by black agents." January 17. *The Washington Post.* www.washingtonpost.com/politics/secret-servi... ...rees-to-pay-24-million-to-settle-decades-old-race-bias-case-brought-by-black-agents/2017/01/17/b386006e-dd23-11e6-ad42-f3375f271c9c_story.html?utm_term=.e575f49d688a (accessed January 24, 2017).

Lonsway, Kim, Michelle Wood, Megan Fickling, Alexandria De Leon, Margaret Moore, Penny Harrington, Eleanor Smeal, and Katherine Spillar. (2002). "Men, Women, and Police Excessive Force: A Tale of Two Genders." National Center for Women and Policing. www.womenandpolicing.com/PDF/2002_Excessive_Force.pdf (accessed July 8, 2013).

Maciag, Mike. (2015). "Why Police Don't Mirror Communities and Why It Matters." August 28. *Governing the States and Localities—Public Safety & Justice.* www.governing.com/topics/public-justice-safety/gov-police-department-diversity.html (accessed January 23, 2017).

Mallory, Christy, Amira Hasenbush, and Brad Sears. (2013). "Discrimination against Law Enforcement Officers on the Basis of Sexual Orientation and Gender Identity 2000 to 2013." November. The Williams Institute. http://williamsinstitute.law.ucla.edu/wp-content/uploads/Law-Enforcement-Discrim-Report-Nov-2013.pdf (accessed February 14, 2017).

Matthies, Carl, Kirsten Keller, and Nelson Lim. (2012). "Identifying Barriers to Diversity in Law Enforcement Agencies." RAND Corporation. www.rand.org/content/dam/rand/pubs/occasional_papers/2012/RAND_OP370.pdf (accessed February 7, 2017).

McGinnis, Brian. (2016). The Workforce Diversity Network. "Transgender Police Officer Wins Title VII Claim against

School District." October 11. www.workforcediversity network.com/res_articles_TransgenderPoliceOfficer WinsTitleVIIClaimAgainstSchoolDistrict.aspx (accessed October 25, 2016).

Miraglia, Greg. (2016). "Coming Out from behind the Badge: The People, Events, and History That Shape Our Journey." Out to Protect Incorporated. www.comingoutfrombehind thebadge.com/about-us/about-greg-miraglia/(accessed February 7, 2017).

More, Harry. (1992). *Male-Dominated Police Culture: Reducing the Gender Gap.* Cincinnati, OH: Anderson Publishing, pp. 113–137.

Myatt, Mike. (2012). "5 Keys of Dealing with Workplace Conflict." February. *Forbes.* www.forbes.com/sites/mikemyatt/2012/02/22/5-keys-to-dealing-with-workplace-conflict/#fdd8a4215a06 (accessed January 4, 2017).

National Center for Transgender Equality. (2016). "The Report of the U.S. Transgender Survey 2015." www.transequality .org/sites/default/files/docs/usts/Executive%20Summary %20-%20FINAL%201.6.17.pdf (accessed January 2, 2017).

National Center for Women & Policing. (2003). "Under Scrutiny: The Effect of Consent Decrees on the Representation of Women in Sworn Law Enforcement." Spring. www .womenandpolicing.org/pdf/Fullconsentdecreestudy.pdf (accessed January 10, 2017).

National Center for Women & Policing. (2005). "Workplace Issues." www.womenandpolicing.org (accessed May 5, 2009).

National Crime Prevention Council. "Conflict Resolution Tips." www.ncpc.org/topics/conflict-resolution/conflict -resolution-tips (accessed July 7, 2013).

Obergefell v. Hodges. (2015). Supreme Court of the United States, October Term, 2014. (October 2014). www.supreme court.gov/opinions/14pdf/14-556_3204.pdf (accessed January 24, 2017).

Ocamb, Karen. (2013). "LAPD Sgt. Ronald Crump Finally Gets His $1.5 M." January 16. *LGBTQ Nation.* www.bilerico .lgbtqnation.com/2013/01/lapd_sgt_ronald_crump_finally _gets_his_15m.php (accessed February 17, 2017).

Orlov, Rick. (2013). "Sgt. Ronald Crump, Gay LAPD Officer, to Receive $1.5 Million Settlement in Harassment Lawsuit." March 18. *The Huffington Post.* www.huffingtonpost .com/2013/01/16/ronald-crump-gay-lapd_n_2487071 .html (accessed February 17, 2017).

Polisar, J. and D. Milgram. (1998, October). "Recruiting, Integrating and Retaining Women Police Officers: Strategies That Work." *Police Chief,* pp. 46–60.

Reaves, Brian. (2015). "Local Police Departments, 2013: Personnel, Policies, and Practices." U.S. Department of Justice, Bureau of Justice Statistics. www.bjs.gov/content/pub /pdf/lpd13ppp.pdf (accessed January 6, 2017).

Rose, Suzanna. (2000). "Lesbian Partner Violence Fact Sheet." National Violence against Women Prevention Center, University of Missouri at St. Louis. www.mainweb-v.musc .edu/vawprevention/lesbianrx/factsheet.shtml (accessed February 7, 2017).

Schulz, Dorothy M. (1995). *From Social Worker to Crime Fighter: Women in the United States Municipal Policing.* Westport, CT: Praeger, p. 5.

SFPD. (2017). San Francisco Police Department. "Pledge." http://notonmywatchsfpd.org/pledge/ (accessed February 20, 2017).

Simons, George, Carmen Vazquez, and Philip Harris. (2011). *Transcultural Leadership—Empowering the Diverse Workforce.* New York, NY: Routledge.

Smith, Betsy B. (2017). Retired Sergeant, Naperville (Illinois) Police Department, owner of The Winning Mind LLC Tucson, AZ, personal communication, February 17.

Spillar, Katherine. (2017). Co-Founder of the National Center for Women and Policing and Executive Director, Feminist Majority Foundation, personal communication, January 5.

Trank, Mark. (2014). "Employee Retaliation Claims Continue to Rise." November. http://www.swflemploymentlawblog .com/2014/11/05/employee-retaliation-claims-continue -to-rise/ (accessed February 17, 2017).

U.S. Bureau of Labor Statistics. (Winter 2013–2014). "Occupational Outlook Quarterly." www.bls.gov/ooq/ooqindex .htm (accessed March 25, 2014).

U.S. Department of Justice. (2016). "Law Enforcement and the Transgender Community—CRS Roll Call Training Video." www.justice.gov/opa/pr/justice-department-releases -new-training-video-law-enforcement-interacting -transgender (accessed February 14, 2017).

U.S. Department of Labor, Bureau of Labor Statistics. (2015). "Women in the Labor Force: A Databook." 2015 Edition. Report 1059. www.bls.gov/opub/reports/womens -databook/archive/women-in-the-labor-force-a -databook-2015.pdf. (accessed January 7, 2017).

U.S. Equal Employment Opportunity Commission. "Facts about Retaliation." www.eeoc.gov/laws/types/retaliation .cfm (accessed February 12, 2017).

U.S. Equal Employment Opportunity Commission. "Pregnancy Discrimination & Temporary Disability." www .eeoc.gov/laws/types/pregnancy.cfm (accessed August 4, 2013).

U.S. Equal Employment Opportunity Commission. (2010). "Facts about Sexual Harassment." www.eeoc.gov/eeoc /publications/fs-sex.cfm (accessed July 1, 2013).

U.S. Equal Employment Opportunity Commission. (2016). "EEOC Releases Fiscal Year 2016 Enforcement and Litigation Data." January 18. www.eeoc.gov/eeoc/newsroom /release/1-18-17a.cfm (accessed June 20, 2017).

Vasquez, Kate. (2012). "Historic LAPD Transgender Guidelines and Procedures." April 15. Trans-Interactions Support Project. https://sites.google.com/site/transinteractions/tsp -publications/tsp-48-historic-lapd-transgender-guidelines -and-procedures (accessed May 12, 2017).

Wilson, Charles and Shirley Wilson. (2014). "Are We There Yet? Perceptive Roles of African American Police Officers in Small Agency Settings." *The Western Journal of Black Studies,* 38(2): 123–136. www.questia.com/library /journal/1G1-387060483/are-we-there-yet-perceptive -roles-of-african-american (accessed February 16, 2017).

Women's Justice Center. (2010). "Increasing Women's Numbers and Influence in Policing." www.justicewomen.com /pw_increasingwomensnumbers.html (accessed October 21, 2016).

Woolsey, Shannon. (2010, October). "Challenges for Women in Policing." *Law and Order.* Hendon Publishing— Law Enforcement Publications and Conferences. www .hendonpub.com/resources/article_archive/results /details?id=1614 (accessed February 6, 2017).

3 Multicultural Representation in Law Enforcement
Recruitment, Retention, and Promotion

LEARNING OBJECTIVES

After reading this chapter, you should be able to:

- Recognize the historical perspectives of women and minorities in law enforcement.
- Discuss the ongoing challenges of recruitment trends with respect to women and minorities in law enforcement agencies.
- Explain recruitment difficulties and strategies for success.
- Describe the importance of retention and promotion of minorities and women in law enforcement careers.
- Identify promotional policies and practices in law enforcement agencies that demonstrate the valuing of differences in our workplaces and communities.

OUTLINE

- Introduction
- Recruitment of a Diverse Workforce
- Attracting and Retaining Women and Minorities
- Selection Processes
- Retention and Promotion of a Diverse Workforce
- Summary
- Discussion Questions and Issues
- References

INTRODUCTION

Our increasingly diverse society has created a demand for law enforcement officers and agents who can work effectively with many different types of people. For this reason, hiring and retaining qualified employees, especially women, African Americans, Asians, Hispanics, and members of other nontraditional groups, continues to be a concern and a priority of law enforcement agencies nationwide. Diversity is a very important element in establishing and increasing trust between law enforcement and the community served; however, many agencies have had difficulty finding qualified applicants, which has led to a recruitment crisis. Although influenced by economic circumstances, the crisis appears to be primarily the result of changing societal and demographic trends.

RECRUITMENT OF A DIVERSE WORKFORCE

The recruitment of women and members of diverse groups is not a new issue in the history of U.S. law enforcement. In 1967, for example, the President's Crime Commission Report recommended that more minorities be hired, and that they receive opportunities for advancement. Soon after the Watts riots in Los Angeles, the 1968 Kerner Commission Report identified the underrepresentation of African Americans in law enforcement as a serious problem. The report recommended improved hiring and promotion policies and procedures for minorities. The Warren Christopher Commission Report on the Los Angeles Police Department (LAPD), released soon after the 1992 riots following the first Rodney King trial, cited problems of racism and bias within the LAPD. The Commission recommended, among other things, improved hiring and promotion processes that would benefit all groups. In 2014, President Obama established the Task Force on 21st Century Policing as a partnership between law enforcement and communities that reduces crime and increases trust. Among its recommendations, the task force identified increasing the diversity of the nation's law enforcement agencies as an important aspect in developing that trust. The task force was created after several years of officer-involved shootings and attacks on law enforcement, which led to demonstrations and protests in many major cities in the United States.

Even with the recommendations over the years that criminal justice agencies become more diverse, statistics still reveal that racial and ethnic minorities are underrepresented by an average of 24 percentage points compared with census estimates for the general public (Maciag, 2015).

Recruitment Crisis and Trends

The past three decades have seen major shifts in employment trends in law enforcement agencies nationwide, including a new challenge in recruiting qualified candidates for law enforcement positions. This can be attributed not only to the economy but also to significant societal changes during this period.

ECONOMIC FACTORS AND RECRUITMENT In the late 1990s and into 2000, the unemployment rate in the United States was approximately 4 percent, the lowest experienced unemployment rate in 30 years. Although there were plenty of jobs in law enforcement, the number of applicants was substantially lower than in the past. As a result, those seeking jobs could be very selective. Many jobs in private industry, especially high-tech jobs, came with high salaries, stock options, signing and year-end bonuses, company cars, and broader opportunities for advancement. Public sector employers had difficulty competing with such incentives and opportunities; thus, public safety occupations seemed less attractive. Court decisions (and pretrial settlements) against such companies as Coke, Texaco, and Wall Street's Smith Barney in race bias lawsuits also factored into recruitment difficulties during this time. Many large companies, aware that the populations within their recruitment areas were diversifying, knew that their employee demographics had to match those of the world outside or they, too, would be subject to lawsuits and/or criticism. As a result, they scrambled to recruit and promote talented women and minorities. This was particularly true of companies that sell products or services to the public. The wide-open market also made for transitory employees, especially those with experience, causing retention problems for employers. During this period, smaller law enforcement agencies lost staff as larger agencies lured experienced officers away with promises of better benefits. The recruitment effort, in which everyone was competing for the same pool of qualified candidates, has been compared to the National Football League Draft.

At the same time, police departments experienced a reduction in staff because many officers who had been hired in the police expansion wave of the 1960s and 1970s (known as the baby boomers) began to retire. Most law enforcement officers retire before age 55, earlier than is typical in civilian occupations. As the baby-boom-era officers began retiring at an accelerated rate, due in part to improved retirement benefits that became an industry standard during the early 2000s, the result was a shortage of employees. The September 11 terrorist attacks put further strain on law enforcement agencies and their ability to recruit as police departments were asked to assume new homeland security and intelligence duties in addition to their normal, ongoing public safety responsibilities. Another consequence of the September 11 attacks was that law enforcement agencies began to face competition for recruits from an expanding number of federal and private security jobs created by the wars in Afghanistan and Iraq. In addition, the national military response to terrorism also affected the ability of existing police officers to meet traditional and new police missions, particularly in small and rural police departments where the call-up of even one or two officers who serve in the National Guard or Reserves can have a noticeable impact.

The number of law enforcement jobs was growing in availability over the years previously mentioned. Then in late 2007, the United States experienced what some economists describe as the worst economic downturn since the Great Depression, seriously impacting local, state, and federal governments. The unemployment rate in December 2007 was at 5 percent and by October 2009 at 10 percent, according to the Bureau of Labor Statistics (U.S. Department of Labor, 2016). Between 2009 and 2010, there was a 3 percent reduction in the number of sworn officers, and students graduating from criminal justice programs found no jobs available to them (Fisher, 2011). From the beginning of 2008 until about 2013, cities and counties were forced to reduce personnel through layoffs and attrition, due to the faltering economy or recession. Reductions were also accomplished by freezing department size and limiting the number of trainees in academies. In 2010, the Georgia Police Academy near Atlanta was closed after 35 years because of the shrinking economy. Unfortunately, layoffs disproportionately affect employees who were the most recently hired, so that women and people of diverse ethnic and racial groups are often the first to lose their jobs, canceling any gains made in achieving a multicultural and multiracial workforce.

One of the causes of the economic woes of city and county agencies was that tax revenues were shrinking while costs for police and firefighters' wages and benefits were escalating. Some municipalities were saddled with labor contracts they could no longer afford to maintain. For example, some government agencies entered into contracts with their law enforcement and firefighters' unions that called for enhanced retirement benefits known as "3-at-50." This benefit allows employees to retire at age 50 with retirement pay of 3 percent of their highest annual salary multiplied by the number of years they served. If any agency in each region offers this benefit, others must follow suit to stay competitive and retain personnel. As more and more eligible employees reached the age of 50, a major exodus of workers took place, severely impacting the budgets of many public agencies and creating vacancies that could not be filled because of the poor economy. In short, there were conflicting trends. Cost-cutting throughout local, state, and federal governments forced layoffs, cutbacks in service, and unfillable vacancies. At the same time, there was public pressure for more effective services and protection from terrorist threats.

After five years of cutbacks and layoffs, in 2013 law enforcement agencies across the country began to see a turnaround. However, most agencies are still operating with a reduced workforce and staffing levels are never expected to return to what they were prior to the recession. Due to the impact of the recession, many agencies across the country negotiated contracts to require officers to pay into their pension plans, something they never had to do before. Supporters of better police benefits point to the deterioration of those benefits as a huge stumbling block to recruitment and retention efforts (Moore, 2011). Not only were pension contributions implemented or increased, but also allowances for uniform maintenance and other incentives were reduced or eliminated.

Because so many people had been laid off from downsizing manufacturing industries, there was an abundance of applicants, diverse and better educated, trying to get into law enforcement. There were more "free agents," students not already hired by a law enforcement agency, putting themselves through police academies. Agencies could once again hire the very best of those who applied. However, there have been continuing recruitment difficulties to fill law enforcement jobs.

Recruitment Difficulties

These shifting economic forces, combined with social and demographic changes, and more recently the unflattering image and danger of law enforcement, have led to challenges for agencies in recruiting qualified workers. These challenges are intensified by strict qualifications or recruitment standards set by local, state, and federal law enforcement agencies, which have historically eliminated many candidates. With jobs in the private sector often offering higher pay and less stress, many potential candidates are forgoing jobs in law enforcement. As a result, police recruiters are seeing a decrease in the quality of the applicant pool and applicants with credit problems or a history of drug and criminal activity waived (Moore, 2011). Agencies around the country report that out of the total number of applicants, very few make it through the testing process, which includes a thorough background and credit check, physical, psychological, and polygraph test. The numbers are again cut by those that drop out of the training academy or leave before completing the field training program after they are hired.

A study by the U.S. Department of Defense shows that an alarming 71 percent of Americans, ages 17–24, would not qualify for military service today because they are physically unfit, failed to finish high school, or have criminal records ("Ready, Willing, and Unable to Serve," Department of Defense, 2015). The percentage is only 4 percent lower than the same study performed in 2009. Because law enforcement organizations recruit from the same demographic groups, the ramifications for hiring are clear. According to the report, those findings are particularly true in low-income areas. The study cites three important reasons that young Americans cannot join the military: poor education (approximately one out of four lack a high school diploma); involvement in crime (approximately one in 10 have at least one prior conviction for a felony or serious misdemeanor); and poor health (nearly 32 percent have health problems, including asthma, vision or hearing problems, mental health issues, or recent treatment for attention deficit hyperactivity disorder). In addition to those health issues, weight problems disqualify 27 percent of young people from joining the military. Because law enforcement organizations recruit from the same demographic groups, the ramifications for hiring are clear.

Like the military, law enforcement agencies screen job applicants using standards that address age, height, weight, education, drug use, criminal history, credit rating (departments don't want recruits who may be hounded by creditors or lawsuits), and physical and mental fitness. Because many of those interested in a career in law enforcement cannot meet these rigorous standards, some standards have had to change in response to social forces. In the past, for example, a previous misdemeanor conviction may have been an automatic disqualifier; however, that is no longer the case for most agencies today.

AGE, HEIGHT, AND WEIGHT   Most law enforcement agencies, at federal, state and levels, do not consider age a crucial factor, provided that the candidate is physically fit and can demonstrate he or she can handle the physical demands of being a police officer. As the population has aged, some agencies have raised their upper age limit for new hires, including the Boston Police Department (from age 32 to 40), the Indiana State Police (from 35 to 40), and the Houston Police Department (from 36 to 44). There are even agencies that have no upper age limit, usually out of fear of age-discrimination lawsuits. However, older job candidates are still required to meet the same physical fitness requirements during the testing processes and in the academy as their younger colleagues. Most agencies have also eliminated height requirements, requiring only that the candidate's weight be proportional to height and that they pass the training academy. In the past decade, the national obesity epidemic has also had an impact on law enforcement and military recruitment. While weight is a genuine issue when screening applicants for law enforcement careers, there are federal laws that ban discrimination based on weight if the candidate can pass the physical fitness test the agency utilizes.

DRUG USE AND CRIMINAL HISTORY   For many years, most law enforcement organizations would not consider job candidates who had any history of drug use. However, agencies have found it increasingly difficult to locate suitable applicants unaffected by the drug culture, and have therefore eased their standards. The trend is that agencies no longer disqualify candidates for minor drug use or even drug convictions that occurred well prior to their application. Numerous studies have found that teenaged girls are just as likely to use illegal drugs as their male counterparts and have difficulty passing background investigations. Today, more women are being incarcerated for offenses that make them ineligible for law enforcement careers, creating a challenge to law enforcement agencies desiring to increase the number of women in their departments. For all these reasons, many criminal justice agencies no longer require that job candidates have a perfectly clean criminal record.

EDUCATION   Despite years of research by academics and practitioners into the relationship between higher education and policing skills, there has been little agreement concerning the optimal extent of education recommended for an entry-level officer. A high school education is usually required of applicants for most police departments and, historically, these officers have performed well. An increasing number of departments require 1 or 2 years of college coursework or more, and a few expect a 4-year college degree. This trend is based on the argument that the movement from traditional policing to community-oriented problem solving requires skill sets, such as critical and analytical reasoning, enhanced understanding of socioeconomic causes of crime, and advanced interpersonal and intercultural communications, that are best developed in higher education programs (Hilal and Erickson, 2010).

Department of Education graduation rates published in 2015 showed that not only more U.S. students were graduating from high school, but also nearly every racial and ethnic subgroup had seen a growth in graduation rates that outpaced that of white students. The graduation rates for African American and Hispanic students increased by 3.7 and 4.2 percentage points, respectively, in two years, compared with 2.6 percentage points for white students, according to the report (U.S. Department of Education, 2015). However, the 2015 "Ready, Willing and Unable to Serve" study found that approximately one out of four young Americans lacks a high school diploma (Council for a Strong America, 2015).

Although the graduation trend appears to be improving, there are still concerns about the eligibility of minority officers, especially in diverse urban areas from which an agency may be trying to recruit. For this reason, only a small fraction of agencies now requires candidates to hold a four-year college degree. Typically, those recruits who do possess such a degree can expect a higher salary than their peers with fewer years of education. Most potential applicants do not have a college degree, however, and those who do are attracted to careers other than law enforcement for many reasons, including salary and benefits.

To increase their applicant pools, agencies such as St. Petersburg and Tampa, Florida, have eliminated the requirement of two years of college if the candidate has military or law enforcement experience. The relaxation of standards has been prompted in large part by a dire need to fill vacancies. At the same time, agencies are attempting to recruit candidates who are wiser, worldlier, and coolheaded in a crisis.

Although the number of high school students graduating has increased throughout the country, employers should be aware that requirements in some schools for a diploma have been reduced. A high school diploma might not mean that the student learned the basic skills needed for higher education or a job requiring one.

ADDITIONAL FACTORS   There are other reasons why many individuals have been deterred from or are reluctant to seek a career in law enforcement. Highly publicized scandals and other negative publicity involving police departments in some major cities have had a diminishing effect on recruitment. In addition, because of an acrimonious history between police and communities of color, members of those communities—the very people law enforcement seeks to attract—may shy away from a career in law enforcement, fearing disapproval from their peers.

In addition, the growing anti-police climate of recent years, punctuated by shootings of police officers, further reduced the number of candidates of any race or ethnicity wanting to enter a law enforcement career. Some potential applicants decided to not pursue careers in law enforcement due to the risks involved and salaries, which were lower than in private industry.

Hispanics are underrepresented in law enforcement (Maciag, 2015). According to Andrew Peralta, 2014–2016 past president of the National Latino Peace Officers Association and lieutenant with the Las Vegas Metropolitan Police Department:

> One possible contributing factor to the disparity is that Hispanics may want nothing to do with police if they were born or lived in countries notorious for police corruption. Just convincing them to call police is challenging, so it may take a generation or two before their children view law enforcement as a career. (Peralta [NLPOA], 2017)

Hispanic/Latino community members' distrust or a lack of understanding of the role of law enforcement in the United States is discussed in more detail in Chapter 1. These perceptions are passed on to their children who are born in the United States; in many cases, they are also too reluctant to apply for criminal justice jobs. Thus, although Hispanics are the nation's largest minority group, the criminal justice system does not attract a large pool of applicants.

According to criminal justice educator and author David Barlow, "...strategies for hiring Latino/a police officers to represent a subset of the United States population may be more complex than for other minority groups" (Barlow, 2017). He cited a Pew Research Hispanic Center report that found that a majority of Hispanic/Latino respondents reject the notion that there is a common "Hispanic" culture. Instead, the study found that most Latinos are connected by a common appreciation for the Spanish language, but their experiences vary widely based upon their country of origin, when their families came to this country, and where they live in the United States. The report indicated that many prefer to be identified not as Hispanic or Latino but by their family's country of origin, such as Mexican, Puerto Rican, Cuban, or Salvadorian. These factors need to be taken into consideration when planning recruitment strategies that will appeal to the Latino/a population. David Barlow said that "[at] a minimum, police leaders should make it a point to know the demographic makeup of their community and seek the appropriate cultural representation."

Departments with employees who match in ratio the demographics of their community secure legitimacy for the agency and promote the democratic principle of representation. Although Latino/a officers should not be required to work only in Hispanic communities, when they do they may be more likely to receive cooperation and support from the community than non-Hispanic officers.

Finally, another reason for the reluctance of young people to apply for careers in law enforcement is that the hierarchical paramilitary structure of most agencies may be unappealing to today's youth. In addition, most young people do not like to be micromanaged. For these reasons, policing has become a less attractive profession.

ATTRACTING AND RETAINING WOMEN AND MINORITIES

The President's Task Force on 21st Century Policing includes the recommendation and action items pertaining to creating a more diverse workforce:

- 1.8 Recommendation: Law enforcement agencies should strive to create a workforce that contains a broad range of diversity including race, gender, language, life experience, and cultural background to improve understanding and effectiveness in dealing with all communities.
- 1.8.1 Action Item: The Federal Government should create a Law Enforcement Diversity Initiative designed to help law enforcement departments to reflect the demographics of the community.
- 1.8.2 Action Item: The department overseeing this initiative should help localities learn best practices for recruitment, training, and outreach to improve the diversity as well as the cultural and linguistic responses of law enforcement agencies. (U.S. Department of Justice, 2015)

The 2017 publication entitled *Hiring for the 21st Century Law Enforcement Officer: Challenges, Opportunities, and Strategies for Success* (Morrison, 2017), developed by Community Oriented Policing Services (COPS) and Police Executive Research Forum (PERF), presents three major themes regarding the need to

- Hire candidates who share the values and vision of the community and the department.
- Make the hiring process more efficient.
- Advance diversity and inclusiveness in the hiring process. (Ibid.)

This document is an excellent resource for law enforcement agencies to use in their recruitment efforts.

The National Center for Women and Policing (NCWP) developed a self-assessment guide to assist agencies seeking to recruit and retain more women in sworn law enforcement positions. The resulting publication, *Recruiting and Retaining Women: A Self-Assessment Guide for Law Enforcement*, aids federal, state, and local law enforcement agencies in examining their policies and procedures to identify and remove obstacles to hiring and retaining women at all levels of the organization. The guide also provides a list of resources for agencies to use when they plan or implement changes to their current policies and procedures. The guide recommends increasing the number of women in all ranks of law enforcement as a strategy to strengthen community policing, reduce the use of excessive force, enhance police response to domestic violence, and provide balance to the workforce (NCWP).

Army recruiting offices across the nation as of the summer of 2015 not only had more women assigned but also had fitness tests to apply to candidates. Prospective soldiers will now have to demonstrate that they can run, jump, lift a weight, and throw a heavy ball to help determine if the potential recruits are physically capable of performing various military jobs. The same procedures would be useful for law enforcement recruiters to evaluate candidates on essential physical abilities required to perform job duties.

RECRUITMENT OF NON-SWORN PERSONNEL Not everyone wants or is well suited for a career that involves arresting people, and for those, there are non-sworn careers within the criminal justice system that do not require someone to become a police officer. Departments hire civilian staff for essential but nonenforcement positions such as dispatch, public information, community relations, evidence collection, research, and records positions. Yet, the same factors that reduce the number of sworn personnel who are successfully recruited to agencies apply to non-sworn law enforcement staff. For example, most agencies today have a shortage of civilian dispatchers. This is a highly stressful job where sound judgment and remaining calm under pressure are crucial. Candidates for dispatcher typically must pass a written and an oral test, a criminal background check, a polygraph, and a psychological exam. The job is so stressful that retention of good dispatchers is difficult. The need to work long hours, nights, weekends, and holiday shifts contribute to the high turnover rate for this position. Competition among agencies for seasoned dispatchers is fierce, and openings are frequent.

Recruitment Strategies

Recruitment strategies to attract diverse candidates for both law enforcement and civilian jobs within the department involve the following:

1. *Commitment:* The chief executive and the department must demonstrate a genuine commitment to hiring a diverse pool of applicants.
2. *Marketing plan:* A strategic marketing plan must be developed that includes action steps, objectives, goals, budget, accountability, and timetables.
3. *Resources:* Adequate resources, including budget, personnel, and equipment, must be made available to the recruitment effort.
4. *Social media platforms:* Recruiters must make use of social media to attract and pre-screen applicants for department jobs.
5. *Selection and training of recruiters:* Recruiters are ambassadors for the department and must be selected carefully, be trained to reflect the diversity within the community, and include women.
6. *Recruiting incentives:* Police executives should consider using financial and other incentives to recruit women and minorities.
7. *Community involvement:* The community should be involved in recruiting and testing processes of women and minorities for sworn and non-sworn positions.
8. *Military involvement:* Efforts should be made to network with the various military branches to recruit discharged veterans.
9. *Internship, cadet, reserve, explorer scout, and high school citizen police academy programs:* High school and college students are potential future recruits, so programs should be available that address these groups.

To build a diverse workforce, recruitment strategies of the past are no longer sufficient and will not provide agencies with high-quality applicants. Agencies with maximum success in recruiting women and minorities have had specific goals, objectives, and timetables in place; these policies must be established at the top level of the organization. The U.S. Department of Justice in conjunction with the International Association of Chiefs of Police in 2009 created a *Law Enforcement Recruitment Toolkit*, which is still useful today and should be referred to by recruiters (U.S. Department of Justice, 2009).

COMMITMENT Recruiting minority and women applicants, especially in highly competitive labor markets, requires commitment and effort. Police executives must communicate that commitment to their recruiting staff and devote the resources necessary to achieve recruitment goals. This genuine commitment must be demonstrated both inside and outside the organization. Internally, chief executives should develop policies and procedures that emphasize the importance of a diverse workforce. Affirmative action and/or programs that target certain applicants (where legal) will not work in a vacuum. Chief executives must integrate the values that promote diversity and affirmative action into every aspect of the agency, from its mission statement to its roll-call training. Externally, police executives should publicly delineate the specific hiring and promotion goals of the department to the community through both formal (e.g., media) and informal (e.g., community-based policing, networking with organizations representing the diverse groups) methods. While chief executives promote the philosophy, policies, and procedures, committed staff members, who are sensitive to the need for affirmative hiring and promotions, carry them out. Executives should also build partnerships with personnel officials so that decisions clearly reflect the hiring goals of the department. It is recommended that police executives audit the personnel selection process to ensure that neither the sequencing of the testing stages nor the length of the selection process hinders the objective of hiring women and minorities.

Although chiefs may be genuine in their efforts to champion diversity and affirmative action hiring, care must be taken that their policies and procedures do not violate Title VII of the Civil Rights Act of 1964. Also, agencies in states that have enacted laws prohibiting affirmative action hiring programs and the targeting of "protected classes" (e.g., California's Proposition 209, passed in 1996, discussed later in this chapter) must adhere to these regulations. A knowledgeable personnel department or legal staff should review policies and procedures prior to implementation. ("Protected Classes" is defined in the Glossary.)

MARKETING PLAN A strategic marketing plan should be developed that includes the action steps that commit the objectives, goals, budget, accountability, and timetables for the recruitment campaign to paper. Demographic data should form one of the foundations for the plan, which must also take into account the current political, social, and economic conditions of the department and the community. Deputy Chief Chris Skinner of the Hillsboro Police Department in Oregon researched what attracts candidates for law enforcement to a particular agency.

> One way agencies can differentiate themselves is to achieve law enforcement "brand" as related to their position in the marketplace, to become the brand name when people discuss law enforcement services in the area. More important, each department should strive to have prospective officers consider it the brand name to work for. (Skinner, 2010)

According to Deputy Chief Skinner, "Creating the brand name or look is easy; the real challenge is creating a unique brand experience" (ibid.). This involves establishing a positive emotional connection between a potential applicant and the agency so that applicants evaluate the agency on more than just factual information, like salary, benefits, and demographics of a community, that applies to every law enforcement organization. The agency must create a special allure that presents itself as a great place to work and thus the better choice among others. Some examples of how to achieve this include ride-along programs; introductions to role models within the department, especially those of the same gender and/or background of the candidate; an informative and attractive Website; and positive press releases about the department.

To avoid losing qualified applicants to other agencies or private industry, the marketing plan should provide for fast-tracking the best candidates through the testing and screening processes. Fast-tracking is an aggressive recruitment strategy wherein a preliminary, qualifying check quickly takes place concerning the driving, credit, and criminal history of the applicant before any other screening occurs. Applicants who do not meet established standards are immediately notified. The remaining applicants are then interviewed by a trained ranking officer or civilian holding the position for which the candidate is applying. Applicants earning a passing score on the personal interview immediately receive a letter advising them that they passed, giving them tangible evidence that the agency is seriously considering hiring them. The letter also informs them that they must pass additional qualifying steps, including a background investigation. The applicant must complete the final testing within 10 days or the agency may withdraw the offer.

To streamline the process, background investigators have established blocks of time for other testing such as polygraphs and psychological and medical evaluations. Streamlining is important because in today's labor market, the best-qualified applicants will not wait for months while testing proceeds at a slow pace; they will get hired and take positions elsewhere.

Additionally, the strategic recruitment plan should include an advertising campaign that targets

- High school seniors
- Colleges and universities, including Reserve Officers' Training Course (ROTC) and sports departments
- Military bases and reserve units
- Churches, temples, mosques, synagogues, and other places of worship
- Community centers in minority neighborhoods and associations for Hispanics, Native Americans, Asians, and African Americans
- Gymnasiums, fitness and martial arts studios, athletic clubs, and the like

Participation of women and minority officers within the department is crucial in recruitment efforts (see "Recruiting Incentives"), as is the involvement of groups and organizations that represent the target groups. If there are high-profile minorities and women, such as athletes and business executives, in the community, they should be enlisted to promote police work as a career through media releases and endorsements on flyers and brochures. Application packages should be made available at police departments and on the agency's Website 24 hours a day, 7 days a week, so that they are available to potential candidates even when the personnel office is closed.

RESOURCES   Adequate resources, including money, personnel, and equipment, must be made available to the recruitment effort. Financial constraints challenge almost every organization's recruitment campaign. The size or financial circumstances of an agency may necessitate less expensive—and perhaps more innovative—approaches. For example, many small law enforcement jurisdictions can combine to implement regional testing. One large county on the West Coast successfully formed a consortium of agencies and implemented regional testing three times per month for law enforcement candidates. To participate, each agency pays into an account based on the population of its jurisdiction. Alternatively, each agency can pay according to how many applicants it hired from the list. The pooled money is then used for recruitment advertising (billboards, radio, television, newspapers) and the initial testing processes (reading, writing, and agility tests, including proctors). The eligibility list is then provided to each of the participating agencies, which continue the screening process for applicants in whom they have an interest. By combining their efforts, they may be able to

- Save money.
- Develop a larger pool of applicants.
- Become more competitive with private industry and other public agencies.
- Test more often.
- Reduce the amount of time from application to hire.

In terms of recruiting a diverse workforce, the second benefit listed above—developing a larger pool of applicants—is central to reaching beyond the traditional applicant pool. Law enforcement agencies can post openings on their Websites to recruit individuals with a wide variety of backgrounds and skills. Department Websites have been found to be valuable recruiting tools when used to highlight the work of women and minorities within an agency, and can be used to attract returning military veterans.

Law enforcement career fairs, usually lasting no more than 2 or 3 hours, should be held on a weekend or an evening, so that people who are already employed have the opportunity to attend. A media and publicity campaign should be used to attract women and minorities to the event. At the career fair, women and minority officers from a variety of assignments within the agency can describe their jobs and answer questions. The sort of information that might be provided by the panel could include the following:

- The history of the agency
- What the testing processes are and how they can prepare
- Programs available to assist them in preparation for tests
- Information about agency volunteer programs, civilian positions, cadets, explorers, internships, and reserves
- Academy requirements, dates, expectations, location and contact information
- Information about the field training program for new hires and expectations
- Examples of work schedules and career ladders
- Availability of, if possible, ride-along programs with the agency
- The importance of problem-solving and communications skills—community policing
- What the department is looking for in a candidate for employment

A high-ranking minority or female officer should also address those in attendance to persuade them to consider becoming employees. Information about the application and selection process, the physical agility test, and the academy should also be available. In addition, law enforcement agencies should give applicants the opportunity to complete an application and register for scheduled testing online to speed up the hiring process and increase the number of prospective hires.

SOCIAL MEDIA PLATFORMS The Internet has become the number-one way that candidates for law enforcement careers learn about job openings and agencies across the country. According to one study, 18 percent of recruits in their survey were first motivated to contact their current employer because of an Internet ad, and that 80 percent reported accessing the Internet at least daily (Weber and Ridgeway, 2010).

Up-to-date agencies advertise openings and career fairs on their own platforms and Websites such as YouTube, Facebook, Twitter, and Craigslist, as well as continuing to utilize more traditional venues. This technology is an inexpensive way to reach thousands of potential candidates in many demographic groups for both sworn and non-sworn positions. It provides an opportunity for the agency to give job-hunters in-depth information about the department and the recruitment and selection process. Social media platforms provide a way to announce testing dates and locations for picking up and returning applications, and can also refer users to the department Website and promote careers in law enforcement. One agency on the West Coast discovered that in the year they created a women's section on their recruitment Website, the percentage of women in the academy jumped from 8 to 50 percent. The Website featured biographies and photos of the department's diverse workforce.

Modern technology offers other benefits as well. Video conferencing using Skype or other platforms can be used by agencies to prescreen applicants for law enforcement jobs to determine if they are eligible and meet all the requirements, so that neither the department nor the candidate's time is wasted. Skype is also useful for background investigators, who can perform interviews long-distance, saving the agency time and money for travel.

SELECTION AND TRAINING OF RECRUITERS A recruiter is an ambassador for the department and must be selected carefully; the recruiter should reflect the diversity within the community and include women. Full-time recruiters are a luxury most often found only in large agencies. The benefit of a full-time recruiter program is that frequently the employees in this assignment receive some training in marketing techniques. They have no other responsibilities or assignments and can therefore focus on what they do, and develop the contacts, resources, and skills to be effective. Whether recruiters are full time, part time, or assigned on an as-needed basis, however, the following criteria should be considered when selecting them:

- Commitment to the goal of recruiting
- Belief in a philosophy that values diversity
- Ability to work well in a community policing environment

- Belief in and ability to market a product: law enforcement as a career
- Comfort with people of all backgrounds and ability to communicate this comfort
- Ability to discuss the importance of entire community representation in police work and its advantages to the department without sounding patronizing

Recruiters must be given resources (such as a budget and equipment) and must have established guidelines. They must be highly trained with respect to their role, market research methods, public relations, and cultural awareness. They must also understand, appreciate, and be dedicated to organizational values and ethics. They must be aware of and in control of any biases they might have toward individuals, or groups of people, who might be different.

Almost every state's Commission on Peace Officer Standards and Training (POST) has developed a course on the techniques and methods of recruitment. Large, progressive agencies (or a consortium of agencies) could develop an in-house program patterned after these model courses. The Institute for Women in Trades, Technology and Science (IWITTS) can provide resources and training programs on recruiting and retaining women. The organization conducts national workshops as well as provides technical assistance to departments via personal contact or the Internet. Their materials include a law enforcement environmental assessment tool (LEEAT) involving institutional checklists and data collection methods to help determine the best recruiting strategies for a particular law enforcement agency.

RECRUITING INCENTIVES Employee referral systems (ERS) are a very effective recruitment technique that sometimes involves incentives. ERS success requires that officers informally assess an applicant to determine if he or she could perform well within the organization, and if so, make a recommendation to the agency. Research has suggested that officers who are recruited through ERS are more likely to succeed in the selection process, be hired, and stay with the agency.

To implement ERS, it is recommended that police executives consider using financial and other incentives, after first determining that such programs are lawful in their jurisdiction (monetary incentive programs may be adversely affected by Fair Labor Standards Act considerations). The percent of state and local law enforcement officers employed by agencies offering selected incentives to recruit applicants for sworn positions in 2008, the most recent statistics available, is shown in Exhibit 3.1.

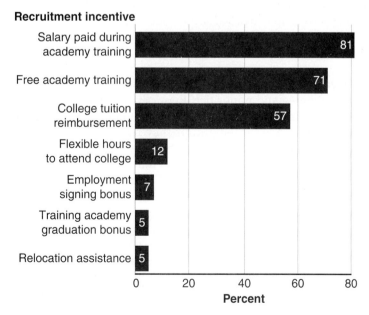

EXHIBIT 3.1 Agencies Incentives to Recruit Applicants for Sworn Positions, 2008

Source: Reaves, Brian A., Ph.D. (2012). "Hiring and Retention of State and Local Law Enforcement Officers, 2008." October. NCJ 238251. www.bjs.gov/index .cfm?ty=pbdetail&iid=4514.

Financial and other incentive programs are especially useful to agencies that cannot afford full-time recruiters. They are used to encourage officers to recruit bilingual whites, women, and ethnically and racially diverse candidates while on or off duty. One possible program would give officers overtime credit for each person they recruit in those categories who makes to the eligibility list, additional credit if the same applicant is hired, and further credit for each stage the new officer passes until the probation period ends. Some departments offer officers who are not specifically assigned to recruiting up to 20 hours of compensatory time for recruiting a lateral police officer. Department members can also receive an additional 40 hours of compensatory time for recruiting a lateral who is bilingual or from a protected class. An agency on the West Coast offers sign-on bonuses for difficult-to-recruit positions. If a recruit successfully completes a POST-certified academy and enters the field training program, the person who referred them receives $1,500. Once the recruit completes probation and receives a "meets standards" evaluation, the person making the referral receives $3,500. Department employees also receive $1,000 if they refer a dispatcher who is hired and another $1,500 once the dispatcher successfully completes the probationary period.

One East Coast agency awards $250 to employees who recruit applicants (of any racial or ethnic group) if they complete all phases of the background process, are hired, and start the academy. The same department awards $250 to employees who recruit lateral police officer candidates once they complete all phases of the background process, are hired, and report for duty. When these recruits make it through probation, the employee who recruited them receives $250 as an additional incentive. Encouraging all department members to be involved in the recruitment effort, including the promotion of law enforcement as a career, is usually effective.

To be competitive in recruiting employees, especially minorities and women, agencies must offer incentives just as corporations do. Some cities and counties offer signing bonuses to experienced officers from other agencies. Some departments offer academy-trained applicants a $3,000 signing bonus. The amounts vary, but the practice of offering these bonuses has been used in cities and counties across the nation by agencies that can afford it. Some jurisdictions also offer law enforcement officers help with down payments and interest-free loans on their first home. Such offers are used not only to encourage current police officers to stay with the department but also to recruit new hires who might not be able to live in a high-cost community. Watching personnel leave for greener pastures can be frustrating for the department that invested time and money in the employee. It takes about a year to hire a new officer, at a cost of approximately $4,000 for the screening processes, and thousands more for academy training. Thus, the use of incentives to attract and retain personnel with experience ultimately saves the agency money.

COMMUNITY INVOLVEMENT   Successful law enforcement agencies involve the community in recruiting and hiring women and minorities. Representatives from protected classes should be involved in initial meetings to plan a recruitment campaign. They can assist in determining the best marketing methods for the groups they represent, and can help by personally contacting potential candidates. They should be provided with recruitment information (such as brochures and posters) that they can disseminate at religious institutions, civic and social organizations, schools, and cultural events. Community-based policing also offers the best opportunity for officers to put the message out regarding agency recruiting.

Community leaders representing the diversity of the community should also be involved in the selection process, including sitting on oral boards for applicants. The San Francisco Police Department utilizes community leaders in all the processes mentioned. Many progressive agencies have encouraged their officers to join community-based organizations, in which they interact with residents and are able to involve them in recruitment efforts for the department.

MILITARY VETERANS   Some law enforcement agencies commit time and resources to recruiting veterans who discharge, separate, or retire from military service. Veterans often make excellent law enforcement employees because of their experience within a military organizational structure.

As the wars in Iraq and then Afghanistan came to a close, an increasing number of military veterans looked for criminal justice jobs. In 2012, the military continued to downsize by reducing recruitment and asking fewer members to reenlist after they served their tours of duty. Unlike prior wars, many of these troops have been formally trained in techniques used in inner-city combat. Referred to as "peacekeeping," these techniques are much like policing, such as the searching and "clearing" of houses and other structures. Today's military veterans have also received training on one of the largest tasks of sheriff's departments and correctional personnel—detention. The International Association of Chiefs of Police published a study in 2011, "Employing Returning Combat Veterans as Law Enforcement Officers—Recruitment Strategies," which provides useful approaches to recruiting combat veterans.

In 2012, the U.S. Department of Justice, Community Oriented Policing Services (COPS), provided funding to begin a hiring program aimed at recent military veterans. The COPS Hiring Program (CHP) has many resources for both military veterans and law enforcement agencies in support of veteran hiring activities (U.S. Department of Justice, 2012a). In addition, Police Career and Promotion Services, LLC, a private company started in 1985, also provides resources and information to help returning U.S. veterans enter law enforcement careers nationwide. More information about the company can be found at https://officer.us.com/.

INTERNSHIP, CADET, RESERVE, EXPLORER SCOUT, AND HIGH SCHOOL CITIZEN POLICE ACADEMY PROGRAMS Law enforcement agencies should have various programs available to high school students and recent graduates. Many agencies already have paid police internship and cadet programs as well as police explorer scout or cadet programs for youth from 14 to 20 who are interested in a career in law enforcement. These are often referred to as "grow your own cops" programs.

In 2015, the Oakland Police Department expanded their existing cadet program. The Oakland Police Department cadet program involves high school graduates who are at least 17 and a half years old at the time of their application and cadets who are 18 to 21 years old. Both are part-time, hourly employees. The city, in conjunction with the Oakland Unified School District, encouraged eligible candidates to apply for the cadet positions, with a focus on recruiting Oakland residents and, in particular, minorities. Having more minority police officers who reflect the demographic make-up of the community contributes to a more positive image of the department.

As a part of a high school police academy, or of other programs geared toward this age group, role model and mentoring components should be incorporated. Mentoring would involve police officers associating themselves with youth in positive ways before the latter make the decision to use drugs, commit crimes, or drop out of school. Such programs would include an emphasis on the importance of developing good speaking and writing skills; weakness in these areas disqualifies many candidates from careers in law enforcement. Police Athletic Leagues, which have operated in many agencies across the nation for decades, have also traditionally filled this mentorship role.

Numerous law enforcement agencies, in conjunction with a college or university justice administration program, have developed classes designed to provide training and experiences for those interested in pursuing criminal justice careers. Retired Oakland police chief Howard Jordan commenced teaching a 13-week elective course at Merritt College in Oakland, California, in the fall of 2015. According to Chief Jordan,

> The primary purpose of the program is to take inner city, local youths and expose them to police work and provide information about what they would be expected to do if hired. Subjects include report writing, radio procedures, defensive driving, police ethics, community relations, background investigations, and tips on how to clean up their credit history. The participants are introduced to the military-style-chain-of-command system and the importance of showing up on time, which, for some students, is the first exposure to structure in their lives. An emphasis is placed on steering locals into the program because they are familiar with their city or county, its customs, culture, and history. The belief is that once on the job, local recruits are more sensitive to the ethnic and racial groups in the community because it is where they grew-up and are better prepared to win the cooperation of citizens during investigations, in reporting crimes, and in the event of a critical incident. (Jordan, 2017)

Young people are clearly a very important part of any recruitment effort, so law enforcement agencies should develop and use surveys of the demographics and attitudes of this age group. Such surveys can help gauge the level of interest in law enforcement careers, and help determine what changes law enforcement agencies need to make to attract the best candidates. The surveys can also provide an opportunity to promote police intern, cadet, explorer, and high school academy programs.

Some city police departments and sheriffs' offices also offer Citizen Police Academies in order to make residents more familiar with police work. Usually the academy is a 10-week course where participants learn about crime scene investigations, use of police dogs, patrolling in cars, firearms, report writing, court room testimony, jail operations, and grand jury functions. Departments see this program as a recruiting tool for its volunteer program. It has also served as an entry point for careers in law enforcement for some participants. The Federal Bureau of Investigation (FBI) also has a Teen/Youth Academy that allows high school students an opportunity to participate in classes where FBI instructors provide presentations on topics pertaining to the operations of a typical FBI field office. The FBI has a Citizens' Academy, a six-to-eight evening program that gives business, religious, civic, and community leaders an inside look at the FBI. The purpose is to provide attendees a greater understanding of the role of federal law enforcement in the community. Candidates are nominated by FBI employees, former Citizens' Academy graduates, and community leaders, and are ultimately selected by the special agent in charge of the local FBI field office. Since 2008, the FBI's Washington Field Office (WFO) has also hosted an annual Future Agents in Training (FAIT) program, which provides a hands-on approach to educating area high school juniors and seniors on the Bureau's operations. With a focus on becoming a special agent, the program presents a cross section of the FBI, including its criminal, counterterrorism, intelligence, and administrative divisions ("U.S. Federal Bureau of Investigation," 2016). Those students that attend the program gain an understanding of what the job involves, commitment required, and the character needed.

SELECTION PROCESSES

Prior to initiating any selection process, law enforcement agencies must assess the satisfaction level of current employees and the workplace environment of the department.

Satisfaction Level of Employees

The first step before outreach recruitment can take place is for the department to look inward. Are any members, sworn or non-sworn, experiencing emotional pain or suffering because of their race, ethnicity, nationality, gender, or sexual orientation? A department seeking to hire applicants from these groups cannot have internal problems—either real or perceived—related to racism, discrimination, or hostility toward any groups considered minorities, including African Americans, Hispanics, Asians, Muslims, and members of the LGBT community. A department with a high turnover rate or a reputation for not promoting women, minorities, or gays and lesbians will also deter good people from applying. The department must resolve any internal problems before meaningful recruitment can occur. To determine the nature and extent of any such problems, law enforcement agencies can perform an assessment of all their employees through anonymous surveys about their work environment. There should be a review of policies and procedures (especially those related to sexual harassment and gender discrimination) and an examination of statistical information such as the number of officers leaving the department and their reasons for doing so, as well as which employees are promoted. The goal is not only to evaluate the workplace environment for women and minorities but also to determine what steps need to be taken to dissolve barriers confronting them.

Supervisors and managers must talk with all members of their workforce on a regular basis to find out if any issues are disturbing them. They must then demonstrate that they are taking steps to alleviate the sources of discomfort, whether this involves modifying practices or simply discussing behavior with other employees.

The field training program for new recruits should also be reviewed and evaluated to ensure that new officers are not being arbitrarily eliminated or subjected to prejudice or discrimination. By the time a recruit has reached this stage of training, much has been invested in the new officer; every effort should be made to see that he or she completes the program successfully. Negligent retention, however, is a liability to an organization. When it is well documented that a trainee is not suitable for retention, release from employment is usually the best recourse regardless of race, ethnicity, sexual orientation, or gender.

Role models, networking and mentoring programs should be established to give recruits and junior officers the opportunity to receive support and important information from senior officers of the same race, ethnicity, gender, or sexual orientation. Many successful programs, however, include role models of different backgrounds than the recruits.

Applicant Screening (Employment Standards)

There has been a movement, albeit controversial, over the years to establish a cultural change in law enforcement which de-emphasizes the "warrior" mind-set or model of policing and changing it to a "guardian" model which emphasizes communications and problem solving. (See Chapter 1 for a detailed discussion.) Historically, law enforcement was considered a male occupation, with screening procedures that put an emphasis upon physical strength ("warrior") and little upon communications skills or problem solving ("guardian"). Now most agencies have removed obstacles that prevented most women and some men from becoming law enforcement officers. According to Kathy Spillar, executive director, Feminist Majority Foundation:

> All too often the physical agility test components are designed to favor upper body strength/brute strength and so wipe out qualified women and qualified men of slighter stature. We would argue they are not only discriminatory, but are not bonafide occupational qualifications for the job of policing. Departments should be testing for general physical fitness with tests adjusted for age, height, weight, etc … and more importantly the testing should emphasize critical thinking and problem solving skills/communication skills. Too much emphasis is placed on physical attributes, and not enough on mental attributes. (Spillar, 2017)

A lawsuit against the Corpus Christi, Texas, Police Department claimed that the agency discriminated against women in its hiring practices. The lawsuit asserted that, from 2005 to 2011, 80 percent fewer females than males passed the physical agility test. The lawsuit postulated that the tests, therefore, violated Title VII of the 1964 Civil Rights Act, amended in 1991. In September of 2012, the Department of Justice settled the sex discrimination lawsuit against the police department, resulting in a consent decree implementing the settlement terms. The consent decree mandated three overall terms: (1) that the Corpus Christi Police Department develop a new selection procedure complying with Title VII; (2) that some women who failed the test be compensated; and (3) that the others who failed receive priority employment offers with retroactive seniority and benefits (U.S. Department of Justice, 2012b).

Testing and preemployment screening now involve assessing skills, abilities, and fitness required of today's law enforcement officers in their use of community policing. Departments across the country are seeking employees who can communicate and cooperate with citizens and use problem-solving skills.

Pertaining to applicant screening, a bad hire, in any occupation, can be very costly to an organization. There have been multiple examples of officers fired or forced to resign from one department who were hired by another agency that did not perform an adequate background investigation. If they did, they may have quickly realized that hiring these officers may very well be a huge liability. A U.S. Justice Department program established a database in 2009 to track officers stripped of their policing powers to reduce these occurrences. But only a few years later, the program was halted due to lack of funding. Law enforcement agencies, therefore, must create a complete plan to recruit, screen, and hire solid candidates to fill openings. The hiring agency must have an accurate, up-to-date job description and an understanding of current standards for the position(s) for which they are hiring. An applicant should know exactly what the standards for employment are and what the job requires so there are no surprises. Those agencies needing assistance in establishing effective and defensible standards for the employment and training of peace officers should contact the International Association of Directors of Law Enforcement Standards and Training (IADLEST).

Law enforcement agencies must assess applicants along a range of dimensions (employment standards) that include, but are not limited to

- Basic qualifications such as education, requisite licenses, and citizenship
- Intelligence and problem-solving capacity
- Psychological fitness
- Physical fitness and agility
- Current and past illegal drug use
- Character as revealed by criminal record, driving record, work history, military record, credit history, reputation, and polygraph examination
- Aptitude and ability to serve others (see U.S. Department of Justice, 2006)
- Racial, ethnic, gender, sexual orientation, and cultural biases

The last dimension, testing for biases, deserves particular attention. An agency whose hiring procedures screen for unacceptable biases demonstrates to the community that it seeks police officers who will carry out their duties with fairness, integrity, diligence, and impartiality—officers who will respect the civil rights and dignity of the people they serve and with whom they work. Such screening should include not only the use of psychometric testing instruments developed to measure attitudes and bias but also careful background investigation of the candidate by personnel staff. The investigation should consider the applicant's own statements about racial issues, as well as interviews with personal and employer references that provide clues about how the applicant feels about and treats members of other racial, ethnic, gender, and sexual-orientation groups. These interviews would include questions such as

- How the applicant has interacted with other groups?
- What members of diverse groups say about the applicant?
- Whether the applicant has ever experienced conflict or tension with members of diverse groups or individuals, and how he or she handled the experience?

Because of the emphasis on community policing, law enforcement recruiters must also seek applicants who are team players and demonstrate the mentality and ability to serve others. Recruiters therefore are looking for candidates who are adaptable, analytical, communicative, compassionate, courageous (both physically and morally), courteous, culturally sensitive, decisive, disciplined, ethical, goal-oriented, incorruptible, mature, responsible, respectful, and self-motivated. Agencies also expect officers to have good interpersonal and communication skills, as well as sales and marketing abilities—a person who does the right thing when no one is around and thinks independently and quickly. Applicants should be screened for these attributes, as well as their desire to continue learning and ability to work in a rapidly evolving environment. More and more, officers are encountering the challenges of different languages, cultural and generational differences, and the diverse opinions of members of the communities they serve; therefore, they must develop a means of generating trust among these groups. The importance of bilingual officers and officers with cultural understanding is paramount in today's communities. Law enforcement agencies today must seek not only women and diversity in their recruiting efforts but also employees who can speak other languages or dialects.

Today, effective law enforcement officers work closely with neighborhood groups, social welfare agencies, housing code officials, and a host of others in partnerships to control crime and improve quality of life. Law enforcement agents must be eager to understand a task, draw up a plan, and follow it through to completion in concert with others. Without an agreeable nature, officers and deputies faced with today's changing attitude toward crime fighting would not have a chance. Thus, the search for recruits should focus on those who demonstrate an ability to take ownership of problems and work with others toward solutions. These potential officers must remain open to people who disagree with them or have opinions that differ from their own. Law enforcement agencies should make their goals and expectations clear to candidates for employment, recognizing that some candidates will not match the department's vision, mission, and values, and therefore should be screened out at the beginning of the process. Screening should include determining the applicants' (1) emotional stability, (2) extroversion versus introversion, (3) openness to experience, (4) agreeableness versus toughness, and (5) conscientiousness.

It is in the best interest of law enforcement agencies to complete a job analysis before implementing tests. Although it is a time-consuming process, the result is a clear description of the job for which applicants are applying and being screened. Utilizing the job analysis data, tests and job performance criteria can be developed and made part of the screening process. Applicants when provided with a copy of the job analysis can decide in advance if they fit the criteria.

Aptitude for a law enforcement career can also be determined from structured oral interviews. The oral interview panel should be gender- and racially diverse, and include members of the local community to reduce the possibility of bias. The panel should also include both sworn and civilian law enforcement employees. It is important that all raters are supportive of women and protected classes in policing, and thoroughly trained in the rules of the interview process. Questions should be developed in advance for the oral interview, and should test for the skills and abilities needed for community policing, including the ability to work with all types of people, to de-escalate violence, to mediate disputes, and to solve problems. The same questions should be asked of each candidate, regardless of whether the candidate is male or female.

The authors believe that one of the most useful new tools for law enforcement recruitment, one that represents a paradigm shift in recruitment philosophy, comes from the findings of the federally funded project Hiring in the Spirit of Service (HSS). The project's recommendations represent a major change in recruitment strategy because the focus is on hiring service-oriented law enforcement personnel.

HIRING IN THE SPIRIT OF SERVICE   The HSS program, developed in the late 1990s, suggests ways of recruiting applicants who are drawn to a career in law enforcement not because they want to "fight crime" but rather because they want to help people. Recruitment should be not just for those who are educated but for those who will work well within community-oriented policing (COP) and problem-oriented policing (POP) philosophies. These philosophies require intelligent individuals who can solve problems. The individuals' size (a move away from recruiting "big tough cops") should not matter if they have interpersonal and service-oriented skills. Those recruited must be able to accept diversity not only within the community they work but also within their own workforce.

A revisit by the Community Policing Consortium of the HSS approach to recruiting in 2006 focused primarily on women and minorities. The evaluation determined that increasing the applicant pool with diverse candidates, the goal of the HSS program, was successful in increasing recruitment of women and people of color within some of the trial agencies and not in others. What was successful was that the trial agencies involved in HSS took on new and proactive approaches in minority and women recruitment. In general, the continuing modifications and study of the HSS program discovered that

- Minority candidates benefit from tutoring and mentoring throughout the testing process, especially those with English as a second language as they had trouble with written examinations.
- Mentoring helps recruits, particularly those from diverse communities, adapt to the police culture and fostered awareness of how they could get into the profession and succeed.
- Mentoring is equally important in retaining recruits, thus protecting the hiring agencies' investment.
- A career as a police officer may not be attractive for women who want to start a family due to shift work schedules and lack of flexibility.
- Many potential women recruits question whether they can pass the physical tests required and the potential physical confrontations on the job.
- Minority candidates for employment for many departments don't see a lot of officers that look like them, resulting in a lack of role models.
- Media coverage of negative incidents involving law enforcement officers is an image barrier to those considering the profession.
- Many minorities come from communities where law enforcement has an unfavorable perception.

- The law enforcement agency administrative support in recruitment is critical. (U.S. Department of Justice, 2006)

Other useful resources include

Recruitment and Retention of Qualified Police Personnel—A Best Practices Guide, published by the International Association of Chiefs of Police (IACP, 2011).

Hiring and Keeping Police Officers, the findings of a study that examined experiences of police agencies nationwide in hiring and retaining sworn officers, published by The National Institute of Justice (NIJ, 2004).

Tearing down the Wall, by the National Center for Women and Policing, which also provides insights on physical agility testing (Lonsway, Spillar, Tejani, Aguirre, Dupes, Moore, Harrington, & Smeal, 2003).

A program, "Vermont Works for Women's Step Up to Law Enforcement," has been successful in preparing women (of all races and ethnicities) for criminal justice jobs. The three key components of the program are physical conditioning geared to the physical exam administered by the police academy and taught by licensed trainers at a local gym; a focus on the soft skills of career planning in law enforcement professions; and training in technical topics specific to law enforcement, taught by policing and corrections partners (Tuomey and Jolly, 2009). The percent of state and local law enforcement officers employed by agencies using selected methods to recruit applicants for sworn positions in 2008, most recent statistics available, is shown in Exhibit 3.2.

Legal Issues and Affirmative Action

In some states or jurisdictions, there may be some controversial and even legal aspects of recruitment efforts that target women and protected class candidates for law enforcement jobs. Generally, it is not permissible to recruit only members of a particular race, ethnicity, or gender. Federal law prohibits programs that require meeting specific *hiring* goals for any particular group except when necessary to remedy discrimination. However, outreach programs and recruiting efforts seeking to broaden the pool of potential candidates by reaching a greater number of qualified individuals that includes women and members of diverse groups would be lawful. Such programs and efforts should be designed to make employment opportunities known to all potential applicants regardless of their race, ethnicity, national origin, sexual orientation, or gender.

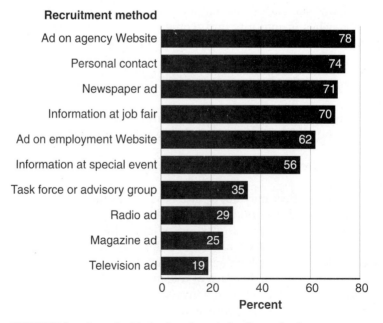

EXHIBIT 3.2 Agencies Methods to Recruit Applicants for Sworn Positions, 2008

In California, Proposition 209, which outlawed governmental discrimination and preferences based on race, sex, color, ethnicity, or national origin, was passed in 1996. The law provides that any government agency that offers preferential treatment in hiring or promoting employees could be penalized by having its revenue cut. In September 2000, the California Supreme Court affirmed that Proposition 209 was legal and, therefore, placed strict limits on employers regarding the types of outreach programs they can legally use to recruit employees. As a result, any outreach program that gives minorities and women a competitive advantage is a violation of Proposition 209. Many other states followed California's example by enacting similar legislation, but not all. Agencies need to research what strategies are legal and appropriate within their state and jurisdiction. The percent of state and local law enforcement officers employed by agencies targeting specific applicant groups with special recruitment efforts in 2008, most recent statistics available, can be seen in Exhibit 3.3.

Affirmative action and consent decrees have enjoyed only moderate success in attempts toward achieving parity in the hiring of women and individuals from ethnically and racially diverse backgrounds. There has been even less success with promotions of members of these groups to command ranks. An unfortunate problem that can be associated with the promotion of women and nonwhites is that doubts are raised about their qualifications: Are they qualified for the job, or are they products of affirmative action? Peers may subtly or even explicitly express to each other that the promotion was not the result of competence, and the promoted candidate may feel that his or her success is not based entirely on qualifications. Consequently, employees may experience strained relationships and lowered morale. There is no denying the potential for a strong negative internal reaction in an organization when court orders have mandated promotions. Some white and/or male employees feel anger or frustration with consent decrees or affirmative action–based promotions. Clearly, preventive work must be done to avoid such problems.

The National Organization of Black Law Enforcement Executives (NOBLE) has consistently endorsed affirmative action to increase the numbers of minorities in the profession. NOBLE has met with recruiters and other representatives of law enforcement across the nation to discuss potentially successful minority recruitment strategies. One such strategy involves the creation of a pilot project with 10 historically black colleges to increase the number of graduates pursuing law enforcement careers. The project includes workshops, lectures, and mini-conferences, as well as internships in law enforcement. NOBLE has also sponsored job fairs that attract prospective candidates for employment, who then meet with representatives from participating agencies.

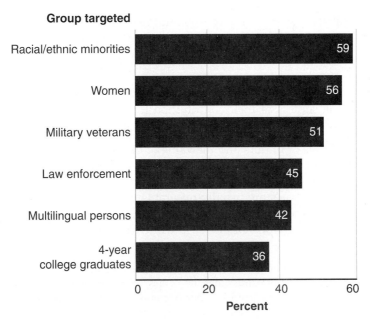

Group targeted

EXHIBIT 3.3   Agencies Targeting Specific Applicant Groups with Special Recruitment Efforts, 2008

Mini Case Study: What Would You Do?

You are the new personnel sergeant responsible for a department with 50 sworn officers. The department has one African American, two Hispanic, and two women officers. There has never been a large number of minority or women candidates applying for sworn positions in the department, and your agency does not reflect the demographics of the city.

Your city has an affirmative action program, but to date no outreach programs have been initiated to recruit women and minorities. Draft a list of strategies you would suggest to your chief as a way to recruit women and minorities. What other departmental processes should take place prior to applicant testing?

RETENTION AND PROMOTION OF A DIVERSE WORKFORCE

Recruiting officers who reflect the gender, racial, ethnic, and sexual orientation demographics of the community is one important challenge for law enforcement agencies. Retention and promotion of these officers are equally important. Employees leave their agencies for a variety of reasons and exit interviews should be conducted of sworn and civilian employees to determine why. Most often the decision to leave is based on either a promotional opportunity elsewhere or to pursue a career that doesn't require shift work or danger.

Retention

Retention of any employee is usually the result of good work on the part of the employee and a positive environment wherein all employees are treated with dignity and respect. In fact, once an agency earns a reputation for fairness, talented men and women of all ethnicities, races, and sexual orientations will seek out that agency and will remain longer. Job satisfaction, thus retention of employees, including women and protected classes, can often be attributed not only to fair compensation and benefits but also to the following:

- Leadership
- Mentoring
- Training and development
- Addressing bias, discrimination, and harassment
- Communication
- Performance evaluations
- Job descriptions

LEADERSHIP   Job satisfaction and employee commitment are often attributed to good leadership. There are three leadership functions that significantly impact employee satisfaction and engagement. An atmosphere needs to be created in which employees:

1. see the value of their work.
2. have access to the leader (supervisor or manager) and feel valued and appreciated.
3. can measure the success of their contribution to the mission of the organization and particularly of the employee's assigned unit. (Lencioni, 2007)

Employees who don't see or understand the value of their work sometimes think, therefore, that it is irrelevant. If they don't have communication with their leader, they feel invisible. If they don't know how to measure their contribution to the unit in which they work, they are frustrated. Such employees are usually miserable because they want to be appreciated by their superiors for the job they do. Leaders who look for these signs and make necessary changes can transform an unhappy employee into one who is satisfied and less likely to leave the organization.

> Law enforcement leaders who get out from behind the desk from time to time and work alongside their members, too, can demonstrate that the "brass" still knows what it's like to do the job. In order to reduce attrition of their officers, departments should have robust and meaningful employee recognition programs…to show them they care and recognize the important job they do. (Roufa, 2013)

MENTORING   The importance of mentoring, supporting, and informal networking programs for women and members of diverse groups is covered in Chapter 2. Mentoring, which is not a new concept or practice, can be both formal and informal. Formal mentoring involves establishing policy and procedures, defining roles and responsibilities, and training senior members who will become mentors on the processes and goals of the organization. Mentoring involves providing a system wherein less experienced employees receive information, advice, support, and encouragement from more senior colleagues. Mentoring involves leading, developing, and guiding by example to facilitate the protégé's personal development, for the benefit of both the individual and the organization. Because mentoring and providing networking opportunities contribute to employee satisfaction, there is a greater likelihood of retention.

It should be noted that the role of a mentor and that of a field training officer (FTO) are not the same. The FTO is responsible for the training and development of an effective new officer and evaluates his or her effectiveness continually during the process. The role of a mentor for the same officer is supportive, relational, and does not involve performance evaluation. The mentor maintains contact with the officer not only during his or her field training but also upon completion to provide continuing support, guidance, and encouragement.

Mentoring and support programs are intended not only for new officers but also for veterans. Even seasoned officers exposed to or involved in violence or distressing cases, such as those involving child pornography, pedophiles, rape, major traffic accidents and deaths, need support. Support programs are particularly important when a death involves a fellow officer. Officers typically learn to compartmentalize or hold in their feelings. They need a way to vent and share, but typically do not turn to spouses, intimate others, friends, or family members. Some departments have peer counseling programs that provide support for those members, both sworn and civilian, who need help. Such programs are another means of providing a working environment that is more conducive to retaining employees.

More information about mentoring is available in publications from the International Association of Chiefs of Police, such as "Best Practices Guide for Institutionalizing Mentoring into Police Departments" (Sprafka and Kranda). Another source, produced by Catalyst, a non-profit organization, is "Optimizing Mentoring Programs for Women of Color" (Catalyst).

TRAINING AND DEVELOPMENT   In-service training, educational opportunities, and access to special assignments within an organization are three factors that help develop employees, leading to job knowledge, experience, and satisfaction—and therefore to retention. Departments with programs that help their employees obtain advanced degrees find that such a practice often results in happy and productive members who stay with that agency.

"To be successful in a constantly changing occupation, employees must increase their skills," notes Mark J. Terra in *The FBI Law Enforcement Bulletin*. "If they work for an organization that does not provide such benefits, they will go elsewhere to find them" (Terra, 2009). Community policing and advances in technology, the emergence of domestic security threats, and the growth of cybercrime and identity theft mean that officers' skills must be constantly updated.

Training for officers of all ranks should continue throughout their careers. Such training should not only address the necessary, practical skills involving search and seizure, firearms, defensive tactics, arrest procedures, and so on but also include current issues, especially when it comes to interacting with a diverse community. Development of employees is important for meeting the requirements for special assignments that increase the chances of promotion within the organization. Special assignments include such highly sought-after positions as SWAT, gang, narcotics, canine, or motorcycles units, horse patrol, and field training.

Some law enforcement agencies have formed partnerships with higher education institutions. One example is the Phoenix Police Department that partnered with a university where officers can earn a master's degree in leadership in two years. Participants can receive almost $4,000 per year in tuition reimbursement as part of their compensation package (ibid.). Other agencies increase job satisfaction by offering incentives for those pursuing a degree.

Departments that provide incentives and encouragement for college education will find that the opportunities correlate with improved performance. Those officers with degrees often have an advantage in promotions over officers without. Conversely, if an agency does not provide these opportunities, officers will look for agencies that do. Online courses are now making it even easier to acquire knowledge and degrees.

ADDRESSING BIAS, DISCRIMINATION, AND HARASSMENT A department seeking to retain employees cannot have internal problems, either real or perceived, related to racism, harassment, discrimination, or hostility toward women, gay male, or lesbian officers. Ethnic slurs, racial or gender jokes, offensive or derogatory comments, or other verbal or physical conduct are unlawful and interfere with the individual's work performance.

Law enforcement agencies or their human relations or personnel departments should analyze statistical information pertaining to the number of officers leaving and their reasons for doing so. Another way to determine the nature and extent of bias problems is to perform an assessment of all employees through an anonymous survey. The goal is not only to evaluate the workplace environment for women and minorities but also to gather information so that steps can be taken, if needed, to eliminate discrimination within the organization.

COMMUNICATIONS Retention is also higher within agencies where supervisors and managers talk with all members of their workforce on a regular basis. Supervisors and managers are then able to act to alleviate the sources of discomfort, whether this involves modifying practices or simply discussing behavior with other employees.

Communication between supervisors and employees should be both formal and informal. Formal feedback most often takes the form of a performance evaluation, but it might also take the form of a commendation or even a thank-you note commending the good work of the employee. Positive reinforcement is often achieved by recognizing good performance, and when this is not done, the employee may become unhappy and his or her performance may suffer.

It is important not only that an agency has effective top-down communications but also communication that flows freely in both directions. Employees who cannot communicate upward become frustrated and angry, which negatively affects their performance level, and may lead to their disengagement from the organization, figuratively or literally.

PERFORMANCE EVALUATION A good employee performance evaluation system is an important factor in personnel satisfaction and retention. Evaluation systems should be used that involve factors that are job-related and objective rather than subjective. To be objective, the evaluation must focus on traits and behaviors that are measurable and related to the position's job description. It must also be related to the goals of the department or unit to which the officer is assigned. A performance evaluation, which should be done annually, requires giving accurate feedback to the employee that helps him or her determine personal strengths and weaknesses. It should be a vehicle to encourage improvement and provide guidelines to do so. The evaluation should also focus on the employee's short- and long-term goals so that the officer receives help not only in his or her own professional development but also in becoming the kind of officer that meets the organization's needs.

JOB DESCRIPTIONS Every sworn and non-sworn employee should have a job description that identifies the position title and describes the essential functions, duties, and tasks the position performs for the employer. The job description lists the knowledge, skills, and abilities required of the position. Further, it delineates the qualifications, such as education and/or experience, license/certificates, and working conditions. The job description is a living document and should be updated when there are changes in the position that impact the employee. It should be reviewed by the employee and his or her supervisor each year at the time of the employee's annual performance evaluation to insure the document provides adequate directions to achieve success in the job. The job description is an excellent tool in eliminating bias and discrimination in the workforce.

Promotion

The limited number of promotions of protected classes and women to supervisor and command ranks has been cited as a severe problem in policing for over four decades by scholars and police researchers alike. Some officers leave an organization when they develop a sense that they will not be able to rise through the ranks at a certain agency. That is due to agencies that don't provide leadership training opportunities or only provide them to those who are on a promotion list. Agencies that have a succession plan in place and offer opportunities and training to all employees who choose or aspire to be leaders create an environment that encourages participation in the promotion process. Given the right motivation and tools for self-improvement, even some poor test-takers can make good leaders.

Authors and advocates for the promotion of women have used the term "glass ceiling" to describe an unacknowledged barrier that inhibits women from reaching ranks above entry level. Whether there is a glass ceiling or not, women still constitute only a small proportion of police supervisors and managers. Within organizations, women and other individuals of diverse backgrounds are frustrated when promotional opportunities seem more readily available to white males than to them. The disenchantment that often accompanies frustration frequently leads to low productivity and morale, early burnout, and resignation; to those individuals, opportunities appear better elsewhere. Lack of attention to equal opportunity and lack of transparent promotion policies and practices at some law enforcement agencies have resulted in court-ordered promotions. These have a negative impact on a department's operations and relationships, both internally and externally, and often lead to distrust and dissatisfaction. The dearth of mentors and role models for women and members of diverse groups has also been cited as a reason these employees fail to learn what it takes to get promoted within an organization.

Chief executives need to measure results of efforts to promote women and minorities by determining if these groups are applying for promotions in numbers that are proportional to their numbers in the department. If not, it could be that women and minority officers need to be encouraged to pursue a higher rank, through encouragement from their supervisors, mentors, or informal network associates. It is also possible that the promotion process disproportionately screens out female and minority officers. Some safeguards against bias include weighting the process toward "hands-on" tasks (e.g., assessment center testing), conducting structured interviews, selecting board members who represent different races and both sexes, and training the board members on interviewing techniques.

Failure to promote qualified candidates who are representative of the diverse populations agencies serve, including women, can result in continued distrust of police by communities. Underrepresentation within police departments also aggravates tensions between the police and residents. Some scholars and criminal justice experts argue that underrepresentation at all levels within law enforcement agencies hurts the image of the department in the eyes of the community.

Police executives and city or county managers cannot afford to minimize the consequences of poor retention and inadequate promotional opportunities for women and diverse members of their organizations. Some departments have done very well in recruiting and hiring women, but, for reasons that are yet to be established, women have left departments more quickly than men. The reasons vary, but family pressures are the most frequently cited cause.

GENERATION Y In Chapter 1, the authors introduced the subject of "Generation Y" or Millennials referring to those persons between the ages of 18 and approximately 30. Employers, managers, and supervisors wishing to recruit and retain members of this generation will benefit from understanding their characteristics, learning styles, and work attitudes (NAS Insights, 2006). One particular characteristic that sets apart members of this generation is their technological proficiency, especially when compared to preceding generations. Other characteristics include a generally higher level of education than previous generations (especially women); an expectation of equality and a strong social conscience; an assumption of promotion in less than two years; and the expectation that they will move on from their job within five years (Eisner and Harvey, 2009). These generational differences impact not only how recruiters attract new law enforcement personnel but also how supervisors and managers interact and direct their work and provide an environment in which they will stay and be promoted. Good leaders are aware of these differences and develop and use leadership strategies that work best with these employees.

Mini Case Study: How Would You Handle It?

You are a male lieutenant in charge of the special weapons and tactics unit. The first female officer will soon be assigned to your unit. The special weapons and tactics team members are voicing negative opinions about having a female officer in the unit. They are complaining that standards will be lowered because women are not as physically fit as men. When you have overheard these conversations, or when they have been addressed to you directly, you have refuted them by pointing to the women in the department who are in outstanding physical shape. This strategy has not been effective, as the squad members continue to complain that women officers can't do the job and that their personal safety might be in jeopardy. What would you do?

Summary

- Population changes, particularly those that result in greater diversity, create a demand for law enforcement personnel who can work with different types of people. The nature of policing has also broadened, requiring officers to master a complex set of skills. The adoption of the community policing model requires departments to be more representative of and responsive to the communities served.

- Recruiting, hiring, retaining, and promoting a diverse workforce will remain a challenge in law enforcement for a long time. The number of people available and qualified for entry-level jobs will continue to decrease; more employers, both public and private, will be vying for the best candidates. Negative images of law enforcement due to officer-involved shootings and the dangers of the job decrease the number of applicants. Hiring and promoting women and minorities for law enforcement careers are achievable goals.

- Successful recruiting involves *commitment* by the chief executive; *planning*, including an assessment of current recruitment practices; adequate *resources*; properly selected and trained *recruiters*; the use of *incentives*; and *community involvement*. Law enforcement will have to use innovative and sophisticated marketing techniques and advertising campaigns to reach the desired population of potential applicants, and it must develop fast-track hiring processes.

- The Hiring in the Spirit of Service (HSS) program suggests that to recruit applicants who historically would not be targeted by law enforcement agencies, departments must seek service-minded individuals having qualifications consistent with professions such as teaching, nursing, and counseling. In the past, candidates who did not fit the "crime fighter" image were discouraged from applying or disqualified during the testing process.

- Law enforcement is still in transition away from the aggressive, male-dominated (and predominantly white) culture or the "warrior" model of the past, so it must now overcome the common perception that policing is a profession that requires only physical strength. With the shift to community policing or "guardian" model, women can thrive. Departments are looking for people with good interpersonal skills who are community and service-oriented, and they are finding that women meet these qualifications. Law enforcement executives should seek minority employees for the same reasons.

- Prior to initiating any recruitment effort, every agency must assess the satisfaction level of the current employees and evaluate the workplace environment. A department seeking to hire applicants from women and minority groups must first resolve internal problems, either real or perceived, related to racism, discrimination, or hostility toward female, gay male, or lesbian officers. A high turnover rate or a reputation for not promoting women, minorities, or gays and lesbians will also deter potential applicants.

- Retention of employees is crucial and requires a positive environment wherein all employees are treated with dignity and respect. Retention also requires good supervisors and managers and an agency in which there is two-way communication and job-related performance evaluations. A high rate of retention is most likely to occur in organizations that meet the basic needs of employees, offer reasonable opportunities for ongoing professional career development, and have mentoring and networking programs. It is important that the agency addresses any claims of bias, discrimination, and harassment within the organization. Once an agency earns a reputation for fairness, talented men and women of all ethnicities and races will seek out that agency and will remain longer.

- Opportunities for promotion of protected classes and women to supervisor and command ranks must be available within the organization. This is accomplished through providing leadership training and mentoring to those who seek advancement. Promotional processes that disproportionately screen out females and minorities should be identified and removed. Failure to promote qualified candidates who are representative of the diverse populations agencies serve, including women, can result in continued distrust of the police by the community and hurt the image of the department.

- Employers, managers, and supervisors wishing to recruit and retain members of the "Gen Y" or Millennial generation will need to understand their unique characteristics, learning styles, and work attitudes.

Discussion Questions and Issues

1. *"Warrior" to "Guardian" Style of Policing.* A fundamental change in law enforcement has been taking place over the past few decades. It involves a policing mindset change from the "warrior" or physical model to the "guardian" problem-solving style of policing. If you serve in a police department, discuss your observations of your agency's style and whether it tends toward "warrior" or "guardian" style, and/or whether it is undergoing a transition. If you are a student, try to get an interview with a police manager or executive. Learn about which style is more prevalent; present to the class examples that you have learned about in the interview.

2. *Employment of a Diverse Workforce and Police Practices.* How has the employment of a diverse workforce affected police practices in your city or county? Is there evidence that significant changes in the gender, ethnic, or racial composition of the department alter official police policy? Can the same be said of gay male and lesbian employment? Does employment of protected classes have any significant effect on the informal police subculture and, in turn, on police performance? Provide examples to support your conclusions.

References

Barlow, David E. (2017). Professor Department of Criminal Justice, Fayetteville State University, Fayetteville, NC, personal communication, February 6.

Catalyst. "Optimizing Mentoring Programs for Women of Color." www.catalyst.org/system/files/Optimizing_Mentoring_Programs_for_Women_of_Color.pdf (accessed May 17, 2017).

Council for a Strong America. (2015). "Ready, Willing, and Unable to Serve." June 3. www.strongnation.org/articles/21-ready-willing-and-unable-to-serve (accessed October 31, 2016).

Eisner, Susan P. and Mary Ellen O'Grady Harvey. (2009). "C-change? Generation Y and the Glass Ceiling." *SAM Advanced Management Journal, 74*(1). www.highbeam.com/doc/1G1-197233637.html (accessed October 13, 2016).

Fisher, Chad. (2011). "Law Enforcement and the Weak Economy." *Business Insider*. www.businessinsider.com/law-enforcement-and-the-weak-economy-2011-12 (accessed October 31, 2016).

Hilal, Susan M. and Timothy E. Erickson. (June 2010). "The Minnesota Police Education Requirement—A Recent Analysis." *FBI Law Enforcement Bulletin, 79*(6).

IACP. (2011). *Best Practices Guide: Recruitment, Retention, and Turnover in Law Enforcement*, International Association of Chiefs of Police. *Employing Returning Combat Veterans as Law Enforcement Officers—Recruitment Strategies.* Bureau of Justice Assistance Grant No. 2009-D2-BX-K008.

Jordan, Howard. (2017). Retired Oakland (California) Chief of Police, Criminal Justice Faculty, Merritt and Diablo Valley Colleges, Oakland/Pleasant Hill, CA, respectively, personal communication, April 10.

Lencioni, Patrick. (2007). *The Three Signs of a Miserable Job.* San Francisco, CA: Jossey-Bass, p. 217.

Lonsway, Kim, Katherine Spillar, Sharyn Tejani, Patricia Aguirre, Hannah Dupes, Margaret Moore, Penny Harrington, and Eleanor Smeal. (2003, Spring). "Tearing Down the Wall: Problems with Consistency, Validity, and Adverse Impact of Agility Testing in Police Selection." http://womenandpolicing.com/pdf/physicalagilitystudy.pdf (accessed May 17, 2017).

Maciag, Mike. (2015). "Where Police Don't Mirror Communities and Why It Matters." *Governing.* www.governing.com/topics/public-justice-safety/gov-police department-diversity.html (accessed November 29, 2016).

Moore, Carole. (2011). "The Changing Face of the Law Enforcement Career." www.officer.com/article/10272710/the-changing-face-of-the-law-enforcement-career (accessed November 29, 2016).

Morrison, Kevin. (2017). "Hiring for the 21st Century Law Enforcement Officer: Challenges, Opportunities, and Strategies for Success." U.S. Department of Justice, Office of Community Oriented Policing and Police Executive Research Forum. www.ric-zai-inc.com/Publications/cops-w0831-pub.pdf (accessed May 15, 2017).

NAS Insights. (2006). "Generation Y: The Millennials. Ready or Not, Here They Come." NAS Recruitment Communications. www.nasrecruitment.com/talenttips/NASinsights/GenerationY.pdf (accessed February 14, 2009).

NCWP. "Recruiting and Retaining Women: A Self-Assessment Guide for Law Enforcement." *National Center for Women and Policing.* A Division of the Feminist Majority Foundation. https://www.ncjrs.gov/pdffiles1/bja/185235.pdf (accessed May 17, 2017).

NIJ. (2004). "Hiring and Keeping Police Officers." August. National Institute of Justice. www.ncjrs.gov/pdffiles1/nij/202289.pdf (accessed May 17, 2017).

Peralta, Andrew [NLPOA]. (2017). Past President of the National Latino Peace Officers Association. www.nlpoa.com (accessed January 4, 2017).

Police Career and Promotion Services, LLC. "The Web's Best Resources for Returning U.S. Veterans Seeking Law Enforcement Employment and Promotion." www.officer.us.com/(accessed November 4, 2016).

Roufa, Timothy. (2013). "What to Do about Police Retention Problems." *The Balance*, April 5. www.thebalance .com/what-to-do-about-police-retention-problems-974770 (accessed November 8, 2016).

Skinner, Chris. (2010). "Recruiting with Emotion and Market Positioning." *FBI Law Enforcement Bulletin, 79*(7), 20–27.

Spillar, Katherine. (2017). Executive Director, Feminist Majority Foundation, personal communication, January 9.

Sprafka, Harvey and April H. Kranda. "Best Practices Guide: Institutionalizing Mentoring into Police Departments." International Association of Chiefs of Police. http://www .theiacp.org/Portals/0/pdfs/Publications/BP-Mentoring .pdf (accessed May 17, 2017).

Tejani, Sharyn, Patricia Aguirre, Hannah Dupes, Margaret Moore, Penny Harrington, and Eleanor Smeal. (2003, Spring). http://womenandpolicing.com/pdf/physicalagilitystudy .pdf (accessed May 17, 2017).

Terra, Mark. (2009). "Increasing Officer Retention through Educational Incentives." February. *FBI Law Bulletin*. https:// leb.fbi.gov/2009-pdfs/leb-february-2009 (accessed May 17, 2017).

Tuomey, Lianne and Rachel Jolly. (2009). "Step Up to Law Enforcement: A Successful Strategy for Recruiting Women into the Law Enforcement Profession." *The Police Chief*. International Association of Chiefs of Police. www .policechiefmagazine.org (accessed April 4, 2009).

U.S. Department of Education. (2015). "U.S. High School Graduation Rate Hits New Record High." www.ed.gov/news /press-releases/us-high-school-graduation-rate-hits-new -record-high-0 (accessed December 3, 2016).

U.S. Department of Justice. (2006). "Innovations in Police Recruiting and Hiring: Hiring in the Spirit of Service." Office of Community Oriented Policing Service. www.// ric-zai-inc.com/Publications/cops-p090-pub.pdf (accessed December 5, 2016).

U.S. Department of Justice. (2009). Law Enforcement Recruitment Toolkit. COPS/IACP Leadership Project. Office of Community Oriented Policing Services. cops.usdoj.gov /pdf/vets-to-cops/e080921223-RecruitmentToolkit.pdf (accessed November 3, 2016).

U.S. Department of Justice. (2012a). "Vets to Cops." Office of Community Oriented Policing Service. www.cops.usdoj .gov/Default.asp?Item=2630 (accessed May 15, 2017).

U.S. Department of Justice. (2012b). "Justice Department Settles Sex Discrimination Lawsuit against City of Corpus Christi, Texas, Police Department." September 19. www.justice .gov/opa/pr/justice-department-settles-sex -discrimination-lawsuit-against-city-corpus-christi-texa s (accessed May 15, 2017).

U.S. Department of Justice. (2015). "President's Task Force on 21st Century Policing." www.themarshallproject.org /documents/2082979-final-report-of-the-presidents-task -force-on#.vUnDUGJmC (accessed December 1, 2016).

U.S. Department of Justice. (2016). "Advancing Diversity in Law Enforcement," Equal Employment Opportunity Commission. www.eeoc.gov/eeoc/interagency/police -diversityreport.com (accessed November 29, 2016).

U.S. Department of Labor. (2016). "Labor Force Statistics from the Current Population Survey." Bureau of Labor Statistics. www. data.bls.gov/timeseries/LNS14000000 (accessed October 30, 2016).

U.S. Federal Bureau of Investigation. (2016). "Future Agents in Training—High School Students Get Inside Look at FBI Careers." www.fbi.gov/news/stories/high-school-students -get-inside-look-at-fbi-careers (accessed November 2, 2016).

Weber, Laura and Greg Ridgeway. (2010). The RAND Corporation. www.rand.org/content/dam/rand/pubs/monographs /2010/RAND_MG992.pdf (accessed November 9, 2016).

CHAPTER

4 Cross-Cultural Communication
for Law Enforcement

LEARNING OBJECTIVES

After reading this chapter, you should be able to:

- Identify language barriers in law enforcement work and skills to address these.
- Describe cultural frameworks influencing communication, including hierarchy and "context."
- Explain typical communication dynamics in cross-cultural, cross-racial, and cross-ethnic encounters.
- Describe how communication can prevent and de-escalate confrontation across cultures.
- List key interviewing and data-gathering skills that contribute to an officer's effectiveness.
- Provide examples of verbal and nonverbal communication style differences across cultures.
- Demonstrate understanding of appropriate male-female communication in law enforcement settings.

OUTLINE

- Introduction
- Language Barriers
- Attitudes toward Limited English Speakers
- Cross-Cultural Communication Insights
- Cross-Cultural/Racial Communication Dynamics
- The Importance of Verbal De-Escalation
- Interviewing and Data-Gathering Skills
- Nonverbal Communication
- Male-Female Communication in Law Enforcement
- Summary
- Discussion Questions and Issues
- References

INTRODUCTION

It is not possible to modify behavior according to the norms or cultural expectations of all groups, and officers do not need to learn the details of myriad groups' culturally influenced communication styles. When officers respond to emergencies, the first order of business is to gain control of the situation and to quickly assess what is happening. In such situations, there is no time to think about, for example, whether a particular group has an indirect style of communication or whether a group is extremely expressive on the continuum of emotionalism across cultures. When officers say that the key to effective communication with citizens is respect, they are correct; additionally, an overall goal in police communication, regardless of whom, is the prevention and de-escalation of confrontation for the benefit of everyone's safety. That said, there are generalities related to cross-cultural communication, including interacting with people for whom English is a second language. Recognition of these generalities will enhance officers' overall understanding of the way people communicate, including some of the normal variations across cultures and ethnic groups. Officers do not need to learn scores of different details about communicating with diverse groups. However, there are some basic principles and cultural specifics that will render law enforcement personnel more prepared when they encounter citizens whose backgrounds differ from their own. It is also essential to understand the principles of effective communication, and those that apply to all people.

After years of working with citizens from nearly every background, the late Dr. George Thompson, former police officer and founder of the Verbal Judo Institute, expressed a belief that there are certain communication essentials that contribute to effectiveness regardless of background. Exhibit 4.1 outlines these items.

To paraphrase Thompson, the default is always respectful communication. Thompson took the key concept of respect one step further: "Talking about respecting people [from all cultural backgrounds] is vague. But treating people with respect is an act that is highly specific" (Thompson, 2009).

In minor situations, an officer's calm, nonaggressive tone and nonthreatening physical stance will communicate respect regardless of the cultural or racial background of citizens, immigrants, or foreign visitors. However, displays of respect can vary from culture to culture especially in cultures where a hierarchy is strongly emphasized. Since, for most Americans, sustained eye-contact signals respect, an officer's ability to read *others'* intent around eye-contact is important cross-culturally. In some cultures, for example, respect is offered through indirect eye contact; in many parts of Asia, Africa, and the Middle East, people often show respect by making intermittent eye contact or by looking off into space ("sustained indirect" eye contact). Some officers interpret this behavior as defiant or as a sign of dishonesty, but first-generation refugees or immigrants from these parts of the world are, in fact, communicating respect in the default way that they have learned. Former FBI agent, Joe Navarro, says, "Little or no eye contact is erroneously perceived by some as a classic sign of deception, especially during questioning, while the truthful should 'lock eyes.' This is not supported by research or experience and is completely false" (Navarro, 2009). In addition, when citizens speak in a certain tone of voice or are talking loudly, an officer may assume that they are exhibiting aggression or going out of control. Because of learned ethnocentrism, any officer can easily fall into the trap of making judgments about citizens just by the way they talk or use body language.

Not knowing how to cope with communication style differences can add stress to situations that are already tense. Human beings are programmed and signaled to be "on alert" when something strange or unexpected occurs. It is as if there is a bell or alarm that sounds loudly when people are faced with diversity such as a group of people to which they are not accustomed. This mechanism for alertness and alarm results in stress. Thus, for law enforcement officials whose work by nature can be tense and stressful, it is all the more crucial to know how to read others, both, individually and cross-culturally.

Understanding cultural differences and how they impact communication is critical. But there is a huge caveat. Let us also understand how we are similar and what kinds of communication works with people of all backgrounds:

1. Remember that everyone, in all cultures, wants to be respected.
2. For all cultural, racial, or ethnic groups, it is better to provide options than to make threats.
3. All people would like a second chance. Ask: "Is there anything I (we) can say or do to get your cooperation? I (we) would like to think there is."

EXHIBIT 4.1 Effective Communication across All Backgrounds
Source: Adapted with permission of George Thompson, Founder of Verbal Judo, personal communication, 2009.

LANGUAGE BARRIERS

In dealing with individuals who are not native speakers of English, these three points should be kept in mind:

- A listener can easily misinterpret speech patterns: intonation, in particular, can be perceived to carry emotion and intentionality. What one hears is not always what is intended.
- A listener can easily misunderstand spoken words when he or she is not fluent in English.
- A listener should use multiple indicators for interpreting correctly what a limited English speaker is attempting to say.

Since there is the potential for misunderstanding with limited English speakers, police officers will often need to modify their use of English to achieve the goals of clear and simple communication. Exhibit 4.3 on p. 105 illustrates an interaction between a police officer and an individual; the officer has not modified his English in this interaction, making it difficult for the listener to follow. With the increasing emphasis on community policing and staff diversity in law enforcement, language and cross-cultural communication skills have become more and more essential not only in establishing good relationships with citizens, but also with professional colleagues. In developing cross-cultural communication and competency skills, police officers who were not born in this country or who spoke another language at home can be a valuable resource, offering insights that can alleviate frustration in encounters with those who are not fluent in English. The following is a personal account of a Vietnamese police officer and his struggles with English when he first came to the United States:

> For the first few months of being here, I was always tired from speaking the language. I had to strain my ears all day long and all my nerves were bothered. It was hard work to make people understand my broken English and to listen to them. Sometimes, I just could not communicate anymore and I just stopped speaking English. Sometimes I had to pretend I understood what others said and why they were laughing. But inside I felt very depressed. I am an adult and my language sounded worse than a child's. Sometimes it was better not to say anything at all.

Nationwide, changing demographics have resulted in the need for law enforcement to deal increasingly with a multicultural population that includes speakers of other languages who do not have equivalent skills in English. From citizens who report crimes using limited English to crime witnesses, suspects, and victims, there is no absolute assurance that officers will understand them. Officers are justifiably frustrated by language barriers and find it difficult to do their jobs in the way they have been trained. On a "good day" some officers make it a point to modify their English so that they will be better understood; on a stressful day, many officers are frustrated at having to slow down their speech and listen more patiently. Some law enforcement officers are noticeably impatient when they deal with non-native English speakers. Even citizens who do not speak English well may sense when police are not listening to their side of the story. As a result, citizens who face language barriers are often not successful at communicating even the minimum amount of necessary information. Perhaps most difficult is the situation in which a person with limited English skills is traumatized, further affecting the victim's ability to speak English. Officers need to be aware of the potential for inadvertent discrimination based on a citizen's language background, which could fall under "language and national origin discrimination" (Ho, 2013).

In one case in Oregon, the friends of an Asian man named Hung Minh Tran were accused of involvement in a barroom assault. One miscommunication led to another; eventually Tran was hauled outside and knocked into some chairs by a female police officer. "Tran said [the officer] was giving him confusing commands, such as go against the wall, back up against the wall, and back away from the wall. He didn't understand what she wanted so he did what he's seen on TV: got down on his knees, with his hands locked behind his head, facing away from her, 'so I'm not a threat.'" At that point, the officer used a Taser on Tran. In the end, over $80,000 was paid out in a federal civil rights suit for police conduct that was "unnecessary, unreasonable and an excessive use of force" (Bernstein, 2011). Had the officer used good cross-cultural communication skills from the start, this situation might have been avoided.

Clearly, the higher the number of bilingual officers a department has, the more efficient and effective the contact is with non-English-speaking citizens. Many agencies subsidize foreign-language training for their personnel or seek recruits with multiple language skills. When the resources are not available for such programs, however, there can be serious and sometimes tragic consequences. Non-English-speaking citizens may not understand why they are being arrested or searched. They may not know their rights if they are unfamiliar with the legal system, as is the case with many recently arrived immigrants and refugees. Using the wrong interpreter can mislead officers, so much so that a victim and his or her interpreter might give two completely different versions of a story—for example, using the friend of a suspected child abuser to translate the allegations of the child who has been abused. As further illustrated in a Department of Justice notice, ... when police officers respond to a domestic violence call ... use of family members or neighbors to interpret for the alleged victim, perpetrator, or witnesses may raise serious issues of competency, confidentiality, and conflict of interest and is thus inappropriate (U.S. Department of Justice, 2002).

Language barriers can lead to serious problems for those who cannot speak English. In some cases there is no sensitivity when it comes to language obstacles. For example, in a largely Spanish-speaking area of Los Angeles, a deputy, according to witnesses, asked a Hispanic male to get out of his car. The man answered in Spanish, "I'm handicapped," and reached down to pull his left leg out of the car. The deputy apparently believed that the man was reaching for a weapon and consequently "struck him on the head with the butt of his gun" (Kolts, 1992). This incident, while dated, is a lesson for all existing and future generations of police officers not to overreact on a motorist traffic stop.

Another Spanish language example has to do with the word *molestar*, which means "to bother" or "to annoy." In the extreme, a Spanish-speaking individual could answer "yes" to an officer's question "Did you molest your niece?" The answer could be "yes" if the non-English-speaking individual thought there was something about his behavior that irritated or annoyed his niece. Certainly, the greater the number of bilingual officers there are, the better. However, even without learning another language, officers can learn about features of other languages that may confuse an interaction when a limited English speaker communicates with a police officer. For example, some languages do not have verb tenses (e.g., most dialects of Chinese and certain languages of India), and thus you might hear, "I eat tomorrow," or "I eat yesterday." When recounting a crime observed, individuals not fluent in English might make verb-tense errors, potentially leading officers to think that they are not reliable witnesses or that they are not telling the truth. Similarly, in some Asian languages such as Tagalog (one of the main languages spoken in the Philippines), there are no terms to distinguish gender in the he/she form. Thus, when speaking English, some Filipinos mix up gender, again potentially giving the impression that they are dishonest or confused about the facts.

Intolerance of language differences and difficulties is sometimes voiced by police officers in cultural diversity in-service training workshops; similarly, recruit police officers attending cultural diversity classes in police academies echo this sentiment. It is not uncommon to hear, "Why do I have to learn about their language and their customs?" In response to such questions, students need to be challenged and asked, "Who benefits in citizen/police contacts when police officers have effective communication skills?" The response clearly would be that the community, police officers, and the non- or limited English speaking individual all benefit.

Communication across cultures and with people for whom English is a second language can be frustrating and exacts a great deal of patience from officers. Exhibit 4.2 lists basic guidelines for communicating with others for whom English is a second language. Sensitivity to the difficulties of those who do not speak English is in order, but that is only a partial solution to the problem. In attempting to cope with the problem of dealing with non-English-speaking citizens, suspects, and criminals, many departments not only have increased the number of bilingual officers in their forces but have also begun to utilize telephone interpreting services, several of which operate in multiple languages around the clock. Some 911 emergency centers have interpreters available 24 hours a day for many languages.

1. Speak slowly and enunciate clearly.

2. Face the person and speak directly even when using an interpreter.

3. Avoid concentrated eye contact if the other speaker is not making direct eye contact.

4. Do not use jargon, slang, idioms, or reduced forms (e.g., "gonna," "gotta," "wanna," "couldja").

5. Avoid complex verb tenses (e.g., "If I would have known, I might have been able to provide assistance").

6. Repeat key issues and questions in different ways.

7. Avoid asking questions that can be answered by yes or no; rather, ask open-ended questions (e.g., instead of "Will you do this?" ask "How will you meet this requirement?").

8. Use short, simple sentences; pause between sentences.

9. Use visual cues such as gestures, demonstrations, and brief written phrases.

10. Use the active rather than the passive tense (e.g., "I expect your attention" [active] rather than "Your attention is expected" [passive]).

11. Have important written and online materials in languages other than English.

12. Pause frequently and give breaks. Monitor speed when talking.

13. Limit the amount of information you have in each sentence.

14. Respect the silence that limited English speakers need to formulate their sentences and translate them in their minds.

15. Check comprehension by having the listener repeat material or instructions, and summarize frequently.

16. Provide encouragement and positive feedback on the person's ability to communicate.

17. Listen even more attentively than when communicating with a native speaker of English.

18. Be patient. Every first-generation immigrant struggles with the acquisition of English.

19. Do not speak more loudly than usual. It will not help!

EXHIBIT 4.2   Basic Guidelines for Communicating with People for Whom English Is a Second Language

---

The following dialogue takes place when an officer pulls a car over, gets out of his car, and approaches the driver. The driver, a nonnative speaker of English, says, in poor English, "Why you stop me?"

OFFICER: I pulled you over because you ran a red light.

CITIZEN: (*Blinking; no response*)

OFFICER: This is a traffic violation (*Receives no feedback*). Do you understand?

CITIZEN: (*Nodding*) Yes.

OFFICER: I'm going to have to issue you a traffic citation.

CITIZEN: (*Looking through the front windshield of the car; no response*)

OFFICER: Let me see your registration and driver's license.

CITIZEN: License? Just a minute (*Leans over to open glove compartment, but finds nothing; gets out of car and goes to trunk*).

OFFICER: (*Irritated and slightly nervous*) Hey! (*In a loud voice*) What's going on here? I asked to see your driver's license. Are you the registered owner of this car?

CITIZEN: Yes. I get my license.

OFFICER: (*Speaking much louder*) Wait a minute. Don't you understand? Are you not the owner of this car? Do you even have a license?

CITIZEN: Wait (*Finds license in trunk and produces it for officer*).

OFFICER: Okay. Would you mind getting back into the car now?

CITIZEN: (*Does nothing*) Yes.

OFFICER: (*Pointing to the front seat*) Back into the car!

CITIZEN: (*Gets back into the car*)

EXHIBIT 4.3   How Would You Rate the Officer's Use of English?

Note: See Discussion Question 3 at the end of the chapter to analyze the language and communication that the officer used in this encounter.

ATTITUDES TOWARD LIMITED ENGLISH SPEAKERS

It is important not to stereotype those who speak with accents or have little knowledge of English. An individual might have immigrated to the United States after the age at which people lose their accents (usually in the early teens). Many immigrants speak broken English, and may give all appearances of being "foreign" because their English is not perfect—yet they may be intelligent and highly educated. People who speak English poorly might be diplomatic personnel from another country or tourists. Treating any of these people with less than the utmost patience and respect can have serious consequences for the community, not to mention the reputation of the local police force. The key is to avoid making inferences about individuals based on their accents or levels of fluency; this includes avoiding assumptions as to whether they are documented or undocumented immigrants.

Citizens' use of a second language and the accompanying frustrations for officers can be overwhelming. In some cases, whether the society at large (or police as a microcosm of society) is concerned about a particular group's use of their native language seems to be directly related to the population size of that group. For example, when large groups of Cubans or Puerto Ricans speak Spanish there is often a higher level of anxiety among the dominant white population than when a few Armenians speak their native language. In other cases, U.S. citizens who do not speak any languages other than English sometimes take it personally when people speak other languages around them, expressing concern that people are talking about them "behind their backs" or—particularly in the case of law enforcement situations—strategizing about criminal activity. While this might be true, it is always more likely *not* to be the case.

Virtually every immigrant group is said to resist learning English, yet the pattern of language acquisition among the generations of immigrants follows a predictable course. Members of the second and third generations of an immigrant family almost always become fluent in English, while many first-generation immigrants (the grandparents and the parents) struggle, sometimes partly learning English and sometimes not learning it at all. This is because most first-generation immigrants arrive in the United States as adults, and thus face the same problem learning English that many Americans face in foreign-language classrooms—that is, they begin their studies as teens or adults, when it is more difficult to learn a new language, rather than as children. Because of this, adults often believe that they are "no good" at the new language and give up trying to learn it.

Many immigrants, however, are extremely motivated to learn English and become productive members of society. In urban areas, access to English classes is often limited (e.g., there have been known to be 4- and 5-year waiting lists for English programs at Los Angeles community colleges). Newcomers are fully aware that without English they will not be able to integrate into society.

Nevertheless, some people, including established immigrants, tend to overgeneralize their observations about newcomers. It is true that some people do not want to learn English and that even some middle-class U.S.-born Americans do not make efforts to improve their language abilities. How often do we hear that high school graduates who are native English speakers have not learned to write or speak well? In such cases, laziness or lack of high-quality education or both may have contributed to this aspect of illiteracy. In fairness, all groups have a percentage of lazy people, but people tend to stereotype others. Although not all first-generation immigrants learn English, there is a great deal of mythology around the "masses" of immigrants who hold on to their native languages. Interestingly, in the reverse, many people born in the United States find it completely normal for an American business executive who is sent to work in Japan, for example, to learn little or no Japanese during his entire stay in the country. In other words, many Americans are tolerant of other Americans who struggle to learn a foreign language but are intolerant of immigrants who struggle with English. Other languages seem "difficult," while one's own language seems "easy." *Any* language can be challenging to master.

The native language of an immigrant family is the language of communication for that family, and speaking it is essential if children in the family are to communicate with relatives who might still be living in the family's country of origin. It is not uncommon to hear comments from U.S.-born citizens such as, "They'll never learn English if they insist on speaking their native tongue at home." But most individuals are severely challenged to express affection, resolve conflicts, show anger, and even to simply relax in a second language. In addition, language is an integral part of a person's identity. During the initial months, and even years, of communicating in a second language, a person does not truly feel like himself or herself. Initially, an individual often has a feeling of play acting or taking on another identity when communicating in a second language.

From a physiological perspective, communicating in a foreign language and adjusting to life in a new culture can be exhausting. Everyday tasks require tremendous mental energy to accomplish. Listening to a foreign language for extended periods of time is absolutely draining, as shown in the case of the Vietnamese police officer presented earlier in this chapter. And in speaking any given language, a person uses a set of muscles to articulate the sounds of that language. Changing to another language, particularly as an adult, requires the use of an entirely new set of muscles. Doing so causes mental strain and facial tension. All of these things combined can lead to a person's "shutting down"—the result of which is an inability to communicate in the new language. It is no wonder that in the multicultural workforce, clusters of people from different ethnic groups can be seen having lunch and taking breaks together. Simply put, it conserves mental and physical energy to be able to speak one's own language.

Sometimes police officers say, "I know they speak English because they speak it among themselves" (i.e., when the group is culturally mixed). "The minute I'm on the scene, it's 'No speak English.' Why do they have to play dumb? What do they think I am—stupid?" It would be naïve to say that this situation does not occur. There will always be some people who try to deceive others and use or not use English to their own advantage. However, there may be other reasons that people "feign" not knowing English. Several factors affect an immigrant's ability to use English at any given moment. A few of these are of significance to law enforcement officers. Generally, an immigrant's ability to express himself or herself in English is at its best when that person is comfortable with the officer. So, the more intimidating an officer is, the higher the likelihood that anxiety will affect the speaker's ability in English. Language breakdown is one of the first signs that a person is ill at ease and stressed to the point of not being able to cooperate and communicate. It is in the officer's best interest to increase the comfort level of the citizen, whether a victim, a suspect, or simply a person requiring help. However, language breakdown in a person who is otherwise conversationally competent in English can also occur as a result of illness, intoxication, fatigue, and trauma.

If officers do not feel favorably toward immigrants and nonnative English speakers, whether on a conscious or unconscious basis, this attitude is likely to affect communication. This is especially true when an officer is under pressure; negative attitudes are more likely to surface under this circumstance. A calm demeanor and sincere efforts to listen and understand, though requiring more time and patience, are equally beneficial to the citizen (immigrant) and to the officer. Limited English speakers in a high anxiety state do not tend to perform as well in English when they are agitated.

Finally, if people are hesitant to speak English with a police officer, this may be due to instinctive self-preservation. If they have experienced corrupt or brutal treatment by law enforcement officers in their own countries their fear may overcome their ability to speak English. (See Chapter 1 for more information.)

CROSS-CULTURAL COMMUNICATION INSIGHTS

To understand the need for skillful communication with members of culturally and ethnically diverse groups, officers should recognize some of the special characteristics of cross-cultural communication in the law enforcement context (Exhibit 4.4). To best protect and serve communities made up of individuals from many different racial and cultural backgrounds, officers as peacekeepers, crime fighters, and law enforcement representatives need to look beyond the "mechanics" of policing and examine what takes place in the process of cross-cultural communication. Communication, in general, is a challenge because "although the words are the same the meaning can be completely different. The same expression can easily have a different connotation or emotional emphasis. Misinterpretation is so common and consistent that eventually we develop limiting perspectives of each other" (Gray, 2002). Most people think that talking to others, making one's points, and giving explanations should not be so difficult. Effective communication, however, results in *mutual* understanding; it is not a one-way process.

- Officers have traditionally used styles of communication and language that at one time were considered acceptable. Now, because of diverse groups within the police agency and within our cities, the unspoken rules about appropriate and inappropriate communication are changing.
- Communication can be tense in crises and in culturally unfamiliar environments.
- Officers' perceptions of a cultural group may be skewed by the populations they encounter.
- Communication will be enhanced when officers are aware of
    1. Perceptions
    2. Cultural filters
    3. High- and low-context communication styles (see explanation in text)
    4. Possible biases and stereotypes
- Through communication, officers have tremendous power to influence the behavior and responses of the citizens they contact. A lack of knowledge of the dynamics of cross-cultural communication will diminish this power.
- Improved communication with all citizens will result in safer interactions for officers.

EXHIBIT 4.4   Key Cross-Cultural Areas in Communication

Every communication act involves a message, a sender, and a receiver. Given that any two human beings are fundamentally different, there will always be a psychological distance between the two involved (even if they have the same cultural background). Professional police officers are usually trained in various methods of bridging the gap, or psychological distance, between the two very different worlds of sender and receiver. In instances of cross-cultural communication, including cross-racial and cross-ethnic interactions, in which the sender and receiver are from different cultures, officers have an even greater gap to try to bridge. Exhibit 4.4 summarizes key factors that can potentially contribute to cross-cultural and cross-racial communication challenges. Psychological distance exists between any two human beings because every individual is "wired" differently from the next. Styles of communication that differ across cultures can contribute to perceptions or misperceptions and incorrect filtering of communication "data."

The Influence of Hierarchy and Formality on Communication

Hierarchy   A deeply embedded system of societal structure whereby people are organized according to how much status and power they have. Hierarchical societies have specific and defined ways in which people must behave toward those lower and higher on the hierarchy. Communication is restricted in hierarchical societies, and people are always aware of where they stand in terms of status and power vis-à-vis other individuals.

One of the key characteristics of a communication style where hierarchy is predominant is the inability to say, "No," to authority because of a desire that an individual may have to say what authority wants to hear. This characteristic applies to many members of *traditional* Asian cultural groups who are first- and sometimes second-generation immigrants. It is also a style that can be seen in other parts of the world (e.g., Latin America) where there is a great **"power distance"** between subordinates and higher ups or between ordinary citizens and people in positions of authority. (This specific tendency is discussed in further detail in the Communication Styles section of Chapter 5.) Power distance between two individuals has a very strong bearing on the **Communication Context** (see next section).

Power Distance   Refers to the way that power is viewed and distributed, with significant variations across cultures. Behavior and communication in "higher power distance" cultures vary, depending on an individual's place in the hierarchy; in "lower power distance" cultures, there is an appearance of equality, with behavior and communication consistent across power distances, and markedly less emphasis on status differences.

Denmark and Israel are "low power distance cultures" where bosses, subordinates, ordinary citizens and those in authority do not perceive a marked hierarchical distance between them. In higher power distance cultures such as in China, Venezuela or Mexico, people in different positions in society accept as normal a distance between them, and this affects behavior and communication. People in high power distance cultures tend to take it as a fact of life that people are not equal and that power and authority are normal.

The military and law enforcement are examples of **high power distance** professional cultures. Information technology, such as in the Silicon, are examples of **low power distance** professional cultures. How people tend to communicate with authority differs tremendously between these sets of professional cultures.

Most Americans, to some extent, believe in equality and reject notions of hierarchy; interpreting hierarchy as the idea that one person is better than another. (Hence the saying, "Everyone puts on their pants one leg at a time.") Related to this belief is an emphasis in American culture on informality. But differences in communication style due to cultural beliefs about hierarchy and formality are not truly foreign to Americans. For example, they tend to communicate differently with their bosses as compared to their siblings or best friends—especially when the topic under discussion is emotionally charged. Communication in *every* culture is influenced by hierarchy and formality to one degree or another.

For people who come from cultures in which differences in hierarchy and formality are emphasized rather than downplayed, communication styles vary widely depending on the status of the person to whom they are speaking. Law enforcement officials who randomly encounter people from cultures in which hierarchy and formality are emphasized must realize that an officer's status is that of a stranger, requiring formality, and of an authority figure, requiring deference based on hierarchy. Relationship building, at least in the initial stages, may be challenging. Law enforcement should recognize that "opening up" can take longer, and that the need to gain trust, a critical step with all citizens, may take more effort.

There is a strong link among the elements of hierarchy, formality, and communication. This has implications for law enforcement workforce interaction not only because agencies are hierarchical, but also because of workforce cultural diversity within an agency and attitudes that may be brought to work by first-generation immigrants and refugees.

High- and Low-Context Communication

Communication Context   The "environment" in which communication takes place. It includes the circumstances of the communication, the relationships involved as well as cultural and social influences. These factors constitute the **context of the communication,** impacting *how* people communicate. For example, the fear of deportation impacts the way an undocumented immigrant will respond to questions by a police officer. Cultural influences can also have a bearing on indirectness, directness and specificity with officers. In all cases where any variables within the **context** inhibit individuals (such as fear or high power distance relationships), officers will have to work harder at establishing rapport and building trust to open the communication.

High-Context/Low-Context Communication   Frameworks of communication, largely influenced by culture, related to how much speakers rely on messages other than from words to convey meaning; explicit and specific communication is valued in the low-context style; conversely, a relatively indirect style with less reliance on the spoken word characterizes high-context communication.

Edward Hall is the author of three dated but still seminal books in the field of cross-cultural communication: *The Silent Language, Beyond Culture,* and *The Hidden Dimension* (Hall, 1959, 1966, 1976). He coined the terms *high-context* and *low-context* to describe very different frameworks of communication across cultures and individual styles. (Exhibit 4.5 depicts a view of the high- to low-context communication spectrum across regions.) An understanding of this spectrum of high- to low-context communication—which can be related to hierarchy—will contribute to officers' understanding of direct/indirect or explicit/implicit communication.

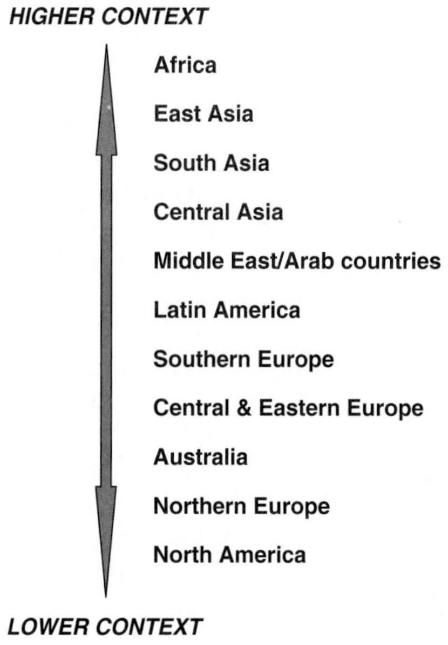

HIGHER CONTEXT

Africa

East Asia

South Asia

Central Asia

Middle East/Arab countries

Latin America

Southern Europe

Central & Eastern Europe

Australia

Northern Europe

North America

LOWER CONTEXT

EXHIBIT 4.5   High- and Low-Context Spectrum across Regions
Sources: Adapted from Edward Hall, *Beyond Culture* (1976), Geert Hofstede and Michael Minkov (2010).

In low-context (or direct/explicit) communication, people depend on words to create meaning, and rely little on other factors such as the setting, people's body language, the levels of hierarchy involved in the discussion, and so on. High-context (or indirect/implicit) communicators, in contrast, take many of their cues from the context rather than from words. In communication, people or cultural groups who tend toward the high-context end of this communication spectrum exhibit the following characteristics, to varying degrees:

- "Yes" means "I'm listening"; tendency to avoid saying no directly
- Desire to maintain harmony and avoid disagreement/conflict
- Difficulty answering yes/no and either/or type questions; awareness of shades of gray and broad context or scope
- Concern about maintaining face (theirs and others)
- Preference for getting to the point slowly and/or indirectly
- Appearance of "beating around the bush" (i.e., this is a low-context communicator's perception and filter of the higher-context style); in high-context communication, beating around the bush is seen as a polite style of communication and the "right" way to communicate

Lower-context communication tendencies include the following:

- "Yes" equals "yes" and "no" equals "no"
- Ease with direct communication and responding directly to conflict
- Belief that "the truth" is more important than issues of "face"
- Preference for getting right to the point; "beating around the bush" seen as negative

Exhibit 4.6 expands on these tendencies and provides a list of other cultural behavior associated with them.

As officers know, rapport-building with all citizens is essential for building trust, and this is often preliminary to people's willingness to communicate freely with the officers. This is especially true when communicating with people who have higher-context communication styles. Typically, these styles are more characteristic of Asian and Latin American cultures. Within any given culture, there are gender differences as well (i.e., women tend to have a higher-context style than do men). The style of communication in law enforcement is essentially a lower-context communication style, but police officers should at least be able to identify when individuals are using a higher-context communication style.

High-Context Cultures	Low-Context Cultures
Relationships among people and the situation (or "context") determine, in large part, how communication should take place.	Styles of communication are similar among people regardless of their relationships or the setting. People do not generally speak more formally to an authority figure.
• There is deference to authority. • There is formality between people in authority and others. • This formality often manifests itself in restrained and polite communication.	• There is an emphasis on equality. • It is acceptable for casual and informal communication to take place between people at differing levels of a hierarchy.
Individuals who are subordinate tend to offer respectful silence and/or statements of agreement in the presence of an authority figure.	Open and transparent communication is characteristic of low-context cultures, in general. (Organizations, however, can still be hierarchical, even in low-context cultures.)
• In a high-context culture, people tend to tell authority figures what they think the authority figures want to hear.	• There is less emphasis on pleasing authority than on speaking one's mind.
There is a greater focus on the importance of relationships rather than on completion of tasks.	There is greater focus on completing tasks than on nurturing relationships.
• Accordingly, timing allows for interruptions and attention to people (vs. tasks).	• Accordingly, there is a high value placed on task achievement and getting things done.
To a low-context, task-oriented person, constant interruptions may appear unfocused, and the communication style may seem digressive.	To a high-context individual, task orientation may appear cold and rude, and can interfere with rapport building.

EXHIBIT 4.6 Characteristics of High- and Low-Context Cultures
Source: Adapted from Edward Hall (1976). *Beyond Culture.* Garden City, NY: Doubleday.

One of the key tools for building rapport in law enforcement is neurolinguistic programming (NLP), a communication model and a set of techniques for establishing rapport. Officers have successfully used this communication tool to build rapport in interviews with witnesses and victims of crimes. The techniques involved have to do with a fundamental principle in interpersonal relationships, which is the need to create harmony with others in order to establish rapport. As such, one type of communication used with NLP is that of "modeling," or matching nonverbal and verbal behavior with a witness, victim, or interviewee. Doing so may prove to be especially challenging with people from different cultural backgrounds, but it is useful as a way to minimize the cultural gap between the officer's style and that of the citizen with whom he or she is interacting. It is beyond the scope of this chapter to detail the theory behind and steps involved in NLP. For additional information, see the FBI Law Enforcement Bulletin article entitled, "Subtle Skills for Building Rapport" (Sandoval & Adams, 2001).

CROSS-CULTURAL/RACIAL COMMUNICATION DYNAMICS

Officers do not need to try too hard to demonstrate cultural understanding. An officer should accommodate differences in communication style where they exist, but should not act unnaturally in an attempt to "get it right." With cultural groups that may appear very different from one's own, or when sensitivities may be high, law enforcement representatives should think about increasing the comfort levels of those they approach. This means not beginning with the assumption that others are foreign and strange, and avoiding the idea that "I have to know too many cultural details before I can communicate with members of this group." Respect toward fellow human beings, with some knowledge of cultural detail, will lead to effective communication. If officers have had limited contact with people from diverse backgrounds, they may inadvertently communicate a lack of cross-cultural competence and comfort. In the next few sections, we exemplify typical ways people attempt to accommodate or react to cultural or racial differences and how they may cover up their discomfort in communication across cultures.

Using Language or Language Style to Become Just Like One of "Them"

Black officer to a white officer: "Hey, what kind of arrest did you have?"
White officer: "Brotha-man was trying to front me ... "

> Police Chief Darryl McAllister from the Union City, California, Police Department uses the preceding example to illustrate how obviously uncomfortable some white people are when communicating cross-racially. One of his pet peeves is hearing other officers trying to imitate him in speech and trying to act like a "brother." He explains that this type of imitative language is insincere and phony. The artificiality makes him feel as if people are going overboard to show just how comfortable they are when, in fact, they may not be. He explained that he does not feel that this style of imitation is necessarily racist but that it communicates others' discomfort with his "blackness." (McAllister, 2013)

Similarly, officers attempting to establish rapport with citizens should not pretend to have familiarity with the language and culture or use words selectively to demonstrate how "cool" they are (e.g., using *señor* with Spanish-speaking people, calling an African American "my man," or referring to a Native American as "chief"). People of one cultural background may find themselves in situations in which an entire crowd or family is using a particular dialect or slang. If officers lapse into the manner of speaking of the group, they will likely appear to be mocking that style. Ultimately, police officers should be sincere and natural. "Faking" another style of communication can have extremely negative results.

Walking on Eggshells

When in the presence of people from different cultural backgrounds, some people have a tendency to work hard not to offend. Consequently, they are not able to be themselves or do what they would normally do. In a cultural diversity session for city government employees, one white participant explained that he normally has no problem being direct when solicitors come to the door trying to sell something or ask for a donation to a cause. His normal response would be to say, "I'm not interested," and then he would promptly shut the door. He explained, however, that when a black solicitor comes to the door, he engages the person in conversation, and most of the time ends up making a donation to whatever cause is being promoted. His inability to be himself and communicate directly stems from his concern about appearing to be racist. It is not within the scope of this subsection to analyze this behavior in depth, but simply to bring into awareness some typical patterns of reactions in cross-cultural and cross-racial encounters. A person must internally recognize the tendency to overcompensate in order to eventually reach the goal of communicating in a sincere and authentic manner with people of all backgrounds (Exhibit 4.7).

"Some of My Best Friends Are ... "

In an attempt to show how tolerant and experienced they are with members of minority groups, some people feel the need to demonstrate this strongly by saying things such as, "I'm not prejudiced," or "I have friends who are members of your group," or "I know ... people," or, worse, "I once knew someone who was also [for example, Jewish/Asian/African American]." Although the intention may be to break down barriers and establish rapport, these types of statements often sound patronizing. To a member of a culturally or racially

---

- Self-awareness about one's early life experiences that helped to shape perceptions, filters, and assumptions about people
- Self-awareness about how one feels toward someone who is "different"
- Management of assumptions and discomfort in dealing with people who are different (e.g., do I try to deny that differences exist and laugh differences away, or imitate "them" in order to appear comfortable?)
- Ability to be authentic in communication with others by modifying communication style when necessary

EXHIBIT 4.7   Key Areas of Self-Awareness

different group, this type of comment comes across as extremely naïve. In fact, many people would understand such a comment as signifying that the speaker actually does have preju- dices toward a particular group. Minority-group members would question a nonmember's need to make a reference to others of the same background when there is no context for doing so. These types of remarks indicate that the speaker is probably isolated from members of the particular group. Yet the person making a statement such as "I know someone who is Asian" is trying to establish something in common with the other person and may even go into detail about the other person he or she knows. As one Jewish woman reported in a cross- cultural awareness session, "Just because a person I meet is uncomfortable meeting Jews or has very little experience with Jews doesn't mean that I want to hear about the one Jewish person he met ten years ago while traveling on a plane to New York!"

"You People" or the We/They Distinction

Some may say, "I'd like to get to know you people better," or "You people have made some amazing contributions." The use of "you people" may be another signal of prejudice or divi- siveness in a person's mind. When someone decides that a particular group is unlike his or her own group (i.e., not part of "my people"), that person makes a simplistic division of all people into two groups: "we" and "they." Often accompanying this division is the attribution of positive traits to "us" and negative traits to "them." Members of the "other group" (the out-group) are described in negative and stereotypical terms (e.g., "They are lazy," "They are criminals," "They are aggressive") rather than neutral terms that describe cultural or ethnic generalities (e.g., "They have a tradition of valuing education," or "Their communication style is more formal than that of most Americans"). The phenomenon of stereotyping makes it very difficult for people to communicate with each other effectively because they do not perceive others accurately. By attributing negative qualities to another group, a person cre- ates myths about the superiority of his or her own group. Cultural and racial put-downs are often attempts to make people feel better about themselves.

"You Stopped Me because I'm ... " or Accusations of Racial Profiling

There are three recurring situations in which an officer may hear the accusation: "You stopped me because I'm [black, Arab, etc.]." The first situation is when citizens from a neighborhood with residents predominantly from one race or culture are suspicious of any person who shows up in their neighborhood who is obviously from a different cultural or racial back- ground. Therefore, they may call 911 reporting a "suspicious character" and may even add such statements as, "I think he has a gun," when there is no basis for such an accusation. In this situation, the police officer must understand the extreme humiliation and anger the "sus- picious characters" feel when they are the object of such racist perceptions. Once the officer determines that there is no reason to arrest the citizen, it is most appropriate for the officer to apologize for having made the stop and to explain that department policy requires that officers are obliged to investigate all calls.

Indeed, incidents occur all over the country in which citizens call a police department to report a "suspicious character" just because he or she does not happen to fit the description of the majority of the residents in that area. Given that there is a history of stopping minori- ties for reasons that are less than legitimate, the officer must go out of his or her way to show respect to the innocent citizen who does not know why he or she has been stopped and is caught totally off guard. Many people reported to be "suspicious" for merely being of a dif- ferent race would appreciate an officer's making a final comment such as "I hope this kind of racism ends soon within our community" or "It's too bad there are still people in our com- munity who are so ignorant." Comments such as these, said with sincerity, may very well get back to the community and contribute to improved future interactions with members of the police department. Of course, some people who are stopped will not appreciate any attempt that the officer makes to explain why the stop was made. Nevertheless, many citizens will react favorably to an officer's understanding of their feelings.

A second situation in which an officer may hear, "You stopped me because I'm ... " may occur not because of any perceived racist intentions of the officer but rather as a "reflex response" of the citizen (in other words, it has no bearing on reality). Many people have been stopped without reason in the past or know people who have; they carry this baggage into each encounter with an officer. One police officer explained: "I don't consider myself prejudiced. I consider myself a fair person, but let me tell you what happens almost every time I stop a black in city X. The first words I hear from them are 'You stopped me because I'm black.' That's bugging the hell out of me because that's not why I stopped them. I stopped them because they violated the traffic code. It's really bothering me and I'm about to explode."

Officers accused of racially or ethnically motivated stops truly need to remain professional and not escalate a potential conflict or create a confrontation. Law enforcement officials should not only try to communicate their professionalism, both verbally and nonverbally, but also try to strengthen their self-control. The best way to deal with these types of remarks from citizens is to work on one's own reactions and stress level. One could potentially receive such remarks on a daily basis. People react to officers as symbols and are using the officer to vent their frustration.

Let's assume that an officer did not stop a person because of his or her ethnicity or race and that the officer is therefore not abusing his or her power. The late George Thompson, founder and president of the Verbal Judo Institute, believed that in these situations, people bring up race and ethnicity to throw the officer off guard. According to Thompson (who was white and a police officer), the more professional an officer is, the less likely he or she is to let this type of statement become a problem. Newer officers, especially, can be thrown off guard by such allegations of racism when, in fact, they are simply upholding the law and keeping the peace as they have been trained to do. Thompson advocated using "verbal deflectors" when citizens make such remarks as "You stopped me because I'm … " He recommended responses such as "I appreciate that, but you were going 55 miles an hour in a 25-mile-per-hour zone," or "I hear what you're saying, but you just broke the law." Verbal deflectors: (1) are readily available to the lips, (2) are nonjudgmental, and (3) can be said quickly. Thompson believed that statements from citizens should not be ignored. Silence or no response can make people even more furious than they already were because they were stopped (Thompson, 2009).

> Pay attention to what citizens say, but deflect their anger. You are not paid to argue with citizens. You are paid to keep the peace. If you use tactical language and focus every word you say so that it relates to your purpose, then you will sound more professional. The minute you start using words as defensive weapons, you lose power and endanger your safety. If you "springboard" over their arguments and remain calm, controlled, and nonjudgmental, you will gain voluntary compliance most of the time. The results of this professional communication are that: (1) you feel good, (2) you disarm the citizen, and (3) you control them in the streets (and in courts and in the media). Never take anything personally. Always treat people with respect and explain the "why" in your communication with them. (ibid.)

The third and final situation in which an officer may hear "You stopped me because I'm … " is when the individual is correct and, indeed, racial profiling is taking place. Police department personnel are not immune from the racism that still exists in our society. Reflecting biased attitudes outside the law enforcement agency, some officers use their positions of power to assert authority in ways that cannot be tolerated. We are referring not only to the white officer who subjugates citizens from different backgrounds, but also, for example, to an African American officer who has internalized the racism of the dominant society and may actually treat fellow group members unjustly. Alternatively, this abuse of power could take place between, for example, a black or Latino officer and a white citizen. (See culture-specific chapters for further examples of racial profiling, and Chapter 12 for in-depth coverage of the topic.)

Officers must consider the reasons a citizen may say, "You stopped me because I'm … " and respond accordingly. The situations described above (i.e., citizens call in because of racist perceptions and the "suspicious character" is innocent; the citizen stopped is simply "hassling" the officer, and may or may not have been unjustly stopped in the past; and the citizen making the accusation toward the officer is correct) call for different responses on the part of the officer. The officer would do well, in all three situations, to remember the quote included in the final section of Chapter 1: "Remember the history of law enforcement with all groups and ask yourself the question, 'Am I part of the past, or a part of the future?'" (Berry, 2017).

THE IMPORTANCE OF VERBAL DE-ESCALATION

> **Verbal De-Escalation**   refers to the act of decreasing the intensity, volume, or magnitude of a conflict or confrontation through a communication style that deflects anger and calms a potentially aggressive or violent situation.

Many officers recognize the importance of communicating in a manner that prevents and de-escalates confrontation. Law enforcement training, however, does not consistently provide sufficient training for officers to master this critical skill in people-to-people and cross-racial/ethnic communication.

Officers facing unsafe or even life-threatening situations need to establish dominance and even use force where appropriate. This is part of the police officer role. That said, there are also many situations where a display of dominance and force lead to unnecessary escalation and confrontation. Many minor incidents do not have to turn aggressive or violent; the officer often has the power to prevent escalation of tensions. Following are some words of advice from retired officer Ronald Hampton whose experience comes from 23 years with the Metropolitan DC Police Department:

> We work for the people. These are our "customers." Our job is to de-escalate and not escalate situations. When police officers are called to a scene, it is the officer who needs to use professional skills to bring calm, to figure out what is going on, to assess who is the perpetrator, and to make decisions as to the best course of action. The officer's respectful style will—most of the time—calm people. If we come on to a scene, heatedly pushing people, we will trigger them. If we grab people and tell them we are going to arrest them, we will trigger them, and things will only get worse. We do not need to go into situations showing that we are tougher than the individuals we encounter, or approach people with our hand on our gun. We want the people we encounter to show respect for the law. That won't happen if we approach them in an aggressive and confrontational manner. (Hampton, 2017) (Review section entitled, "Conflict Resolution Tips" in Chapter 2, p. 50, for a summary of guidelines on managing conflict.)

Deflecting Anger

We mentioned "Verbal Judo" above in relation to individuals' responses to *perceived* racial profiling. Verbal Judo involves deflecting anger, i.e., turning others' words around in a way that cools them off. Officer Hampton agrees that officers need to acquire the kinds of communication skills that will calm situations rather than heat them up, and provides a specific example from his own experience:

> CITIZEN: "I am going to hit him in the face." (*"Him," referring to another individual on the scene.*)
> OFFICER HAMPTON: "Why are you going to hit him in the face if you know that I will have to arrest you for that?" (*Citizen is quiet.*)
> OFFICER HAMPTON: "I want you to think about why this fight is not a good idea. I am hoping that you will come to the conclusion that it is a better choice to show respect for the law." (Hampton, 2017)

Officer Hampton deflected or turned aside the individual's anger, and in doing so, slowed down this individual's reaction time. Hampton encourages officers to make it a goal to gain "command and control of themselves" by thinking about what triggers them to anger or aggression (ibid.). A trigger, for example, could be a defiant tone of voice or the shouting of disrespectful language, such as the use of the word "pig." Self-awareness before entering a heated situation and self-control while entering the situation are equally important.

Limited English Speakers—Communication Considerations

Interactions with citizens, immigrants, and foreign-born residents who do not speak English fluently are particularly challenging for both the officer and the individual. As noted earlier in the chapter, limited English speakers in a high anxiety state do not tend to communicate well when they are agitated.

Officers need more patience than usual in these situations. It takes longer for nonnative or limited English speakers to absorb and process speech because they are mentally translating at several stages of the interaction. Breaking down the process, it looks like this:

- An officer speaks in English to a limited English speaker.
- He or she mentally translates the officers' words to the native language.
- He or she mentally constructs the response in the native language.
- He or she then translates the response to English (i.e., another mental step).
- He or she responds in English to the officer.

Of course, emergency and life-threatening situations that call for quick decision-making and immediate instructions or commands do not often allow the luxury of patience. However, a great deal of police contact is not at the level of an emergency. In more minor incidents, consider that the extra time and patience spent with a limited English speaker will also be beneficial to the officer. When individuals are limited by language, an officer's patience allows better language processing which, in turn, can keep situations calm and prevent escalation of conflict.

Effective communication helps to keep officers safe. Listening, too, can deflect anger and de-escalate confrontation. This is obviously essential in communication with all people, regardless of background and language ability. However, the officer's ability to listen is even more critical with those who are not fluent in English. When people feel that they have not been able to tell their side of a story or express emotions, their frustration and anger can also trigger or escalate conflict.

Reducing Defensiveness

Law enforcement training has not typically been focused as much on communication skills as on other components of policing such as weapons training. All types of training are needed to develop a well-balanced officer. One highly respected model of communication training, is the LEED model (Exhibit 4.8), developed in 2011 by Former Sherriff, Sue Rahr, of King County, Washington, and the Executive Director of The Washington State Criminal Justice Training Commission. LEED stands for "Listen and Explain with Equity and Dignity, comprising what the Washington State Criminal Justice Training Commission refers to as the Four Pillars of *Justice-Based Policing*, a strategy that " … strengthens community trust and confidence in the police and increases future cooperation and lawful behavior by citizens" (Washington State Criminal Justice Training Commission, 2017).

Acquiring skills to reduce defensiveness, including "Listening and Explaining with Equity and Dignity" will serve officers well, especially where individuals who, because of their history with the police, may be on the slightest defensive, and triggered easily. While officers are not responsible for the injustices in the past, negative history with members of minority communities is a fact. Although officers can easily be triggered by individuals' disrespect, they—the officers—are the ones who must be held to a higher standard of behavior.

- *Listen:* Allow people to give their side of the story. Give them a voice, and let them vent. Listening is the most powerful way to demonstrate respect.
- *Explain:* Explain what you're doing, what they can do, and what's going to happen.
- *Equity:* Tell them why you are taking action. The reason must be fair and free of bias, and show that their side of the story was considered.
- *Dignity:* Act with dignity, and leave them with their dignity. Treat every person with basic human decency.

EXHIBIT 4.8   LEED: Listen and Explain with Equity and Dignity
Source: Washington State Criminal Justice Training Commission Website, Justice Based Policing Course.

Communication Strengths Associated with Gender

Katherine Spillar, co-founder of The National Center for Women and Policing and executive director of the Feminist Majority Foundation, is a strong advocate for the recruitment and hiring of female police officers in law enforcement. She argues that much of women's strength lies in the ability to de-escalate conflict and confrontation (Spillar, 2017). Generally speaking, and according to more than 40 years of research, women have been shown to demonstrate a style of policing that is markedly different from men's, characterized by less authoritarianism than the average male officer's style. Much of this assertion is related to the communication skills that many women possess. Spillar asserts, and data show, that female police officers respond with less aggression even when encountering challenging or threatening situations with citizens than do male officers. For example, women tend not to use confrontational language or resort to force as an immediate response to threatening situations. The very presence of women can often influence people away from violence. According to Spillar, the research also shows that women generally tend to have better relations with the public, and keep a focus on community engagement more than on a paramilitary style of policing (ibid.). Captain Teresa Ewins of the San Francisco Police Department agrees that the communication skillset that many women bring to policing represents an important strength that law enforcement should leverage:

> Female officers have a tendency to know how to defuse situations rather than provoking the people involved. Negotiation, listening, persuading are all part of the communication toolkit that women make great efforts to use as a major strategy. Without these skills, otherwise minor incidents might escalate to the point of confrontation. (Ewins, 2017)

INTERVIEWING AND DATA-GATHERING SKILLS

Interviewing and data-gathering skills form the basic techniques for problem-solving and intervention work with multicultural populations. For the officer, the key issues in any interviewing and data-gathering situation are as follows:

- Establishing interpersonal relationships to gain trust and rapport for ongoing work
- Bringing structure and control to the immediate situation
- Gaining information about the problems that require the presence of the law enforcement officer
- Giving information about law enforcement guidelines, resources, and assistance available
- Providing action and intervention as needed
- Bolstering and supporting the different parties' abilities and skills to solve current and future problems on their own

Listed in Exhibit 4.9 are helpful guidelines for providing and receiving information in appropriate ways in a multicultural context.

In the area of data gathering and interviewing, the officer in a multicultural law enforcement situation cannot assume that his or her key motivators and values are the same as those of the other parties involved. Recognizing such differences in motivation and values will result in greater effectiveness. For example, the values of maintaining face and/or preserving one's own honor as well as the honor of one's family are extremely strong motivators for many people from Asian, Latin American, and Mediterranean cultures. An Asian gang expert from the Oakland, California, Police Department illustrated this value system with the case of a niece who had been chosen by the police to translate for her aunt, who had been raped. The values of honor and face prevented the aunt from telling the police all the details of the crime of which she was the victim. Her initial story, told to the police through her niece's translation, contained very few of the facts or details of the crime. Later, through a second translator who was not a family member, the rape victim gave all the necessary information. Precious time had been lost, but the victim explained that she could not have revealed the true story in front of her niece because she would have shamed her family.

Exhibit 4.10 lists key values or motivators for police officers. In any given situation, these values may be at odds with what motivates the victim, suspect, or ordinary citizen of any background. However, when the officer and the citizen are from totally different backgrounds, additional cultural or racial variables may also be in conflict.

1. Be knowledgeable about who is likely to have information. Ask questions to identify the head of a family or respected community leaders.

2. Consider that some cultural groups have need extra efforts at rapport and trust building before they are willing to share information. Do not consider the interval that it takes to establish rapport a waste of time.

3. Provide background and context for questions, information, and requests. Cultural minorities differ in their need for contextual (i.e., background) information before getting down to the issues or business at hand. Remain patient with those who want to go into more detail than you think is necessary.

4. Expect answers to be formulated and expressed in culturally different ways. Some people tend to be linear in their answers (i.e., giving one point of information at a time in a sequential or chronological order); some present information in a zigzag fashion (i.e., they digress frequently); and others tend to present information in a spiral or circular style (i.e., they may appear to be avoiding the point). And, of course, in addition to cultural differences, there are individual differences in ways of presenting information.

5. It is important to speak simply, but do not make the mistake of using simple or "pidgin" English. Remember, people's comprehension skills are usually better than their speaking skills.

6. "Yes" does not always mean "yes"; do not mistake a courteous answer for the facts or the truth or even for understanding.

7. Remember that maintaining good rapport is just as important as coming to the point and getting work done quickly. Slow down!

8. Silence is a form of speech; do not interrupt it. Give people time to express themselves by respecting their silence.

EXHIBIT 4.9   Interviewing and Data Gathering in a Multicultural Context

1. Survival or injury avoidance
2. Control and structure
3. Respect and authority
4. Use of professional skills
5. Upholding laws and principles
6. Avoiding conflict and tension
7. Harmony and peacekeeping
8. Conflict resolution and problem solving
9. Self-respect and self-esteem

EXHIBIT 4.10   Key Values or Motivators in Law Enforcement

Interviewing after Hate Incidents or Crimes

When interviewing and gathering data on hate incidents and crimes targeted at individuals from particular backgrounds (including threats conveyed by phone calls or letters), officers may encounter highly emotional and even hysterical reactions from other community members. In officers' attempt to control the situation, they must consider that there is also a community needing reassurance. For example, an officer must be willing to respond sensitively to heightened anxiety on the part of group members and not downplay their fears. Interviewing and data gathering may therefore last much longer when the officer is required to deal with multiple community members and widespread fears.

Detecting Deception across Language and Cultural Lines

Police officers are trained in interviewing skills, and these include the ability to identify when suspects or witnesses are lying. Trying to assess truthfulness when an individual is a nonnative speaker of English adds another layer of challenge. A team of experts consisting of a psychology professor, a research scientist, and a retired FBI agent and polygraph examiner, conducted a novel study, whose results were reported in a 2015 FBI Law Enforcement Bulletin (Sandoval, Matsumoto, Hwang, & Skinner, 2015). The study subjects were from four different language and ethnic groups: Chinese, Hispanic, Middle Eastern, and European American. They were instructed to participate in a simulated scenario in which some were asked to steal a check from a file room and then, lie to the investigators about what they did. The others were instructed not to steal the check and to be truthful about this when they answered the investigators' questions. It turned out that the same "verbal markers of deception" were used by the nonnative speaking subjects (i.e., those who stole the check) as by native speakers of English (ibid.).

The study analyzed language and grammatical features known as "Statement Analyses" (Matsumoto, Hwang, & Sandoval, 2015). The following are some of the verbal markers of deception that researchers looked at when analyzing the nonnative English responses to their "investigation."

- Using intentionally vague words, such as:
  ○ Maybe, believe, kind of, around (e.g., around 8 PM), sort of, to the best of my knowledge
- Telling things that were not prompted by an investigator, specifically "non-prompted negation"—for example:
  ○ Investigator: "Tell me about your morning."
  ○ Suspect: "I didn't talk to anyone."
- "Editing adverbs"—using words to edit or omit information: "I *then* drove home." "*Later* I spoke with my mother." "*While* I did that, I … "
- Providing extraneous information:
  ○ "On my way home, after I went to work, I listened to some really cool music from my playlist."
- Not remembering: "I really can't remember."
- Using imprecise language: "I didn't do much else."
- Using "intensifying adverbs" such as "truthfully," "honestly" and "really" (Sandoval et al., 2015).

The hope, with the above-noted study findings, is that investigators working across linguistic and ethnic lines will be able to analyze confidently the use of nonnative English responses in investigations with the same verbal markers of deception used to analyze native-speaker English (ibid.).

NONVERBAL COMMUNICATION

Up to this point in the chapter, we have primarily discussed verbal communication across cultures and its relevance to the law enforcement context. Nonverbal communication, including tone of voice, plays a key role in the dynamics between any two people. Dr. Albert Mehrabian of the University of California, Los Angeles, described in the classic and highly quoted book *Silent Messages* (1971) the general impact on the interaction between two or three people when a person's verbal and nonverbal messages contradict each other. In this scenario, it is almost always tone of voice and body language, including facial expressions that convey an individual's true feelings. Obviously, low-context (direct/explicit) people pay attention to other aspects of communication in addition to words; it is simply a matter of degree of emphasis. Officers have to, of course, attend to citizens' words; however, tone of voice and body language can reveal much more. In addition, across cultures, there are other considerations that relate directly to the interpretation of meaning.

Consider the following examples of reactions to differences in nonverbal communication across cultures and their implications for day-to-day police work:

> *He didn't look at me once. I know he's guilty. Never trust a person*
> *who doesn't look you in the eye.*
> AMERICAN POLICE OFFICER

> *Americans seem cold. They seem to get upset when you stand close to them.*
> JORDANIAN TEACHER

As in the first example, if an officer uses norms of eye contact as understood by most Americans, he or she could make an incorrect judgment about someone who avoids eye contact; or, as in the second example, an officer's comfortable distance for safety might be violated because of a cultural standard defining acceptable conversational distance. The comments demonstrate how people can misinterpret nonverbal communication when it is culturally different from their own. Misinterpretation can happen even with two people from the same background, but it is more likely when there are cultural differences. Universal emotions such as happiness, fear, and sadness are expressed in similar nonverbal ways throughout the world; however, nonverbal variations across cultures can cause confusion.

Take the example of the way people express sadness and grief. In many cultures, such as Arab and Iranian cultures, people express grief openly and out loud. In contrast, in other parts of the world (e.g., in China and Japan), people are generally more subdued or even silent in their expressions of grief. In Asian cultures, the general belief is that it is best to contain one's emotions (whether sadness or happiness) if it is not an appropriate time or place to express them, and so that others will feel comfortable in one's presence. Without this cultural knowledge, in observing a person who did not openly express grief, for example, one might conclude that he or she is not in emotional distress. This would be an incorrect and ethnocentric interpretation based on one's own culture.

The expression of friendship is another example of how cultural groups differ in their nonverbal behavior. Feelings of friendship exist everywhere, but their expression varies. In some cultures, it is acceptable for men to embrace and kiss each other (in Saudi Arabia and Russia, for example) and for women to hold hands (in China, Korea, Egypt, and other countries). Russian gymnasts of the same sex have been seen on television kissing each other on the lips; this is an acceptable gesture in their culture and does not imply that they are gay or lesbian. What is considered "normal" behavior in one culture may be viewed as "abnormal" or unusual in another.

The following areas of nonverbal communication have variations across cultures; the degree to which a person displays nonverbal differences depends, in part, on the age of the person and the degree of his or her acculturation to the United States.

1. **Gestures:** A few American gestures are offensive in other cultures. For example, the OK gesture is obscene in Germany and Latin America—and in France, it means "zero"; the crossed-fingers-for-good-luck gesture is offensive in Vietnam; and the "come here" gesture (beckoning with a curled index finger and with the palm up) is very insulting in most of Asia and Latin America.

2. **Position of feet:** A police sergeant relaxing at his desk with his feet up, baring the soles of his shoes, would most likely offend a Thai or Saudi Arabian (and other groups as well) coming into the office. To show one's foot is insulting in many cultures because the foot is considered the dirtiest part of the body. (Another example of this was the intended insult toward Saddam Hussein when Iraqis hit a statue of him with their shoes.) Officers need to be mindful of this taboo with respect to the feet, and should refrain, whenever possible, from making physical contact with their feet when, for example, someone is lying on the ground.

3. **Facial expressions:** Not all facial expressions mean the same thing across cultures. The smile is a great source of confusion for many people in law enforcement when they encounter people from Asian cultures. A smile or giggle can cover up pain, humiliation, and embarrassment. Some women (e.g., Japanese, Vietnamese) cover their mouths with their hands when they smile or giggle. Upon hearing something sad, a Vietnamese person may smile. Similarly, an officer may need to communicate something that causes a loss of face to a person, resulting in the person smiling. This smile does not mean that the person is trying to be a "smart aleck"; it is simply a culturally conditioned response.

4. **Facial expressiveness:** People in law enforcement have to be able to "read faces" in certain situations in order to assess situations correctly. The degree to which people show emotions on their faces depends, in large part, on their cultural background. Whereas Latin Americans, African Americans and people from Mediterranean regions tend to show emotions facially, other groups, such as many of the Asian cultural groups, tend to be less facially expressive and less emotive. An officer may thus incorrectly assume that a person is not being cooperative or would not make a good witness.

5. **Eye contact:** In many parts of the world, eye contact is avoided with authority figures. In parts of India, for example, a father would discipline his child by saying, "How dare you look me in the eye when I'm speaking to you"; whereas an American parent would say, "Look me in the eye when I'm talking to you." Direct eye contact with some citizens

can be perceived as threatening to that citizen; for a citizen to maintain direct eye contact with a police officer would be disrespectful in some cultures. A security officer in a large store in San Jose, California, offered the example of officers looking directly at Latino/Hispanic young people suspected of stealing items from the store. On a number of occasions, the officers' direct eye contact was met with a physical reaction (i.e., the young person attempting to punch the officer). He explained that the Latino/Hispanic individual mistook the eye contact as confrontation and a challenge for a fight.

6. **Physical or conversational distance:** All people subconsciously keep a comfortable distance around them when communicating with others, resulting in invisible walls that keep people far enough away. (This subcategory of nonverbal communication is called *proxemics.*) Police officers are perhaps more aware than others of the distance they keep from people in order to remain safe. When someone violates this space, a person often feels threatened and backs away or, in the case of an officer, begins to think about protective measures. Although personality and context also determine interpersonal distance, cultural background comes into play. In general, Latin Americans and Middle Easterners are more comfortable at close distances than are northern Europeans, Asians, and the majority of Americans. In some cultures, the amount of acceptable space depends on whether the other person is of the same sex or the opposite sex. A male police officer should not necessarily feel threatened, for example, if approached by an Iranian or Greek male in a manner that feels uncomfortably close. While maintaining a safe distance, the officer should also consider cultural background. Consider the example of a Middle Eastern suspect who ignores an officers' command to "step back." The social distance for interacting in the Middle East (as in many other areas of the world) is much closer than it is in the United States. For officers, for whom safety is paramount, this could easily lead to misinterpretation. Generally, Americans are comfortable at a little more than an arm's distance from each other.

For the law enforcement professional, nonverbal communication constitutes a major part in all aspects of peacekeeping and enforcement—but as an FBI article on interviewing skills cautions, "Investigators must remember that no 'silver bullet' for identifying deception exists" (Matsumoto, Hwang, Skinner, & Frank, 2011). A combination of two skills: (1) the detection of micro-expressions (fleeting expressions of emotions observed in the face) and (2) "statement analysis" (examination of word choice and grammar) are said to be reliable indicators of truthfulness, but training and practice are necessary for officers to employ these skills reliably (ibid.). In addition, while some micro-expressions are believed to be fairly consistent across cultures, they must be interpreted within the context of a situation, and statement analysis is most likely to be reliable only when applied to native speakers. Thus, when working with multicultural populations, it is crucial for officers to be aware of the variety of nuances and differences that may exist from one group to another (Exhibits 4.11 and 4.12).

---

1. Body language and nonverbal messages can override an officer's verbal content in high-stress and crisis situations. For example, the officer's statement that he or she is there to help may be contradicted by a body posture of discomfort and uncertainty in culturally unfamiliar households.

2. For people of different ethnic backgrounds, stress, confusion, and uncertainty can communicate unintended messages. For example, an Asian may remain silent and look nervous and anxious at the scene of a crime. He or she may appear to be "uncooperative" when in fact this person may have every intention of helping the officer.

3. For people with limited English skills, the nonverbal aspects of communication become even more important. Appropriate gestures and nonverbal cues help the nonnative English speaker understand verbal messages.

4. It is important for officers to learn about and avoid offensive gestures and cultural taboos. However, immigrants and international visitors are quick to forgive and overlook gestures and actions made out of forgetfulness and ignorance. Officers should realize, too, that, in time, newcomers usually learn many of the nonverbal mannerisms with which officers are more familiar. Nevertheless, learning about offensive gestures can help officers avoid interpersonal offenses.

EXHIBIT 4.11 Nonverbal Communication: Key Points for Law Enforcement

Note: Each of the culture-specific chapters (Chapters 5–9) contain information about nonverbal characteristics of culture-specific groups.

- When is touch appropriate and inappropriate?
- What is the comfortable physical distance between people in interactions?
- What is considered proper eye contact? What do eye contact and lack of eye contact mean to the people involved?
- What cultural variety is there in facial expressions? For example, does nodding and smiling mean the same in all cultures? If someone appears to be expressionless, does that mean he or she is uncooperative?
- What are appropriate and inappropriate gestures for a particular cultural group?
- Is the person in transition from one culture to another and, therefore, lacking knowledge of American-style communication?

EXHIBIT 4.12 Key Questions concerning Nonverbal Communication across Cultures

Officers must be authentic in their communication with people from various backgrounds. When learning about both verbal and nonverbal characteristics across cultures, officers do not need to feel that they must communicate differently each time they are in contact with someone of a different background. However, understanding that there are variations in communication style will help the officer interpret people's motives and attitudes more accurately and, overall, assess situations without a cultural bias.

MALE-FEMALE COMMUNICATION IN LAW ENFORCEMENT

> You have to go along with the kind of kidding and ribbing that the guys participate in; otherwise, you are not one of them. If you say that you are offended by their crass jokes and vulgar speech, then you are ostracized from the group. I have often felt that in the squad room men have purposely controlled themselves because of my presence, because I have spoken up. But what I've done to them is make them act one way because of my presence as a woman. Then they call me a prude or spread the word that I'm keeping track of all their remarks for the basis of a sexual harassment suit down the road. I have no interest in doing that. I simply want to be a competent police officer in a professional working environment. (Comments by a female police officer at a Women Peace Officers' Association [WPOA] Conference)

With the changing workforce, including increasing numbers of women in traditionally male professions, many new challenges related to male-female communication are presenting themselves. A strong camaraderie exists in law enforcement among the male members of police forces, although, in some cases, women are part of this camaraderie. Women allowed into what has been termed the "brotherhood" or "the good old boys' network" (also discussed in Chapter 2) have generally had to "become one of the guys" to gain acceptance into a historically male-dominated profession. Many of these women have learned to communicate in a more male style—more directly and assertively. Some early sociolinguistic research on the differences between the way men and women speak illustrate the following:

> It is frequently observed that male speakers are more likely to be confrontational by arguing, issuing commands, and taking opposing stands for the sake of argument, whereas females are more likely to avoid confrontation by agreeing, supporting, and making suggestions rather than commands ... fighting with each other and banding together to fight others can create strong connections among males ... (Tannen, 2001)

Camaraderie results when a group is united because of a common goal or purpose; the glue cementing and reflecting the camaraderie is the easy communication among its members. The extracurricular interests of the members of the group, the topics selected for conversation, and the jokes that people tell all contribute to the cohesiveness or tightness of members of police departments and other law enforcement agencies.

In some departments, women find that they or other women are the objects of jokes about sexual topics or that there are simply numerous references to sex. Because certain departments within cities have consisted mostly of men, they have not had to consider the inclusion of women on an equal basis and have not had to examine their own communication with each other.

Young women who are new to a department feel that they must tolerate certain behaviors to be accepted. A female sheriff participating in a WPOA conference said that she confronts, on a daily basis, vulgar language and sexual references in the jail where she works. Her list was long: "I am extremely bothered about the communication of the men where I work. Without mincing words, I'll tell you—at the county jail, officers are very degrading to women. They sometimes make fun of rape victims, they are rude and lewd to female inmates, and they are constantly trying to get me to join into the 'fun.' A woman is referred to as a 'dyke,' a 'cunt,' a 'douche bag,' a 'whore,' a 'hooker,' a 'bitch,' and I'm sure I could come up with more. The guys don't call me those names, but they use them all the time referring to other women." This sheriff also noted that she did not experience the disrespectful verbal behavior in one-on-one situations with male deputies, but only when they were in a group. She wondered out loud, "What happens to men when they get together in groups? Why is there the change?"

It is not only the male grouping phenomenon that produces this type of rough, vulgar, and sexist language. One study of a large urban police department conducted for California Law Enforcement Command College documented inappropriate communications from patrol cars' two-way radios and computers. The language on the official system was often unprofessional—rough, vulgar, offensive, racist, and sexist. Obviously, both discipline and training were needed in this agency.

Certainly, not all men behave and talk in offensive ways, but the phenomenon is frequent enough that women in traditionally male work environments mention this issue repeatedly. Some women join in conversations that make them uneasy, but they do not let on that their working environment is uncomfortable and having an impact on morale and productivity. Some women seem to be comfortable with the sexual comments of their male counterparts and may not object to the use of certain terms that other women find patronizing (e.g., sweetie, honey, babe). Furthermore, women can also speak in vulgar terms to other women, perpetuating the offensive behavior and degrading their peers. A California deputy probation officer shared that when she began her job (in 2017), a female supervisor sat her down and said, "If you want to be successful in law enforcement, you can be a bitch, a whore or a dyke. You pick. It's that or get fired."

This same officer also shared how women still, in the year 2017, fear retribution if they speak up. She said that after she got married, her male boss assumed that it would be OK to joke about sex, and asked, "Now that you are married, are you worn out?" And since this officer married her boyfriend only after a few months of knowing him, the boss assumed it would be OK or funny to ask, "Are you pregnant?" Although the officer was extremely irritated by these questions, she did not have the confidence to report her boss for fear of being ostracized. In male-dominated institutions, vocations, and professions, women find that being vocal about this type of talk and joking not only creates discomfort, but it puts them in a double bind. A female police officer at a cross-cultural training workshop on discrimination in the workplace said she felt that women's choices regarding communication with fellow male officers were limited. She explained that when a woman objects or speaks up, she risks earning a reputation or label that is hard to shed. If she remains quiet, she must tolerate a lot of verbal abuse and compromise her professionalism. This police officer decided to speak up in her own department, and, consequently, earned a reputation as a troublemaker. In fact, she had no interest in going any further than complaining to her supervisor, but nevertheless was accused of preparing for a lawsuit. She explained that a lawsuit was the farthest thing from her mind and that all she wanted was professional respect.

Though there have been gains in recent years with respect to women having more legal protection against harassment or a hostile work environment, we also know that women in all professions are still reluctant to come forward to report inappropriate conversation and communication (see Chapter 2 for a detailed discussion of sexual harassment in the law enforcement workforce).

Some women who have objected to certain mannerisms of their male counterparts' communication say that when they come into a room or office, the men stop talking. The result is that the communication that normally functions to hold a group together is strained and tense. The ultimate result is that the workplace becomes segregated by gender. When shut out from a conversation, many women feel excluded and unempowered; in turn, many men feel resentful about having to modify their style of communication.

Women in traditionally male work environments such as police, fire, and corrections find that they are sometimes put in a position of having to trade their professional identity for their personal one. A woman officer who proudly tells her sergeant about the arrest she made may be stunned when he, totally out of context, compliments the way she has been keeping in shape and tells her how good she looks in her uniform. This is not to say that compliments are never acceptable. But in this context, the woman is relating as a professional and desires reciprocal professional treatment. Men and women often ask, "Where do I draw the line? When does a comment become harassment?" In terms of the legal definition of sexual harassment, when the perpetrators are made aware that their comments are uninvited and unwelcome, then they must be reasonable enough to stop making them. It is not within the scope of this chapter to detail sexual harassment and all its legal implications (see Chapter 2). However, it should be noted that everyone has his or her own limits. What is considered harassment to one individual may be appreciated by another. When communicating across genders, each party must be sensitive to what the other party considers acceptable or insulting (see Exhibit 4.13).

Through sexual harassment policies, officers learn that patronizing terms and sexual innuendoes contribute to hostile working environments. It is the responsibility of the individual who has been offended, whether male or female, to make it clear that certain types of remarks are offensive.

Not all male-female communication difficulties fall within the realm of sexual harassment. Differences in directness and other subtleties can also play a part. Women tend to apologize more than men—for interrupting, for not being clear, or simply as a soothing phrase to make others feel comfortable. Statements from female witnesses or victims that include apologies, for example, should not necessarily be interpreted by police officers as being any less reliable than statements from males that do not include such apologies. The way women and men present themselves in professional settings also differs. "Ask a man to explain his success and he will typically credit his own innate qualities and skills. Ask a woman the same question and she will attribute her success to external factors, insisting she did well because she 'worked really hard,' or 'got lucky,' or 'had help from others'" (Sandberg, 2013).

Clearly, communication skills are vital tools for law enforcement professionals in interaction with colleagues, citizens and non-citizens alike. Effort as well as observation of and sensitivity to how other individuals "hear" or receive messages are essential components of effective communication across gender, interpersonal, and cross-cultural/racial differences.

- Use terms that are inclusive rather than exclusive. Examples: "police officer," "chairperson," "commendations" (instead of the informal "atta boys").
- Avoid using terms or words that many women feel diminish their professional status. Examples: "chick," "babe," honey, sweety, sweetheart.
- Avoid using terms or words that devalue groups of women or stereotype them. Example: Referring to women officers as "dykes"
- Avoid sexist jokes, even if you think they are not offensive. (Someone is bound to be offended; the same applies to racist jokes.)
- Avoid using terms that negatively spotlight or set women apart from men. Examples: "For a woman cop, she did a good job." This implies that this is the exception for women rather than the rule (This applies equally to references about other cultural groups: "He's Latino, but he works hard." "He's black, but he's really skilled.")

EXHIBIT 4.13 Inclusive Workplace Communication

Summary

- Communication with people for whom English is a second language can exact a great deal of patience from officers. The language barriers can lead to serious problems for non-English speakers and law enforcement. Using inappropriate interpreters can mislead officers, so much so that a victim and his or her interpreter may give two completely different versions of a story. In some cases, extra sensitivity on the part of law enforcement is needed when it comes to language obstacles. Increasing bilingual hires is one of the most practical solutions if budget allows; as an additional advantage, bilingual officers often have a better understanding of the communities they serve. At a minimum, officers should know what the basic guidelines are for communicating with speakers of other languages. In addition, officers can become sensitive to features of other languages that frequently cause confusion when limited or non-English speakers attempt to communicate in English.

- Officers' attitudes about immigrants and nonnative English speakers, whether positive or negative, are likely to affect their interaction with them. One important guideline is to refrain from making inferences about individuals based on their accent or level of fluency. From a physiological perspective, communicating in a foreign language can be exhausting and cause mental strain, potentially resulting in a person's "shutting down" or not being able to communicate in the new language. In general, limited English-speaking individuals' ability to express themselves in the second language is at its best when they are comfortable with officers. Language breakdown is one of the first signs that a person is ill at ease and stressed to the point of not being able to cooperate and communicate. It is in the officers' best interest to increase the comfort level of the people with whom they interact, whether victims, suspects, or simply people requiring help.

- Rapport-building with all citizens is essential for building trust, and this is often preliminary to people's willingness to communicate freely with officers. This is especially true when communicating with people who have relatively "high context" (indirect/implicit) communication styles. Typically, these styles are characteristic of cultural groups coming from Asian, African, and Latin American cultures. There are gender differences within cultures as well (i.e., women tend to have a higher-context style than do men). The style of communication in law enforcement is a relatively low-context (direct/explicit) communication style; police officers must understand the framework of "context" when interacting with individuals who exhibit different styles than their own.

- Officers' own filters and perceptions influence the responses they choose to exhibit in cross-cultural and cross-racial encounters. As with all people, officers have blind spots and emotional "hot buttons" that may negatively affect communication with individuals from races, ethnicities, and backgrounds different from their own. Officers may unknowingly communicate biases or a lack of comfort with members of certain groups.

- Many officers know about the importance of communicating in a manner that results in the prevention and de-escalation of confrontation. Law enforcement training, however, does not consistently or sufficiently focus on skill training designed to help officers gain mastery of de-escalation skills. Officers' facing unsafe or even life threatening situations need to establish dominance and even use force, where appropriate; this is part of the police officer's role. That said, there are also many situations where dominance and force are not needed or helpful, and only lead to escalation and major confrontation.

- Interviewing and data-gathering skills form the basic techniques for communication and intervention work with multicultural populations. For the officer, key issues include establishing interpersonal relationships to gain trust and rapport; bringing structure and control to the immediate situation; gaining information about the problems that require the presence of a law enforcement officer; giving information about law enforcement guidelines, resources, and assistance available; providing action and interventions as needed; and supporting the different parties' abilities and skills to solve current and future problems on their own.

- Nonverbal communication across cultures can have a direct impact on police/citizen interaction and police perception of behavior. Body language can include gestures, eye contact, physical or conversational distance, and the degree to which an individual is facially expressive. For law enforcement professionals working within multicultural populations, it is important to be aware of a variety of nuances and differences that may exist from one group to another.

- Officers have used styles of communication and language in the past that were considered acceptable not only within the police agency but with citizens as well. Because of cultural diversity in the population and the accompanying need to respect all individuals, the unspoken rules about what is appropriate have changed dramatically. This includes the need to use inclusive communication with women within the law enforcement profession. Through communication, officers have tremendous power to influence the behavior and responses of the citizens with whom they have contact. This is true of all citizens, regardless of background. A lack of knowledge of the cross-cultural aspects of communication will diminish that power with people whose backgrounds differ from that of the officer.

Discussion Questions and Issues

1. *Communicate with Respect.* The introduction to this chapter discusses the need to respect people from all cultural backgrounds. Ultimately, the respect an officer shows, both in verbal communication and nonverbal stance, allows people to have dignity. Describe in detail behavior that defines, for you, "respectful communication." What does it mean to give a person his or her dignity? Provide examples with your answer.

2. *The Origins of Stereotypes.* In this chapter, we argue that officers need to recognize how their early experiences in life and later adult experiences shape their perceptions and "filters" about people from groups different from their own. What do you remember learning about various ethnic and racial groups when you were young? Did you grow up in an environment of tolerance, or did you hear statements such as "That's the way they are," or "You've got to be careful with those people" or "They are lazy [or dishonest, etc.]"? Also, discuss your experiences as an adult interacting with people from different ethnic or cultural groups and how those experiences may be affecting your perceptions.

3. *Police Officer Interaction with Speakers of Other Languages.* The dialogue in Exhibit 4.3 illustrates an interaction between a police officer and a nonnative speaker of English. How would you evaluate the officer's use of English?
   A. Comment on at least the following four areas:
      (1) choice of words,
      (2) manner of asking questions,
      (3) use of idioms (there are at least two or three that could be changed to simple English), and
      (4) tone and attitude.
   B. Rewrite the officer's lines so that his English would be more easily understood by the limited English speaker.

4. *Police Officers' "Hot Buttons."* What emotionally laden language sets you off? If you are a police officer, discuss how individuals (e.g., suspects, victims, complainants) affect your reactions and communication. Specifically, what words have individuals used or attitudes have they displayed that have triggered your responses?

5. *Professional Communication with Citizens.* After you have discussed Question 4, participate in role-plays with fellow officers/students involving situations in which you must respond professionally to abusive language. Think of scenarios that you have experienced or can imagine. Then, in pairs and with an observer, act out the situation, switching roles. Have the observer comment on the quality of the officer's communication. Was it professional? Did it serve to de-escalate the situation? Did it calm the other person down?

6. *Discomfort with Unfamiliar Groups.* Try to recall a situation in which you found yourself in a culturally unfamiliar environment (e.g., responding to a call in an ethnically different household or being the only person of your background among a group of people from another cultural or ethnic group). How much discomfort, if any, did you experience? If the situation was uncomfortable, did it affect your communication effectiveness or professionalism?

7. *Accusations of Racially or Ethnically Motivated Stops.* Have you encountered, "You stopped me because I'm [any ethnic group]?" If so, how did you handle the situation? How effectively do you think you responded?

References

Bernstein, Maxine. (2011). "Portland Officers Use Tasers on 2 Men Who Had Surrendered, Costing City Almost $140,000 to Settle Lawsuits." *The Oregonian*, February 27.

Berry, Ondra. (2017). Retired Assistant Police Chief, Reno, NV, Police Department, personal communication, February.

Ewins, Teresa. (2017). Captain, San Francisco Police Department; President of SFPD Pride Alliance. San Francisco, CA, personal communication, January 24.

Gray, John. (2002). *Mars and Venus in the Workplace.* New York, NY: Harper Collins, p. 23.

Hall, Edward. (1959). *The Silent Language.* Garden City, NY: Doubleday.

Hall, Edward. (1966). *The Hidden Dimension.* Garden City, NY: Doubleday.

Hall, Edward. (1976). *Beyond Culture.* Garden City, NY: Doubleday.

Hampton, Ronald E. (2017). Retired Police Officer, DC Metropolitan Police Department. Former Executive Director of National Black Police Association. Former Adjunct Criminal Justice Professor, University of the District of Columbia, personal communication, February 2.

Ho, Christopher. (2013). Senior Staff Attorney for the Language Rights Project, Employment Law Center/Legal Aid Society, San Francisco, CA, personal communication, August.

Hofstede, Geert and Michael Minkov. (2010). *Cultures and Organizations: Software of the Mind.* New York, NY: McGraw-Hill.

Kolts, James G. and Staff. (1992, July). *The Los Angeles County Sheriff's Department*, p. 199.

Matsumoto, David, Hyi S. Hwang, Lisa Skinner, and Mark Frank. (2011, June). "Evaluating Truthfulness and Detecting Deception." *FBI Law Enforcement Bulletin.*

Matsumoto, David, Hyisung C. Hwang, and Vincent A. Sandoval. (2015, March). "Ethnic Similarities and Differences in Linguistic Indicators of Veracity and Lying in a Moderately High Stakes Scenario." *Journal of Police and Criminal Psychology*, 30(15). http://link.springer.com/article/10.1007/s11896-013-9137-7#%20-tool-for-cross-cultural-interviewing (accessed February 19, 2017).

McAllister, Daryl. (2013). Chief of Police of Union City, California Police Department, personal communication, February 28.

Mehrabian, Albert. (1971). *Silent Messages.* Belmont, CA: Wadsworth Publishing.

Navarro, Joe. (2009). "The Body Language of the Eyes." *Psychology Today*, December 11.

Sandberg, Sheryl. (2013). *Lean In: Women, Work, and the Will to Lead.* New York, NY: Alfred A. Knopf, p. 30.

Sandoval, Tony, David Matsumoto, Hyisung C. Hwang, and Lisa Skinner. (2015, July). "Exploiting Verbal Markers of Deception across Ethnic Lines: An Investigative Tool for Cross-Cultural Interviewing." *FBI Law Enforcement Bulletin*. https://leb.fbi.gov/2015/july/exploiting-verbal-markers-of-deception-across-ethnic-lines-an-investigative-tool-for-cross-cultural-interviewing (accessed February 19, 2017).

Sandoval, Vincent A. and Susan H. Adams. (2001, August). "Subtle Skills for Building Rapport." *FBI Law Enforcement Bulletin*, pp. 1–5.

Spillar, Katherine. (2017). Co-Founder of the National Center for Women and Policing and Executive Director, Feminist Majority Foundation, personal communication, January 5.

Thompson, George. (2009). Founder of the Verbal Judo Institute. http://verbaljudo.com/, personal communication, March.

Tannen, Deborah. (2001). *Talking from 9 to 5: How Women's and Men's Conversational Styles Affect Who Gets Heard, Who Gets Credit, and What Gets Done at Work*. New York, NY: Harper Collins Publishers, p. 236.

U.S. Department of Justice. (2002). "Guidance to Federal Financial Assistance Recipients Regarding Title VI Prohibition against National Origin Discrimination Affecting Limited English Proficient Persons." June 1. *Federal Register, 67*(117).

Washington State Criminal Justice Training Commission. (2017). "Justice Based Policing, Course # 1995." https://fortress.wa.gov/cjtc/www/index.php?option=com_content&view=article& (accessed April 26, 2017).

PART TWO

Cultural and Community Specifics for Law Enforcement

The first five chapters of Part Two present information on Asian/Pacific, African American, Latino/Hispanic, Arab American/Middle Eastern, and Native American cultures relevant to law enforcement and criminal justice personnel. These cultural groups were selected for one or more of the following reasons: (1) the broad group categories represent ethnic or racial groups in the United States; (2) the traditional culture of the group differs widely from that of mainstream American culture; and/or (3) typically or historically there have been problems between group members and law enforcement officials.

Chapters 5–9 present general information on demographics, historical background, and diversity within each cultural group. Also included is specific information related to stereotypes, communication styles, family structures, and key policing issues, such as racial profiling and hate crimes.

Chapter 10 discusses law enforcement contact with gangs, victims of human trafficking, the homeless, and the mentally ill, that is, groups representing additional facets of America's multicultural communities and cities. This chapter, like the previous five, raises awareness of specific group characteristics as well as issues of concern to law enforcement. The content provides officers with insight into group member behavior as well as effective interaction with members of vulnerable groups.

Important note: Part Two presents content on specific cultural, racial, and community groups. We remind readers that individuals rarely fall into neat group categories. The generalizations we present in these chapters are intended to serve as a framework only for increased awareness. These generalizations are important for basic understanding, as is the recognition that individuals may not reflect the broad descriptions of the groups to which they belong.

Each chapter ends with summary points, discussion questions, and a list of references.

- Appendix C, *Listing of Selected Gangs and Identifying Characteristics*, corresponds to content in Chapter 10.
- Appendix D, *Resources for Law Enforcement: Gangs and Human Trafficking*, corresponds to content in Chapter 10.

5 Law Enforcement Contact with Asian/Pacific Americans

LEARNING OBJECTIVES

After reading this chapter, you should be able to:

- Describe the historical background of Asian/Pacific American communities in the United States.
- Highlight selected demographic features and diversity within the population.
- Discuss the implications of group identification terms for Asian/Pacific Americans.
- Identify myths and stereotypes associated with Asian/Pacific Americans.
- Understand characteristics of traditional Asian/Pacific American extended family structures as they relate to law enforcement contact.
- Recognize communication styles used by Asian/Pacific Americans.
- Discuss key issues associated with law enforcement contact in Asian/Pacific American communities.

OUTLINE

- Introduction
- Asian/Pacific American Defined
- Historical Information
- Demographics: Diversity among Asian/Pacific Americans
- Labels and Terms
- Myths and Stereotypes
- The Asian/Pacific American Family
- Communication Styles of Asian/Pacific Americans
- Key Issues in Law Enforcement
- Summary
- Discussion Questions and Issues
- References

INTRODUCTION

For over five decades, the Asian/Pacific American (sometimes referred to as Asian American/ Pacific Islander) population has experienced the largest proportional increases of any ethnic minority population in the United States, with over 100 percent growth for the decades from 1960 to 1990, 76 percent growth for the decade from 1990 to 2000, and 46 percent growth from 2000 to 2010. This growth can be attributed to: (1) steady immigration from Pacific Rim countries; (2) relative longevity; and (3) admission of immigrants with special skills and expertise for work in high-technology industries in the United States. The numbers of Asian/Pacific Americans now living in major urban areas is particularly striking, with the highest concentrations found in New York City, Los Angeles, San Jose (CA), San Francisco, Honolulu, San Diego, Chicago, Houston, Seattle, Philadelphia, Fremont (CA), and Sacramento (CA). Increasing numbers of Asian/Pacific Americans are engaged in politics, business, education, community leadership, and public service areas. Law enforcement contact with people from the Asia/Pacific region has likewise increased because of their greater presence in communities. Asian/Pacific Americans have one of the highest naturalized citizenship rates among all foreign-born groups: approximately 58 percent of the immigrants from Asian/Pacific countries are naturalized citizens. Estimates for 2010 to 2015 show population growth slowing to approximately 30 percent (U.S. Census Bureau, 2015).

ASIAN/PACIFIC AMERICAN DEFINED

The term *Asian/Pacific Americans* is a contraction of two terms: *Asian Americans* and *Pacific Islander* peoples. Although used throughout this chapter as referring to a single ethnic/cultural group, *Asian/Pacific Americans* is, in fact, a convenient summary label for a very heterogeneous group—an ever-changing, ethnic mosaic of people from diverse backgrounds. Groups are added and removed based on self-definition and needs for self-choice. In our definition, we have not included immigrants or refugees from the South Central Asian nations of Kazakhstan, Kyrgyzstan, Tajikistan, Turkmenistan, or Uzbekistan (i.e., countries that were republics of the former Soviet Union). We also do not include certain countries that are physically located on the Asian continent even though they are listed as such in the "World Population Data Sheet" (Population Reference Bureau, 2016) because of the self-choice issue. (People from Jordan or Israel, for example, might not identify with the term "Asian.") Clearly, the pooling of separate Asian and Pacific Islander groups under the label of Asian/Pacific Americans emerged, in part, out of the necessity to have a collective whole when a large numerical count might make a difference—especially in political and community issues.

At least 40 distinct ethnic and cultural groups can be included under the Asian/Pacific American designation.

1. Bangladeshi
2. Bhutanese
3. Bruneian
4. Cambodian
5. Guamanian/Chamorro
6. Chinese
7. Fijian
8. Hawaiian (or Native Hawaiian)
9. Hmong
10. Indian (Asian)
11. Indonesian
12. Japanese
13. Kiribati
14. Korean
15. Laotian
16. Malaysian
17. Maldivian
18. Marshallese (of the Marshall Islands, to include Majuro, Ebeye, and Kwajalein)
19. Micronesian (to include Kosrae, Pohnpei, Chuuk, and Yap)
20. Mongolian
21. Myanmarese/Burmese
22. Nauruan
23. Nepalese
24. Ni-Vanuatu
25. Okinawan
26. Palauan (formerly Belauan)
27. Pakistani
28. Filipino
29. Saipan Carolinian (or Carolinian, from the Commonwealth of the Northern Marianas)
30. Samoan

31. Singaporean		**36.** Tibetan	
32. Solomon Islander		**37.** Tongan	
33. Sri Lankan (formerly Ceylonese)		**38.** Thai	
34. Tahitian		**39.** Tuvaluan	
35. Taiwanese		**40.** Vietnamese	

Exhibit 5.1 shows the six largest Asian groups in the United States, with Chinese and Filipino comprising nearly 43 percent of more than 17 million U.S. Asian groups.

While there are marked differences among the groups listed, individuals *within* any of these groups may also differ in a vast number of ways. From the viewpoint of law enforcement, it is important to recognize some of the factors that may either diverge or be common to all Asian/Pacific ethnic groups. Certain aspects of culture might be similar, for example, while English-language abilities might vary widely.

One research study (Pew Research Center, 2013) found that "62% [of Asians] say they most often describe themselves by their country of origin" (e.g., "Korean" for those whose ancestry is from Korea, or "Vietnamese" for those whose ancestry is from Vietnam); however, there may be other demographic variables of greater importance than that of nationality. For example, whether a person of Chinese descent is from the Central Asian nation of Uzbekistan, the Southeast Asian nation of Vietnam, or the Pacific Island nation of Micronesia, the demographic variable of ethnicity (being Chinese) may be a more important identifier than national origin. As another example, religion might be a more important group identifier than either ethnicity and/or nationality, as seen with some Muslims (i.e., people who practice Islam). Given that the four countries with the largest Muslim populations—Indonesia, India, Pakistan, and Bangladesh (Pew Research Center, 2015)—are in southern Asia, Asian/Pacific American people who practice Islam might see religion as a more important identifier than ethnicity or nationality.

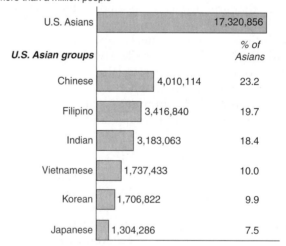

The six largest country of origin groups each number more than a million people

U.S. Asian groups		% of Asians
U.S. Asians	17,320,856	
Chinese	4,010,114	23.2
Filipino	3,416,840	19.7
Indian	3,183,063	18.4
Vietnamese	1,737,433	10.0
Korean	1,706,822	9.9
Japanese	1,304,286	7.5

EXHIBIT 5.1 The Largest U.S. Asian Groups

Source: Pew Research Center, 2013, based on Pew Research Center, 2013; U.S. Census Bureau, March 2012.

HISTORICAL INFORMATION

The first Asians to arrive in the United States in sizable numbers were the Chinese in the 1850s, who immigrated to work in the gold mines in California and later on the transcontinental railroad. In the late 1800s and early 1900s, the Chinese were followed by the Japanese and Filipinos (and in smaller numbers by Koreans and South Asian Indians). Large numbers of Asian Indians eventually entered the United States as a result of Congressional action in 1946 for "persons of races indigenous to India," as well as Filipinos, to have the right of naturalization—although both Indians and Filipinos were limited to 100 persons per year becoming naturalized citizens (Hayes, 2012). Most immigrants in those early years were men, and most worked as laborers and at other domestic and menial jobs. Until the change of the immigration laws in 1965, the number of Asian and Pacific Islander peoples coming into the United States was severely restricted, and families often had to wait a decade or longer before members could be reunited. With the change in the immigration laws, large numbers of immigrants came to the United States from Hong Kong, Taiwan, China, Japan, Korea, South Asia (e.g., India, Sri Lanka, Bangladesh), the Philippines, and other parts of Southeast Asia (e.g., Vietnam, Thailand, Singapore, Cambodia, Malaysia). After the Vietnam War, large numbers of Southeast Asian refugees were admitted in the late 1970s and early 1980s. The need for engineering and scientific expertise and skills in high-tech and Internet companies resulted in many Asian/Pacific nationals immigrating under special work visas to the United States in the late 1990s and early 2000s.

Law Enforcement Interactions with Asian/Pacific Americans

Early experiences of Asians and Pacific Islanders were characterized by the majority population's wanting to keep them out of the United States and putting tremendous barriers in the way of those who were already here. Many Asian/Pacific Americans found the passage and enforcement of "anti-Asian" federal, state, and local laws to be more hostile and discriminatory than racially motivated community incidents. It was the role of law enforcement and criminal justice agencies and officers to carry out these laws. Thus, from the beginning, the interactions of Asian/Pacific Americans with law enforcement officials were fraught with conflicts, difficulties, and mixed messages.

ANTI-ASIAN FEDERAL, STATE, AND LOCAL LAWS   Almost all early U.S. federal immigration laws were written such that their enforcement made Asian newcomers feel neither welcomed nor wanted. Following the large influx of Chinese in the 1850s to work in the gold mines and on the railroad, many Americans were resentful of the Chinese for their willingness to work long hours for low wages. With mounting public pressure, the Chinese Exclusion Act of 1882 banned the immigration of Chinese laborers for 10 years, and subsequent amendments extended this ban indefinitely. Because of this ban and because the Chinese population in the United States was predominantly male, the Chinese population in the United States dropped from 105,465 in 1880 to 61,639 in 1920 (Takaki, 1998). But the Chinese Exclusion Act applied only to the Chinese; Japanese immigration arrived in large numbers in the 1890s to work as laborers and in domestic jobs on farms on the West Coast. Similar to the case of the Chinese, public pressure to restrict Japanese immigration ensued. In the case of the Japanese, however, the Japanese government did not want a "loss of face" or loss of international prestige through having its people "banned" from immigrating to the United States. Rather, a "Gentlemen's Agreement" was negotiated with President Theodore Roosevelt in 1907, which resulted in the Japanese government voluntarily restricting the immigration of Japanese laborers to the United States. Family members of Japanese already in the United States, however, were allowed to enter. Under the Gentlemen's Agreement, large numbers of "picture brides" began entering the United States, resulting in a substantial increase in the Japanese American population—from 25,000 in 1900 to 127,000 in 1940 (Daniels, 1988). Subsequent laws banned or prevented immigration from Asian countries. The Immigration Act of 1917 banned immigration from all countries in the Pacific Rim except for the Philippines (a U.S. territory at the time). The Immigration Act of 1924 restricted migration from all countries to 2 percent of the countries' national origin population living in the United States in 1890; this went unchanged until 1965. Moreover, it was not until 1952 that most Asian immigrants were eligible to become naturalized citizens of the United States and therefore have the right to vote. (African and Native Americans were able to become citizens long before Asian/Pacific Americans were given the same rights.)

While Filipinos had been immigrating to the United States since the early 1900s, large numbers of Filipino laborers began entering in the 1920s because of the need for unskilled laborers—and due in part to the unavailability of Chinese and Japanese immigrants whose entry was restricted by law. Similar to the immigration of previous Asian groups, Filipino immigration was soon limited to a quota of 50 immigrants per year with the passage of the Tydings-McDuffie Act of 1934. Moreover, Congressional resolutions in 1935 reflected clear anti-Filipino sentiment by providing free, one-way passage for Filipinos to return home on the agreement that they would not come back to the United States.

Anti-Asian immigration laws were finally repealed starting with the removal of the Chinese Exclusion Act in 1943. Other laws were repealed to allow immigration of Asians and Pacific Islanders, but the process was slow. It was not until 1965 that amendments to the McCarran-Walter Act opened the way for Asian immigrants to enter in larger numbers (a fixed quota of 20,000 per country, as opposed to 2 percent of the country's national origin population living in the United States in 1890). The 1965 amendment also established the "fifth preference" category, which allowed highly skilled workers needed by the United States to enter. Under this category, a second major wave of immigrants from Hong Kong, Taiwan, India, Korea, the Philippines, Japan, Singapore, and other Asian countries entered in the mid-1960s. An earlier wave of South Asian immigrants (from India, Pakistan, and Sri Lanka) with expertise to help in America's space race against the Soviets led to large numbers of professional and highly educated South Asians immigrating into the United States under the "fifth preference" category after 1965. For example, 83 percent of the Asian Indians (about 60,000) who immigrated under the category of professional and technical workers between 1966 and 1977 were engineers (about 40,000) and scientists with PhDs (about 20,000) (Prashad, 2001).

The third major wave of close to one million refugees and immigrants arrived in the United States from Vietnam and other Southeast Asian countries starting in the mid-1970s and lasting through the mid-1980s. The Refugee Act of 1980: (1) established the definition for "refugee"; (2) reduced limits on the numbers of refugees entering the United States; (3) created the Office of Refugee Resettlement; and (4) permitted refugees to adjust their statuses after one year to become permanent residents, and after four more years to become U.S. citizens (Povell, 2005). From the mid-1990s to the early 2000s, the need for personnel with high-tech, engineering, and Internet skills led to an additional influx of immigrants from India, Pakistan, Singapore, Korea, China (including Hong Kong), Taiwan, and other Asian locales. Further changes in immigration policies, such as the American Competitiveness in the Twenty-First Century Act of 2000 and the H-1B Visa Reform Act of 2004, contributed to the immigration increase, particularly for immigrants with advanced degrees.

Although many immigrant groups (e.g., Italians, Jews, Poles) have been targets of discrimination, bigotry, and prejudice, Asian/Pacific Americans, like African Americans, have experienced historic legal discrimination, hindering their ability to participate fully as Americans. This discrimination has gravely affected their well-being and quality of life. Some states had laws that prohibited intermarriage between Asians and whites. State and local laws imposed restrictive conditions and taxes specifically on Asian businesses and individuals. State courts were equally biased; for example, in the case of *People v. Hall*, heard in the California Supreme Court in 1854, Hall, a white defendant, had been convicted of murdering a Chinese man on the basis of testimony provided by one white and three Chinese witnesses. The California Supreme Court threw out Hall's conviction on the basis that state law prohibited blacks, mulattos, or Indians from testifying in favor of or against whites in court. The court's decision read:

> Indian as commonly used refers only to the North American Indian, yet in the days of Columbus all shores washed by Chinese waters were called the Indies. In the second place the word "white" necessarily excludes all other races than Caucasian; and in the third place, even if this were not so, I would decide against the testimony of Chinese on the grounds of public policy. (*People v. George W. Hall*, 4 Cal. 399 [October 1854])

This section on anti-Asian/Pacific American laws and sentiments cannot close without noting that Japanese Americans are the only immigrants in the history of the United States who have been routed out of their homes and interned without due process. President Roosevelt's Executive Order 9066 resulted in the evacuation and incarceration of 100,000 Japanese Americans in 1942. For Asian/Pacific Americans, the internment of Japanese Americans represents how quickly anti-Asian sentiments can result in victimization of innocent people.

DEMOGRAPHICS: DIVERSITY AMONG ASIAN/PACIFIC AMERICANS

As noted in the section defining Asian/Pacific Americans, this is an extremely heterogeneous population comprising many different ethnic and cultural groups with educational and socioeconomic diversity as well as other background, generational, and life experience differences. (See Appendix A, "General Distinctions among Generations of Immigrants.")

Asian/Pacific Americans are currently estimated at 22.5 million and represent just over 6.5 percent of the U.S. population (U.S. Census Bureau, 2015). While longevity and birth rates have contributed to population increases, the major contributor to the growth of the Asian/Pacific American population is immigration from Pacific Rim countries. Currently, as evident in Exhibit 5.2, Chinese are the largest group comprising 23.4 percent of the total Asian/Pacific American population, followed by Asian Indians (18.9 percent) and then Filipinos (18.5 percent), Vietnamese (9.4 percent), Koreans (8.6 percent), Japanese (6.7 percent), and 14.5 percent for "all other Asian/Pacific groups." In the "all other" category, the four largest groups are, in order of their numbers: Pakistani, Cambodian, Hmong, Thai, Laotian, and Bangladeshi.

According to a Bureau of Justice report (Reaves, 2015), as of 2013 the proportion of Asian/Pacific American law enforcement officers was 2.4 percent in local police departments and 1.6 percent in sheriff offices. One way for officers to compensate for a mismatch with the population profile is to gain cultural understanding of specific cultural groups that are found in any location. Overall, the key Asian/Pacific American groups to understand are the six largest groups: Chinese, Asian Indian, Filipino, Vietnamese, Korean, and Japanese (considering, in addition, local community trends and unique qualities of the community's populations). Knowledge of growing trends among these Asian/Pacific American populations is also important for officer recruitment and other human resource considerations. Currently, the Asian/Pacific Americans involved in criminal justice careers are largely Japanese, Chinese, and Korean Americans. To accommodate the changing Asian/Pacific American population base, in certain locations it will be critical to recruit and develop officers from the Filipino, Vietnamese, and Asian Indian communities. Moreover, given the anticipated growth of the world population in the coming decades, it would be wise to recruit and develop officers with cultural knowledge, languages, and skills pertaining to China, India, Indonesia, and Pakistan—Asian nations with the largest populations (Population Reference Bureau, 2016).

More than half of all Asian/Pacific Americans are foreign-born (12.4 million) and comprise over 29 percent of the foreign-born population in the United States (U.S. Census Bureau, 2015). Five countries contributed the largest numbers of foreign-born Asian/Pacific Americans, as seen in Exhibit 5.3.

As noted earlier, foreign-born Asian/Pacific Americans constitute the second highest percentage of immigrants becoming naturalized citizens at just over 58 percent; only those born in Europe had a higher rate (U.S. Census Bureau, 2015). Many Japanese, Filipinos, Cambodians, and Indonesians reside in the western states. Chinese, Koreans, Vietnamese,

Asian/Pacific American Groups	Percentage of Total Asian/Pacific American Population
Chinese (including people from Taiwan)	23.4
Asian Indian	18.9
Filipino	18.5
Vietnamese	9.4
Korean	8.6
Japanese	6.7
All other Asian/Pacific groups	14.5
All Asian/Pacific Americans	100.00

EXHIBIT 5.2 Asian/Pacific American Population by Groups

Source: Calculated from American Community Survey data (U.S. Census Bureau, 2015).

Location of Birth	Number of Foreign-Born
China, Hong Kong, Taiwan	2,444,610
India	2,114,754
Philippines	1,902,486
Vietnam	1,291,135
Korea	1,078,555

EXHIBIT 5.3   Distribution of Foreign-Born Asian/Pacific Americans by Country of Birth
Source: American Community Survey data (U.S. Census Bureau, 2015).

Laotians, and Thais are widely distributed in the large urban areas of the United States. Many Asian Indians and Pakistanis live in the eastern states, with a secondary concentration in Texas. The cities of Minneapolis, Minnesota, and Fresno, California, have the largest Hmong populations in the country (Pfeifer, Sullivan, Yang, & Yang, 2012). Proficiency in English language varies within groups: groups that have immigrated most recently (Southeast Asians) have the largest percentage of those unable to speak English well.

Law enforcement officers, depending on their jurisdictions, need to determine what additional languages and skills training might be appropriate in their work with Asian/Pacific American communities.

For many Asian/Pacific American groups, especially those that have recently immigrated into the United States, the law enforcement system is somewhat of a mystery. Thus, some Asian/Pacific American newcomers may initially hesitate to communicate openly or cooperate with police.

> In Vietnam, if you are arrested, then the work of the attorney is to prove that you are innocent. You remain locked up in jail until your innocence is proven. In the United States, a suspect who is arrested is released either upon posting bail or on their own recognizance, usually within 24 hours. To the Vietnamese immigrant, it would seem that if you have the money, you can buy your way out of jail! (Vietnamese community advocate's comments at a community meeting about a local merchant's reluctance to cooperate with police)

LABELS AND TERMS

As noted earlier, the term *Asian/Pacific Americans* is a convenient summarizing label used to refer to a heterogeneous group of people. There is no universal acceptance of this labeling convention, but for practical purposes it has been adopted frequently, with occasional variations (e.g., Asian and Pacific Americans, Asian Americans/Pacific Islanders, Asians and Pacific Islanders). As of 1997, the U.S. government divided this group into two categories: "Asian" and "Native Hawaiian and Other Pacific Islander." Which particular terms are used is based on the principle of self-designation and self-preference. Asian and Pacific Islander people are sensitive about the issue because until the 1960 census, the population was relegated to the "Other" category. With the ethnic pride movement and ethnic minority studies movement in the late 1960s, people of Asian and Pacific Islands descent began to designate self-preferred terms for group reference. The terms were chosen over the previous term *Oriental*, which many Asian/Pacific Americans consider to be offensive. *Oriental* symbolizes to many the past references, injustices, and stereotypes of Asian and Pacific people. It was also a term designated by those in the West (i.e., the Occident/Western Hemisphere) for Asian people, and reminds many Asian/Pacific Americans of the colonial mentality and its effects on Pacific Rim countries (not to mention that it is most often used to refer to carpets!).

By individuals within any of the groups, as previously mentioned, often the more specific names for the groups are preferred (e.g., Chinese, Japanese, Vietnamese, Pakistani, Hawaiian). Some individuals may prefer that the term *American* be part of their designation (e.g., Korean American, Filipino American). For law enforcement officers, it is best to ask individuals which ethnic or cultural group(s) they identify with and what they prefer to be called.

The use of slurs such as "Jap," "Chink," "Gook," "Chinaman," "Flip," and other derogatory ethnic slang terms is never acceptable in crime fighting and peacekeeping, no matter how provoked an officer may be. The use of other stereotype depictions, including "Chinese fire drill," "DWA (Driving While Asian)," "Fu Man Chu mustache," "Kamikaze kid," "yellow cur," "yellow peril," "Bruce Lee Kung Fu type," "slant-eyed," "towel head," "Vietnamese bar girl," and "dragon lady," does not convey the professionalism and respect for community diversity important to law enforcement and must be avoided. Officers hearing these words used in their own departments (or with peers or citizens) should immediately provide helpful feedback about such terms to those who use them. Officers who, out of habit, routinely use these words may find themselves or their superiors in the embarrassing situation—in other words, on the evening news—of having to explain to offended citizens and communities why these terms were used.

MYTHS AND STEREOTYPES

Knowledge of and sensitivity to Asian/Pacific Americans' concerns, diversity, historical background, and life experiences will facilitate the crime-fighting and peacekeeping missions of law enforcement officers. It is important to have an understanding about some of the myths, environmental messages, and stereotypes of Asian/Pacific Americans that contribute to the prejudice, discrimination, and bias they encounter. Many Americans do not have much experience with the diversity of Asian/Pacific American groups and learn about these groups only through stereotypes, often perpetuated by movies and the media. The effect of myths and stereotypes is to reduce Asian/Pacific Americans to simplistic, one-dimensional characters whom people then lump into one stereotypic group. Often, the complexities of the diverse Asian/Pacific American groups in terms of language, history, customs, cultures, religions, and life experiences become confusing and threatening, and it is easier to deal with stereotypes. Nonetheless, it is important for law enforcement officers to be aware of the different stereotypes of Asian/Pacific Americans. The key to effectiveness with any ethnic or racial group is not the complete elimination of myths and stereotypes about the group, but rather the awareness of these stereotypes and management of one's behavior when the stereotypes are not true of the person with whom one is dealing.

Some of the stereotypes that have affected Asian/Pacific Americans in the law enforcement context include the following:

1. *Viewing Asian/Pacific Americans as "all alike."* That is, because there are many similarities in names, behavior, and physical features, many law enforcement officers make comments about their inability to tell people apart, or may deal with Asians in group fashion (e.g., they are all "inscrutable"; involved in gangs).

2. *Viewing Asian/Pacific Americans as successful "model minorities" or as a "super minority."* Some hold the stereotype that Asian/Pacific Americans are all successful, which is further reinforced by the media (Kawai, 2005; Wang, 2015). This has resulted in intergroup hostilities and hate crimes directed toward Asian/Pacific Americans and has served to mask true differences and diversity among the various Asian and Pacific Islander groups. Some Asian/Pacific American groups have had to highlight the inaccurate perceptions of the "model minority" stereotype. The language barriers and adjustment issues associated with new immigrant groups affect the cohesiveness of some Asian families, contributing to delinquency among youth and high crime rates (e.g., Southeast Asian youth in the San Francisco Bay Area). Thus, the model minority stereotype does not apply across the board, yet is a common stereotype when people do not recognize distinctions among and within groups.

   Clearly, no group of people can be "all successful" or "all criminals." Nonetheless, the educational or financial "success" and the "model minority" stereotypes have affected Asian/Pacific Americans negatively. For example, because of their implied success, law enforcement organizations may not spend the time to recruit Asian/Pacific American individuals for law enforcement careers (assuming that they are more interested in other areas such as education and business pursuits). This stereotype also hides the existence of real discrimination for those who are successful, as seen in glass (or "bamboo") ceilings in promotional and developmental opportunities, for example. The success stereotype has resulted in violence and crimes against Asian/Pacific persons. One example etched in the memories of many Asian/Pacific Americans is representative of issues very salient to Asian/Pacific Americans today.

> The murder of Vincent Chin, and the subsequent inability of the court system to bring the murderers to justice, is now a well-known case among Asian/Pacific American communities. The perpetrators in this case, Ronald Ebens and Michael Nitz, were two white automobile factory workers who blamed Vincent Chin (a Chinese American) for the success of the Japanese automobile industry that was, in turn, blamed for taking away American jobs in the automobile factory. (Takaki, 1989)

More recent examples include a 2010 attack on Asian American high school students in Philadelphia which necessitated the hospitalization of 13 students (Thompson, 2009), and a series of robberies and other crimes targeting Asian American residents of the Sacramento, California, area in 2016 (Chang, 2016).

3. *Viewing some Asian/Pacific Americans as possible "foreign" terrorists because of their skin color, religious affiliation, and/or native dress.* Many Asian/Pacific Americans immigrate from countries with large populations that practice Islam (e.g., Indonesia, Pakistan, Bangladesh, and India) and stay close to their cultural traditions and native dress. It is unfortunate that people sometimes come to inappropriate conclusions about who might be a "foreign" terrorist based solely on such outward appearances. In addition, Sikhs—who wear turbans and grow beards—originate in India and Pakistan and are often mistaken for Muslims. These types of examples spiked following the 9/11 tragedy—one of the first suspects detained for questioning was a Sikh who was wearing a turban and was misidentified as an Afghani Taliban member (who also wear turbans, but different kinds); additionally, South Asians (e.g., Bengalis) with dark skin tones were misidentified as Arabs and detained for questioning on homeland security issues.

   In one widely publicized 2012 case, a Sikh temple in Wisconsin was the scene of a shooting that left six people dead and three others wounded (Yaccino, Schwirtz, & Santora, 2012). A separate incident in 2017 involved a Navy veteran who believed that he was shooting "two Iranians" in a bar in Olathe, Kansas; the two men were from India. One was killed and the other wounded (Young & DiGiacomo, 2017).

   From a law enforcement perspective, many hate crimes against Asian/Pacific Americans are related to the stereotyping of the group as foreigners and not Americans.

4. *Misunderstanding Asian/Pacific cultural differences and practices and viewing differences as a threat to other Americans.* The more than 40 Asian/Pacific American groups encompass great differences in languages, backgrounds, cultures, and life experiences. When we lack specific information about any group, it is natural to draw conclusions based on our own stereotypes, assumptions, and filtering systems. Most of the time, inappropriate assumptions and stereotypes are modified by favorable contact and actual interpersonal relationships with Asian/Pacific American people. From a law enforcement perspective, the thrust of community policing, as well as cultural competency training, is to provide opportunities to modify stereotypes and learn about ethnic communities. Law enforcement agencies, however, have to intervene in situations in which individuals and/or groups view Asian/Pacific American cultural differences as perceived threats. Stereotypical and racially biased views of Asian/Pacific Americans as threats require the ongoing attention of law enforcement agencies.

THE ASIAN/PACIFIC AMERICAN FAMILY

With so many different cultural groups falling under the label of Asian/Pacific Americans, great differences exist in how families operate within the various subgroups. There are, however, certain common characteristics of Asian/Pacific American families that might be of value in crime fighting and community peacekeeping. These families generally exhibit very strong ties among family members, and it is not unusual for three to four generations of the same family to live under one roof. Moreover, the extended family can have an ongoing relationship network that spans great geographic distances. For example, family members (all of whom consider themselves as one unit) can be engaged in extensive communications and activities with members of the same family in the United States, Canada, Hong Kong, and Vietnam, all simultaneously. It is not uncommon for an officer to come into contact with members of the extended Asian/Pacific American family in the course of servicing these communities.

Culture Shock and the Asian/Pacific American Family

Because the traditional cultures of Asia and the Pacific Islands are so very different from that of the United States, many Asian/Pacific American families (whether refugees, immigrants, businesspersons, students, or tourists) experience some degree of culture shock when they enter and reside in the United States. Culture shock results not only from differences in values and traditions but also from differences in urbanization, industrialization, and modernization owing to technology that may be different from that in their homeland. Police officers need to be aware that Asian/Pacific Americans may cope with their culture shock by becoming "clannish" (e.g., Chinatowns, Koreatowns). Other survival mechanisms include avoiding contact and interaction with those who are different, including police officers. One key to the success of law enforcement officers in working with Asian/Pacific Americans is the knowledge of how best to communicate with families residing in these "clannish" communities, and which family members to speak to for information, help, and referral.

The Roles of Family Members

In most traditional Asian/Pacific American families, relationship and communication patterns tend to be hierarchical, with an elder such as a parent or grandparent as the head of the household. Although many decisions and activities may appear to be determined by the elder, other individuals may be influential. Generally, if there are grandparents in the household, the parent might act as the spokesperson for the family, but would consult the grandparents and others regarding any major decision. It is important in any kind of law enforcement contact that requires a decision and/or choice to allow the family time to discuss issues in, as much as feasible, a "private" manner. This might involve giving the family members an extensive amount of time to speak among themselves in their native language, which some Americans find excruciatingly uncomfortable. In addition, self-control and keeping things within the family are key values for Asian/Pacific Americans. An officer thus may find that there is more leverage in a situation by allowing an Asian/Pacific American to come to the same conclusion as the officer with respect to a situation. For example, the officer can explain an arrest situation to an elder family member, and instead of saying directly to the individual to be arrested that he or she has to leave with the officer, the officer can allow the elder to suggest to the family member that he or she leave with the officer. What may appear to be a minor consideration in this case can result in a great degree of persuasion, control, and cooperation by all parties concerned.

Although there are no clear-cut rules as to whether one goes to a male head of the household or to a female head to make a law enforcement inquiry, it should be noted that for most Asian/Pacific American families, the role of the mother in discipline and decision-making is very important. In other words, even when a household appears to be controlled by a father or grandfather, the women's roles could be major.

Children, Adolescents, and Youths

Most Asian/Pacific American families comprise at least two or more individuals within the same household working outside of the home. Thus, if young children are present, there is a high reliance on either family members or others to help care for them while the parents are at work. It is not uncommon for older children to care for younger children within a household.

In recent immigrant and refugee families, Asian/Pacific American children have a special role in being the intermediaries between parents and the external community because of the ability of the younger individuals to learn English and American ways of doing things. Children often serve as interpreters for officers in their communication and relations with

Asian/Pacific American families comprising recent immigrants and refugees, which can put the children in extremely awkward situations. Officers should review the role expected of a young family member and determine how sensitive any translated content might be to the different family members and the consequences if messages are interpreted incorrectly. For example, asking a juvenile to interpret for his or her parents who speak no English when the juvenile has been involved in a sexual abuse situation at school may result in significant omissions and/or changed content because of shame. Likewise, due to the emphasis on hierarchy in most Asian families, children will dutifully tell police officers whatever an elder family member says at the time, even if the child knows the information to be false. Thus, it is extremely wise to procure the services of an interpreter when interviewing Asian families. And in all cases, even when a child is acting as an interpreter, officers should direct communication to elder family members lest they view the officers' lack of attention to them as an insult.

Asian/Pacific American Family Violence

Research studies on family violence (e.g., spousal physical abuse, child abuse, sexual abuse) by Asian/Pacific Americans show an increasing trend. Possible explanations for this increase include the overall growth of the Asian/Pacific population in the United States, improved data collection efforts and methods, and enhanced awareness of family violence issues within various ethnic groups. In any case, it is only during recent decades that researchers and community advocates have begun collecting nationwide data on family violence among Asian/Pacific Americans. The National Latino and Asian American Study, conducted in 2002–2003, found that over 10 percent of Asian Americans had experienced "minor violence" (e.g., shoving, slapping) and about 2 percent had experienced "major violence" (e.g., choking, threatening with a weapon) (Chang et al., 2009). A study released in 2010 (Dabby, Patel, & Poore) showed that 78 percent of homicides involving Asian/Pacific Americans were perpetrated by intimate partners of their victims. (Only 10 percent of perpetrators were female; 90 percent were male.)

One factor that limits data collection attempts is that keeping sensitive issues within the family and using self-help and personal effort strategies are part of Asian/Pacific cultural values and norms. As one researcher explains, " … social science research reveals shared cultural norms among Asian American women that may inhibit help-seeking behavior, and a common context of patrilocality [physical proximity to one's patrilineal family], economic dislocation, and isolation related to immigration" (Lee, 2015). And unfortunately, as researchers Cho and Kim (2012) point out, "Asian victims of IPV [intimate partner violence] are less likely to use mental health services than any other racial groups. The odds of other racial groups seeking mental health services [are] more than four times those for Asians." The availability of multilingual outreach services is of key importance to the Asian/Pacific American community.

The role of officers in detecting, assessing, and intervening in family violence situations within Asian/Pacific American communities is a critical one given this area of increasing needs and problems. The sensitivity of law enforcement representatives to cultural influences and patterns of communication (as noted in the next section) will be significant in the effective gathering of initial information and subsequent referral and interventions with Asian/Pacific American families involved in domestic violence and other issues of abuse.

COMMUNICATION STYLES OF ASIAN/PACIFIC AMERICANS

There are key generalizations that can be made concerning Asian/Pacific American verbal and nonverbal communication styles. Misunderstandings resulting from style differences can lead to conflicts and perceptions of poor service from police agencies, as well as safety and control issues for officers.

1. It is important that officers take the time to get information from witnesses, victims, and suspects even if individuals speak limited English. The assistance of interpreters, language-bank resources, and officers who speak Asian/Pacific dialects or languages can greatly enhance this process. Often Asian/Pacific Americans have not been helped

in crime-fighting and peacekeeping situations because officers could not or did not take information from individuals who could not speak English well.

2. Asian/Pacific Americans tend to hold a greater "family" and/or "group" orientation than mainstream Americans. As such, the lack of the use of "I" statements and/or self-reference should not be evaluated as being evasive. Officers may be concerned because an Asian/Pacific American may use the pronoun "we" when the situation calls for a personal observation involving an "I" statement. For example, concerning a traffic accident, the Asian/Pacific American may describe what he or she saw by saying, "We saw . . . . " Using such group statements to convey what the individual saw is consistent with the family and group orientation of Asian/Pacific Americans. Another area of some concern to law enforcement is the tendency of certain Asian-language speakers to confuse pronouns, switching back and forth between "he" and "she" to refer to an individual. One reason for this is that in some languages, such as various spoken dialects of Chinese, there is no difference in the pronunciation of "he" and "she." Be patient when taking witness statements or during interrogations; Asian Americans are not trying to be deceptive, and any nervousness on their part—or any sense that an officer is becoming impatient—will only make matters worse.

3. Officers should be aware that for many Asian/Pacific Americans, it is considered rude and involves a "loss of face" (for the officers; not for the speaker) to directly say "no" to an authority figure. Officers must understand the following possibilities when an answer of "yes" is heard from an Asian/Pacific American. It can mean (1) "Yes, I heard what you said (but I may or may not agree with you)"; (2) "Yes, I understand what you said (but I might not do it)"; (3) "Yes, I can see this is important for you (but I do not share your sense of urgency)"; or (4) "Yes, I agree (and will do what you said)." Because both the context of the communication and nonverbal aspects of the message are equally meaningful, it is vital for law enforcement officers to be sure of the "yes" answers received, as well as of other language nuances from Asian/Pacific Americans. Two examples might be illustrative: (a) If an Asian/Pacific American says that he or she will "try his or her best to attend," this generally means that he or she will not be there, especially for voluntary events and situations such as community neighborhood safety meetings. (b) If an Asian/Pacific national says in response to a question "It is possible," this generally means, "Do not wait for it to happen." Such communications, as noted previously, may be more applicable to some Asian/Pacific Americans than others, but sensitivity on the part of law enforcement officers to these language nuances will facilitate understanding. In a communication situation in which the response of "yes" may be ambiguous, it is suggested that law enforcement officers rephrase the question so that the requested outcome in action and understanding is demonstrated in the verbal response. For example:

   Asking a yes/no question that prompts an ambiguous response:

   OFFICER: "I need you to show up in court on Tuesday. Do you understand?"

   ASIAN WITNESS: "Yes!"

   (*Providing context and rephrasing the question to elicit a response that shows understanding and outcome:*)

   OFFICER: "It is important to tell this information to a judge. How will you come to court on Tuesday?"

   ASIAN WITNESS: "Yes. My brother has a car. He will take me to court on Tuesday."

4. Asian/Pacific Americans tend to be "high context" (indirect; implicit) in communication style. This means that officers must provide both interpersonal and situational context for effective communication. Context for Asian/Pacific Americans means that members of the community know the officers in the community. Community members may have had previous working relationships with the officers (e.g., crime prevention meetings; police athletic league). Moreover, other members of the community may help to provide information and context for police cooperation based on past relationships. Context also means providing explanations and education to Asian/Pacific American individuals or groups about procedures and laws before asking them questions and/or

requesting their participation in an activity. By providing background information and establishing prior community relationships, Asian/Pacific American individuals have context for cooperating with law enforcement agencies and officers.

5. Be aware of nonverbal and other cultural nuances that may detract from effective communication between officers and members of the Asian/Pacific American community. Many Asian/Pacific Americans find it uncomfortable and inappropriate to maintain eye contact with those of higher status, or with authority figures like police officers. As such, many Asian/Pacific Americans look down at the ground and/or avert their eyes while talking. Police officers should not automatically read this nonverbal behavior as indicating a lack of trust or respect, or as dishonesty. Likewise, police officers should be aware of possible nonverbal gestures and actions that may detract from their professional roles. For example, in many Asian cultures, gesturing with a curled index finger for a person to come forward is used primarily for servants, children, and/or dogs. It would be more polite for an officer to call someone over using all fingers together in a sweeping motion rather than use the index finger only.

6. Asian/Pacific Americans may not display emotions in ways that officers expect. The central thesis guiding some Asian/Pacific Americans is the Confucian notion of "walking the middle road." This means that extremes—too much or too little of anything—are not good. As such, Asian/Pacific Americans tend to moderate displays of positive and/or negative emotion. Often, in crisis situations, nonverbal displays of emotions are controlled to the point that the affect of the Asian/Pacific American appears "flat." However, it is not uncommon for Asians to laugh when nervous, which is the opposite of what most Americans expect. Under such circumstances, the officer needs to correctly understand and appropriately interpret unemotional or unexpected behavior. For example, just because the parent of a murder victim does not appear shaken by an officer's report does not mean that the person is not experiencing a severe emotional crisis.

KEY ISSUES IN LAW ENFORCEMENT

Underreporting of Crimes

Asian/Pacific Americans, because of their past experiences with certain law enforcement agencies (e.g., anti-Asian immigration laws; health and sanitation code violations in restaurants; perceived unresponsiveness by police), are often reluctant to report crimes and may not seek police assistance and help. Many Asian/Pacific Americans remember how police in their home countries brutalized and violated them and others (e.g., in Southeast Asian and other Asian countries). Crimes that occur within a family's home (e.g., home invasion; family violence) or within the confines of a small family business (e.g., robbery of a Chinese restaurant) often go unreported unless these crimes are connected to larger criminal activities.

Many immigrants and refugees are simply not knowledgeable about the legal system of the United States and therefore avoid any contact with law enforcement personnel. Outreach and community-policing efforts will enhance the contact and relationship with Asian/Pacific American communities, helping to correct the underreporting of crimes.

Asian/Pacific American Community and Law Enforcement Interaction

Increasingly, when there are collaborative and cooperative efforts among law enforcement, criminal justice, and community advocacy systems, Asian/Pacific American communities begin to gain trust and confidence resulting from effective multicultural and multidisciplinary law enforcement actions. Numerous "Citizen Police Academies" exemplify how police, community advocates, and citizens join together to collaborate on police services in the Asian community. The programs are intended to open lines of communication with the police and to help individuals and communities understand the complexities of its policies and regulations.

The Los Angeles Police Department Airport Police Bureau was one of the first units to establish storefront outreach efforts that resulted in improved police–community relationships and better service benefits to the Asian/Pacific American neighborhood in the Korean area of Los Angeles (Chin, 1985). Storefront outreach efforts are now utilized in most urban centers with large Asian/Pacific American communities such as San Francisco, New York, Oakland, Chicago, Boston, and Seattle. (Chapter 1 presented information on various types of community policing outreach.) Another example of an outreach approach is the use of Asian/Pacific American bilingual community service officers (CSOs)—nonsworn officers with badges and uniforms—who provide police department supportive services to Southeast Asian communities in San Diego, California.

Increasing Asian/Pacific American Police Officers

There is a noticeable underrepresentation of Asian/Pacific Americans in federal, state, and local law enforcement and criminal justice positions. According to a survey conducted by the Bureau of Justice Statistics, of over 477,000 full-time local police officers, less than 3 percent were Asian/Pacific Islanders (Reaves, 2015). Additional research comparing EEOC (U.S. Equal Employment Opportunity Commission) and Bureau of Justice data with Census results found underrepresentation of Asian Americans in police departments averaging 31–33 percentage points relative to local area populations (Governing, 2015; U.S. Department of Justice/EEOC, 2016).

The small numbers of Asian/Pacific American officers have hampered many departments in neighborhoods with large Asian/Pacific American populations in serving those communities effectively with appropriate role models and bicultural expertise. A variety of reasons exist for such underrepresentation, including: (1) the history of law enforcement relationships with Asian/Pacific American communities; (2) interest (or more specifically, the lack thereof) of Asian/Pacific Americans in law enforcement careers, to some extent due to the perception of a "bamboo ceiling" of limited career advancement possibilities; (3) the image of law enforcement personnel in Asian/Pacific American communities; (4) a lack of knowledge about the different careers and pathways in law enforcement (again, exacerbated by the "bamboo ceiling" perception); (5) concern with and fear of background checks, physical requirements, and the application process; and (6) a limited number of role models and advocates for law enforcement careers within Asian/Pacific American communities. With growing Asian/Pacific American populations in areas throughout the United States, law enforcement has begun to emphasize the importance of diversity in its recruitment efforts.

Tailored recruitment and hiring efforts can take a variety of forms, such as the use of social media, outreach to K-12 schools, and a presence at community events (U.S. Department of Justice/EEOC, 2016). Cities that have responded to the specific need for more Asian/Pacific American police officers include Des Moines, Iowa, which created the full-time position of Asian Outreach Resource Officer in 2007. In Austin, Texas, a former 911 operator who is Vietnamese is now in charge of the police department's Asian Immigrant Outreach Program, coordinating police presence at events such as Chinese new year celebrations; efforts to hire Asian officers are ongoing (Fan, 2015).

Hate Crimes against Asian/Pacific Americans

By far, the greatest number of hate crimes motivated by racial bias is targeted toward black Americans (see Chapter 6). However, such crimes extend beyond racism associated with skin color. Immigrant Americans and those who are *perceived* to be immigrants are often scapegoated as responsible for the poor state of the economy, a lack of jobs, and the failure of some to get ahead. Asian/Pacific immigrants, whether first-, second-, third- or fourth-generation Americans, are often lumped into one category—"immigrant."

> In examining the underlying and historical context for these hate crimes, it is important to note that the persistent stereotype of Asian Americans as "perpetual foreigners" has fueled discrimination, hostility, and even violence against Asian American and NHPI [Native Hawaiian and Pacific

Islander] individuals. Political or economic tensions between the U.S. and Asian countries during rough economic times have also led to increased violence against Asian Americans and NHPIs in the past. More recently, inflammatory rhetoric targeting immigrants has instigated an increase in hate-based violence against those perceived to be immigrants—including Asian Americans and NHPIs. (APALC, 2012)

In August 2013, the Department of Justice announced that a number of additional groups would be included in the national program that tracks hate crime, that is, the Uniform Crime Reporting Program (discussed in Chapter 11). These groups include individuals from South Asia such as Sikhs and Hindus, as well as Buddhists who are from many different parts of Asia. Speaking as a member of the Congressional Asian Pacific American Caucus (CAPAC), California Congressman Ami Bera stated:

> I am pleased that Director Mueller has approved the FBI Advisory Policy Board's recommendation to add several categories in its tracking of hate crimes, including offenses committed against Sikh, [and] Hindu … Americans. As we near the one-year anniversary of the tragic Oak Creek shootings where six Sikh Americans were killed in a horrific hate crime, I am confident this change will protect domestic civil rights and aid law enforcement in securing our communities. By ensuring that all Americans—regardless of religion, race, gender or creed—feel safe in their communities, we can heal our families and honor the memories of those killed in Oak Creek. (CAPAC, 2013)

In 2015, there were just over 6,800 hate crime offenses motivated by racial bias (i.e., single-bias), based on data collected and presented in this new format. More than 3 percent of those offenses were targeted toward Asian/Pacific Americans (i.e., there were other hate crimes reported vis-à-vis individuals reporting to be more than one race). Additional data shows that among the more than 1,300 religious-bias offenses, 22 percent were anti-Islamic (Muslim). Small percentages were anti-Sikh, anti-Hindu, or anti-Buddhist (under 1 percent each) (FBI, 2015).

Crimes within Asian/Pacific American Communities

Many crimes committed in Asian/Pacific American communities, particularly among Asian/Pacific refugee and Asian/Pacific immigrant groups, are perpetrated by members from within the same community. Law enforcement officials have often found it difficult to get cooperation from refugee and immigrant victims of human trafficking, extortion, home robbery, burglary, theft, and other crimes. In part, the lack of cooperation stems from a fear of retaliation by the criminals, who are often known to the victims. Other concerns of Asian/Pacific American victims include: (1) the perceived level of responsiveness of officers and agencies; (2) a lack of familiarity with and trust in police services; (3) the perceived level of effectiveness of law enforcement agencies; and (4) prior stereotypes and images of law enforcement agencies as discriminatory (e.g., immigration laws) and unresponsive to crimes against Asian/Pacific Americans. Recent Asian/Pacific American refugees and immigrants are often prime targets, in part because of their distrust of most institutions (e.g., banks; police departments; hospitals). As a result, they are more inclined to hide and store cash and other valuables in their homes. A key challenge for police agencies is to educate this group and to work cooperatively with Asian/Pacific Americans to reduce crime within these communities.

Human trafficking has been highlighted as one of the crimes perpetrated by Asian/Pacific Americans on others within their own communities. The International Labour Organization estimates that more than 20.9 million people worldwide (including 11.7 million from the Asia-Pacific region) are victims of forced labor (ILO, 2012). (See Chapter 10 for further discussion of cultural groups and nationalities affected by human trafficking.) The largest flow of human trafficking to the United States comes from East Asia (United Nations, 2016).

Human trafficking The transportation of persons for sexual exploitation, forced labor, or other illegal or criminal activities.

Human trafficking has become a global business, with many victims coming from Asian countries; such illegal activities "generate vast profits from the exploitation of victims in myriad ways" (United Nations, 2016). Because of its secretive and hidden nature, human trafficking is likely to remain an increasingly underreported crime. Victims, especially those who are sexually exploited, are typically brainwashed by traffickers into thinking that they are criminals instead of victims. Many women—and sometimes men—brought to the United States have been told that they will be given legitimate, relatively lucrative jobs; financial conditions at home leave them desperate to believe the traffickers' tales. A rather rosy image of life in America, portrayed via television and other media, raises their hopes. In one case in Minnesota:

> [Tieu] Tran recruited a woman from Vietnam to travel to the United States using false promises of legal immigration status and a high-paying job. In reality, Tran smuggled the victim and two other Vietnamese nationals across the southern U.S.-Mexico border, imposed a significant debt upon the victim and forced the victim to pay down the smuggling debt by working at Tran's son's Vietnamese restaurant … (U.S. Department of Justice, 2014)

Law enforcement officers' involvement with Asian/Pacific American communities on human trafficking has emerged as one of the major areas of their work. Estimates range from 100,000 to 300,000 American-born children, annually, who are sold into the sex trade. The FBI and other law enforcement agencies have initiated numerous national programs to help combat this phenomenon. In 2016, the FBI led an international collaboration—"Operation Cross Country X"—resulting in 82 minors being rescued, and over 200 traffickers and their associates being arrested (FBI, 2016). (Further details about Operation Cross Country X can be found in Chapter 10, section on Victims of Human Trafficking.)

Many trafficking victims are young immigrants or the children of immigrants whose parents face extreme poverty in the United States and continue to be traumatized by memories of war or genocide. In northern California, a particular demand for Cambodian American girls has been reported (Brown, 2011). These girls and young women are from families whose parents and grandparents experienced or escaped from one of the worst tragedies in modern history. (The Cambodian genocide resulted in the killing of 1.7 million people or 21 percent of the population [CGP, 2013].) Within a Cambodian family, the emotional scars from genocide are likely to be passed on from generation to generation, and the fallout affecting family dynamics is considerable. Human trafficking abusers can be family members (e.g., brothers as pimps). Many domestic minors forced into the sex trade still live with parents, and end up working in massage parlors or strip clubs, with escort services, or even as acupuncturists (Professor Richard J. Estes, University of Pennsylvania, as quoted in Brown, 2011).

Families whose members have been victims of violence and genocide often fear law enforcement and do not ask for help. Law enforcement professionals have to work hard at building relationships and encouraging such victims to open up.

> Perhaps most important in these cases is earning the trust of the victims of commercial sexual exploitation. These cases often require the victims' willingness to cooperate in the investigation and, ultimately, testify against these defendants. Where trust is established with the victim, these victims will often notify detectives with new cell phone numbers, addresses and changes in work status. Even simple changes in outreach can make a difference. For example, recognizing that most of these individuals are awake at night and have cell phone contact that is viable at night means regular contact is more likely. Limiting victim outreach to the 8 a.m. to 5 p.m. workday, on the other hand, precludes most reasonable chances of staying in touch with the victims in these cases. (Tiapula & Turkel, 2008)

Worldwide efforts to end this situation are being led by the United Nations with the "Trafficking in Persons Protocol," which entered into force in 2003. As of October 2016, 170 countries had ratified the Protocol (United Nations, 2016).

Summary

- As a result of early immigration laws and other discriminatory treatment received by Asian/Pacific Americans in the United States, the experiences of Asian/Pacific Americans with law enforcement officials have been fraught with conflicts, difficulties, and mixed messages. Some Asian/Pacific Americans remember this history and carry with them images of police services as something to be feared and avoided. Law enforcement officials may need to go out of their way to establish trust and to win cooperation in order to accomplish their goals effectively when serving and protecting Asian/Pacific Americans.

- The label Asian Americans/Pacific Islanders encompasses over 40 very diverse ethnic and cultural groups. Significant differences exist among these groups (e.g., different cultures and languages) in addition to differences *within* the groups as a result of individual life and generational experiences. While it is difficult to understand individual subtleties within these communities, officers can learn about the various motivational determinants of individuals within different generational and immigrant groups.

- The preferred term for referring to Asian/Pacific Americans varies with context, groups, and individual preferences. Law enforcement officials need to be aware of terms that are unacceptable and derogatory as well as terms that are preferred. When in doubt, officers should ask Asian/Pacific Americans which terms they prefer. Officers are advised to provide helpful feedback to peers when offensive terms, labels, and/or actions are used concerning Asian/Pacific Americans. This will reduce the risk of misunderstanding and improve the working relationships between officers and Asian/Pacific American communities. Moreover, it will enhance the professional image of the department within those communities.

- The complexities of the diverse Asian/Pacific American groups in terms of language, history, customs, cultures, religions, and life experiences can be confusing and threatening. Accordingly, it can be easy to fall back on stereotypes of these groups. A key stereotype of great concern to Asian/Pacific Americans is that they are regarded by mainstream Americans as being very much alike. It is important that police officers show awareness of diversity among Asian/Pacific Americans. Some hold the stereotype that Asian/Pacific Americans are all successful; this stereotype is further reinforced by the media. Such stereotypes have resulted in intergroup hostilities and hate crimes directed toward Asian/Pacific Americans.

- With so many cultural groups falling under the label of Asian/Pacific Americans, we find great differences in how families operate within the various subgroups. There are also commonalities. Asian/Pacific American families generally exhibit very strong ties among extended family members. It is not unusual for three to four generations of the same family to live under one roof. One key to the success of law enforcement officers in working with Asian/Pacific American families is knowledge of how best to address family members for information, help, and referral. Police officers need to be aware that Asian/Pacific Americans may cope with culture shock by seeking solace within the family or community; in other words, becoming "clannish" (e.g., Chinatowns, Koreatowns).

- Many Asian/Pacific Americans are concerned with their inability to communicate clearly, and this is of particular concern among Asian/Pacific Americans who are immigrants and refugees. Officers must recognize that bilingual individuals and nonnative English speakers want to communicate effectively with them, and officers must take the time to allow them to do so. Maintaining contact, providing extra time, using interpreters, and being patient with speakers will allow Asian/Pacific Americans to communicate their concerns. Officers should be aware of nonverbal aspects in the communication styles of Asian/Pacific Americans, including eye contact, touch, gestures, and affect (show of emotions). Accents, limited vocabulary, and incorrect grammar may give officers the impression that Asian/Pacific Americans are unintelligent or do not understand what is being communicated. It is important to remember that the English listening and comprehension skills of Asian/Pacific American immigrants and refugees are usually better than their speaking skills.

- In most Asian/Pacific American families, relationship and communication patterns tend to be hierarchical, with a parent or grandparent as the head of the household. Elder family members are typically consulted regarding any major decision. In recent immigrant and refugee families, Asian/Pacific American children have a special role in being interpreters or intermediaries between parents and the external community because of their English-language abilities and awareness of the American ways of doing things. In law enforcement encounters, however, it is better to employ the services of professional interpreters than to rely on young family members.

- Asian/Pacific Americans, because of their past experiences with law enforcement agencies along with concerns about privacy and other factors, are reluctant to report crimes and may not seek police assistance and help. Law enforcement departments and officials need to build relationships and working partnerships with representative groups from Asian/Pacific American communities. Relationship building is often helped by outreach efforts such as community storefront offices, bilingual officers, and participation of officers in community activities.

Discussion Questions and Issues

1. *Law Enforcement Interactions.* Many anti-Asian/Pacific American laws and events leave Asian/Pacific Americans with the view that law enforcement agencies are not user-friendly. What are the implications of this view for law enforcement? Suggest ways to counteract negative points of view.

2. *Diversity among Asian/Pacific Americans.* The Asian/Pacific American category comprises over 40 diverse ethnic and cultural groups. Which groups are you most likely to encounter in crime fighting and peacekeeping? Based on trends within your community, which groups do you anticipate encountering in your future work?

3. *How Asian/Pacific American Groups Differ.* In Chapter 1 and in Appendix A, an outline and descriptions are presented of some behavioral differences among generations of immigrants and refugees. How might you apply these descriptions to better understand (a) an Asian/Pacific American refugee involved in a traffic moving violation? (b) an Asian/Pacific American immigrant involved as a victim of a house robbery? (c) an Asian/Pacific national involved as a victim of a burglary? (d) Southeast Asian youths involved in possible gang activities?

4. *Choice of Terms.* The term *Asian Americans and Pacific Islanders* is used in many publications and by many people to refer to members of the diverse groups included in this category. How might you find out which is the best term to use in reference to an individual if ethnic and cultural information of this kind is necessary?

5. *Effects of Myths and Stereotypes.* Myths and stereotypes about Asian/Pacific Americans have greatly affected this group. What are some of the Asian/Pacific American stereotypes that you have heard of or encountered? What effects might these stereotypes have on Asian/Pacific Americans? Suggest ways to manage these stereotypes in law enforcement. How might awareness of Asian/Pacific American stereotypes be helpful in an interview with an Asian/Pacific American about homeland security issues?

6. *Communication Style Variations among Cultures.* How do you think that the information in this chapter about verbal and nonverbal communication styles can help officers in their approach to Asian/Pacific American citizens? Does understanding the cultural components of the styles and behavior help you to become more sensitive and objective about your reactions? Provide some examples of rephrasing questions to elicit responses that show understanding and intended actions on the part of Asian/Pacific Americans.

7. *Self-Monitoring and Avoidance of Law Enforcement.* Why do you think many Asian/Pacific Americans keep to their own communities and express the desire for self-monitoring and community resolution of their problems? When are such efforts desirable? When are they ineffective? How can police agencies be of greater service to Asian/Pacific American communities in this regard?

8. *Human Trafficking and Other Populations.* This chapter highlights human trafficking within the context of Asian Americans or Asians brought to the United States for trafficking purposes. It is well known that criminals use the massage industry as a means for sex trafficking in the United States, and that many owners and workers in such "massage" parlors are of Asian origin. However, human trafficking in the United States is not limited to Asians. Do some research about the jurisdiction in which you live or work (or choose the nearest metropolitan area), and list demographic characteristics of other trafficking victims (e.g., age, gender, ethnic group, and national origin).

References

APALC: Asian Pacific American Legal Center. (2012). Statement of APALC. Hearing on Hate Crimes and the Threat of Domestic Extremism, September 17. www.advancingjustice-la.org/sites/default/files/Senate%20Judiciary%20Committee%20Hearing%20on%20Hate%20Crimes%20and%20Domestic%20Extremism%20(Sept%202012)%20-%20APALC%20Written%20Comments.pdf (accessed January 15, 2013).

Brown, Patricia Leigh. (2011). "In Oakland, Redefining Sex Trade Workers as Abuse Victims." May 23. *The New York Times.*

CAPAC: Congressional Asian Pacific American Caucus. (2013). "CAPAC Applauds New FBI Hate Crime Tracking Data." August 2. Press release.

CGP: Cambodian Genocide Program, a Program of the Genocide Studies Program of Yale University. (2013). http://gsp.yale.edu/case-studies/cambodian-genocide-program (accessed March 31, 2017).

Chang, D. F., Shen, B. J., & Takeuchi, D. T. (2009). "Prevalence and Demographic Correlates of Intimate Partner Violence in Asian Americans." *International Journal of Law and Psychiatry, 32*, 167–175.

Chang, Richard. (2016). "Community Vigilantes Step Up Patrols in Face of Crime Wave Targeting Sacramento Asians." *The Sacramento Bee*, October 1.

Chin, James. (1985). "Crime and the Asian American Community: The Los Angeles Response to Koreatown." *Journal of California Law Enforcement, 19*, 52–60.

Cho, Hyunkag and Woo J. Kim. (2012). *Intimate Partner Violence among Asian Americans and Their Use of Mental Health Services: Comparisons with White, Black, and Latino Victims*, April 22. Springer Science and Business Media, LLC.

Dabby, C., Hetana Patel, and Grace Poore. (2010). *Shattered Lives: Homicides, Domestic Violence and Asian Families*, February. San Francisco, CA: Asian & Pacific Islander Institute on Domestic Violence, APIA Health Forum.

Daniels, Roger. (1988). *Asian America: Chinese and Japanese in the United States since 1850*. Seattle, WA: University of Washington Press.

Fan, Gloria. (2015). "Lone Liaison Works to Link Austin Police with Growing Asian Communities." *Reporting Texas*, April 10.

FBI: Federal Bureau of Investigation. (2015). "Hate Crime Statistics, 2015." *Uniform Crime Report*. U.S. Department of Justice.

FBI. (2016). "Operation Cross-Country X: Recovering Underage Victims of Sex Trafficking and Prostitution." October 17. *FBI News*. https://www.fbi.gov/news/stories/operation-cross-country-x (accessed September 9, 2017).

Governing. (2015). *Diversity on the Force: Where Police Don't Mirror Communities—A Governing Special Report*, September. Washington, D.C.

Hayes, Patrick. (Ed.). (2012). *The Making of Modern Immigration: An Encyclopedia of People and Ideas*. Santa Barbara, CA: ABC-CLIO, LLC.

ILO: International Labour Organization. (2012). *ILO 2012 Global Estimate of Forced Labour: Executive Summary*. Geneva, Switzerland: ILO Special Action Programme to Combat Forced Labour.

Kawai, Yuko. (2005). "Stereotyping Asian Americans: The Dialectic of the Model Minority and the Yellow Peril." *The Howard Journal of Communications, 16*, 109–130.

Lee, Donna. (2015). "Intimate Partner Violence against Asian American Women: Moving from Theory to Strategy." *CUNY School of Law*. http://academicworks.cuny.edu/cgi/viewcontent.cgi?article=1125&context=cl_pubs (accessed September 9, 2017).

Pew Research Center. (2013). *The Rise of Asian American*, April 4. Washington, D.C.

Pew Research Center. (2015). *10 Countries with the Largest Muslim Populations, 2010 and 2050*, April 2. Religion & Public Life. Washington, D.C.

Pfeifer, Mark E., John Sullivan, Kou Yang, and Wayne Yang. (2012). "Hmong Population and Demographic Trends in the 2010 Census and 2010 American Community Survey." *Hmong Studies Journal, 13*(2), 1–31. http://hmongstudies.org/PfeiferSullivanKYangWYangHSJ13.2.pdf (accessed January 13, 2013).

PRB: Population Reference Bureau. (2016). *World Population Data Sheet*. Washington, D.C.

Povell, Marc. (2005). *The History of Vietnamese Immigration*. Washington, D.C.: The American Immigration Law Foundation. www.saigonecho.us (accessed March 31, 2017).

Prashad, V. (2001). *The Karma of Brown Folk*. Minneapolis, MN: University of Minnesota Press.

Reaves, Brian A. (2015). "Local Police Departments, 2013: Personnel, Policies, and Practices," May. U.S. Department of Justice, Office of Justice Programs. Bureau of Justice Statistics Bulletin NCJ 248677.

Takaki, R. (1989). "Who Killed Vincent Chin?" by G. Yun, *A Look beyond the Model Minority Image: Critical Issues in Asian America*. New York, NY: Minority Rights Group, Inc., pp. 23–29.

Takaki, R. (1998). *Strangers from a Different Shore: A History of Asian Americans*. Boston, MA: Little, Brown and Company.

Thompson, George. (2009). Founder of the Verbal Judo Institute. http://verbaljudo.com/, personal communication, March.

Tiapula, Suzanna and Allison Turkel. (2008). "Identifying the Victims of Human Trafficking, April/May/June 2008." *The Prosecutor*.

United Nations. (2016). *Global Report on Trafficking in Persons 2016*. Vienna: United Nations Office on Drugs and Crime.

U.S. Census Bureau. (2012). *The Asian Population: 2010, 2010 Census Briefs, March, 2012*. https://www.census.gov/prod/cen2010/briefs/c2010br-11.pdf (accessed August 12, 2017).

U.S. Census Bureau. (2015). *American Community Survey*. Washington, D.C.

U.S. Department of Justice. (2014). *Minnesota Woman Pleads Guilty to Human Trafficking for Holding Victim in Forced Labor in Restaurant*, March 26. Office of Public Affairs, Washington, D.C.

U.S. Department of Justice; U.S./EEOC (Equal Employment Opportunity Commission). (2016). *Advancing Diversity in Law Enforcement*, October. Washington, D.C.

Wang, Yanan. (2015). "Asian Americans Speak Out against a Decades-old 'Model Minority' Myth." *The Washington Post*, October 20.

Yaccino, Steven, Michael Schwirtz, and Marc Santora. (2012). "Gunman Kills 6 at a Sikh Temple near Milwaukee." *The New York Times*, August 5.

Young, Ryan and Janet DiGiacomo. (2017). "Kansas Shooting Survivor Recalls Deadly Night: 'I still feel this is not reality.'" *CNN*, March 2.

6 Law Enforcement Contact with African Americans

LEARNING OBJECTIVES

After reading this chapter, you should be able to:

- Describe the historical background of African Americans, especially as it relates to the dynamics between citizens and police.
- Recognize key aspects of diversity within African American communities, including those of class, culture, and religion.
- Explain selected African American identity movements.
- Understand the impact of African American stereotypes on law enforcement and cross-racial perceptions.
- Identify selected characteristics of African American youth, parents, and other family members as they relate to contact with law enforcement.
- Illustrate the potential for cross-cultural misunderstanding by describing characteristics of African American verbal and nonverbal communication styles.
- List and discuss key issues associated with law enforcement contact in African American communities.

OUTLINE

- Introduction
- Historical Information
- Demographics: Diversity among African Americans
- Identity and Selected Movements
- Stereotypes and Cross-Racial Perceptions
- The African American Family
- Language and Communication
- Key Issues in Law Enforcement
- Summary
- Discussion Questions and Issues
- References

INTRODUCTION

> There is no point in telling Negroes to observe the law…It has almost always been used against them.
>
> —*Senator Robert Kennedy after visiting the scene of the Watts riots, 1965 (Schlesinger, 1978)*

In a speech entitled, "Hard Truths: Law Enforcement and Race," former FBI director James Comey said:

> We must better understand the people we serve and protect—by trying to know, deep in our gut, what it feels like to be a law-abiding young black man walking on the street and encountering law enforcement. We must understand how that young man may see us. We must resist the lazy shortcuts of cynicism and approach him with respect and decency. (Comey, 2015)

The impact of slavery, racism, and discrimination plays a significant role in black/white relations. A history of intimidation of African Americans by police continues to affect the dynamics of law enforcement with members of many black communities today; implicit bias and cultural differences also play a role. Understanding both the history and culture of African Americans is especially important for criminal justice agencies and their employees as they work toward improving relations and changing perceptions. Most African Americans are fifth and sixth generation Americans. Aspects of black culture are heavily influenced by African culture, and those of white culture by European culture. The historical, cultural, and racial barriers between African Americans and police officers pose significant challenges. Officers who are willing to make special efforts toward understanding African American communities, having close contact with individuals within them, will then be working towards breaking a cycle of aggression and negative historical baggage.

HISTORICAL INFORMATION

Many African Americans or blacks (terms used interchangeably) in the United States trace their roots to western or interior Africa. For some, African relatives had been kidnapped originally by Europeans, especially in the earliest days of the slave trade; others were prisoners of war due to tribal conflicts; yet others were sold into slavery by their families or traded off by mercenary tribal leaders. They were torn from their families and cultures of origin between the seventeenth and the nineteenth centuries when they were brought to the United States as slaves. Blacks represent the only migrants to have come to the Americas, North and South, against their will. This experience has made African Americans, as a group, very different from immigrants who chose to come to the United States to better their lives, and different from refugees who fled their homelands to escape religious or political persecution. Slavery is the centerpiece of many of the societal dynamics we see today among blacks and whites; law enforcement bears a particular burden because of the role it has played in the treatment of African Americans.

Historically, in the United States, slaves were considered "inferior" beings; a slave was, by definition, entirely under the domination of some influence or person. While most slave owners likely understood that treating people as animals to be owned, worked, and sold was immoral, they wanted to think of themselves as good, religious, moral people. Hence they had to convince themselves that their slaves were not really human, but a lower form of life. They focused on racial differences such as skin color and hair texture as "proof" that black people were not really people after all. Racism began, then, as an airtight alibi for a horrifying injustice. A slave was counted as three-fifths of a person during census-taking as dictated by the Constitution, the foundation of the U.S. judicial system. Many slave owners routinely and brutally raped their female slaves, often before puberty, as well as forced their healthiest slaves to couple and breed regardless of the slaves' own attachments and preferences. The fact that many African Americans' genetic background is part Caucasian is testimony to slave owners' violations of slave girls and women.

This historical notion of the slave, and by extension, any African American, as less than human has created psychological and social problems for succeeding generations of black citizens. Slavery and the system of apartheid that followed (i.e., Jim Crow laws) led to legalized discrimination—inferior housing, schools, health care, and jobs for black people—the impact of which is still felt today.

Although the institution of slavery formally ended in 1865, many racist ideas borne of slavery persisted. These ideas continue even now to leave deep scars on many African Americans from all socioeconomic classes. The psychological heritage of slavery, as well as current discrimination, continues to prevent equal opportunity and protection in many realms of life.

The history taught in American educational institutions has tended to present a distorted, incomplete picture of black family life, emphasizing familial breakdown during the slave era. This version of history has generally ignored the moral strength of the slaves and the community solidarity and family loyalty that arose after emancipation. There is no doubt that these attributes have positively affected the rebuilding of the African American community.

Despite many slave owners' attempts to destroy black family life, most slaves managed to form lasting families headed by a mother and a father, and slave couples typically enjoyed long marriages. Although white slave masters would often do everything possible to pull families apart, including the selling of slaves, there is evidence that slaves maintained their family connections as best as they could and produced stable units with admirable values. According to U.S. historian Char Miller, "Despite the fact that slavery tore apart many families, blacks maintained links, loves, and relationships just as anyone else would under these circumstances" (Miller, 2017).

African American survival, and consequently, African American contributions to U.S. society, testify to a people's great strength and thus deserve a high level of respect. It is not within the scope of this chapter to discuss African American contributions to society, but suffice it to say that the perceptions of some people in law enforcement are conditioned by exposure to the black underclass, for whom crime is often a way of life.

Law Enforcement Interaction with African Americans: Historical Baggage

> Many of the police and African-American problems in our communities today go way back into our history. Some of the issues can be traced directly from the Civil War reconstruction era, in slavery days, when police and the military were required to return runaway slaves.
>
> (Patton, 2017)

During the late seventeenth and eighteenth centuries, prior to and following slave uprisings in a number of colonies, colonists created strict laws to contain slaves. Even minor offenses were punished harshly, setting a negative tone between law enforcement and blacks. American police were called on to form "slave patrols" and to enforce racially biased laws (Williams & Murphy, 1990). In many areas of the country, police were expected to continue enforcing highly discriminatory laws including those setting curfews for blacks and barring blacks from many facilities and activities.

Most police officers have been exposed to the historical precedents of poor relationships between police and minority communities, and to institutional bias in law enforcement. This historical "baggage" cannot be dismissed as, for some individuals, it is a trigger, contributing to a challenging dynamic between individuals police officers.

DEMOGRAPHICS: DIVERSITY AMONG AFRICAN AMERICANS

As of 2015, blacks comprised about 13.3 percent of the U.S. population (U.S. Census Bureau, 2015b). Originally living mostly in the southeastern United States, the First Great Migration involved the movement northward and westward of over 1.3 million blacks and took place between 1916 and 1930. The Second Migration occurred between 1941 and 1970, and involved 5 million blacks who migrated initially to the north and then to the west coast, largely seeking better job opportunities (Lemann, 1991). Although this was one of the primary reasons for such a mass exodus from the South, it was not the main reason. Many blacks left the South for the sole purpose of escaping racism and discrimination.

Historically, over 50 percent of the black population has lived in urban areas. The rural black population has decreased, in large part because of the great migrations; the shifting flow has contributed to the increase in numbers in suburban areas (some rural blacks may migrate directly into the inner city while others may move to more suburban areas; the flow is not actually known). In any case, urban cores experience cycles of repopulation, mainly by blacks, Latinos, and various new immigrant groups such as asylum-seekers from Central Africa (Bidgood, 2013). One of the most vivid examples is the city of Detroit, where over 82 percent of the population is black (U.S. Census Bureau, 2015a) while many whites and immigrant groups have settled in outlying areas (although there has been a slight increase in the white population of Detroit in recent years). Similarly, other cities such as Washington, D.C., St. Louis, Chicago, and Cleveland, are populated mainly by blacks and new immigrants, creating layers of tension when diverse groups with conflicting values and customs, and competing for resources, suddenly find themselves crowded into the same urban settings. Another layer of urban tension has resulted from gentrification, diversifying the population further. Where local law enforcement is not prepared for population changes, including a greater racial mix, there can be additional stresses on police (Jordan, 2017).

As with whites, there are cultural differences among African Americans related to the region of the United States in which they have lived longest, including "southern" and "northern" as well as urban, suburban, and rural characteristics.

Although many African Americans are among the lower socioeconomic class, they are represented in all the socioeconomic classes, from the underclass to the upper class, and have moved increasingly into the suburban middle class. Despite this, discrimination against blacks in a number of important areas of life remains a fact of life, with a significantly greater percentage of blacks, in comparison to whites, perceiving unfair treatment in several domains of life (see Exhibit 6.1).

As with all racial/ethnic groups, there are significant class-related differences among blacks that affect values and behavior. However, color, more than class, tends to determine how the larger society reacts to and treats blacks. For example, many blacks who are successful professionals complain that they are stopped just because they look like they do not belong in a certain neighborhood. Thus, economic success does not shield an individual

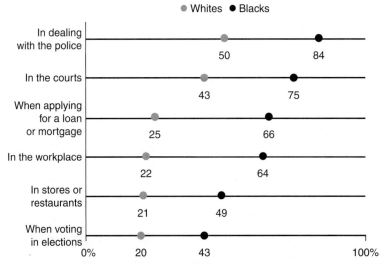

EXHIBIT 6.1   Perceptions of How Blacks Are Treated in the United States Vary Widely by Race

Percentage saying blacks are treated less fairly than whites in the country, 2016

Source: Pew Research Center. (2016). "On Views of Race and Inequality, Blacks and Whites Are Worlds Apart." June 27.

from discrimination, including treatment by law enforcement. The racial experience of many African Americans in the United States is, in many ways, similar, regardless of an individual's level of prosperity or education.

Despite the commonalities of racial experience, there is a great deal of cultural diversity among African Americans. Over the past 400 years, black families have come from many different countries (e.g., Jamaica, Trinidad, Belize, Haiti, and Puerto Rico, to name a few). By far the largest group's forebears came directly to the United States from Africa. New immigrant groups from Africa continue to arrive. Africans constitute an increasingly large segment of the black immigrant population; the increase between 2000 and 2013 was 137 percent (Anderson, 2015).

The largest groups of African immigrants have come from Nigeria, Ethiopia, Egypt (i.e., North Africa), Ghana, and Kenya, and have settled primarily in the following states, each of which is home to at least 100,000:

- New York
- California
- Texas
- Maryland
- New Jersey (ibid.)

> Black African immigrants generally fare well on integration indicators. Overall, they are well educated, with college completion rates that greatly exceed those for most other immigrant groups and US natives. Black African immigrants' earnings are on par with other immigrants and lag those of natives, despite their higher levels of human capital and their strong English skills. The underemployment of highly skilled African immigrants has been documented, and may be explained by factors such as a recent date of arrival, difficulty in transferring home-country credentials, and labor market discrimination. Cape Verde has the longest history of any African nation in sending migrants to the United States, almost all of whom enter through family reunification channels, but educational attainment, employment, and earnings are the lowest for immigrants from Cape Verde as well as several refugee-source countries—most notably Somalia. Refugees from Somalia have among the lowest levels of formal education and most difficulties integrating of any US immigrant group. (Capps, McCabe, & Fix, 2011)

Religious backgrounds vary, as shown in Exhibit 6.2, but the majority of American-born blacks are Protestant from historically black churches, and largely Baptist, with a minority being Methodist, Pentecostal, and Holiness to name a few (Pew Research Center, 2014b). The first black-run, black-controlled denomination in the country was the African Methodist Episcopal church. It was created because churches in the North and South either banned blacks or required them to sit apart from whites. A significantly smaller percentage of African Americans belongs to the black Muslim religions, including the Nation of Islam and American Muslim Mission. There are also sizable and fast-growing black populations among members of the Seventh-Day Adventists, Jehovah's Witnesses, Pentecostals (particularly among Spanish-speaking blacks), and especially among religious groups of Caribbean origin—Santeria, Candomble, Voudun, and similar sects, blending Catholic and West African (mainly Yoruba) beliefs and rituals. Rastafarianism has spread far beyond Jamaica, where it originated, to become an influential religious movement among immigrants, including whites, from many other English-speaking Caribbean nations.

- 75% of African Americans in all states said that religion is very important.
- African Americans identified as the most religious of the racial and ethnic groups polled.
- 79% of African Americans identified as Christian.
- 53% of Christian African Americans identified as Protestant (e.g., from historical black churches); 14% identified as Evangelical Protestant.
- 5%, identified as Catholic; 2% Jehovah Witness; 1% Mormon (small percentages also identified as Muslim, Jewish, Hindu, and Buddhist).

EXHIBIT 6.2 Religiosity and Diversity

Source: Pew Research Center. (2014a). *Religious Landscape Study.* http://www.pewforum.org/about-the-religious-landscape-study/

Religion, spirituality and the church have always played important roles in the lives of African Americans. The love of the church, in particular, is shared by many African Americans across religions and class. It is a pillar of the black community, and is often a center for political or social protest. The minister is often held in high esteem in African communities; religion, for many is a foundation of life that contributes to family cohesion. In the days of slavery, time at church was the only time off work, and it was here that the Negro spiritual flourished. The church's centrality in African American community life, has also meant that it is a target of hate crimes; anything done against the church has always been an attack on the soul of the community (see Hate Crimes section, beginning on p. 171).

IDENTITY AND SELECTED MOVEMENTS

In the 1960s and 1970s, the Civil Rights Movement and the Black Pride Movement marked a new direction in black identity. The Civil Rights Movement resulted in improved educational and employment opportunities as well as active political involvement. Some adults marched in the Civil Rights Movement knowing that they themselves might never benefit directly from its advances; they hoped that their efforts in the struggle would better the lives of their children. Many middle-class youths who attended community churches and black colleges became leaders in the movement for equal rights (McAdoo, 1992).

Both American-born and Caribbean-born blacks, inspired by a growing sense of community identification and increased pride in racial identity, have also placed an emphasis on learning more about and identifying with African cultures. Despite the great differences in culture between African Americans and Africans, blacks throughout the western hemisphere are discovering that they can take pride in the richness of their African heritage, including its ethical values and community cohesiveness. Examples of African cultural values that have influenced American black culture or are held in high esteem by many African Americans are (Walker, 1992):

- Cooperative interdependence among and between peoples (focus on the group), in contrast with Western individualism (focus on the individual)
- Partnership with nature and with the spirit world reflected in the approach to ecology and communication with the spirit world, similar to Native American beliefs
- Balance and harmony among all living things, reflected in the placing of human relations as a priority value—as contrasted with the Western view of "doing" (achievement) as a priority over the nurturing of human relations
- Joy and celebration in life itself
- Time as a spiral and focused on "now," which can be contrasted with the Western view of "time is money" and time running away from us
- Giving of self to community
- Renewed interest in respecting elders

The combination of the Black Pride Movement of the 1960s and 1970s and the more current focus on cultural roots has freed many African Americans from the "slave mentality" that haunted the African American culture long after emancipation. Pride in race and heritage has, for some, replaced the sense of inferiority fostered by white racial supremacist attitudes.

Several ethnic groups, including African Americans, in a positive evolution of their identity and pride, have initiated name changes for their group. Although it can be confusing, it represents, on the part of group members, growth and a desire to name themselves rather than be labeled by the dominant society. Until approximately the early 1990s, the most widely accepted term was *black*, having replaced *Negro* (which, in turn, replaced *colored people*). *Negro* has been out of use for several decades, although some older blacks still use the term (as do some younger African Americans among themselves). To many, the term *Negro* symbolizes what the African American became under slavery. The replacement of *Negro* with *black* came to symbolize racial pride. Exceptions to the avoidance of the terms *Negro* and *colored* can be found in titles such as United Negro College and National Association for the Advancement of Colored People (NAACP). *African American*, a term preferred by many, focuses on positive historical and cultural roots rather than on race or skin color.

In the 1990s, the use of the term *African American* grew in popularity. (It is the equivalent of, for example, Italian American or Polish American.) Many feel that the word *black* is no more appropriate in describing skin color than is white. Yet, some Americans who are black do not identify with African American because it does not fully represent their background, which may be Caribbean or Haitian. Since the 1980s and early 1990s, the term *people of color* has sometimes been used, but this catchall phrase has limited use for police officers because it is used to describe anyone who is not white and can include Asian/Pacific Americans, Latino/Hispanic Americans, and Native Americans.

Black Lives Matter

Many police officers have deeply visceral and negative reactions to the BLM (Black Lives Matter) movement because of video footage and media reports showing extreme antipolice sentiment expressed by some activists. Understandably, images of individuals chanting hateful antipolice slogans have not positively promoted BLM's objectives or ideals in the eyes of law enforcement personnel, and much of the public. Nor does the antipolice focus of some activists take into account the communities around the country where law enforcement and black community organizations have positive partnerships and collaborative strategies for improving relationships. BLM arose in response to police killings and beatings of black individuals. Social and traditional media have both created powerful and sometimes distorted images of the movement. Law enforcement is all too familiar with the mixed impacts that conventional and social media can convey, as police actions often are the subject of similar kinds of coverage.

The following is a view of BLM from the perspective of retired Metropolitan D.C. police officer Ronald Hampton, who for 23 years was also the executive director of the National Black Police Association:

> It is a powerful movement of young people who have observed what is happening with excessive and disproportionate use of violence against blacks. Too many innocent blacks are killed by the police. The young people are experiencing the frustration of injustice. They are not afraid and will stand up for justice. They have the benefit of technology and are communicating with each other. They are organizing and can mobilize quickly. (Hampton, 2017)

Hampton further comments on the phrasing "Black Lives Matter," and people's objections to it:

> Black Lives Matter does not mean that other lives do not matter. Blue lives matter. White lives matter. This is obvious. But Black lives do *not* matter *less* than other lives. People started responding, "All lives matter," only after the movement started. Black Lives Matter started as a social movement to bring attention to unjust killings, and to make people aware of the lack of justice for black people. (Ibid.)

With respect to the lives of police officers, a prominent African American writer and educator wrote: "Blue lives matter expresses a fact in our society. Black lives matter exists as a reminder" (Cobb, 2016a).

BLM is an ideological, political movement that emerged after the 2012 shooting death of Trayvon Martin, an unarmed 17-year-old African American youth, by George Zimmerman, a white Neighborhood Watch volunteer. Mr. Zimmerman was found not guilty of second-degree murder by a Florida jury. Shortly after his acquittal, Alicia Garza, who later cofounded BLM, posted on Facebook, *"Black people. I love you. I love us. Our lives matter"* (based on The Guardian, 2015; Cobb, 2016b). Approximately one year later, 18-year old Michael Brown was killed by a white police officer in Ferguson, Missouri. Intense debate ensued within and outside of law enforcement as to whether the officer's lethal action was justified (U.S. Department of Justice, 2016). (It is beyond the scope of this book to delve into the legal standards for the use of excessive force, or the discussion surrounding police training in use of force.) Garza organized "freedom rides" to Ferguson from major cities in the United States under the hashtag #blacklivesmatter. Ultimately, a grand jury found the officer's shooting of Michael Brown to be justified (U.S. Department of Justice, 2015). BLM became particularly visible and vocal after that, and whenever subsequent police killings of unarmed blacks occurred.

Many antipolice protests in the United States have been attributed to the BLM movement even if BLM was not the organizer. Regardless, the perspectives of white and black officers on the protests differ considerably:

> Black and white officers, more so than blacks and whites in the general population, are highly divided in their views of the protests that followed the officer-involved killings of blacks. Almost 70% of black officers felt that these protests were held in part in order to hold police accountable for their action (Morin, Parker, Stepler, & Mercer, 2017). On the other hand, under 30% of white officers held this view. (Ibid.)

The core messages of BLM center around "the ways in which Black lives are deprived of … basic human rights and dignity" (blacklivesmatter.com). Although the movement began in response to the killing of unarmed black men, its ideals and objectives have broadened substantially. There is strong feminist leadership within BLM, in contrast to previous black pride movements, such as the Black Panthers. The movement's Web site lists 10 commitments and affirmations, focusing broadly on justice for all black people, including those who have been marginalized (ibid.). For example:

> We are committed to collectively, lovingly and courageously working vigorously for freedom and justice for Black people and, by extension all people. As we forge our path, we intentionally build and nurture a beloved community that is bonded together through a beautiful struggle that is restorative, not depleting.

One consequence is that there is confusion about what the movement stands for. BLM has been criticized for not having a singular focused message or centralized leadership (Cobb, 2016b). At one extreme, BLM is seen as a hate group. Some believe that BLM has created an unnecessary rift between officers and the community, and that the movement gave people an excuse to use race as the *only* reason as to why an officer would stop them (Jordan, 2017). Others see it as a positive voice for justice and equality, and an affirmation of contributions of blacks to society, including those who have been marginalized (e.g., LGBTQ, disabled, and undocumented black immigrants). Others credit the movement with influencing policy decisions around transparency, including the use of body cameras, and the creation of a statewide database to collect and analyze police use of force incidents (ibid.). The different ways in which BLM is characterized reflect highly polarized political and personal perspectives. Whichever way it is viewed, BLM is a multi-faceted movement. And, just as it is unjustified to stereotype police officers, the individuals active in the movement represent great diversity and perspectives.

STEREOTYPES AND CROSS-RACIAL PERCEPTIONS

Many of the impressions people in society and law enforcement form about African Americans come from their exposure to messages and images in the media. The phenomenon of stereotyping is as much at work as when citizens see all police officers as repressive and capable of brutality (see Chapter 1, Introduction). Police officers know that law enforcement, in general, takes a beating nationwide whenever there is publicity about an instance of police brutality against blacks or reports of racial profiling. These public perceptions do not differentiate between police departments and officers, doing an injustice to the majority of police professionals who have chosen their careers in order to serve communities.

Racist whites' views of blacks reflect the same problem. Those who are bent toward prejudice may feel that their racism is justified whenever a crime involving an African American makes the news or hits social media. A suburban African American mother addressing a community forum on racism pointed out:

> Every time I hear that there has been a murder or a rape, I pray that it is not a black who committed the crime. The minute the media reports that a black person is responsible for a crime, all of us suffer. When something negative happens, I am no longer seen as an individual with the same values and hopes as my white neighbors. I become a symbol, and even more so my husband and sons become feared. People treat us with caution and politeness, but inside we know that their stereotypes of the worst criminal element of blacks have become activated.

Frequent depictions of black criminals in the media, particularly television and movies, further reinforce this image:

> This image often contributes to a police officer's decision to pull over black motorists in nice cars or in affluent neighborhoods; the pedestrian's decision to cross the street or clutch her purse when approaching a black male; the salesperson's decision to follow a black customer throughout the store for fear of theft; and the politician's decision to use a black face to kindle fears that crime is out of control. (Johnson, 2013)

Harboring unreasonable fears about black people is a result of the prevalence of stereotypes associated with criminality (sometimes referred to as a "black crime association"). These stereotypes produce labels about the "other," and the racial divide dramatically highlights how stereotypes play into completely different perceptions. O.J. Simpson's criminal trial and subsequent acquittal in the mid-90s are excellent examples of stereotypes and their relationship to opposing racial perceptions about whether O.J. was innocent or guilty (Jordan, 2017). According to polls referencing the mid-90s, most African Americans believed O.J. to be innocent, while the majority of whites thought he was guilty.* (Ross, 2016).

The consequences of stereotyping are common phenomena known in the fields of both sociology and criminology, and have clear implications for law enforcement behavior (see Chapter 12, Racial Profiling).

While George Zimmerman, the neighborhood volunteer in the 2012 Trayvon Martin tragedy, was not a police officer, and the Trayvon case is not a specific example of *police stereotyping*, it is an illustration of what many believe to be a common cross-racial perception, characterizing conscious and subconscious stereotypical beliefs. The critical learning from the Trayvon case is the understanding of the relationship between stereotypes, bias (defined in Chapter 1), and subconscious decision-making that in turn influences action and behavior.

Prejudice, lack of contact, and ignorance lend themselves to groups' developing perceptions about the "other" that are often based on biased beliefs. Unfortunately, perceptions are then seen as reality or "the truth," whether or not they are valid. Exhibit 6.3 illustrates differing images that some members of the dominant society have toward black and white males.

Likewise, African Americans have attached certain negative connotations to the actions of police officers, even though most officers do not exhibit overt racism. Furthermore, many officers are being trained to understand that every human being carries biases and prejudices, and that this is as much a problem in society as it is in law enforcement (Fridell, 2017a). The perceptions listed in Exhibit 6.4 were presented to Northern California police officers in the early 1990s by then vice president of the Alameda, California, NAACP chapter (the late Al Dewitt). When Dewitt presented this list to police officers, he explained that, over time, African Americans had formed perceptions about police behavior that led to riots, race problems, and a lack of trust. According to Skipper Osborne, former president of the Portland NAACP, and to Greg Patton (African American, former Washington State patrol trooper),

Black Male	White Male
Arrogant	Confident
Chip on shoulder	Self assured
Aggressive	Assertive
Strong personality	Natural leader
Violence prone	Wayward
Naturally gifted	Smart
Sexual prowess	Sexual experimentation

EXHIBIT 6.3 Are Blacks and Whites Viewed in Equal Terms?

---

*In recent years, the racial gap has narrowed regarding perceptions of O.J. Simpson's guilt or innocence. (Ross, 2016).

Police Action	Black Perception
Being stopped or expelled from so-called "white neighborhoods."	Whites want blacks to "stay in their neighborhoods."
Immediately suspecting and reacting to blacks without distinction between drug dealer and plainclothes police officer.	Police view black skin itself as probable cause.
Using unreasonable force; beatings; adding charges.	When stopped, blacks must be submissive; many fear they will be shot if not compliant.
Negative attitudes; jokes; body language; talking down to people.	Officers are racists.
Quick trigger; take-downs; accidental shootings.	Bad attitudes will be exhibited because "I am black."
Slow response; low priority; low apprehension rate.	Crime in low income black neighborhoods is not important.
Techniques of enforcing local restrictions and white political interests.	Police are the strong arm for the status quo.
Police stick together, right or wrong.	Us-against-them mentality; they stick together, so we have to stick together.

EXHIBIT 6.4   Perceptions of Police Officers' Actions by Some Blacks

the items presented in Exhibit 6.3 are entirely valid today. Improving cross-racial perceptions, and preventing racial misperceptions will inevitably benefit all concerned by way of increased cooperation and safety (Patton, 2017).

THE AFRICAN AMERICAN FAMILY

American families from all backgrounds are highly diverse, with children being raised by grandparents, foster parents, relatives, married or unmarried parents, and LGBTQ parents. LGBTQ African American families, growing in number, face challenges of acceptance by both the larger society and within their own communities. According to data gathered from multiple polls, in 2012, estimates of same-sex African American couples were 84,000 with a third of those raising children (Kastanis & Gates). Over half of the same-sex couples were female and young (ibid.). Most African American families enjoy very strong ties among extended family members, especially among women. Female relatives often substitute for each other in filling family roles; for example, a grandmother or an aunt may raise a child if the mother is unable to do so. Sometimes several different family groups share one house. When a problem occurs (i.e., an incident that has brought an officer to the house), extended family members are likely to be present and offering help. An officer may observe a number of uncles, aunts, brothers, sisters, cousins, and boyfriends or girlfriends who are loosely attached to the household. Enlisting the aid of any of these household members, no matter what the relationship, can be beneficial.

The Roles of Men and Women

In some U.S. urban core areas, and in particular in housing projects, it is not uncommon to find a majority of African American women living alone with children; thus the widespread view that African American families are matriarchies in which women are typically the heads of the household. Over time, a variety of theories have been formulated to explain this. Some point to evidence that certain tribes in Africa were (and/or currently are) matriarchies, influencing modern African American culture. During the days of slavery, black women played a crucial role in the family because of repeated attempts by slave owners, police, and others to break down "black manhood" (Bennett, 1989). Yet an additional explanation is that the "system" of women running the household has mostly come about by default because of the absence of fathers.

Similar to the dynamic in many cultures, African American fathers usually view themselves as heads of the household, and often the mother is the behind-the-scenes head of the family even as she works one or two jobs outside the home (Jordan, 2017). It is insulting and disrespectful for officers to direct questions to and focus on just the father or the mother when both parents are present. A mother's assertiveness does not mean that the father is passive or indifferent and thus should be ignored; nor does a father's silence indicate agreement with the officer's action. It may be worthwhile to get his view of the situation first.

The Single Mother and African American Women

The single mother, particularly in the inner city, does not always receive the respect that she is due; outsiders may be critical of the way she lives—or the way they think she lives. She is often stereotyped by officers who doubt their own effectiveness in the urban black community. For instance, in theory, an unmarried African American mother on welfare who has just had a fight with her boyfriend should receive the same professional courtesy that a married white suburban mother is likely to receive from an officer; however, in practice this is not always the case. African American women sometimes complain that white officers in general treat them aggressively, using coarse language or obscenities. This type of behavior can also be attributed to a lack of respect for women, in general (Jordan, 2017).

Ondra Berry, retired deputy police chief, Reno, Nevada, and an African American, offers advice regarding relations between police officers and single mothers. He advises officers to go out of their way to establish rapport and trust. Following are his suggestions for assisting the single mother (Berry, 2017):

- Offer extra assistance to low-income mothers, for example, connect them with community resources.
- Proactively engage youth and encourage them to participate in organized social activities.
- Give your business card to the mother to show that you are available for further contact.
- Make follow-up visits when there are no problems so that the mother and the children can associate the officer with good times.
- Make sure that you have explained to the mother her rights.
- Use the same discretion you might use with another minor's first petty offense (e.g., shoplifting); consider bringing the child home and talking with the mother and child rather than sending the child immediately to juvenile hall.

All of these actions will help to build trust between officers and African American single mothers. Retired Metropolitan D.C. Police Officer Ronald Hampton also advises officers to be aware of stereotypes and perceptions they may have based on class. A professional, single white woman may decide to have children on her own, and is viewed differently, sometimes being treated with more respect than poor African American women with children (Hampton, 2017). His advice:

> Treat all women you encounter in the projects or low-income neighborhoods in the same way as you treat women in middle and upper class neighborhoods. (Ibid.)

An additional area related to African American women is particularly worthy of attention. Historically, the sexual assault of an African American woman has not been considered as serious by law enforcement as the sexual assault of a white woman; past and current perceptions and experiences may contribute to lower reporting rates. The Department of Justice estimates that black women refrain from reporting rapes at significantly higher rates than white women. According to Brooke Axtell, a writer and advocate for survivors of sexual assault and domestic violence, there are multiple reasons for this—by seeking help after a rape, some African American women may wish to avoid compromising their community, and particularly African American men about whom society has held stereotypical beliefs related to sexuality. Additionally because of police injustice, historically against black communities, some African American women are more reluctant to report sexual assault (Axtell, 2012).

Children/Adolescents/Youth

Because some black households, especially in the inner city, have absent fathers, young boys in their middle childhood years (ages seven to eleven) are at risk for serious behavioral problems, and school is often where these problems show up. According to Berry, some single mothers unwittingly place their young sons in the position of "father," giving them the message that they have to take care of the family. These young children can get the mistaken impression that they are the heads of the household, and in school situations may try to control the teacher—who is often female and often white. Officers who refer these children to agencies that can provide role models, even on a limited-time basis, stand better chances of gaining the family's and community's trust and respect. Eventually, cooperation will be earned from community members (Berry, 2017).

Among older African American male children, especially in inner cities, statistics indicate a disproportionately high crime rate, in large part stemming from the difficult economic conditions of their lives as well as a lack of positive role models actively involved in their lives (Jordan, 2017). This fact notwithstanding, the majority of African American teenagers are law-abiding citizens. There are strong emerging youth organizations in urban America, such as "Youth Uprising" in Oakland, California, and other youth empowerment programs (ibid.) that are focusing on youth leadership and community transformation.

Young people form some of their impressions of police because they have heard about individuals who are stopped for no apparent reason and they have heard reports about how officers have interacted with those stopped. The negative and collective impact of unjustified stops cannot be emphasized enough. African American teens and young adults report being stopped on a regular basis by police officers when they are in predominantly "white neighborhoods" (including those where they happen to live). For example, a 19-year-old African American male living in an upper-middle-class suburban neighborhood in Fremont, California, reported that he was stopped and questioned four times in two weeks by different officers. On one occasion, the conversation went this way:

OFFICER: What are you doing here?

TEEN: I'm jogging, sir.

OFFICER: Why are you in this neighborhood?

TEEN: I live here, sir.

OFFICER: Where?

TEEN: Over there, in that big house on the hill.

OFFICER: Can you prove that? Show me your I.D.

Parents of African American young people have to deal with the possibility that their children may get stopped for no reason, necessitating warnings to their children of the consequences of inappropriate behavior towards officers. Ronald Hampton shared his personal perspective regarding the different ways that black and white parents speak about police to their children and teenagers.

> At the dinner table, white families typically tell children that police are there to help, and that they should call the police when they need to. When I used to speak to my young daughter about encounters with the police, my message to her over and over was about how she had to interact with the police. What she should do and not do. How she should behave. How polite she had to be. Our children have something to fear if they don't act appropriately with police. (Hampton, 2017)

Hampton also provided a long view of ways to bridge the gap between black youth and law enforcement, strongly suggesting that police recruitment start with African Americans at a young age. He encourages black youth to consider the law enforcement profession as a way to help African American community members to have more of a voice, and to model positive and respectful policing within the communities (ibid.).

LANGUAGE AND COMMUNICATION

Racial conflicts between African Americans and other citizens can cover up communication style differences, which until the 1990s had been largely ignored or minimized. Yet many would acknowledge that cultural differences between, for example, a white officer and a Vietnamese citizen could potentially affect their respective communication styles as well as their perceptions of each other. Similarly, language comes into play when looking at patterns of communication among many African Americans.

"Ebonics" or African American Vernacular English

What Is Ebonics?

At its most literal level, Ebonics simply means "black speech" (a blend of the words ebony "black" and phonics "sounds"). The term was created in 1973 by a group of black scholars who disliked the negative connotations of terms like "Nonstandard Negro English" that had been coined in the 1960s when the first modern large-scale linguistic studies of African American speech-communities began. (Rickford)

African American Vernacular English (AAVE) a term used interchangeably with Ebonics, is considered to be a dialect of English by some and a language by others; AAVE meets all of the requirements of a language; it possesses a coherent system of signs; it has a grammar of elements and rules; and it is used for communication and social purposes (based on Patrick, 2006).

Many African Americans speak, or speak some of the time, what has been called *Black English*, *African American Vernacular English* (AAVE), *African American English*, *Black Vernacular*, or *Black English Vernacular*. Academics and sociolinguists tend to use AAVE, and colloquially, it is known as *Ebonics*. Individuals often "code switch," a linguistic term that means to go back and forth flexibly between standard English and Ebonics, speaking the latter among peers and family members, while switching to the former when the situation calls for it (e.g., at work, in interviews, and with nonblack friends and colleagues).

Linguists have done years of research on the origins of Ebonics, and have made significant findings. With roots from West African languages, AAVE or Ebonics evolved as slaves "learned" English from their masters and as they communicated among themselves despite their many tribal language differences. Thus, Ebonics appears to be derived from the early varieties of English spoken in the United States, mixed together with certain grammatical patterns common to several West African tribal languages (Wolfram & Torbert, 2004, 2005).

Many people hold on to an unscientific view of these language varieties spoken among African Americans. Ebonics has been ridiculed by people, including educators, who have no understanding of its foundation and legitimacy (Rickford, 2009). There are many varieties of *non-standard* English that are *not* "substandard," "deficient," or "impoverished" versions of the language. Instead, most have a complete and consistent set of grammatical rules. For example, Asian Indians speak a variety of English that is unfamiliar to some, while people in England speak numerous dialects of British English, each containing distinctive grammatical structures and vocabulary not used by Americans. Similarly, some African Americans speak a version of English that historically has been labeled substandard because of a lack of understanding of its origins.

Some individuals regularly use Ebonics and others do not use it at all or rarely use it. People who are both educated and uneducated speak it. It is not exclusively spoken by African Americans; some Ebonics speech patterns can also be heard by some white southerners. There has been an intense and complex controversy around the status of Ebonics (i.e., whether it is a separate language or a dialect); one of the most important aspects of the use of Ebonics has to do with the need for teachers to respect the language variety that children use while also teaching them standard English.

Discrimination associated with the use of Ebonics has been referred to as language or linguistic profiling. "As with racial profiling, linguistic profiling can have devastating consequences for [individuals] who are perceived to speak with an undesirable accent or dialect"

(Baugh, undated). It is not uncommon for nonblacks to assume that Ebonics is "bad" English; an individual or officer's view of this way of speaking can lead to negative perceptions of or judgments about the person using it (Makoni, Smitherman, Ball, & Spears).

When attempting to establish trust, and rebuild relations with people who have historically had few reasons to trust the police, officers should not try to imitate black accents, dialects, or styles of speaking. These imitations can be viewed as very insulting and may give blacks the impression that they are being ridiculed, or that the officer is seriously uncomfortable with them (see Chapter 4, Cross-Cultural/Racial Communication Dynamics). It is important to be authentic and sincere when communicating with African Americans, without pretending to be "cool," by using slang or imitating a style that is not authentic for the officer.

Nonverbal Communication: Interaction with and Reactions to Authority

Communication, verbal and nonverbal, can easily be escalated if either party misreads the intention of the other. Misinterpretation can turn the most benign situations into hostile encounters, which could otherwise be de-escalated by both officers and citizens. "Police have the power and the badge. A friendlier approach, accompanied by smiling and a clear show of respect can go a long way towards improving interaction with African Americans" (Osborne, 2017). An officer's aggressive stance can inflame a situation just as a citizen's threatening stance can. However, it is incumbent on the officer to learn how to disarm heated situations though verbal and nonverbal skills. A police officer, and male in particular, might approach a young black male or female, using a posture that may be interpreted as aggressive, and even more so if the officer has his hand on his gun or is reaching for it when there is no provocation to do so (ibid.) (see Chapter 4, Importance of Verbal De-Escalation).

Eye contact during conversation is another area in which African American and mainstream styles can differ and have the potential to lead to miscommunication. In one research study (Hecht, Jackson II, & Ribeau, 2003), it was found that, "...while speaking, [white] Americans look less and African Americans look more, and while listening, African Americans look less and European Americans look more." A police officer may misinterpret the listening style of a black citizen, incorrectly inferring that less eye contact during listening equates to a lack of engagement or rudeness. In addition, officers are specifically trained that a lack of eye contact is also a sign of deception (Jordan, 2017). Likewise, the steady gaze of an African American who is talking with a police officer could be misinterpreted as a display of aggression.

The pattern of avoiding eye contact with authority figures can be explained from a couple of different perspectives. It could signal intentional defiance as in, "You stopped me for no reason, and I don't have to look at you" (Osborne, 2017). At the same time, some people have grown up hearing parents or other authority figures admonishing them to *not* look at them in the eye when they are being spoken to, and especially when being disciplined. According to Osborne, this submissiveness is less common than it was in the past (ibid.).

Verbal Expressiveness and Emotionalism

The Ebonics vernacular style of speech emphasizes emotional response—being "real" is the term. This means it is okay to express one's indignation, to be emotional, and to express to someone how you feel. Many African Americans perceive that the mainstream culture is taught to be reserved and to temper their emotions. This is a cultural difference that can be misread by law enforcement.

(Patton, 2017)

Linguist and sociologist Thomas Kochman has devoted his professional life to studying differences in black and white culture that contribute to misunderstandings and misperceptions. Of historical significance, Chicago's African American mayor Harold Washington passed out copies of Kochman's book *Black and White Styles in Conflict* (1981) to the city hall press corps because he believed that he was seriously misunderstood by the whites of the city. According to Kochman, "If a person doesn't know the difference in cultures, that's ignorance. But if a person knows the difference and still says that mainstream culture is best, that 'white is right,' then you've got racism" (ibid.).

In his book, Kochman explains that blacks and whites have different perspectives and approaches to many issues, including conversation, public speaking, and power. This notion is supported in the following advice given to police officers by former Reno assistant police chief Ondra Berry:

> Don't get nuts when you encounter an African American who is louder and more emotional than you are. Watch the voice patterns and the tone. Blacks can sound militant [even when they are not]. Blacks have been taught [i.e., socialized] to be outwardly and openly emotional. Sometimes we are emotional first and then calm down and become more rational. Whites may be more rational at first, but then become more emotional as they lose control. (Berry, 2017)

This cultural difference has obvious implications for overall communication, including how to approach and react to angry citizens. Kochman explains that many "whites [are] able practitioners of self-restraint [and that] this practice has an inhibiting effect on their ability to be spontaneously self-assertive." He also states that, "the level of energy and spiritual intensity that blacks generate is one that they can manage comfortably but whites can only manage with effort" (Kochman, 1981). The problems in interaction come about because neither race understands that there is a cultural difference between them. Kochman states: "Blacks do not initially see this relative mismatch, because they believe that their normal animated style is not disabling to whites…Whites are worried that blacks cannot sustain such intense levels of interaction without losing self-control [because that degree of 'letting go' of emotions for a white would signify a lack of control]" (ibid.). In other words, a nonblack person, unaware of the acceptability in black culture of expressing intense emotion, including anger, might not be able to imagine that he himself could express such intense emotion without losing control. He may feel threatened, convinced that the ventilation of such emotion will surely lead to a physical confrontation.

While racism may also be a factor in communication breakdowns, differing conventions of speech contribute in ways that are not always apparent. In several cultural awareness training sessions, police officers have reported that white neighbors, upon hearing highly emotional discussions among African Americans, called to report fights. When the police arrived on the scene of the "fight," the individuals involved responded that they were not fighting, just talking. While continuing to respond to all calls, officers can be aware of different perceptions of what constitutes a fight. This awareness of style differences will have an impact on how officers approach citizens, and while remaining vigilant, can even assist with the understanding of calls to dispatch in which "fights" are reported.

> We like to get together and play cards and dominoes. We slam them on the table. We make noise. We are loud and expressive. It may sound like we are fighting. We are hyperbolic when we talk and we enjoy this. This behavior may be misunderstood. (Osborne 2017)

Pastor Ronald Griffin, a prominent African American leader in Detroit who later joined the Detroit Police Department Board of Commissioners, also referring to socializing and playing cards, saying, "If anyone was listening to us from the outside, they would have heard us, at times, laughing, and, at times, talking loudly and pounding the table. These are intense moments of fellowship, and if you were there, you would have understood" (Griffin, 2009).

Berry illustrated how a white police officer can let his or her own cultural interpretations of black anger and emotionalism influence judgment. He spoke of a fellow officer who made the statement: "Once they [i.e., blacks] took me on, I wanted to take control." This officer, working in a predominantly black area for a three-month period, made 120 stops and 42 arrests, mainly petty offenses such as prowling and failure to identify. He then worked in a predominantly white area for the same period of time, made 122 stops and only 6 arrests. The officer went on to say that "one group will do what I ask; the other will ask questions and challenge me." His need to take control over people whom he perceived to be "out of place" was so extreme, it resulted in his being sued (Berry, 2017). His perception of the level of threat involved was much higher in the black community than in the white.

One of the factors involved was the officer's inability to deal with having his authority questioned or challenged. If he had used appropriate communication skills, he might have been able to work situations around to his advantage rather than creating confrontations. Listening professionally, instead of engaging in shouting matches with citizens of other backgrounds, can require a great deal of self-control, but it will usually bring the best results. As one African American police officer said in a media interview, "I make sure that whatever the 'perp' says I don't pay attention to. Most police brutality cases arise from cops who can't control their emotions in the face of insults" (NewsOne, 2010).

Threats and Aggressive Behavior

Kochman, who has conducted cultural awareness training sessions for police departments nationwide, asks the question, "When does a fight begin?" Many whites, he notes, believe that "fighting" has already begun when it is "obvious" that there will be violence ("when violence is imminent"). Therefore, to whites, a fight begins as soon as the shouting starts. According to whites, then, the fight has begun whenever a certain intensity of anger is shown, along with an exchange of insults. If, in addition, the shouting includes threats, many whites would tend to agree that violence is surely on its way (Kochman, 2013).

Kochman explains that while verbal confrontation and threats may indeed be a prelude to a fight, they may also be a surrogate or substitute for a fight. Many blacks tend to make a clear distinction between what may appear to be verbal threats and physical confrontations. Kochman explains that fighting, for some blacks, does not begin until one person does something physically provocative (ibid.). Thus, loud conversation, *accompanied by* nonverbal signs, such as a hand going into a pocket or closer interpersonal distance, can indicate more of a threat.

Officers who are trained to think about officer safety, however, might have a problem believing that they "got nothing to worry about" when encountering two belligerent individuals of a different culture than their own. Similarly, a threat in today's society, where anyone may be carrying weapons, may be just that—a very real threat that will be carried out. A threat must always be taken seriously by officers. However, there can be instances when cultural differences are at work, and extreme anger can be expressed without accompanying physical violence. When this is the case, an officer can actually escalate hostilities with an approach and communication style that demonstrates a lack of understanding of culturally/racially different modes of expression.

KEY ISSUES IN LAW ENFORCEMENT

Racial Perceptions, Prejudice, and the Code of Silence

The results of a national survey comparing attitudes involving a total of 8,000 black and white sworn officers showed race to be a divisive issue, and in some areas "racial differences among the police are considerably more pronounced than they are among the public as a whole" (Gramlich, 2017). In particular, black and white officers differed significantly as to how they viewed the fatal shootings of African Americans (i.e., in 2015 and 2016). African American police officers were twice as likely to view the deaths as part of a larger pattern in law enforcement whereas white officers saw these as "isolated incidents"—57 percent vs. 27 percent of white officers (ibid.). The perception among whites and blacks in the public also differed, with whites perceiving less of a broad pattern of abuse than blacks, but the disparity between the races was not as great as it was for law enforcement (79 percent blacks vs. 50 percent whites). The life experiences of black and white officers are not the same, and therefore, the perspectives of each racial group, despite in-group diversity, have been shaped by completely different realities. Race is a divisive issue for members of the law enforcement profession because it is a divisive issue in the larger environment.

In the wake of publicized allegations and Department of Justice reports detailing differential treatment of minority groups, officers who hold biases and prejudices have to face them and recognize when these result in action. "I am not prejudiced. I treat all citizens fairly." This statement holds true for many officers, although explicit utterance of this type of statement often signals prejudice. Prejudice may have outward and explicit manifestations, as with someone who is obviously and openly racist, or it may manifest in more subtle ways. "While all people have biases of one sort or another, officers have to be able to suspend their biases when they are called upon to take action" (Jordan, 2017). The following is an African American officer's observation of bias on the part of his white partner:

My partner and I several years ago went to an all-white nightclub. He found cocaine on this white couple. He poured it out and didn't make an arrest. Later we were at an all-black nightclub. He found marijuana on one individual and arrested him. I was shocked, but I didn't say anything at the time because I was fairly new to the department. He had told me on two occasions that he "enjoyed" working with black officers and "has no difficulty" with the black community.

Dr. James Johnson, researcher on criminal justice and minority group issues, reacted to the above-noted incident: "This officer validated and legitimized his white partner's prejudicial behavior by exercising the 'Blue Code of Silence.'* Because the black officer did not say anything, the white officer saw no need to face or recognize his racially biased behavior" (Johnson, 2013).

It is this very code of silence that destroys trust between African Americans and law enforcement, and holds individuals back from cooperating with the police. "When officers break the blue code of silence, we will break our code of silence, that is, we will speak up as witnesses and will be more willing to provide leads. Community members often don't want to be snitches on people from our own communities. But we are ready to break that code of silence once we see that officers are willing to break their code of silence…" (Osborne, 2017).

Retired Chief of Police Howard Jordan, from the Oakland, California PD, notes that most police departments have policies that require officers to report fellow officers who engage in misconduct. For example, the presumptive discipline for an Oakland police officer that has failed to report another officer for misconduct is termination (Jordan, 2017).

Implicit Bias and Implications for Law Enforcement

The topic of bias** and policing is a highly sensitive one, but in recent years has been acknowledged and highlighted in law enforcement training. High-profile police shootings and beatings of unarmed black men have been the impetus for a great deal of social science research on bias. The Department of Justice and other organizations have documented patterns of excessive force with and racial profiling of minorities in various U.S. police department, such as Baltimore and Chicago (U.S. Department of Justice, Civil Rights Division, 2016, 2017a).

Researchers in the last couple of decades have looked at racial background, perception of threat, and officer behavior (Correll, Park, Judd, Wittenbrink, Sadler, & Keesee, 2007). For example, in the first experimental study of this kind, results showed how the stereotype associating blacks with crime and violence ("black crime association") can have a subliminal effect on perception of threat (Payne, 2004). Study participants were asked to identify an object either as a gun or a tool, such as a wrench in less than a second (i.e., ½ second) after seeing images of black and white faces. The research showed a correlation between the speed and identification of an object as a gun with a black face, and the speed and identification of a tool with a white face. Thus, in this early study, people were more likely to "misidentify tools as guns when linked to a black face" (ibid.). In interpreting his study results, Payne made the statement, "People don't have to be bigots to be under the influence of racial bias…" (ibid.).

In a later study (Plant et al., 2005), participants looked at images of individuals' faces with objects that popped up and were superimposed on the faces. These objects were either guns or other objects that were not weapons. The study subjects had to either hit the "Shoot" or "Don't Shoot" key. The first phase of the study showed that both officers and non-officers were more likely to erroneously shoot at a black individual even when the superimposed object was not a gun (ibid.). More research has taken place in the last decade in which results have shown that, compared to non-officers, police officers' "high quality use of force training has made a difference in terms of accuracy (i.e., with respect to *the shoot/don't shoot* response), which is what one would expect" (Fridell, 2017a). For example, in a key study exploring the effects of law enforcement weapons training (Correll et al., 2007), researchers looked at two dimensions of officer performance: accuracy and speed of decision-making regarding the *shoot/don't shoot response*. The study compared an equal number of police officers as community members (i.e., approximately 125 subjects in each group).

---

*Blue Code of Silence—the unspoken rule said to exist in police culture, resulting in officers' not reporting the misconduct, errors or crimes of fellow officers.

**The Community Relations Service Department of the DOJ has produced an excellent "toolkit" for policing entitled, *Understanding Bias: A Resource Guide.* (U.S. Department of Justice)

With respect to accuracy, community members showed a definite pattern of racial bias, making incorrect decisions by shooting at representations of unarmed black targets. Police also occasionally shot at unarmed targets, but showed less of a pattern of racial bias in that they were as likely to shoot at an unarmed white as an unarmed black. However, both police and nonpolice showed "clear, robust evidence of bias" in…response times, i.e., the measure of decision-making speed. With regard to outcome and accuracy, police had fewer errors because of their training, and their errors were less likely than those of community members to be linked to bias (ibid.).

The Fair and Impartial Policing (FIP) curricula, introduced in Chapter 1, presents key conclusions, including those described above, from years of social science research on implicit bias. We review core FIP principles here:

–Bias is a normal human attribute.
–Biases are often unconscious or "implicit."
–Implicit biases manifest even in individuals who, at the conscious level, reject prejudices and stereotyping.
–Implicit biases can influence our actions.
–Understanding how implicit bias can affect our perceptions and behavior is the first step in "overriding" implicit bias. (FIP website, 2017)

In her book entitled, *Producing Bias-Free Policing: A Science-Based Approach* (Fridell, 2017b), Dr. Fridell explains that when a threat is ambiguous, there is more likelihood that implicit biases will be operative.

> An example is the shooting by [an] officer in Columbia, South Carolina, in 2014. The state trooper pulled over a young Black male and, after the man was out of the car, asked him for his driver's license. The young man quickly turned and reached into the car. The officer, clearly fearful, fired. This ambiguous behavior on the part of a Black male produced perceptions of threat; likely if a professionally dressed, White woman had acted the same way, the perception (and outcome) would have been different. (Ibid.)

The opposite of implicit bias is *explicit* bias (see Chapter 1). Racist comments and racists acts, such as hate speech and hate crimes, are examples of explicit bias. People who are explicitly biased know that they have prejudices against certain groups. They do not hesitate to use racial epithets with peers, and have such strong prejudicial feelings that they risk sending racist messages by e-mail or text, including in professional settings. They often scapegoat other groups and elevate their own ethnic group. Nevertheless, an individual with explicit biases may still state, "I am not racist," but then will send text messages containing racial slurs and vilify all people from one race, religion, and so on.

Behaviors resulting from both explicit and implicit biases are based on stereotypes. In the case of implicit biases, individuals do not know that they hold stereotypical images of people from other groups, and do not have an awareness that, one day, there is a high probability that they will act out with discriminatory behavior.

Retired police chief Howard Jordan, currently a criminal justice instructor, often gets questions from his students related to differentiating between a racist and someone with racist tendencies. "Some officers deny being a racist, but find it very normal to share racist jokes with co-workers, thus exhibiting racist tendencies" (Jordan, 2017).

A Case of Officer Error and Implicit Bias—Example for Discussion

Ronald Hampton, retired Metropolitan D.C. police officer/former executive director of National Black Police Association taught criminal justice to students in the '90s and beyond at the University of the District of Columbia. A highly publicized shooting of a black off-duty officer by a white officer took place; Hampton proceeded to use the incident as a teaching tool in his criminal justice class.

Background: A black plainclothes officer, who had ended his shift at 11 PM, was on his way home when he passed a taxi cab driver being robbed by an unarmed black man. Onlookers called 911 before the off-duty officer passed by, but on-duty officers had not yet arrived. The off-duty officer stopped his car, and got out to intervene in the robbery. With his weapon in hand, he restrained the robber, and held a gun to him. At that moment, the on-duty officers pulled up to the scene, and parked across the street from the taxi cab. From there, they saw the black plain clothes officer holding a gun to the robber. The off-duty officer turned toward one of the white officers who was across the street, and was immediately shot. (Hampton, 2017).

(As an aside, a debate ensued as to whether the on-duty white officer said, "Police drop your gun." The officer claims that he did, whereas the taxi driver said that the on-duty just got out of the car and started shooting (ibid.). The focus of the discussion questions below is not on the details of the ensuing investigation, but rather on the action that the white officer took when he saw a black man holding a gun to another individual.)

The assignment given to Hampton's criminal justice students: Shortly after the shooting, Hampton had his students conduct a very brief and informal poll just outside Safeway, near the scene of the shooting. The incident was fresh in the minds of the public.

Half of the students were asked to poll white customers coming out of the nearby store, using question A immediately below; the remaining half of the students were asked to poll white customers, using question B. Respondents were encouraged to answer honestly.

Questions asked of white customers:

A. If you saw a black man holding a gun in the same scenario (i.e., as described in the real-life incident above), what would you automatically assume about who this individual is? The "police officer" or the "criminal committing the robbery?"

B. If you saw a white man holding a gun in the same scenario (i.e., as described in the real-life incident above), what would you automatically assume about who this individual is? The "police officer" or the "criminal committing the robbery?"

Responses were completely consistent—the white customers who responded to the first question all said that the black man holding the gun would be the one committing a robbery; the white customers who responded to the second question all said that the white man holding the gun would be the police officer.

Discuss the following questions:

- Re-read the chapter section on implicit bias (pp. 165–166) and discuss the shooting. The officer called to the scene claimed that he did not recognize the black man with the gun as a fellow police officer.
- How could the erroneous shooting have been prevented?
- The D.C. community and Metropolitan D.C. police department were deeply affected by the erroneous shooting of a police officer. If you were the police chief in that community, what would you suggest as an appropriate follow up with both officers and the community?

Racial Profiling

Skipper Osborne, former President of Portland NAACP, and civil rights activist had plans to temporarily stay in the home of friends in an upscale, mainly white neighborhood outside of Portland, Oregon. He feared that, because the neighbors did not know him, someone would call the police. Since he felt that he needed to protect himself from being profiled, he called the local Chief of Police prior to his stay in this neighborhood. Skipper had already had the experience of being stopped multiple times for being in the "wrong neighborhood," and he wanted to avoid this humiliation during his stay in his friend's neighborhood. After talking with the Chief of Police ahead of time, he felt confident that officers would know not to respond to any "suspicious person" calls from the neighbors.

(Osborne, 2017)

"You stopped me because I am black." The truth may, at times, lie between the categorical denial of some police officers and the statement, "We're always being stopped only because we're black." Undoubtedly, there are police procedures of which citizens are unaware, and they do not see all the other people whom an officer stops in a typical day. However, the citizen is not getting paid to be professional, truthful, or even reasonable with the officer. We know that some officers feel that they are doing "good policing" when they stop citizens whom they feel will be guilty of a crime. However, this "feel" for who may be guilty can actually be a reflection of a bias or an assumption that substitutes for real "data." Observing and selecting "guilty-looking" motorists can be the result of subconscious biased thinking. (Refer to "Ladder of Inference" in Chapter 12 as it relates to racial profiling.)

The Trayvon Martin case, mentioned earlier in this chapter, is not an example of *police* racial profiling (it was a Neighborhood Watch volunteer), but it escalated discussions of racial profiling to the highest office in the land. One week after the verdict, President Obama shared with the nation that he was not immune to the stigma of "suspiciousness" associated with his black skin. President Obama acknowledged, "Trayvon Martin could have been me 35 years ago." Before becoming a senator, like many African American men, he too experienced "…being followed… in a department store…getting on an elevator [with] a woman clutching her purse…hearing the locks click on the doors of cars…" (Federal News Service, 2013).

Dr. James Johnson, social science analyst for the Administrative Office of the U.S. Courts, lives in the Washington, D.C. metro area. He and other black men he knows, both professional and nonprofessional, have had the experience of being stopped by the police and subjected to the following line of questioning: "Do you have any ID? Where are you going? Do you have any drugs on you?" The justification for these stops, according to Johnson, is "we fit a description." Officers will typically say, "There have been some robberies in this neighborhood and you fit the description of one the suspects." Johnson explains, "When this happens, we are being treated as if we have already committed a crime."

Officers treat suspects differently than they treat persons whom they believe are innocent of any wrongdoing. We don't get the benefit of the doubt. It is assumed that we don't belong in a particular neighborhood merely because of our skin color, so we are profiled as "suspects." When asked if police officers have made progress in managing racial biases over the years, Johnson replies, "We as black Americans would like to believe so, but some of our experiences remind us that we have a long way to go. It seems like whenever this nation takes one step forward, something happens that causes it to take two steps back. You can roll off the names of African Americans who have been unjustly profiled and injured or even killed because of the color of their skin. That's not progress" (Johnson, 2013).

In essence, the freedom for black Americans to travel to any neighborhood is denied when officers' biases "kick in" and they stop minorities based on their color rather than their behavior. Johnson suggests that officers slow down their thinking process and challenge some of their personal biases and prejudices, particularly when there are no obvious signs of wrongdoing. Officers are advised to go through the following mental steps before acting on racial biases and prejudices (see also last paragraph in this section, reminding readers that the public often does not understand the context for a police stop):

- If I see an individual simply walking down the street, let me first acknowledge to myself that I am not sure whether there is any reason to stop this person.
- I will ask myself the following questions:

  "Why do I think this person should be stopped?"

  "What is this person doing that makes me think he/she is suspicious?"

  "Could this person be lost or in the need of help?"

  "Is this person's race a part of the reason why I want to stop them?"

- If I decide that I should, for whatever reason, stop this individual, would there be merit in my saying something like:

  "There has been a robbery in the neighborhood and I want you to be aware of the potential dangers. You look a little lost, so I was wondering if you need any help or directions." *This only applies if there have actually been recent robberies in the neighborhood. If the person lives in that neighborhood, being dishonest can negatively affect the officer's credibility.* (Ibid.)

In the process of slowing down one's mental processes, the officer makes a conscious decision to recognize potential bias if it is there, and refrains from making inferences or jumping to conclusions based on racial bias or prejudice. Officers can increase cooperation with respectful communication, and, at the same time, assess the *behavior* of the person they are stopping.

The majority of officers do not act on racial biases and prejudices, and, at the same time, the public frequently does not understand the full context (e.g., "reasonable suspicion") as to why an individual may be stopped by the police (Jordan, 2017). We remind readers of the importance of verbal de-escalation (see Chapter 4) so that a citizen's unjustified protest at being stopped does not trigger the officer and lead to unnecessary confrontation.

Perceptions of Treatment by Police/Authority

Research has shown that the psychological experience of many blacks during police encounters differs significantly from that of whites who are stopped by the police (Najdowski, Bottoms, & Goff, 2015). In one study, researchers asked both black and white men to describe what they would be thinking in an encounter with the police. Twenty-seven percent of the black men interviewed felt that the officer would profile them as criminals. In contrast, only

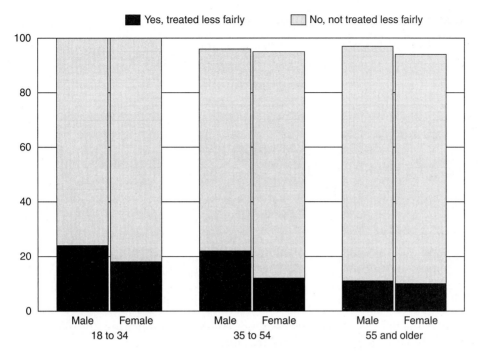

EXHIBIT 6.5   Black Perceptions of Police Treatment in Last 30 Days

Source: Newport, Frank. Gallup Poll: Minority Rights and Relations Poll (June 13–July 5, 2013). All rights reserved. The content is used with permission; however, Gallup retains all rights of republication.

3 percent of white men felt that they would be profiled. Perceiving that officers would see them as threats, some blacks stated that they would "freeze up, look nervous, try to avoid looking nervous or avoid making eye contact in the encounter" (ibid.). This self-conscious behavior, in turn, could lead officers to the conclusion that the individuals were indeed deceptive and suspicious, resulting in a vicious cycle of communication.

Exhibit 6.5 shows the results of a 2013 Gallup Poll in which the following question was asked: "Can you think of any occasion in the last thirty days when you felt you were treated unfairly in dealings with the police, such as [in] traffic incidents?" Nearly 4,400 adults were surveyed; 24 percent of young black men under the age of 35 reported that their dealings with police were unfair, and results were similar for black men between the ages of 35–54. Responses by gender and age differed, with men and women 55 and older reporting significantly fewer unfair dealings with police (10 percent and 11 percent, respectively). Exhibit 6.6 shows results for the same survey question from 1997 to 2013. The high point in 2004 represents 25 percent of blacks of all ages reporting unfair dealings with the police. By 2013, that number had dropped to 17 percent (Newport, 2013).

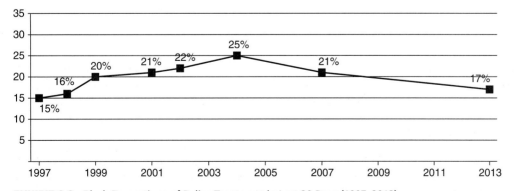

EXHIBIT 6.6   Black Perceptions of Police Treatment in Last 30 Days (1997–2013)

Source: Gallup Poll: Minority Rights and Relations Poll (Historical View 1997–2013). All rights reserved. The content is used with permission; however, Gallup retains all rights of republication.

Excessive and Discriminatory Use of Force

The technical and policy aspects of excessive use of force are outside the scope of this textbook; however, because reports and studies have shown that there is a history of discriminatory use of force against minorities, and especially African Americans, we include content around the need for better screening of police officer applicants, better training in de-escalation strategies as well as an understanding of excessive use of force as a basic human rights violation. It is also advisable that, through community policing programs, citizens be better educated on the complexities and nuances of when force is justified and when it is not, as there is a great lack of information or misinformation in the public.

DOJ report details on police departments such as Baltimore and Chicago (2016 and 2017), respectively, do not describe the actions of each department's entire police workforces. That said, discriminatory behavior is not yet something that can be referred to as "history." Providing a historical perspective that is no less relevant today than it was 25 years ago, the following is one of the key issues presented from a *1994* National Institute of Justice research report:

> …Excessive force needs to be considered a result not only of individual personality traits but also of organizational influences. It is symptomatic of a system wide problem that implicates administrative policies as well as such departments they work for, and it will be increasingly important to the success of community policing initiatives. (Scrivner, 1994)

In August 2016, the Justice Department presented its findings on the Baltimore Police Department (BPD). The findings showed that the department

> …engages in a pattern or practice of conduct that violates the First and Fourth Amendments of the Constitution as well as federal anti-discrimination laws. BPD makes stops, searches and arrests without the required justification; uses enforcement strategies that unlawfully subject African Americans to disproportionate rates of stops, searches and arrests; uses excessive force…[this] has exacerbated community distrust of the police, particularly in the African American community. (U.S. Department of Justice, Civil Rights Division, 2016)

> In January, 2017, the Justice Department published its report on the Chicago Police Department: "Justice Department Finds a Pattern of Civil Rights Violations by the Chicago Police Department" (U.S. Department of Justice, Civil Rights Division, 2017a).

> > The Justice Department announced today that it has found reasonable cause to believe that the Chicago Police Department (CPD) engages in a pattern or practice of using force, including deadly force, in violation of the Fourth Amendment of the Constitution. The department found that CPD officers' practices unnecessarily endanger themselves and result in unnecessary and avoidable uses of force. The pattern or practice results from systemic deficiencies in training and accountability, including the failure to train officers in de-escalation and the failure to conduct meaningful investigations of uses of force…the department's findings further note that the impact of CPD's pattern or practice of unreasonable force falls heaviest on predominantly black and Latino neighborhoods, such that restoring police-community trust will require remedies addressing both discriminatory conduct and the disproportionality of illegal and unconstitutional patterns of force on minority communities. (Ibid.)

The larger context of excessive and discriminatory force against African Americans can be seen in the context of human rights violations. The Inter-American Commission on Human Rights published a report examining contributors to excessive and discriminatory use of police force from an international human rights perspective (Inter-American Commission on Human Rights, 2016). This report was a written submission supporting a hearing on the theme of "Excessive Use of Force by the Police against Black Americans in the United States." The following statement from the report highlights the need for appropriate training for police officers as an "obligation under human rights law" (ibid.):

> **Proper training of police officers is an obligation under international human rights law.**

> As agents of the State, police officers bear the burden to protect and ensure the rights to life, to freedom from torture and ill treatment, and to freedom from discrimination, among others. Violations of these rights are often attributable to inadequate police training. To ensure that police officers are equipped to perform their jobs without putting themselves at risk or violating others' rights, they must be adequately trained, and their training must fulfill minimum essential components required by international standards and domestic laws designed to safeguard human rights.

The Inter-American Court considers international standards to encompass international guidelines and principles, including the Code of Conduct and the Basic Principles. In the words of the Committee on the Elimination of Racial Discrimination, "[l]aw enforcement officials should receive intensive training to ensure that in the performance of their duties they respect as well as protect human dignity and maintain and uphold the human rights of all persons without distinction as to race, color or national or ethnic origin." (Ibid.)

The case of Rodney King, in 1992, brought public attention to the fact that excessive force and brutality are serious problems in America. The existence of brutality has been a problem that blacks and other racial and ethnic groups have asserted, but until the early 1990s when several cases were highly publicized, many whites either did not believe or closed their eyes to this reality—or thought these were an anomaly when considering the number of arrests made without brutality across the nation. Another was the brutality against a black American of Haitian origin, Abner Louima, who, in 1997, was arrested and sodomized with a broomstick inside a restroom at the 70th Precinct station house in Brooklyn. "The case became a national symbol of police brutality and fed perceptions that New York City police officers were harassing or abusing young black men as part of a citywide crackdown on crime" (Chan, 2007).

In 2006, readily available video cameras on smart phones have changed the landscape with respect to visibility and police accountability of excessive use of force, including fatal shootings. The killing of Philando Castile is one of several high-profile cases occurring between 2014 and 2016. During a traffic stop for a broken taillight, Castile was shot seven times in front of his girlfriend, Diamond Reynolds, and her daughter. Ms. Reynolds captured his last moments of life on her cell phone, live-streaming the video on Facebook. The graphic footage went viral and received immediate, nationwide news coverage. The officer responsible for his death was charged and convicted of second-degree manslaughter, having escalated a minor situation to one involving the unjustified use of deadly force (based on Capechi & Smith, 2016; Berman, 2016).

As U.S. Attorney Jenny Durkan commented during an investigation into allegations of excessive force by the Seattle Police Department, "Police officers are taught how to win fights but not how to avoid them" (Pulkkinen, 2011). Police department leaders and DOJ representatives from across the country attended a 2015 program sponsored by PERF (Police Executive Research Forum), entitled: "Re-Engineering Use of Force" (PERF, 2015). Methods of de-escalation must be a priority training issue in all police departments across the country (see Chapter 4). At this program, concerns were voiced that the law enforcement "guardian" rather than "warrior" role must be strengthened with the objective of improving communication skills, and officers' ability to assess and respond to threats. Former police chief Howard Jordan adds that the term, "guardian," is now commonly used to describe the type of police officer that many departments are seeking to recruit and hire (Jordan, 2017). Police departments also need to recognize that stress-reduction techniques must be addressed as frequently and effectively as are traditional topics such as self-defense. Abusive behavior from citizens constitutes one of the worst aspects of the job, but it is not citizens who are required to behave like professionals.

Clearly, the majority of U.S. police officers refrain from using excessive force though we know from examples that continue to occur that police brutality is not yet a phenomenon of the past. Great strides have been made to bring law enforcement and minority communities closer. The overwhelming majority of law enforcement representatives have chosen their profession in order to help people and to be of service to communities.

Hate Crimes against Individuals and Institutions

Hate crimes can trigger racial conflict that extends deep into communities and has repercussions nationwide, including riots and civil disturbances. Communities terrorized by hate crimes require frequent communication with law enforcement representatives, and the assurance that everything possible is being done to prevent further terror. (Chapter 11 provides extensive information on victim needs and response strategies.)

U.S. law enforcement agencies reported 4,216 single-bias hate crime incidents in 2015, according to the FBI:UCR *Hate Crime Statistics Report* (FBI:UCR, 2015). Based on this report, over half of the hate crime victims (52.2 percent) were African Americans though they account for only 13.3 percent of the U.S. population. Racist hate crimes are often vicious, and are intended to intimidate individuals based on a key dimension of their identity such as skin color.

> From lynching, to burning crosses and churches, to murdering a man by chaining him to a truck and dragging him down a road for three miles, anti-black violence has been and still remains the prototypical hate crime, intended not only to injure and kill individuals but to terrorize an entire group of people. Hate crimes against African Americans have an especially negative impact upon society for the history they recall and perpetuate, potentially intimidating not only African Americans, but other minority, ethnic, and religious groups. (LCCREF, 2009)

Throughout history, African Americans have consistently been the victims of hate crimes and marginalization. Following the Civil War, the KKK specifically targeted black churches as a way of terrorizing entire communities. The church has always been a pillar of the black community. Destroying churches or committing hate crimes within them desecrates buildings as well as damages individuals and communities at a very deep and personal level (ADL, 2015).

> In June 2015, a white supremacist, an unemployed ninth grade dropout, opened fire at a black church during a prayer meeting. This horrendous act of racism and assault on the right to worship took place in one of the oldest black churches in the U.S. In December 2015, Dylan Storm Roof was charged with firing more than 60 bullets and was convicted of 33 counts of federal hate crimes for the murder of nine black congregants during their church bible study. In Roof's testimony where he admitted guilt, he claimed that that he "had to do it…that someone had to do it." When asked why, Roof quoted a 2005 FBI statistic about blacks killing and raping white women daily. He further explained that what he did was "miniscule" compared to what blacks did. He felt that he "had to do it" because there was no one brave enough to do it anymore. He said that in the 80s and 90s, skinheads would do it, and someone needed to do it now. The U.S. attorney who prosecuted Roof, said that Roof targeted black congregants, and chose to kill them in a church in order to enhance his message of hate. According to reports, he did not show any remorse, but rather animosity toward African Americans. (Based on Waters & Sullivan, 2016; Jarvie, 2016)

It has been noted that this hate crime took place at the historic Emanuel African church in the heart of Charleston, the same city in which the civil war began, and at a time when the state of South Carolina was also being criticized for flying the Confederate flag from the State Capitol. Roof was heard to have said that he committed the crime for the white race and that he wanted to start a civil war. Roof was convicted of the murders and hate crimes (based on Greene, 2015; Bentley, 2017).

Inner City and Community Policing

African Americans and other racial and ethnic groups have criticized law enforcement for under-policing their communities, despite progress that has been made to improve relations between police and community members in some inner cities. Officers experience a vicious cycle in urban areas, where citizens have become increasingly armed with highly sophisticated weapons; officers, consequently, have to take more self-protective measures. The negative cycle of fear and animosity often operates; police and citizen frequently approach the other with extreme defensiveness. Former police officer Ronald Hampton, who in addition to having served on the Metropolitan D.C. force for 23 years, was the executive of the National Black Police Officer Association. He underscores the importance of taking a community policing approach in the inner city:

> As police officers, we work for the people, both in the inner city and in upscale areas. The people in all neighborhoods are our customers. But in the inner city, we are often ready for battle. When we approach people on the street, we need to see ourselves as others see us. Do we need to put our hand on our gun when we walk towards the people we are serving? Do we have command and control of ourselves and do we know what triggers us? Have we learned about the communities we are going into to serve? We need to understand that when we don't understand, our fear takes over and we rely on our gun because that is what we feel protects us. Instead, we need to connect with respect even if citizens are not being respectful toward us. Walking the footbeat, and getting to know people is one of the best ways to increase our safety margin. The more we do, the more we *increase* our security, and at the same time, we turn the public towards us. (Hampton, 2017)

In summary of Hampton's key points:

• Get to know how people live and work in your jurisdiction.
• Show respect, and you will eventually earn it back.
• Introduce yourself to community members.

- Engage in community meetings and listen to what the needs are.
- Be responsive whenever and wherever you can to try to make a difference. (Ibid.)

Illustrating the last point from his own experience: "Citizens told me that a city street light was not working in back alley streets, causing fear when they walked in those areas. I decided that I could help solve this problem, and approached city officials. Eventually, the problem was taken care of. It was a small gesture, but it made a big difference" (ibid.).

In the inner city and in impoverished areas especially, it is critical to develop positive police–youth relationships early in a child's life. This early interaction can have a lifelong impact on individuals' relationship with law enforcement. A model program is the Police Athletic League (PAL) of Jacksonville, Inc., one of the oldest police/citizen partnerships in the United States, which has served a majority of African American youth in much of Jacksonville for more than 40 years. PAL of Jacksonville…"is built on the idea that a young person who respects police officers is much more likely to respect the laws they enforce" (PAL of Jacksonville, 2017).

Further, PAL's philosophy is that, "…if a young person respects a police officer on the ball field, gym or classroom, the youth will likely come to respect the laws that police officers enforce. Such respect is beneficial to the youth, the police officer, the neighborhood and the business community." Lieutenant Matt Nemeth, former executive director of PAL in Jacksonville, Florida, explained that, in many cases, police officers work as teachers, mentors and coaches, becoming surrogates for those parents who are incapable of or unwilling to fulfill their parental responsibilities. The program serves children and youth in areas of the city that have the highest rate of violence, crime and high school drop-out rates. Children as young as five years old through 17-year-old teens participate in programs including sports, after-school mentoring, and homework classes. Lieutenant Nemeth cited many cases in which young adults return 10 years after participating in PAL with a "grateful heart." He describes the PAL partnership with Jacksonville's minority and nonminority community members as a "long-term investment in prevention. PAL provides opportunities to youth who are at a fork in the road. It provides them with direction that they would not have otherwise had" (Nemeth, 2013).

Programs such as PAL, where positive relations with officers are fostered, can eventually lead some young people to consider law enforcement. Retired Police Chief Howard Jordan talks about the role of Law Enforcement "Pre-Academy" Programs to further inspire and attract youth to policing as a career. Such programs, run by police professionals and trainers, help young people to decide if policing is a good choice for them, and, if so, how the career affords the opportunity to give back to their communities (Jordan, 2017).

Efforts toward Positive Relationships between Police and Community

Community members and police departments differ widely in the way they build positive relationships with each other. Ideally, every law enforcement agency would pursue personal and face-to-face opportunities for building trust; especially with community groups that have not had a history of positive relations with law enforcement. However, community policing is not an absolute guarantee of positive community relations, though effort should always go first toward making it successful. Many inappropriate police actions within African American and other minority communities have resulted in the implementation of federal "consent decrees." Some police leaders believe that a consent decree is not a symbol of a positive relationship; at the same time, many community leaders have supported them. However the consent decree is viewed, its aim is to force a change of prejudicial or unjust behavior or actions by legal means.

Consent Decree—Police Agencies

Consent Decree Upon finding that a police agency has a "pattern or practice" of biased policing, the Department of Justice will reach a legal agreement with that agency, designed to bring about positive change in the areas of recruiting, training, use of force and discipline. Consent decrees are enforceable by the courts.

As of April 2017, 14 police departments around the country were operating under Consent Decrees (U.S. Department of Justice, Civil Rights Division, 2017b). These contracts are viewed by many as important tools to address such issues as excessive force and discriminatory practices. The Los Angeles Police Department is a good example of how a consent decree, over a 12-year period until 2012, changed it from what was once a major metropolitan police department with a pattern of "excessive force, false arrests and unreasonable searches and seizures" (LAPD, 2017) to a model for big city agencies (Orlov, 2013). The consent decree ended up being a guide that helped transform organizational culture that was clearly discriminatory against African Americans and other minority groups to one that eventually won back the public trust.

While there is controversy around consent decrees, with some officers' feeling that they add too much paperwork and bureaucracy to their already demanding jobs, they serve a purpose. Consent decrees are an attempt, on the part of the federal government as well as local and state police departments and communities, to try to improve community/police interaction in a quick and dramatic manner. Some outcomes can be influenced informally and others by consent decrees.

With or without consent decrees, the key to improved relationships with community deeply rests on the following:

- Leadership;
- Organizational culture and vision of department;
- Goals and strategies;
- Understanding of mutual benefits for police and community;
- Effective communication, on the part of both law enforcement professionals and community members; and
- Mutual understanding and education to break down stereotypes and replace them with positive images.

Police officers, community members and leaders need to develop opportunities for one-on-one and police department-community interaction to break down cycles of aggressive communication and dispel stereotypes. They need to develop ongoing relationships before crises occur. This is especially important in African American communities, where people have historically not had trust in law enforcement.

Summary

- The experiences of both slavery and racism have shaped African American culture and continue to leave psychological scars on many African American communities and individuals. Law enforcement represents a part of a system that has, in the past, explicitly oppressed African Americans and other minorities. Protecting as well as ensuring that justice is served in African American communities across the United States often necessitate extra effort on the part of officers in order to establish trust and win cooperation.
- African Americans are represented in all socioeconomic classes, from the underclass to the upper class, and have moved increasingly into the middle class. As with all racial and ethnic groups, there are significant class-related differences among blacks affecting values and behavior. However, color, more so than class, determines how the larger society reacts to and treats blacks. Therefore, the racial experience of many African Americans in the United States is similar, regardless of an individual's level of prosperity or education.
- The Civil Rights and Black Pride Movements, along with positive identification with African culture, have for some replaced the sense of inferiority fostered by white racist supremacist attitudes. The changing terms that African Americans have used to refer to themselves reflect stages of racial empowerment and cultural growth. The Black Lives Matter (BLM) movement is one that has empowered youth, in particular, and has broad goals of affirming the contributions of all African Americans, including those previously marginalized. BLM grew out of community reaction to multiple high-profile fatal shootings of unarmed blacks by police.
- Single mothers, particularly in the inner city, do not always receive the respect that they are due. An officer who takes the time to establish rapport and make

appropriate and helpful referrals will stand a good chance of gaining both family and community's trust, respect and cooperation. Officers are advised to treat single mothers in impoverished areas with as much respect as they would treat single mothers in middle and upper class areas.

• Many African Americans switch back and forth between language styles or use what is commonly referred to as *Ebonics* or *African American Vernacular English.* Acceptance of another person's variety of English can go a long way toward establishing rapport. Use of Ebonics, which is a nonstandard variety of English, does not signal ignorance. Many African Americans from all classes speak Ebonics among peers and family members, while switching to standard English when the situation calls for it (e.g., at work, in interviews, and with white friends and colleagues).

• Regarding communication style, within African American cultural norms it is acceptable to be highly expressive and emotional in speech. This is in contrast to an unspoken white mainstream norm that discourages the open and free expression of emotion, and especially anger. Therefore, officers from different backgrounds should not over-interpret a style, which may differ from their own, as being aggressive and leading to violence. Similarly, people in positions of authority can misinterpret certain ways of walking, standing, and dressing, and perceive these styles as defiant.

• Police departments are microcosms of the environments that surround them; black and white officers often have significant differences in perceptions regarding racial matters. The issues of implicit bias, differential treatment, racial profiling, excessive force, and hate crimes are still realities in policing and law enforcement interaction with African Americans. Acts of bias, injustice and hate cause suffering in communities and in entire police departments. Bridging the gap that has hindered relationships between the police and African Americans involves far reaching changes and special efforts on the part of police officers to break cycles of aggressive communication and dispel stereotypes.

Discussion Questions and Issues

1. *Racism: Effects on Blacks and Whites.* Under the "Historical Information" section in this chapter, the authors state that slavery has created great psychological and social problems for succeeding generations of black citizens. How does the legacy of slavery continue to impact both blacks and whites? What are the implications for law enforcement?

2. *Offensive Terms.* Officers should refrain from using racial epithets at all times, even when there are no African Americans present. What are the reasons for this?

3. *Blue Code of Silence.* Discuss the example on p. 000 in which an African American officer, who was fairly new to a department, did not speak up when it came to his partner's differential treatment of black citizens in a nightclub. Questions to discuss:

   • What do you think held this officer back from speaking up?

   • What might the consequences of his silence be with respect to the ongoing relationship between black and white officers?

   • How should this example of differential treatment have been handled?

   • After you have answered these questions, discuss how departments, in community-policing forums with African American and other ethnic communities, can convey their commitment to police professionalism and ethics—a step that is crucial in rebuilding trust with communities that have historically not had positive relations with law enforcement.

4. *Excessive and Discriminatory Use of Force.* Since the police shooting of Michael Brown in Ferguson, Missouri, the phrase, "The Ferguson Effect" (also known as "de-policing") has come into existence. Research this phrase, explain what it means, and explain the controversy that surrounds it.

5. *Inner Cities.* Toward the end of the chapter, the authors mention the vicious cycle that is created in urban areas, especially where citizens have become increasingly armed with highly sophisticated weapons. Consequently, officers must take more self-protective measures. Each views the other with fear and animosity and approaches the other with extreme defensiveness. Obviously, there is no simple answer to this widely occurring phenomenon, and police alone cannot solve it. Discuss your observations of the way officers cope with the stresses of these potentially life-threatening situations and how the coping or lack thereof affects relations with African Americans and other minorities. What type of support do police officers need to handle this aspect of their job? Do you think police departments are doing their job in providing the support needed?

6. *When Officers Try to Make a Difference.* Many young African American children live without a father in the household. This means that they do not have a second parental figure as a role model and are consequently deprived of an important source of adult support. No one can take the place of a missing parent, but there are gestures of support that a police officer can do to make an impression in the life of a child. Compile a list of actions officers can take to demonstrate caring for children in this type of environment. Brainstorm in one list suggestions, including ones that are ideal, but may not be realistic. Your second list can be more realistic and include actions that can be taken even when there are minimal resources. Compile both sets of suggestions (i.e., the realistic and ideal suggestions). Post these lists as reminders of how officers can attempt to make a difference in their communities, not only with African American children but with others as well.

References

ADL. (2015). "ADL Expresses Concern about Spate of Fires at African-American Churches and Commends Attorney General for Investigating." July 1. Anti-Defamation League. www.adl.org/news/press-releases/adl-expresses-concern-about-spate-of-fires-at-african-american-churches-and (accessed April 2, 2017).

Anderson, Monica. (2015). "African Immigrant Population in U.S. Steadily Climbs." February 14, 2017. www.pewresearch.org/fact-tank/2015/11/02/african-immigrant-population-in-u-s-steadily-climbs/ (accessed January 5, 2017).

Axtell, Brooke. (2012). "Black Women, Sexual Assault and the Art of Resistance." *Forbes*, April 25.

Bennett, Lerone, Jr. (1989). "The 10 Biggest Myths about the Black Family." *Ebony*, November, pp. 1–2.

Bentley, Rosalind. (2017). "After Dylann Roof, What's the Fate of the Confederate Flag?" *The Atlanta-Journal Constitution*, January 9. www.ajc.com/news/crime–law/after-dylann-roof-what-the-fate-the-confederate-flag/HaCtiPvplkXOdQbn6jAhAN/ (accessed April 17, 2017). www.ajc.com/news/crime–law/after-dylann-roof-what-the-fate-the-confederate-flag/HaCtiPvplkXOdQbn6jAhAN/

Berman, Mark. (2016). "Minnesota Officer Charged with Manslaughter for Shooting Philando Castile during Incident Streamed on Facebook," November 16. https://www.washingtonpost.com/news/post-nation/wp/2016/11/16/prosecutors-to-announce-update-on-investigation-into-shooting-of-philando-castile/?utm_term=.dc81003acf17 (accessed March 3, 2017).

Berry, Ondra. (2017). Retired Assistant Police Chief, Reno, Nevada, Police Department, personal communication, March 15, 2017.

Bidgood, Jess. (2013). "Helping Immigrants Warm to Winter." *The New York Times*, March 6.

Capechi, Christina and Mitch Smith. (2016). "Officer Who Shot Philando Castile Is Charged with Manslaughter." *The New York Times*, November 16. www.nytimes.com/2016/11/17/us/philando-castile-shooting-minnesota.html (accessed February 20, 2017).

Capps, Randy, Kristen McCabe, and Michael Fix. (2011). *New Streams: Black African Migration to the United States*. Washington, D.C.: Migration Policy Institute. www.migrationpolicy.org/pubs/CBI-AfricanMigration.pdf (accessed December 15, 2016).

Chan, Sewell. (2007). "The Abner Louima Case, 10 Years Later." *The New York Times* (New York/Region section), August 9. https://cityroom.blogs.nytimes.com/2007/08/09/the-abner-louima-case-10-years-later/commen (accessed January 2, 2016).

Cobb, Jelani. (2016a). "Honoring the Police and Their Victims." *The New Yorker*, July 25. www.newyorker.com/magazine/2016/07/25/baton-rouge-st-paul-and-dallas (accessed February 16, 2017).

Cobb, Jelani. (2016b). "The Matter of Black Lives." *The New Yorker*, March 14. www.newyorker.com/magazine/2016/03/14/where-is-black-lives-matter-headed (accessed February 16, 2017).

Comey, James B. (2015). "Hard Truths: Law Enforcement and Race," Former FBI Director speech at Georgetown University, Washington, D.C., February 12. www.fbi.gov/news/speeches/hard-truths-law-enforcement-and-race (accessed December 1, 2016).

Correll, J., B. Park, C. Judd, C.M. Wittenbrink, B. Sadler, M.S., and T. Keesee. (2007). "Across the Thin Blue Line: Police Officers and Racial Bias in the Decision to Shoot." *Journal of Personality & Social Psychology, 92*(6), 1006–1023.

FBI:UCR. (2015). *Hate Crime Statistics Report*. Federal Bureau of Investigation. https://ucr.fbi.gov/hate-crime/2015 (accessed January 21, 2017).

Federal News Service. (2013). "Transcript: Obama's Remarks on Trayvon Martin Case, Race in America." *The Wall Street Journal*, July 19.

FIP website. (2017). "Fair and Impartial Policing," UJSDOJ COPS supported training programs for Law Enforcement (*Command Level, Supervisor, Patrol and Train the Trainer* developed between 2008–2014); 2017 update FIP, LLC. www.fairimpartialpolicing.com/ (accessed December 15, 2016).

Fridell, Lorie. (2017a). Former Director of Research at the Police Executive Research Program (PERF); National Expert on Biased Policing, personal communication, January 31, 2017.

Fridell, Lorie. (2017b). Producing Bias-Free Policing: A Science Based Approach, Springer Publishers, New York, NY.

Gramlich, John. (2017). Pew Research Center. "Black and White Officers See Many Aspects of Policing Differently." January 12. www.pewresearch.org/fact-tank/2017/01/12/black-and-white-officers-see-many-key-aspects-of-policing-differently/ (accessed January 18, 2017).

Greene, Leonard. (2015). "Charleston Massacre Suspect Wanted to 'Start a Civil War'." *New York Post*, June 18. http://nypost.com/2015/06/18/suspect-in-church-shooting-had-apartheid-era-jacket-patches/ (accessed April 17, 2017).

Griffin, Ronald P. (2009). Detroit-Based Pastor and Community Leader, Vice Chair of Detroit Board of Police Commissioners, personal communication, July 13, 2009.

The Guardian. (2015). "#BlackLivesMatter: The Birth of a New Civil Rights Movement," July 19. www.theguardian.com/world/2015/jul/19/blacklivesmatter-birth-civil-rights-movement (accessed April 27, 2017).

Hampton, Ronald. (2017). Retired Police Officer, DC Metropolitan Police Department. Former Executive Director of National Black Police Association. Former Adjunct Criminal Justice Professor, University of the District of Columbia, personal communication, February 2.

Hecht, Michael, Ronald Jackson II, and Sidney Ribeau. (2003). *African American Communication: Exploring Identity and Culture*. Mahwah, NJ: Lawrence Erlbaum Associates, Inc.

Inter-American Commission on Human Rights. (2016). "Excessive Use of Force by the Police against Black Americans in the United States," February 12. http://rfkcenter.org/media/filer_public/7d/84/7d8409c1-588f-4163-b552-1f6428e685db/iachr_thematic_hearing_submission_excessive_use_of_force_by_police_against_black_americans.pdf (accessed January 30, 2017).

Jarvie, Jenny. (2016). "Jurors find Dylann Roof guilty of all 33 Counts in Hate-crime Shootings at South Carolina Church." *Los Angeles Times*, December 15. www.latimes.com/nation/la-na-south-carolina-dylann-roof-20161215-story.html (accessed January 4, 2017).

Johnson, James L. (2013). Social Science Analyst, Administrative Office of the U.S. Courts, personal communication, July 13.

Jordan, Howard. (2017). Retired Oakland (California) Chief of Police, Criminal Justice Faculty, Merritt and Diablo Valley Colleges (Oakland/Pleasant Hill, California, respectively) personal communication, April 10, 2017.

Kastanis, Angeliki and Gates, Gary. "LGBT African-Americans and African-American Same-Sex Couple." Williams Institute. http://williamsinstitute.law.ucla.edu/wp-content/uploads/Census-AFAMER-Oct-2013.pdf (accessed December 30, 2016)

Kochman, Thomas. (1981). *Black and White Styles in Conflict.* Chicago, IL: University of Chicago Press, p. 121.

Kochman, Thomas. (2013). Founder and Chief Operating Officer of KMA Associates; internationally known diversity specialist, personal communication, July 13.

LAPD. (2017). "Consent Decree Overview." Los Angeles Police Department. http://www.lapdonline.org/search_results/content_basic_view/928 (accessed January 25, 2017).

LCCREF: Leadership Conference on Civil Rights Education Fund. (2009). *Confronting the New Faces of Hate: Hate Crimes in America, 2009.*

Lemann, Nicholas. (1991). *The Promised Land: The Great Black Migration and How It Changed America.* New York, NY: Vintage Books.

Markoni, Sinfree, Geneva Smitherman, Arnetha F. Ball, and Arthur K. Spears. (Eds.). "Black Linguistics: Language, Society, and Politics in Africa and the Americas." http://web.stanford.edu/~jbaugh/Black%20Linguistics.pdf (accessed January 15, 2017)

McAdoo, Harriet P. (1992). "Upward Mobility and Parenting in Middle Income Families." *African American Psychology.* Newbury Park, CA: Sage.

Miller, Char. (2017). (Former) Professor of History, Trinity College, San Antonio, Texas, personal communication, February 15, 2017.

Morin, Rich, Kim Parker, Renee Stepler, and Andrew Mercer. (2017). "Behind the Badge." January 11. Pew Research Center. http://www.pewsocialtrends.org/2017/01/11/behind-the-badge/ (accessed January 15, 2017).

Najdowski, Cynthia J., Bette L. Bottoms, and Phillip A. Goff. (2015). "Stereotype Threat and Racial Differences in Citizens' Experiences of Police Encounters." *Law and Human Behavior 2015, 39*(5), 463–477. www.apa.org/pubs/journals/features/lhb-lhb0000140.pdf (accessed January 19, 2017).

Nemeth, Matt, Lieutenant. (2013). Executive director, PAL, Jacksonville, FL, personal communication, July 29.

Newport, Frank. (2013). "In U.S., 24% of Young Black Men Say Police Dealings Unfair." *Gallup Politics*, July 16. http://www.gallup.com/poll/163523/one-four-young-black-men-say-police-dealings-unfair.aspx (accessed February 13, 2017).

NewsOne. (2010). "Black Police Officer Talks Police Brutality, Racism in Interview," August 13. https://newsone.com/669975/black-police-officer-talks-police-brutality-racism-in-interview/ (accessed February 3, 2017).

Orlov, Rick. (2013). "LAPD Consent Decree Dismissed, Federal Oversight End." *Los Angeles Daily News*, May 16. www.dailynews.com/article/zz/20130516/NEWS/130519159 (accessed January 25, 2017).

Osborne, A.L. "Skipper." (2017). Former President, Portland Branch NAACP #1120, Civil Rights Advocate, Founder/CEO of Truth and Justice for All, personal communication, January 26.

Pal of Jacksonville. (2017). https://jaxpal.com/about-us/ (accessed January 15).

Parton, Heather Digby. (2015). "'The Law Is the Enemy': What RFK Can Remind America about Police Brutality." *Salon*, April 29. http://www.salon.com/2015/04/29/the_law_is_the_enemy_what_rfk_can_remind_america_about_police_brutality/ (accessed September 12, 2017).

Patrick, Peter L. (2006). *Answers to Some Questions about Ebonics.* University of Essex, U.K.

Patton, Greg. (2017). Retired Criminal Justice Cultural Diversity Instructor at Portland Community College, personal communication, January 17.

Payne, Keith. (2004). "Whites More Likely to Misidentify Tools as Guns When Linked to Black Faces," https://researchnews.osu.edu/archive/gunbias.htm (accessed January 15, 2017).

PERF. (2015). "Re-Engineering Training on Police Use of Force." *Police Executive Research Forum*, August. www.policeforum.org/assets/reengineeringtraining1.pdf (accessed April 25, 2017).

Pew Research Center. (2014a). "Religious Landscape Survey." *2014 U.S. Religious Landscape.* http://www.pewforum.org/religious-landscape-study/racial-and-ethnic-composition/Study;www.pewforum.org/about-the-religious-landscape-study; www.pewforum.org/religious-landscape-study/racial-and-ethnic-composition/ (accessed January 26, 2017).

Pew Research Center. (2014b). "Racial and Ethnic Composition by Religious Group." http://www.pewforum.org/religious-landscape-study/racial-and-ethnic-composition/ (accesses January 26, 2017).

Pew Research Center. (2016). "On Views of Race and Inequality, Blacks and Whites Are Worlds Apart." Perceptions of How Blacks Are Treated in the U.S. Vary Widely by Race, June 27, 2016.www.pewsocialtrends.org/2016/06/27/on-views-of-race-and-inequality-blacks-and-whites-are-worlds-apart/ (accessed January 18, 2017).

Plant, E.A., B.M. Peruche, and D.A. Butz. (2005). "Eliminating Automatic Racial Bias: Making Race-On Diagnostic for Responses to Criminal Suspects." *Psychological Science*, 16, pp. 180–183.

Pulkkinen, Levi. (2011). "Feds: Seattle police show 'pattern of excessive force.'" *Seattlepi.com*, December 16 (accessed October 13, 2011).

Rickford, John R. "What Is Ebonics (African American English)." Linguistic Society of America. www.linguisticsociety.org/content/what-ebonics-african-american-english (accessed January 21, 2017).

Rickford, John R. (2009). Linguistics Professor; specialist in African American Vernacular English, personal communication, June.

Ross, Janell. (2016). "Two Decades Later, Black and White Americans Finally Agree on OJ Simpson's Guilt," March 4, 2016. Washington Post ABC News-poll. https://www.washingtonpost.com/news/the-fix/wp/2015/09/25/black-and-white-americans-can-now-agree-o-j-was-guilty/?utm_term=.d2871ff6b703 (accessed April 27, 2017).

Schlesinger, Arthur M., Jr. (1978). *Robert Kennedy and His Times, A Mariner Book.* Boston, New York, p. 780.

Scrivner, Ellen M. (1994). "Controlling Police Use of Excessive Force: The Role of the Police Psychologist." https://www.ncjrs.gov/pdffiles1/Digitization/150063NCJRS.pdf

U.S. Census Bureau. (2015a). Quick Facts Detroit, Michigan. http://www.census.gov/quickfacts/table/PST045215/2622000 (accessed January 18, 2017).

U.S. Census Bureau. (2015b). Quick Facts United States. https://www.census.gov/quickfacts/ (accessed January 18, 2017).

U.S. Department of Justice. "Understanding Bias: A Resource Guide," Community Relations Service Toolkit for Policing. www.justice.gov/crs/file/836431/download (accessed January 10, 2017).

U.S. Department of Justice. (2015). "Attorney General Holder Delivers Update on Investigations in Ferguson, Missouri," March 4. Office of Public Affairs. https://www.justice.gov/opa/speech/attorney-general-holder-delivers-update-investigations-ferguson-missouri (accessed April 27, 2017).

U.S. Department of Justice. (2016). "Justice Department and City of Ferguson, Missouri, Resolve Lawsuit with Agreement to Reform Ferguson Police Department and Municipal Court to Ensure Constitutional Policing," March 17. Office of Public Affairs. www.justice.gov/opa/pr/justice-department-and-city-ferguson-missouri-resolve-lawsuit-agreement-reform-ferguson (accessed April 27, 2017).

U.S. Department of Justice. Civil Rights Division. (2016). "Investigation of the Baltimore Police Department," August 10. www.justice.gov/opa/file/883366/download (accessed February 17, 2016).

U.S. Department of Justice. Civil Rights Division. (2017a). "Investigation of the Chicago Police Department," January 13. www.justice.gov/opa/file/925846/download (accessed February 17, 2017).

U.S. Department of Justice. Civil Rights Division. (2017b). "Police Reform and Accountability Accomplishments." https://www.justice.gov/opa/file/797666/download (accessed April 5, 2017).

Walker, Samuel. (1992). *The Police in America*. New York, NY: McGraw-Hill.

Waters, Dustin and Kevin Sullivan. (2016). "Dylann Roof Guilty on 33 Counts of Federal Hate Crimes for Charleston Church Shooting." *The Washington Post*, December 15. www.washingtonpost.com/national/dylann-roof-guilty-on-33-counts-of-federal-hate-crimes-for-charleston-church-shooting/2016/12/15/0bfad9e4-c2ea-11e6-9578-0054287507db_story.html?utm_term=.ba19ab376182 (accessed March 3, 2017).

Williams, Hubert, and Patrick Murphy. (1990). *The Evolving Strategy of Police: A Minority View*. Washington, D.C.: U.S. Department of Justice, Office of Justice Programs, National Institute of Justice.

Wolfram, Walt and Benjamin Torbert. (2004). "African American English." *Language Magazine, 3*(6), 40–45.

Wolfram, Walt and Benjamin Torbert. (2005). *The Linguistic Legacy of the African Slave Trade*. PBS, American Varieties: African American English. http://www.pbs.org/speak/seatosea/americanvarieties/AAVE/worldscollide/ (accessed January 5, 2017).

7 Law Enforcement Contact with Latino/Hispanic Americans

LEARNING OBJECTIVES

After reading this chapter, you should be able to:

- Discuss the implications of group identification terms for Latino/Hispanic Americans.
- Describe the historical background of Latino/Hispanic American communities in the United States.
- Highlight the demographic features and diversity of Latino/Hispanic communities.
- Identify myths and stereotypes associated with Latino/Hispanic Americans.
- Understand selected characteristics of traditional Latino/Hispanic American extended family structure as it relates to law enforcement contact.
- Recognize communication styles used by Latino/Hispanic Americans.
- Highlight key law enforcement issues related to Latino/Hispanic Americans.

OUTLINE

- Introduction
- Latino/Hispanic Americans Defined
- Historical Information
- Demographics: Diversity among Latino/Hispanic Americans
- Myths and Stereotypes
- The Latino/Hispanic American Family
- Communication Styles of Latino/Hispanic Americans
- Key Issues in Law Enforcement
- Summary
- Discussion Questions and Issues
- References

INTRODUCTION

Many police officers have little knowledge of Latino/Hispanic people, communities, language, or culture and there is little to no training in police academies on these subjects. With a growing population in many states around the country, academy trainers, field training officers, and instructors of advanced officer courses would benefit from understanding more about the cultural backgrounds of Latinos. Officers who have a solid grasp of issues facing Latinos in the United States, including fear of law enforcement and language, will be able to better serve these communities by developing trust and obtaining more collaboration from residents.

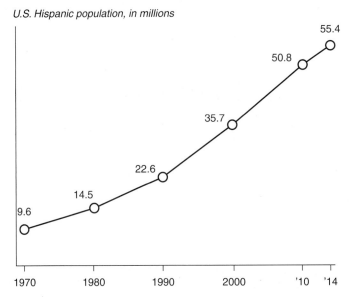

U.S. Hispanic population, in millions

EXHIBIT 7.1 Hispanic Population Growth

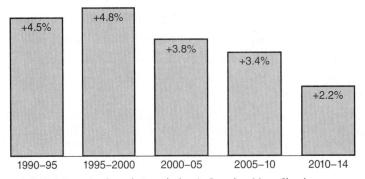

Average annual percent change in U.S. Hispanic population

EXHIBIT 7.2 U.S. Hispanic Population Is Growing More Slowly

Latino or Hispanic Americans are the fastest growing cultural group in the United States in terms of overall numbers of people. The Hispanic population reached 55.4 million in 2014, an increase of 1.2 million (2.1 percent) from the year before (see Exhibit 7.1) (Krogstad & Lopez, 2015). However, the 2.2 percent rate in 2014 continues a trend of slower growth that began in 2007

> …when the Great Recession started, immigration from Latin America cooled and Latino fertility rates declined sharply. Immigration, which in the 1980s and 1990s was the principal driver of Hispanic population growth, began to slow in the mid-2000s. And, in the case of Mexico, immigration has now reversed back toward Mexico since 2009. (Stepler & Lopez, 2016) (see Exhibit 7.2)

The projected Hispanic population in the United States in 2060 is 119 million which will constitute 28.6 percent of the nation's population (U.S. Census Bureau, 2015).

Terminology

In this text, we use "Latino" and "Hispanic" interchangeably as well as "Latino/Hispanic." Following are additional definitions from the U.S. Census Bureau, the Department of Homeland Security, and academic researchers (refer also to Chapter 1 for additional definitions related to types of immigrants).

Foreign-born   Refers to an individual who is not a U.S. citizen at birth or who is born outside the United States, Puerto Rico, or other U.S. territories, and whose parents are not U.S. citizens.

U.S.-born Describes those who are U.S. citizens at birth, including people born in the United States, Puerto Rico, or other U.S. territories, as well as those born elsewhere to parents who are U.S. citizens.

Legal immigrant An individual granted legal permanent residence, granted asylum, admitted as a refugee, or admitted under a set of specific authorized temporary statuses for longer-term residence and work. This group includes "naturalized citizens," legal immigrants who have become U.S. citizens through naturalization; "legal permanent resident aliens," who have been granted permission to stay indefinitely in the United States as permanent residents, asylees, or refugees; and "legal temporary migrants," who are allowed to live and, in some cases, work in the United States for specific periods of time (usually longer than one year).

Sanctuary city, county, or state There is no official definition for "sanctuary" as applied to cities, counties, and states. However, it is a term applied by some to jurisdictions that have adopted policies designed to protect unauthorized immigrants by not prosecuting them solely for violating federal immigration laws.

Unauthorized/Undocumented immigrants All foreign-born non-citizens residing in the country who are not "legal immigrants" and who entered the country without valid documents or arrived with valid visas but stayed past their visa expiration date or otherwise violated the terms of their admission (these two terms are used interchangeably) (Passel & Cohn, 2016).

Undocumented Immigrants in the United States

Chapter 1 presents general issues related to undocumented immigrants. The Pew Hispanic Center estimated that the total number of undocumented immigrants in the United States as of 2014, the most recent statistics available, was 11.1 million, which represented a two-year decline from the peak of 12 million in 2007. The trend of fewer undocumented immigrants coming from Mexico between 2007 and 2014, a decline of about 6.5 million, are:

- The numbers of people from Mexico leaving the United States almost matched the numbers entering. It was attributed to the U.S. recession or economic downturn and fewer jobs available,
- Stepped-up enforcement at the Mexico border,
- Increasing dangers of illegal crossings,
- Improvements in the economic conditions in Mexico. (Passel & Cohn, 2016)

Undocumented immigrants from Mexico make up about half (52 percent) of the nation's immigrant population (ibid.).

It was the first significant reversal in a two-decade pattern of growth (ibid.). The nativity and legal status of the Mexican-origin population as of 2011 is shown in Exhibit 7.3.

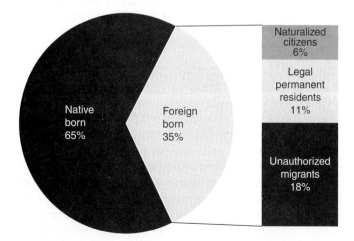

EXHIBIT 7.3 Nativity and Legal Status of Mexican-Origin Population in the United States, 2011

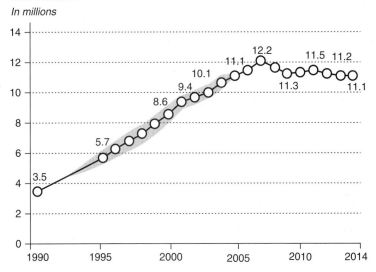

Estimated unauthorized immigrant population in the U.S. rises, falls, then stabilizes

In millions

EXHIBIT 7.4 Estimates of the U.S. Undocumented Immigrant Population, 1990–2014

Source: http://www.pewresearch.org/fact-tank/2017/04/27/5-facts-about-illegal -immigration-in-the-u-s/

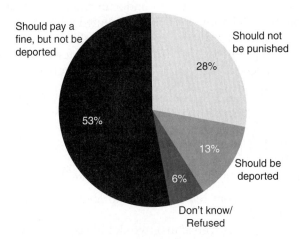

EXHIBIT 7.5 Latinos Are Divided over What to Do about Unauthorized Immigrants

Source: "Illegal Immigration Backlash Worries, Divides Latinos." Mark H. Lopez, Rich Morin, and Paul Taylor. Pew Research Center. October, 2010.

Estimates of the undocumented immigrant population in the United States between 1990 and 2014, from 3.5 to 11.1 million, is shown in Exhibit 7.4.

Latinos are divided over what to do about unauthorized immigrants (see Exhibit 7.5).

Chapter 1 presents information about a federal program, 287(g), which allows the U.S. Immigration and Customs Enforcement (ICE) administration to enter into partnerships or joint Memoranda of Agreement with state and local law enforcement agencies. Under this agreement, officers can enforce federal immigration laws within their jurisdiction if the state or local agency has entered into an agreement with ICE. There have been complaints by immigrant rights groups and within the general public about the 287(g) immigration enforcement program. The program itself is a controversial one, with arguments for and against, nationwide. Arguments against allowing state and local law enforcement officers to enforce federal immigration laws include: (1) it diverts resources from state and local agencies to do federal enforcement work; (2) there is the potential for officers to racially profile people suspected of being undocumented; and (3) increased enforcement has not led to decreased crime (Miles & Cox, 2014).

Across the country, law enforcement agencies vary as to whether to partner with ICE in enforcing immigration laws believing that involvement with ICE corrodes their relationship with immigrant communities, who are already less likely to report crimes. The same was true of participation in the Secure Communities program that existed from 2008 to 2014 when it was replaced by Priority Enforcement Program (PEP), which focuses on convicted criminals and others who pose a danger to public safety.

Some cities, counties, and states have enacted policies that make them, what has been called, a sanctuary jurisdiction or more commonly, "Sanctuary City." The 1980s was the first appearance of sanctuary policies when cities, and churches, offered "sanctuary" to immigrants that had come to the United States due to civil wars in Latin America. The Regan administration was planning to deport those who had fled and some cities created policies to provide protection for the immigrants.

> Civil-rights advocates argue that some of the biggest proponents for sanctuary policies are police departments, many of whom rely on communities for tips about crime.

> A 2013 statement by the Major Cities Police Chiefs group declared that immigration enforcement was a "major concern" for departments working to build trust with communities. President Barack Obama's 21st Century Policing report also found that decoupling policing and immigration enforcement was key to improving community policing. (Ibid.)

The murder of a young woman in San Francisco in 2015 by an undocumented immigrant who had been deported seven times resulted in the introduction of legislation in U.S. Congress that would punish cities that refused to enforce immigration laws (Rasmussen Reports, 2015). Neither bill passed. On January 3, 2017, H.R. 83—Mobilizing Against Sanctuary Cities Act was introduced in Congress, which, if passed and signed into law, would prohibit any federal funding for a minimum period of one year to any state or local government which has a policy or law that prevents them from assisting immigration authorities in enforcing federal immigration law. At the time, the Immigration and Customs Enforcement agency listed about 300 state and local governments that were considered sanctuary jurisdictions (H.R. 83, 2017). The above is covered here because, although "sanctuary cities" and policies and laws pertaining to them are applied to all undocumented immigrants, the largest impact is upon the Hispanic/Latino population. The impact and backlash has even included those who were born in the United States or who immigrated legally (Lopez, Moran, & Taylor, 2010). See Chapter 1, section entitled, Fear of Deportation, Law Enforcement and ICE (pp. 21–24), for more information.

LATINO/HISPANIC AMERICANS DEFINED

The word *Hispanic* does not describe a racial group; for example, a person can be white, black, or Asian and still be considered Hispanic. *Hispanic* is a generic term referring to all Spanish-speaking people who reside within the United States and Puerto Rico or people whose ancestors came from Latin America. *Latino* is generally the preferred label on the West Coast, parts of the East Coast, and the Southeast. The term *Latino* is a Spanish word indicating a person of Latin American origin, and it reflects the gender-specific nature of its Spanish-language derivation: Latino, for men, and Latina, for women. Hispanic is generally, although not universally, preferred on the East Coast, specifically within the Puerto Rican, Dominican, and Cuban communities (although individual members within each of these communities may prefer the specific term referring to their country of heritage). A new Pew Research Center survey of multiracial Americans finds that, for two-thirds of Hispanics, their Hispanic background *is* a part of their racial background—not something separate. This suggests that Hispanics have a unique view of race that doesn't necessarily fit within the official U.S. definitions (Gonzalez-Barrera & Lopez, 2015). The U.S. government Census Bureau specifically distinguishes Hispanic and Latino as terms to define ethnic origin and not a person's race.

Sometimes, the term *Spanish-surnamed* may be used to recognize that one may have a Spanish surname and have ethnic roots in Latin America but may not speak Spanish (which is the case for a large number of Latino/Hispanic Americans). *La Raza* is another term used, popularized by the Latino civil rights movements of '70s in the United States to express a pride and solidarity among people from Latin America; the word *raza* literally means "race." Like La Raza, *Chicano* is another term that grew out of the ethnic pride in the late 1960s. Chicano refers specifically to Mexican Americans, and it is used primarily on the West Coast, in the Southwest, and in the Midwest. Historically, "Chicano" was considered a derogatory term, but has in more recent years been embraced as a source of pride by a younger generation of Mexican Americans.

United States Census—Hispanic and Latino Survey Category

In 1976, Congress passed Public Law 94-311, which required the inclusion of a self-identification question on Spanish origin or descent in government surveys and censuses. As such, *Hispanic* is the official term used in federal, state, and local governmental writings and for demographic references. Federal standards implemented in 2003 allow the terms *Latino* and *Hispanic* to be used interchangeably (Office of Management and Budget, 1997). As of 2013, the U.S. Census Bureau has proposed a change of wording from "Hispanic" to "Hispanic Race" for the census that will take place in 2020 (Ayala & Huet, 2013). The reason for the change of wording is that many Hispanics do not identify with or see themselves fitting into the standard racial categories from which to select. For example, when it comes to race, according to a Pew Hispanic survey, half (51 percent) of Latinos identify themselves as "some other race" or volunteer "Hispanic/Latino." Meanwhile, 36 percent identify their race as white, and 3 percent say their race is black. Those completing the survey were able to mark one or more race, but only one Hispanic ethnicity category. One of the purposes of the proposed change is to reduce the number of nonresponses to the survey question and, thus, improve accuracy of the census pertaining to the numbers of Hispanic/Latino in the U.S. population (Taylor, Lopez, Martinez, & Velasco, 2012). In planning stages is that eventually the U.S. Census Bureau will eliminate Hispanic as a category altogether and classify Hispanics as their own racial category such as white, black or African American, Asian, Native Hawaiian, or Other Pacific Islander, thus no longer focus on ethnic labels. The Census Bureau in 2020 plans to not use the words "race" or "origin" on the form, but instead the questionnaire will ask the respondent the check categories that describe them (U.S. Census Bureau, 2014a).

Labels and Terms

As noted earlier, the term *Latino/Hispanic* American is a convenient summarizing label to achieve some degree of agreement in referring to a very heterogeneous group of people. As with Asian/Pacific Americans, the key to understanding which terms to use is based on the principle of self-preference. Sensitivity is warranted in the use of the term *Hispanic* with the Latino/Hispanic American community. For those who have origins in the Caribbean (e.g., Puerto Rican, Cuban, Dominican), the term *Latino* may be equally problematic for self-designation and self-identification.

Until 2003, federal and other governmental designations used only Hispanic; Latino and Hispanic are now used interchangeably. The governmental designations are used in laws, programs, and regulations, and in most reports and publications. According to a Pew Research Center report, over 51 percent of those surveyed described themselves as "Mexican," "Cuban," "Puerto Rican," "Argentinean," "Salvadorian," or "Dominican," depending on the country from which their family came. Only 24 percent used the terms *Hispanic* or *Latino* to describe their identity. Twenty-one percent said they use the term *American* most often (Taylor et al., 2012). "Spanish speakers may take offense if law enforcement officials describe them as Latino[s] or Hispanic[s] or categorize them with citizens from countries other than their own." It is incorrect to assume that all Spanish speakers hold the same political views, especially if they are from different countries and don't "share the same identity, whether cultural or national. And they often feel great pride in their regional or national identities to the point that they may resent being grouped with those from other parts of the Spanish-speaking world" (Natella & Madera, 2008). For law enforcement officers, the best term to use in referring to individuals is the term that those individuals prefer to be called. It is perfectly acceptable to ask people what nationality they are. Never ask "what race are you?" because neither term [Latino or Hispanic] describes a race. In some situations, asking this question would be considered rude and, in the workplace, possibly even illegal and can expose you to potential liability under antidiscrimination laws.

The use of slurs like "wetback," "Mex," "spic," "beaner," "nacho," "border nigger," or other derogatory ethnic slang terms is never acceptable by law enforcement officers, no matter how provoked an officer may be. These and other stereotypic terms do not convey the kind of professionalism and respect for community diversity important to law enforcement and peacekeeping, and must be avoided in law enforcement work. Officers hearing these or similar words used in their own departments (or with peers or citizens) should provide immediate feedback about the inappropriateness of the use. Officers who, out of habit, routinely use these or other derogatory terms may find themselves or their superiors in the embarrassing situation of explaining to offended citizens and communities why they used the term and how they intended no bias, stereotype, or prejudice. Officers should avoid culturally-loaded terms like "macho" because while it can be used to praise someone's masculinity, strength and chivalry, it has also been associated with male aggression and violence.

HISTORICAL INFORMATION

This brief historical review focuses primarily on the larger Latino/Hispanic communities in the United States, specifically those with Mexican, Puerto Rican, and Cuban ethnic and historical roots.

In the 1800s, under the declaration of Manifest Destiny, the United States began the expansionist policy of annexing vast territories to the south, north, and west. As Lopez y Rivas (1973) noted, the United States viewed itself as a people chosen by "Providence" to form a larger union through conquest, purchase, and annexation. With the purchase and annexation of the Louisiana Territories in 1803, Florida in 1819, Texas in 1845, and the Northwest Territories (Oregon, Washington, Idaho, Wyoming, and Montana) in 1846, it seemed nearly inevitable that conflict would occur with Mexico. The resulting Mexican–American War ended in 1848 with the signing of the Treaty of Guadalupe Hidalgo, in which Mexico received $15 million from the United States for the land that is now Texas, New Mexico, Arizona, and California, with more than 100,000 Mexican people living in those areas. As is obvious from this portion of history, it makes little sense for many Mexican Americans to be stereotyped as "unauthorized immigrants," especially since more than a million Mexican Americans can trace their ancestry back to families living in the southwestern United States in the mid-1800s. Moreover, for Latino/Hispanic Americans (especially Mexican Americans), the boundaries between the United States and Mexico are seen as artificial. "The geographic, ecological, and cultural blending of the Southwest with Mexico is perceived as a continuing unity of people whose claim to the Southwest is rooted in the land itself" (Montiel, 1978).

While one-third of Mexican Americans can trace their ancestry to families living in the United States in the mid-1800s, the majority of this group migrated into the United States after 1910 because of the economic and political changes that occurred as a result of the Mexican Revolution.

Puerto Rico, on the other hand, was part of Spain until 1897, at which time it was allowed the establishment of a local government. The United States invaded Puerto Rico and annexed it as part of the Spanish–American War (along with Cuba, the Philippines, and Guam) in 1898. Although Cuba (in 1902) and the Philippines (in 1949) were given their independence, Puerto Rico remained a territory of the United States. In 1900, the U.S. Congress passed the Foraker Act, which allowed the president to appoint a governor, to provide an Executive Council consisting of 11 presidential appointees (of which only five had to be Puerto Rican), and to elect locally a 35-member Chamber of Delegates. In reality, the territory was run by the U.S. president-appointed governor and the Executive Council. The Jones Act of 1917 made Puerto Ricans citizens of the United States. It was not until 1948 that Puerto Rico elected its first governor, Luis Munoz Marin. In 1952, Puerto Rico was given Commonwealth status, and Spanish became the language of instruction in the schools again (with English taught as the second language). Following World War II, large numbers of Puerto Ricans migrated to the United States. With citizenship status, Puerto Ricans could travel easily, and they settled in areas on the East Coast, primarily New York City (in part because of the availability of jobs and affordable apartments).

Cubans immigrated into the United States in three waves. The first wave occurred between 1959 and 1965 and consisted of primarily white, middle-class or upper-class Cubans who were relatively well-educated and had business and financial resources. The federal government's Cuban Refugee Program, Cuban Student Loan Program, and Cuban Small Business Administration Loan Program were established to help this first wave of Cuban immigrants achieve a successful settlement (Bernal & Estrada, 1985). In 1958 and 1960, embargos involving blocking of commercial, economic, and financial trade with Cuba were imposed. Exports and imports were stopped (Hufbauer, Schott, Elliott, & Cosic, 1960).

The second wave of Cuban immigrants occurred between 1965 and 1973, spurred by the Cuban government's the opening of the Port of Camarioca and allowing all who wished to leave Cuba to do so. Those who left tended to be more working class and lower middle class, primarily white men and women.

The third wave of Cuban immigrants occurred from the summer of 1980 to early 1982, and is known as the Mariel Boat Lift. This wave was the largest and brought about 125,000 to the United States, primarily of working-class persons, more reflective of the Cuban population than were previous waves. Most immigrated into the United States with hopes for better economic opportunities. Within this group of "Marielitos" were many criminal and mentally ill people considered undesirable by Fidel Castro (Glass, 2009; Springer, 1985).

In addition to the three major groups that have immigrated to the United States from Mexico, Puerto Rico, and Cuba, there are immigrants from 21 countries of South and Central America, as well as the Caribbean. Arrival of these immigrants for political, economic, and social reasons began in the early 1980s and has added to the diversity of Latino/Hispanic American communities in the United States. The total number of some groups, such as the Dominicans (a rapidly growing group on the East Coast), is difficult to determine because of their unauthorized entry status within the United States.

In 2015, President Obama urged Congress to reopen the American embassy in Cuba and lift the U.S. trade embargos. Despite resistance from a Republican-controlled Congress, the United States opened an embassy in Havana, its first in more than 50 years, while the Cubans opened an embassy in Washington, D.C. However, as of the writing of this edition, the embargo barring tourism and financial transactions between the two countries remains in effect.

DEMOGRAPHICS: DIVERSITY AMONG LATINO/HISPANIC AMERICANS

The historical information shows that despite a common language for most, Latinos in the United States span a wide spectrum of countries of origin, socioeconomic groups and educational levels. Moreover, the language of Brazil is Portuguese, not Spanish, and thus the language connection for Brazilian Latino/Hispanic Americans is unique. The following are some demographic highlights of the Hispanic/Latino population in the United States, illustrating both commonalities and differences:

1. *Age:* The Latino/Hispanic American population tends to be younger than the general U.S. population (see Exhibit 7.6). In 2014, the Hispanic population younger than 18 was 32 percent in contrast to 26 percent for black, 20 percent for Asian, and 19 percent for white (Patten, 2016). Hispanics were the nation's youngest major racial/ethnic group in 2014 (see Exhibit 7.7).

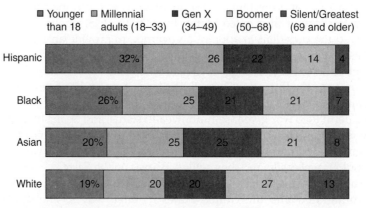

EXHIBIT 7.6 Nearly Six in Ten Hispanics Are Millennials or Younger

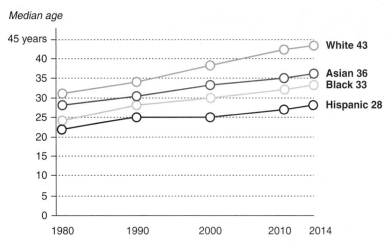

Median age

EXHIBIT 7.7   Hispanics Are the Nation's Youngest Racial/Ethnic Group

2. *Birthrate:* Nearly a quarter of all births nationwide among women ages 15 to 44 in 2011, were to Hispanics (Hispanic Population Trends, 2013) (see Exhibit 7.7). The overall birth rate in the United States declined 8 percent from 2007 to 2010 to its lowest level ever recorded by 2011. "The birth rate for U.S.-born women decreased 6 percent during these years, but the birth rate for foreign-born women plunged 14 percent. …The birth rate for Mexican immigrant women fell even more, by 23 percent," ("U.S. Birth Rate Falls to New Lows," 2013). The decrease, according to some demographers and sociologists, has been linked to changes in views among many Hispanic women about motherhood, size of family, desire to have a career, and use of contraception. Another factor suggested was the prolonged recession, which, historically, results in drops in birthrates.

3. *Language:* Latino/Hispanic American self-identification is most strongly demonstrated in the knowledge and use of Spanish. The Spanish language is often the single most important cultural aspect retained by Latino/Hispanic Americans. The 2014 U.S. Census indicated that of the 54 million Latino/Hispanics in the United States, 68.4 percent spoke English at home or indicate they speak English "very well," up from 59 percent who said the same in 1980. "Most of the growth in English proficiency had been driven by U.S. born Hispanics, mostly millennials, whose English proficiency has grown from 72 percent in 1980 to 89 percent in 2014" (Stepler & Brown, 2016).

  Eighty-seven percent of Hispanics surveyed say adult immigrants need to learn English to succeed in the United States. At the same time, 95 percent want future generations to be able to speak Spanish, indicating a preference for bilingualism (Taylor et al., 2012).

4. *Poverty rate:* The nation's official poverty rate in 2013 was 14.5 percent, a decline from the previous year. Hispanics were the only group among the major race and ethnic groups to experience a statistically significant change in their poverty rate and the number of people in poverty, both the rate and number, declined, down 2.1 percent from 2012 (U.S. Census Bureau, 2014b).

5. *Education:* In 2014, the percentage of Hispanics 25 years and older that had
   • at least a high school education was 61.7 percent compared to 52 percent in 2000.
   • at least a bachelor's degree or higher was 14 percent compared to 10 percent in 2000.
   (Patten, 2016)

Place of Birth and Regional Distribution of Latino/Hispanic Origin Groups in the United States

In 2015, 63.3 percent of people who identify as either Latino or Hispanic were of Mexican background, 9.5 percent were of Puerto Rican background, 3.7 percent Cuban, 3.7 Salvadoran, 3.1 percent Dominican, and 6 percent South American origin (U.S. Census Bureau, 2015).

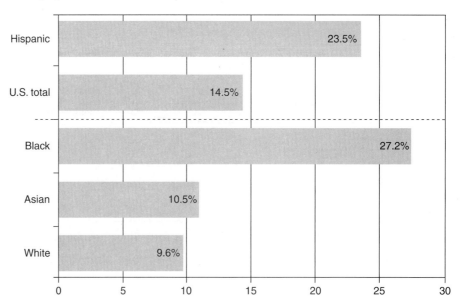

EXHIBIT 7.8   The Hispanic Poverty Rate Is Higher than the U.S. Poverty Rate Overall
Source: U.S. Census Bureau, 2014b.

Hispanic Concentration in the United States

Two-thirds of Hispanics live in just five states—California, Texas, Florida, New York, and Illinois (see Exhibit 7.9) although the fastest growth of Latinos is in South Carolina, Kentucky, Arkansas, Minnesota, and North Carolina, according to the U.S. Census Bureau (Exhibit 7.10). The same report indicates:

- People of Mexican, Salvadoran, and Guatemalan heritage or who were born in those countries make up the highest number of Latinos in California, while in Florida, Latinos tend to hail from Cuba, Colombia, Honduras, and Peru. In New York, Puerto Ricans, Dominicans, and Ecuadorians dominate, although of course there are people from all countries in every state.
- Mexicans make up the single largest group of Hispanic origins, with approximately 12 million in California and another 8.4 million in Texas. Together, these two states contain 61 percent of the total Mexican population in the United States (Motel & Patten, 2012).

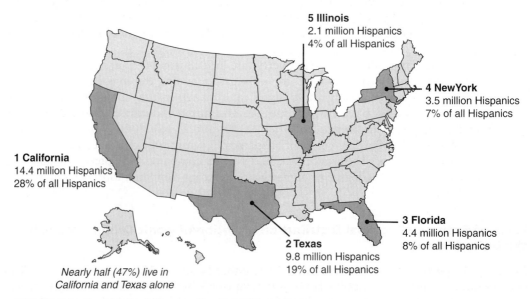

EXHIBIT 7.9   Two-Thirds of Hispanics Live in Just Five States
Source: Hispanic Population Trends, 2013.

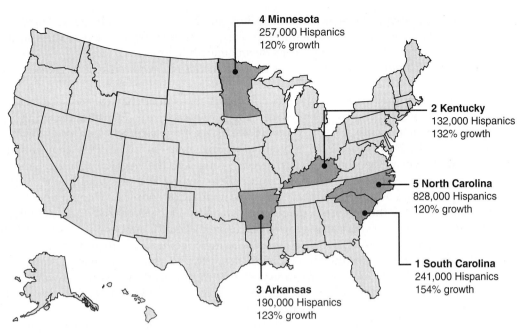

4 **Minnesota**
257,000 Hispanics
120% growth

2 **Kentucky**
132,000 Hispanics
132% growth

5 **North Carolina**
828,000 Hispanics
120% growth

1 **South Carolina**
241,000 Hispanics
154% growth

3 **Arkansas**
190,000 Hispanics
123% growth

EXHIBIT 7.10 Five States with Fastest Growth since 2010
Source: Hispanic Population Trends, 2013.

General Distinction among Generations of Immigrants

In Appendix A, we describe general behavior and characteristics of five immigrant types associated with different generations. The framework and descriptions are intended to help law enforcement, criminal justice, and public safety personnel distinguish among groups in the broad category called "immigrant." Additionally, the information can help prepare law enforcement personnel for contact with immigrant/community members who have been in the United States for varying periods of time. People often use the label "immigrants" which does not convey distinctions, and, therefore, lends itself to overgeneralizations and stereotypes.

MYTHS AND STEREOTYPES

Many law enforcement officers do not have much experience with the diversity of Latino/Hispanic American groups and learn about these groups only through stereotypes (often perpetuated by movies) and through the very limited contact involved in their law enforcement duties. Stereotypic views of Latino/Hispanic Americans reduce individuals within this group to simplistic, one-dimensional characters and have led many Americans to lump members of these diverse groups into calling everyone "Mexicans." Knowledge of and sensitivity to Latino/Hispanic Americans' concerns, historical background, and life experiences will help law enforcement in the crime-fighting and peacekeeping mission. The key to effectiveness with any ethnic or racial group is that we understand that certain cultural generalizations are valid, but that misleading stereotypies exist and may influence our thinking in subtle ways.

Some of the stereotypes that have affected Latino/Hispanic Americans include the following:

1. *Viewing all Latino/Hispanic Americans as "illegal aliens:"* Although many may argue over the number of unauthorized immigrant Latino/Hispanic people in the United States, most do not fall into this category; the vast majority are U.S. citizens or legal residents.
2. *Viewing Latino/Hispanic Americans as lazy and as poor workers:* It is difficult to understand why some people continue to hold this stereotype or what factors continue to perpetuate it, given what we know about the Latino/Hispanic American workforce in the United States and globally. Latino/Hispanic American community advocates

make the argument that it is difficult to imagine anyone being labeled as "lazy" or "poor workers" when they are willing to work as laborers from dawn to dusk in the fields or in many other jobs Americans deem beneath them.

3. *Perceiving Latino/Hispanic Americans as uneducated and uninterested in educational pursuits:* In 2014, the percentage of Hispanics 25 years and older that had at least a high school education was 61.7 percent, while 14 percent of Hispanics have at least a bachelor's degree or higher, with both categories seeing increases each year (Stepler & Brown, 2016).

4. *Seeing Latino/Hispanic American young males as gang members and drug dealers:* Some hold the stereotype, especially about young males in inner cities, that Latino/Hispanic Americans are commonly involved in gangs and the illegal drug trade. Latino/Hispanic cultures are group oriented, and people, young and old, tend to congregate and be identified as groups rather than as individuals or couples. "Hanging out" as a group tends to be the preferred mode of socialization. However, given the stereotype of Latino/Hispanic American young males as being gang members, it is easy to perceive five young Latino/Hispanic males walking together as constituting a "gang." Such stereotypes have resulted in suspicion, hostility, and prejudice toward Latinos and have served to justify improper treatment such as routine traffic stops and unwarranted searches. Such stereotypes can also lead law enforcement officers to unfairly associate Latino/Hispanic Americans with criminal activity.

5. *Assuming that all Latino/Hispanic Americans speak Spanish:* In 2014 over 68.4 percent of Latino/Hispanics 5 to 17 years of age who spoke Spanish in the home also spoke English "well" or "very well" (ibid.). Additionally, many Latino/Hispanic American families have been in the United States for six generations or more—longer than many other ethnic groups—and English is the only language they speak and write. Therefore, it could be considered both insulting and ignorant to tell a Latino that their English is good without knowing more about them and their background.

6. *Assuming that all unauthorized immigrants are from Mexico:* Most of the unauthorized immigrants do come from Mexico and account for the largest percentage of people in the United States illegally. However, there are also a substantial number of undocumented immigrants who are from Central and South America as well as Asia, Europe and Canada, and Africa (Nittle, 2016).

THE LATINO/HISPANIC AMERICAN FAMILY

Names

Non-Latino/Hispanic persons, including police officers, are often confused when people from Spanish-speaking countries use two last names in contrast to those from English-speaking countries in which the last name is the family name and name of record. For example, a person named Octavio Chavez Hernandez may use Chavez as his last name of record rather than Hernandez, which is his mother's last name. Some Latino/Hispanics may inadvertently mislead criminal justice authorities by telling them that the second of their two names are their name of record, while others do this intentionally. This confusion can result in having to initiate a records check, issuing a citation, or even charging an individual using the wrong name. Another source of confusion is the fact that, traditionally, Latino/Hispanic married women add their husbands' last name to their maiden name. They would insert the Spanish word *de* (which means "of") before their married name, thus Octavio's wife, Ana Maria, would become Ana Maria de Chavez. There is some variation to this practice whereby women do not take on their husbands' last name.

Importance of Family

Understanding the importance of family for Latino/Hispanic Americans might be of significant value in community peacekeeping and crime fighting. Obviously, with over 25 different cultural groups that make up the Latino/Hispanic American category, many differences exist among the groups in their family experiences.

La familia is perhaps one of the most significant considerations in working and communicating with Latino/Hispanic Americans. (In places where we use the Spanish term, we have done so to indicate the additional cultural meanings that are not captured in the English term *family*.) The Latino/Hispanic American family is most clearly characterized by bonds of interdependence, unity, and loyalty, and includes nuclear and extended family members as well as networks of neighbors, friends, and community members. Primary importance is given to the history of the family, which is firmly rooted in the set of obligations tied to both the past and the future. In considering the different loyalty bonds, the parent–child relationship emerges as primary, with all children owing *respeto* to parents (*respeto* connotes cultural meanings beyond those in the English term *respect*).

Traditionally, the role of the father has been that of the disciplinarian, decision maker, and head of the household. The father's word is law, and he is not to be questioned. The father tends to focus his attention on the economic and well-being issues of the family and less on the social and emotional issues. The mother, on the other hand, is seen as balancing the father's role by providing for the emotional and expressive issues of the family. Extended family members such as grandmothers, aunts and uncles, and godparents (*padrinos*) may supplement the mother's emotional support. In the Latino/Hispanic American family, the oldest son is traditionally the secondary decision maker to the father and the principal inheritor (*primogenito*) of the family. Because of the central importance of the entire extended family, police officers can expect to come into contact with victims' or suspects' cousins, aunts, uncles, and grandparents in the course of working in Latino/Hispanic communities. Additionally, godparents have traditionally carried significant expectations of financial, emotional, and other types of support. In the United States, however, the mainstream cultural focus is highly individualistic, and, as such, extended support beyond the nuclear family may be decreasing.

The Role of the Man and the Woman in a Latino/Hispanic American Family

Despite an overall patriarchal family structure, the father may appear to be the sole decision maker, but many other individuals may come into the picture. Generally, if there are grandparents in the household, the father may consult them as well as his wife, on major decisions. Latina women are more likely to become employed in the United States, due to increased opportunities and sometimes more facility with English, leading to more independence as well as stress. For these reasons, a husband or father who is used to being the head of the family is sometimes forced to adjust the way he views himself within the family unit, which may be difficult in a culture where a father has ultimate authority.

In the case of law enforcement matters, it may be of great importance if officers can provide the father and the family with some privacy to discuss key issues. With central values like *respeto* and *machismo* (see later) in the Latino/Hispanic American culture, it is critical for the father and other family members to demonstrate control in family situations. Thus, law enforcement officers may find that the best way to maintain control in a situation is by allowing the citizen to think through a decision, come to the same conclusion as that of the officer, and exercise self-control in behaving in the best interests of all parties concerned.

Within the Latino/Hispanic American family, the sex roles are clearly defined; boys and girls are taught from childhood two different codes of behavior (Comas-Diaz & Griffith, 1988). Traditional sex roles can be discussed in the context of the two codes of gender-related behaviors: *machismo* and *marianismo*. *Machismo* literally means maleness, manliness, and virility. Within the Latino/Hispanic American cultural context, *machismo* means that the male is responsible for the well-being and honor of the family and is in the provider role. Machismo is also associated with having power over women, as well as responsibility for guarding and protecting them. Boys are seen as strong by nature and do not need the protection that is required by girls, who are seen as weak by nature.

Women are socialized into the role of *marianismo*, based on the beliefs about the Virgin Mary, in which women are considered spiritually superior to men and therefore able to endure all suffering inflicted by men (Stevens, 1973). Women are expected to be self-sacrificing in favor of their husbands and children. Within the context of the Latino/Hispanic American family, the role of the woman is as homemaker and caretaker of the children. In the current U.S. context, the traditional gender roles of women and men in the Latino/Hispanic American community have undergone much change, which has resulted in conflicts. Since women have begun to work, earn money, and have some of the financial independence men have (e.g., they can go out and socialize with others outside of the family), they have started pursuing many experiences inconsistent with the traditional Latino/Hispanic female role.

Because of these changes, there are no clear-cut rules as to whether law enforcement officers should go to the male head of the household or to the female family member; however, officers would probably be more correct if they address the father first in law enforcement inquiries.

Children, Adolescents, and Youth

Within the Latino/Hispanic American family, the ideal child is obedient and respectful of his or her parents and other elders. Adults may at times talk in front of the children as if they are not present and as if the children cannot understand the adults' conversations. Children are taught *respeto*, or respect, which dictates the appropriate behavior toward all authority figures, older people, parents, relatives, and others. If children are disrespectful, they are punished and scolded. In many traditional families, it is considered appropriate for parents and other relatives to physically discipline a disrespectful and misbehaving child.

In Latino/Hispanic American households, there is a high reliance on family members (older children and other adults) to help care for younger children. Both parents often work. As such, it is not uncommon for Latino/Hispanic American families to have latchkey children or have children cared for by older children in the neighborhood. In homes where English is a second language, children often serve as intermediaries for parents when dealing with teachers, going to medical appointments, and interacting with police and other authority figures in the community.

Although the use of children and family members as translators is viewed as professionally and culturally inappropriate, often it is the only means available to the law enforcement officer. Keep in mind that parents may be upended when children understand and speak English better than their parents as the children then hold inappropriate power as translators and negotiators with the outside world. Additionally, the officer needs to see how sensitive a topic might be for different family members. The consequences of an incorrect translation must also be evaluated. For example, asking a juvenile to translate to his or her parents, who speak no English, that the juvenile has been involved in drinking and riding in a stolen vehicle may result in significantly changed content. Because of the embarrassment and fear of punishment on the part of the juvenile, and possibly a sense of shame or embarrassment to the parents, the message may be altered by the child to avoid negative ramifications. In all cases, when a child is acting as a translator for parents, the officer should direct all verbal and nonverbal communication to the parents. Otherwise, the parents may view the officer's lack of attention to them as an insult. Such sensitivity by the peace officer is particularly important because of the cultural value of *personalismo*, which emphasizes the importance of the personal quality of any interaction. This cultural concept implies that relationships occur among individuals as people, not as representatives of institutions or merely as individuals' performing a role.

COMMUNICATION STYLES OF LATINO/HISPANIC AMERICANS

Although we do not wish to create stereotypes of any kind, key features of Latino/Hispanic American verbal and nonverbal communication styles necessitate explanation. Misunderstanding resulting from style differences can result in perceptions of poor community services from police agencies, conflicts resulting from such misunderstandings, and safety and control issues for the peace officer.

1. Latino/Hispanic Americans' high cultural value for *la familia* results in a very strong family and group orientation. As such, officers should not view frequent "eye checking" with family members before responding to questions or the lack of "I" statements as dishonesty. An example of "eye checking" would be a break in eye contact with the officer as the person being interviewed glances quickly at a family member. The officer may be concerned because a Latino/Hispanic American witness may wish to use the pronoun "we" when the situation may call for a personal observation involving an "I" statement. For example, a Latino/Hispanic American family member who witnessed a store robbery may first nonverbally check with other family members before describing

what he or she saw. Such verbal and nonverbal behavior is consistent with the family and group orientation of Latino/Hispanic Americans.

2. Speaking Spanish to others in the presence of a law enforcement officer, even though the officer requested responses in English, should not automatically be interpreted as an insult or an attempt to hide information from the officer. In times of stress, such as when interacting with police officers, those who speak English as a second language automatically revert to their first language, which is more accessible and comfortable for them. Moreover, speaking Spanish gives the individual a greater range of expression (to discuss and clarify complex issues with other speakers and family members), thus yielding clearer, more useful information to law enforcement personnel about critical events.

3. It is important for officers to take the time to get information from witnesses, victims, and suspects even if the individuals have limited skills in speaking English (the use of officers who speak Spanish, translators, and language bank resources will help). Often Latino/Hispanic Americans have not been helped in crime-fighting and peacekeeping situations because officers could not or did not take information from nonnative English speakers.

4. Although Latino/Hispanic Americans may show respect to law enforcement officers because of police authority, they do not necessarily trust the officers or the organization. *Respeto* is extended to elders and anyone who is perceived to be in a position of authority. This respect is denoted in the Spanish language by the use of *Usted* (the formal you) rather than *Tu* (the informal you). Showing respect, however, does not ensure trust. The cultural value of *confianza* (or trust) takes some time to develop. Like many from ethnic minority communities, Latino/Hispanic Americans have experienced some degree of prejudice and discrimination from the majority community, and citizens with such experiences need time to develop trust with law enforcement officers, who are identified as being a part of the majority community.

5. The cultural value of *personalismo* emphasizes the importance of the person involved in any interaction. Latino/Hispanic Americans take into strong consideration not only the content of any communication but also the context and relationship of the communicator. This means, for effective communications, it is important for the officer to provide information about why questions are asked, who is the person asking the question (i.e., information about the officer), and how the information will be used. Additional contextual elements, such as providing explanations and information to Latino/Hispanic Americans about procedures, laws, and so forth before asking them questions or requesting their help, will ease the work of the officer. By providing background information and establishing prior relationships with community members, law enforcement agencies and officers build a context for cooperation with Latino/Hispanic American individuals.

6. Officers should recognize nonverbal and other cultural nuances that may detract from effective communication. Many Latino/Hispanic Americans, especially younger individuals, find it uncomfortable and sometimes inappropriate to maintain eye contact with authority figures such as police officers. Strong eye contact with someone who is of higher position, importance, or authority is considered a lack of respect in Latin/Hispanic American cultures. As such, many citizens from this background may deflect their eyes from police officers. It is important that officers not automatically read this nonverbal behavior as indicative of a lack of trust or as a dishonest response.

7. Latino/Hispanic Americans may exhibit behaviors that appear evasive, such as claiming not to have any identification or saying that they do not speak English. In some of the countries from which many Latino/Hispanic Americans have emigrated, the police and law enforcement agencies are not considered public service agencies, but are aligned with a politically repressive government. Because many Latino/Hispanic Americans may fear interactions with law enforcement, officers should take the time to explain the need for identification and cooperation, and that they acknowledge the importance of comprehension on the part of the Latino/Hispanic American individual(s) involved.

8. Latino/Hispanic people from Latin America and Spain can be extremely expressive in their body language and facial expressions and tend to converse in close proximity to others. Officers should not, in most cases, believe that the expressive gestures are a threat to their personal safety (Natella & Madera, 2008).

KEY ISSUES IN LAW ENFORCEMENT

Machismo

The term *machismo*, discussed earlier in the chapter, comes from the Spanish word *macho*. It refers to a strong sense of masculine pride or exaggerated sense of power or strength, a combination of attitudes basic to the Spanish-speaking world (Webster's New World Dictionary). Criminal justice officers, especially those in law enforcement, need to be aware of this potential trait found in Latino/Hispanic males they encounter. Criminal justice trainers (academies and in-field) should prepare students and probationary employees for the possibility that they may encounter a higher degree of resistance from Latino/Hispanic men due to machismo. It can be difficult to deal with individuals manifesting this trait or attitude. For example, in domestic violence incidents in which the man is the responsible party, he might not understand that hurting his spouse constitutes a criminal offense and is not just a matter of family, but a matter of civil control (Natella & Madera, 2008).

Underreporting of Crimes and Cooperation with Law Enforcement

Law enforcement officials may encounter difficulty getting cooperation from Latino/Hispanic American crime victims (see Chapter 1 for an expanded discussion). This lack of cooperation by immigrants, in particular, is in part connected to a fear of retaliation within the Latino/Hispanic community. Their past experiences with some law enforcement agencies in their countries of origin (e.g., repressive military force in their native country) may result in a reluctance to report crimes. Others may not seek police assistance or help feeling that doing so is pointless. Finally, many immigrants and refugees are simply not knowledgeable about the United States' legal system and may try to avoid any contact with law enforcement personnel. Outreach and community policing efforts will enhance relationships with Latino/Hispanic American communities and may help alleviate the underreporting of crimes and improve relationships and cooperation.

Hate Crimes and Discrimination against Latino/Hispanic Immigrants

In 2015, 4,029 single-bias hate crime offenses were reported in the country, of which approximately 9 percent were hate crimes specifically aimed at Latinos. ("Hate Crime Statistics, 2015," 2016). Per a Pew Research Center survey on race in America, "About half of Hispanics in the U.S. (52%) say they have experienced discrimination or have been treated unfairly because of their race or ethnicity" (Krogstad & Lopez, 2016):

> Hispanics' experience with discrimination or being treated unfairly varies greatly by age. Among Hispanics ages 18 to 29, 65% say they have experienced discrimination or unfair treatment because of their race or ethnicity. By comparison, only 35% of Hispanics 50 and older say the same—a 30-percentage-point gap… In addition, Hispanics born in the U.S. (62%) are more likely than immigrants (41%) to say they have experienced discrimination or unfair treatment. There are also differences by race. For example, 56% of nonwhite Hispanics say this has happened at some point in their lives, a higher share than that among white Hispanics (41%). (Ibid.)

Racial Profiling of Latino/Hispanics

Many incidents of racial profiling in policing have been recorded in recent history. These include "stop and frisk" policies in New York City that predominantly targeted young Latino and African American men by allowing police to question them and then search for contraband and weapons. In 90 percent of instances, no such contraband was found, but the practice had a disastrous impact on community relations and was found to be unconstitutional in 2013. It was later challenged by the NYPD union, who later dropped the appeal.

In 2011, the Department of Justice concluded that the East Haven (New Jersey) Police Department targeted and abused Latino drivers during traffic stops. The abuse included false arrests as well as assault, illegal searches, and, ultimately obstruction of the investigation (Associated Press, 2014; Lips, 2014).

Latino/Hispanic Americans must be able to trust that they will be treated fairly and protected as part of their involvement and association with local law enforcement and public safety and law enforcement must do everything within their power to make sure that trust is not broken See Chapter 12, Racial Profiling).

Increasing Police Services to the Latino/Hispanic American Community

The Police Neighborhood Resource Center, started in 1991 in the largely Hispanic community of Rolling Meadows, Illinois, showed positive results of cooperation among the police department, the Latino/Hispanic American community, and local and regional businesses. During that time, crime rates in Rolling Meadows were significantly reduced, but after the Police Neighborhood Resource Center closed, the number of reported shootings, stabbings, robberies, aggravated batteries, and other crimes in the East Park Apartments increased. In 2008, the Police Department received 73 calls for such crimes; that number rose to 86 in 2009, 94 in both 2010 and 2011, and 119 in 2012. However, when the department hired a bilingual social worker in 2013 whose job it was to work with families in the neighborhood, the crime rate dropped once again. Rolling Meadows Police Chief David Scanlan noted at the time that "we've been working very hard to establish communication, get the program up and running, mitigate crime problems in that area and make it a place where families want to live and where kids can play comfortably" (Owens-Schiele, 2013).

The outreach approach of using bilingual community service officers (CSOs) who are nonsworn officers to serve the ethnic communities in San Diego, California, provides yet another viable and effective model for the Latino/Hispanic American community as a whole. There, the community service officers provide referrals, educate residents about various programs, and help them report crimes when the need arises. Likewise, the assistance of Latino/Hispanic American police outreach coordinators is successfully used in some communities to liaison and outreach with residents of the community.

Law enforcement should be aware of the need to bridge the service gap between the Latino/Hispanic American community and law enforcement and public safety agencies. To this end, meetings between police executives and Latino/Hispanic American leaders of community-based and advocacy agencies have been found to be helpful when there are issues to resolve or allegations of misconduct by officers. These include a Citizens' Police Academy held entirely in Spanish in Durham, North Carolina, an area with a high number of Latinos. Spanish-language version of their Citizens Police Academy includes a brochure and registration form printed in Spanish. The classes, free to the public, meet twice each week to give residents first-hand knowledge of police operations ("Citizens Police Academy," 2017). Another way to bridge the gap is to have officers learn Spanish. Some officers will attest that even "survival" Spanish-language training, such as greetings and basic phrases, have a positive effect on community relations because they indicate an officer's respect toward Latinos (see Chapter 4 for a discussion of language training in police departments).

Increasing the Number of Latino/Hispanic American Police Officers

Police officers of color can increase police effectiveness through the specific knowledge, skills, experience, and image that they bring to their departments (Barlow, 2017). In the past decade, the number of Latino/Hispanic Americans has significantly increased in federal, state, and local law enforcement positions (discussed in Chapter 2). Despite these improving numbers, Latino/Hispanic Americans are still underrepresented in local police departments and sheriffs' offices. Local law enforcement's attempts to effectively serve states, cities, and community neighborhoods with large Latino/Hispanic American populations are hampered by the still small number of Latino/Hispanic American officers, despite the immense growth of this community. Reasons for underrepresentation include (1) the history of law enforcement relationships with Latino/Hispanic American communities; (2) the limited interest in and lack of knowledge about careers in law enforcement among Latino/Hispanic Americans; (3) the image that many in Latino/Hispanic American communities hold of law enforcement personnel; (4) the concerns that members of the community have regarding background checks and immigration status, physical requirements, and the application process; (5) ineffective and misdirected law enforcement recruitment and outreach efforts within the Latino/Hispanic American community; and (6) the lack of role models and advocates for law enforcement careers for Latino/Hispanic Americans.

Law enforcement agencies have clearly seen the need for increasing their ability to serve the Latino/Hispanic American community with more bilingual/bicultural personnel and more visible role models. The President's Task Force on 21st Century Policing includes Recommendation 1.8, which, although not just specific to Latinos, states: "Law enforcement agencies should strive to create a workforce that contains a broad range of diversity including race, gender, language, life experience, and cultural background to improve understanding and effectiveness in dealing with all communities." Combined with the recommendation are action items 1.8.1: "The Federal Government should create a Law Enforcement Diversity Initiative designed to help communities diversity law enforcement departments to reflect the demographics of the community," and 1.8.2: "The department overseeing the initiative should help localities learn best practices for recruitment, training, and outreach to improve the diversity as well as the cultural and linguistic responses of law enforcement agencies" ("President's Task Force on 21st Century Policing," 2016).

Summary

- The label Latino/Hispanic American encompasses over 25 diverse ethnic, cultural, and regional groups from North, Central, and South America. Law enforcement officials must be aware of the differences between these groups (e.g., nationality, native cultural and regional differences and perceptions, and language dialects), as well as the within-group differences that may result from individual life experiences. Since stereotypes of Latinos by mainstream Americans are often more negative than positive, it is important that police officers make a special effort to extend respect and dignity to this community of proud people with a culturally rich heritage.

- The preferred term for referring to Hispanic people depends on the individual and can include Chicano, Mexican American and Latino/a. However, Pew research survey results indicate that the majority prefer to be identified with their family's country of origin rather than with pan-ethnic terms. When in doubt and a designation is required, officers should ask individuals which term they prefer. Spanish speakers and people from Latino/Hispanic backgrounds may take offense if law enforcement officers describe them as a Latino or Hispanic or incorrectly associate them with a country other than their own.

- Officers should also never assume that a Latino is an immigrant, as many have been in the country for generations and may not even speak Spanish. Officers are advised to provide feedback to their peers whenever offensive terms, slurs, labels, and/or actions are used with Latino/Hispanic Americans. Such feedback will help reduce the risk of misunderstanding and improve the working relationships of officers within the Latino/Hispanic American communities.

- The experience of Latino/Hispanic Americans with law enforcement officers in the United States has been complicated by their perceptions of immigration law enforcement against undocumented or unauthorized immigrants, by the discriminatory treatment they have received in the United States, and by perceptions of police ineffectiveness and unresponsiveness. Some citizens may still remember this history and view police as something to be feared and avoided.

- The projected Hispanic population in the U.S. in 2060 is 119 million which will constitute 28.6 percent of the nation's population (U.S. Census Bureau, 2015). The number of undocumented immigrants in the United States has fluctuated from a peak in 2007 of 12 million to an estimated 11.1 million in 2014. Americans are deeply divided on immigration issues and hate crimes and hate speech toward many minority groups have increased. The tendency to generalize about Latinos, both documented and undocumented immigrants, has resulted in discrimination, hate speech, and hate crimes against Latino/Hispanic Americans who are citizens of the United States.

- It is important to have an understanding about some of the myths and stereotypes of Latino/Hispanic Americans that contribute to the prejudice, discrimination, and bias this group encounters. The key to effective community relations with any ethnic or racial group is to be aware of stereotypes and to monitor our thinking and behavior when interacting with individuals.

- Many differences exist among the groups collectively described as Latino/Hispanic. However, *la familia* is perhaps the most significant concept to understand in working and communicating with these communities. The Latino/Hispanic American family is often characterized by bonds of interdependence, unity, and loyalty, and includes nuclear and extended family members as well as networks of neighbors, friends, and community members. To interact effectively with Latino/Hispanic individuals, law enforcement personnel should understand traditional gender roles in the family structure, although these have started to change as more women work outside the home.

- According to recent research on race in America, "slightly over half of Hispanic/Latinos in the United States indicated that they experienced discrimination or unfair treatment because of their race or ethnicity."

- Some Latino/Hispanic Americans may be concerned with their inability to communicate clearly or about possible reprisals from the police, based on their experiences in politically repressive countries. To communicate effectively, peace officers should maintain contact, provide extra time, use translators, and be patient with speakers. Officers must recognize the nonverbal aspects of some Latino/Hispanic Americans' communication styles, such as eye contact, touch, and gestures. When dealing with people for whom English is a second language, it's important to remember that listening and comprehension skills are usually better than speaking skills.

- For a variety of reasons, Latino/Hispanic Americans may be reluctant to report crimes and may not seek police assistance and help. It is important for law enforcement departments and officials to build relationships and working partnerships with Latino/Hispanic American communities using strategies such as community offices, bilingual officers, and participation by officers in community activities. Law enforcement officials need to go out of their way to establish trust, provide outreach efforts, and win cooperation to effectively serve Latino/Hispanic Americans. Building partnerships focused on community collaboration in the fight against crime is key to effectiveness.

Discussion Questions and Issues

1. *Diversity among Latino/Hispanic Americans.* Latino/Hispanic Americans comprise more than 25 diverse regional, national, ethnic, and cultural groups. Which groups are you most likely to encounter in crime fighting and peacekeeping in your work? Which groups do you anticipate encountering in your future work?
2. *Choice of Terms.* Terms such as *Latino, Hispanic, Chicano, Mexican, La Raza, Puerto Rican*, and so forth is confusing for many people. How might you find out which term to use when referring to an individual if ethnic and cultural information of this kind is necessary? What would you do if the term you use appears to offend the person with whom you are speaking?
3. *Offensive Terms and Labels.* What would you do or say if a fellow police (or fellow student) made a racially or ethnically insensitive statement? How should police department management respond?
4. *Effects of Myths and Stereotypes.* Describe some of the Latino/Hispanic American stereotypes that you have heard of or encountered. What effect might these stereotypes have on Latino/Hispanic Americans? Suggest ways to manage these stereotypes in law enforcement.

In what ways can you help an officer who uses stereotypes about Latino/Hispanic Americans to become aware of the effects of such stereotypes?
5. *Verbal and Nonverbal Communication Style Variations among Cultures.* How do you think verbal and nonverbal communication styles can help officers in their approach to Latino/Hispanic American citizens? Does understanding culture-specific behavior help you to become more sensitive when dealing with people? In what ways might you use your understanding about Latino/Hispanic American family dynamics in law enforcement?
6. *Avoidance of Law Enforcement and Underreporting of Crimes.* Why do you think many Latino/Hispanic Americans keep to their own communities and underreport crimes of violence? How can police agencies be of greater service to Latino/Hispanic American communities in this regard?
7. *The Future of Latino/Hispanic Americans and Law Enforcement.* The Latino/Hispanic American population is the fastest-growing segment of the U.S. population. What implications do you see for law enforcement in terms of services, language, recruitment, and training?

References

Associated Press. (2014). "East Haven Settles Suit on Civil Rights." *New York Times, June 9.* www.nytimes.com/2014/06/10/nyregion/east-haven-settles-suit-on-civil-rights.html (accessed May 16, 2017).

Ayala, Elaine and Ellen Huet. (2013). "Hispanic May Be a Race on 2020 Census." *San Francisco Chronicle,* February 4. www.sfgate.com/nation/article/Hispanic-may-be-a-race-on-2020-census-4250866.php (accessed August 11, 2013).

Barlow, David E. (2017). Professor Department of Criminal Justice, Fayetteville State University, Fayetteville, North Carolina, personal communication, February 6.

Bernal, G. and Alejandrina Estrada. (1985). "Cuban Refugee and Minority Experiences: A Book Review." *Hispanic Journal of Behavioral Sciences, 7*, 105–128.

Comas-Diaz, L. and Ezra E.H. Griffith. (1988). *Cross-Cultural Mental Health.* New York, NY: Wiley.

Glass, Andrew. (2009). "Castro Launches Mariel Boatlift, April 20, 1980." *Politico.* http://www.politico.com/story/2009/04/castro-launches-mariel-boatlift-april-20-1980-021421 (accessed May 16, 2017).

Gonzalez-Barrera, Ana and Mark H. Lopez. (2015). "A Demographic Portrait of Mexican-Origin Hispanics in the United States." Pew Research Center. http://www.pewhispanic.org/2013/05/01/a-demographic-portrait-of-mexican-origin-hispanics-in-the-united-states/ (accessed May 17, 2017).

Gonzalez-Barrera, Ana and Mark H. Lopez. (2015). "Is Being Hispanic a Matter of Race, Ethnicity or Both?"

June 15. Pew Research Center. www.pewresearch.org /fact-tank/2015/06/15/is-being-hispanic-a-matter-of-race -ethnicity-or-both/ (accessed January 12, 2017).

Hispanic Population Trends. (2013). Used by permission of Pew Research Center. www.pewhispanic.org/topics /population-trends/ (accessed May 17, 2017).

H.R. 83. (2017). "Mobilizing against Sanctuary Cities Act." 115th Congress, January 3. www.congress.gov/115/bills /hr83/BILLS-115hr83ih.pdf (accessed January 17, 2017).

Hufbauer, Gary, Jeffrey Schott, Kimberly Elliott, and Milica Cosic. (1960). "Case Studies in Economic Sanctions and Terrorism." Case 60-3. U.S. v. Cuba (1960–: Castro). Updated 2011. Peterson Institute for International Economics. https://piie.com/publications/papers/sanctions -cuba-60-3.pdf (accessed May 1, 2017).

Krogstad, Jens and Mark Lopez. (2015). "Hispanic Population Reaches Record 55 Million, but Growth Has Cooled." June 25. Pew Research Center. www.pewresearch .org/fact-tank/2015/06/25/u-s-hispanic-population -growth-surge-cools/ft_15-06-25_hispanic_trend/ (accessed December 10, 2016).

Krogstad, Jens and Gustavo Lopez. (2016). "Roughly Half of Hispanics Have Experienced Discrimination." June 29. Pew Research Center. http://www.pewresearch.org /fact-tank/2016/06/29/roughly-half-of-hispanics-have -experienced-discrimination/ (accessed December 10, 2016).

Lips, Evan. (2014). "East Haven Settles Civil Rights Lawsuit for $450,000, Changes in Treatment of Immigrants." June 9. *New Haven Register News.* www.nhregister.com/general -news/20140609/east-haven-settles-civil-rights-lawsuit -for-450000-changes-in-treatment-of-immigrants (accessed May 16, 2017).

Lopez, Mark H., Rich Moran, and Paul Taylor. (2010). "Illegal Immigration Backlash Worries, Divides Latinos, 2010." Pew Research Center. www.pewhispanic.org/2010/10/28 /illegal-immigration-backlash-worries-divides-latinos/ (accessed April 28, 2017).

Lopez y Rivas, G. (1973). *The Chicanos: Life and Struggles of the Mexican Minority in the United States,* trans. Elizabeth Martinez and Gilberto Lopez y Rivas. New York, NY: Monthly Review Press.

Miles, Thomas and Adam Cox. (2014, November). "Does Immigration Enforcement Reduce Crime? Evidence from 'Secure Communities.'" *The Journal of Law & Amp; Economics, 57*(4), 937–973. http://www.jstor.org /stable/10.1086/676011 (accessed December 13, 2016)

Montiel, Miguel. (1978). *Hispanic Families: Critical Issues for Policy and Programs in Human Services.* Washington, D.C.: National Coalition of Hispanic Mental Health and Human Services Organizations.

Motel, Seth and Eileen Patten. (2012). "The 10 Largest Hispanic Origin Groups: Characteristics, Rankings, Top Counties." June 27. Pew Hispanic Center. www .pewhispanic.org/2012/06/27/the-10-largest-hispanic -origin-groups-characteristics-rankings-top-counties/ (accessed August 8, 2012).

Natella, Arthur, Jr. and Pablo P. Madera. (2008, December). "Law Enforcement Training: Factors in the Spanish-Speaking Community." *FBI Law Enforcement Bulletin, 77*(12), 12–15.

Nittle, Nadra. (2016). "Myths and Stereotypes about Hispanics and Immigration. Diversity Matters." August 1. *ThoughtCo.* https://www.thoughtco.com/hispanics-and -immigration-myths-stereotypes-2834527 (accessed December 10, 2016).

Office of Management and Budget. (1997). "Revisions to the Standards for the Classification of Federal Data on Race and Ethnicity." October 30. *Federal Register, 62*(280), 58782–85790

Owens-Schiele, Elizabeth. (2013). "Crime Drops at Apartment Complex after Police Hire Social Worker." *Chicago Tribune*, May 30. www.articles.chicagotribune.com/2013 -05-30/news/ct-tl-nw-rolling-meadows-social-services -outreach-20130530_1_east-park-apartments-scanlan -social-worker (accessed August 28, 2013).

Passel, Jeffrey and D'Vera Cohn. (2016). "Unauthorized Immigrant Population Stable for Half a Decade." September 21. Pew Research Center. www.pewresearch.org/fact -tank/2016/09/21/unauthorized-immigrant-population -stable-for-half-a-decade/ (accessed December 10, 2016).

Patten, Eileen. (2016). "The Nation's Latino Population Is Defined by Its Youth." April. Pew Research Center— Hispanic Trends. www.pewhispanic.org/2016/04/20/the -nations-latino-population-is-defined-by-its-youth/ (accessed December 12, 2016).

Pew Research Center. (2016a). "Nearly Six-in-Ten Hispanics Are Millennials or Younger." April 14. www.pewhispanic .org/2016/04/20/the-nations-latino-population-is -defined-by-its-youth/ph_2016-04-20_latinoyouth-01/ (accessed May 17, 2017).

Pew Research Center. (2016b). "Unauthorized Immigrant Population Trends for States, Birth Countries and Regions." November. Pew Research Center. www.pewhispanic.org /interactives/unauthorized-trends/ (accessed December 29, 2016).

Rasmussen Reports. (2015). "Voters Want to Punish Sanctuary Cities." July 10. www.rasmussenreports.com /public_content/politics/current_events/immigration /july_2015/voters_want_to_punish_sanctuary_cities (accessed April 28, 2017).

Springer, Katie. (1985). "Five Years Later, Overriding Crime Is Mariel Legacy." *Sun-Sentinel Newspaper*, September 26. www .articles.sun-sentinel.com/1985-09-26/news/8502100720_1 _mariel-boatlift-criminals (accessed May 16, 2017).

Stepler, Renee and Anna Brown. (2016). "Statistical Portrait of Hispanics in the United States." April. Pew Research Center. www.pewhispanic.org/2016/04/19/statistical -portrait-of-hispanics-in-the-united-states-key-charts /-hispanic-language (accessed December 12, 2016).

Stepler, Renee and Mark Lopez. (2016). "U.S. Latino Population Growth and Dispersion Has Slowed since Onset of Great Recession." September. Pew Research Center. www .pewhispanic.org/2016/09/08/latino-population-growth -and-dispersion-has-slowed-since-the-onset-of-the-great -recession/ (accessed December 10, 2016).

Stevens, E. (1973). "Machismo and Marianismo." *Transaction-Society, 10*(6), 57–63.

Taylor, Paul, Mark H. Lopez, Jessica Martinez, and Gabriel Velasco. (2012). "When Labels Don't Fit: Hispanics and Their Views of Identity." April 4. Pew Hispanic Center. www .pewhispanic.org/2012/04/04/when-labels-dont-fit-hispanics -and-their-views-of-identity/ (accessed June 26, 2013).

"U.S. Birth Rate Falls to New Lows." (2013). Pew Research Center. www.pewresearch.org/daily-number/u-s-birth -rate-falls-to-new-lows/ (accessed August 21, 2013).

U.S. Census Bureau. (2014a). "Preparing for the 2020 Census: Measuring Race and Ethnicity in America." October 6. http://www.directorsblog.blogs.census.gov/2014/10/06/preparing-for-the-2020-census-measuring-race-and-ethnicity-in-america/(assessed January 11, 2017).

U.S. Census Bureau. (2014b). "Income, Poverty and Health Insurance Coverage in the United States: 2013." Release Number: CB14-169. www.census.gov/newsroom/press-releases/2014/cb14-169.html (accessed December 14, 2016).

U.S. Census Bureau. (2015). "Hispanic Heritage Month, September 4, 2016." www.census.gov/newsroom/facts-for-features/2016/cb16-ff16.html (accessed December 12, 2016).

U.S. Department of Justice. (2016). "President's Task Force on 21st Century Policing." www.themarshallproject.org/documents/2082979-final-report-of-the-presidents-task-force-on#.vUnDUGJmC (accessed December 23, 2016).

U.S. Federal Bureau of Investigation. (2015). "Hate Crime Statistics, 2015." www.ucr.fbi.gov/hate-crime/2015/topic-pages/incidentsandoffenses_final (accessed December 17, 2016).

Law Enforcement Contact with Arab Americans and Other Middle Eastern Groups

LEARNING OBJECTIVES

After reading this chapter, you should be able to:

▥ List the groups belonging to the category "Middle Easterners," and define "Arab" and "Muslim."

▥ Describe the reasons for Arab/Middle Eastern immigration to the United States.

▥ Provide examples of similarities and differences among Middle Eastern groups.

▥ Explain the impact of Arab/Middle Eastern stereotypes on law enforcement.

▥ Identify basic ways that law enforcement can show respect toward Muslims.

▥ Understand selected characteristics of traditional Arab American/Middle Eastern extended family structure as related to law enforcement contact.

▥ Define characteristics of traditional Arab/Middle Eastern communication styles and cultural practices.

▥ List and discuss key issues associated with law enforcement contact with Arab American and other Middle Eastern groups.

OUTLINE

- Introduction
- Middle Easterners and Related Terminology Defined
- Historical Information and Arab American Demographics
- Differences and Similarities
- Stereotypes
- Islamic Religion
- Family Structure
- Communication Styles and Cultural Practices
- Key Issues in Law Enforcement
- Summary
- Discussion Questions and Issues
- References

INTRODUCTION

Middle Easterners come to the United States for numerous reasons: to gain an education and begin their careers; to escape unstable political situations, including war and violence; and to invest in commercial enterprises with the goal of gaining legal entry into the country. Many law enforcement personnel have contact with Middle Easterners from different countries; thus, basic knowledge about past and present world events is beneficial. Attitudes among Americans toward Middle Easterners, as well as geopolitical events in the Middle East, have ongoing implications for law enforcement.

Second-, third-, and fourth-generation Americans of Arab origin are sometimes treated as if they have just arrived from the Middle East and might be potential terrorists. These stereotypes significantly affect people's perceptions of who Arab-Americans and other Middle Easterners are. Such perceptions increased significantly after 9/11; high-profile terrorist incidents continue to be followed by increased incidents of bias hate against Middle Easterners. The rise in anti-Muslim hate groups as well as hate crimes against Arab Americans and others perceived to be Arab, Muslim, or Middle Eastern constitute important ongoing concerns of law enforcement. An understanding of Arab American and Middle Eastern heterogeneity as well as the impact of related societal stereotypes will assist police officers in their approach and relationships with people from these diverse backgrounds.

MIDDLE EASTERNERS AND RELATED TERMINOLOGY DEFINED

Among the general U.S. population, there is considerable confusion as to who Middle Easterners are and, specifically, who Arabs are. Although commonly thought of as Arabs, Iranians and Turks are not Arabs. Many people assume that all Muslims are Arabs, and vice versa. In fact, many Arabs are also Christians, and the world's Muslim population is actually composed of dozens of ethnic groups. The country with the largest Muslim population is Indonesia, which is located in Southeast Asia—not in the Middle East. The second largest Muslim population is in India, which is in South Asia.

The predominant religion among Arabs is Islam, and its followers are called *Muslims*. They are also sometimes called *Moslems*, but *Muslim* is the preferred term because it is closer to the Arabic pronunciation. There are two major sects of Islam: Sunni and Shia (the people are referred to as Sunnis and Shiites). The following excerpt is from *100 Questions You Have Always Wanted to Ask about Arab Americans*, compiled in 2001 by the Detroit Free Press staff in consultation with Arab American community members. (The Detroit Metropolitan area is described as the "center of Arab American life in the U.S." Michigan is said to have a quarter million people with roots in the Middle East.) (Warikoo, 2014).

> SHOULD I SAY ARAB, ARABIC, OR ARABIAN?
>
> Arab is a noun for a person and is used as an adjective as in "Arab country." Arabic is the name of the language and generally is not used as an adjective. Arabian is an adjective that refers to Saudi Arabia, the Arabian Peninsula, or the "Arabian horse." When either ethnicity or nationality is relevant, it is more precise and accurate to specify the country by using Lebanese, Yemeni, or whatever is appropriate.

What all Arabs have in common is the Arabic language, even though spoken Arabic differs among countries (e.g., Algerian Arabic is different from Jordanian Arabic). The following countries are generally considered to constitute the Middle East and all are Arab countries with the exception of three, noted below:

- Aden
- Bahrain
- Egypt
- Iran (non-Arab country)
- Iraq
- Israel (non-Arab country)
- Jordan
- Kuwait
- Lebanon

- Oman
- Palestinian Authority (also referred to as Palestine)
- Qatar
- Saudi Arabia
- Syria
- Turkey (non-Arab country)
- United Arab Emirates
- Yemen

There are other Arab countries that are not located in the Middle East (e.g., Algeria, Tunisia, Morocco, Libya), in which the majority population speaks Arabic and adheres to the religion Islam. In this chapter we primarily cover information on refugees and immigrants from Arab countries in the Middle East. They constitute the majority of Middle Eastern newcomers who bring cultural differences and special issues requiring clarification for law enforcement. Issues related to the established Arab American community (i.e., people who began arriving in the United States in the late nineteenth century) are covered as well. We begin with a brief description of the populations from the three non-Arab countries.

Iranians and Turks

Iranians use a variation of the Arabic script in their writing but for the most part speak Farsi (Persian) and not Arabic. Turks speak Turkish, although there are minority groups in Turkey that speak Kurdish, Arabic, Greek, and Armenian. Nearly 100 percent of Iranians and Turks are Muslim. In Iran, approximately 90 percent are "Shiite" Muslims or of the "Shia" branch of Islam, and the remaining are "Sunni" Muslims (World Factbook, 2017c). In Turkey, nearly 100 percent of the Muslims are "Sunni" (ibid.). Armenians, who are largely Christian, were a persecuted minority in Turkey. The Armenian genocide, between 1915 and 1923, claimed the lives of between 1 and 1.5 million people. Animosity still exists between some Armenians and Turks. Turkey continues to deny that the Armenians were the victims of genocide during World War I (Arango, 2015; Today's Zaman, 2012). In April 2015, the 100th anniversary of the Armenian genocide was remembered in many capital cities around the world. The Turkish government acknowledges that there were atrocities against the Armenians, but denied that there was any systematic attempt to eliminate the entire population of Armenians (ibid.).

Many Iranians in the United States are Jewish or Bahai, both of which groups are minorities in Iran. Of the Muslim population in Iran, most belong to the Shi'a sect of Islam, which is the state religion. Persians are the largest ethnic group in Iran, but there are other ethnic populations, including Azeris, Kurds, Arabs, and Turkmen tribes (World Factbook, 2017a).

Many Iranian Americans and Turkish Americans came to the United States in the 1970s and were from upper-class professional groups such as doctors, lawyers, and engineers. During the Iranian hostage crisis in 1979, Iranians in the United States were frequently targets of hate crimes and anti-Iranian sentiment; the same attitudes prevailed against other Middle Easterners (Arabs) and South Asians (Indians from India) who were mistakenly labeled as Iranian. Many Jewish Iranians who now live in the United States left Iran after the fall of the Shah; there are large Iranian Jewish populations in the San Francisco Bay Area, Los Angeles, and New York. Also, populations of Muslim Iranians are found in major U.S. cities, such as New York, Chicago, and Los Angeles. Although Iranians and Turks are not Arabs, some of their family values with respect to pride, dignity, and honor are similar to those in the traditional Arab world.

Israelis

Israel is the only country in the Middle East in which the majority of the population is not Muslim. Nearly 20 percent of the population in Israel is made up of Arabs, both Christian and Muslim. Approximately three-quarters of the Israeli population is Jewish (World Factbook, 2017b), with the Jewish population divided into two main groups: Ashkenazim and Sephardim. The Ashkenazim are descended from members of the Jewish communities of Central and Eastern Europe. The Sephardim, now slightly over 50 percent of the Jewish population, came in the Middle Ages, from Spain or other Mediterranean countries, including

Arab countries of the Middle East. Israeli immigrants in the United States may be either Ashkenazi, Sephardic, or a mixture of both; their physical appearance will not indicate to an officer what their ethnicity is. An Israeli may look like an American Jew, a Christian, or a Muslim Arab—or none of these.

There are many extreme political and religious divisions among Israeli Jews; moreover, many Israeli Jews are secular. The political divisions among Israeli Jews are huge; some of these involve ongoing tension and hostility related to Jewish settlements in Palestinian-occupied territory.

Most Arabs who live within Israel proper are Palestinians whose families remained in Israel after the Arab–Israeli war of 1948, when armies from five Arab states attacked Israel. The Six-Day War in 1967 resulted in the occupation of lands that formerly belonged to Egypt, Syria as well as Jordan, in which the majority of the population was Palestinian. Thus, Israel occupied territories with a population of approximately 1 million Palestinians following the Israeli Independence War in 1948. Israel Independence Day is referred to in most of the Arab world, as the "nakba" which means "catastrophe."

The Palestinian/Israeli situation in the Middle East has created a great deal of hostility on both sides as well as in the region as a whole. In the fall of 2000, failure to reach a negotiated agreement required by the Oslo accords of 1993 resulted in a period of increased conflict. The tension continued and intensified during what is referred to as the second *intifada* or Palestinian "uprising," which took place between approximately 2000 and 2005. Hostilities continued in 2006 with the outbreak of war involving Israel and Lebanon, associated with rocket attacks into Israel proper. Similarly, violence in Gaza beginning in 2005, and continuing off and on through 2009, started with rocket attacks into Israel and had repercussions around the world, including the United States. Although Israel withdrew from Gaza in 2009, another Gaza-Israeli war lasting 50 days broke out in 2014. Currently, the continued expansion of settlements, often by extremely religious Jewish "settlers" in the West Bank where many Palestinians aspire to establish their own independent state, continues to inflame tensions in the region.

These political tensions have definite implications for law enforcement officials in the United States, especially in communities that contain large populations of Jews and Arabs, or where Israelis and Palestinians reside in large numbers (e.g., Los Angeles, New York, Chicago). All law enforcement agencies should become knowledgeable about how Palestinian-Israeli tensions may manifest among Americans. Public events such as Israel Independence Day celebrations and Israeli or Palestinian political rallies have the potential for confrontation; the political climate at some college campuses has become increasingly tense and heated around the issue of Israel and Palestine. Police presence is required at such events, but as with other situations, excessive presence can escalate hostilities. Current events in the Middle East have significant ripple effects across the world.

The impact of the "Arab Spring" in Arab-majority countries in the Middle East and North Africa at the end of 2010 was also felt in major cities around the world in demonstrations and other various forms of public protest. For the most part, U.S. cities experienced only minor demonstrations. However, it appeared that the 2011 Occupy Wall Street protestors modeled their demonstrations after those of the Arab Spring (Knafo, 2011).

The monitoring of world events and community trends will help police officers take a preventive posture that can ultimately avoid confrontation among various Middle Eastern ethnic groups in this country. Chapter 11 goes into more depth on the importance of such monitoring.

HISTORICAL INFORMATION AND ARAB AMERICAN DEMOGRAPHICS

Although many recent Middle Eastern immigrants and refugees in the United States left their countries due to political reasons, not all Arab Americans did so. There have been two major waves of Arab immigration to the United States. The first wave came between 1880 and World War I, and was largely from Syria and what is known today as Lebanon (at the time these areas were part of the Turkish Ottoman Empire). Of the immigrants who settled during this wave, approximately 90 percent were Christian. Many people came to further themselves economically (thus they were immigrants, and not refugees forced to leave their countries);

but in addition, many of the young men wanted to avoid military service for the Ottoman Empire (Samhan, 2006). A substantial percentage of these immigrants were farmers or artisans, and they became involved in the business of peddling their goods to farmers, moving from town to town. In the way of crime statistics, not much is reported, partly because in the Arab immigrant community, people took care of their own (ibid.).

In sharp contrast to the first wave of immigrants in terms of motivation and compositional characteristics, the second wave of Arab immigration to the United States, beginning after World War II, came in large part as students and professionals. They came seeking to escape economic instability and political unrest in their home countries. As a result, these groups brought a "political consciousness unknown to earlier immigrants" (John Zogby, 2013). The largest group of second-wave immigrants was made up of Palestinians, many of whom came around 1948 (the time of the partition of Palestine which resulted in Israel's independence). In the 1970s, after the Six-Day War among Israel, Egypt, Syria, and Jordan, another large influx of Palestinians was witnessed by the United States. In the 1980s, a large group of Lebanese came as a result of the civil war in Lebanon. Yemenis (from Yemen) have continued to arrive throughout the twentieth century; also many Syrians and Iraqis have made the United States their home since the 1950s and 1960s because of political instability in their countries (ibid.). Thus, these second-wave immigrants came largely because of political turmoil in their respective home countries and have been instrumental in changing the nature of the Arab American community in the United States.

The most dramatic example of how immigration from the Middle East has affected the United States is the Detroit area in Michigan. Arabs began to arrive there in the late nineteenth century, but the first huge influx was between 1900 and 1924, when the auto industry attracted immigrants from all over the world (Woodruff, 1991). Today the Detroit/Dearborn area has the largest Arab community in the United States, with Arab Americans constituting about 30 percent of the population of Dearborn. In addition, a large percentage of the Detroit area's Middle Eastern population is Chaldean, i.e., Christian Iraqis who speak the Chaldean language. While they are from the heart of the Middle East, most do not identify themselves as Iraqi; some are even offended by being labeled "Iraqi" as they wish to maintain their own cultural identity (Haddad, 2017).

Selected Arab American Demographics

Immigrants from all over the Arab world have continued to settle in the United States although beginning with the Trump administration in 2017, attempts to ban immigration and travel from several predominantly Muslim countries made immigration more challenging. Prior to the attempted travel bans, the Obama administration had enabled an increase in immigration from Middle Eastern countries. From 2013 to 2014, the Department of Homeland Security granted 32 percent more green cards (i.e., lawful permanent resident) to immigrants from the Middle East than the year before (U.S. Department of Homeland Security, 2014).

According to the 2013 Migration Policy Institute, and based on U.S. Census research, the total number of Middle Eastern immigrants in that year was nearly 700,000 (Zong & Batalova, 2015). Based on 2013 estimates, the greatest numbers of Middle Eastern immigrants came from Iraq, Lebanon, and Saudi Arabia. The U.S. war in Iraq began in 2003, and it took several years for the surge of Iraqi refugees or asylees to reach the United States.

Although in 2010 the U.S. Census Bureau estimated that the U.S. Arab American population was under 2 million people, the Arab American Institute Foundation (AAIF) suggests that a more accurate estimate is over 3.7 million (AAIF, 2014). Between 2010 and 2014, immigrants to the United States from Saudi Arabia increased by 93 percent, which represented the largest increase of immigrants from any country of origin (Camarota, 2016). Refugee status was given to approximately 12,000 Syrian refugees in 2016 (Pew Research Center, 2016), all of whom were vetted over a period of 18–24 months by multiple U.S. intelligence agencies (see Chapter 1, pp. 000–000).

The communities with the largest Arab American populations are located in Los Angeles, Detroit, the greater New York area, Chicago, and Washington, D.C. According to Zogby International research, the five states with the largest Arab American populations in 2010 were California, Michigan, New York, Texas, and Florida (AAIF, 2014).

DIFFERENCES AND SIMILARITIES

Differences

There is great diversity among Arab American groups. Understanding this diversity will encourage people to move away from thinking in stereotypes. As previously mentioned, Arabs from the Middle East come from at least 13 different countries, many of which are vastly different from each other. The governments of Arab countries also differ, ranging from monarchies to emirates to republics. Arab visitors such as students, tourists, businesspeople, and diplomats to the United States from the Gulf countries (e.g., Saudi Arabia, Qatar, Oman, Bahrain, United Arab Emirates) are typically wealthy, but their Jordanian, Lebanese, and Palestinian brethren do not generally bring wealth to the United States; in fact, many are extremely poor. Another area of difference is clothing. In some countries in the Middle East, many older men wear head-dresses, but it is less common among young men. Similarly, young women in the Middle East may choose not to wear head coverings and long dresses that cloak them from head to toe.

The younger generation of Arab Americans may display entirely different behavior from what is expected of them from parents and grandparents, this phenomenon is typical in most immigrant and refugee groups. In addition, as with other immigrant groups, there are Arab Americans who have been in the United States for generations and have completely assimilated into American culture. Consequently, they may not identify in any way with their roots. Others, although they have also been in the United States for generations, consciously try to keep Arab traditions alive and pass them on to their children. (See "Selected Distinctions Among Generations of Immigrants," in Chapter 1 with further detail in Appendix A, pp. 000.) Officers should not treat established Arab Americans as if they are newly arrived Americans.

There are broad differences among Arab American groups in terms of social class and economic status. Although many Arab Americans living in the United States are educated professionals—for example, as of 2011, more than 50 percent of foreign-born adults from Saudi Arabia, Egypt, and Kuwait had bachelor's degrees (Terrazas, 2011)—a percentage comes from rural areas (e.g., peasants from southern Lebanon, West Bank Palestinians, Yemenis), and they differ in outlook and receptiveness to modernization. On the other hand, despite holding traditional values, many newcomers are modern in outlook. For example, although people in the United States tend to have a stereotypical image of the Arab woman, many women of Arab descent do not adhere to this image. John Zogby, president of Zogby International, describes the modern Arab women who defy the stereotype: "Among the upper-class, educated Palestinian population, for example, you can find many women who are vocal and outspoken. You might see the young husbands wheeling the babies around in strollers while the women are discussing world events" (John Zogby, 2013).

Some Arab governments (e.g., that of Saudi Arabia) place restrictions on women, mandating that they do not mix with men, and that they must always be veiled. Saudi Arabian men, in general, are guardians for women, making the most critical decisions about women's lives for them (Human Righs Watch, 2016). Women from less restrictive Arab countries (e.g., Lebanon and Jordan) may exhibit very different behavior from those whose governments grant them fewer freedoms. Nevertheless, women in traditional Muslim families from any country typically have limited contact with men outside their family and wear traditional dress. Some implications of these traditions, as they relate to Arab women and male police officers in the United States, are discussed further in this chapter.

Examining people's motivation for coming to the United States can help to avoid stereotyping. There is a distinction between immigrants and refugees. Some refugees, having been forced to leave their country of origin, believe that they are here temporarily, because they are waiting for a conflict to end. As a result, they may be hesitant to change their traditional ways, and relationship building by law enforcement personnel may take extra time.

Similarities

Despite many differences, whether apparent in socioeconomic status, levels of traditionalism, or motivation for coming to the United States, there are values and beliefs associated with Arab culture that law enforcement officials should understand in order to establish rapport and trust. Officers will recognize that some of the information listed later does not apply only to Arab cultures. At the same time, the following will help officers understand deeply held beliefs that many Arab Americans would agree are keys to understanding traditional Arab culture.

TRADITIONAL ARAB VALUES

1. Traditional Arab society upholds honor (in Arabic, *ayb*); the degree to which an Arab can be shamed publicly is foreign to the average Westerner. Officers recognize that dignity and respect should be shown to all individuals, but citizens from cultures emphasizing shame (*sharam*) and loss of honor (e.g., Middle Eastern, Latin American) may react even more severely to loss of dignity and respect than do other individuals. To avoid shame, some people will not report crimes. That said, Arab Americans, increasingly, have embraced community policing engagement and are generally much more willing than a decade ago, for example, to work together with authorities to be able to prosecute successfully (Haddad, 2017).
2. Loyalty to one's family takes precedence over other personal needs. A person is completely intertwined with his or her family; protection and privacy in a traditional Arab family often overrides relationships with outsiders. Generally, members of Arab families tend to avoid disagreements and disputes in front of others, preferring to resolve issues on their own (ibid.).
3. Communication is expected to be courteous and hospitable, and harmony between individuals is emphasized. Too much directness and candor can be interpreted as extremely impolite. From a traditional Arab view, it may not be appropriate for a person to give totally honest responses if they result in a loss of honor, especially for self or family members (this may not apply to established Arab Americans). This aspect of cross-cultural communication is not easily understood by most Westerners and is often criticized. Certainly, officers will not accept anything but the whole truth, despite arguments rationalized by cultural ideals of honor. However, this should not lead officers to draw attention explicitly to an indirect communication style. Officers would be well advised to work around this style rather than insinuating that a citizen is not being honest.

STEREOTYPES

The Arab world has been perceived in the West in terms of negative stereotypes, and these have been transferred to Americans of Arab descent. As with all distorted information about ethnic groups, it is important that police officers recognize how stereotypes interfere with true understanding.

Movies and Television

Perhaps the most offensive Arab stereotypes come from the media; television programs, video games, and movies routinely portray Arabs in a negative light. Even films and programs aimed at children propagate the stereotype of Arabs as villains. Because many Americans do not know Arabs personally, media images become embedded in people's minds. In a talk at the Levantine Cultural Center in Los Angeles in late 2012, Jack Shaheen, author of *Reel Bad Arabs: How Hollywood Vilifies a People*, recounted how in his research he "has found the same stereotypes repeated since the early days of Hollywood—the belly dancer, the terrorist, the dangerous but incompetent Arab, the lecherous sheikh, the submissive woman…the constant repetition of negative images of Arabs, even in fictional movies or television shows, has a tendency to desensitize the public and entrench harmful stereotypes" (Lohmann, 2013).

Shaheen has argued that the atmosphere created by Hollywood contributed to the recorded 326 hate crimes against Arab Americans in the first month alone following the terrorist attacks in 2001. Though military retaliations after the attacks were labeled "antiterrorist" rather than "anti-Islamic," the movie industry has continued the negative stereotyping of Arabs and Muslims. In Shaheen's view, "There certainly should be movies based on what happened, but if [images of Arabs as terrorists] are the only images we see from now on, if we continue to vilify all Muslims and all Arabs as terrorists instead of making clear this is a lunatic fringe, what are we accomplishing?" (Shaheen, 2001).

While some filmmakers and studios have become more sensitive to the potential they have in terms of perpetrating stereotypes, a number of Muslim and Arab American organizations feel that there is room for improvement.

The "Terrorist" Stereotype, Post-9/11 Backlash, and Ongoing Challenges

Even prior to the attacks of 9/11, Arabs had often been stereotyped as terrorists. A most convincing example of the persistence of discrimination against Arabs occurred after the Oklahoma City bombing in April 1995. Immediately following the bombing, many journalists and political leaders said that the tragedy appeared to be the work of Muslim terrorists. This was an initial conclusion made without any supporting evidence; the arrest and conviction of Timothy J. McVeigh proved them wrong. The paranoia that had led to that conclusion gave way to Arab-bashing, including many hate calls to Arabs; scapegoating of Arabs spread pervasively across the country.

The rage that ensued after 9/11 turned into general Arab and Muslim bashing. Within the first nine weeks following the attacks, there were more than 700 reported violent crimes against Arab Americans and Muslim Americans, or those who were perceived to be. Even Sikhs, who may have simply been dark-skinned and wore turbans but were neither Muslim nor Middle Eastern, were targets and victims of hate crimes in the aftermath of the attacks. (Sikhs continue to be the targets of hate crimes, such as in the 2012 shootings at a Sikh temple in Wisconsin; see Chapter 5).

The attacks of 9/11 were a pivotal point in the history of Arab Americans in this country. The impact, more than a decade later, is no less important to understand as it was immediately following the attacks:

> What remained [after the attacks] was primarily a heightened self-consciousness (including a heightened sense of vulnerability) on the part of Arab Americans, and a much more widespread cognition in the rest of American society of the existence of these communities (although this recognition was…accompanied by a degree of antipathy). Arab American individuals and organizations would, for the foreseeable future, be placed under a microscope of intense scrutiny for disloyalty and covert sympathy with those who attacked the United States. (ADC Research Institute, 2008)

Law enforcement needs to be aware of the heightened risk of threats and hate crimes toward Arab Americans when criminal acts around the world are committed by terrorists in the name of Islam. The ADC report cited above includes two examples of global news and its impact on hate crimes against those perceived to be Arab Americans in the United States. When global events occur, fear and anger can be ignited among some highly intolerant individuals who then lash out at people who appear to be Middle Eastern. This type of fear that spreads throughout communities creates ongoing anxiety,

Increased understanding will benefit all concerned. Arab contributions to civilization have been significant in numerous areas, including mathematics, astronomy, medicine, architecture, geography, and language. Arab Americans participate in all sectors of the professional world; organizations such as the National Arab American Medical Association and the Michigan Arab American Legal Society have highly respected and substantial membership (Haddad, 2017). In the last 10 years, Arab Americans have become much more involved and astute politically (AAI, 2012). With respect to business and entrepreneurialism, including information technology in Silicon Valley, "The list is long of outstanding tech innovators and leaders of Middle Eastern origin" (Kumar, 2016).

Current stereotypes that can affect law enforcement officers' perceptions include the myth that all terrorists as having Arab and Middle Eastern nationality or Muslim religious background as a result of 9/11, the Boston marathon bomb explosions, and other incidents in the United States.

Knowledge of the concerns, diversity, and historical backgrounds of various multicultural communities will facilitate the public safety and peacekeeping mission of law enforcement officers in dealing with terrorism. It is important to have an understanding about some of the myths and stereotypes that are held of groups associated with terrorism and how these stereotypes might contribute to prejudice, discrimination, and biased encounters with members of these populations. Stereotypic views of multicultural groups who might be potential terrorists reduce individuals within those groups to simplistic, one-dimensional caricatures and as either "incompetent cowards" who can't fight face to face or "suicidal bogey persons" who can't be stopped. It is important for law enforcement officers to be aware of the different stereotypes of potential terrorists. The key to effectiveness in multicultural law enforcement with any group is to intelligently discern the myths and stereotypes about that group. Further, police officers need to be aware of these stereotypes and be able to monitor their thinking and behaviors when the stereotypes do not apply to the persons with whom they are interacting.

ISLAMIC RELIGION

Misunderstanding between Americans and Arab Americans can often be traced, in part, to religious differences and to a lack of tolerance of these differences. Islam is practiced by some Muslim newcomers to the United States as well as by Muslim African Americans. Many Muslims in the United States *identify* culturally with their religion, but this does mean that they are "religious." "Islamic" is not necessarily connected to culture or ethnicity. Muslims, or those who practice or identify with Islam, come from all over the world. "Islamic" does not mean "Arabic," nor does it mean "Middle Eastern" (demographic groups were explained earlier in the chapter). "Islamic" is merely an adjective referring to the religion of Islam. A large percentage of Muslims in the United States are African American, and not Arab or Middle Eastern. Many Arab Americans, especially those from the first wave of Arab immigration, are Christian, although non-Arab Americans tend to assume that they are Muslim simply because they are Arabs. *Muslims* refer to those who practice the religion, Islam. (See pp. 000–000 for further definitions and related distinctions.)

By and large, most Americans do not understand what Islam is and, because of stereotyping, wrongly associate Muslims with terrorists or fanatics. Many, but by no means all, Arab Muslims in the United States continue to practice traditional aspects of their religion, which are intertwined with daily life. However, some Muslims attend mosques only on holy days. Some do not have any "official" affiliation at all.

Islam means submission to the will of God, and for traditional, religious Muslims, the will of God (which is somewhat similar to the Western notion of fate) is a central concept. Islam has been called Mohammedanism, which is an incorrect name for the religion because it suggests that Muslims worship Mohammed* rather than God (Allah). It is believed that God's final message to man was revealed to the prophet Mohammed. *Allah* is the shortened Arabic word for the God of Abraham, and is used by both Arab Muslims and Arab Christians.

The Qur'an (Koran) and the Pillars of Islam

The Qur'an is the holy text for Muslims, and is regarded as the word of God. There are five Pillars of Islam, or central guidelines, that form the framework of the religion:

1. Profession of faith in God
2. Prayer five times daily
3. Giving of alms (concern for the needy)
4. Fasting during the month of Ramadan (sunrise to sunset)
5. Pilgrimage to Mecca (in Saudi Arabia) at least once in each person's lifetime

There are several points where law enforcement officials can show respect for a Muslim's need to practice his or her religion. The need to express one's faith in God and to be respected for it is one area. Usually, people pray together as a congregation in a mosque, which is the Islamic equivalent of a church or synagogue. People, however, can pray individually if a congregation is not present. Religious Muslims in jails, for example, will continue to pray five times a day and should not be ridiculed for or prevented from doing so. Remember that

---

*An alternate spelling is Muhammad, which is closer to the Arabic pronunciation of the name.

prayer, five times a day, is a "pillar" of Islam and that practicing Muslims will want to uphold this "command" no matter where they are. Call to prayer takes place at the following times:

- One hour before sunrise
- At noon
- Midafternoon
- Sunset
- Ninety minutes after sunset

Taboos in the Mosque

Police officers convey respect to the Muslim community if they can avoid, where possible, entering mosques and interrupting prayers (emergencies may occasionally make this impossible). Religion is vital in Arab life; one of the quickest ways to build rapport with the Muslim community is to show respect for Islamic customs and beliefs. Thus, other than in emergency situations, officers are advised to:

- Never step on a prayer mat or rug with shoes on.
- Avoid walking in front of people who are in the midst of prayer.
- Speak softly while people are praying.
- Dress conservatively (both men and women are required to dress conservatively; shorts are not appropriate).
- Invite people out of a prayer area to talk to them.
- Never touch a Qur'an, place it on the floor, or put anything on top of it.

Proper protocol in a mosque (also referred to as a *masjid*) requires that people remove their shoes before entering, but this must be left to the officer's discretion. Officer safety, of course, comes before consideration of differences.

Ramadan: The Holy Month

One of the holiest periods in the Islamic religion is the celebration of Ramadan, which lasts for one month. There is no fixed date because, like the Jewish and Chinese calendars, the Islamic calendar is based on the lunar cycle, related to the phases of the moon, with dates varying from year to year. During the month of Ramadan, Muslims do not eat, drink, smoke, or satisfy certain other "physical needs" from sunrise to sunset. Muslims fast during Ramadan to practice self-discipline and to experience and demonstrate unity with Muslims all over the world who identify with their religion. On the 29th night of Ramadan, when there is a new moon, the month of fasting is officially over. The final fast is broken and for up to three days, people celebrate with feasting and other activities. Throughout the month of Ramadan, Muslim families tend to pray in mosques more often than during other times of the year.

For Muslims, Ramadan is as important and holy as Lent and Christmas are for Christians; this fact is appreciated when others who are not Muslim recognize its importance. One city with a sizable Arab American population (Dearborn, Michigan) puts up festive lights in its business district during Ramadan as a gesture of acceptance and appreciation for the diversity that Arab Americans bring to the city. The Arab American community has reacted favorably to this symbolic gesture.

Knowledge of Religious Practices

Knowledge of religious practices, including what is considered holy, will help officers avoid problems and conflicts. For example, in a suburb of San Francisco, California, police officers and a group of Muslims from Tunisia were close to violence when police entered a morgue to obtain a hair sample from a person who had just been killed in a car accident. Apparently, the body had already been blessed by an *Imam* (a religious leader) and, according to the religion, any further contact would have been a defilement of the body that had already been sanctified and was ready for burial. The police officers were merely doing what they needed to do to complete their investigation and were unaware of this taboo. This, together with a language barrier, created an extremely confusing and confrontational situation in which officers lost control. A better course of action would have been to explain what had to be done and request permission to handle a body that had already been sanctified. If the citizens had not granted permission, the police would then have had to decide how to proceed. Most members of the Arab American community would comply with the wishes of police officers. As in many other situations involving police/citizen communication, the initial approach sets the tone for the entire interaction. To further officers' understanding of taboos related to death, Islam forbids what it views as any type of mutilation of bodies; thus autopsies are not performed unless they are mandated in conjunction with a crime investigation (CAIR, 2005). Some experts explain that "bodily intrusion violates beliefs [in Islam] about the sanctity of keeping the human body complete, although religion itself does not strictly forbid autopsies…[but, rather]…it is a matter of interpretation of the doctrines which have changed over time" (Burton, 2012).

Similarities between Christianity, Judaism, and Islam

When reading the above tenets of the Muslim faith, notice that certain practices and aspects of Islam are also found in Christianity and Judaism. All three religions are monotheistic, that is, each believes in only one God. Followers of these religions believe that God is the origin of all, and is all-knowing as well as all-powerful. Because God is merciful, it is possible for believers to be absolved of their sins, though the practices for obtaining absolution vary in the different ideologies. All three religions have a Holy Book central to the faith: Judaism has the Torah (the first five books of the Old Testament), Christianity the Bible, and Islam the Qur'an (Koran). All three religions regard their texts to be either the direct word of God or inspired by the word of God. There are similarities between the three books. For example, the concept of the Ten Commandments is present in each. All three contain stories about many of the same people, such as Adam, Noah, Abraham, Moses, David, and Solomon. Also, both the Bible and the Qur'an contain stories about Mary, Jesus, and John the Baptist. The oral reading or recitation of each book constitutes part of regular worship.

Prophets exist in each tradition and are revered as those who transmit the word of God to people. Chronologically, Judaism became a religion first, followed by Christianity and then Islam. Islam builds upon the foundations of Judaism and Christianity and believes in the authenticity of the prophets of earlier books. For example, Islamic belief sees both Moses and Jesus as rightful prophets and as precursors to Mohammed, who is believed to be the final prophet of God. As there are different interpretations of Christianity and Judaism, so do followers of Islam, too, interpret the religion in different ways. Differing readings of the Qur'an can lead to more (or less) tolerance within the religion. Lastly, both the Islamic and the Judeo-Christian traditions are said to stem from the same lineage; Abraham was father to both Isaac, whose progeny became the people of Israel, and Ishmael, who started the Arab lineage.

Definition of Further Terms: "Islamist" and "Jihad"

The term "Islamist" refers to Muslims who identify with the religion and believe its tenets should directly influence political life. "Islamist" does not automatically equate to "terrorist," which is a common misconception. There are many degrees of Islamism or political affiliation, as well as many nuanced definitions (Khan, 2013).

One way to understand "Islamist" (the person) and "Islamism" (the ideology) is to think about some Christian political coalitions. There are political Christian movements that may be considered fundamentalist or conservative in their religious beliefs, but they are not in any way terrorists. Members of Christian political organizations in the United States identify religiously and have political agendas which vary among Christian political coalitions just as they do among Islamists (ibid.).

The media frequently uses the word "Islamist" to mean "fundamentalist," or extremist, and often the two words (Islamist extremist) are used together. According to Humera Khan, an expert on preventing radicalization and violent extremism in the American Muslim community and who also consults to the Federal Bureau of Investigation (FBI) and the Justice Department on counter-terrorism:

> The word "Islamist" is always political—but that word does not indicate how conservative or extreme a particular group or individual is; Islamist conveys a political position. In contrast with the word "Islamic," Islamist is not about a way of life—that is, rather, "Islamic." Your personal identity as a Muslim is related to Islam, and you identify with things "Islamic," but politically you could still be very secular. (Ibid.)

Another term that is frequently linked with extremism is *jihad*, which means "struggle" in Arabic. ("Jihadi" or "jihadist" are adjectives, as in "Jihadist movement," or can pertain to an individual, as in "a jihadist.") Jihad refers to both the notion of an inner spiritual religious struggle as well as to an external struggle against oppression and enemies of Islam. The latter concept is sometimes described in mainstream American media as a "holy war," and is a distorted variation of the ideological foundation for terrorist organizations such as al-Qaida. Because of widespread media coverage of terror groups, many people are probably aware only of the notion of violent jihad (which is inaccurately used as a synonym for terrorism), though the internal personal struggle is often referred to as the more significant jihad and physical conflict as the lesser jihad.

Fundamentalism

Some attribute the acts of radical Muslims to "different readings" of the Qur'an—which often entail literal interpretations of certain passages. For example, one scholar points to certain modern writings or interpretations of the Qur'an, such as "The Way of a Muslim," which is used to indoctrinate young men in fundamentalism (Wallace & Effron, 2010). However, other religions and sects have also produced extremists who commit violence under the rubric of faith, such as the Ku Klux Klan. Islamic fundamentalism or extremism is not synonymous with terrorism. Humera Khan has observed:

> In fact, scholars from different schools of Islamic thought sometimes associated with "extremism," such as Wahabism and Salafism, have issued *fatwas* (opinions or rulings on points of Islamic law by a recognized authority) condemning terrorism. Wahabis and Salafis, for example, may be more conservative in their leanings and practice, but this does not mean that the way they practice Islam directly leads to terrorism. Terrorism is a deviation from Islam. (Khan, 2013)

Khan emphasizes that law enforcement officials should not infer that a visibly religious person has terrorist tendencies. "Law enforcement sees the outer veneer of what a person practices, and then stereotypes can often play out" (ibid.). She further explains that people who don't know much about Islam are often the ones who are more likely to join terrorist groups. "We are seeing a younger and younger age group involved. They don't know what religion is to start with, and when they learn about a deviant ideology, they can't filter out what Islam truly is and what it is not" (ibid.).

FAMILY STRUCTURE

Arab Americans typically have close-knit families in which members have a strong sense of loyalty and fulfill obligations to all members, including extended family (aunts, uncles, cousins, grandparents). Traditionally minded families also believe strongly in the family's honor, and members try to avoid behavior that will bring shame or disgrace to the family. The operating unit for Arab Americans (which may be less true for people who have been in the United States for generations) is not the individual but the family. Hence, if a person behaves inappropriately, the entire family is disgraced. Similarly, if a family member is assaulted in the Arab world, there would be some type of retribution. For police officers, three characteristics of the Arab family will affect their interaction with family members:

- Extended family members are often as close as the "nuclear family" (mother, father, children) and are not seen as secondary family members. If there is a police issue, officers can expect that several members of the family will become involved in the matter. Although officers might perceive this as interference, from an Arab cultural perspective, it is merely involvement and concern. The numbers of people involved are not meant to overwhelm an officer.
- Family loyalty and protection are seen as one of the highest values of family life. Therefore, shaming, ridiculing, insulting, or criticizing family members, especially in public, can have serious consequences.
- Newer Arab American refugees or immigrants may be reluctant to accept police assistance. Because families are tightly knit, they can also be closed "units" within which members prefer to keep private matters or conflicts to themselves. As a result, officers will have to work harder at establishing rapport if they want to gain cooperation.

There is an important point of contact between all three of these characteristics and law enforcement interaction with members of Arab American families. Former Dearborn Police Department Corporal Berro explains: "When we respond to a call at a home, the police car is like a magnet. Every family member comes out of the house and everyone wants to talk at once. It can be an overwhelming sensation for an officer who doesn't understand this background" (Berro, 2013).

Police officers who are not trained in understanding and responding appropriately and professionally to cultural differences could alienate the family by: (1) not respecting the interest and involvement of the family members and (2) attempting to gain control of the communication in an authoritarian manner. The consequences are likely to be that the officers would have difficulty establishing the rapport needed to gain information about the conflict at hand and would not be trusted or respected. To do their jobs effectively, law enforcement officials must demonstrate respect for Arab family values, along with communication style differences (the latter will be discussed shortly).

Head of the Household

As in many cultures with a traditional family structure, the man in the Arab home is the head of the household and his role and influence are strong. The wife has a great deal of influence, too, but it can more often be "behind the scenes" in traditional marriages. An Arab woman does not always defer to her husband in private as she would in public. However, as mentioned earlier in the chapter, there are many women who have broken out of the traditional mold and tend to be more vocal, outspoken, and assertive than were their mothers or grandmothers. A Middle Eastern woman's country of origin might also be a factor in determining her public behavior.

Traditionally, in many Arab countries, fathers maintain their status by being strict disciplinarians and demanding absolute respect, thus creating some degree of fear among children and even among wives. Once again, Arab Americans born and raised in this country have, for the most part, adopted a middle-class "American" style of child raising whereby children participate in some of the decision-making and are treated in an egalitarian manner. In addition, as with changing roles among all kinds of families in the United States, the father as traditional head of the household and the mother as having "second-class" status is no longer prevalent among established Arab Americans in the United States. Wife abuse and child abuse are not considered respectable practices by educated Arab Americans, but the practices still occur, just as they do in mainstream American society.

In traditional Arab society, displays of power and influence are common among males. While this can be viewed in a negative light from certain Western perspectives, this trait can be helpful in securing the compliance of the family in important matters. The husband or father can be a natural ally of authorities. Officers would be well advised to work with both the father and the mother, for example, in matters where children are involved. On family matters the woman frequently is the authority, even if she seems to defer to her husband. Communicating with the woman, even if indirectly, while still respecting the father's need to maintain his public status, will win respect from both the man and the woman.

Children and Americanization

Americanization, which involves both assimilation in and acculturation to U.S. society, involves adapting to different behaviors, attitudes, and values. Younger immigrant and refugee children typically adapt more quickly than their parents, and learn the new language with relative ease. In addition, peer influence and pressure in American society overshadow parental influence, especially beginning in the formative and teen years (AbuHamda, 2017). Arab children, cherished by their parents, often face challenges bridging the cultural gap between their parents' culture of origin and the expectations of their new adopted country. Children may rebel and reject their language, customs, and traditions of origin to be more "American" than "Arab" (ibid.).

Children in Arab families are taught to be respectful of their parents, elders and people in authority. Preserving a family's dignity and reputation brings honor to the family; reputation is highly regarded. Parents worry about and strongly oppose certain types of behaviors in American society, and especially those associated with alcohol and physical relations between the sexes (Ismail, 2017). "When young people engage in these behaviors, shame is brought to the family that can bring distress, conflict, and restrictions on the child. However, when a child's, and especially a girl's, behavior involves what is seen as sexual misconduct, the family's honor is ruined. When this happens, *all* members of the family suffer" (ibid.).

There is very little that police officers can do to change the attitudes of parents who restrict their children's behavior. However, if officers respond to calls during which they notice that the family has become dysfunctional because of children's behavior, it is a service to the family to initiate some sort of social service intervention or make a referral. If a family is already at the point of needing police assistance in problems involving children and parents, then, more likely than not, they need other types of assistance as well. At the same time, newer immigrants and refugees will not necessarily be open to social service interventions, especially if the case workers do not speak Arabic. According to Lobna Ismail, President of Connecting Cultures, a Washington, D.C., firm specializing in Arab American cross-cultural understanding, some individuals may reveal more information to people outside their own community than to people within the community. "Hesitation to disclose personal family matters or struggles to people from their own cultural, religious, or ethnic group may be a preference so as to minimize embarrassment or shame" (ibid.).

COMMUNICATION STYLES AND CULTURAL PRACTICES

As with all other immigrant groups, the degree to which people preserve their cultural practices varies. The following descriptions of everyday behavior will not apply equally to all Arab Americans, but they do not necessarily apply only to newcomers. Immigrants may preserve traditions and practices long after they come to a new country by conscious choice or sometimes because they are unaware of their cultural behavior (i.e., it is not in their conscious awareness).

Greetings, Names, Approach, and Touching

Americans of Arab heritage have been coming to the United States since the late 1800s; second-, third-, and fourth-generation Arab Americans are the children and grandchildren of immigrants who settled in the United States over 100 years ago. For Arab American newcomers, however, there are some customs of which to be aware, including the use of titles to address someone who is older or in a position of authority. "Most commonly, people would be addressed by a title, Sir or Ma'am or 'Mr./Mrs.' followed by the last name or first name (i.e., in some Arab countries, the first name is used after 'Mr.' or 'Mrs.'). It is customary for Arab women to preserve their names after marriage. Therefore, the distinctions between the terms 'maiden' name and 'married' name may cause confusion for some" (Ismail, 2017).

Arabic is a phonetic language, but you may see the same name spelled in two different ways. For example, "Mohamed" can also be spelled "Muhammad" and "Lobna," can be spelled "Lubna." In English, using a different vowel would usually change the pronunciation. In the case of these Arabic names, the "o" and the "u" are interchangeable, with the pronunciation of each name remaining the same despite the different spellings (ibid.).

Many Arab Americans who have retained their traditional customs shake hands and then place their right hand on their chest near the heart, which signifies warmth, deep respect, and gratitude. When visiting the Middle East, Americans are advised to reciprocate whenever they observe this gesture. Officers can decide whether they are comfortable using this gesture—most people would not expect it from an officer, but might appreciate the gesture as long as the officer was able to convey sincerity. Generally, when Arabs from the Middle East shake hands, they do not shake hands briefly or firmly. (The expression "He has a dead fish handshake" is unfamiliar to many cultural groups!) Traditional Arab style is to hold hands longer than other Americans do and shake hands more lightly. Older children are taught to shake hands with adults as a sign of respect. Many Arabs would appreciate an officer shaking hands with their older children. With a recent immigrant or refugee Arab woman, it is generally not appropriate to shake hands unless she extends her hand first. This would definitely apply to women who wear head coverings.

Many Arabs of the same sex greet each other by kissing on the cheek. Two Saudi Arabian men, for example, might greet each other by kissing on both cheeks a number of times. Public touching of the opposite sex is forbidden in the traditional Arab world, and male officers should make every effort not to touch Arab women, even casually—unless, as noted above, a woman extends her hand first for a handshake.

Police officers should be aware that some Arab American citizens (e.g., Lebanese) who are new to the United States may react to a police officer's approach in unexpected ways. For example, an officer who has just asked a person to give his driver's license may find the person getting out of his car to be able to talk to the officer. From the person's perspective, he or she is simply trying to be courteous (because this is how it is done in the person's home country). An officer, always conscious of safety issues, may simply have to explain that in the United States, officers require citizens to remain in their cars.

Hospitality

Hospitality is a byword among Arabs, whatever their station in life. Guests are generally treated to the kindest and most lavish consideration. Hospitality in the Arab culture is not an option; it is more of an obligation or duty. In some parts of the Arab world, thanking someone for hospitality might be answered with a common expression meaning, "Don't thank me. It's my duty." (Here the word *duty* has a more positive than negative connotation.) To be anything but hospitable goes against the grain of Arab culture. Officers need to understand how deeply ingrained the need to be hospitable is and should not misinterpret this behavior. Whether in the home or in a business owner's shop or office, when an officer enters, an Arab American may very well offer coffee or tea and something to eat. This is not to be mistaken for a bribe and, from the Arab perspective, carries no negative connotations. According to Berro, most people would be offended if officers did not accept their offers of hospitality. The period of time spent socializing and extending hospitality gives Arab Americans a chance to get to know and gauge the extent to which the other person should be trusted. Obviously, on an emergency call, there is no time for such pleasantries. However, with the trend toward increasing community policing practices, officers may find that they are involved in more situations in which they may decide to accept small gestures of hospitality, within departmental policy (Berro, 2013).

Verbal and Nonverbal Communication

Arabs in general are very warm and expressive people, both verbally and nonverbally, and appreciate it when others extend warmth to them. There are some areas in the realm of nonverbal communication in which Americans, without cultural knowledge, have misinterpreted the behavior of Arab Americans simply because of ethnocentrism (i.e., the tendency to judge others by one's own cultural standards and norms).

CONVERSATIONAL DISTANCE Acceptable conversational distance between two people is often related to cultural influences. Officers are very aware of safety issues and keep a certain distance from people when communicating with them. Generally, officers like to stand about an arm's length or farther from citizens to avoid possible assaults. This distance is similar to how far apart "mainstream Americans" stand when in conversation. When this distance is "violated," officers can feel threatened (either consciously or subconsciously). Many Arabs, especially if they are new to the country, tend to have a closer acceptable conversational distance than do Americans. In Arab culture, it is not considered offensive to "feel a person's breath." Yet many Americans, unfamiliar with this intimacy in regular conversation, have misinterpreted the closeness. While still being conscious of safety, law enforcement officers can keep in mind that this closer-than-normal behavior (i.e., "normal" for the officer) does not necessarily constitute a threat.

When Americans travel to the Middle East, they often notice this tendency for people to stand closer to each other as compared to mainstream U.S. cultural norms. This is relevant to police officers in the United States, especially in the context of communicating with recent immigrants and refugees. (It is recommended not to back away when an Arab stands very close while speaking to you in order to maintain rapport.) Some Arabs may stare into other people's eyes, watching the pupils for an indication of the other person's response (e.g., dilated pupils mean a positive response). Male police officers, however, should avoid staring directly into a woman's eyes.

GESTURES   There are some distinct gestures and body language in some Arab countries that first generation immigrants may exhibit. For example:

- *Indicating that something is not understood.* The right hand is held up, with the palm up, and is twisted back and forth.
- *Indicating to someone to hold on or to wait.* Fingers and thumb are touching with the palm up.
- *Indicating, "Never."* The right forefinger is pointed up and moved from left to right quickly and repeatedly.
- *Saying, "No."* The head moves back slightly, eyebrows are raised as is the chin; there is also a sound that may be made by clicking the tongue on the roof of the mouth.
- *Motioning to someone to leave.* The right hand is held out with the palm down and moved as if pushing something away from you.

As with many other cultural groups, pointing a finger directly at someone is considered rude and can be taken as a sign of contempt. Arab immigrants, especially older ones, will often use their entire hand to point. The "OK" or "thumbs-up" gesture is considered obscene. Again, this applies only to people who have not yet been acculturated to mainstream America.

Emotional Expressiveness

Some Arab Americans may express themselves in a highly emotional manner, and this can be threatening for some police. Upon seeing a family member in trouble, it would be most usual and natural for a woman to put her hands to her face and say something like, "Oh, my God" frequently and in a loud voice. While other Americans can react this same way, it is worth pointing out that in mainstream American culture, there is a tendency to subdue one's emotions and not to go "out of control." What some Americans consider "out of control," Arabs (like Mexicans, Greeks, Israelis, and Iranians, among other groups) consider perfectly "normal" behavior. In fact, the lack of emotionalism that Arabs observe among mainstream Americans can be misinterpreted as lack of interest or involvement.

Although a communication-style characteristic never applies to all people in one cultural group (and we have seen that there is a great deal of diversity among Arab Americans), there are group traits that can apply to many. Arabs, especially the first generation of relatively recent newcomers, tend to display emotions when talking (as seen in the previous example). Unlike many people in Asian cultures (e.g., Japanese), Arabs have not been "taught" to suppress their emotions. Arabs, like other Mediterranean groups such as Israelis or Greeks, tend to shout when they are excited or angry and are very animated in their communication. They may repeatedly insert expressions into their speech such as "I swear by God." This is simply a cultural mannerism.

Westerners, however, tend to judge this "style" negatively. To some Westerners, the emotionalism, repetition, and emphasis on certain statements can give the impression that the person is not telling the truth or is exaggerating for effect. An officer unfamiliar with these cultural mannerisms may feel overwhelmed, especially when involved with an entire group of people. With large groups of people (e.g., multiple extended family members), the officer needs to determine the spokesperson for the group, and to refrain from showing impatience or irritation at this culturally different style.

SWEARING, OBSCENITIES, AND INSULTS   Officers working in Arab American communities should know that for Arabs, words are extremely powerful. If an officer displays a lack of professionalism by swearing at an Arab (using even words like "damn"), it will be nearly impossible to repair the damage.

Officers who understand professionalism are aware that this type of language and interaction is insulting to all persons. The choice to use obscenities and insults, especially in conjunction with one's ethnic background, however, means that officers risk never being able to establish trust within the ethnic community. This can translate into not being able to secure cooperation when needed. Even a few officers exhibiting this type of behavior can damage the reputation of an entire department for a long period of time.

ENGLISH LANGUAGE PROBLEMS   If time allows, before asking the question "Do you speak English?" officers should try to assess whether the Arab American is a recent arrival or an established citizen who might react negatively to the question. A heavy accent does not necessarily mean that a person is unable to speak English (although that may be the case). There are specific communication skills that can be used with limited-English-speaking persons (see Chapter 4), which should be applied with Arab Americans. Officers should proceed slowly and nonaggressively with questioning and, wherever possible, ask open-ended questions. An officer's patience and willingness to take extra time will be beneficial in the long run.

KEY ISSUES IN LAW ENFORCEMENT

Perceptions of and Interactions with Police

It is not possible to generalize Arab Americans' perception of the police, but it is fair to say that a large part of the Arab American community has great respect for law enforcement. On the other hand, some immigrants, such as Jordanians and Palestinians, do not understand the American system and have an ingrained fear of police because of political problems in their own region of the world (James Zogby, 2013). Given that they distrust the government, they are more likely to reject help from the police, and this puts them at a decided disadvantage in that they can more easily become victims. Their fear, in combination with the interdependence and helpfulness that characterize the extended family, results in families not wanting assistance from the police. Thus, police will encounter some families that would prefer to handle conflicts on their own when police intervention is clearly needed. Some of the newer immigrants and refugees feel that it is dishonorable to have to go outside the family (e.g., to police and social service providers) to get help, and, if given a choice, they would choose not to embarrass themselves and their families in this manner. On the other hand, community partnerships in recent years have served to re-educate new Americans; thus, there is less reluctance today than a decade ago to see the police as a resource (Haddad, 2017).

   Unlike community policing engagement in the United States where citizens can approach the police, such models of law enforcement are, for the most part, unheard of in the Middle East. While there are major differences in governments in this world region, some are repressive regimes. Commenting on an extreme with respect to law enforcement in the Middle East, Police Chief Haddad says, "One can only imagine how law enforcement in Syria is under the Assad regime, and how it contrasts with community policing in the United States today" (ibid.). During the rule of Saddam Hussein, Iraqi immigrants in the United States used to complain that "Saddam's enforcers robbed them of their jewelry, even if it meant cutting off their fingers to get it" (ibid.).

Modesty, Women's Dress, and Diversity among Women

Modesty is highly valued in Arab and Muslim cultures. Based on both faith and cultural customs, Arab women may cover their hair and wear loose fitting clothing. However, there is tremendous diversity and contrast in women's attire. It is important to resist stereotyping based on images of Muslim women and "the veil." Cross-Cultural specialist Lobna Ismail describes a contrast: "Two Arab American women are talking to each other, one is wearing a black cloak or *abaya*, her hair covered with a black scarf. The other is wearing ripped jeans and her kneecaps are exposed." These two women are dressed very differently. Nevertheless, it is not possible to draw conclusions about a woman's degree of religiosity, political affiliation, or education level simply by outward appearance.

   Ismail has frequently encountered the assumption that, if a woman covers her hair, she is a newcomer to the United States, is uneducated, and speaks no or little English. This can be quite contrary to the reality (ibid.). According to Ismail, a range of factors plays into one's identity and clothing preferences, including family background, generation, personality, experiences, and education. In some cases, a young woman may decide to dress more modestly than her mother, and, yet, identifies as a feminist and progressive.

As an officer, if the need to search requires that a woman remove her head covering, it is important to explain the reason (e.g., safety or security risk). Berro, an Arab American, routinely gave this advice to officers: "Approach this matter sensitively. Don't overpower the woman, intimidate her, or grab her 'hijab' (head covering). Ask her to go into a private room and have her remove it, and get a female officer to help with the procedure" (Berro, 2013).

American officers may have difficulty understanding the violation that a woman feels when her head covering is taken away forcibly. Even if a woman is arrested for something like disorderly conduct, it is a great offense on the part of the officer to remove her head cover or touch her in any way. When police procedures require that a head cover be removed, the officers should explain why this is taking place, what the procedure is and, offer an apology to convey empathy and respect. Having dealt with this same issue, the department of U.S. Citizenship and Immigration Services (USCIS) states its regulations in the following way:

> USCIS will ask individuals to remove headwear that is not religious at the time of photograph capture. However, USCIS will accommodate an individual who wears headwear as part of their religious practices. Religious headwear can be worn if a reasonable likeness can be obtained from an individual, the full face is visible and the religious headwear does not cast a shadow on the face. Therefore, USCIS will ask an individual to remove or adjust portions of religious headwear that covers all or part of the individual's face…. (U.S. Citizenship and Immigration Services, 2012)

Thus, USCIS officials accept photographs of Muslim women with their head coverings on. Because police departments deal with safety issues (such as concealed weapons), they may not have the liberty to accommodate this particular cultural practice in the same way that USCIS does. The matter of women and head coverings must be handled with extreme sensitivity. Ismail reinforces the importance of Berro's message: if a woman must remove her head covering for an extensive search, the officer should first ask her to remove it herself in a private area with a female officer in attendance. Moreover, this should be done out of view of any unrelated male (Ismail, 2017).

Arab Small Business Owners

Racial and ethnic tensions exist between Arab grocers and liquor store owners in low-income areas and members of other minority groups. The dynamics between Arab store owners and African Americans are similar to those between Koreans and African Americans in inner cities. The non-Arab often views the Arab as having money and exploiting the local residents for economic gain. Dr. James Zogby explains that this perception is reinforced because, in some locales, one rarely sees a non-Arab working in an Arab-owned store. The local resident, according to Zogby, does not understand that the Arabs, for the most part, are political refugees (e.g., Palestinians) and have come to the United States for a better life. Despite stereotypes that these store owners have connections to "Arab money" (i.e., oil money), when they first arrive, the only work that they can do is to operate small "marginal" businesses. Most of the small Arab-run grocery stores, liquor stores, and gas stations are family-operated businesses where two brothers, or a father and two sons, for example, are managing the operation. It would not be economically possible for them to hire outside the family (James Zogby, 2013). Police officers, in the midst of conflicts between store owners and residents, can attempt to explain the position of the refugees, but of course, the explanation by itself cannot take care of the problem. Many poor American-born citizens harbor a great deal of animosity toward immigrants and refugees because of scarce resources.

Alcohol is forbidden in the Muslim religion, yet Arab liquor store owners sell it to their customers. There has been a debate in the Arab American community as to whether Muslim immigrants and refugees should go into this type of business. For the majority of newcomers, however, the choices are very limited. Members of other ethnic groups have also owned mom-and-pop stores throughout the years.

Finally, there is another dimension to the problem of Arab store owners in inner cities. Many inner-city residents (Arab Americans and African Americans included) do not feel that law enforcement officials take the needs of the inner city as seriously as they do elsewhere. A pattern has emerged in the Arab American community whereby Arab American store owners feel that they themselves have to take on problems of crime in their stores (John Zogby, 2013). If an Arab store owner is robbed and is treated in an unsupportive or harsh way by police, he feels that he needs to defend himself and his store all by himself. In some cases, Arab store owners have assaulted shoplifters in their stores, potentially risking becoming victims themselves. Like many other minority group members, some Arab shop owners in the inner city have given up on the police. Police officers cannot solve the social ills that plague the inner city, but, at a minimum, need to instill the confidence that they will be as supportive as possible when dealing with the crimes that immigrant/refugee store owners experience. In addition, Arab shop or gas station owners often assist their more recently arrived relatives in opening similar businesses. Many of these recent immigrants do not know the system or all the regulations for running a business. There have been instances of store owners being chastised for running "illegal" businesses, when in fact they were not familiar with the complete process required for proper licensing (Haddad, 2017).

Hate Crimes against Arab and Muslim Americans

Two Sacramento, California area Islamic Centers were the targets of hate crimes, where explicit intolerance of Muslims and Islam was manifested by the desecration of the Quran, the Islamic holy book. In one case, pages were torn out of a Quran and thrown at an Islamic Center. At a second Islamic Center, the hate crime perpetrators burned a Quran, filled it with bacon (a food that is forbidden in Islam) and then handcuffed the holy book to a fence of the Center.

(Glover, 2017; Rocha, 2017)

"Islamophobia" is similar to the word xenophobia, which means fear or hatred of strangers or foreigners. The term "Islamophobia"—meaning fear or hatred of Muslims—was coined in the early 1990s in the context of Muslims in the United Kingdom (Runnymede Trust, 1996). Hostility toward Muslims has existed in Western cultures for many centuries, but it has become more extreme and violent since 9/11 (CAIR, 2015), and "has increased in notoriety and frequency" (Gallup, 2011). The weeks and months following the 9/11 attacks were accompanied by a huge spike in unofficial (i.e., non-DOJ) reporting of hate crimes directed at Arab Americans, Muslim Americans, and those thought to be of the same background. There were more than 700 violent crimes against Arab Americans reported within the first nine weeks after the tragedy of 9/11, and 165 reported hate crimes from January 1, 2002, through October 11, 2002, a figure higher than most years in the previous decade (ADC Research Institute, 2003). However, the American-Arab Anti-Discrimination Committee (ADC) emphasized that this did not represent the actual total number of hate crimes; many cases had not been made public because victims feared additional violence against them. Dearborn, Michigan, Police Chief Ronald Haddad points out that fear is a universal human emotion when one is victimized, and this fear factor plays an important role in why many hate crimes go unreported. In explaining the lack of reporting to police, it is also important to recognize the Arab value of honor and maintaining harmony whenever possible (ibid.).

Prior to the terrorist attacks of 9/11, "single-bias" hate crimes (with a single motivation) against people from one ethnic or national group were the second *least* reported of the hate crimes. The initial spike in post-9/11 hate crimes against Arab Americans or those perceived to be Arab or Muslim had declined significantly as community members and law enforcement officers work together to curb the number of incidents.

Weeks before the war with Iraq, the FBI warned of a similar potential surge in hate crimes. Top FBI officials met with Arab and Muslim leaders in the United States to assure them of the FBI's priority to prevent and investigate hate crimes. This was a step that they had *not* initially taken in the aftermath of 9/11. The targeted interviews of thousands of Iraqis living in the United States were also organized in part to reassure the Iraqi community that law enforcement officials would not tolerate any ethnic backlash in the case of a war ("FBI: War Could...," 2009).

In 2008, the ADC reported on hate crimes and discrimination against Arab Americans between the years 2003 and 2007. While the actual number of hate crimes was down as compared to the immediate post-9/11 period, there were nevertheless significant numbers of hate crimes, acts of discrimination (especially at airports and at the workplace), and border and customs issues targeted toward Arab Americans. Vandalism and destruction of property at mosques and Islamic centers were on the rise during the years 2003–2007 (ADC Research Institute, 2008).

Hate crimes against Arab and Muslim Americans increased again beginning in 2010. The Southern Poverty Law Institute summarized FBI data by reporting "that there were 157 anti-Muslim hate crimes in 2011, down very slightly from the 160 recorded in 2010. The 2011 crimes occurred during a period when Islam-bashing propaganda, which initially took off in 2010, continued and even intensified" (Southern Poverty Law Center, 2013).

In August 2013, the Department of Justice announced that a number of additional groups would be included in the national program that tracks hate crime, i.e., the Uniform Crime Reporting Program, discussed in Chapter 11. These groups included Arab Americans as well as individuals from South Asia, such as Sikhs and Hindus (also, Buddhists who are from all parts of Asia).

Arab Americans and others perceived to be Arab, Muslim, or Middle Eastern are frequently targets of hate speech and hate crimes after high profile terror attacks, and, as such, require additional police vigilance. Additional factors contribute to the anti-Muslim/anti-Arab bias and acts of hate. Throughout 2015, news reports came in of nearly 1 million Syrian refugees fleeing war and destruction, and seeking asylum mainly in Europe; views on immigration became increasingly divisive with many equating the words "refugee" and "terrorist." Around the same time, U.S. presidential campaign rhetoric in 2015–2016 called for a "total and complete shutdown of Muslims entering the United States," furthering the stereotype of Muslims as terrorists. (Travel bans against Muslim majority countries, issued by executive order in 2017, were challenged and blocked by federal appeals courts on the basis of discrimination against religion; the case was brought to the Supreme Court, which ruled to allow partial enforcement of the ban. Full review of the travel ban case will have taken place after the publication of this edition.)

FBI data in 2015 showed that assaults against Muslims, Arabs, or those perceived to be from the Middle East reached the levels that had been seen after the 9/11 attacks (FBI UCR, 2015). Anti-Muslim hate groups rose by almost 200 percent in 2016 (Southern Poverty Law Center, 2016). (See also "Anti-Arab/Muslim Victimization" in Chapter 11.)

Law Enforcement, Federal Agencies, and Arab/Muslim Americans

According to a study released by the Vera Institute of Justice in 2006, "In the aftermath of September 11, Arab Americans have a greater fear of racial profiling and immigration enforcement than of falling victim to hate crimes." Nearly 100 Arab Americans and over 100 law enforcement personnel (FBI agents and police officers) participated in the study, which was conducted from 2003 to 2005. Interviewees in the study, both from the Arab American community and from the law enforcement agencies, felt that cooperation and trust post-9/11 had deteriorated. Arab Americans reported an "increasing sense of victimization, suspicion of law enforcement, and concerns about protecting their civil liberties" (Henderson, Ortiz, Sugie, & Miller, 2006). Interview inquiries confirmed that:

> September 11 had a substantial impact on Arab American communities. In every site, Arab Americans described heightened levels of public suspicion exacerbated by increased media attention and targeted governmental policies (such as special registration requirements, voluntary interviews, and the detention and deportation of community members). Although community members also reported increases in hate victimization, they expressed greater concern about being victimized by federal policies and practices than by individual acts of harassment or violence. Among law enforcement, the most notable change was a new pressure to incorporate counterterrorism into their work. Local police and FBI participants alike reported that this pressure had frequently resulted in policies that were poorly defined or inconsistently applied. (Ibid.)

In 2014, the U.S. Commission on Civil Rights published a report of a briefing entitled, "Federal Civil Rights Engagement with Arab and Muslim-American Communities," with the objective of examining U.S. government efforts to counter civil rights violations after the terrorist attacks on 9/11. The findings, based on expert testimony, included (U.S. Commission on Civil Rights, 2014):

- Many Americans of Muslim background continue to feel discrimination from stereotyping and profiling, and are reluctant to report violations, including those at the workplace;
- There continues to be "widespread religious and racial profiling" by Customs and Border Patrol, the Transportation and Safety Administration, and the FBI;
- Some federal government agencies' training programs on the American Muslim community fall short of presenting Muslims as a heterogeneous group, and do not adequately present distinctions and cultural diversity;
- Muslim Americans are concerned about being placed on government watch lists; fear of surveillance by U.S. Intelligence has limited Muslims' freedom of expression and association at universities and at religious institutions;
- American Muslims' confidence and trust in law enforcement has been affected by "overzealous government monitoring programs." (Ibid.)

Haris Tarin, Director of the Muslim Public Affairs Council DC Office, testified before the above-noted Commission, stressing the importance of creating law enforcement partnerships with Arab Americans and other Muslims to address a variety of issues related to religious and racial discrimination. He noted that there are two trends with respect to law enforcement engagement of members of minority communities (MPAC, 2014):

1. Treating members of minority communities as suspect.
2. Treating community members as partners.

The briefing report characterizes these as the "suspect trend of engagement" versus the "partnership trend of engagement" (ibid.). Community policing research points to strong evidence that effective policing must include partnering and developing relationships with community members and organizations. The International Association of Chiefs of Police maintain that solving crimes and maintaining order depends on the cooperation of people in the community, including immigrants of all kinds (IACP, 2015).

Recruitment of Arab Americans in Law Enforcement

NYPD Muslim Officer's Society was the first fraternal organization in the country to represent Muslim Americans in law enforcement. In 2015, NYPD announced an initiative to recruit more Muslim police officers in the hope that they could assist with relationship building between officers and the community, in addition to increasing efforts to combat extremism. (Jenkins, 2015; Rankin, 2015). By 2016, the 36,000 officer force had approximately 1,000 Muslim officers, up a couple of hundred from the previous year. Many Muslim organizations encourage their members to pursue law enforcement, but there are significant recruitment obstacles (CAIR, 2005). Recent immigrants, who come from repressive regimes, have frequently internalized negative views of corrupt police, and therefore require a great deal of re-education to begin to see police differently. Some Arab Americans feel that an anti-Muslim bias is tolerated in law enforcement due to a history with federal surveillance programs as well as extensive profiling in in the name of security (ibid.).

With 42 percent of the population Arab American, the Dearborn Police Department, Michigan, recruits Arab Americans for all levels of police work, including sworn officers, interns, and cadets, in addition to having excellent and diverse officer representation in the city's high schools. Dearborn's Chief of Police, Ronald Haddad, has 20 Arab American officers out of 190. He states that having this representation is "one less bridge to walk over with community members" (Haddad, 2017).

The Need to Rebuild Trust

Major events in the past three decades have contributed to Islamophobia and, on the part of some Muslim and Arab American community members, a collective mistrust of law enforcement. Beginning with the Gulf Wars, and continuing with 9/11, acts of violence in the name of Islam, the 2015–2016 presidential campaign and 2017 executive orders specific to mainly Muslim-majority countries, community members have felt that law enforcement representatives automatically view them as suspects. Ismail characterizes the collective blame of and backlash toward the vast majority of law abiding Arab Americans as both "psychologically and physically damaging. As a result, community members may hesitate to call the police when they are victims of crimes, fearing treatment as suspects rather than victims of a crime" (Ismail, 2017).

While there has been a great deal of progress bridging the cultural gap with police in some jurisdictions after 9/11, mutual distrust between some Arab American communities and law enforcement lingers. Between 2002 and 2014, the NYPD, with the help of the CIA, created a surveillance unit, called the Demographics Unit, whose objective was to catalog information on Muslim communities. Undercover police officers monitored mosques, Muslim-owned businesses and other Islamic institutions in the New York region. This resulted in mass spying of individuals on the basis of religion only. The unit, which did not result in any leads, was dropped in 2014 after two federal law suits and public criticism (Boyette, 2014).

Some immigrants already bring with them a fear of law enforcement from their native countries where widespread police corruption as well as police brutality were and continue to be a normal part of life. It is therefore imperative to consider the importance of building trust, rapport, and relationships with Arab Americans and people from the Middle East. According to Dr. James Zogby, president of the Arab American Institute Foundation in Washington, D.C., the more a community-policing mindset has developed in a particular jurisdiction, the more easily communication barriers come down between law enforcement and Arab Americans. "We have found that when FBI and police department leadership are willing to sit down and dialogue with community leaders, then it is much more likely that citizens will be willing to share information and provide tips because officers have gone out of their way to build trust" (James Zogby, 2013).

Summary

- There is some confusion as to who Arabs and Middle Easterners are; although commonly thought of as Arabs, Iranians and Turks are not Arabs, and they do not speak Arabic. Many people assume that all Muslims are Arabs, and vice versa. Many Arabs are also Christians; the world's Muslim population is composed of dozens of ethnic groups. Nevertheless, the predominant religion among Arabs is Islam, and its followers are called Muslims. Israel is the only country in the Middle East in which the majority of the population is Jewish; there are also Arabs living in Israel who are Christians or Muslims.

- The first wave of Arab immigrants, largely from Syria, came between 1880 and World War I to further themselves economically. The second wave of Arab immigrants to the United States, beginning after World War II, came in large part as students and professionals seeking to escape economic instability and political unrest in their home countries. The communities with the largest Arab American populations are in Los Angeles/Orange County, Detroit, the greater New York area, Chicago, and Washington, D.C., California has the largest "cluster" of Arab American communities.

- There is great diversity among Arab American groups. Understanding this diversity will assist officers in not seeing Arabs as homogeneous and will encourage people to move away from thinking in stereotypes. Nevertheless, there are several basic Arab cultural values that officers should keep in mind when interacting with Arab American citizens, and these are shared across the various cultural groups. The cultural value of honor is of paramount importance. Family loyalty often takes precedence over other needs. Communication should be courteous and hospitable; honor and the avoidance of shame govern interpersonal interactions and relationships.

- Arab Americans have been wrongly characterized and stereotyped by the media; as with all stereotypes, inaccurate perceptions have affected people's thinking about Arab Americans. Officers should be aware of stereotypes that may influence their judgment. Scapegoating Arabs, Muslims and those perceived to be Muslims often spreads pervasively across the country after high-profile terrorist incidents. Additionally, the political rhetoric in 2015 and 2016 that explicitly targeted Muslims created a more open environment for backlash with a spike in hate speech and hate crimes against Muslims.

- Officers can demonstrate to Muslim Arabs a respect for their religion by refraining from interrupting people in the mosque, and during prayers, unless absolutely necessary; maintaining courteous behavior in mosques, such as not stepping on prayer mats, not walking in front of people who are praying, and not touching a Qur'an. Finally, officers should attempt to work out solutions with community members regarding such issues as noise and parking associated with religious celebrations.

- The basic unit for Arab Americans, especially for recent arrivals and traditional families, is not the individual but the family, including the extended family. If a family member is involved in a police incident, officers should expect that other family members will become actively involved; this is not an attempt to interfere with police affairs. Traditionally and outwardly, the father is the head of the household and much of the conversation should be directed toward him; this does not mean that the officer should ignore any women who are present.

- There are a number of specific cultural practices and taboos that officers should consider when communicating with Arab Americans who have preserved a traditional lifestyle. Be respectful of the preference of some Arab women to be modest. Male officers should not touch a woman at all, and should be mindful of her modesty in front of male officers.

Traditional Arabs deeply value hospitality; it is a hallmark of culture in the Middle East. There are cultural differences in communication style that can affect officers' judgment and reactions. Becoming highly emotional (verbally and nonverbally) and speaking loudly is not looked down upon in the Arab world.

- Law enforcement needs to be continually vigilant as to the potential for hate crimes against Arab Americans and other Middle Eastern groups. In addition, some Middle Eastern immigrants bring negative perceptions of the police from their own experiences, and these contribute to difficulty in trusting the police.

- Many Arab Americans feel that they are automatic suspects when approached by law enforcement representatives. Since 9/11, there has been collateral damage to the entire Arab American community that persists today. They may hesitate to call the police when they are victims of crimes, and they fear being treated as suspects rather than victims of a crime. While there has been progress bridging the cultural gap with police in some jurisdictions after 9/11, mutual distrust between some Arab American communities and law enforcement lingers.

Discussion Questions and Issues

1. *Police/Ethnic Community Relations.* Discuss the following incident that took place at the end of the holy month of Ramadan in a city close to Detroit: officers ticketed many cars parked across the street from a mosque. According to community people, the stores adjacent to the parking lots were closed, and although parking was technically for customers only, Arab Americans did not anticipate that there would be a problem utilizing the parking lot after hours. From a community relations point of view, the mass ticketing created some very negative feelings and a collective perception that "They (meaning the police) don't respect us; they don't want to understand us." What is your opinion regarding the way things were handled? Do you have any suggestions as to how this situation could have been avoided? Comment on what both the community and the police could have done to prevent the problem.

2. *Who Is the Head of the Household?* The stated head of the household in most traditional Arab families is the father, although the mother actually has a great deal of power within the family. Although in public many Arab women will defer decision-making to their husbands, a police officer should not discount what the woman might have to offer in various police-related situations. How can the police officer, while respecting the status of the father, still acknowledge the mother and get input from her?

3. *Nonverbal Variations across Cultures.* When Arab Americans greet each other, they sometimes shake hands and

then place their right hand on their chest near their heart. This is a sign of sincerity. In your opinion, should officers greet Arab Americans using this gesture if a person greets them in this way? What would be the pros and cons of doing this?

4. *Hospitality toward Officers: A Cultural Gesture.* Hospitality is a virtue in Arab culture and also functions to help people get to know (and see if they can trust) others with whom they are interacting. Given this cultural emphasis on being hospitable, what should an officer do if offered a cup of coffee and something to eat? Should department policy regarding the acceptance of hospitality be reexamined in light of this cultural tendency? Would your answer be different for departments that have adopted a community-based policing philosophy?

5. *"But It's the Custom in My Country."* In January 1991, the Associated Press reported that a Stockton, California, man originally from Jordan was arrested for investigation of "selling his daughter into slavery" because he allegedly accepted $25,000 for her arranged marriage. After police officers had taken the girl to a shelter, a police lieutenant reported on the father's protest claiming that "he was within his rights to arrange his daughter's marriage for a price." The father contacted the police and explained that it was the custom in his country and was perfectly acceptable. The police explained that he couldn't do that in this country: "It is slavery...." The father then went to the shelter where the

daughter was being held and was arrested for creating a disturbance. If you were investigating this case, how would you proceed? How might you assess the validity of what the father was saying? If you found out that the act was indeed "perfectly acceptable in his country," how would you explain practices in the United States? Comment on the statement that the police made ("It is slavery"). From the perspective of needing cooperation from this man, what type of approach should be taken?

6. ***Officer Discretion: To Let Her Go?*** In the section on the perceptions of police, the authors mention an incident involving a Saudi Arabian woman who was caught shoplifting in a 7–Eleven store. She begged the officer to let her go because she feared being sent home, and there she would receive a harsh punishment (typically, in Saudi Arabia, a person's hand is cut off if he or she steals). The officer decided that since this was her first offense, he would let her go. What is your reaction to the officer's decision? What would you have done?

References

AAI. (2012). "Arab American Political Participation Under Attack." June 24. Arab American Institute. http://www.aaiusa.org/arab-american-political-participation-under-attack (accessed April 24, 2017).

AAIF. (2014). "Demographics." Arab American Institute Foundation. http://www.aaiusa.org/demographics (accessed April 7, 2017).

AbuHamda, Mona Dr. (2017). Clinical Psychologist, McLean, VA, personal communication, May 5.

ADC Research Institute. (2003). *Report on Hate Crimes and Discrimination against Arab Americans: The Post-September 11 Backlash, Tracking Crimes from September 11, 2001 through October 11, 2002.* Washington, D.C.: American-Arab Anti-Discrimination Committee.

ADC Research Institute. (2008). *2003–2007 Report on Hate Crimes and Discrimination against Arab Americans.* Washington, D.C.: American-Arab Anti-Discrimination Committee.

Arango, Tim. (2015). "A Century after Armenian Genocide, Turkey's Denial Only Deepens," April 16. https://www.nytimes.com/2015/04/17/world/europe/turkeys-century-of-denial-about-an-armenian-genocide.html (accessed April 7, 2017).

Berro, Mohammed. (2013). Former Corporal, Dearborn, MI, Police Department, personal communication, February 13.

Boyette, Chris. (2014). "New York Police Department Disbands Unit That Spied on Muslims." April 16. *CNN.* www.cnn.com/2014/04/15/us/nypd-muslims-spying-ends/ (accessed April 15, 2017).

Burton, Elizabeth C. (2012). "Religions and the Autopsy." March 20. Medscape. http://emedicine.medscape.com/article/1705993-overview (accessed April 25, 2017).

CAIR. (2005). "Law Enforcement Official's Guide to the Muslim Community." Council on American Islamic Relations. https://www.cair.com/images/pdf/law_enforcement_guide.pdf (accessed April 17, 2017).

CAIR. (2015). "Challenging Islamophobia Pocket Guide." Council on American-Islamic Relations. https://www.cair.com/images/pdf/Islamophobia-Pocket-Guide.pdf (accessed March 30, 2017).

Camarota, Steven A. (2016). "Immigrants in the United States, 2016." October. Center for Immigration Studies. http://cis.org/Immigrants-in-the-United-States (accessed April 7, 2017).

CBS News. (2009). "FBI: War Could Trigger Hate Crimes." February 11. www.cbsnews.com/2100-500164_162-543781.html (accessed August 30, 2013).

Conner, Phillip. (2016). "U.S. Admits Record Number of Muslim Refugees." October 5. Pew Research Center. www.pewresearch.org/fact-tank/2016/10/05/u-s-admits -record-number-of-muslim-refugees-in-2016/ (accessed April 1, 2017).

Detroit Free Press. (2001). *100 Questions and Answers about Arab Americans: A Journalist's Guide.* Detroit, MI.

FBI UCR. (2015). "2015 Hate Crime Statistics, Criminal Justice Information Services Division." Uniform Crime Reporting. https://ucr.fbi.gov/hate-crime/2015 (accessed April 16, 2017).

Gallup. (2011). "Islamophobia: Understanding Anti-Muslim Sentiment in the West." http://www.gallup.com/poll/157082/islamophobia-understanding-anti-muslim -sentiment-west.aspx (accessed May 1, 2017).

Glover, Mark. (2017). "Officials Investigate Possible Hate Crimes at Islamic Centers in Sacramento, Davis." June 24. *Sacramento Bee.* http://www.sacbee.com/news/local /crime/article158102329.html (accessed June 28, 2017).

Haddad, Ronald. (2017). Chief of Police, City of Dearborn, Michigan Police Department, personal communication, April 24.

Henderson, Nicole, Christopher Ortiz, Naomi Sugie, and Joel Miller. (2006, June). *Law Enforcement and Arab American Community Relations after September 11, 2001: Engagement in a Time of Uncertainty.* New York, NY: Vera Institute of Justice.

Human Rights Watch. (2016). "Boxed In: Women and Saudi Arabia's Male Guardianship System." July 16. www.hrw.org/report/2016/07/16/boxed/women-and-saudi-arabias -male-guardianship-system (accessed April 9, 2017).

IACP. (2015). "IACP National Policy Summit on Community-Police Relations: Advancing a Culture of Cohesion and Community Trust." January. International Association of Chiefs of Police. http://www.iacp.org/Portals/0 /documents/pdfs/CommunityPoliceRelationsSummit Report_web.pdf (accessed February 15, 2017).

Ismail, Lobna. (2017). President of Connecting Cultures, a training and consulting organization specializing in Arab American culture, personal communication, April 18.

Jenkins, Jack. (2015). "NYPD Announces Plan to Recruit More Muslim Police Officers." June 9. Think Progress. https://thinkprogress.org/nypd-announces-plan-to-recruit-more -muslim-police-officers-bd678772d80 (accessed April 13, 2017).

Khan, Humera. (2013). Executive Director of Muflehun. http://muflehun.org/personal communication, August 20, 2013.

Knafo, Saki. (2011). "Occupy Wall Street: Protesters Gather for Demonstration Modeled on Arab Spring." September 18. *Huffington Post.* http://www.huffingtonpost.in/entry/occupy -wall-street-protesters_n_968589 (accessed August 9, 2017).

Kumar, N. P. Krishna. (2016). "The Entrepreneurs of Silicon Valley with Arab Roots." June 26. Arab America. http://

www.arabamerica.com/entrepreneurs-silicon-valley-arab -roots/ (accessed April 24, 2017).

Lohmann, Ashley. (2013). "Sheikhs and Stereotypes in American Media." January 24. Fair Observer. https:// www.fairobserver.com/region/north_america/sheikhs -and-stereotypes-american-media/ (accessed April 10, 2017).

MPAC. (2014). "MPAC's Tarin Testifies at U.S. Commission on Civil Rights." September. Muslim Public Affairs Council. http://www.mpac.org/programs/government-relations /dc-news-and-views/mpacs-tarin-testifies-at-us -commission-on-civil-right.php (accessed April 9, 2017).

Rankin, Kenra. (2015). "NYPD Announces Plan to Recruit Muslim Officers." June 11. *Colorlines.* http://www.colorlines .com/articles/nypd-announces-plan-recruit-muslim -officers (accessed April 16, 2017).

Rocha, Veronica. (2017). "Bacon Strips and Broken Window at Davis Islamic Center Investigated as Hate Crime." January 23. *Los Angeles Times.* http://www.latimes.com/local /lanow/la-me-ln-hate-crime-mosque-davis-20170123-story .html (accessed June 28, 2017).

Runnymede Trust. (1996). "Islamophobia: A Challenge for Us All." Report of the Runnymede Trust: Commission on British Muslims and Islamophobia. Chair of the Commission, Professor Gordon Conway. www.runnymedetrust.org /companies/17/74/Islamophobia-A-Challenge-for-Us-All .html (downloadable report accessed May 1, 2017).

Terrazas, Aaron. (2011). "Middle Eastern and North African Immigrants in the United States." March 8. Migration Policy Institute. http://www.migrationpolicy.org/article /middle-eastern-and-north-african-immigrants-united -states-1 (accessed April 15, 2017).

Samhan, Helen. (2006). Executive Director, Arab American Institute, Foundation, Washington, D.C., personal communication, August 23.

Shaheen, Jack. G. (2001). *Reel Bad Arabs: How Hollywood Vilifies a People.* New York, NY: Olive Branch Press.

Southern Poverty Law Center. (2013). "FBI: Bias Crimes against Muslims Remain at High Levels." Spring. *Intelligence Report*, 149.

Southern Poverty Law Center. (2016). "Anti-Muslim Groups 2010–2016." www.splcenter.org/fighting-hate/extremist -files/ideology/anti-muslim (accessed April 15, 2017).

Today's Zaman. (2012). *Turkish Minister: I Deny the Armenian Genocide, Come Arrest Me.* January 29. www.todayszaman. com/news-269907-turkish-minister-i-deny-the-armenian -genocide-come-arrest-me.html (accessed July 23, 2013).

U.S. Citizenship and Immigration Services. (2012). "Policy Memorandum: USCIS Policy for Accommodating Religious Beliefs during Photograph and Fingerprint Capture." July 23. Title 8, Code of Federal Regulations (8CFR), sections 103.2 and 333. www.uscis.gov/sites/default/files/USCIS /Laws/Memoranda/2012/August2012/Accommodating Religious (accessed April 25, 2017).

U.S. Commission on Civil Rights. (2014). "Federal Civil Rights Engagement with Arab and Muslim American Communities Post 9/11." A Briefing Before the U.S. Commission on Civil Rights, Washington, D.C. www .usccr.gov/pubs/ARAB_MUSLIM_9-30-14.pdf (accessed April 9, 2017).

U.S. Department of Homeland Security. (2014). "2014 Yearbook of Immigration Statistics." https://www.dhs.gov /immigration-statistics/yearbook/2014/table2 (accessed April 7, 2017).

Wallace, Rob and Lauren Effron. (2010). "Does the Koran Advocate Violence?" October 1. *ABC News.* http:// abcnews.go.com/2020/violence-islam-diane-sawyer-asks -scholars-passages-koran/story?id=11760637 (accessed August 18, 2017)

Warikoo, Niraj. (2014). "A Quarter Million Michiganders have Roots in the Middle East." October 24. *Detroit Free Press.* http://www.freep.com/story/news/local/michigan /wayne/2014/10/24/arab-american-chaldean-diversity -future-metro-detroit/17804861/

Woodruff, D. (1991). "Letter from Detroit: Where the Mideast Meets the Midwest—Uneasily". *Business Week*, February 4, p. 30A.

The World Factbook. (2017a). Middle East: Iran. Washington, D.C.: Central Intelligence Agency.

The World Factbook. (2017b). Middle East: Israel. Washington, D.C.: Central Intelligence Agency.

The World Factbook. (2017c). Middle East: Turkey. Washington, D.C.: Central Intelligence Agency.

Zogby, James, Ph.D. (2013). Director, Arab American Institute Foundation, Washington, D.C., personal communication, August 20.

Zogby, John, Ph.D. (2013). President, Zogby International, New York, NY, personal communication, August 27.

Zong, Jie and Batalova, Jeanne. (2015). "Middle Eastern and North African Immigrants in the United States." June 3. Migration Policy Institute. http://www.migrationpolicy .org/article/middle-eastern-and-north-african-immigrants -united-states (accessed April 7, 2017).

9 Law Enforcement Contact with Native Americans

LEARNING OBJECTIVES

After reading this chapter, you should be able to:

- Describe the historical background of Native Americans, especially as it relates to the dynamics between law enforcement representatives and Indians today.
- Define the terms *reservation*, *Indian Country*, and *federally recognized tribe*.
- Understand cultural commonalities shared by most traditional Indian tribes.
- Recognize characteristics of traditional Native American communication styles, including aspects of verbal and nonverbal interaction.
- Provide examples of terms, labels, and stereotypes that have been used to refer to or disparage Native Americans.
- Identify characteristics of the traditional Native American extended family, as well as assimilation problems of those who lack cultural and family support.
- List and discuss key issues associated with law enforcement contact with Native Americans.

OUTLINE

- Introduction
- Historical Information and Background
- Native American Populations, Reservations, Tribes, and Identity
- Similarities among Native Americans
- Language and Communication
- Offensive Terms, Labels, and Stereotypes
- Family and Acculturation Issues
- Key Issues in Law Enforcement
- Summary
- Discussion Questions and Issues
- References

INTRODUCTION

"It's just a bunch of Indians—let them go!"

(Cox, 2017)

Retired chief Jim Cox, a Comanche Indian formerly with the Midwest City Police Department in Oklahoma, heard a police officer utter these words in the context of a traumatic moment he experienced as a youth in Oklahoma. He was riding with other Native American teenagers in an old Nash automobile. Police officers stopped the car and discovered that the teens had been drinking. Instead of taking appropriate action, which would have been to arrest the young people or at least to call the parents to pick up the kids, the officers let them go. Cox recalls to this day his feeling that Indians were not worth the time or bother: he interpreted the officer's statement to mean that if the young people had killed themselves, it did not matter because they were "just Indians" (ibid.). This impression of biased and prejudicial treatment of Indians* remained with him even after he had become a police officer. Dr. Peggy Bowen-Hartung, Native American and associate professor of Psychology and Counseling and Criminal Justice, expressed the sentiment that "as distasteful as the remark was then, it is absolutely still the reality today" (Bowen-Hartung, 2017).

JOSE RIVERA, NATIVE AMERICAN CALIFORNIA STATE PEACE OFFICER (RETIRED)

When an officer contacts an Indian person, there is often 500 years of frustration built up… Officers should be aware of the "baggage" that they bring to the encounter. (Rivera, 2013)

SITTING BULL [LAKOTA], IN THE SPIRIT OF CRAZY HORSE

What treaty that the whites have kept has the red man broken? Not one. What treaty that the white man ever made with us have they kept? Not one. When I was a boy the Sioux owned the world; the sun rose and set on their land; they sent ten thousand men to battle. Who slew [the warriors]? Where are our lands? Who owns them? What white man can say I ever stole his land…? Yet, they say I am a thief. What white woman, however lonely, was ever captive or insulted by me? Yet they say I am a bad Indian. What white man has ever seen me drunk? Who has ever seen me…abuse my children? What law have I broken? Is it wicked for me because my skin is red? (Matthiessen, 1992)

HISTORICAL INFORMATION AND BACKGROUND

Recorded history disputes the origins of the first "Indians" in America. Some researchers claim that they arrived from Asia more than 40,000 years ago; others claim that they arose spontaneously. Recent DNA research indicates that Native Americans came to North America in waves from Siberia; anthropological findings estimate the timing at 15,000 years ago (Powell, 2012). In any case, despite their long history in North America and the fact that they were the first "Americans," traditional U.S. history books simply mentioned their existence upon the arrival of Christopher Columbus in 1492. The depiction of native peoples as insignificant reflects an ethnocentric and Eurocentric view of history.

Even the word *Indian* is not a term that Native Americans* originally used to designate their tribes or communities. Because Columbus did not know that North and South America existed, he thought he had reached the Indies, which then included India, China, the East Indies, and Japan. In fact, when he arrived in what is now called the West Indies (in the Caribbean), he referred to the people he met as *Indians (los Indios)*. Eventually, this became the name for all the indigenous peoples in the Americas. However, before white settlers came to North and South America, almost every "Indian" tribe had its own name, and despite some

---

*The authors use the terms *Native American, American Indian,* and *Indian* interchangeably. *Native American* is often preferred as the generic name; however, government agencies often break down this overly broad category into American Indian and Alaska Native. In modern usage, the term *Native Americans* can also include Native Hawaiians, Chamorros (native people of Guam), and American Samoans. This chapter does not include information about these cultural groups.

shared cultural values, Native Americans did not see themselves as one collective group or call themselves *Indians*. Over the years, most tribes have referred to themselves in their own languages as "The People," "The Allies," or "The Friends." Some of the terms that whites use for various tribes are not even authentic names. For example, the label *Sioux*, which means enemy or snake, was originally a term given to that group by an enemy tribe and then adopted by French traders. Traditionally, rather than being described as part of the American people's common legacy, Native American cultural heritage has often been presented as bits of colorful "exotica."

Genocide, or the killing of entire tribes, is not a feature of U.S. history that is taught in most schools. The reality is that Euro-American and Indian relations have long been characterized by hostility, contempt, and brutality. Native peoples have generally been treated by Euro-Americans as less than human or as "savages," and their rich cultures have been ignored or crushed. For this reason, many American Indians do not share in the celebrations of Thanksgiving or Christopher Columbus Day. To say that Columbus discovered America implies that Native Americans were not considered "human enough" to be of significance.

Ignoring the existence of Native Americans before 1492 constitutes only one aspect of ethnocentrism. American Indians' experience with the "white man" has largely been one of exploitation, violence, and forced relocation. This historical background has shaped Native American views of Euro-Americans and their culture. While most people in the United States have a sense that Native Americans were not treated with dignity in U.S. history, many are not aware of the extent of current societal prejudices against them. Overall, the American Indian and Alaska Native grouping is a small and traditionally "forgotten minority" in the United States, constituting just over 5.4 million people or about 2 percent of the overall population (U.S. Census Bureau, 2015).

It would not be accurate to say that no progress at all has been made in the United States with respect to the awareness and rights of our nation's first Americans. Today in public schools across the United States, some educators are beginning to discuss in realistic terms the nature of contact with Native Americans in early American history. At the government level, former President Bill Clinton renewed his commitment to tribal sovereignty by issuing Executive Order 13175 on consultation with tribal governments. The purpose of the Order was "to establish regular and meaningful consultation and collaboration with tribal officials in the development of Federal policies that have tribal implications, to strengthen the United States government-to-government relationships with Indian tribes, and to reduce the imposition of unfunded mandates upon Indian tribes" (Federal Register, 2000). President Obama's speech to the Crow Indian Nation on their reservation in Montana acknowledged the failure of the U.S. government to keep its promises to Native Americans, referring to a "tragic history."

> Few have been ignored by Washington for as long as Native Americans—the first Americans… I understand the tragic history… Our government has not always been honest or truthful in our deals. (Zeleny, 2008)

In 2013, President Obama signed an executive order establishing the White House Council on Native American Affairs "as a means of promoting and sustaining prosperous and resilient tribal communities" (White House, 2013). Regular meetings with Native American tribal leaders were held during Obama's tenure; the eighth joint meeting occurred in September of 2016 (Editorial Board, 2016).

The U.S. government has often not acted in good faith toward its Native American citizens, instead seriously and repeatedly disregarding Indian rights that have been guaranteed in the form of binding treaties. Consequently, individuals and tribes are reluctant to trust the words of the government or people representing "the system." Whether they are aware of it or not, law enforcement agents are perceived in the same light and carry this "baggage" into encounters with Native Americans. Historically, the police officer from outside the reservation has been a symbol of rigid and authoritarian governmental control that has affected nearly every aspect of Indian life. Officers, like most citizens, have only a limited understanding of how the government, including the criminal justice system, caused massive suffering by not allowing Indians to preserve their cultures, identities, languages, lands, rituals, and sacred sites. Because of this, officers have a responsibility to educate themselves about the history of the treatment of Indian peoples in order to deal with them effectively and fairly today. Law enforcement officers must understand Indian communities and put forth extra effort to establish rapport. Doing so will increase the possibility of success in gaining cooperation and respect from people who, historically, have not had any reason to trust representatives of the government.

One example of a process of building trust between Native Americans and law enforcement occurred in Seattle after an Indian wood carver was shot on the street by a police officer for not putting his small carving knife down quickly enough. As tensions rose in the community, a mediated discussion was held among family members of the deceased, other Native Americans, and local law officials. "The [wood] carvers expressed anger over what they perceived to be a lack of respect shown by many newer officers for First Nations/Native American people, other minorities, and the homeless, as well as about the way the 'command and control' approach demands obedience and escalates quickly and unnecessarily into use of force to punish those the police don't like or who don't obey. As [the deceased man's brother] asked bluntly: 'Who gives you the right to play God?'" (Brenneke, 2012). While this discussion and others held later were mostly successful at calming community tensions, the City of Seattle Police Department was nevertheless put under investigation by the Department of Justice for "a pattern and practice of unconstitutionally excessive use of force and a need for serious structural reform in training, supervision, and discipline" (ibid.). It was a painful situation for all concerned; a situation that could have been avoided if ample levels of trust had existed on all sides.

Native Americans and Military Service

For some American Indians, an additional phenomenon aggravates the repeated breach of trust by the federal government. There is a very proud tradition of American Indians serving in the armed services. For more than 200 years, they have participated with distinction in U.S. military actions. American military leaders, beginning with George Washington in 1778, have recognized American Indians to be courageous, determined, and as having a "fighting spirit" (CEHIP, 1996). American Indians contributed to military efforts in the 1800s and participated on an even larger scale beginning in the 1900s. In World War I, it is estimated that 12,000 American Indians served in the military, with even more serving in World War II.

> More than 44,000 American Indians, out of a total Native American population of less than 350,000, served with distinction between 1941 and 1945 in both European and Pacific theaters of war. Native American men and women on the home front also showed an intense desire to serve their country, and were an integral part of the war effort. More than 40,000 Indian people left their reservations to work in ordnance depots, factories, and other war industries. American Indians also invested more than $50 million in war bonds, and contributed generously to the Red Cross and the Army and Navy Relief societies… The Native American's strong sense of patriotism and courage emerged once again during the Vietnam era. More than 42,000 Native Americans, more than 90 percent of them volunteers, fought in Vietnam. (Ibid.)

No description of Native American participation in war would be complete without mentioning the Navajo Code Talkers, whose efforts on behalf of the U.S. Marine Corps completely stumped expert Japanese code breakers during World War II. Kept secret for over two decades due to security concerns, the service of these Navajo veterans was revealed to the public in the late 1960s, and finally honored in a moving ceremony held at the White House (Jevec, 2001).

In Desert Storm, Bosnia, and the wars in Afghanistan and Iraq, Native Americans continued to serve in the U.S. Armed Forces with the estimated number having exceeded 12,000 American Indians (ICMN Staff, 2003). Exhibit 9.1 shows the number and percentage of American Indians/Alaska Natives in the U.S. military by their period of service as of 2012 (see first two columns). The second two columns show the contrast with all other races (U.S. Department of Veterans Affairs, 2012). As can be seen, American Indians and Alaska Natives have contributed greatly to the military by their service over many years. As of 2012, there were over 22,000 American Indians and Alaska Natives on active duty (U.S. Department of Defense, 2012).

Period of Service	AIAN	Percent	All Other Races	Percent
Gulf War II (Sept. 2001 to present)	17,570	11.4	2,261,573	10.5
Gulf War I (Aug. 1990 to Aug. 2001)	21,380	13.9	2,522,033	11.7
Vietnam Era	56,543	36.6	7,205,748	33.3
Korean Conflict	9,801	6.4	2,295,464	10.6
World War II	5,007	3.2	1,865,559	8.6
Peacetime Only	44,004	28.5	5,470,503	25.3
Total	154,305	100.0	21,620,880	100.0

EXHIBIT 9.1   American Indian Alaska Native (AIAN) Veterans by Period of Service and Race

NATIVE AMERICAN POPULATIONS, RESERVATIONS, TRIBES, AND IDENTITY

According to Bureau of Indian Affairs (BIA) figures, there are 567 federally recognized tribal governments in the United States (the words *tribe* and *nation* may also be used), and these include native groups of Alaskans such as Aleuts (Bureau of Indian Affairs, 2016). The three states with the largest Native American populations in 2015 were, in descending order, California, Oklahoma, and Arizona (U.S. Census Bureau, 2015).

Each federally recognized tribe has a distinct history and culture and often a separate language. Each has its own government, schools, and law enforcement and economic systems. The previously mentioned executive order signed by President Obama underscores this issue: "The United States recognizes a government-to-government relationship, as well as a unique legal and political relationship, with federally recognized tribes" (White House, 2013). However, there are still many tribes that, for historical and political reasons, do not benefit from federally recognized status. Members of such tribes are not necessarily eligible for special benefits under federal Indian programs. On the other hand, fraud in this area is quite rampant whereby people falsely claim Indian ancestry to take unfair advantage of governmental benefits and other perceived opportunities. Some tribes may be state recognized or in the process of seeking federal recognition, while others may not seek recognition at all. The issue of increasing rivalry among some Indian groups seeking recognition is reflected in the sentiment that some Indian tribes are pitted against each other over government benefits and resources.

Indian "…all persons of Indian descent who are members of any recognized Indian tribe now under Federal jurisdiction, and all persons who are descendants of such members who were, on June 1, 1934, residing within the present boundaries of any Indian reservation, and shall further include all other persons of one-half or more Indian blood… Eskimos and other aboriginal peoples of Alaska shall be considered Indians" (U.S. Code, 2017b).

Indian tribe "…any Indian tribe, organized band, pueblo, or the Indians residing on one reservation. The words 'adult Indians'… shall be construed to refer to Indians who have attained the age of twenty-one years" (ibid.).

Indian Country "…all land within the limits of any Indian reservation under the jurisdiction of the United States Government…, all dependent Indian communities within the borders of the United States whether within the original or subsequently acquired territory thereof, and whether within or without the limits of a state, and all Indian allotments, the Indian titles to which have not been extinguished…" (U.S. Code, 2017a).

An Indian reservation is land that a tribe has reserved for its exclusive use through statutes, executive order, or the course of treaty-making. It may be on ancestral lands or on the only land available when tribes were forced to give up their original territories through federal treaties. A reservation is also land that the federal government holds in trust for the use of an Indian tribe. The BIA administers and manages over 56 million acres of land that are held in trust for American Indians, Indian tribes, and Alaska natives. Census results have shown that over 1.1 million Indians and Alaska Natives live on reservations (Perry, 2016). It should be noted, however, that approximately 4.8 million people live on American Indian reservations or in Alaska Native villages; thus, about 78 percent of these residents are *not* American Indian or Alaska Natives (ibid.).

The largest of the American Indian reservations is that of the Navajo Nation which extends into three states—Arizona, Utah, and New Mexico. Indians are not forced to stay on reservations, but many who leave have a strong desire to remain in touch with and be nourished by their home cultures. For this reason and because of culture shock experienced in urban life, many later returned to reservations. The 1950s "Relocation Program" (Urban Indian Relocation Program) of the federal government had been created to entice Indians to move off of the reservation with the promise of economic opportunities and, thus, eventual integration into mainstream U.S. culture. As an outcome of this program, the government's responsibilities to Indians on reservations, as outlined in treaties with Indian tribes, were significantly reduced (PRRAC, 1996). Indians' moved off the reservations in great numbers after the second world war. The promise of a good life was both enticement and coercion that resulted in massive migration from the reservations, lessening the U.S. government's obligation to tribal Indians on reservations (NCUIH, 2017 and PRRAC, 1996).

The cultural differences that Indians experienced once they moved to the city were so immense that it became difficult to impossible for American Indians, in general, to maintain their cultural cohesiveness (NCIUH, 2017). The government's relocation program resulted in the extreme weakening or complete destruction of Indian family life. The culture in America's cities was vastly different from the culture on the reservations. Cultural values from the reservation to the city completely clashed. Indians were suspended between two cultural worlds, with very little means for survival. Consequently, Indians became a part of America's underclass (ibid.). Urban Indians have been referred to as an "invisible minority (PRRAC, 1996)."

In general, the Indian population is characterized by constant movement between the reservation and the city, and sometimes relocation from city to city. In urban areas, when officers encounter American Indians, they will not necessarily know how acculturated to city life those individuals are. In rural areas it is easier for officers to get to know the culture of a particular tribe. In the city, one's tribal background may be less significant than the fact that the person is an American Indian.

Since the early 1980s, more than half of the Native American population has been living outside of reservation communities; many have left to pursue educational and employment opportunities, as life on some of the reservations can be very bleak. Although a large number returns home to the reservation to participate in family activities and tribal ceremonies, many attempt to remake their lives in urban areas.

As with other culturally or ethnically defined categories of people (e.g., Asian, African American), it would be a mistake to lump all Native Americans together and to assume that they are homogeneous. For example, in Arizona alone, one finds a number of different tribes with varying traditions: there are Hopis in the northeast, Pimas and Papagos (Tohono O'odham) in the south, Apaches in the north-central region, and Yuman (Quechan) groups in the west. All of these descend from people who came to what is now called *Arizona*. The relative "newcomers" are the Navajos and Apaches, who arrived about 1,000 years ago. Overall, these six tribes represent differences in culture, with each group having its own history and life experiences.

Broadly speaking, in the United States there are distinct cultural groups among Native Americans. Every tribe has evolved its own sets of traditions and beliefs, and each sees itself as distinct from other tribes despite some significant broad similarities. However, since the governmental removal of entire tribes* from their homelands, tribes ended up spread out across

---

*Some readers may have heard of the "Trail of Tears," the Cherokee nation's description of their forced migration in 1838 and 1839 from Georgia, Tennessee, and North Carolina to an area in present-day Oklahoma. They called this journey the "Trail of Tears" because of the tragic effects of hunger, disease, and exhaustion on the forced march during which several thousand Cherokee men, women, and children died. The bitterness remains today among some descendants of the original people of the "Trail of Tears." While no records have been kept, there are also many stories of people who refused to go on the forced march and were killed by federal authorities.

the country as forced migrants from their homes. For example, as a result of the Indian Removal Act of 1830, five tribes—Cherokee, Choctaw, Chickasaw, Creek, and Seminole—were forced to relocate to Oklahoma in an area designated as Indian Territory. Some of these tribes were traditional enemies, though in current times, they have learned to coexist peacefully.

Law enforcement officials may find themselves confused about who an American Indian is. The issue of identity is important for law enforcement because of jurisdictional laws governing which police departments, tribal or state/local, may arrest and prosecute criminals (i.e., whether Indian or non-Indian; jurisdiction is discussed later in this chapter). Individuals may claim to have "Indian blood," but tribes have their own criteria for determining tribal membership. Because the determination of tribal membership is a fundamental attribute of tribal sovereignty, the federal government generally defers to tribes' own determination when establishing eligibility criteria under special Indian entitlement programs.

In the reverse, individuals may claim to be Indian when they are not. When a tribal member leaves the reservation, he or she is subject to the laws of the surrounding county and state as anyone else would be. But the question of Indian identity arises when an Indian is in "Usual and Accustomed" (U&A) places where Native Americans may exercise treaty rights such as hunting or fishing. If, for example, hunting season is not open for non-Native Americans, and a state wildlife officer sees someone with a rifle, the officer might question that individual and request identification. Non-Native Americans may claim to be Indian when they are not, in order to take advantage of Native Americans' rights on U&A lands. If officers have any doubt about whether the individual they encounter is truly an Indian, they should ask to which tribe the person belongs and then contact the tribal headquarters to verify that person's identity. Every tribe has its own administration and authority, the members of which will be able to answer questions of this nature. By verifying information about the individual's identity with tribal authorities rather than making personal determinations of "Indianness," officers will help create good rapport between tribal members and law enforcement officials (Becker, 2013).

In another potentially confusing area of identity determination, some Native Americans in the southwest have Spanish first or last names (because of intermarriage or because they adopted or were given these names by early *conquistadores*—conquerors—from Spain) and may "look" Hispanic or Latino (e.g., Hopis). Identification can be difficult for officers, so they should not assume that a person is Latino just because of the name or appearance. Many Native Americans do not want to be grouped with Latinos because (1) they are not Latinos; (2) they may resent that some Latinos deny their Indian ancestry and instead identify only with the Spanish part of their heritage; and (3) many tribes have a history of warfare with the *mestizo* (mixed ancestry) populations of Mexico. As an aside, the majority population in Mexico, Central America, and South America is of "Indian" ancestry (U.S. CIA World Factbook, 2017).

SIMILARITIES AMONG NATIVE AMERICANS

Significant differences exist among the cultures, languages, history, and socioeconomic status of Native American tribes, communities, and individuals. Yet, it is still possible to talk about general cultural characteristics of Native American groups without negating their diversity. The cultural characteristics described in the following sections apply to Native Americans who are traditionally "Indian" in their orientation to life. While being aware of tribal differences, the law enforcement officer should also understand that there is a strong cultural link among the many worlds and tribes of Native Americans and their Indian counterparts throughout the American continent.

Philosophy toward the Earth and the Universe

"The most striking difference between… Indian and Western man is the manner in which each views his role in the universe. The prevailing non-Indian view is that man is superior to all other forms of life and that the universe is his to be used as he sees fit…an attitude justified as the mastery of nature for the benefit of man [characterizes Western philosophy]" (Bahti, 1982). Through its contrast with Western philosophy (that people have the capacity to alter nature), we can gain insight into the values and philosophies common to virtually all *identifying* Native Americans. While acknowledging the character of each Indian tribe or nation, there is a common set of values and beliefs involving the earth and the universe, resulting in a deep respect for nature and "mother earth." According to American Indian philosophy, the earth is sacred and is a living entity. By spiritual involvement with the earth, nature, and the universe, individuals bind themselves to their environment. Indians do not see themselves as superior to all else (e.g., animals, plants) but rather as part of all creation. Through religious ceremonies and rituals, Indians are able to transcend themselves to be in harmony with the universe and connected to nature.

The inclination of people who do not understand this philosophy might be to dismiss it as primitive and even backward. The costumes, the rituals, the ceremonies, and the dances are often thought of as colorful but strange. Yet from an Indian perspective, "It is a tragedy indeed that Western man in his headlong quest for Holy Progress could not have paused long enough to learn this basic truth—one which he is now being forced to recognize (with the spoilage of the earth), much to his surprise and dismay. Ever anxious to teach 'backward' people, he is ever reluctant to learn from them" (ibid.). Many non-Indians now embrace certain Native American beliefs regarding the environment; what people once thought of as primitive, they now see as essential in the preservation of our environment. Native Americans speak of "earth wisdom," a cultural legacy from their traditions that all people should embrace for the future of the environment.

An Indian prayer

Oh our Mother the earth, Oh our Father the sky,
Your children are we, and with tired backs
We bring you the gifts you love.
Then weave for us a garment of brightness…
May the fringes be the falling rain.
May the border be the standing rainbow.
That we may walk fittingly where birds sing… and where grass is green
Oh our mother earth, Oh our father sky. (Author unknown)

When law enforcement officers make contact with people who are in the midst of celebrating or praying, whether on reservations or in communities, it is vitally important to be as respectful as possible. Officers must refrain from conveying an air of superiority and ethnocentrism, or an attitude that "those rituals" are primitive. Native American prayers, rituals, and ceremonies represent ancient beliefs and philosophies, many of which have to do with the preservation of and harmony with the earth. Thus, officers should, at all costs, try to avoid interrupting prayers and sacred ceremonies, just as one would avoid interrupting church services. (Officers should also be aware that taking photographs during ceremonies would constitute an interruption and is forbidden. In general, officers should seek permission before taking photos of American Indians; this is true for many tribes. Visitors to some reservations are told that their cameras will be confiscated if they take pictures.)

In certain parts of the country, people are revitalizing Native American culture rather than letting it die. For some tribes and individuals, the result is a sense of "pan-Indianism" in which there is a growing pride around ethnic Indian identity. Members of tribes or communities with very different traditions identify as a group by following certain practices that are associated with Indians. Examples include males wearing long hair, a symbol of strength and power—if you shame yourself, you cannot have long hair (Bowen-Hartung, 2017); the use of the sacred pipe (i.e., the pipestone pipe, sometimes called the *peace pipe*); and participation in rituals, sweat lodges, and the sacred sun dance for purification. Many tribes have these elements in their traditions, and tribes practice them to varying degrees, gravitating more toward one tradition over another (Rivera, 2013).

It should be noted that the pan-Indian movement is not necessarily viewed positively by all Indians; some believe that there is a strong possibility of misusing a tradition or diluting the meaning of a ritual. There are some tribes that are reviving their own identities by emphasizing their unique customs and strengths rather than identifying with the pan-Indian movement (ibid.).

LANGUAGE AND COMMUNICATION

It is possible to make generalizations about the way a group of people communicates, even when there is great diversity within the group. The following contains information about nonverbal and verbal aspects of communication as well as tips for the law enforcement officer interacting with Native Americans. The paragraphs that follow describe patterns of communication and behavior as exhibited by some American Indians who are traditional in their outlook. No description of communication traits, however, would ever apply to everyone within a group, especially one that is so diverse.

Openness and Self-Disclosure

Many Native Americans, in early encounters, use caution in their interactions with others in order to demonstrate humility and create harmony. Too much openness is to be avoided, as is disclosing personal and family problems. This often means that an officer must work hard to establish rapport and gain trust. In contrast, within mainstream American culture, appearing friendly and open is highly valued—especially in certain regions such as the West Coast and the South. Because different modes of behavior are expected and accepted, non-Indians may view Indians as aloof and reserved. The Indian perception can be that Euro-Americans, due to their excessive openness, are superficial and thus untrustworthy. American core or mainstream cultural style encourages the importance of "speaking up," with an emphasis on the importance of words and self-disclosure (with variations among groups and individuals). While there are also differences among tribes and individuals, American Indian culture encourages calmness and quiet; silence is deeply embedded in *traditional* cultural style. A core cultural value centers around the cherished belief, "Listen and you will learn" (Rice; Richardson, 2012).

Silence and Interruptions

> *"What are the fruits of silence? They are self-control, true courage or endurance, patience, dignity and reverence. Silence is the cornerstone of character."*
>
> *(Lakota Sioux)*

The ability to remain quiet, to be still, and to observe is highly valued in Native American culture; consequently, silence is truly a virtue. (In mainstream American culture, it is said that "silence is golden," but this is probably more an expression of an ideal than a description of a fact.) Indians are taught to study and assess situations and only act or participate when one is properly prepared (Bowen-Hartung, 2017). When law enforcement officials contact Native Americans, they may mistake this reticence to talk as sullenness or a lack of cooperation. The behavior must not be misinterpreted or taken personally. A cultural trait must be understood as just that: a behavior, action, or attitude that is not intended to be a personal insult. The officer must also consider that interrupting an Indian when he or she speaks is seen as very aggressive and should be avoided whenever possible. As a survival skill on the reservation, Dr. Peggy Bowen-Hartung, as a child, learned to remain silent and especially to avoid speaking directly to a male. Direct communication was perceived as a challenge to authority. While this has changed to a certain extent because of the influence of the media, a reticence to talk directly to authority is still prevalent (ibid.).

Talking and Questions

Talking just to fill silence is not seen as important. The small talk that one observes in mainstream society ("Hi, how are you? How was your weekend?" and so on) is traditionally not required by Native Americans. Words are considered powerful and are therefore chosen carefully. This cultural trait may result in a situation in which Native Americans retreat and appear to be withdrawn if someone else is dominating a conversation. When law enforcement officials question Native Americans who exhibit this tendency (i.e., preferring formality and/or silence), the officers should not press aggressively for answers. Aggressive behavior, both verbal and physical, is traditionally looked down upon. Questions should be open-ended, with the officer being willing to respect the silence and the time it may take to find out the needed information.

Nonverbal Communication: Eye Contact, Touching

With respect to American Indian cultures, people often make the statement that Indians avoid making direct eye contact. Although this is true for some tribes, it does not hold true for all. Some Indian tribes believe that looking directly into another person's eyes for a prolonged period of time is disrespectful, just as pointing at someone is considered impolite. Direct eye contact can be viewed as an affront or an invasion of privacy by some tribes. Navajo tribe members tend to stare at each other when they want to express anger. An Indian who adheres to the unspoken rules about eye contact may appear to non-Indians to be shifty and evasive. Officers and other law enforcement officials must not automatically judge a person as guilty or suspicious simply because that person is not maintaining direct eye contact. To put a person at ease, the officer can decrease eye contact if it appears to be inhibiting the Native American citizen. Avoidance of eye contact with the officer can also convey the message that the officer is using an approach that is too forceful and demanding.

With regard to their sense of space, most Native Americans are not comfortable being touched by strangers, whether a pat on the back or the arm around the shoulder. Either no touching is appropriate or it should be limited to a brief handshake. Married couples tend not to show affection in public. In addition, people should avoid crowding or standing too close. Keep in mind that Indian relations with strangers are more formal than those of the mainstream culture; therefore, officers might be viewed as overly aggressive if they do not maintain a proper distance. Officers who are going to pat down or search a Native American should first explain the process.

Law enforcement officials may experience particular difficulty when trying to communicate with female Native Americans. Dr. Bowen-Hartung recalls that until she left the reservation, she was unable to maintain direct eye contact with authority because it was never a behavior that was reinforced. As with speaking directly to males, girls and women could get into trouble if they attempted direct eye contact with men. This is still the case, to a certain extent, particularly on reservations that are relatively isolated (ibid.).

For law enforcement officials in the United States, holding back on judging Native American cultural styles of communication is key to establishing good rapport.

Language

Some Native Americans are able to converse in one of the 149 Native North American languages that are spoken in the United States today. The language with the largest number of speakers is Navajo. Some Native American languages are known to have disappeared, and others are currently endangered: at least 14 of these 149 languages have fewer than 50 speakers each (U.S. Census Bureau, 2015).

English, for some, is a second language; those who do not speak English well may be inhibited from speaking. In addition, because many Native Americans tend to speak quietly and non-forcefully, law enforcement agents must demonstrate patience and allow extra time for discussions; interaction must not be rushed. The Native American who is not strong in English needs to spend more time translating from his or her own language to English when formulating a response (this is true of all second-language speakers who are not yet fluent). As with other languages, English words or concepts do not always translate exactly into the various Indian languages. Indian languages are rich and express concepts reflecting unique views of the world. It is mandatory that the utmost respect be shown when Native Americans speak their own languages; in other words, officers would do well to resist the temptation to force them to speak only English in public. Remember that Indians have a long history of forced assimilation into Anglo society, during which, among other things, many were denied the right to speak their native languages.

OFFENSIVE TERMS, LABELS, AND STEREOTYPES

> Native American Indians are a people in transition between history and contemporary America. The challenge for Native Americans is to maintain their heritage, erase a stereotype and adjust recognition in society. Native Americans are too often stereotyped by antiquated and discriminatory attitudes...
>
> *(Seven Fires Council, 2017)*

In the interview cited in the opening of this chapter, retired chief of police Jim Cox, a Comanche Indian, described a situation in which police officers referred to him and his friends as "just a bunch of Indians" in his presence. Proud of his heritage, he was deeply offended by this insensitive communication (Cox, 2017). In addition, the use of racial slurs toward any group is never acceptable in crime fighting and peacekeeping, no matter how irritated an officer might become. When officers hear others use disrespectful terms and stereotypical statements about Native Americans, they should speak up about this lack of professionalism and disrespect for community diversity.

There are a number of words that are offensive to Native Americans: *chief* (a leader who has reached this rank is highly honored), *squaw* (extremely offensive), *buck, redskin*, Indian *brave*, and *skins*. (Some young Indians may use the word *skins* to refer to themselves but would be offended if others use the term.) Words such as *braves, chiefs, squaws*, and *papooses* are not native Indian terms, but have come about as mistranslations, mispronunciations, or as shortened terms, and are "perpetuated by non-Native Americans" (Seven Fires Council, 2013). In addition, the use of Indian tribal names or references as mascots for sports teams is highly objectionable to many Native Americans.

Other terms used to refer to Native Americans are *apple* (a slightly dated term referring to a highly assimilated Indian: "red" on the outside, "white" on the inside) and *the people* (more commonly used by some groups of Indians to refer to themselves). In some regions of the country, a reservation is called a *rez* by Indians, but this word would not be appreciated when uttered by those who are not Native Americans (Bowen-Hartung, 2017). It is also patronizing when non-Indians use certain kinship terms, such as *grandfather* when talking to an older man, even though other Indians may use those terms. As a rule of thumb, it is advisable to ask Native Americans how *they* would like to be addressed, and then respect their preferences. The key is to avoid making assumptions about the names used to directly call or indirectly refer to an individual (ibid.).

Other offensive and commonly used terms include *sitting Indian style* to refer to sitting in a cross-legged position on the floor; *Indian giver* to characterize someone who takes back a present or an offer; *wild Indians* to describe misbehaving children; *powwow* to mean a discussion; or *bottom of the totem pole* to mean lowest ranking. In addition, it is worth noting that some American Indians deliberately choose not to reveal their ethnic identity in the workplace because of concerns about stereotypes about Indians. Coworkers may make comments about Indians or use offensive expressions because they do not "see one in the room." People can be deeply offended and hurt by "unintentional" references to American Indians.

Indians find it offensive when non-Indians make claims that may or may not be true about their Indian ancestry, such as "I'm part Indian—my great-grandfather was Cherokee." Although this may be an attempt to establish rapport, it rings of, "Some of my best friends are Indians" (i.e., to "prove" that one does not have any prejudice). People should not assume affinity with American Indians based on novels, movies, a vacation trip, or an interest in silver jewelry. These are among the most offensive, commonly made errors when non-Indians first encounter an American Indian person or family. Another is a confidential revelation that there is an Indian "princess" in the family tree—tribe unknown, identity unclear, but a bit of glamour in the family myth. The intent may be to establish rapport, but to the Indian these types of statements reveal stereotype images.

Many people growing up in the United States can remember the stereotypical depiction of an Indian as a wild, savage, and primitive person. In older textbooks, including history books recounting Native American history, Indians were said to "massacre" whites, whereas whites simply "fought" or "battled" the Indians (Harris, Moran, & Moran, 2004). Hollywood has to take some responsibility for the promotion of stereotypes as well. "Native Americans have a long history of one-sided portrayals in Hollywood, including such stereotypical characters as the war whooping savage or the grunting tribesman" (Bull, 2009).

Other common stereotypical or disparaging statements include "All Indians are drunks" (an argument has been put forth that the white man introduced "fire water" or alcohol to the Indian as a means of weakening him); "You can't trust an Indian"; "Those damn Indians"; and "The only good Indian is a dead one"—a remark that can be traced back to a statement made by a U.S. military general in 1869 (Harris et al., 2004).

Despite the persistence of many social problems, progress has been made with respect to education and political participation among Native Americans. Law enforcement officials must not hold on to the stereotype of American Indians as being uneducated. There is a growing Native American population attending colleges and rising to high positions in education, entertainment, sports, and industry. President Obama's "Generation Indigenous" initiative further stimulated increases in the resources available to Native American educators and students (U.S. Department of Education, 2016).

FAMILY AND ACCULTURATION ISSUES

Respect for Elders

"Nothing will anger an Indian more than them seeing [his or her] grandmother or grandfather being spoken to belligerently or being ordered around with disrespect. If that happens, that's a firecracker situation right there" (Rivera, 2013). Unlike mainstream American culture, Indian cultures value aging because of the respect they have for wisdom and experience. People do not feel that they have to cover up signs of aging because this phase of life is highly revered. The elders of a tribe or the older people in Native American communities must be shown the utmost respect by people in law enforcement. This includes acknowledging their presence during a home visit, even if they are not directly involved with the police matter at hand. In some tribes (e.g., the Cherokee), the grandmother often has the maximum power in the household and is the primary decision maker. It is advisable for people in law enforcement to include elders in discussions so they can give their advice or perspective on a situation. The elders are generally respected for their ability to enforce good behavior within the family and tribe.

It should also be noted, however, that because of assimilation or personal preference among some Native Americans, the elders in any given household may tend to avoid interfering with a married couple's problems. And although the elders are respected to a higher degree than in mainstream American culture, they may withdraw in certain situations in which there is police contact, letting the younger family members deal with the problem. If in doubt, it is advisable to begin the contact more formally, deferring to the elders initially. Officers can then observe the extent to which the elders participate and whether the younger family members include them.

Extended Family and Kinship Ties

In mainstream American society, people usually think of and see themselves first as individuals, and, after that, they may or may not identify with their families or various communities and groups with which they are affiliated. In traditional Native American culture, a person's primary identity is related to his or her family and tribe (i.e., a group orientation). Some law enforcement agents may be in positions to make referrals when there is a problem with an individual (e.g., an adolescent) in a family. A referral for counseling for that person alone may be culturally alienating; family counseling might be a more appropriate alternative. From a traditional cultural perspective (as in many other cultures), Western-style individual counseling or therapy is often viewed as a foreign way to treat problems. "…research has found that Native American men and women who meet the criteria for depression, anxiety, or substance abuse disorders are significantly more likely to seek help from a spiritual healer than from specialty or other medical sources" (American Psychiatric Association, 2010).

Today, some of this family and tribal cohesiveness has lessened because of assimilation, extreme levels of poverty, and lack of education and employment. However, many Native Americans still have large networks of relatives who live in close proximity to each other. It is not uncommon for children to be raised by someone other than the father or mother (e.g., grandmother, aunts). When law enforcement officials enter an Indian's home and, for example, ask to speak to the parents of a child, they may end up talking to someone who is not the biological mother or father. Various other relatives can function exactly as a mother or father would in mainstream culture. This does not mean that Indian "natural" parents are lazy about their child-rearing duties, even when the child is physically living with another relative (and may be raised by several relatives throughout childhood). The intensely close family and tribal bonds allow for this type of child raising. The officer must not assume that something is abnormal with this type of arrangement or that the parents are neglecting their children.

Children and Separation from Parents

It is crucial that police officers understand the importance of not separating children from family members if at all possible. Many Native American families in urban areas and on reservations have memories of or have heard stories from elder family members that involved the federal government's routine and systematic removal of Indian children from their homes; in many cases, children were placed in boarding schools operated by the BIA that were often hundreds of miles away. This phenomenon, including education for the children that stripped them of their language and culture, began in the late nineteenth century. The underlying premise was that Indians were savages and did not know how to treat children. Children were punished for speaking their own languages and for saying prayers from their own religious traditions. They were basically uprooted and placed in an alien environment in an attempt by the government to eliminate the Indian population (Bowen-Hartung, 2017).

Although for many families the severe trauma of children's forced separation from parents took place years ago, the effects linger (Rivera, 2013). In the early twentieth century, there was a famous case in which Hopi Indian fathers were sentenced to hard labor on Alcatraz Island. Their crime was hiding their children from BIA officials because they did not want the children to be taken to the BIA boarding schools. By hiding the children, the Hopi fathers violated federal law and were arrested and charged with sedition. This case is still talked about today (ibid.). The memory of a "uniform coming to take away a child" is an image that can be conjured up easily by some Indians. It is this "baggage" that law enforcement officers encounter today when interacting with Native Americans. Some officers may be totally unaware of the power of Native Americans' memories of the tragedies that took place in the past with respect to forcible removal of children.

Given that Native American parents can be very protective of their children, an officer is well advised to let the parents know about any action that needs to be taken with regard to a child. Law enforcement officers must become knowledgeable about the Indian Child Welfare Act (ICWA), passed by Congress in 1978. Prior to the passage of this Act, Indian children removed from their homes were placed with white foster parents. There were no Indian foster homes, and the tribes did not have any way to deal with cases involving children. With the passage of ICWA, the mandate exists to find viable homes in which to place the children, first with a tribal member, and, if that is not possible, then in a Native American home. How the ICWA works in practice is being tested in courts; the case of *Adoptive Couple v. Baby Girl* went all the way to the Supreme Court (Wolf, 2013). When officers go out on calls to pick up children, there can be serious consequences if officers are not aware of the ICWA and its implications. Law enforcement officials are likely to establish good rapport with Indian families if they treat the children well (i.e., in contact off the reservation), which includes understanding the legal rights of Indian children (Bowen-Hartung, 2017).

Issues of Mental Health and Adaptation

People who are caught between two cultures and are successful in neither run the risk of contributing to family breakdown, often becoming depressed, alcoholic, drug dependent, and/or suicidal. However, Indian group members who have remained tightly identified with their culture and religion and who have close-knit extended families tend to exhibit this type of behavior less. With cultural and family support, their isolation from mainstream culture is not as pronounced as it is with individuals and families who lack this support (Bowen-Hartung, 2017).

In studies on suicide and ethnicity in the United States, much has been written about patterns of what can be described as self-destructive behavior. This has been generalized to those Indian groups whose lives are characterized by despair, and, for many, a loss of ethnic identity. According to Psychologist Dr. Jon Perez, former director of the Behavioral Health Unit of the Indian Health Service (IHS):

> The intergenerational trauma, compounded by extreme poverty, lack of economic opportunity and widespread substance abuse has shattered these communities. Suicide is a single response to a multiplicity of problems. If you have these things going on, and you don't see any hope for the future, suicide seems like an option. (Meyers, 2007)

The national Centers for Disease Control and Prevention has reported that the rate of suicide "among American Indian/Alaska Native adolescents and young adults ages 15 to 34…is 1.5 times higher than the national average for that age group," and that within that age group, suicide is the second leading cause of death (Centers for Disease Control and Prevention, 2015). In October 2016, a bill introduced by North Dakota Senator Heidi Heitkamp was signed into law to create a commission that will examine and make recommendations for accommodating the unique educational as well as physical and mental health needs of Native American children (Flower, 2016). A primary aim of this bill is to find ways to reduce the suicide rate on Indian reservations.

While for decades many studies have reported comparatively high alcohol consumption rates by Native Americans, some researchers—by examining multiple, current databases and adjusting for certain factors—have found that consumption levels are actually similar to those of white Americans (Izadi, 2016). The use of crystal methamphetamine (CM) and other drugs on some reservations, however, is an issue of epidemic proportions, creating tremendous problems associated with domestic violence and neglect of children.

> The use of illicit drugs leads to impaired personal behavior that often results in violence and other criminal behavior. While crime rates on some reservations continue to be five times (in some cases more) higher than the national averages, the widespread availability and abuse of drugs coupled with trafficking by multiple criminal groups and gangs operating in Indian Country, contribute to a wide range of violent and property crime… The number of drug cases worked by Indian Country law enforcement programs increased seven-fold between FY2009 and FY2014; drug arrests increased eleven-fold during that time. (Drug Enforcement Administration, 2015)

The cause of so many problems for Native Americans dates back to the way the government has handled and regulated Indian life. The dominant society in no way affirmed the cultural identity of Indians; thus, many Indians have internalized the oppression that they experienced from the outside world. The following quote reflects the sentiments of a Native American law enforcement officer in a Southern California police department: "I know very little about my roots. My mother and grandmother were denied the opportunity to learn about their culture [due to forced assimilation] and nothing was passed on. I feel empty and have intense anger toward those who held the power to decide that certain traditions were not worth preserving. Forced denial of our ethnicity has resulted in extremely high alcohol, illegal drug use and suicide rates as a collective response."

While some would question the long-lingering effects of stress and oppression, there is growing evidence within the scientific field of epigenetics that such effects are physiologically inheritable. In a presentation delivered in San Diego in 2013, Dr. Lee Bitsóí of Harvard University reported that "…scientific research in epigenetics has begun to demonstrate that intergenerational trauma is real and has an impact on present day populations… Native healers, medicine people and elders have always known this and it is common knowledge in Native oral traditions" (Bitsóí, 2013).

Furthermore, many young people feel the stresses of living between two cultural worlds, and feel alienated when it comes to their own identity. They are not fully part of the traditional Indian world as celebrated on the reservation or in a community that honors traditions; neither are they fully adapted to the dominant American culture.

KEY ISSUES IN LAW ENFORCEMENT

Perception of Police

The general distrust of police held by Native Americans stems from a history of negative relations with "the system," which can refer to federal, state, and local governments. In the view of Native Americans, officers represent a system that has not supported Indian rights, tribes, or communities; most contact with law enforcement has been negative in nature. Thus, many Native Americans have never had a chance to build relationships of trust and cooperation with people in law enforcement.

Victimization Rates/Comparisons with Other Groups

According to a National Crime Victimization Survey, between 1992 and 2001, American Indians experienced violence at rates more than twice that of blacks, two-and-a-half times that of whites, and four-and-a-half times that of Asians (Perry, 2004). American Indians comprised 0.5 percent of the U.S. population but 1.3 percent of all violent crime victims. These crimes affected both males and females; victims were from all geographies, age groups, and economic levels.

Beginning in 2009, the issue of public safety for Native Americans was pronounced a priority by Attorney General Eric Holder and brought to the attention of congressional leaders. President Obama signed the Tribal Law and Order Act in 2010 to "address crime in tribal communities and [place] a strong emphasis on decreasing violence against American Indian and Alaska Native women." Early results show promise (see Exhibit 9.2), but violent victimization rates against American Indians and Alaska Natives are still woefully high. "Federal law and policy is [sic] primarily responsible for deplorable reservation conditions, where crime rates generally are more than twice the national average, and, in some places, soar to over twenty times the national average... On some reservations, the murder rate of Native women is ten times the national average" (Riley, 2016).

Native American Women and Rape

Concern had begun to build when a report was issued in the early 2000s, citing that the rate of violent crime victimization for Native American women was at least twice as that of other women (Perry, 2004). Amnesty International picked up the thread in 2007 with its report titled, "Maze of Injustice," issuing a follow-up report one year later that cautioned, "this is not simply a public health or criminal justice issue, but a serious human rights issue, that the U.S. government is obligated to address under internationally recognized human rights standards" (Amnesty International, 2008). A report examining data from 2010 to 2012 showed that 28.9 percent of American Indian or Alaska Native women had "experienced rape at some point during their lifetime," as opposed to 19.9 percent of white women (Smith, Chen, Basile, Gilbert, Merrick, Patel, Walling, & Jain, 2017).

The epidemic of rape in Indian Country has been due, in large part, to "a maze of archaic laws that prevent tribes from arresting and prosecuting offenders" (Sullivan, 2009). Chickasaw Nation Tribal Police Chief, Jason O'Neal, had explained that if a woman was Indian on Indian land and her attacker was Indian, he [O'Neal] could help her. If not, there is not much that he could do (ibid.). O'Neal described the attackers as almost "untouchable... 80% of victims describe their offenders as people from outside the reservation" (ibid.).

> Two years ago, the Standing Rock Sioux Reservation, which straddles North and South Dakota, had five Bureau of Indian Affairs officers to patrol an area the size of Connecticut. Officials there, and on many reservations nationwide, described a rampant problem of rape where hundreds of cases were going unreported, uninvestigated and unprosecuted. According to the Justice Department, one in three Native American women will be raped in her lifetime. Tribal leaders say predators believe Native American land is almost a free-for-all, where no law enforcement can touch them. (Ibid.)

	2002	2010	2013
Whites	32.6	18.3	22.2
Blacks	36.1	25.9	25.1
American Indian/Alaska Native	62.9	77.6	56.3
Asian/Native Hawaiian/other Pacific Islanders	11.7	10.3	7.0

EXHIBIT 9.2   Rate of Violent Victimization per 1,000 Persons Aged 12 or Older

Source: Truman, Jennifer L. and Lynn Langton. (2014). *Criminal Victimization, 2013.* U.S. Department of Justice, Office of Justice Programs, Bureau of Justice Statistics.

In 2013, the U.S. Congress passed the Violence Against Women Reauthorization Act, the aim of which was to allow Native American tribes "to exercise their sovereign power to investigate, prosecute, convict, and sentence both Indians and non-Indians who assault Indian spouses or dating partners or violate a protection order in Indian country" (U.S. Department of Justice, 2013). President Obama stated, "Previously, tribes had no jurisdiction over non-tribal members, even if they are married to Native women or reside on native lands. But as soon as I sign this bill, that ends" (ICMN Staff, 2013).

In reality, progress has been slow. Two years passed before implementation of the modified Act began (Bendery, 2015). Some tribes must change their laws in order to meet U.S. federal requirements; in some cases, these changes are complicated and expensive. While grants have been promised to help tribes meet these expenses, funding has been slow to be released (McClung, 2015); further programs and funds were promised one year later (White House, 2016). In addition, the Act unfortunately does not cover a variety of other crimes such as crimes between two strangers—including sexual assaults. Obviously, the need to serve and protect Native American women must be a priority for law enforcement officials at all levels in the years to come.

Hate Crimes against Native Americans

In 2015, 3.3 percent of hate crimes involving racial or ethnicity bias were directed at American Indians or Alaska Natives. This percentage is relatively large given that Native Americans comprise only about 2 percent of the overall national population. Many of these crimes are quite violent, and seem to be "misdirected" as crimes toward people of color, in general, rather than Native Americans specifically. In some cases, Native American victims have been referred to by their attackers using the "N—word," and in one case were mistaken for Pacific Islanders. The attacker wrote on his Facebook page, "Just laid the fists and boots to some 6' 5" Tongan dude" (Kain, 2011).

Many Native Americans feel that the crimes against them are not investigated in a fair or timely way. The previously mentioned victim who had been mistaken for a Tongan suffered a broken nose and sinus cavities after being hit with a baseball bat, yet was held in jail for six days with no medical treatment; his wife was told by a guard "that if he wanted to receive medical treatment he'd need to 'get his Indian doctor'" (ibid.).

Jurisdiction

> Investigating crimes on native lands poses a unique challenge for FBI personnel and their law enforcement partners. Working in Indian Country, as we call it, often means operating in isolated, forbidding terrain where cultural differences abound. Some older Native American people, for example, do not speak English… On many reservations there are few paved roads or marked streets. Agents might be called to a crime scene in the middle of the night 120 miles away…
>
> *(Federal Bureau of Investigation, 2012)*

The FBI, since its beginnings in 1908, has played an important role in the investigation of crimes committed on Indian Country lands. History dating even further back helps to explain the role of the U.S. government in law enforcement in Indian Country. In 1885, the Major Crimes Act was passed in the United States. This gave exclusive jurisdiction to the federal government on major crimes committed on reservations. The 1994 Crime Act expanded federal criminal jurisdiction in Indian Country because of the sovereign status of federally recognized Indian tribes, which precludes most states from exercising criminal jurisdiction in Indian Country over Indian persons. Jurisdiction resides with the tribes themselves, on a limited basis, or with the federal government. Federal criminal jurisdiction in Indian Country is derived from the U.S. Code, Title 18, U.S.C. 1152 (General Crimes Act) and Title 18, U.S.C. 1153 (Major Crimes Act).

In addition to the FBI, the Department of the Interior's Bureau of Indian Affairs (BIA) plays a significant role in enforcing Federal law, including the investigation and presentation for prosecution of cases involving violations of 18 U.S.C. 1152 and 1153… In short, numerous Federal and tribal law enforcement agencies are necessary for the efficient administration of criminal justice in Indian country. Determining which law enforcement agency, Federal or tribal, has primary responsibility for investigation of a particular crime may depend on the nature of the crime committed and any applicable local guidelines, which vary across jurisdictions. (U.S. Department of Justice, 2015)

Adding to the situational nature of law enforcement responsibility in Indian Country, due to changes enacted in 1953 under Public Law 280 (PL280), certain matters fall under state (rather than federal or tribal) jurisdiction in places such as Alaska, California, Minnesota, Nebraska, Oregon, and Wisconsin. The Tribal Law and Order Act (TLOA) of 2010 was meant to clarify a handful of jurisdictional issues but did not change the status of the PL280 states. Five years after TLOA enactment, a roundtable discussion involving tribal and federal government representatives revealed mixed results in terms of the Act having produced measures of clarity (Lee, 2016).

Resources allocated by the FBI to various locations throughout the country are based on a number of factors, including identified crime problems; jurisdictional responsibilities; and the availability of non-FBI investigative resources. Also, by virtue of the Indian Gaming Regulatory Act (IGRA) enacted in 1988, the FBI has federal criminal jurisdiction over acts directly related to casino gaming in Indian Country gaming establishments, including those locations on reservations under state criminal jurisdiction.

Four Indian Country divisions (Albuquerque, Minneapolis, Phoenix, and Salt Lake City) of the FBI accounted for about 71 percent of all Indian Country investigation closures in 2015 (U.S. Department of Justice, 2015). In that same year, there were "approximately 127 Special Agents dedicated full-time and 41 FBI Victim Specialists working in support of Indian country investigative matters in more than 20 FBI Field Offices" (ibid.). Despite these efforts and application of resources, in recent years there has been a feeling of bias against Indian Country in terms of follow-through on cases (Patterson, 2016; Williams, 2012). As one law journal article stated, "…the federal government's limited resources combined with an array of disincentives to investigate and prosecute Indian country crimes means that remarkably few are ever even superficially pursued" (Riley, 2016).

In terms of other areas of federal involvement in Indian Country law enforcement, occasionally the FBI joins forces with the BIA to hold regional training conferences for Indian Country officials. But since the mid-90s, most training has been held at the United States Indian Police Academy, which is co-located with the Department of Homeland Security at the Federal Law Enforcement Training Center in Artesia, New Mexico. Specialized training for Indian Country includes "courses in the Indian Child Welfare Act, Indian Country jurisdictional issues, and the challenge of working alone without assistance of backup for an extended period of time due to the ruralness of where they work" (Wright, 2010).

Interview with Former Chief Jason O'Neal, Chief of Police, Chickasaw Nation Lighthorse Police (Ada, Oklahoma), May 19, 2009*

Q. *What are the most important ways for civilian police to show respect on Indian lands?*

A. First, it is important for civilian police to understand tribal sovereignty as well as the tribes and their history. It's equally important for tribal police to understand the issues facing civilian police. This helps to build cooperation. Tribal police need to make it a priority to build relationships with all the agencies in their jurisdictions, including state and local.

Q. What, in particular, should civilian police be learning about Indian culture?

A. They should become familiar with religious practices, and should understand that every tribe is unique, and has its own customs and beliefs. They also need to get a basic understanding of Indian jurisdiction. We have worked with the state [of Oklahoma] to ensure that the state academy presents information of this kind. Civilian police have issues facing Indian Country, and require dedicated training in this area.

Q. Is there anything that you can think of that Native Americans find frustrating when it comes to dealing with civilian police?

(continued)

A. It is frustrating for Native Americans and tribal police that some law enforcement agencies do not recognize tribal police as equal or even perceive tribal police as police. Many of our officers attend a Police Academy. We work with outside agencies to achieve common goals, and we have worked on cross-deputization agreements. We all need to recognize each other.

It can also be frustrating when civilian police are working operation in and around Indian Country, and do not coordinate with tribal police. Cooperation and mutual recognition are key. For example, we have cross-training with the Oklahoma Bureau of Narcotics and Dangerous Drugs; we have assigned an investigator to their office and vice versa.

Q. *What do Native Americans say about civilian police?*

A. We mainly receive calls from the Native public who have dealings with civilian police and who want our department to be part of the investigation. When civilian police are working in Indian Country, they should consult us during an operation. We might be able to assist them or come up with an even more effective alternative to a problem.

Q. Is there a particular message you would like to be passed on to the readers of our text regarding law enforcement interaction with Native Americans?

A. We have to be interconnected. There is a maze of jurisdictional rules in and around Indian Country. The only way to achieve public safety is through cooperative law enforcement efforts. It benefits everyone.

Communication is the key. During any calls for service, it is critical that officers take the time to communicate with the population they serve, and in this way officers also learn how to do their jobs more effectively.

---

*Jason O'Neal, Chickasaw Nation Lighthorse Police Chief, was recognized for his pioneering work in cooperative law enforcement as he was awarded Chief of Police of the Year ...at the national conference of the National Native American Law Enforcement Association in Las Vegas ("Lighthorse Chief Named Police Chief of the Year," 2008).

Tribal and Civilian Police

Law enforcement activities in Indian Country are managed by the BIA, under which falls the Office of Justice Services (OJS). The problems these groups face are immense. "The OJS continues to address the issues prevalent in Indian communities which are diverse, dispersed, and spread over large geographic expanses. These communities often face socioeconomic challenges such as high levels of unemployment and drug abuse, which can cause severe challenges for emergency services personnel" (U.S. Department of the Interior, 2013). In addition, tribal police and criminal justice services are chronically short-handed. Exhibit 9.3 shows that while the situation is improving slightly due to diligent efforts in recruitment, training, and retention, still only 52 percent of tribal law enforcement agencies had adequate levels of staffing in 2015. A report released by the U.S. Government Accountability Office neatly summarized the plight:

> In [a DOJ] study, researchers estimated that there are fewer than 2 officers per 1,000 residents in Indian country compared to a range of 3.9 to 6.6 officers per 1,000 residents in non-tribal areas such as Detroit, Michigan and Washington, D.C. The challenge of limited law enforcement resources is exacerbated by the geographic isolation or vast size of many reservations. In some instances officers may need to travel hundreds of miles to reach a crime scene. For example, the Pine Ridge Indian Reservation in South Dakota has about 88 sworn tribal officers to serve 47,000 residents across 3,466 square miles, which equates to a ratio of 1 officer per 39 square miles of land... (U.S. Government Accountability Office, 2011)

2006	36%
2008	59%
2010	52%
2012	52%
2014	50%
2015	52%

EXHIBIT 9.3 Percent of BIA/Tribal Law Enforcement Agencies on Par with Recommended National Ratio of Staffing

Source: U.S. Department of the Interior. *Budget Justifications and Performance Information: Indian Affairs.* Figures for 2006 from Fiscal Year 2011 report; figures for 2008–2010 from Fiscal Year 2013 report. Figures for 2012–2015 from Fiscal Year 2017 report.

While tribal law enforcement obviously cannot handle everything given available staffing and geographic constraints, policing on tribal lands can also cause confusion and friction between tribal and civilian law enforcement. Jurisdiction of the tribal police may be limited, and the non-Indian is not always subject to Indian tribal law. Some tribes have decriminalized their codes and taken on civil codes of law (e.g., for basic misdemeanors, civil fines may go to the tribal court), yet still conduct a trial of the non-Indian in a tribal court (Tribal Court Clearinghouse, 2017; www.tribal-institute.org/lists/jurisdiction.htm).

Police officers can be put into an unusual situation when it comes to enforcing the law among Indians. They may make an arrest in an area that is considered to be "Indian land" (on which tribal police have jurisdiction). The land may be adjacent to non-Indian land, sometimes forming "checkerboard" patterns of jurisdiction. In the case of an Indian reservation on which tribal police usually have authority, civilian law enforcement agencies are challenged to know where their jurisdiction begins and ends. With the multijurisdictional agreements that many tribes have signed with local and state officials, nontribal police officers may have the right to enter reservations to continue business. It is not uncommon for a person suspected of a crime to be apprehended by a nontribal police officer on a reservation. (Bowen-Hartung, 2017).

It is expected that civilian law enforcement agents inform tribal police or tribal authorities when entering a reservation, but this does not always happen. Going onto reservation land without prior notice and contacting a suspect or witness directly is an insult to the authority of the tribal police (ibid.). Civilian police should see themselves as partners with tribal police. Obviously, in dangerous or emergency situations, time may prevent civilian authorities from conferring with the tribal police. Where possible, it is essential that the authority of the reservation be respected.

Levels of cooperation and attitudes toward civil and tribal law enforcement partnerships differ from area to area. Retired police chief Cox, who served as executive director of the Oklahoma chiefs of police, spoke of the progress his state had made with respect to legislation associated with jurisdictional issues and the cross-deputization of local, state, and tribal police officers (e.g., Sac and Fox, Cherokee, Creek, Comanche, and Chickasaw Nations). Further progress came on November 1, 2013, when the Oklahoma state legislature passed House Bill 1871, giving the same authority to tribal law enforcement officers as other peace officers.

> A Bureau of Indian Affairs law enforcement officer or a tribal law enforcement officer of a federally recognized Indian tribe who has been commissioned by the tribe, has a law enforcement contract or compact with the Bureau of Indian Affairs and who has been certified by the Council on Law Enforcement Education and Training shall have state police powers limited to tribally owned land or land defined as Indian country...to enforce state laws or municipal ordinances on tribal land. (State of Oklahoma, 2013)

In the past several years, the increasing use of GPS devices has contributed to better identification of location, jurisdiction, and resources. This cross-training and cooperation are especially critical in the complex geography of the state (Cox, 2017). In Oklahoma, Indian Country spans approximately 8,000 miles, and there is no contiguous border (out of 77 counties, 63 are in Indian Country). The patchwork Indian land and non-Indian land, therefore, lends itself to an uneven system of arrests and prosecutions, depending on whether a crime takes place on Indian land, with an Indian victim, and/or with an Indian perpetrator. Cross-deputization, which is now fairly widespread in Oklahoma, enables both tribal and civilian police to make arrests in each other's jurisdiction. Retired chief Cox hopes that the models and progress he has seen in Oklahoma will benefit other states as well (ibid.).

Police departments around the country, such as in New Mexico and Washington State, have also been working intensively to form relationships with local Indian tribes. Tribal police officers in Oregon are federally commissioned and state-certified police officers with full law enforcement authority. In Oregon, if a tribal police officer arrests a non-Indian, the non-Indian will be lodged in the county jail and arraigned in the county circuit court. If the same tribal police officer arrests an Indian, the Indian will be lodged in the tribal jail, usually housed in the county jail, and arraigned in tribal court. If there is a will to work cooperatively, police departments and Indian tribal departments can be of tremendous benefit to each other. Initiating this type of effort means, for both Indians and non-Indians, putting aside history and transcending stereotypes.

Finally, cross-cultural contact between civilian officers and tribal members occurs fairly frequently on small Indian reservations. Former deputy chief Larry Becker worked with the Port Gamble S'Klallam Tribe, a tribe consisting of 1,300 members in 2013 on a reservation of 8–10 square miles in Northwest Washington. This tribe is a sovereign, self-governing tribe with its own courts, laws, prosecutor, public defender, and police department. The county and the state have no authority over this small tribe's reservation, and thus its members are free to use or not use tribal law officers. Becker explained that only civilian officers, that is, non-Native American officers, police the reservation. Because small tribes may consist primarily of family members, members have a higher level of comfort when police officers from outside the reservation are hired by the tribe to enforce laws. Becker said that this scenario, that is, non-Native American officers' policing reservations, was common for many of the (then) Washington's 26 (of 32 total tribes) sovereign, self-governing tribes (Becker, 2013).

Racial Profiling of Native Americans

Just as other groups such as Latinos and African Americans have routinely been victims of profiling, so have Native Americans (see Chapter 12 for extensive information on racial profiling). If a group of Native Americans is riding in a poorly maintained car, or a car with a license plate that indicates Indian reservation residence, there is the potential that they will be stopped simply because they are perceived as suspicious and because negative stereotypes are operating (Loevy, 2015). Negative biases against Native Americans are strong and have persisted for generations. In one study conducted in Arizona, it was shown that "The highway patrol was 3.5 times more likely to search a stopped Native American than a White…" (The Leadership Conference, 2011). When there is no legitimate reason to stop a car, the next step is for officers to check their own stereotypes of whom they think is a criminal. Like members of other ethnic groups, Indians have repeatedly reported being stopped for no reason, adding to their distrust of police.

Among some minority groups in the United States, encounters with law enforcement that involve what is perceived as excessive force and/or end in death for a minority individual are often thought to be based on racial issues. Incidents that receive media attention, such as the shooting in Denver of a mentally ill Native American named Paul Castaway, stoke tensions between minorities and law enforcement (Roberts, 2016). While incidents involving the use of deadly force tend to alarm and anger Native Americans, at least one well-researched report indicates that, "Ratios of admitted and fatal injury due to legal police intervention per 10,000 stops/arrests did not differ significantly between racial/ethnic groups" (Miller, Lawrence, & Carlson, 2017). Other data from the Centers for Disease Control and Prevention indicate that "legal intervention deaths" of Native Americans occur at a higher rate than those of African Americans when calculated relative to racial group population size (Lyons, Fowler, Jack, Betz, & Blair, 2016; U.S. Census Bureau, 2015). A legal intervention death is defined as "injuries inflicted by the police or other law-enforcing agents…in the course of arresting or attempting to arrest lawbreakers, suppressing disturbances, maintaining order, and other legal action" (ICD-9, 2016).

Peyote

Many states have specific laws exempting the traditional, religious use of peyote by American Indians from those states' drug enforcement laws. Following is a definition of peyote:

> Peyote is a small turnip-shaped, spineless cactus [containing] nine alkaloid substances, part of which, mainly mescaline, are hallucinogenic in nature; that is, they induce dreams or visions. Reactions to peyote seem to vary with the social situation in which it is used. In some it may merely cause nausea; believers may experience optic, olfactory and auditory sensations. Under ideal conditions color visions may be experienced and peyote may be "heard" singing or speaking. The effects wear off within twenty-four hours and leave no ill aftereffects. Peyote is non-habit forming. (Bahti, 1982)

There have been a variety of uses associated with peyote: (1) as a charm for hunting, (2) as a medicine, (3) as an aid to predict weather, (4) as an object to help find things that are lost (the belief being that peyote can reveal the location of the lost object through peyote-induced visions;

peyote was even used to help locate the enemy in warfare), and (5) as an object to be carried for protection. People have faith in peyote as a powerful symbol and revere its presence (ibid.).

Dried peyote charms are carried in small bags or pouches, which are then typically placed inside a "peyote box." (Peyote boxes contain items for use in religious ceremonies, as well as personal objects. See Swan, 2010, for more information.) Peyote charms and other medicinal items can be "ruined" if touched.* Police officers may need to confiscate peyote but should do it in a way that is appropriate and respectful. It is far better to ask the Native American politely to remove a bag containing peyote rather than forcibly take it away.

In a 1990 freedom-of-religion case, the Supreme Court ruled that state governments could have greater leeway in outlawing certain religious practices. The ruling involved the ritual use of peyote by some American Indians who follow the practices of the Native American Church of North America (NACNA), which had an estimated membership of 250,000 people at that time (Morris, 2010). Until then, the U.S. government had allowed for the religious use of peyote among Native Americans based on the Bill of Rights' Free Exercise of Religion guarantee; in other words, peyote use was generally illegal except in connection with bona fide American Indian religious rituals.

From a law enforcement perspective, if drugs are illegal, no group should be exempt, and indeed, officers must uphold the law. For example, a few fringe organizations have called themselves Native American churches, and their members have tried to claim that marijuana and other substances are used in Native American religious ceremonies. The NACNA responded by issuing a formal statement that declares, "We do not recognize, condone, or allow the use of marijuana, or any substance other than peyote, in any of our religious services" (Native American Churches, 2016).

From a civil rights perspective, religious freedom applies to all groups and no group should be singled out for disproportionately burdensome treatment. Historically, legal and illegal status of peyote has been complex. There have been many attempts to prohibit the use of peyote on the federal level, and many states passed laws outlawing its use. However, several states have modified such prohibitions to allow traditional American Indians to continue using peyote as a sacrament. Moreover, in some states, anti-peyote laws have been declared unconstitutional by state courts insofar as they burden the religious practice of American Indians.

This historic ambiguity on the state level, together with the 1990 ruling on the federal level, causes confusion and resentment on the part of many Native Americans. Recognizing that the existing Act of August 11, 1978 (42 U.S.C. 1996), commonly called the American Indian Religious Freedom Act, was no longer adequate in protecting Native Americans' civil rights in their traditional and cultural religious use of peyote, Congress passed, and President Clinton signed into law, the American Indian Religious Freedom Act Amendments of 1994. Following are select portions of this federal law (American Indian Religious Freedom Act, 1994):

Section 3. The Congress finds and declares, among other issues, that:

1. for many Indian people, the traditional ceremonial use of the peyote cactus as a religious sacrament has for centuries been integral to a way of life, and significant in perpetuating Indian tribes and cultures;
2. since 1965, this ceremonial use of peyote by Indians has been protected by Federal regulation;
3. while at least 28 States have enacted laws which are similar to, or are in conformance with, the Federal regulation which protects the ceremonial use of peyote by Indian religious practitioners, 22 States have not done so, and this lack of uniformity has created hardship for Indian people who participate in such religious ceremonies; and
4. the lack of adequate and clear legal protection for the religious use of peyote by Indians may serve to stigmatize and marginalize Indian tribes and cultures, and increase the risk that they will be exposed to discriminatory treatment.

---

*Native Americans from many tribes across the country wear small medicine bags, considered to be extremely sacred. The medicine bags do not carry drugs or peyote, but hold symbols from nature (e.g., corn pollen, cedar, sage, tree bark), and are believed to have certain powers. If it becomes necessary, law enforcement officers should handle these as they would handle any sacred symbol from their own religion. Ripping into the bags would be an act of desecration. The medicine contained in the bags has often been blessed and therefore must be treated with respect.

The use of peyote outside the NACNA (established in 1918) is technically forbidden and generally regarded by church members as sacrilegious. Within the NACNA, there are very specific rules and rituals pertaining to its sacramental use. But within the judicial system, the issue eventually arose as to whether peyote use by non-Indian members of the NACNA would be legally allowed, such as in the Utah case of James "Flaming Eagle" Mooney (who is not a Native American). Some church members say that to limit peyote use to Native Americans constitutes racial discrimination. Officers who have regular contact with Native American communities should stay informed about court rulings as to whether NACNA membership or "Indianness" is the critical factor in allowing the use of peyote. Establishing respectful communication with the leaders of the NACNA can also assist officers in determining whether peyote is being abused in certain circumstances.

Law enforcement officials would do well to understand the importance and place of peyote in the culture from a Native American point of view. It is not the intent of the authors to recommend a particular course of action with regard to enforcement or lack thereof. When the use of peyote is understood from an Indian perspective, officers will be more likely to communicate a respectful attitude toward an ancient ritual that some researchers say dates back over 5,000 years. If police officers suddenly enter a prayer meeting or drumming ceremony where peyote is being used and aggressively make arrests, it will be very difficult to establish trust with the community. When peyote is an issue, officers must recognize their own ethnocentrism (i.e., subconsciously viewing other cultures or cultural practices as primitive, abnormal, or inferior). Law enforcement personnel working in communities where peyote use is an issue should anticipate the problems that will occur and should discuss it with members of the Indian community. Officers should also know the laws pertaining to peyote use in their jurisdictions and the policy of their agencies regarding enforcement if it is illegal. Historically, the federal government actively tried to suppress and change Native American cultures. The banning of peyote was and has been viewed by Native American groups as a failure of the Bill of Rights to truly guarantee the freedom to practice one's own religion.

Trespassing and Sacred Lands

In a number of states, traditional Indian harvest areas or sacred burial and religious sites are now on federal, state, and, especially, private lands. Indians continue to visit these areas just as their ancestors did to collect resources or to pray. The point of concern for law enforcement involves conflicts occurring among ranchers, farmers, and homeowners on what Indians consider their holy ground. How officers react to allegations of trespassing determines whether there will be an escalated confrontation (Rivera, 2013). When there is a dispute, officers can alienate Indians by choosing an authoritarian and aggressive method of handling the problem (e.g., "You're going to get off this land right now"). Alternatively, officers could show empathy and the Native American may very well be more supportive of efforts to resolve the immediate conflict. If there is no immediate resolution, the officers can, at a minimum, prevent an escalation of hostilities.

As a leading Native American law scholar wrote in the Harvard Law Review, "The inconvenient fact is that the United States continues to occupy Indian lands" (Washburn, 2017). Given that police officers cannot solve this complex and very old problem, the only tool available is the ability to communicate sensitively and listen well. "The officer is put between a rock and a hard place. If the officer is sensitive, he could try to speak to the landowner and describe the situation, although often the landowners don't care about the history, claiming, 'It's my land now.' However, there have been some people who have been sensitive to the needs of the Native Americans and who have worked out agreements" (ibid.).

In one case in Fargo, North Dakota, escalation was less about property ownership and more about ignorance concerning the use of a religious site and officers taking an aggressive stance. Police officers spotted a fire burning unattended in a distant field. The fire, as it turned out, had been used by local Native Americans to heat rocks for an Indian sweat lodge ceremony. Although the sweat lodge had been in place for a long time, an unknowing first-year officer initiated a raid on the structure and dragged at least one Native American through the snow in handcuffs after perceiving resistance to arrest. The Native American had no weapon and was dressed only in undershorts. Charges against the Native American were dropped, and the Fargo Police Department made plans for cultural competency training for its officers (Hagen, 2017; Johnson, 2017).

Land and Water Issues—Standing Rock, 2016

In April of 2016, Native Americans set up camp in North Dakota to protest the installation of an oil pipeline by a company called Energy Transfer Partners. By August, two additional camps had been established, in total housing over 3,000 protesters made up of members of federally recognized Native American tribes and other supporters of the cause. Standing Rock caught the attention of individuals and organizations around the world, including members of the U.S. Congress, movie stars, military veteran groups, Amnesty International, and a Norwegian bank investor in the project; all made public statements of support for the Native American cause. The media, including social media, presented and reported the events at Standing Rock in different ways.

Law enforcement on the scene included the North Dakota Highway Patrol and the Morton County Sheriff's Department. In August, the governor of North Dakota declared a state of emergency in order to procure relief funds for providing security, and Morton County officials quickly followed suit. Eventually, law enforcement details from six different states and the North Dakota National Guard, as well as a private security company, became involved (Dresslar, 2016).

At issue was a lengthy stretch of land over which the pipeline would pass. This land, jutting northward from the Standing Rock Reservation, had originally been carved out for the Great Sioux Nation via the 1851 Treaty of Fort Laramie; the U.S. government had unilaterally taken the land back in 1889. Essentially, local Native Americans believe that the Treaty is still valid, and that there are burial and sacred grounds on the territory (Young, 2015).

Interactions between the protesters and law enforcement escalated, with reports of officers using tear gas, rubber bullets, fire hoses, and armored personnel carriers. The private security company unleashed attack dogs and tear gas on the crowd after protesters burst through a fence carrying "wooden posts and flagpoles" (Cone, 2016; Eckroth, 2016). Late October saw law enforcement make efforts to clear one camp of protesters from private property; protesters countered that it was tribal property. In November, as protesters attempted to clear a barricade from a bridge, police sprayed them with fire hoses and tear gas (Wong, 2016). After a tribal representative sought the assistance of the United Nations Human Rights Council, it issued a statement in November of 2016 that read in part:

> Law enforcement officials, private security firms and the North Dakota National Guard have used unjustified force to deal with opponents of the Dakota Access pipeline… Tensions have escalated in the past two weeks, with local security forces employing an increasingly militarized response to protests… The use of violence by some protesters should not be used as a justification to nullify the peaceful assembly rights of everyone else. (U.N. Human Rights, 2016)

Overall, the situation was fraught with emotion on the part of the Native American protesters, who felt that their traditions and sovereign status were once again being ignored and their history eradicated by bulldozers. LaDonna Brave Bull Allard, the Historic Preservation Officer for the Standing Rock Sioux Tribe and the initiator of the protest camps wrote, "If we allow an oil company to dig through and destroy our histories, our ancestors, our hearts and souls as a people, is that not genocide?" (Allard, 2016). Certainly, the situation was more complex than can be conveyed here in a few paragraphs. But when dealing with Native Americans, it is wise to avoid an overly aggressive stance and, whenever possible, seek the counsel and support of Native American leaders, legislators, and law enforcement officials.

Native American Sites—Use of, Desecration, and Looting

The Native American Free Exercise of Religion Act of 1993 was an attempt by Senator Inouye and his cosponsors to return authority over religious sites on Indian lands to Native American tribes. A scaled-down version was signed that year by President Clinton, which mostly applied to the use of peyote (see previous section). It took two more years for an executive order to be signed concerning the protection of Native American heritage sites. Excerpts:

Section 1. Accommodation of Sacred Sites.

a. In managing Federal lands, each executive branch agency with statutory or administrative responsibility for the management of Federal lands shall, to the extent practicable, permitted by law, and not clearly inconsistent with essential agency functions, (1) accommodate access to and ceremonial use of Indian sacred sites by Indian religious practitioners and (2) avoid adversely affecting the physical integrity of such sacred sites. Where appropriate, agencies shall maintain the confidentiality of sacred sites.

b. For purposes of this order… (iii) "Sacred site" means any specific, discrete, narrowly delineated location on Federal land that is identified by an Indian tribe, or Indian individual determined to be an appropriately authoritative representative of an Indian religion, as sacred by virtue of its established religious significance to, or ceremonial use by, an Indian religion, provided that the tribe or appropriately authoritative representative of an Indian religion has informed the agency of the existence of such a site. (Federal Register, 1996)

Even more degrading to Native Americans than the violation of sacred lands is the taking of human remains (skulls and bones) from Indian reservations and public lands. Most often, this type of looting has been done to make a profit on Native American articles and artifacts. Vandalism of archeological sites often occurs without any criminal prosecution. Officers in certain parts of the country may enter non-Indian homes and see such remains "displayed" as souvenirs of a trip into Indian Country. The Native American Graves Protection and Repatriation Act of 1990, passed by Congress and signed by former President George H. W. Bush, resulted as a response to such criminal acts. When officers see human remains, they must investigate as to foul play. Officers should contact state agencies established to enforce laws that protect Indian relics to determine how to proceed in such situations.

Indian Casinos and Gaming

Native American reservations in the United States are considered to be sovereign nations, and as such, leaders are responsible for providing and securing financing in order to pay for basic infrastructure and services as leaders would in any city. To date, the most successful source of public funds for Indian reservations has been casinos and other types of gaming for profit. The legal wording on most documents referring to this industry uses the term *Indian gaming.*

Legalized gambling on reservations dates back to a landmark case in 1976 in which the Supreme Court ruled that states no longer could have regulatory jurisdiction over Indian tribes. Because of the lawsuits that followed, it was later ruled that states did not have the right to prohibit Native American tribes from organizing and participating in for-profit legalized gambling. The Indian Gaming Regulatory Act became law in 1988. For the first time, Native Americans were given the right to regulate all gaming activities on their sovereign lands.

There is a great deal of controversy around the Indian gaming industry. On the one hand, according to one research study, "Four years after tribes open casinos, employment [increases] by 26 percent, and tribal population [increases] by about 12 percent… The increase in economic activity appears to have some health benefits in that four or more years after a casino opens, mortality [falls] by 2 percent." On the other hand, according to the same study, "bankruptcy rates, violent crime, and auto thefts and larceny are up 10 percent in counties with a casino" (Evans & Topoleski, 2002).

As a whole, American Indians have made significant gains and progress through the gaming industry as it has enabled a certain amount of economic self-reliance for some tribes. As of 2013, about 240 recognized tribes operated more than 400 Indian gaming operations in 28 states, "from bingo halls to multimillion dollar casinos" (U.S. Government Accountability Office, 2015). However, "The majority of [these] tribes, 57%, generate less than $25 million per year in gross gaming revenue. And 20% …produce less than $3 million per year" (National Indian Gaming Commission, 2016).

Fishing

"If you ever want to get into a fight, go into a local bar [e.g., in parts of Washington State] and start talking about fishing rights. The fishing issue is a totally hot issue" (Rivera, 2013).

The wording of treaties with regard to the fishing rights of Native Americans is clear and unequivocal in English as well as in the languages of the specific tribes concerned. For example, the treaty with Indians of the Northwest regarding fishing rights on the rivers gives these rights to the Indians "for as long as the rivers shall flow" (Reference is from an American Indian Prayer for Peace; author unknown). The rivers in the Northwest are still flowing, and Indians are still struggling with the state of Washington about the state's violations of the treaty's terms, even on Indian property (ibid.).

Indians continue to say, "We have treaties with the government allowing us to fish here." Commercial and sports fishermen, on the forefront of trying to prevent Native Americans from exercising their treaty rights, claim that Indians are destroying the industry. From the Native Americans' perspective, they are providing sustenance to their families and earning extra money for themselves or their tribes to make it through the year. (For 150 years, there had been no industry on many, if not most, of the reservations.) Once again, the officer on the front line will be unable to solve a problem that has been raging for generations. The front-line officer's actions, in part, depend on the sensitivity of his or her department's chief executive. Admittedly, the commander is in a difficult position, caught between the state fish and game industry and the people trying to enforce federal treaties. Nevertheless, he or she can communicate to officers the need for cultural sensitivity in their way of approaching and communicating with Native Americans. The alternative could be dangerous, as illustrated by at least one situation when, in northern California, peace officers with flak jackets and automatic weapons resorted to pursuing Native Americans with shotguns up and down the river (ibid.).

Similar issues arise concerning fishing and general water use rights. After a decade of negotiations, a formal agreement meant to sort out water rights in western Montana was stalled by local farmers and ranchers. Regional agriculture depended on adequate water supplies for crops and livestock, and farmers accused the state of colluding with Native Americans interested in protecting fishing rights. "Generations of misunderstanding have come to a head," said Robert McDonald, the communications director for the Confederated Salish and Kootenai Tribes. "It's starting to tear the fabric of our community apart" (Healy, 2013).

There are many complex dimensions to cases involving Native Americans "breaking the law" when, in parallel, the federal government is not honoring its historical treaties with them. Native Americans are frustrated by what they see as blatant violations of their rights. The history of the government's lack of loyalty to its American Indian citizens has caused great pain for this cultural group. Clearly, sensitivity and understanding on the part of law enforcement officials are required. Officers should demonstrate patience and tact, remembering that history has defined many aspects of the current relationships between law enforcement and American Indians. Being forceful and displaying anger will alienate Native Americans and will not result in the cooperation needed to solve issues that arise.

Summary

- Historically, the police officer from outside the reservation has been a symbol of rigid and authoritarian governmental control that has affected nearly every aspect of Indian life, especially on reservations. Officers, like most citizens, have only a limited understanding of how the government, including the criminal justice system, caused massive suffering by not allowing Indians to preserve their cultures, identities, languages, rituals, lands, and sacred sites.
- Each federally recognized tribe has a distinct history and culture, and often a separate language. Each has its own government, schools, law enforcement, and economic systems. Federal recognition means that a legal relationship exists between the tribe and the federal government. "Indian Country" refers to all land that is within the limits of an Indian reservation under the jurisdiction of the U.S. government, and to all dependent Indian communities within the borders of the United States. An Indian reservation is land that a tribe has reserved for its exclusive use through statutes, executive order, or treaty-making.

- Significant differences exist among the cultures, languages, history, and socioeconomic status of Native American tribes, communities, and individuals. Yet, there is a strong cultural link among the many worlds and tribes of Native Americans. There is a common set of values and beliefs involving the earth and the universe, resulting in a deep respect for nature and "mother earth." According to American Indian philosophy, the earth is sacred and is a living entity. Indians do not see themselves as superior to animals and plants, but rather as part of all of creation. Through religious ceremonies and rituals, traditional Native Americans are able to transcend themselves so that they are connected to nature and in harmony with the universe.
- Many American Indians who favor traditional styles of communication tend toward formality and slow building of rapport with strangers. Behavior that appears aloof or hostile may be part of a cultural style; police officers should not automatically attribute a lack of cooperation to the behavior observed. Aggressive questioning can result in withdrawal of responses. In addition, direct eye contact for some traditional tribal members is an affront or invasion of privacy. Holding back on judging cultural styles of communication is key to establishing good rapport.
- There are many offensive terms for and stereotypes of Native Americans. The terms *chief, redskin, buck, squaw, braves,* and *skins* are examples of these, especially when used by a non-Indian. The use of Indian tribal names or references as mascots for sports teams is highly objectionable to many Native Americans.
- The traditional extended family is close-knit and interdependent, and a great deal of respect is paid to the elderly. Police officers should remember to ask elders for their opinions or advice, as they are often the major decision makers in the family. A particularly sensitive area in family dynamics relates to the separation of children from families. This can bring back memories of times when children were forcibly taken from their parents. Native Americans who have close-knit extended families, and who identify with their tribal cultures, tend to be better adjusted than those who lack family and cultural support. In the case of the latter, social and health problems can be severe, and include depression, alcoholism, drug use, and suicidal tendencies.
- Key issues for law enforcement with respect to Native Americans include jurisdiction, victimization, fishing, the use of peyote, allegations of trespassing, sacred sites violations, and Indian gaming and casinos. Some of these involve matters in which Native Americans feel they have been deprived of their rights: in the case of peyote, the right to religious expression; in the case of trespassing, the right to honor their ancestors; and in the case of fishing, the ability to exercise their rights as guaranteed by treaties made with the U.S. government.

Discussion Questions and Issues

1. *Popular Stereotypes.* List some of the commonly held stereotypes of Native Americans. What is your personal experience with Native Americans that might counter these stereotypes? How have people in law enforcement been influenced by popular stereotypes of Native Americans?

2. *Recommendations for Effective Contact.* If you have had contact with Native Americans, what recommendations would you give others regarding effective communication, rapport building, and cultural knowledge that would be beneficial for officers?

3. *The Government's Broken Promises to American Indians.* The famous Lakota chief, Sitting Bull, spoke on behalf of many Indians when he said of white Americans, "They made us many promises...but they never kept but one: They promised to take our land, and they took it." There was a time when many acres of land in what we now call the United States were sacred to Native American tribes. Therefore, today many of us are living on, building on, and in some cases destroying the remains of Indian lands where people's roots run deep. How would you deal with the problem of an Indian "trespassing" on someone's land when he or she claims to be visiting an ancestral burial ground, for example? What could you say or do so as not to alienate the Native American and thereby risk losing trust and cooperation?

4. *Jurisdiction.*
   a. What should law enforcement agents do when state law is in conflict with a federal law that has been based on treaties with Native Americans signed by the federal government? How can officers who are on the front line win the respect and cooperation of Native Americans when they are asked to enforce something that goes against the treaty rights of the Indians?
   b. A special unit in the early 1990s was established by the San Diego Sheriff's department to patrol Native American reservations, overrun from the outside by drugs and violence. Federal Public Law 280 transferred criminal jurisdiction and enforcement on reservations to some states. Conduct research on law enforcement jurisdiction issues and tribal lands in your region or state (if applicable); note whether there are still unresolved areas or areas of dispute.

5. *Protests at Standing Rock.* If you were the head of the Morton County Sheriff's department, what would you have done to prevent or minimize escalation?

References

Allard, LaDonna B. B. (2016). "Why the Founder of Standing Rock Sioux Camp Can't Forget the Whitestone Massacre." September 3. *Yes! Magazine.* http://www.yesmagazine.org/people-power/why-the-founder-of-standing-rock-sioux-camp-cant-forget-the-whitestone-massacre-20160903 (accessed May 12, 2017).

American Psychiatric Association. (2010). "Mental health disparities: American Indians and Alaska Natives." www.integration.samhsa.gov/workforce/mental_health_disparities_american_indian_and_alaskan_natives.pdf (accessed May 17, 2017).

Amnesty International. (2008, Spring). *Maze of Injustice: The Failure to Protect Indigenous Women from Sexual Violence in the USA.* https://www.amnestyusa.org/pdfs/mazeofinjustice.pdf (accessed May 2, 2017).

American Indian Religious Freedom Act. (1994). *Amendments of 1994, Public Law 103–344 [H.R. 4230].* October 6. 103rd Congress. http://uscode.house.gov/statutes/pl/103/344.pdf (accessed May 2, 2017).

Bahti, Tom. (1982). *Southwestern Indian Ceremonials.* Las Vegas, NV: KC Publications.

Becker, Larry. (2013). (Former) Deputy Chief of S'Klallam Tribes in Kingston, Sequim, and Port Angeles, Washington, D.C., personal communication.

Bendery, Jennifer. (2015). "At Last, Violence against Women Act Lets Tribes Prosecute Non-Native Domestic Abusers." March 6. *The Huffington Post.* http://www.huffingtonpost.com/2015/03/06/vawa-native-americans_n_6819526.html (accessed May 2, 2017).

Bureau of Indian Affairs. (2016). *Federal Register, 81*(86), May 4. https://www.bia.gov/cs/groups/xraca/documents/text/idc1-033010.pdf (accessed May 2, 2017).

Bitsóí, Lee, Ph.D. (2013). *Bridging the Gap and Democratizing Scientific Research for Native Americans.* Presentation delivered at XSEDE13: Gateway to Discovery, July 24, San Diego, CA. https://www.xsede.org/web/xsede13/presentations (accessed May 2, 2017).

Bowen-Hartung, Dr., Peggy. (2017). Associate Professor of Psychology and Counseling and Criminal Justice; Alvernia College, Reading, PA, personal communication, May 15.

Brenneke, Andrea. (2012). "A Restorative Circle in the Wake of a Police Shooting." February 1. *Tikkun.* http://www.tikkun.org/nextgen/a-restorative-circle-in-the-wake-of-a-police-shooting (accessed May 4, 2017).

Bull, Brian. (2009). "For Native Americans, Old Stereotypes Die Hard." May 4. National Public Radio, *All Things Considered.* http://www.npr.org/s.php?sId=103711756&m=1 (accessed May 4, 2017).

Carr, Gwen. (1996). "Urban Indians. The Invisible Minority." Poverty & Race, March/April 1996. www.prrac.org/full_text.php?item_id=3563&newsletter_id=25 (accessed November 9, 2017).

Centers for Disease Control and Prevention. (2015). *Suicide Facts at a Glance.* National Center for Injury Prevention and Control, Division of Violence Prevention. https://www.cdc.gov/violenceprevention/pdf/suicide-datasheet-a.pdf (accessed May 12, 2017).

CEHIP. (1996). "20th Century Warriors: Native American Participation in the United States Military." Washington, D.C.: CEHIP Incorporated, in partnership with Native American advisors Rodger Bucholz, William Fields, and Ursula P. Roach. Department of Defense. https://www.history.navy.mil/research/library/online-reading-room/title-list-alphabetically/t/american-indians-us-military.html (accessed May 4, 2017).

Cone, Allen. (2016). *Dakota Access Pipeline Construction Resumes after Protest Turns Violent.* September 5. United Press International. http://www.upi.com/Dakota-Access-Pipeline-construction-resumes-after-protest-turns-violent/8381473002285 (accessed May 5, 2017).

Cox, Jim. (2017). Retired Police Chief, Midwest City, Oklahoma; Retired Executive Director of Oklahoma Chiefs of Police, Midwest City; Deputy in the Oklahoma Law Enforcement Museum and Hall of Fame, personal communication, June 12.

Dresslar, Thomas. (2016). "How many Law Enforcement Agencies Does It Take to Subdue a Peaceful Protest?" November 30. American Civil Liberties Union. https://www.aclu.org/blog/speak-freely/how-many-law-enforcement-agencies-does-it-take-subdue-peaceful-protest (accessed April 1, 2017).

Drug Enforcement Administration. (2015, October). *2015 National Drug Threat Assessment Summary.* Washington, D.C.: U.S. Department of Justice. https://www.dea.gov/docs/2015%20NDTA%20Report.pdf (accessed May 11, 2017)

Eckroth, Leann. (2016). "North Dakota Pipeline Protesters Break through Fence Line at Alternate Construction Site." September 4. *Bismarck Tribune.* http://www.duluthnewstribune.com/news/4108250-north-dakota-pipeline-protesters-break-through-fence-line-alternate-construction-site (accessed May 5, 2017).

Editorial Board. (2016). "Mr. Obama Honors a Pledge to American Indians." September 30. *The New York Times*, p. A26

Evans, William N. and Julie H. Topoleski. (2002, September). *The Social and Economic Impact of Native American Casinos.* National Bureau of Economic Research, Working Paper 9198. http://www.nber.org/papers/w9198.pdf (accessed May 4, 2017).

Federal Bureau of Investigation. (2012). *Journey through Indian Country—Part 1: Fighting Crime on Tribal Lands,* June 1. https://www.fbi.gov/news/stories/journey-through-indian-country (accessed May 4, 2017).

Federal Register. (1996). "Executive Order 13007: Indian Sacred Sites." May 24. 61 FR 26771. https://www.gpo.gov/fdsys/pkg/FR-1996-05-29/pdf/96-13597.pdf (accessed May 12, 2017).

Federal Register. (2000). "Executive Order 13175—Consultation and Coordination with Indian Tribal Governments." November 9. 65 FR 67249. https://www.federalregister.gov/documents/2000/11/09/00-29003/consultation-and-coordination-with-indian-tribal-governments (accessed May 12, 2017).

Flower, Ruth. (2016, October 18). *Alyce Spotted Bear and Walter Soboleff Commission on Native Children.* Washington, D.C.: Friends Committee on National Legislation.

Gross, Lawrence. (2014). *Anishinaabe Ways of Knowing and Being.* Ashgate Publishing Limited. Doreset Press, United Kingdom, p. 58.

Hagen, C. S. (2017). "Fargo Police Arrest Native American from Sweat Lodge." February 24. *High Plains Reader*. http://hpr1.com/index.php/feature/news/fargo-police-arrest-native-american-from-sweat-lodge (accessed May 3, 2017).

Harris, Philip R., Robert T. Moran, and Sarah V. Moran. (2004). *Managing Cultural Differences: Global Leadership Strategies for the 21st Century*, 6th ed. Oxford, UK: Butterworth-Heineman.

Healy, Jack. (2013). "Water Rights Tear at an Indian Reservation." April 21. *The New York Times*. http://www.nytimes.com/2013/04/22/us/bitter-battle-over-water-rights-on-montana-reservation.html (accessed May 4, 2017).

ICD-9. (2016). *International Classification of Diseases*, 9th ed. American Medical Association (definition of "legal intervention deaths").(E-970-E977).

ICMN Staff. (2003). "First American Female and Native Soldier Killed in Iraq War Is Remembered." April 11. *Indian Country Today*. https://indiancountrymedianetwork.com/news/first-american-female-and-native-soldier-killed-in-iraq-war-is-remembered (accessed May 4, 2017).

ICMN Staff. (2013). "President Obama Signs Violence against Women Act into Law." March 7. *Indian Country Today*. https://indiancountrymedianetwork.com/news/politics/president-obama-signs-violence-against-women-act-into-law (accessed May 4, 2017).

Izadi, Elahe. (2016). "Your Assumptions about Native Americans and Alcohol Are Wrong." February 12. *The Washington Post*. https://www.washingtonpost.com/news/post-nation/wp/2016/02/12/your-assumptions-about-native-americans-and-alcohol-are-wrong/?utm_term=.8bae507ef17b (accessed May 4, 2017).

Jevec, Adam. (2001, Winter). "Semper Fidelis, Code Talkers." *Prologue Magazine, 33*(4).

Johnson, Ryan. (2017). "Arrest of Native American Using Sweat Lodge Was 'Misunderstanding,' Fargo Mayor Says." February 26. *Inforum*. http://www.inforum.com/news/4225354-arrest-native-american-using-sweat-lodge-was-misunderstanding-fargo-mayor-says (accessed May 3, 2017).

Kain, Erik. (2011). "Did Police Turn a Blind Eye to Attack on Native American Family in Nevada?" July 6. *Forbes*. https://www.forbes.com/sites/erikkain/2011/07/06/did-police-turn-a-blind-eye-to-attack-on-native-american-family-in-nevada/#9d0dca42ec20 (accessed May 12, 2017).

The Leadership Conference on Civil and Human Rights. (2011, March). *Restoring a National Consensus: The Need to End Racial Profiling in America*. Washington, D.C. http://www.civilrights.org/publications/reports/racial-profiling2011/racial_profiling2011.pdf (accessed May 12, 2017).

Lee, Tanya H. (2016). "Tribal Law and Order Act Five Years Later: What Works and What Doesn't." March 8. *Indian Country Today*. https://indiancountrymedianetwork.com/news/politics/tribal-law-and-order-act-five-years-later-what-works-and-what-doesnt (accessed May 3, 2017).

"Lighthorse Chief Named Police Chief of the Year." (2008, October 20). *The Ada News*. http://www.theadanews.com/news/local_news/lighthorse-chief-named-police-chief-of-the-year/article_116d0246-5e06-5ba4-86d3-1a08f0e83fd9.html (accessed May 12, 2017).

Loevy, Debra. (2015). "Do Indian Lives Matter? Police Violence against Native Americans." October 29. *CounterPunch*. http://www.counterpunch.org/2015/10/29/do-indian-lives-matter-police-violence-against-native-americans (accessed May 12, 2017).

Lyons, Bridget, Katherine A. Fowler, Shane P. D. Jack, Carter J. Betz, and Janet M. Blair. (2016). *Surveillance for Violent Deaths—National Violent Death Reporting System, 17 States, 2013*. August 19. Morbidity and Mortality Weekly Report, Centers for Disease Control and Prevention. https://www.cdc.gov/mmwr/volumes/65/ss/ss6510a1.htm#T19_down (accessed May 2, 2017).

Matthiessen, Peter. (1992). *The Spirit of Crazy Horse*. New York, NY: Penguin Books.

McClung, Kassie. (2015). "Domestic Abuse Law Slow to take Root on Oklahoma Tribal Land." July 28. *The Oklahoman*. http://newsok.com/article/5436214 (accessed May 12, 2017).

Meyers, Laurie. (2007, February). "A Struggle for Hope." *Monitor on Psychology, 38*(2), p. 30. American Psychological Association. http://www.apa.org/monitor/feb07/astruggle.aspx (accessed May 12, 2017).

Miller, Ted, R., Bruce A. Lawrence, Nancy N. Carlson. (2017). *Science News*. July 17. https://www.sciencedaily.com/releases/2016/07/160725223820.htm (accessed September 15, 2017).

Morris, Nomi. (2010). "Rituals of Native American Church Offer Comfort, Sustenance." October 30. *Los Angeles Times*. http://articles.latimes.com/2010/oct/30/local/la-me-beliefs-peyote-20101030 (accessed May 12, 2017).

NCUIH. (2017). "Relocation" (downloadable document). National Council of Urban Indian Health. www.ncuih.org/action/document/download?document_id=120 (accessed March 3, 2017).

National Indian Gaming Commission. (2016). *Live from Indian Country, The NIGC Announces Largest Tribal Revenue Gain in 10 Years*. July 19. Press Release. https://www.nigc.gov/news/detail/live-from-indian-country-the-nigc-announces-largest-tribal-revenue-gain-in (accessed May 12, 2017).

Native American Churches. (2016). "National Council Does Not Condone Faux Native American Churches or Marijuana Use." February 18. *Indian Country Today*. https://indiancountrymedianetwork.com/history/events/national-council-does-not-condone-faux-native-american-churches-or-marijuana-use (accessed May 12, 2017).

O'Neal, Jason (2009, May). Chief of Police, Chickasaw Nation Lighthorse Police, Ada, OK, personal communication.

Patterson, Jacob. (2016). "This Native Teen's Death Speaks to a Larger Crisis on Indian Reservations." June 10. *Fusion*. http://fusion.net/this-native-teen-s-death-speaks-to-a-larger-crisis-on-i-1793857444 (accessed May 3, 2016).

Perry, Steven W. (2004, December). *A BJS Statistical Profile, 1992–2002: American Indians and Crime*. Washington, D.C.: Department of Justice, Bureau of Justice Statistics. NCJ 203097. https://www.bjs.gov/content/pub/pdf/aic02.pdf (accessed May 12, 2017).

Perry, Steven W. (2016, July). *Tribal Crime Data Collection Activities, 2016*. U.S. Department of Justice, Office of Justice Programs, Bureau of Justice Statistics. Technical Report NCJ 249939. https://www.bjs.gov/content/pub/pdf/tcdca16.pdf (accessed May 12, 2017).

Powell, Alvin. (2012). "Mystery of Native Americans' Arrival." July 24. *Harvard Gazette*. http://news.harvard.edu/gazette/story/2012/07/mystery-of-native-americans-arrival (accessed May 12, 2017).

Rice, Marah. "Differences in Communication." Union College Native Americans http://unioncollegenativeamericans.weebly.com/cultural-differences-in-communication.html (accessed May 1, 2017)

Richardson, W.J. Buck, Jr. (2012). Cultural Awareness to Help While Serving Native Veterans. Office of Rural Health Webinar, June 27. Veteran's Rural Health Resource Center-Western Region. https://www.ruralhealth.va.gov/docs/webinars/richardson-cultural-sensitivity-062712.pdf (accessed April 5, 2017).

Riley, Angela R. (2016, August). "Crime and Governance in Indian Country." *UCLA Law Review, 63*(6). http://www.uclalawreview.org/wp-content/uploads/2016/08/Riley-63-6.pdf (accessed May 4, 2017).

Rivera, Jose. (2013, August). Retired California State Peace Officer, Manager of Audience Development and Community Partnerships of Bay Area Discovery Museum, personal communication.

Roberts, Michael. (2016). "Paul Castaway 'Effectively Murdered' by Denver Cop, Attorney Says." July 27. *Westword.* http://www.westword.com/news/paul-castaway-effectively-murdered-by-denver-cop-attorney-says-8115971 (accessed on May 1, 2017).

Seven Fires Council. (2013). *Our People, Our Future*. Kentucky Native American online Web site. www.merceronline.com/Native/native10.htm (accessed April 26, 2017).

Smith, Sharon G., Jieru Chen, Kathleen C. Basile, Leah K. Gilbert, Melissa T. Merrick, Nimesh Patel, Margie Walling, and Anurag Jain. (2017, April). *The National Intimate Partner and Sexual Violence Survey (NISVS): 2010-2012 State Report*. Atlanta, GA: National Center for Injury Prevention and Control, Centers for Disease Control and Prevention.

State of Oklahoma. (2013). *House Bill 1871*. 1st Session of the 54th Legislature, 2013. http://www.ecapitol.net/viewtext.wcs?HB1871_HFLR~54th (accessed May 4, 2017).

Sullivan, Laura. (2009). "Lawmakers Move to Curb Rape on Native Lands." May 3. *National Public Radio.* http://www.npr.org/templates/transcript/transcript.php?storyId=103717296 (accessed May 12, 2017).

Swan, Daniel C. (2010). "Objects of Purpose—Objects of Prayer: Peyote Boxes of the Native American Church." *Museum Anthropology Review, 4*(2). https://scholarworks.iu.edu/journals/index.php/mar/article/view/887/1036 (accessed May 12, 2017).

Tribal Court Clearinghouse. (2017). "General Guide to Criminal Jurisdiction in Indian Country." www.tribal-institute.org/lists/jurisdiction.htm (accessed May 17, 2017).

Truman, Jennifer L. and Lynn Langton. (2014). *Criminal Victimization, 2013*. September 19. U.S. Department of Justice, Office of Justice Programs, Bureau of Justice Statistics. https://www.bjs.gov/content/pub/pdf/cv13.pdf (accessed May 4, 2017).

U.N. Human Rights. (2016). *Native Americans Facing Excessive Force in North Dakota Pipeline Protests—UN Expert*. November 15. Office of the United Nations High Commissioner for Human Rights. http://www.ohchr.org/EN/NewsEvents/Pages/DisplayNews.aspx?NewsID=20868 (accessed May 5, 2017).

U.S. Census Bureau. (2015). *American Community Survey*. Washington, D.C. https://www.census.gov/programs-surveys/acs (accessed May 12, 2017).

U.S. CIA World Factbook. (2017). https://www.cia.gov/library/publications/the-world-factbook/geos/ae.html (accessed May 17, 2017).

U.S. Code. (2017a). "Indian Country Defined." Title 18; Section 1151. uscode.house.gov (accessed April 25, 2017).

U.S. Code. (2017b). "Indians. Definitions." Title 25; Section 5129. uscode.house.gov (accessed April 25, 2017).

U.S. Department of Defense. (2012). "2012 Demographics. Profile of the Military Community." http://download.militaryonesource.mil/12038/MOS/Reports/2012-Demographics-Report.pdf (accessed May 17, 2017).

U.S. Department of Education. (2016). *Obama Administration Announces New Resources to Help Ensure Opportunity for Native Students*. September 27. Press Release. https://www.ed.gov/news/press-releases/obama-administration-announces-new-resources-help-ensure-opportunity-native-students (accessed May 4, 2017).

U.S. Department of the Interior. *Budget Justifications and Performance Information: Indian Affairs*. Fiscal Years 2011, 2013, and 2017 reports. https://www.bia.gov/WhoWeAre/AS-IA/OCFO/TBAC/BDDoc/Greenbook/index.htm (accessed May 4, 2017).

U.S. Department of Justice. (2013). *Violence against Woman Act (VAWA) Reauthorization 2013*. https://www.justice.gov/tribal/violence-against-women-act-vawa-reauthorization-2013-0 (accessed May 4, 2017).

U.S. Department of Justice. (2015). Indian Country Investigations and Prosecutions. https://www.justice.gov/tribal/page/file/904316/download (accessed May 3, 2017).

U.S. Department of Veterans Affairs. (2012, September). American Indian and Alaska Native Servicemembers and Veterans. www.va.gov/TRIBALGOVERNMENT/docs/AIAN_Report_FINAL_v2_7.pdf (accessed May 22, 2017).

U.S. Government Accountability Office, United States Government. (2011, February). *Indian Country Criminal Justice: Departments of the Interior and Justice Should Strengthen Coordination to Support Tribal Courts*. Report to Congressional Requesters. http://www.gao.gov/new.items/d11252.pdf (accessed May 4, 2017).

U.S. Government Accountability Office. (2015, June). *Indian Gaming: Regulation and Oversight by the Federal Government, States, and Tribes*. Report to Congressional Requesters. http://www.gao.gov/assets/680/670603.pdf (accessed May 2, 2017).

Washburn, Kevin K. (2017, April). "What the Future Holds: The Changing Landscape of Federal Indian Policy." *Harvard Law Review*, Forum, *130*(6). http://harvardlawreview.org/wp-content/uploads/2017/04/vol130_Washburn.pdf (accessed May 4, 2017).

White House. (2013). *Executive Order: Establishing the White House Council on Native American Affairs*. June 26. Office of the Press Secretary. https://obamawhitehouse.archives.gov/the-press-office/2013/06/26/executive-order-establishing-white-house-council-native-american-affairs (accessed May 4, 2017).

White House. (2016). *Fact Sheet: North American Working Group on Violence against Indigenous Women and Girls, New Commitments & Accomplishments from the Obama Administration*. October 14. Office of the Press Secretary. https://obamawhitehouse.archives.gov/the-press-office/2016/10/14/fact-sheet-north-american-working-group-violence-against-indigenous (accessed May 4, 2017).

Williams, Timothy. (2012). "Higher Crime, Fewer Charges on Indian Land." February 20. *New York Times*. http://www.nytimes.com/2012/02/21/us/on-indian-reservations-higher-crime-and-fewer-prosecutions.html (accessed May 3, 2017).

Wolf, Richard. (2013). "Court Rules for Adoptive Parents in Baby Veronica Case." June 26. *USA Today*. https://www.usatoday.com/story/news/nation/2013/06/25/supreme-court-baby-veronica-custody-native-american/2382699 (accessed May 4, 2017).

Wong, Julia C. (2016). "Standing Rock Protest: Hundreds Clash with Police Over Dakota Access Pipeline." November 21. *The Guardian*. https://www.theguardian.com/us-news/2016/nov/21/standing-rock-protest-hundreds-clash-with-police-over-dakota-access-pipeline (accessed May 5, 2017).

Wright, Joseph W. (2010). As transcribed in *Examining Bureau of Indian Affairs and Tribal Police Recruitment, Training, Hiring, and Retention*. March 18. Hearing before the Committee on Indian Affairs, United States Senate. Washington, D.C.: U.S. Government Printing Office. https://www.gpo.gov/fdsys/pkg/CHRG-111shrg58266/pdf/CHRG-111shrg58266.pdf (accessed May 4, 2017).

Young, Waste W. (2015). Letter to Army Corps of Engineers. February 25. Standing Rock Sioux Tribe, Tribal Historic Preservation Office, Administrative Service Center. https://puc.sd.gov/commission/dockets/HydrocarbonPipeline/2014/HP14-002/rebuttal/ien/winltr3.pdf (accessed May 5, 2017).

Zeleny, Jeff. (2008). "Obama Adopted by Native Americans." May 19. *The New York Times: The Caucus Section*. https://thecaucus.blogs.nytimes.com/2008/05/19/obama-adopted-by-native-americans (accessed May 4, 2017).

10 Law Enforcement Contact with Gangs, Victims of Human Trafficking, the Homeless, and the Mentally Ill

LEARNING OBJECTIVES

After reading this chapter, you should be able to:

- Describe the three types of major gangs and their level of criminal activity.
- Describe reasons for youth gang formation.
- Identify law enforcement strategies to reduce the gang problem.
- Define human trafficking and its impact on the victim.
- Describe physical and psychological health consequences of human trafficking.
- Identify law enforcement strategies to stop human trafficking.
- Define homelessness.
- Identify law enforcement strategies for responding to homelessness.
- Define mental illness.
- Explain police protocol for responding to mentally ill individuals.

OUTLINE

- Introduction
- Types of Gangs and Criminal Activity
- Reasons for Gang Formation
- Law Enforcement Strategies to Reduce Gang Problems
- Victims of Human Trafficking
- Physical and Psychological Health Consequences on Victims
- Law Enforcement Strategies to Stop Human Trafficking
- The Demographics of Homelessness
- Peacekeeping Responses to the Homelessness Crisis
- Understanding Dimensions of Mental Illness
- Police Protocol in Encounters with People Who Have Mental Illness
- Proactive Response Strategies between Police and People with Mental Illness
- Summary
- Discussion Questions and Issues
- References

INTRODUCTION

Gangs, victims of human trafficking, homeless persons, and people with mental illness are represented in most of America's multicultural cities and communities. Law enforcement officers have continual contact with members of these groups for assorted reasons: gangs—suspected criminal activity; human trafficking—victims; homelessness—loitering complaints by businesses; and people with mental illness—public nuisance complaints. Among people in all of these groups, there is a great deal of diversity; learning about the groups, in general, and then recognizing individual diversity, as with groups of every kind, can help safeguard against negative stereotypes and biases, which can lead to prejudicial law enforcement treatment.

Law enforcement's responsiveness to gang problems, human trafficking, and the challenges of homelessness and mental illness is an essential component of developing strategies for peacekeeping in a diverse society. Ongoing relationships with multicultural community leaders, nonprofit organizations, and other government entities are essential in law enforcement's ability to confront and deal with these societal issues. Community strategies for meeting law enforcement challenges of these multicultural groups and communities are critical to police departments' stated mission of serving the community.

TYPES OF GANGS AND CRIMINAL ACTIVITY

In 1982, only 27 percent of U.S. cities with populations of 100,000 or more had a reported gang problem (Miller, 1982/1992). In the mid-1980s, criminal gangs began to expand from urban cities to suburban areas and then to rural America. In 2017, the Federal Bureau of Investigation (FBI) reported approximately 33,000 criminally active gangs with about 1.4 million members in the United States and Puerto Rico (U.S. Federal Bureau of Investigation, 2017). This estimate has not changed from the 2013 count. U.S. gang composition is approximately 88 percent street gang members (includes neighborhood-based and national gangs), 9.5 percent prison gang members (includes federal and state corrections), and 2.5 percent outlaw motorcycle gang (OMG) members (NGIC, 2013).

Following are some key statistics and facts from a 2015 DOJ National Gang Intelligence Center report, based on gang data analysis and reporting from federal, state, local, and tribal law enforcement (NGIC, 2015):

- Approximately 50 percent of law enforcement agencies reported street gang membership and gang-related crime increases in their jurisdictions.
- Approximately 30 percent of jurisdictions report an increase in threats by gangs to law enforcement.
- Over 68 percent of correctional respondents indicate prison gang membership has increased.
- Approximately 26 percent of jurisdictions and 44 percent of prison facilities report gang members joined domestic extremist groups.
- Gang members' use of technology and social media has increased, enabling gangs to recruit prospects, communicate, locate rivals, and stall law enforcement efforts (social media includes Facebook, YouTube, Instagram, Twitter, and Snapchat).
- Over 54 percent of law enforcement agencies report using social media in gang investigations.

To help mitigate the growth of gangs and their criminal activity, the FBI, at the direction of Congress, facilitated the creation of the National Gang Intelligence Center (NGIC) in 2005. The NGIC compiles gang intelligence from federal, state, and local law enforcement on the growth, migration, criminal activity, and association of gangs that pose a significant threat to the United States. The NGIC consists of representatives from multiple federal departments: FBI, U.S. Drug Enforcement Administration (DEA), U.S. Bureau of Alcohol, Tobacco, Firearms, and Explosives (ATF), U.S. Bureau of Prisons (BOP), U.S. Department of Defense (DOD), and U.S. Customs and Border Protection (CBP). Its mission is to support law enforcement by disseminating timely information and provide strategic/tactical analysis of intelligence.

Definition of Gang

"Gang" is defined in various ways among law enforcement agencies and jurisdictions at all levels of government, from the local to the federal. The National Gang Center (NGC) provides a functional definition for law enforcement, using the five characteristics listed below. While there is some flexibility in the definition, researchers widely accept these five criteria for classifying groups as gangs (Decker & Curry, 2003; Esbensen, Winfree, He, & Taylor, 2001; Klein, 1995; Miller, 1982/1992; Spergel, 1995):

1. The group, particularly street gangs, has three or more members, generally aged 12 to 24.*
2. Members share an identity typically linked to a name, and often have shared symbols, such as style of clothing, graffiti, tattoos, and hand signs.
3. Members view themselves as a gang, and are recognized by others as a gang.
4. The group has some permanence and a degree of organization.
5. The group is involved in an elevated level of criminal activity (NGC, 2010).

Three Most Common Gangs and Definitions

The NGIC defines street gangs, prison gangs, and OMGs as follows:

STREET GANGS Street gangs are criminal organizations that form on the street and operate in neighborhoods throughout the country. Neighborhood-based gangs are confined to specific neighborhoods and jurisdictions, with no known membership beyond their communities. National-level gangs have a presence in multiple jurisdictions (NGIC, 2015).

Street gangs are the most common type of gang and control the greatest geographic area. They are represented in urban centers, rural communities and Indian Country. Street gangs commit violent crimes such as assault, drug trafficking, home invasions, homicide, intimidation, weapons trafficking, sex trafficking, and robbery. Juveniles join street gangs and actively participate in criminal behavior and violence; however, 65 percent of gang members identified by law enforcement agencies are 18 years or older compared to 35 percent who are under 18 (NGC, 2011).

PRISON GANGS A prison gang is a criminal organization that originates and operates in the U.S. penal system. Prison gangs are self-perpetuating criminal entities that extend their operations outside prison (NGIC, 2015).

National, regional, and local prison gangs are prevalent throughout U.S. federal and state prison systems. They are highly structured and organized networks, influencing prison operations and street gang crime. According to the NGIC, national-level prison gangs pose a major crime threat since most maintain some form of relationship with drug trafficking organizations (DTOs). Prison gang leaders strictly enforce established internal rules and codes of conduct (NGIC, 2013).

Because they are institutionalized, prison gang members, for the most part, cannot commit the same type of crimes as street gangs and OMG members. However, they have committed homicides, assaults, and other crimes against inmates and corrections staff. Prison gang members participate heavily in the smuggling of contraband, especially drugs, weapons, cell phones, and tobacco. Prison gang members have ties to DTOs and have control over many street gangs that traffic drugs and commit crimes on their behalf. Incarcerated members communicate to gang members on the outside through visitors, notes, defense attorneys, corrupt prison staff, court sessions, smuggled cell phones, institution phones, social media, and newly released inmates (NGIC, 2013). Moreover, prison gangs are structured along racial and ethnic lines and within state correctional facilities. Bloods, Crips, Sureños, Almighty Latin King and Queen Nation, and Gangster Disciples rank as the five most commonly reported prison gangs (NGIC, 2015).

---

* More common with street gangs.

OUTLAW MOTORCYCLE GANGS Outlaw Motorcycle Gang members must possess and be able to operate a motorcycle to achieve and maintain membership with the group. These gangs of three or more persons typically engage in a pattern of criminal conduct (ibid.).

Typically, OMGs are highly structured, organized networks whose members commit crimes such as violence against people and property, weapons trafficking, and drug trafficking. There are over 300 active OMGs in the United States and many of these chapters pose a serious domestic threat because of their strong associations with transnational DTOs and other criminal enterprises. OMG chapters have been involved in cross-border (Canada and Mexico) drug smuggling operations with major international DTOs (ibid.).

OMGs recruit from street gangs, prison gangs, and extremist groups. Black OMGs, in particular, are known to recruit from street gangs. Membership in an OMG usually results in fights with rival gangs and intra-gang violence. Many OMG members are employed in various white-collar professions and are business owners. Some OMGs use their businesses to facilitate their criminal enterprises. Member-owned businesses include: motorcycle repair shops, tattoo parlors, automobile repair facilities, bars (owner/operator), construction/general contractors, body guard/security/bouncers, and trucking/transportation entities (NGIC, 2015).

Criminal Activity

Exhibit 10.1 lists criminal activity associated with street gangs, prison gangs, and OMGs.

Street Gangs	Prison Gangs	Outlaw Motorcycle Gangs
Alien smuggling	Smuggling of contraband	Alien smuggling
Assault	(drugs, cigarettes, cell	Assault
Burglary	phones, inmates, and	Bribery
Check fraud	weapons)	Burglary
Child sex trafficking	Assault	Child sex trafficking
Counterfeiting	Corruption of prison staff	Counterfeiting
Credit card fraud	Extortion	Credit card fraud
Large-scale drug	Murder	Street-level drug sales
distribution	Prostitution	Large-scale drug distribution
Street-level drug sales	Racketeering	Drug shipment protection
Extortion	Robbery	Drug Manufacturing
Fencing stolen goods	Threats/intimidation	Explosive possession
Hate crimes/civil rights		Manufacturing of/trafficking
violations		in explosives
Home invasions		Extortion
Homicide		Fencing stolen goods
Human trafficking		Hate crimes/civil rights
Identify theft		violations
Larceny/theft		Homicide
Money laundering		Human trafficking
Mortgage fraud		Identity theft
Motor vehicle theft		Insurance fraud
Prescription fraud		Larceny/theft
Prostitution		Money laundering
Robbery		Mortgage fraud
Social Security fraud		Motor vehicle theft
Tax fraud		Prostitution
Threats/intimidation		Robbery
Weapons trafficking		Tax fraud
		Threats/intimidation
		Vandalism
		Weapons possession
		Weapons trafficking

EXHIBIT 10.1 Type of Criminal Activity Committed by Gangs
Source: National Gang Intelligence Center, 2015.

Cartel with strongest trafficking influence	Region
Sinaloa	West Coast, Midwest, Northeast
Gulf, Juarez, and Los Zetas	Southwest Border
BLO	East Coast

EXHIBIT 10.2   Cartel with Strongest Trafficking Influence
Source: Drug Enforcement Administration (2015a).

Mexican Drug Trafficking Organizations

U.S. law enforcement officials at federal, state, and local levels have been combating the flow of illegal drugs from Mexico and Central America's drug cartels or DTOs into the U.S. border states of California, Arizona, New Mexico, and Texas. Street gangs, prison gangs, and OMGs have fostered partnerships with these drug cartels. This remains an ongoing problem; U.S. law enforcement agencies have responded by using drug interdiction and other practices, resulting in countless arrests and drug seizures. Drug trafficking, human trafficking, and, most noticeably, the violence from these criminal activities have spilled over into local U.S. communities across the Mexico border and beyond.

Mexican transnational criminal organizations (TCOs) represent the biggest criminal drug threat to the United States. In 2015, the Drug Enforcement Agency (DEA) identified eight Mexican TCOs that traffic drugs such as heroin, methamphetamine, cocaine, and marijuana in at least 38 of the 50 states. The cells of these cartels include:

1. Sinaloa Cartel
2. Gulf Cartel
3. Juarez Cartel
4. Knights Templar (Los Caballeros Templarios or LCT)
5. Beltran-Leyva Organization (BLO)
6. Jalisco New Generation Cartel (Cartel Jalisco Nueva Generacion or CJNG)
7. Los Zetas
8. Las Moicas

Each cartel has cells throughout the United States. Exhibit 10.2 shows the ones with the strongest trafficking influence in the country's five regions.

According to the DEA's 2016 National Heroin Threat Assessment (NHTA) Summary, there were three times as many people using heroin in 2014 compared to users in 2007. The Centers for Disease Control and Prevention (CDC, 2017) data indicate that:

- Heroin-related overdose deaths more than quadrupled between 2010 and 2017.
- From 2014 to 2015, heroin overdose death rates increased by 20.6 percent, with nearly 13,000 people dying in 2015.
- In 2015, males aged 25 to 44 had the highest heroin death rate at 13.2 per 100,000, which was an increase of 22.2 percent from 2014.

The use of heroin by Mexican TCOs, street gangs, prison gangs, and OMGs have had a tragic impact on thousands of lives in the United States.

National and Regional Gangs

State, county, and city law enforcement agencies in multicultural jurisdictions are increasingly aware of local gangs. Additionally, law enforcement has identified several national-level gangs that are expanding and integrating into neighborhood gangs.

The Bloods were identified as the leader in recruitment, followed by:

- Crips,
- Sureños/La Eme,
- Latin Kings,
- United Blood Nation,

- Gangster Disciples,
- OMGs,
- Norteños/Nuestra Familia,
- Black P. Stone,
- Vice Lords (NGIC, 2013).

National-level Hispanic gangs, such as MS-13, La Eme, Sureños, and True Bloods, are the most criminally active along the southwest border region of the United States (ibid.). Along the entire U.S. northern border region with Canada, all major gang types—street, prison gangs, and OMGs, are criminally active. The northern border region also has several lesser known racially or geographically based gangs. For example, multiple sectors in the region reported the presence of Somali gangs such as the True Somali Blood and Somali Hot Boyz; Caribbean gangs, the Zoe Pound Gang, the Jamaican Posse; and Asian gangs, specifically the Asian Boyz (ibid.).

(See Appendix C for a list of national and regional gangs and their specific characteristics for the three major gangs listed. Appendix C also includes information about the ethnic gangs noted above.)

Gangs in the Military

It is not uncommon to find gang membership among military personnel and their dependents in the U.S. Armed Forces. As of June 2013, the National Gang Intelligence Center had identified at least 54 gangs whose members have served in or are affiliated with the U.S. military. According to the National Gang Intelligence Center, members from nearly every major street gang, as well as prison gangs and OMGs, have been identified in the U.S. military on both foreign and domestic installations. Gangs identified with military-trained members include:

- Bloods
- Crips
- Folk Nation
- Gangster Disciples
- Latin Kings
- MS-13
- Sureños
- Aryan Brotherhood (AB)
- Bandidos
- Hells Angels Motorcycle Club (HAMC)
- Outlaws
- Pagans
- Vagos Motorcycle Club (National Gang Intelligence Center, 2013).

Even though the actual numbers are unknown, military personnel and veterans who are gang members pose a risk to law enforcement, particularly if these gang members provide weapons and tactical training to other members. The military training of individual gang members could result in highly skilled and deadly gangs, as well as lethal attacks on rivals and law enforcement officers. Moreover, military personnel's access to weapons and their ability to move easily across U.S. borders makes them attractive for gang recruitment (NGIC, 2015).

Gangs in the Government

As in the military, gang membership exists in various levels of city, county, state, and federal government. In a report, entitled "OMGs and the Military 2014," the DOJ's Bureau of Alcohol, Tobacco, and Firearms (ATF) states:

> OMGs and their support clubs continue to court active-duty military personnel and government workers, both civilians and contractors, for their knowledge, reliable income, tactical skills and dedication to a cause. Through our extensive analysis, it has been revealed that many support clubs are utilizing active-duty military personnel and U.S. Department of Defense (DOD) contractors and employees to spread their tentacles across the United States. (U.S. Department of Justice, 2014)

It is unknown how many government employees are gang members, but many have been documented working for city, county, state, and federal agencies. The ATF report states that OMG members hold positions such as electricians, bus drivers, police department mechanics, and parking authority officials. The OMG employees may not have access to sensitive documents, but do have access to home addresses and vehicles owned and operated by local, state, and federal law enforcement. Examples of these gangs include:

- Down and Dirty
- Infidels
- Midgard Serpents
- Pagans
- Red Devils
- Wheels of Souls (ibid.).

Juvenile Gangs

The terms *youth* and *street gang* are commonly used interchangeably; however, the use of the term *street gang* rather than *youth gang* often results in confusing the latter with adult criminal organizations (NGC, 2011). Street gangs are composed of juveniles and young adults. Gangs have traditionally recruited juveniles because of their underage status, vulnerability, and the likelihood of their not serving long sentences in correctional facilities. Such groups as Gangster Rap gangs, often composed of juveniles, are being used to launder drug money through decoy legitimate businesses (ibid.).

Gangs in Indian Country

The size and number of criminal street gangs across Indian Country varies. Generally, smaller reservations have fewer active gangs, and membership tends to be low, often ranging from 5 to 25 individuals. However, on Indian Country's larger reservations, gangs are more prevalent. On the Navajo Nation Reservation, 60 to 70 active gangs have been identified, with approximately 1,500 to 2,500 persons claiming gang affiliation (U.S. Department of Justice, 2013). According to the NGIC, some regional gangs such as the Native Mob and Native Pride operate primarily in North Dakota, Minnesota, South Dakota, and Wisconsin. These gangs initially formed in the prison system, and then expanded to reservations.

NGIC data shows that national-level gangs such as the Barrio Azteca, Bloods, Crips, Mexican Mafia, and Norteños are operating on several reservations. In addition, due to the proximity of some reservations to Canada and Mexico, there is an ongoing problem of cross-border drug trafficking associated with gangs (NGIC, 2011). One such example is the Colville Indian Reservation in Washington—due to its border with Canada—it has a constant flow of drug trafficking throughout the reservation. TCOs transport cocaine, marijuana, and methamphetamine north and south through the region with the assistance of Hispanic gangs and OMGs (NGIC, 2013).

Racial and Ethnic Composition of Gangs

Over a period of 15 years, from 1996 to 2011, the racial and ethnic backgrounds of gang members were assessed in 10 National Youth Gang Surveys (NGC, 2011). The report findings throughout those years showed consistency in gang members' race and ethnic composition. Member percentages were disproportionately high for the general population of Hispanic/Latino Americans and African Americans, and extremely low for white Americans (see Exhibit 10.3). Appendix C provides further information on racial and ethnic characteristics of all three types of gangs. It is worth noting that, even though the numbers are reported to be low for white membership in the three major types of gangs, the numbers of white offenders are among the highest in hate/bias crimes in the United States (see Chapter 11).

OMGs and street gangs generally form alliances and rivalries based on race, geography, protection, resources, and control of criminal activities. Prison gangs most often form along racial and ethnic lines in state and federal correctional facilities (NGIC, 2015).

Year	Hispanic or Latino	Black or African American	White	Other
1996	45.2%	35.6%	11.6%	7.5%
1998	46.5%	33.6%	11.8%	8.0%
1999	47.3%	30.9%	13.4%	8.4%
2001	49%	33.7%	10.3%	7%
2002	47%	35.7%	10.4%	6.9%
2004	48.7%	37.8%	7.9%	5.7%
2005	50.1%	32.6%	9.5%	7.7%
2006	49.5%	35.2%	8.5%	6.8%
2008	50.2%	31.8%	10.5%	7.6%
2011	46.2%	35.3%	11.5%	7.0%

EXHIBIT 10.3   Race/Ethnicity of Gangs, 1996–2011
Source: National Gang Center (2011). Latest data available at this seventh edition.

Gender Makeup

In 2010, slightly over 92 percent of gang members were male and approximately 7 percent were female (National Gang Center, 2011). The NGC reported that these percentages had remained somewhat constant over the previous 12 years. The National Youth Gang Survey Analysis showed that nearly half the gangs outside larger cities had female gang members, compared with approximately one in four in the larger cities (ibid.). Females leave gang membership at an earlier age than most males (Gottfredson & Gottfredson, 2001; Thornberry, Krohn, Lizotte, Smith, & Tobin, 2003). Some observers attribute this early departure to maturity, and others to pregnancy. Another phenomenon noted in at least 25 states was the expansion of hybrid gangs that comprise multi-ethnic and mixed-gender members (ibid.).

Gang-Related Homicides

Homicides by drive-by shooting and other means have occurred in almost every city where there are criminal gangs. Exhibit 10.4 shows the number of gang-related homicides from 2007 to 2012. Multiple gang-related homicides usually occur more often in larger cities and suburban counties than in smaller cities and rural counties. The National Youth Gang Survey (NYGS) Analysis highlights gang-related homicides for the period of 2007 to 2012 (NGC, 2014):

1. The total number of gang-related homicides reported by law enforcement respondents in the NYGS sample averaged 2,000 annually from 2007 to 2012. During the same period (2007–2011), more than 15,500 homicides were committed across the United States. These numbers suggest that gang-related homicides typically account for around 13 percent of all homicides annually.
2. Highly populated areas accounted for the clear majority of gang homicides: nearly 67 percent occurred in cities with populations over 10,000, and 17 percent occurred in suburban counties in 2012.

2007	2008	2009	2010	2011	2012	Percent change, from previous 5-year average to 2012
1,975	1,659	2,083	2,020	1,824	2,363	23.6

EXHIBIT 10.4   Number of Gang-Related Homicides
Source: NGC (2014).

3. The number of gang-related homicides decreased 2 percent from 2010 to 2011 and then increased by 28 percent from 2011 to 2012 in cities with populations over 10,000.
4. In a typical year in the so-called "gang capitals" of Chicago and Los Angeles, around half of all homicides are gang-related; these two cities alone accounted for approximately one in four gang homicides recorded in the NGC from 2011 to 2012.
5. Among agencies serving rural counties and small cities that reported gang activity, around 75 percent reported zero gang-related homicides. About 5 percent or less of all gang homicides occurred in these areas annually.

According to multiple media and government sources, Chicago had 4,331 shooting victims and 762 murders in 2016. This is the highest number of homicides in Chicago since 1996. An increase in street gang criminal activity and violence, and a reluctance of the police department to take proactive action because of publicized police shootings were blamed for the increased shootings (Edwards, 2017; Gallagher & Shapiro, 2017).

Gun Use by Gangs

Law enforcement officers know that firearms play a key role in gang violence and that gang members are more likely to carry guns and use them. In a five-year study examining five cities with a high prevalence of gang homicides, the Centers for Disease Control and Prevention (CDC) analyzed data from the National Violent Death Reporting System (NVDRS) for firearms usage. The cities in the CDC study were Los Angeles, California; Oklahoma City, Oklahoma; Long Beach, California; Oakland, California; and Newark, New Jersey. The CDC findings showed that more than 90 percent of the gang-related homicides in each city involved firearms. Further, most of the shootings occurred in public places, which implies that they were quick and retaliatory (CDC, 2012).

REASONS FOR GANG FORMATION

Risk Factors for Gang Membership

Criminal justice professionals should be aware of risk factors that can result in young people becoming vulnerable to gang membership. The following five risk factors were identified by the combined efforts of Thornberry (1998); Esbensen (2000); Hill, Lui, and Hawkins (2001); and Howell and Egley (2005):

- Prior delinquency in violence and alcohol/drug use.
- Poor family management and problematic parent–child relations.
- Low school attachment and academic achievement, and negative labeling by teachers.
- Association with peers who engage in delinquency.
- Disorganized neighborhoods where large numbers of youth are in trouble and where drugs and firearms are readily available.

LAW ENFORCEMENT STRATEGIES TO REDUCE GANG PROBLEMS

In 1992, the FBI developed a National Gang Strategy designed to incorporate the investigative and prosecutorial practices proven successful in the Organized Crime/Drug Program National Strategy. By promoting coordination and information sharing between federal, state, and local law enforcement agencies, the FBI's Safe Streets and Gang Unit can identify violent gang enterprises that pose a significant threat and pursue these criminals with coordinated investigations that support successful prosecutions. The FBI's Safe Streets and Gang Unit administers 160 Violent Gang Safe Streets Task Forces throughout the United States (U.S Federal Bureau of Investigation, 2017). Likewise, state and local law enforcement agencies have been responding to the gang threat since their inception, but have not always maintained a consistent level of responsiveness. There are multiple reasons for this including the lack of budget, political support, effective resources, as well as the challenges of relentless gang threats.

Further resources and strategies to assist federal, state, and local law enforcement agencies in mitigating the gang threat can be found in Appendix D.

Largest Gang Arrest in U.S. History—Cross-Ethnic Example

On May 21, 2009, in the City of Hawaiian Gardens and nearby communities southeast of Los Angeles, California, approximately 1,400 federal, state, county, and city law enforcement officers arrested 88 Latino gang members. According to the Department of Justice, the multiagency operation was connected to several events or phenomena: the murder of a sheriff's deputy, racially motivated attacks on African Americans, and illicit drug trafficking. "Operation Knock Out," the largest gang arrest in U.S. history, led to federal indictments against 147 members and associates of the Latino gang, Varrio Hawaiian Gardens, whose members have ties to the Mexican Mafia. The investigation of the gang began in 2005, following the fatal shooting of L.A. County Sheriff's Deputy Jerry Ortiz by Varrio Hawaiian Gardens' gang member Jose Orozco. This occurred while Deputy Ortiz was attempting to arrest Orozco for the shooting of an African American male. After the shooting, Orozco was arrested for murder, convicted, and placed on death row. Prior to the massive arrests, 10 defendants were already in custody and 49 were still at large as fugitives or waiting to be located. Charges included violation of the federal RICO (Racketeer Influenced and Corrupt Organizations) Act, murder, attempted murder, drug trafficking, carjacking, extortion, kidnapping, and witness intimidation. Seventeen SWAT teams helped make the arrests, and police seized 105 firearms and 31 pounds of methamphetamines. Twenty-six children were taken into protective custody (U.S. Federal Bureau of Investigation, 2009; Glover & Winton, 2009).

This multiagency gang operation illustrates the need for law enforcement officers, especially in certain regions of the country, to familiarize themselves with the cultural, racial, and ethnic dimensions of gangs. Training academies and department management should commit to sustaining a focus on cross-cultural/ethnic gang activity, regularly updating training content.

"The Role of Gangs in Sex Trafficking" in the next section of this chapter supplements the above content on gangs (pp. 266–267).

VICTIMS OF HUMAN TRAFFICKING

Globally, including the United States, human trafficking in 2014 was $150-billion-per-year illicit industry that preyed off approximately 21 million victims of forced labor and sex trafficking (International Labour Organization, 2014). The International Labour Organization (ILO) estimated that 9.1 million (44 percent) victims of human trafficking were moved internally or internationally, while 11.8 million (56 percent) remained in their local areas. On average, human trafficking victims spend 18 months in their slavery; however, this may vary depending on the type of bondage (ibid.).

The available global data on human trafficking is grim, even without representing the true extent of the problem. The ILO identified the largest percentage of victims in Asia Pacific and Africa, but victims are throughout the world, including in North America (ibid.). The following is a global picture of modern-day slaves, victims in three broad categories:

- 7.1 million victims—forced labor in construction, manufacturing, and utilities, (50 percent of all trafficking victims)
- 3.5 million victims—forced labor in agriculture, forestry, and fishing, representing (25 percent)
- 3.4 million victims—domestic forced labor (24 percent) (ibid.)

Human trafficking, and especially sexual exploitation, is prevalent in the United States, though much of it is unreported or underreported, making it a challenge for law enforcement to identify. Victims are not only silenced by their traffickers, they fear going to the police, knowing or believing that they could be charged with a crime, especially prostitution. Yet, the 13th amendment to the United States Constitution, which was ratified in 1865, states the following:

> neither slavery nor involuntary servitude, except as a punishment for crime whereof the party shall have been duly convicted, shall exist with the United States, or any place subject to their jurisdiction. (The Library of Congress, 2015)

Human trafficking, also known as trafficking persons and modern-day slavery, is a crime under state, federal, and international law. The victims of human trafficking can be anyone—regardless of age, disability, race, religion, ethnic background, gender, gender identity, sexual orientation, social class, or citizenship status. Traffickers can also be anyone, including—organized crime, gangs, and family members as well as business owners, pimps, women and men, young and old, and people from any race or ethnic group. (See Chapter 5 for specific examples of human trafficking in Asian/Pacific American communities.)

Myths and Misconceptions of Human Trafficking

Many people are uninformed on the topic of human trafficking and base their views on myths and stereotypes, often perpetrated in movies. Law enforcement personnel specifically need to understand the common misconceptions around human trafficking that contribute to the tremendous degree of prejudice and bias that victims encounter.

The following are some common misconceptions of which law enforcement should be aware (International Association of Chiefs of Police, 2006). Following these myths is an example illustrating the inaccuracy of these assumptions.

Victims:

- …know what they are getting into.
- …commit unlawful acts.
- …are paid for services.
- …have freedom of movement.
- …are able to escape, but choose not to.

Kika Cerpa, was a young woman with an accounting background from Venezuela when she arrived in America as an immigrant. She was introduced to her boyfriend's cousin, Sandra, who promised her a job as a nanny. Sandra took Cerpa's passport and money, telling Cerpa that her boyfriend owed her money; and that Cerpa would have to pay it off by working. The next day, Sandra took Cerpa to a brothel in Queens, New York where Cerpa had sex with 20 men and Sandra kept the money. For one year, Cerpa lived in Sandra's house, unable to leave on her own, and being forced to rely on Sandra for food. Eventually Cerpa escaped, but ended up returning to the brothel because Sandra still had her passport. (Fuchs, 2014; United Nations Human Rights, 2017)

As the above example illustrates, officers need to be nonjudgmental as well as sensitive when it comes to relating to the victim. In addition to the myths noted above, there are other misconceptions about human trafficking that can result in officers' missing cues:

- Trafficking always involves the crossing of borders.
- U.S. citizens cannot be trafficked.
- The trafficker's actions are culturally appropriate (e.g., when the trafficker and victim are from the same background).
- When the trafficker and victim are relatives or are married, it's not trafficking (International Association of Chiefs of Police, 2006).

Federal Law Definition of Human Trafficking

The Trafficking Victims Protection Act of 2000 provides the legal definition of severe forms of trafficking in persons as found under Title 22 U.S.C. Chapter 78, Section 7102.

Signs of Human Trafficking

The Department of Homeland Security provides a checklist, which serves as a guide only, to recognize the signs of a human trafficking victim. Not all indicators are present in every situation, and the presence or absence thereof is not necessarily proof of human trafficking. If a person suspects someone to be a human trafficking victim, the Department of Homeland Security requests that a call be made to their 24/7 law enforcement hotline. Here are some

Extract from the definitions of Title 22 U.S.C. Chapter 78, Section 7102:

- Coercion
  The term "coercion" means

  (A) Threats of serious harm to or physical restraint against any person;
  (B) Any scheme, plan, or pattern intended to cause a person to believe that failure to perform an act would result in serious harm to or physical restraint against any person; or
  (C) The abuse or threatened abuse of the legal process.

- Commercial sex act
  The term "commercial sex act" means any sex act where something of value is given to or received by any person.

- Debt bondage
  The term "debt bondage" means the status or condition of a debtor arising from a pledge by the debtor of his or her personal services or of those of a person under his or her control as a security for debt, if the value of those services as reasonably assessed is not applied toward the liquidation of the debt or the length and nature of those services are not respectively limited and defined.

- Involuntary servitude
  The term "involuntary servitude" includes a condition of servitude induced by means of

  (A) Any scheme, plan, or pattern intended to cause a person to believe that if the person did not enter or continue in such condition, that person or another person would suffer serious harm or physical restraint; or
  (B) The abuse or threatened abuse of the legal system.

- Severe forms of trafficking in persons
  The term "severe forms of trafficking in persons" means

  (A) Sex trafficking in which a commercial sex act is induced by for, fraud, or coercion, or in which the person induced to perform such act has not attained 18 years of age; or
  (B) The recruitment, harboring, transportation, provision, or obtaining of a person for labor or services, by force, fraud, or coercion to subject them to involuntary servitude, peonage, debt bondage, or slavery.

(10) Sex trafficking

  The term "sex trafficking" means the recruitment, harboring, transportation, provision, obtaining, patronizing, or soliciting of a person for a commercial sex act. (U.S. Code, House of Representatives, 2017)

common indicators to help recognize human trafficking (U.S. Department of Homeland Security, 2017):

- Does the person appear disconnected from family, friends, community organizations, or houses of worship?
- Has a child stopped attending school?
- Has the person had a sudden or dramatic change in behavior?
- Is a juvenile engaged in commercial sex acts?
- Is the person disoriented or confused, or showing signs of mental or physical abuse?
- Does the person have bruises in various stages of healing?
- Is the person fearful, timid, or submissive?
- Does the person show signs of having been denied food, water, sleep, or medical care?
- Is the person often in the company of someone to whom he or she defers or someone who seems to be in control of the situation, e.g., where they go or who they talk to?
- Does the person appear to be coached on what to say?
- Is the person living in unsuitable conditions?
- Does the person lack personal possessions and appear to have an unstable living situation?
- Does the person have freedom of movement? Can the person freely leave where they live? Are there unreasonable security measures?

The Role of Gangs in Sex Trafficking

One of the least studied aspects of human trafficking in the United States is the role of gangs in sex trafficking. In a three-year research project, data was analyzed from hundreds of current and former gang members, schools, law enforcement agencies, and victim service providers in San Diego County. The 2016 study involved more than 1,250 subjects, making it, at that time, one of the largest, most comprehensive U.S. human trafficking case studies. The large-scale model of collaborative research conducted by the University of San Diego serves as a national model for designing future research on human trafficking (National Institute of Justice, 2016). Study results include:

- **Gang involvement:** At least 110 gangs were involved in the exploitation of individuals for commercial sex in San Diego. An estimated 85 percent of pimps/sex-trafficking facilitators in the area are gang members.
- **Victimization:** San Diego County had between approximately 9,000 and 12,000 victims/survivors of sex trafficking every year, with an average of nearly 2,000 law enforcement contacts.
- **Regional commercial sex economy:** Sex trafficking produced an estimated $810 million annually in San Diego, making it the second-largest underground economy after drug trafficking ($4.76 billion annually).
- **Clients:** Based on interviews conducted with sex traffickers in prison, demand was widespread and clients of commercial sex came from all socioeconomic and ethnic backgrounds.
- **Recruitment:** Significant recruitment occurred on high school and middle school campuses and the average age of entry into child sexual exploitation for commercial gain was 15. (Ibid.)

Passage of California Senate Bill 1322

To protect juvenile victims from being charged as criminals for commercial sexual exploitation or prostitution, lawmakers in California passed Senate Bill 1322, which became law on January 1, 2017. This new law, the first of its kind in the United States, allows law enforcement officers or judges to place juvenile victims of commercial sexual exploitation with California's Department of Social Services, rather than arrest and charge juveniles with prostitution. It remains unlawful for a person under the age of 18 to consent to sexual intercourse in the State of California. Moreover, California's current Welfare and Institutions Code 300(b)(2) requires that if an officer determines that a minor is in an unsafe situation, he or she is required to remove the child from harm (State of California Legislature, 2016). According to the law's author, California State Senator Holly Mitchell:

> Minors involved in prostitution are victims and we have a moral responsibility to provide them with a safe placement that protects them. Juvenile hall is not that place. Being criminalized as opposed to being treated like a victim of rape through, detainment and criminal charges is not how California treats victims of abuse. It would never occur to us to arrest a victim of rape or domestic violence to keep them safe from their perpetrator. Today, we provide victims with safe shelters and wrap around services. SB 1322 will provide minor victims of human trafficking the same protection. (Mitchell, 2016)

Documenting the Extent of Human Trafficking

Nationally, government reporting or collection of human trafficking data was nonexistent until January 2013, when the Uniform Crime Report Program of the Federal Bureau of Investigation began collecting offense and arrest data regarding human trafficking as

---

Extract is from the U.S. State Department Trafficking in Person's Report, June 2016 on Vacatur

In cases in which trafficking victims have records for crimes committed as a result of being subjected to trafficking, such records should be vacated or expunged. In the United States, several states have enacted provisions that provide survivors the ability to seek a court order vacating or expunging criminal convictions entered against them that resulted from their trafficking situation. In 2010, New York became the first state to pass a law allowing survivors of trafficking to vacate their convictions for prostitution offenses. In 2013, Florida's law went even further providing for the expungement of "any conviction for an offense committed while...a victim of human trafficking."

Vacatur is the formal recognition of "factual innocence." Vacatur laws should apply to both adults and children, given that anyone who has been forced, tricked, or coerced into criminal activity should not be considered as having consented to that activity. States should also ensure these laws cover convictions that encompass the wide variety of nonviolent crimes that victims are forced to commit.

These laws not only allow victims to correct past injustices, but also thereby help trafficking victims reclaim and rebuild their lives. Vacatur increases a survivor's ability to find work, reducing their economic vulnerabilities and the risk of being re-trafficked. In the absence of a vacatur law, trafficking victims are condemned to being perpetually viewed as former criminals, which in numerous ways compromises their efforts to rebuild their lives (U.S. State Department, 2016).

authorized by the William Wilberforce Trafficking Victims Protection Reauthorization Act of 2008. The act required the FBI to collect human trafficking offense data from all states on a voluntary basis and created two additional offenses in the Summary Reporting System and National Incident-Based Reporting System. The Summary Reporting System provides number of offenses, clearances by arrest, juvenile or adult status, gender, race, and ethnicity of the suspect; it doesn't provide victim information or details of the offense. To aid law enforcement in combating human trafficking, the National Incident-Based Reporting System provides victim and suspect details. On the other hand, about 30 percent of law enforcement agencies use this system to submit information to the FBI. Missing in both reporting systems is the category of sexual orientation of both the victim and suspect. This is significant because many victims are LGBTQ. The following definitions for the two additional offenses are adapted from the federal law's definition of "severe forms of trafficking in persons" (FBI: UCR, 2016a):

> **Human Trafficking/Commercial Sex Acts:** inducing a person by force, fraud, or coercion to participate in commercial sex acts, or in which the person induced to perform such act(s) has not attained 18 years of age.

> **Human Trafficking/Involuntary Servitude:** the obtaining of a person(s) through recruitment, harboring, transportation, or provision, and subjecting such persons by force, fraud, or coercion into involuntary servitude, peonage, debt bondage, or slavery (not to include commercial sex acts).

As part of a training program on sex trafficking for law enforcement officers and prosecutors, Prosecutor Glen Ujifusa, a deputy district attorney from the Multnomah County District Attorney's Office, Portland, Oregon, asks his audience four questions to assess if their areas have a sex trafficking problem. The questions are:

1. Do you have Internet in your area?
2. Do individuals in your area have disposable incomes?
3. Do individuals in your area want more money?
4. Do individuals in your area like sex?

Prosecutor Ujifusa indicated that if all four responses are "yes," there is a strong likelihood that sex trafficking is occurring in the law enforcement officers' communities. He added that most major cities and small towns have sex trafficking problems, and as suggested previously, extreme caution should be used when analyzing the statistics. It has been Prosecutor Ujifusa's experience that law enforcement officers often discover sex trafficking victims on other types of calls, including domestic violence, runaway reports, and shoplifting.

FBI UCR Summary and National Incident-Based Reporting Systems—2015

The FBI began collecting human trafficking data in 2013 and, at that time, most states did not submit any information. In 2015 (the most recent year for which data are available), only 20 states submitted data in the UCR Summary Reporting System Program (FBI: UCR, 2016b) and 9 out of 50 states submitted data in the National Incident-Based Reporting System (FBI: UCR, 2016e); therefore, reports of human trafficking don't even begin to reflect the true numbers of cases. The FBI concedes that many of the crimes are never reported to law enforcement. In order to have full understanding of human trafficking, it is necessary to gather information from victim service organizations who try to serve the needs of the victims (FBI: UCR, 2016a).

Federal Law Enforcement Human Trafficking Data

In addition to investigating and enforcing federal laws specific to their agency, the following agencies also investigate and enforce human trafficking crimes: the FBI; the Homeland Security Investigations (HSI) of the Department of Homeland Security; Department of State's Bureau of Diplomatic Security; Department of Labor's Inspector General; and the Department of Defense's Criminal Investigative Service which encompasses the U.S. Armed Forces service members, department contractors, and civilians. The combined total of investigations among the federal agencies was over 2,000, and resulted in 4,113 arrests (U.S. Government Accounting Office, 2016).

Established in 2007, the National Human Trafficking Hotline (NHTH) receives calls, e-mails, and online tip data about human trafficking, and shares information, referrals, and options for victims and survivors. Trained advocates take reports of trafficking and pass information to the appropriate authorities. The toll-free hotline operates 24 hours a day, 7 days a week and offers more than 200 languages to its callers. The NHTH is operated by Polaris, a nonprofit, nongovernmental organization that receives funding by the Department of Health and Human Services and other private donors.

In 2016, the NHTH received nearly 27,000 calls, with approximately 7,500 human trafficking cases being reported. According to hotline data from that year, the following types of human trafficking were tracked (numbers are approximate):

- Sex Trafficking (5,500)
- Labor Trafficking (1,000)
- Sex and Labor (300)
- Other Unspecified Types of Trafficking (700)

The NHTH logged the following characteristics for the 2016 victim callers:

- The majority were female (over 6,000 females; nearly 1,000 males);
- A small percentage were gender minorities (70);
- Nearly twice as many adults as children (nearly 5,000 adults and 2,500 children);
- More U.S. citizens than foreign nationals (approximately 2,000 were U.S. Citizens and 1,400 were foreign nationals).

The top five industries reported for labor trafficking were domestic work, agriculture, traveling sales crews, restaurants/food service, and health/beauty services. Data showed that the top venues for sex trafficking or for marketing sex trafficking included hotels/motels, commercial-front and residential brothels, and online ads (NHTH, 2017).

Why Victims Do Not Self-Report Human Trafficking

Many victims of human trafficking do not report their victimization, causing law enforcement to rely upon investigation and tips from the public. This makes it difficult to investigate and calculate the number of crimes that have taken place. Moreover, many victims do not consider themselves victims. Reasons for the reluctance to self-report include the following (U.S. Department of Justice, 2017):

1. Both minor and adult victims are isolated and have been coached by their trafficker to fear law enforcement, or lie about their circumstances.
2. Victims may fear law enforcement because of their participation in illegal activities, such as prostitution, or, in the case of foreign victims, their undocumented status or experiences with corrupt authorities in their home country.
3. Traffickers exploit these fears by threatening the victim with arrest or deportation if encountered by law enforcement.
4. The victim escapes other problems, such as an abusive family, drug addiction, or extreme poverty; the trafficker exploits these problems to ensure the victim's compliance.
5. Traffickers exploit control specific vulnerabilities of their victims, which can include preexisting psychological trauma, drug dependency, disabilities, homelessness, dislocation, and isolation.
6. Traffickers control their victims through force, fraud, coercion, forced drug use, violence, threats, intimidation, debt bondage, and passport confiscation.

Labor Trafficking Settings

Based on FBI investigations, labor trafficking is generally found in low-skilled or temporary worker labor arrangements—including agriculture, traveling sales crews, and restaurant and food service. About one-third of the FBI's labor trafficking investigations are domestic servitude, such as compelling the victim to work in a home cooking, cleaning, elder care, child care, or other domestic labor. Even though some of the victims are U.S. citizens, most of the FBI's labor investigations involve foreign-born victims. In the FBI's cases, most labor trafficking victims from outside of the United States come from Mexico, China, and the Philippines (ibid.).

Sex Trafficking Settings

Sex traffickers, also known as pimps, use many different venues and contexts for sex trafficking their victims, which include (U.S. Department of Justice, 2016, 2017):

- Street prostitution
- Prostitution facilitated through online advertising
- Escort services to hotels or residences
- Prostitution in cantinas, casinos, group homes, karaoke bars, massage parlors, nightclubs, residences, strip clubs, truck stops, or other entertainment venues

Child Sex Trafficking

To convict an offender of child sex trafficking, a prosecutor only needs to show that the victim is under 18 years old. The prosecutor does not have to prove that the victim was subjected to force, fraud, or coercion, nor does it require that the child victim was moved across state lines. (Of course, if the offender did all these things, the prosecutor will enter this as evidence if it goes to trial.) Traffickers actively recruit children because they are easier to control, receive a higher profit, and usually have fewer sexually transmitted diseases. The most frequent places traffickers recruit victims from are bus stops, train stations, and schools. Generally, traffickers target minors from broken homes or runaways. Victims often succumb to traffickers who attract them with food, clothes, attention, friendship, love, and the perception of a safe place to sleep. Once a trafficker gains control in the relationship through the loyalty of a minor, he or she often uses acts of violence, intimidation, or psychological manipulation to force the child to become and remain a prostitute. Many of the traffickers are gang members and have a history of committing violent crimes (U.S. Department of Justice, 2016).

Homeless Youth and Human Trafficking

Research results from a 2017 study showed that one out of five homeless youth have been victims of human trafficking. Of the approximate 900 individuals, ages 17 to 24, from across 11 U.S. cities and two cities in Canada:

- 19.4 percent of homeless youth were victims of human trafficking—15 percent trafficked for sex, 7.4 percent trafficked for labor, and 3 percent trafficked for both;
- 34 percent of LGBTQ homeless youth had survived human trafficking, although they accounted for only 19 percent of the interview pool;
- 27 percent of LGBTQ youth—more than one in four—had been trafficked for sex;
- 50 percent of LGBTQ homeless youth were engaged in the sex trade at some point in their lives;
- 66 percent of the youth engaged in commercial sex did so when they did not have a safe place to stay (Edward, 2017; Ryan, 2017).

Disparate Treatment toward LGBTQ Youth in Sex Trafficking

Nongovernmental organizations continue to report that runaway and homeless LGBTQ youth have difficulties accessing nondiscriminatory community services. Furthermore, LGBTQ victims are less likely to report their exploitation to local law enforcement or to access needed services (U.S. Department of State, 2016). LGBTQ youth who are not self-sufficient are more susceptible to traffickers' offers of food or shelter in exchange for performing commercial sex acts. Due to societal biases, LGBTQ sex trafficking victims are more likely to be arrested by law enforcement for prostitution compared to heterosexual sex trafficking victims (ibid.). Law enforcement needs to become more aware of the bias against LGBTQ victims, and develop sensitivity and compassion toward these young people.

PHYSICAL AND PSYCHOLOGICAL HEALTH CONSEQUENCES ON VICTIMS

Sex Trafficking Victims

To measure the physical and psychological health consequences of sex trafficking on victims, researchers surveyed 107 surviving victims across 12 U.S. cities. Study results showed that 92 percent of the victims had neurological symptoms and 69 percent reported physical injuries (i.e., from being punched, beaten, kicked, and raped); two-thirds of the victims had contracted a sexually transmitted disease. Additional survey data from the surviving sex trafficking victims showed that:

- 86 percent had at least one symptom impacting their general health
- 67 percent had at least one cardiovascular/respiratory symptom
- 62 percent had at least one gastrointestinal symptom
- 54 percent had at least one dental symptom
- 81 percent experienced depression
- 71 percent felt shame and guilt
- 62 percent had Post-Traumatic Stress Disorder
- 21 percent had attempted suicide (Lederer & Wetzel, 2014)

Mental Health Needs

The physical and psychological abuse human trafficking victims (forced labor and sex) experience from their traffickers often lead to serious mental or emotional health problems. Victims commonly have feelings of severe guilt, post-traumatic stress disorder, depression, anxiety, substance abuse (alcohol or narcotics), and eating disorders. In addition to receiving medical care for physical injuries and illnesses, human trafficking victims often require psychological care as part of their comprehensive medical treatment. Providing culturally appropriate and trauma-informed mental health treatment is complicated. Some of the barriers to and difficulties in helping victims with their trauma include (Office for Victims of Crime, 2017a):

- Limited availability and access to appropriate mental health services.
- Staff challenges in establishing trusting relationships with survivors.
- Mandated mental health treatment efforts, including in locked treatment facilities, can be counterproductive when working with victims.
- Co-occurrence of trauma, diagnosed mental health conditions, and substance abuse or addiction.
- Long history of multiple types of abuse (physical, sexual, mental, etc.).
- Victim perceptions that they have not been abused (and, therefore, did not attempt to escape).
- Cultural, linguistic barriers and isolation from home community.

LAW ENFORCEMENT STRATEGIES TO STOP HUMAN TRAFFICKING

United States Government

The United States is one of 170 countries that has ratified the United Nations Trafficking Persons Protocol. The Protocol became effective in December 2003 and is an international legal instrument, requiring member countries to criminalize and prosecute human trafficking crimes (United Nations, 2016).

President Barrack Obama signed into law the Justice for Victims of Trafficking Act of 2015. The act, among other requirements, mandated that the U.S. attorney general oversee that federal law enforcement officers and prosecutors receive anti-trafficking training; required the Federal Judicial Center, the research and education agency of the federal judicial system, to provide training for judges on ordering restitution for victims of certain trafficking-related offenders under Chapter 77 of Title 18, U.S. Code; mandated that the secretary of Homeland Security implement a human trafficking training program for department personnel; required the U.S. attorney general to implement and maintain a national strategy for combating human trafficking; established the Domestic Trafficking Victim's Fund to supplement existing statutorily authorized grants or activities; and amended the federal definition of child abuse to include human trafficking (U.S. Code, 2017).

Action Agenda Checklist

Police executives and managers need to be proactive in finding ways to stop human trafficking in their jurisdictions. The International Association of Chiefs of Police (IACP) has developed a document, "The Crime of Human Trafficking: A Law Enforcement Guide to Identification and Investigation," containing helpful information for departments (IACP, 2006). The following is an action agenda checklist:

1. Conduct department-wide training, including dispatch, on human trafficking.
2. Educate your community about the crime of human trafficking.
3. Develop foreign-language resources for your department.
4. Identify nonprofit agencies that provide victim assistance.
5. Develop collaborative relationships before a human trafficking case occurs.
6. Assess locations that may serve as fronts for illegal activity.
7. Identify industrial/service-based businesses that employ low-paid workers and learn how they are recruited and treated.
8. Assess the local sex industry in your community and the forms it takes (e.g. street prostitution, massage parlors, strip clubs).
9. Identify escort agencies in your community that advertise foreign or "exotic" women.
10. Ensure officers responding to prostitution offenses address and document possible indicators of human trafficking.
11. Locate neighborhoods or communities where domestic servants are typically employed (ibid.).

Human Trafficking Incident Investigations

Law enforcement agencies must make it a priority to investigate all reports of human trafficking offenses. Agencies must have written policies and procedures to ensure that their officers are properly trained and follow the investigative guidelines for labor and sex trafficking. With this come the expectations that officers be sensitive and responsive to the medical, emotional, and mental health needs of the victim. Requests for victim advocates should be immediate and not delayed. It is essential that police officers, from the responding patrol officer to the assigned detective, be respectful and nonjudgmental toward the victim. The IACP states:

> Victims will need to feel safe before being able to assist in the investigation and prosecution of offenders. Victims may be in danger because of a variety of factors, including the extent of the trafficking operation, the trafficker's perception of how damaging a victim's testimony may be, and the trafficker's propensity to use violence. You will need to work with victims to address and plan for their safety. In instances where the victim's safety or health is at risk, it may be best to remove them from the situation immediately. If arrests are made, take care not to re-traumatize the victim. If no arrests are made, work to build a relationship so the victim will trust you or another officer in the future. (Ibid.)

Protocol for Successful Interviews

To increase the chances of successfully interviewing victims of human trafficking, the IACP makes several recommendations:

1. Be aware that traffickers might not be easy to distinguish from victims and understand that some victims may have had to "collaborate" to survive.
2. Educate yourself on trauma, its impact and effects or collaborate with a trauma specialist to assist with interviews.
3. Adopt a compassionate and nonjudgmental manner.
4. Conduct interviews with victims/witnesses while in plainclothes if possible.
5. Conduct interviews individually and in private, remembering that the victim may need a counselor or attorney present for support.

6. When an interpreter is needed, select a skilled interpreter who you are confident is in no way connected to the traffickers.
7. Do not begin your interview with documentation or legal status as this may frighten or confuse the victim and interfere with building trust.
8. Do not ask "Are you a slave?" or "Are you a trafficking victim?"
9. Allow interviewees to describe what happened to their counterparts before focusing on the victims' own suffering; initially, it is often easier for them to talk about what happened to other people.
10. Provide victims the opportunity to tell their story; it may help them to do so (ibid.).

Police Chiefs, sheriffs, and directors of state law enforcement must collaborate with each other and federal law enforcement agencies in the detection, investigation, arrest, and prosecution of human traffickers in their jurisdictions. If specialized training is required on human trafficking investigations, agency law enforcement executives need to be accountable for their officers receiving that training at the federal or local level. Furthermore, law enforcement leaders should be well versed in the national strategy for combatting human trafficking, and communicate this strategy to their employees and local prosecutors. (Chapter 11, pp. 327–328, presents information on interacting with victims; this information is highly applicable to victims of human trafficking.)

Victim Service Providers

Survivors of human trafficking should be at the center of any response to human trafficking. All victims deserve to feel safe and supported. Quality care, compassionate responses, and essential services are needed to help survivors recover from their victimization. Creating conditions of trust and respect will help victims reclaim their lives and help them move toward self-sufficiency and independence.

Trafficking victims typically need numerous types of emergency and long-term services. These include, but are not limited to, intensive case management, victim advocacy, housing, food, medical and dental care, mental health treatment, substance abuse treatment, support groups, interpretation/translation services, immigration and other legal assistance, literacy education, and employment and training services.

No one agency can respond to all aspects of the crime of human trafficking and the individualized needs of every victim.

A coordinated, community-wide and multidisciplinary response is needed.

Everyone has a role! Victims of human trafficking are regularly identified and served by individuals working in child welfare systems, runaway and homeless youth programs, immigrant and refugee service programs, sexual assault programs, and domestic violence shelters. You do not need to be a specialized human trafficking service provider to provide good services for victims of human trafficking. However, it is critically important that when you do engage with victims, you should know what resources are available within your community and provide services that are trauma-informed, victim-centered, and tailored to the specific needs of trafficking victims.

Source: Office for Victims of Crime, 2017b.

Mini Case Study: FBI Announces Results of Operation Cross County X

Chapter 5 referenced "Operation Cross Country X" as an example of law enforcement's successful efforts to combat human trafficking. Read the following details of this FBI-led operation and answer the questions at the end of the summary.

Details of Operation Cross County X

As a result of "Operation Cross County X," an international law enforcement effort, focusing on underage human trafficking, 82 minors were rescued and 239 traffickers were arrested in the United States. The FBI-led operation ran from October 13 to 15, 2016. Additionally, law enforcement agencies in Cambodia, Canada, the Philippines, and Thailand conducted their own operation.

U.S. operations took place in several locations, including hotels, truck stops, and on the streets. Juveniles rescued during a trafficker arrest were helped by state protective services and victim assistance. Adults arrested on state charges were processed by state and local law enforcement; adults arrested on federal charges were processed by federal law enforcement.

As part of the operation in Georgia, the FBI's Metro Atlanta Child Exploitation Task Force executed two search warrants; seized seven firearms; rescued one juvenile victim in Lake City, Georgia; and arrested 15 pimps/traffickers as well as 54 prostitutes. The ages of those arrested ranged from 19 to 55.

Operations in Athens, Georgia resulted in the arrest of five adults who were traveling in furtherance of having sex with a minor child. Two firearms were seized. The ages of the adults were between 22 and 66. No information was available on the victims.

Operations in Augusta, Georgia, resulted in the arrest of one pimp/trafficker.

Arrests were made in Atlanta of two fugitives, wanted out of Orlando, Florida, for the murder of a 14-year-old sex trafficking victim and the exploitation of a 15-year-old victim. The suspects were a 26-year-old male and a 20-year-old female.

"Operation Cross County X" is part of the FBI's Innocence Lost Initiative, which began in 2003 and operates year-round to rescue trafficking victims that are minors. "Operation Cross County X" is the largest operation in the history of the initiative with 55 FBI field offices and 71 state and local task forces participating in 106 cities across the United States. Internationally, several dozen operations were conducted in Canada, and approximately 10 operations took place in six cities across Cambodia, Thailand, and the Philippines.

Assisting the FBI in Georgia were 12 city police departments, eight county sheriff's departments, two county district attorney offices, Georgia Bureau of Investigation, Georgia Attorney General's Office, Georgia Department of Community Supervision, Georgia Department of Family and Children Services, and four nongovernmental service organizations.

Source: U.S. Federal Bureau of Investigation, 2016.

Answer the following questions:

1. Why was Operation X focused on underage human trafficking?
2. How many adults were arrested for prostitution? Could the adults who were arrested for prostitution have been victims of sex trafficking? What type of questions would you ask to determine if they were sex trafficking victims?
3. What does the age range imply for those adults arrested for sex trafficking?
4. What does the age range imply for those adults arrested for traveling in furtherance of having sex with a minor child?
5. How could the participation of multiple law enforcement agencies illustrate the national strategy for combating human trafficking?
6. What role would the Department of Family and Children Services have in this operation?

THE DEMOGRAPHCS OF HOMELESSNESS

Introduction

Dealing with the homeless is not a new task for U.S. law enforcement. In repeated acts of humane and compassionate treatment, the Philadelphia Police Department offered their station precincts as shelter to more than 100,000 homeless people a year during the 1880s (Monkkonen, 1981). Almost a century later, in the 1980s, U.S. cities started noticing a significant increase of homeless people and blamed the recession as one of the major causes. According to the National Law Center on Homelessness and Poverty (NLCHP), approximately 3.5 million people, including over 1 million school-aged children, experience homelessness each year (NLCHP, 2015).

Estimated Count of Homeless on a Single Night

Every year, the U.S. Department of Housing and Urban Development (HUD) releases its "Point-In-Time" (PIT) estimate on data reported by community-wide organizations across the United States on the scope of homelessness over the course of one night every January. These local planning organizations provide "Continuum of Care" programs, the staff of which are responsible for coordinating homelessness services in a geographic area, which may include a city, county, metropolitan area, or an entire state. The following are 2016 key findings of HUD's estimated number of homeless on a single night (U.S. Department of Housing and Urban Development, 2016):

1. In January 2016, there were nearly 550,000 homeless nationwide, representing a decrease of 3.0 percent from a year earlier; homelessness declined by 15 percent overall between 2007 and 2016. The counting in 2007 was not as comprehensive; in earlier years, it did not include those in unsheltered locations, emergency shelters, transitional housing programs, or safe havens.
2. Individuals (i.e., not families) represented 65 percent of the homeless population, a decline of less than 1.0 percent from 2015.
3. People in family households with children represented 35 percent of the homeless. On average, a homeless family consisted of three people. This is a decline of 6 percent from 2015.

4. Veterans represented about 10 percent of the homeless population. This had dropped by 17 percent since January 2015. This reduction was due, in part, by HUD housing vouchers as well as case management through the Department of Veterans Affairs.
5. People experiencing long-term or chronic homelessness was close to 22 percent, and had declined 7 percent from 2015.
6. Unsheltered homelessness (street homelessness) was 32 percent, representing an increase of 2 percent from 2015.
7. Sheltered homelessness (i.e., emergency shelters, transitional housing programs, or safe havens) was 68 percent. There was a decline of 5 percent from 2015.
8. Five states accounted for almost half of the nation's homeless population in 2016:

   • California, 22 percent (of total homeless population) or approximately 118,000 people;
   • New York, 16 percent or approximately 86,000;
   • Florida, 6 percent or approximately 34,000;
   • Texas, 4 percent or approximately 23,000 people;
   • Washington, with 4 percent or approximately 21,000.

Exhibit 10.5 shows the estimates of homeless people by state.

Criticism on the Estimated Counts of the Homeless

Advocates for the homeless believe the HUD PIT estimates are low and do not accurately track the homeless population numbers. As noted by the National Coalition for the Homeless (NCH), the PIT method only counts those who are homeless at a specific time. The number may stay stable, but the population can change greatly because some homeless may secure housing while others become newly homeless. An alternative to the PIT method would be "Period Prevalence Counts" (PPC), which would examine the number of people who are homeless over a period (National Coalition for the Homeless, 2009). The NCH points out that another problem with studies of the homeless include only counting people who are in shelters or on the streets. Although this approach may provide useful information about the number of people who use services such as shelters and soup kitchens, it can often result in under-reporting the number of homeless who may be living in cars or alternative places (ibid.).

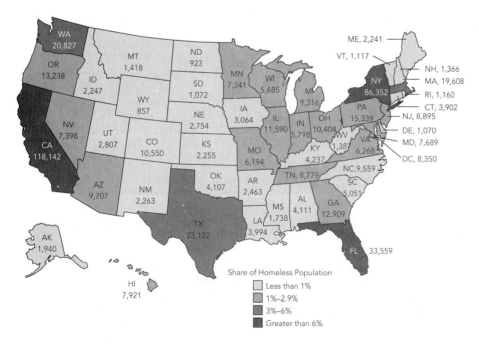

EXHIBIT 10.5 Estimates of Homeless People by State, 2016
Source: U.S. Department of Housing and Urban Development, 2016.

Hunger and Homelessness in U.S. Cities

In December 2016, the U.S. Conference of Mayors released its "Hunger and Homelessness Survey." Thirty-two cities were surveyed in 24 states from September 2015 to August 2016. Key findings include (U.S. Conference of Mayors, 2016):

1. Survey data revealed that 71 percent of the cities surveyed saw an increase in the number of people requesting food assistance for the first time.
2. Among those requesting food assistance:
   - 63 percent were from families
   - 51 percent were employed
   - 18 percent were elderly
   - 8 percent were homeless
3. It was estimated that 14 percent of the people needing emergency food assistance did not receive it.
4. Survey data revealed the three main causes of hunger were low wages, high housing costs, and poverty.
5. In the 32 cities surveyed, the average rate of homelessness was 51 per 10,000 people compared to the national rate of 17 people per 10,000.
6. Most survey cities identified the need for more housing assistance and affordable housing to reduce homelessness.
7. The study cities were only able to provide shelter to approximately 80 percent of their homeless population with emergency shelters.

In 2015, there were 43.1 million people living in poverty in the United States, 3.5 million fewer than in 2014 (U.S. Census Bureau, 2016).

Race, Ethnicity, Gender, and Age

In 2016, the HUD PIT estimated racial and ethnic breakdown of the homeless population to be:

- 48 percent white
- 39 percent African American
- 22 percent Hispanic American
- 7 percent multiracial
- 3 percent Native American
- 2 percent Pacific Islander
- 1 percent Asian American

With respect to gender, HUD estimated the following:

- 60 percent were men
- 40 percent were women
- less than 1 percent was transgender

HUD's estimated age breakdown was as follows:

- 22 percent were under the age of 18 years
- 9 percent were between 18 and 24 years
- 89 percent were over 24 years

Exhibit 10.6 illustrates gender, ethnicity, and race for sheltered and unsheltered people.

LGBTQ Youth

Different studies indicate that LGBTQ youth represent between 20 and 40 percent of homeless youth (Youth, 2017). The 2017 information on homeless LGBTQ youth showed (NAEH, 2017):

- LGBTQ experience higher rates of physical and sexual assault.
- LGBTQ experience a higher incidence of mental health problems, and participate in unsafe sexual practices.

Characteristics	All Homeless People	Sheltered People	Unsheltered People
Gender			
Female	39.5%	44.4%	29.2%
Male	60.2%	55.4%	70.3%
Transgender	0.3%	0.2%	0.6%
Ethnicity			
Non-Hispanic	77.9%	76.7%	80.6%
Hispanic	22.1%	23.3%	19.4%
Race			
European American	48.3%	43.9%	57.7%
African American	39.1%	45.1%	26.4%
Asian American	1.0%	0.9%	1.2%
Native American	2.8%	2.1%	4.2%
Pacific Islander	1.6%	1.2%	2.4%
Multiple Races	7.2%	6.8%	8.1%

EXHIBIT 10.6   Gender, Ethnicity, and Race for Sheltered and Unsheltered Homeless People
Source: 2016 Annual Homeless Assessment Report to Congress (U.S. Department of Housing and Urban Development, 2016).

- LGBTQ homeless youth commit suicide at a higher rate than heterosexual homeless youth (62 percent vs. 29 percent).
- LGBTQ homeless youth report verbal abuse, harassment, and personal criticism from peers and staff in homeless youth shelters and drop-in centers.

Quality-of-Life Concerns

The homeless are constantly in need of food, water, and shelter, so it is not uncommon for many homeless people to panhandle for food or money. Homeless people deal with poor health, inadequate health care, an unsatisfactory diet, poor personal hygiene, and sleep deprivation. The average life expectancy for a chronically homeless adult is between 42 and 52 years of age (O'Connell, 2005). In addition, there are other quality-of-life concerns for the homeless. The 2015 data showed (U.S. Conference of Mayors, 2015):

1. **Mental Health Issues:** 29 percent of homeless adults were severely mentally ill.
2. **Disabled:** 22 percent were physically disabled.
3. **Working Class:** 18 percent were employed.
4. **Domestic Violence:** 17 percent were victims of domestic violence.
5. **HIV Positive:** 4 percent were HIV positive.

Federal Law Definitions of Homelessness

Following are two definitions for homelessness specified in the federal McKinney-Vento Act in U.S. Code, Title 42. One is a general definition of homelessness for adults, and the second definition specifically applies to homeless children and youth. The two definitions and their key elements are as follows:

> **Homeless adult person** (1) An individual or family who lacks a fixed, regular, and adequate nighttime residence; (2) an individual or family who resides in a public or private place not designed for or ordinarily used as a regular sleeping accommodation for human beings, including a car, park, abandoned building, bus or train station, airport or camping ground; (3) an individual or family living in a supervised publicly or privately operated shelter designed to provide temporary living arrangements (including hotels and motels paid for by federal, state, or local government programs for

low-income individuals or by charitable organizations, congregate shelters, and transitional housing); and (4) an individual who resided in a shelter or place not meant for human habitation and who is exiting an institution where he or she temporarily resided (U.S. Code, 2010).

Homeless children and youths This includes similar residency and shelter/transitional housing as a homeless adult, but expands to sharing the housing of other persons due to loss of housing; living in motels, hotels, trailer parks, or camping grounds; or abandoned in hospitals; or are awaiting foster care placement (U.S. Code, 2016).

Causes for Homelessness

There are many interrelated causes for people experiencing homelessness. History shows that a poor economy, coupled with high unemployment, contributes to increased poverty and housing shortages. Personal bankruptcy, chronic alcohol and drug abuse, domestic violence, family breakups, lack of family or government support, and mental illness are contributing factors as well. Being an undocumented immigrant or a runaway can also be causes for homelessness. Unfortunately for LGBTQ youth, family conflict related to their sexual orientation and gender identities are added factors contributing to homelessness (NAEH, 2017).

When asked to list the main causes of homelessness among families with children in 2015, the U.S. Conference of Mayors identified the lack of affordable housing, poverty, and unemployment. Regarding individuals, the top reasons for homelessness were lack of affordable housing, poverty, followed by mental illness and the lack of treatment, and substance abuse and the lack of treatment (U.S. Conference of Mayors, 2015).

Homeless Veterans

Military veterans who experience homelessness have served in World War II, the Korean War, Cold War, Vietnam War, Grenada, Panama, Lebanon, Persian Gulf War, Afghanistan and Iraq, the military's anti-drug efforts in South America, and non-wars. Many homeless veterans suffer from post-traumatic stress disorder (PTSD) and substance abuse. Like other homeless sub-groups, veterans lack a family and social support network. Unfortunately, military occupations and training are not always transferable to the civilian workforce, placing some veterans at a disadvantage when competing for employment (NCHV, 2016).

When There Are No Shelters

People who experience homelessness become creative and adaptive when they need temporary shelter. Exhibit 10.7 shows the many locations where homeless people end up sleeping and congregating. Safety is the first obvious law enforcement concern for homeless people, especially when they are sleeping. The lack of shelter in extreme weather (cold, wet, or hot) leads to a myriad of health problems.

1. Abandoned buildings	12. Parks
2. Alleys	13. Patios
3. Awnings	14. Picnic Tables
4. Benches	15. Rest Areas
5. Bus Stations	16. Sidewalks
6. Cardboard Boxes	17. Subway Stations
7. Cars	18. Tarps
8. Construction Sites	19. Tents
9. Covered Bus Stops	20. Train Stations
10. Homeless Camps	21. Vacant Buildings
11. Overpasses	22. Vacant Houses

EXHIBIT 10.7 When There Is No Shelter, 2017

Criminalizing Homelessness

Homeless people are continually forced to leave from most, if not all, of these temporary locations by the police, business owners, or other government representatives. As a result, the homeless are unable to rest and receive adequate sleep. When homeless people do not leave, they are subject to arrest by police officers for city ordinance offenses such as trespassing or disorderly conduct. This is referred to as criminalizing homelessness. To assess the number and type of municipal codes that criminalize life-sustaining behaviors of homeless people, a survey of 187 cities was conducted, with results showing the following (NLCHP, 2014):

- 57 percent prohibit camping in certain public places.
- 27 percent prohibit sleeping in certain public places, such as in public parks.
- 76 percent prohibit begging in certain public places.
- 65 percent prohibit loitering and vagrancy in certain public places.
- 53 percent prohibit sitting or lying down in certain public places.
- 43 percent prohibit sleeping in vehicles.
- 9 percent prohibit sharing food with homeless people.

Police officers are in a difficult position when they are pressured by government officials to enforce homelessness laws in their jurisdictions. Even with such enforcement, police officers should still be respectful toward and compassionate with homeless individuals. Instead of telling a homeless person to leave a public or privately owned area, police officers should make every effort to locate an emergency shelter and be helpful. In the meantime, advocates for the homeless from across the United States are uniting with homeless people to resolve the issue through public awareness, legislation, and the courts.

In 2014, the UN Human Rights Committee reviewed the treatment of homeless people in the United States. The committee issued a report critical of the criminalization of homelessness life activities, such as eating, sleeping, and sitting, calling it "discriminatory, cruel, inhuman, and degrading treatment" (United Nations, 2014). Furthermore, the United States violated Articles 2, 7, 9, 17, and 26 of the International Covenant on Civil and Political Rights (ibid.). The UN Human Rights Committee called for the United States to take corrective action in its criminalization laws and stated:

The State party (U.S.) should engage with state and local authorities to:

a) Abolish the laws and policies criminalizing homelessness at state and local levels;
b) ensure close cooperation among all relevant stakeholders, including social, health, law enforcement and justice professionals at all levels, to intensify efforts to find solutions for the homeless in accordance with human rights standards; and
c) offer incentives for decriminalization and the implementation of such solutions, by providing continued financial support to local authorities that implement alternatives to criminalization, and withdrawing funding from local authorities that criminalize the homeless (ibid.).

Crime Victimization

The homeless are extremely vulnerable to person and property crimes, and do not have the security and safety that most Americans have. Data from 1999 to 2015 showed there were (NCH, 2016):

- Approximately 1,600 acts of violence against homeless people resulting in nearly 430 murders across 48 states and Puerto Rico, and Washington, D.C.
- On average, the murder victims were over the age of 40 and were males.
- Nearly 80 percent of the perpetrators were younger than 30 and male.

Individual crimes committed against homeless people are not coded and classified by law enforcement agencies because the FBI's Uniform Crime Report does not collect housing status in its crime victimization and suspect statistics. Further, homelessness status is not protected by federal hate/bias crime laws.

State Laws Protecting the Homeless from Hate Crimes

As of July 2016, Alaska, Florida, Maine, Maryland, Rhode Island, Washington, Puerto Rico and the District of Columbia enacted hate crime statutes to protect the homeless (NCH, 2016). Advocates for the homeless reference cases like the one in South Baltimore in 2001, where, over a period of four months, three teenage males attacked and beat to death three homeless men and assaulted several other homeless persons. All three teenagers called their actions "bum stomping" and were sentenced to prison for the brutal murders and assaults (Klein, 2003). According to Megan Hustings, Director of the National Coalition for the Homeless (NCH), passage of these laws allows judges to increase penalties for people who attack the homeless. Director Hustings states, "We need to send a symbolic and practical message that attacks against the homeless will not be tolerated" (Hustings, 2017). NCH recommends an amendment to the federal Hate Crimes Statistics Act to include crimes against the homeless and supports state legislative efforts to add homeless persons as a protected class to state hate crime statutes (ibid.).

PEACEKEEPING RESPONSES TO THE HOMELESSNESS CRISIS

Public trust in government and law enforcement agencies is essential for effective responses to the homelessness crisis. Homeless people in communities must believe they will be protected and treated with respect by the police and local government before relationships can develop. They need to have the confidence that the police and local government are attentive to and responsive in their efforts to help them and that there is no risk of being harassed or assaulted. Further, homeless people and their advocates must see positive behavior from the police and local government that proves their desire to help. Chapter 11 discusses humane law enforcement strategies for responding to victims of hate/bias crimes; the same strategies apply to people experiencing homelessness. The following are just a few examples of jurisdictions that have put forth significant effort to meet the needs of the homeless:

- Seattle, WA. In February 2017, the City of Seattle created a Navigation Team comprised of outreach workers and trained police officers who are working to connect unsheltered homeless people to housing and essential resources. Part of the team's responsibilities are to help homeless people with chemical addictions and mental illness (City of Seattle, 2017).
- Wichita, KS. The Wichita City Police Department has a Homeless Outreach Team (HOT) that is responsible for all 911 calls related to homeless individuals or homeless' calls for service. The team attempts to keep homeless people out of jail by directing them to shelters or services (e.g., mental health, substance abuse, employment). HOT is comprised of three police officers and a sergeant who work adjustable hours to meet the needs of the homeless (City of Wichita, 2017).

Federal Strategic Plan to Prevent and End Homelessness

In June 2010, the United States Interagency Council on Homelessness (USICH) and its 19 federal member agencies initiated *Opening Doors*, the first comprehensive federal strategic plan to prevent and end homelessness. The USICH's goals are to prevent and end all types of homelessness, including chronic homelessness, veterans, individuals, families, youth, and children. Since its inception, the USICH has had wide collaboration across the federal government and among states, local communities, homeless advocates as well as across private and nonprofit homeless organizations (USICH, 2015). The USICH has developed helpful strategies that address five central themes. These themes address the importance of (U.S. Interagency Council on Homelessness, 2015):

1. Increasing leadership, collaboration, and civic engagement
2. Increasing access to stable and affordable housing
3. Increasing economic security
4. Improving health and stability
5. Retooling the homeless crisis system

Themes and Objectives

Theme 1: Increase Leadership, Collaboration, and Civic Engagement

Objective 1: Provide and promote collaborative leadership at all levels of government and across all sectors to inspire and energize Americans to commit to preventing and ending homelessness.

Objective 2: Strengthen the capacity of public and private organizations by increasing knowledge about collaboration, homelessness, and successful interventions to prevent and end homelessness.

Theme 2: Increase Access to Stable and Affordable Housing

Objective 3: Provide affordable housing to people experiencing or most at risk of homelessness.

Objective 4: Provide permanent supportive housing to prevent and end chronic homelessness.

Theme 3: Increase Economic Security

Objective 5: Improve access to education and meaningful, sustainable employment for people experiencing or most at risk of homelessness.

Objective 6: Improve access to mainstream programs and services to reduce people's financial vulnerability to homelessness.

Theme 4: Improve Health and Stability

Objective 7: Integrate primary and behavioral health care services with homeless assistance programs and housing to reduce people's vulnerability to and the impacts of homelessness.

Objective 8: Advance health and housing stability for youth aging out of systems such as foster care and juvenile justice.

Objective 9: Advance health and housing stability for people experiencing homelessness that have frequent contact with hospitals and criminal justice.

Theme 5: Retool the Homeless Crisis Response Team

Objective 10: Transform homeless services to crisis response systems that prevent homelessness and rapidly return people who experience homelessness to stable housing.

EXHIBIT 10.8 Overview of the Federal Strategic Plan to End Homelessness: Themes and Objectives
Source: U.S. Interagency Council on Homelessness (2015).

Exhibit 10.8 identifies the organizational objectives under each theme. USICH amended several of its initial objectives related to youth and education in 2010, illustrating the ability to be responsive to feedback from national advocates and service providers. The objectives are helpful for criminal justice professionals in that they offer problem-solving strategies that can carry over to direct work with the homeless (ibid.).

Soup Kitchens and Emergency Shelters

Soup kitchens are in many cities throughout the United States and provide meals to those who are hungry, poor, and homeless. Many churches, mosques, and synagogues provide emergency shelter during extreme weather periods with congregants' volunteering to stay with the

---

Mini Case Study: What Would You Do?

Consider the following case study, applying it to two different scenarios: (1) the individuals involved are U.S.-born and speak English fluently and (2) the individuals involved are immigrants and speak limited English. Describe the challenges in each scenario, as you answer the questions following the case study.

You are a police officer on duty and having lunch with another police officer at a family-style restaurant in your patrol district. A homeless adult male with a small child walks into the restaurant; both approach your table. The man tells you that he is homeless, and that he and his nine-year-old daughter are looking for temporary shelter and haven't had a meal in

24 hours. He tells you that he had been laid off from his part-time job one month ago, and was evicted from his apartment one week ago. He mentions that he has no family and friends to turn to for assistance. Suddenly, his nine-year-old daughter looks at you and starts crying and pleads, "Please help me and my daddy."

- How do you feel about this situation?
- What are you going to say to the child and her father?
- How are you going to help these individuals with your current knowledge, skills, and resources?

1. Offer food (a meal or food pack), water, or meal vouchers.
2. Generally, refrain from giving cash to homeless individuals unless there are mitigating circumstances.
3. If you choose, donate to a soup kitchen, shelter, rescue mission, or other nonprofit organization to help the homeless.
4. Assist homeless individuals in locating emergency shelter when needed.
5. Find ways to speak to and treat homeless individuals with respect.

EXHIBIT 10.9   Five Tips for Encounters with a Homeless Person on the Street

homeless around the clock. It is extremely beneficial for officers and criminal justice students to volunteer at such soup kitchens and emergency shelters. Having one-on-one contact in a noncrisis mode is one of the best ways to dispel stereotypes about the homeless. This contact allows volunteers to see homeless individuals as human beings and enables positive and reciprocal interaction that, in turn, increases homeless individuals' trust and confidence in law enforcement.

Education and Training

Awareness training on homelessness should be a regular component in police academies and in-service training. At a minimum, the curriculum should include the causes and solutions to homelessness with a strong emphasis on how to interact with homeless people in a humane and respectful manner. Many law enforcement and public safety training programs already include this topic in their cultural diversity courses or community-policing courses. Criminal justice and emergency services, college students, police officers, and other first responders greatly benefit from homelessness awareness instruction. Exhibit 10.9 lists some practical tips that can be included in such instruction and in community meetings.

UNDERSTANDING DIMENSIONS OF MENTAL ILLNESS

In 2014, the Substance Abuse and Mental Health Services Administration (SAMHSA) estimated that about one in five American adults, ages 18 or older (18.1 percent or 43.6 million) suffered from a diagnosable mental disorder or mental illness and 9.8 million (4.1 percent) from a serious mental illness. The percentage of adults with mental illness of any kind remained relatively stable from 2008 to 2014 (SAMHSA, 2015). Additionally in 2014, 11.4 percent or 2.8 million youth ages 12 to 17 had a major depressive episode (ibid.).

> **Mental illness**   A mental, behavioral, or emotional, health disorder which can range from no or mild impact to a serious impairment, affecting one or more major life activities; and meets the diagnostic criteria specified within the 4th edition of the Diagnostic Statistical Manual of Mental Disorders (U.S. Department. of Health and Human Services, National Institute of Mental Health, 2015).

According to a 2016 Alzheimer's Association report, an estimated 5.4 million (11 percent) Americans, age 65 and over, had Alzheimer's disease while approximately 200,000 persons (4 percent) under age 65 had the disease.

> Alzheimer's disease is the most common type of dementia. "Dementia" is an umbrella term describing a variety of diseases and conditions that develop when nerve cells in the brain (called neurons) die or no longer function normally. The death or malfunction of neurons causes memory loss, erratic behavior and lessens one's ability to think clearly. In Alzheimer's disease, these brain changes eventually impair an individual's ability to carry out such basic bodily functions as walking and swallowing. Alzheimer's disease is ultimately fatal. (Alzheimer's Association, 2016)

People with severe mental illness can include anyone—children, teenagers, adults, and senior citizens. Mental illness transcends race, ethnicity, gender, disability, and sexual orientation. Serious mental illness includes major depression, schizophrenia, schizoaffective disorder, bipolar disorder, dissociative disorder, obsessive compulsive disorder (OCD), panic disorder, post-traumatic stress disorder (PTSD), and borderline personality disorder (NAMI, 2017a). Most trained and experienced law enforcement officers are familiar with these disorders and the term "psychotic episode," as they have had encounters with people with mental illness. Police officers know that a psychotic episode is a critical period for the person with a mental illness. Stabilization of the person without injury or loss of life should always be the primary objective in these encounters.

Psychotic episode   A period when a person with a serious mental illness is impaired and at risk of endangering himself or herself, or others.

Mental illness is a significant problem for police, medical, and social services and places a burden on the local community as well. The likelihood of miscommunication and misunderstanding are high when officers encounter people with mental illness and many encounters can quickly turn negative. Encountering individuals afflicted with mental illness requires preparation including an understanding of what types of law enforcement situations can arise, both from mentally ill individuals themselves or people reporting incidents.

Types of Calls

Regardless of the time of day or the size of the agency, law enforcement officers encounter people with mental illness in a variety of situations. According to the U.S. Department of Justice, these types of calls involve criminal offenders, disorderly persons, missing persons, complainants, victims, and persons in need of care. Exhibit 10.10 shows examples for each role.

Type	Examples
Offender	• A person with mental illness commits a person or property crime. • A person with mental illness commits a drug crime. • A person with mental illness threatens to commit suicide. • A person with mental illness threatens to injure someone else in the delusional belief that the other person poses a threat to him or her. • A person with mental illness threatens to injure police as a means of forcing police to kill him (commonly called "suicide by cop").
Disorderly person	• A family or community member reports annoying or disruptive behavior by a person with mental illness. • A hospital, group home, or mental health facility calls for police assistance in controlling a person with mental illness. • A police officer on patrol encounters a person with mental illness behaving in a disorderly manner.
Missing person	• A family member reports that a person with mental illness is missing. • A group home or mental health institution reports that a person with mental illness walked away and/or is missing.
Complainant	• A person with mental illness calls the police to report real or imagined conditions or phenomena. • A person with mental illness calls the police to complain about care received from family members or caretakers.
Victim	• A person with mental illness is the victim of a person or property crime. • A family member, caretaker, or service provider neglects or abuses a person with mental illness.
Person in need of care	• Police are asked to transport a person with mental illness to a hospital or mental health facility. • Police encounter a person with mental illness who is neglecting his or her own basic needs (food, clothing, shelter, medication, etc.).

EXHIBIT 10.10 • Law Enforcement Encounters with Various Types of Mentally Ill Individuals
Source: "People with Mental Illness," U.S. Department of Justice, Office of Community Oriented Policing Services, May 2006.

Individually and collectively, law enforcement officers are trained to handle diverse types of incidents in several types of scenarios. Likewise, police officers will benefit from studying and formulating response strategies to the five most frequent types of mental illness calls, which are (Peck, 2003):

1. A family member, friend, or other concerned person calls the police for help during a psychiatric emergency.
2. A person with mental illness feels suicidal and calls the police as a cry for help.
3. Police officers encounter a person with mental illness behaving inappropriately in public.
4. Citizens call the police because they feel threatened by the unusual behavior or presence of a person with mental illness.
5. A person with mental illness calls the police for help because of imagined threats.

Even though these are the five most frequent scenarios law enforcement officers may have with people with mental illness, no two contacts or encounters are ever the same. Police officers will continually have a variety of contacts with mentally ill persons at places such as parks, schools, colleges, businesses, care facilities, and other locations. Law enforcement officers must always be attentive and sensitive to the behavior and needs of each mentally ill person.

POLICE PROTOCOL IN ENCOUNTERS WITH PEOPLE WHO HAVE MENTAL ILLNESS

Law enforcement officers exercise a great amount of discretion when they encounter a person who has a mental illness. Generally, there are three options: (1) arrest, (2) hospitalization, and (3) informal disposition. Arrest is based on a crime that has been committed.

Arrest

The police officer takes the mentally ill person into custody and transports him or her to jail where the arrested person is booked for the crime and later released, like any other person under the same circumstances. Some officers may believe arresting a mentally ill person may result in treatment for that person in a correctional facility. In almost all cases this is not the reality. All arrests should be made on the probable cause that a crime has been committed and law enforcement officers should always follow the due process protection guarantees of the U.S. Constitution. The arrest of people with mental illness for the sole reason of getting them treatment is discouraged.

Hospitalization

Hospitalization of a person with mental illness is accomplished through voluntary or involuntary commitments. Often law enforcement officers will become involved with helping family members who need assistance in the voluntary commitment of another family member who is then taken to a hospital or clinic for mental health treatment. The police officer generally will stand by until the ambulance arrives to transport the person, or, depending on the law enforcement agency's protocol and the totality of the circumstances, make the transport themselves to the treatment facility. If the person with mental illness refuses a voluntary commitment, the police officer must decide if the individual is a danger to himself, herself, or to others. When it is determined the mentally ill person is indeed a danger to himself, herself, or others, then the officer can legally place a police officer hold on the person to make it an involuntary commitment. In this case, the officer would take the person into custody and depending on the agency, will either transport or plan for an ambulance to transport the person to a local hospital that treats and accommodates people with mental illness. This matter then becomes a civil rather than a criminal matter and will not be reflected on a person's arrest record. Law enforcement officers should follow mental health professionals' guidelines, local laws, and their agency's procedures when making a voluntary or involuntary commitment on any person.

Informal Disposition

Informal disposition is the third alternative to arrests or hospitalizations in encounters between law enforcement officers and persons with mental illness. Usually there is no written report by the police officer as is required in an arrest or hospitalization. Commonly, the only documentation of the informal disposition is in the police officer's notebook and the 911 Center's Computer Aided Dispatch (CAD). Informal dispositions can range from calming down an individual to having a responsible family member or friend watch over the person, or doing nothing at all.

Use of Force

- Bakersfield, CA. On December 12, 2016, after midnight, Bakersfield police officers responded to a 911 call regarding a suspicious man with a gun in a residential area. After failing to obey police commands to remove his hands from his jacket and to stop approaching, a 73-year-old Hispanic man with dementia was shot seven times by a police officer outside his house. The elderly man died at the scene and the police did not find a gun, however, they found a wooden crucifix on him. As of this seventh edition writing, the California Attorney General's Civil Rights Enforcement Section had opened a civil rights investigation into this shooting death (based on Hamilton & Rocha, 2016, and Eversley, 2016).
- San Jose, CA. On December 21, 2015, a federal jury in a civil lawsuit awarded $11.8 million to a 38-year-old Vietnamese man who was shot in the back and left paralyzed below the waist. The officer from the San Jose Police Department wasn't wearing her glasses and was deemed to have used excessive force when she shot the mentally ill man in the back as he was holding a knife to himself and threatening suicide. The man, who had a history of mental illness, was shot in the front yard of his house in January 2014 (based on Kaplan, 2015, and Wadsworth, 2015).
- Dallas, TX. In 2015, the city council of Dallas, Texas, approved a $1.6 million settlement for a 54-year-old, mentally ill white man, who was shot in the stomach in 2013 by a Dallas police officer. The man was sitting in an office chair on his street, holding a knife and acting erratically. As two police officers approached him, he stood up and was told to drop the knife. He remained still and was then shot by one of the officers. Initially, the mentally ill individual was charged with aggravated assault against a public servant, based on a false statement by one of the officers. After a neighbor came forward with a video of the shooting to disprove the false statement, the charges against him were dropped. As a result, Police Chief David Brown suspended one officer and fired the other officer who was later charged with aggravated assault by a public servant. The police department began to explore the use of body cameras after the shooting (based on Hallman, 2015, and Nicholson, 2014).

Communication is the primary tool for de-escalating conflict (see Chapter 4). The idea of officers de-escalating an individual's aggressive communication is especially relevant when they are in contact with people who have mental illnesses. These individuals are easily intimidated and threatened. The officer's approach should be calm and nonthreatening. Once the officer has exhausted all nonphysical means, he or she should use the minimum amount of force necessary to physically restrain the individual.

Many law enforcement agencies across the United States are experimenting with having trained crisis intervention providers ride with officers. These units are dispatched to calls involving mental health issues. Having a provider take the lead on making contact allows the officer to focus on the physical safety of the provider as well as the person in crisis. The specialist can direct the person to appropriate services and situations are more likely to be resolved peacefully.

Police recruits spend an average of eight hours a year on crisis intervention training for mental illness and related de-escalation strategies in police academies nationwide (PERF, 2016). The Police Executive Research Forum recommends that training involving encounters with persons who are mentally ill be scenario-based and that officers be trained to consider

1. Communicate in a respectful manner.

2. Speak in a calm and nonthreatening voice.

3. Be direct in your inquiries and requests.

4. Rephrase your inquiries and requests, if needed.

5. Be patient and take the extra steps to communicate, and over communicate, if needed.

6. Do not argue with, talk down, or belittle the person.

7. Do not make threats toward the individual.

8. Protect the person, others, and yourself from any physical injuries.

9. If the person is having a psychotic episode and requires physical restraint, use the appropriate techniques to minimize any physical injuries to him or her.

10. Only use the minimum amount of force that is necessary and justified if the person becomes violent with you or others.

11. Notify a supervisor and at a minimum, document in your police report any use of physical force against a person with mental illness.

12. Follow your department policy on how to handle the encounter, specifically in the areas of: (1) the arrest, (2) hospitalization, and (3) informal disposition.

13. Always seek medical treatment for a person with mental illness if they are physically injured.

EXHIBIT 10.11   Recommendations for Police Officers Who Encounter Mentally Ill Persons

all of their options in realistic exercises that match the different types of calls on patrol. Police training managers need to examine and highlight what practices and methods have worked well for dealing with individuals with mental illness. Exhibit 10.11 presents selected recommendations.

Having recognized that there was no national data collection of police use of force incidents to have an informed discussion on police-involved citizen shootings, former FBI director James B. Comey announced in 2015 that the FBI would lead efforts to establish a system for all law enforcement agencies to voluntarily report information on use of force incidents. Leaders from law enforcement and other organizations were receptive to the FBI's national proposal, and in early 2016, the National Use of Force Collection Task Force had the first in a series of meetings with the FBI; the members include (FBI: UCR, 2017):

- Local, tribal, and federal agency representatives
- Association of State Criminal Investigative Agencies
- Association of State Uniform Crime Reporting Programs
- International Association of Chiefs of Police
- Major Cities Chiefs Association
- Major County Sheriffs' Association
- National Organization of Black Law Enforcement Executives
- National Sheriffs' Association
- Police Executive Research Forum

According to the FBI, data collection would begin in January 2017 and the FBI's Uniform Crime Reporting (UCR) program would be used.

PROACTIVE RESPONSE STRATEGIES BETWEEN POLICE AND PEOPLE WITH MENTAL ILLNESS

In 1999, the first Conference on Mental Health addressed ways to reduce the stigma of mental illness, discrimination against people with mental disorders, and mental health within the justice system. The attorney general addressed the recurring cycle of people with mental disorders' incarceration for crimes (often minor offenses) and the minimal or complete lack of treatment for their underlying mental health problems. Following the 1999 conference, the Office of Justice Programs, in collaboration with the Department of Health and Human Services, began focusing on multiple new areas:

- the challenges of integrating criminal justice and mental health systems;
- appropriate treatment of mentally ill offenders through mental health court programs;
- the improvement of juvenile justice system mental health services;
- the creation of community partnerships to respond to the needs of mentally ill individuals.

Ongoing awareness of the needs and civil rights of mentally ill individuals must be promoted in police departments along with communication training with this most vulnerable population. As of this text's seventh edition, intense debates about health care reform had been taking place. The debate is beyond the scope of this section; however, with potential changes in the health care system, many more thousands of people could go untreated for their mental illnesses. With or without health care reform, the need for proactive response strategies between police and mentally ill individuals, such as the following, is critical:

1. Partnerships with multicultural community leaders, local faith-based organizations, and other community-based agencies (e.g., homeless shelters, food banks, social services, hospitals/mental health clinics) to provide a network of support for people with mental health problems.
2. Assistance to local multicultural business organizations that wish to work voluntarily on mental health issues within the community.
3. Creation and updating of specific police training programs and continuing education for encounters with people with mental health problems.
4. Development and updating of policies, procedures, and practices within the law enforcement agency for dealing with mental health problems (e.g., crisis intervention teams).
5. Collaboration with local fire departments, emergency medical services, 9-1-1, and surrounding law enforcement agencies to pool resources and strategies to mitigate the mental health challenges.

Treatment for Mental Illness

Mentally ill individuals without adequate family or support systems have limited to no capacity to care for themselves, often experiencing repeated hospitalizations and psychiatric trauma. They are usually not able to track their medication, frequently deny that they are sick, and refuse to be treated. This becomes law enforcement's challenge as these individuals pose threats to others. New York State has enacted legislation that occurred because of Kendra Webdale's death in 1999 when she was pushed in front of a train by a mentally ill individual who was neither taking medication nor receiving treatment for his schizophrenia. "Kendra's Law" in short mandates, via court order, that certain individuals must receive outpatient treatment for their illness (New York State, Office of Mental Health, 2006). Most

---

Mini Case Study: CIT (Crisis Intervention Team)

The strategies of the CIT model in Memphis, Tennessee, explained below are impressive. Read the following and identify and explain at least two barriers that could potentially prevent a police department from adopting the CIT model. After you identify the barriers, discuss ways of overcoming these obstacles so that the model becomes more feasible for a police department.

Memphis, Tennessee

In replicating the success of the CIT program started in Memphis, a national CIT training curriculum model was developed through a partnership between NAMI, the University of Memphis CIT Center, CIT International and the International Association of Chiefs of Police. As of 2017, 2,632 police departments have undergone the 40-hour CIT training program (Crisis Intervention Team Center, 2017). Per the National Alliance on Mental Illness (NAMI), CIT training includes: learning from mental health professionals and experienced officers, personal interaction with people who have recovered from a mental health crisis, verbal de-escalation skills, scenario-based training, and ongoing coordination with mental health providers in the community to transfer individuals in crisis directly to treatment facilities.

Since establishing the CIT model in Memphis, injuries to police officers responding to mental health calls dropped 80 percent. Compared to other jail diversion programs, police officers report CIT is better at minimizing the amount of time they spend on mental crisis calls and CIT is more effective in meeting the needs of people with mental illness. Further, CIT saves public money in jail diversion programs, reduces the number of re-arrests of people with mental illness, and is better at maintaining community safety (NAMI, 2017b).

states have similar laws, but New York has put significant resources into developing this legislation, and a study has shown that patients who must receive treatment (because of laws such as Kendra's Law) are not arrested or hospitalized as frequently as those receiving no treatment (Belluck, 2013). This conclusion is intuitive; officers should become familiar with their state's form of Kendra's Law.

Summary

- There are three major types of gangs: (1) street gangs, (2) prison gangs, and (3) outlaw motorcycle gangs. Typical gang-related crimes for street gangs and outlaw motorcycle gangs include alien smuggling, armed robbery, assault, human trafficking, motor vehicle theft, drug trafficking, extortion, fraud, identity theft, murder, weapons trafficking, and hate crimes. Street gangs have the largest membership and most members are adults, but most youth who join a gang belong to a street gang. The next largest group of gangs is prison gangs, followed by outlaw motorcycle gangs.
- The terms *youth* and *street gang* are commonly used interchangeably, but the use of the term *street gang* for *youth gang* often results in confusing juvenile gangs with adult criminal organizations. There are five general risk factors for youth gang membership: (1) prior delinquency in violence and alcohol/drug use; (2) poor family management and problematic parent–child relations; (3) low school attachment and academic achievement, and negative labeling by teachers; (4) association with peers who engage in delinquency; and (5) disorganized neighborhoods where large numbers of youth are in trouble and where drugs and firearms are readily available.
- By promoting coordination and information sharing between federal, state, and local law enforcement agencies, the FBI has been able to identify violent gang enterprises that pose a significant threat. The agency has also been able to pursue these criminals with coordinated investigations that support successful prosecutions. Major multiagency gang operations involving federal, state, county, and city law enforcement officers illustrate the need for officers to familiarize themselves with the cultural, racial, and ethnic dimensions of gangs.
- Human trafficking is a crime involving inducing a person by force, fraud or coercion to participate in commercial sex acts and involuntary servitude. Globally, human trafficking is a $150 billion-per-year illicit industry that preys on approximately 21 million victims. Many victims of human trafficking do not report their victimization which leaves law enforcement to rely upon investigation and tips from the public to detect the crime.
- Studies on survivors of sex trafficking indicate that the majority had neurological problems and had at least one major medical condition affecting their general health. The physical and psychological abuse trafficking victims experience often lead to serious mental or emotional health problems. Victims commonly have feelings of severe guilt, post-traumatic stress disorder, depression, anxiety, substance abuse and eating disorders. In addition to receiving medical care for physical injuries and illnesses, human trafficking victims often require psychological care as part of their comprehensive medical treatment. Victims may have a history of physical, sexual and/or mental abuse and may not define their experience as abusive. As such, they may not attempt to escape their circumstances with their traffickers and may experience cultural and linguistic barriers as well as isolation from their home community.
- The United States is one of 170 countries that has ratified the United Nations Trafficking Persons Protocol. There is an international legal instrument requiring member countries to criminalize and prosecute human trafficking crimes. Every police department needs to be proactive in finding ways to stop human trafficking in their jurisdiction; the International Association of Chiefs of Police (IACP) has developed an action checklist to help police departments in this pursuit. Police Chiefs, sheriffs, and directors of state law enforcement must collaborate with each other and federal law enforcement agencies in the detection, investigation, arrest, and prosecution of human traffickers in their jurisdictions.
- A homeless person is an individual who lacks a regular and adequate nighttime residence. Homelessness is a growing problem in the United States that impacts all groups in our multicultural society. The main causes for homelessness include a lack of affordable housing or shelter, poverty, and unemployment. People who are homeless are often targeted victims of hate crimes.
- Public trust in government and law enforcement agencies is essential for effective responses to the homelessness crisis. Homeless people in communities must believe they will be protected and treated with respect by the police and local government before relationships can develop. Awareness training

on homelessness should be a regular component in police academy and in-service training. At a minimum, the curriculum should include the causes and solutions to homelessness with a strong emphasis on how to interact with homeless people in a humane and respectful manner.

- Mental illness is a mental, behavioral, or emotional health disorder which can range from no or mild impact—to a serious impairment that affects one or more major life activities. A psychotic episode is a period when a person with a serious mental illness is impaired and at risk of endangering himself or herself or others. People with mental illness can be criminal offenders, disorderly persons, missing persons, complainants, victims, and persons in need of care. Encountering individuals with mental illness requires preparation, including an understanding of what types of law enforcement situations can arise, both from mentally ill individuals themselves or people reporting incidents.

- Most police officers have limited training on dealing effectively with mental health issues. Officers need to be aware that the use and level of force directed against a person with mental illness may be unnecessary unless there is a risk to the officer's safety. Other methods of dealing with the mentally ill are available to law enforcement; more training such as verbal de-escalation is needed at the local, state, and national levels.

Discussion Questions and Issues

1. *Types of Gangs.* Make a list of the specific street gangs and outlaw motorcycle gangs within the law enforcement jurisdiction that you work or live in. Research information regarding each gang's membership and reported criminal activity. After compiling this information, discuss three strategies a police department could use to curtail each gang's membership and criminal activity.

2. *Mini Case Study: How would you respond?* You are a police officer who has just been reassigned to a new neighborhood. You are scheduled to meet with a group of parents in a multicultural neighborhood gathering. The neighborhood has misgivings about your agency because of some police officers' use of profanity toward citizens and disrespect toward African American teenage males during traffic stops. There are a few street gangs in the neighborhood, and one of the biggest complaints from parents is, "Even good kids are being treated by the police as if they are gang members."
   - What would you say at this meeting?
   - How would you respond to the parents' allegations?
   - What recommendations could you make to your fellow officers that would improve their contacts with the young people they encounter?

3. *Human Trafficking.* Compile two lists; one for victims of labor trafficking and one for victims of sex trafficking. Determine what their needs will be once they are physically free from their traffickers. Assess how their needs might be different for the following populations:
   a. Juvenile females
   b. Juvenile males
   c. Adult males
   d. Adult females
   e. LGBTQ
   f. New immigrant (any country)—unable to speak English

4. *Homelessness.* Compile a list of the homelessness conditions and causes in the law enforcement jurisdiction that you work or live in. Research the number of people who are homeless and indicate their race, ethnicity, age, and gender. Identify the number of temporary emergency shelters, rescue missions, and soup kitchens in the area. Also, refer to Exhibit 10.7: "When There Is No Shelter" and identify all the types of places homeless people stay in your area. Upon completing these tasks, identify strategies you could take individually and collectively with other people, to help homeless people in your multicultural community.

5. *Police Encounters with Mental Illness.* Select a city, county, or state law enforcement agency in your community and collect the following information:
   a. How many hours of training do police recruits receive at the academy on mental health issues?
   b. How many hours a year do police officers receive for mental health issues at in-service training?
   c. Review the police department's written policy, procedures, and practices for encounters with people who have mental illness.
   d. Does the police department track and keep record of all police officer contacts with people who have mental illness?
   e. Does the police department follow the five response strategies law enforcement should use to deal with problems of people with mental health issues? You can review the five strategies on p. 287

References

Alzheimer's Association. (2016). "2016 Alzheimer's Disease Facts and Figures." https://www.alz.org/documents_custom/2016-facts-and-figures.pdf (accessed March 3, 2017).

Belluck, Pam. (2013). "Program Compelling Outpatient Treatment for Mental Illness Is Working, Study Says." July 30. *The New York Times.* www.nytimes.com/2013/07/30 /us/program-compelling-outpatient-treatment-for-mental-illness-is-working-study-says.html?pagewanted=all&_r=0 (accessed May 15, 2017).

CDC. (2017). "Heroin Overdose Data." Center for Disease Control and Prevention. www.cdc.gov/drugoverdose /data/heroin.html (accessed February 10, 2017).

City of Memphis. (2017). "Police Services, Crisis Intervention Team."   http://www.memphistn.gov/Government /PoliceServices/CrisisInterventionTeam.aspx   (accessed March 10, 2017).

City of New York, NY, Department of Homeless Services. (2017). "Press: NYPD Management Team to Assist DHS With Management of Security in Homeless Shelters." January 6. http://www1.nyc.gov/site/dhs/about/press-releases/nypd-dhs-security-release.page (accessed March 1, 2017).

City of Seattle, WA, Office of the Mayor. (2017). "City launches Navigation Team, announces Navigation Center, February 8, 2017 by Office of the Mayor." http://murray.seattle.gov /city-launches-navigation-team-announces-navigation-center-location/ (accessed March 1, 2017).

City of Wichita, KS. (2017). "Homeless Outreach Team." http:// www.wichita.gov/government/departments/wpd /fieldservices/HOTTeam/Pages/default.asp (accessed March 1, 2017).

Crisis Intervention Center. (2017). "CIT Center, A Resource for CIT Programs Across the Nation." http://cit.memphis .edu/ (accessed March 10, 2017).

Decker, Scott and G. David Curry. (2003). "Suppression without Prevention, Prevention without Suppression." In S. H. Ecker (Ed.), *Policing Gangs and Youth Violence*. Belmont, CA: Wadsworth/Thompson Learning, pp. 191–213.

Drug Enforcement Administration (DEA). (2015a). "United States: Areas of Influence of Major Mexican Transnational Criminal Organizations." https://www.dea.gov/docs /dir06515.pdf (accessed February 10, 2017).

Drug Enforcement Administration. (2015b). "National Heroin Threat Summary." https://www.dea.gov/divisions/hq/2015/hq052215_National_Heroin_Threat_ Assessment_Summary.pdf (accessed February 10, 2017).

Edward, Roz. (2017). "Largest Ever Research Studies Find One-fifth of Homeless Youth in Atlanta Are Victims of Human Trafficking." April 18. *Atlanta Daily World*. https://atlantadailyworld.com/2017/04/18/largest-ever-research-studies-find-one-fifth-of-homeless-youth-in-atlanta-are-victims-of-human-trafficking/ (accessed May 11, 2017).

Edwards, Breanna. (2017). "Chicago Ends a Violent 2016 with 762 Murders." January 3. *The Root*. http://www .theroot.com/chicago-ends-a-violent-2016-with-762-murders-1791134150 (accessed April 21, 2017).

Esbensen, Finn-Aage. (2000). *Preventing Adolescent Gang Involvement*. Youth Gang Series. Washington, D.C.: U.S. Department of Justice, Office of Juvenile Justice and Delinquency Prevention.

Esbensen, Finn-Aage, L. Thomas Winfree, Jr., Ni He, and Terrance Taylor. (2001). "Youth Gangs and Definitional Issues: When Is a Gang a Gang, and Why Does It Matter?" *Crime and Delinquency, 47*, 105–130.

Eversley, Melanie. (2016). "Unarmed Elderly Man with Dementia Killed by Police in Calif." December 13. *USA Today*. https://www.usatoday.com/story /news/2016/12/13/unarmed-retiree-dementia-fatally-shot-police-ca/95399066/ (accessed May 3, 2017).

FBI: UCR. (2016a). "2015 Crime in the United States: Human Trafficking." Federal Bureau of Investigation. https:// ucr.fbi.gov/crime-in-the-u.s/2015/crime-in-the-u.s.-2015 /additional-reports/human-trafficking/humantrafficking _-2015-_final (accessed April 5, 2017).

FBI: UCR. (2016b). "2015 Crime in the United States: Human Trafficking, Table 2—Offenses and Clearances by State." Federal Bureau of Investigation. https://ucr.fbi.gov/crime-in-the-u.s/2015/crime-in-the-u.s.-2015/additional-reports /human-trafficking/table_2_human_trafficking_offenses_ and_clearances_by_state_2015.xls (accessed April 5, 2017).

FBI: UCR. (2016c). "2015 Crime in the United States: Human Trafficking Table 3—Human Trafficking Arrests by Age by State, 2015." Federal Bureau of Investigation. https:// ucr.fbi.gov/crime-in-the-u.s/2015/crime-in-the-u.s.-2015 /additional-reports/human-trafficking/table_3_human _trafficking_arrests_by_age_by_state_2015.xls (accessed April 5, 2017).

FBI: UCR. (2017). "Use-of-Force." Federal Bureau of Investigation. https://ucr.fbi.gov/use-of-force (accessed March 11, 2017).

Fuchs, Erin. (2014). "This Is What Modern-Day Sex Slavery in America Looks Like." August 11. Business Insider. http:// www.businessinsider.com/a-portrait-of-human-sex -trafficking-in-america-2014-8 (accessed May 4, 2017).

Gallagher, J.J. and Emily Shapiro. (2017). "Chicago's 'Out of Control' Violence Produces 762 Homicides in 2016." January 3. *ABC News*. http://abcnews.go.com/US /chicagos-control-violence-produces-762-homicides-2016 /story?id=44402951 (accessed April 21, 2017).

Glover, Scott and Richard Winton. (2009). "Dozens Arrested in Crackdown on Latino Gang Accused of Targeting Blacks." May 22. *L.A. Times*. http://articles.latimes.com/2009 /may/22/local/me-gang-sweep22 (accessed May 15, 2017).

Gottfredson, G. D. and Gottfredson D. C. (2001). *Gang Problems and Gang Programs in a National Sample of Schools*. Ellicott City, MD: Gottfredson Associates, Inc. www.nationalgang-center.gov/About/FAQ#RefGottfredson2001   (accessed May 15, 2017).

Hallman, Tristan. (2015, September 22). "Update: City Will Pay 1.6 Million to Settle Lawsuit by Mentally Man Shot by Cop." September 16. *Dallas News*. http://www.dallas-news.com/news/crime/2015/09/16/city-and-mentally-ill-man-shot-by-dallas-officer-in-2013-agree-on-settlement (accessed March 9, 2017).

Hamilton, Matt and Veronica Rocha. (2016). "Man, with Dementia Fatally Shot by Police had a Crucifix, Not a Gun, Police Say." December 13. *L.A Times*. http://www.latimes. com/local/lanow/la-me-ln-unarmed-man-dementia -bakersfield-killed-nine-20161213-story.html (accessed March 8, 2017).

Hill, Karl. G., Christina Lui, and J. David Hawkins. (2001). *Early Precursors of Gang Membership: A Study of Seattle Youth*. Bulletin. Youth Gang Series. Washington, D.C.: U.S. Department of Justice, Office of Juvenile Justice and Delinquency Prevention.

Howell, James C. and Arlen Egley, Jr. (2005). "Moving Risk Factors into Developmental Theories of Gang Membership." *Youth and Juvenile Justice, 3*(4), 334–354.

Hustings, Megan. (2017). Director of National Coalition for the Homeless, Washington D.C., personal communication, March 1.

IACP. (2006). "The Crime of Human Trafficking: A Law Enforcement Guide to Identification and Investigation." International Association of Chiefs of Police. www.theiacp. org/portals/0/pdfs/completehtguide.pdf (accessed May 5, 2017).

International Labour Organization. (2014). "Profits and Poverty: The Economics of Forced Labour." http://www.ilo.org/wcmsp5/groups/public/—ed_norm/—declaration/documents/publication/wcms_243391.pdf (accessed May 8, 2017).

Kaplan, Tracey. (2015). "Jury awards Vietnamese Man Shot and Paralyzed by San Jose Police $11.3 Million." December 22. *Mercury News*. http://www.mercurynews.com/2015/12/22/jury-awards-vietnamese-man-shot-and-paralyzed-by-san-jose-police-11-3-million/ (accessed March 9, 2017).

Klein, Allison. (2003). "Friend Testifies Defendant Took Part in Bum Stomping." November 20. *Baltimore Sun*. http://articles.baltimoresun.com/2003-11-20/news/0311200114_1_waterbury-daniel-ennis-holle (accessed May 15, 2017).

Klein, Malcom W. (1995). *The American Street Gang*. New York, NY: Oxford University Press.

Lederer, Laura J., Christopher A. Wetzel. (2014). "The Health Consequences of Sex Trafficking and Their Implications for Identifying Victims in Healthcare Facilities." *Annals of Health Law* 23, pp. 61–91. http://www.globalcenturion.org/wp-content/uploads/2014/08/The-Health-Consequences-of-Sex-Trafficking.pdf (accessed April 11, 2017).

The Library of Congress. (2015). "13th Amendment to the U.S. Constitution." https://www.loc.gov/rr/program/bib/ourdocs/13thamendment.html (accessed April 4, 2017).

Miller, Walter. (1982/1992). *Crime by Youth Gangs and Groups in the United States*. Washington, D.C.: Government Printing Office.

Mitchell, Holly J. (2016). "I Denounce False Claims Made by Republicans on My Bill #SB1322 that Decriminalizes Sexually Exploited Minors." https://twitter.com/HollyJMitchell/status/814997578978689024 (accessed April 13, 2017).

Monkkonen, Eric H. (1981). *Police in Urban America, 1860–1920*. Cambridge, England: Cambridge University Press.

NAEH. (2017). "LGBTQ Youth." National Alliance to End Homelessness. www.endhomelessness.org/pages/lgbtq-youth (accessed February 24, 2017)

NAMI. (2017a). "Mental Health Conditions." National Alliance on Mental Illness. www.nami.org/Learn-More/Mental-Health-Conditions (accessed March 3, 2017).

NAMI. (2017b). "What Is CIT." National Alliance on Mental Illness. www.nami.org/Law-Enforcement-and-Mental-Health/What-Is-CIT (accessed March 10, 2017).

NCH. (2009, July). "How Many People Experience Homelessness?". National Coalition for the Homeless. www.nationalhomeless.org/factsheets/How_Many.pdf (accessed May 15, 2017).

NCH. (2016, July). "No Safe Street: A Survey of Hate Crimes and Violence Committed Against Homeless People in 2014 & 2015." National Coalition for the Homeless. http://nationalhomeless.org/wp-content/uploads/2016/07/HCR-2014-151.pdf (accessed February 25, 2017).

NCHV. (2016). "Media Information." National Coalition for Homeless Veterans. http://nchv.org/index.php/news/media/media_information/(accessed April 27, 2017).

NGC. "Frequently Asked Questions About Gangs." National Gang Center. https://www.nationalgangcenter.gov/About/FAQ#q1 (accessed June 1, 2017).

NGC. (2011). "National Youth Gang Survey Analysis." National Gang Center. www.nationalgangcenter.gov/Survey-Analysis (accessed May 25, 2017).

NGC. (2017). "About the National Gang Center." National Gang Center. www.nationalgangcenter.gov/About (accessed February 8, 2017).

NGIC. (2009). *National Gang Threat Assessment*. Product No. 2009-M0335-001. National Gang Intelligence Center. www.fbi.gov/stats-services/publications/national-gang-threat-assessment-2009-pdf (accessed May 15, 2017).

NGIC. (2013). "National Gang Report 2013." National Gang Intelligence Center. www.fbi.gov/file-repository/stats-services-publications-national-gang-report-2013/view (accessed February 9, 2017).

NGIC. (2014). "National Youth Gang Survey Analysis—Number of Gang Related Homicides." National Gang Intelligence Center. www.nationalgangcenter.gov/Survey-Analysis/Measuring-the-Extent-of-Gang-Problems#homicidesnumber (accessed February 18, 2017).

NGIC. (2015). "2015 National Gang Report." National Gang Intelligence Center. www.fbi.gov/file-repository/national-gang-report-2015.pdf/view (accessed February 3, 2017).

NHTH. (2017). "2016 Hotline Statistics." National Human Trafficking Hotline. https://humantraffickinghotline.org/states (accessed April 6, 2017).

NLCHP. (2014). "No Safe Place: The Criminalization of Homelessness in U.S. Cities." National Law Center on Homelessness and Poverty. www.nlchp.org/documents/No_Safe_Place (accessed April 26, 2017).

NLCHP. (2015). "Homelessness in America: Overview of Data and Causes." National Law Center on Homelessness and Poverty. https://www.nlchp.org/documents/Homeless_Stats_Fact_Sheet (accessed February 20, 2017).

National Institute of Justice. (2016). "Gangs and Sex Trafficking in San Diego." September 20. http://nij.gov/topics/crime/human-trafficking/pages/gangs-sex-trafficking-in-san-diego.aspx (accessed May 24, 2017).

New York State, Office Mental Health. (2006). "An Explanation of Kendra's Law." www.omh.ny.gov/omhweb/Kendra_web/Ksummary.htm (accessed May 15, 2017).

Nicholson, Eric. (2014). "Ex-Dallas Cop Carden Spencer Indicted for Shooting a Mentally Ill Rylie Man." April 30. Dallas Observer. http://www.dallasobserver.com/news/ex-dallas-cop-carden-spencer-indicted-for-shooting-a-mentally-ill-rylie-man-7128509 (accessed May 3, 2017).

O'Connell, James J. (2005, December). *Premature Mortality in Homeless Populations: A Review of the Literature*. Nashville, TN: National Health Care for the Homeless Council, Inc. http://santabarbarastreetmedicine.org/wp-content/uploads/2011/04/PrematureMortalityFinal.pdf (accessed May 15, 2017)

Office for Victims of Crime (OVC). (2017a). "Mental Health Needs." https://www.ovcttac.gov/taskforceguide/eguide/4-supporting-victims/44-comprehensive-victim-services/mental-health-needs/ (accessed May 12, 2017).

Office for Victims of Crime (OVC). (2017b). "Victim Service Providers." https://ovc.ncjrs.gov/humantrafficking/providers.html (accessed May 11, 2017).

Peck, Leonard W. Jr. (2003). "Law Enforcement Interactions with Persons with Mental Illness." *TELEMASP Bulletin*, 10(1), 1–12.

PERF. (2016, March). *Critical Issues in Policing Series, Guiding Principles on Use of Force*. Police Executive Research Forum. www.policeforum.org/assets/30%20guiding%20principles.pdf (accessed March 9, 2017).

Ryan, Kevin M. (2017). "One in Five Homeless Youth Trafficked, New Research Reveals." April 17. *The Huffington Post.* http://www.huffingtonpost.com/entry /one-in-five-homeless-youth-trafficked-new-research _us_58f5032ee4b015669722517d (accessed May 11, 2017).

SAMSHA. (2015, September). "Behavioral Health Trends in the United States: Results from the 2014 National Survey on Drug Use and Health: Mental Health." Substance Abuse and Mental Health Services Administration. www.samhsa.gov/data/sites/default/files/NSDUH-FRR1-2014 /NSDUH-FRR1-2014.pdf (accessed March 3, 2017).

Spergel, Irving A. (1995). *The Youth Gang Problem.* New York, NY: Oxford University Press.

State of California Legislature. (2016). "SB-1311 Commercial Sex Actions: Minors, Version." September 26. https:// leginfo.legislature.ca.gov/faces/billCompareClient. xhtml?bill_id=201520160SB1322 (accessed April 13, 2017).

Thornberry, Terrence. P. (1998). "Membership in Youth Gangs and Involvement in Serious and Violent Offending." In R. Loeber and D. P. Farrington (Eds.), *Serious and Violent Juvenile Offenders: Risk Factors and Successful Interventions,* Thousand Oaks, CA: Sage Publications.

Thornberry, T. P., M. D. Krohn, A. J. Lizotte, C. A. Smith, and K. Tobin. (2003). *Gangs and Delinquency in Developmental Perspective.* New York, NY: Cambridge University Press.

Ujifusa, Glen. (2017). Deputy District Attorney, Multnomah County District Attorney's Office, Portland, OR, personal communication, April 18.

U.S. Census Bureau. (2016). "Income and Poverty in the United States: 2015." www.census.gov/library/publications/2016 /demo/p60-256.html (accessed February 22, 2017).

U.S. Code. (2010). "Title 42 USC—The Public Health and Welfare Chapter 119, Subchapter 1—General Provisions, Section 11302—General definition of homeless individual." www.gpo.gov/fdsys/pkg/USCODE-2010-title42/html /USCODE-2010-title42-chap119-subchapI-sec11302.htm (accessed June 12, 2017).

U.S. Code. (2016). "Title 42 USC Chapter 119, Subchapter VI, Part B: Education for homeless Children and Youths, Definitions, Section 11434a." http://uscode.house.gov/view .xhtml?req=granuleid%3AUSC-prelim-title42-chapter119- subchapter6-partB&edition=prelim (accessed June 12, 2017).

U.S. Code. (2017). "Title 22 USC Chapter 78, Section 7102- Traffic Victims Protection." http://uscode.house.gov/view. xhtml?path=/prelim@title22/chapter78&edition=prelim (accessed April 6, 2017).

U.S. Conference of Mayors. (2015, December). "Hunger and Homelessness Survey: A Status Report on Hunger and Homelessness in America's Cities: A 22-City Survey /December 2015." www.tuw.org/sites/tuw.org/files /US%20Conference%20of%20Mayors%20Hunger %20and%20Homelessness%20Survey_2015.pdf (accessed February 25, 2017).

U.S. Conference of Mayors. (2016, December). "Hunger and Homelessness Survey: A Status Report on Hunger and Homelessness in America's Cities, December 2016." https://endhomelessness.atavist.com/mayorsreport2016 (accessed February 23, 2017).

U.S. Department of Health and Human Services. National Institute of Mental Health. (2015). "Any Mental Illness among U.S. Adults." www.nimh.nih.gov/health/statistics /prevalence/any-mental-illness-ami-among-us-adults.shtml (accessed May 1, 2017).

U.S. Department of Homeland Security. (2017). "Indicators of Human Trafficking." https://www.dhs.gov/blue-campaign /indicators-human-trafficking (accessed April 13, 2017).

U.S. Department of Housing and Urban Development. (2016). "The 2016 Annual Homeless Assessment Report (AHAR) to Congress—Part 1: Point-in-Time Estimates of Homeless." www.hudexchange.info/resources/documents/2016 -AHAR-Part-1.pdf (accessed February 20, 2017).

U.S. Department of Justice. (2006). Office of Community Oriented Policing Services: "People with Mental Illness." www.popcenter.org/problems/pdfs/MentalIllness.pdf (accessed May 15, 2017).

U.S. Department of Justice. (2013). Community Corrections Institute, Office of Justice Programs, Bureau of Justice Assistance. "Native American Involvement in the Gang Subcultures: Current Trends and Dynamics—2013." http:// www.communitycorrections.org/images/publications /NAInvolveinGangs-Trends.pdf (accessed February 17, 2017)

U.S. Department of Justice. (2014). Office of Strategic Intelligence and Information, Bureau of Alcohol, Tobacco, Firearms and Explosives. "OMGs and the Military 2014 ATF Report." https://cryptome.org/2015/05/omgs-ongs. pdf (accessed February 16, 2017).

U.S. Department of Justice. (2016). "The National Strategy for Child Exploitation Prevention & Interdictions: A Report to Congress, April 2016." www.justice.gov/psc/file/842411 /download (assessed April 7, 2017).

U.S. Department of Justice. (2017). "U.S. Department of Justice National Strategy to Combat Human Trafficking, January 2017." www.justice.gov/humantrafficking/page /file/922791/download (accessed April 7, 2017).

U.S. Federal Bureau of Investigation. (2009). "Why Partnerships Matter: In Cases Like Operation Knockout." https://archives.fbi.gov/archives/news/stories/2009 /october/knockout_100509 (accessed May 15, 2017).

U.S. Federal Bureau of Investigation. (2016). "October 18, 2016, FBI Announces Results of Operation Cross Country X." www.fbi.gov/contact-us/field-offices/atlanta/news /press-releases/fbi-announces-results-of-operation-cross- country-x- (accessed April 13, 2017).

U.S. Federal Bureau of Investigation. (2017) "What We Investigate—Gangs." www.fbi.gov/investigate/violent- crime/gangs (accessed February 3, 2017).

U.S. Government Accounting Office. (2016). "Report to Congressional Committees, Human Trafficking: Agencies Have Taken Steps to Assess Prevalence, Address Victim Issues, and Avoid Grant Duplication, June 2016." www .gao.gov/assets/680/678041.pdf (accessed April 6, 2017).

U.S. Interagency Council on Homelessness. (2015). "Opening Doors: Federal Strategic Plan to Prevent and End Homelessness, as Amended 2015." https://www.usich.gov/ resources/uploads/asset_library/USICH_OpeningDoors _Amendment2015_FINAL.pdf (accessed March 1, 2017).

U.S. State Department. (2016). "Trafficking in Persons Report, June 2016." www.state.gov/documents/organiza- tion/258876.pdf (accessed April 10, 2017).

United Nations. (2014). United Nations Human Rights Committee. "Concluding Observation on the Fourth

Periodic Report of the United States of America, 23 April 2014." http://tbinternet.ohchr.org/_layouts/treaty-bodyexternal/Download.aspx?symbolno=CCPR%2fC%2f USA%2fCO%2f4&Lang=en (accessed April 27, 2017).

United Nations. (2016). "United Nations Office on Drugs and Crime Global Report on Trafficking in Persons 2016." www.unodc.org/documents/data-and-analysis/glo-tip/2016_Global_Report_on_Trafficking_in_Persons.pdf (accessed April 12, 2017).

United Nations. (2017). "Human Rights Office of the High Commissioner. (Survivors of Human Trafficking—Breaking the Silence." www.ohchr.org/EN/NewsEvents/Pages /SurvivorstraffickingBreakingthesilence.aspx (accessed May 4, 2017).

Wadsworth, Jennifer. (2015). "Jury Grants $11.3 Million to Man Paralyzed by SJPD." December 22. San Jose Inside. www.sanjoseinside.com/2015/12/22/jury-grants-11-3-million-to-man-paralyzed-by-sjpd/ (accessed May 3, 2017).

Youth. (2017). "Homeless and Runaway: LGBT." http:// youth.gov/youth-topics/runaway-and-homeless-youth /lgbt (accessed February 23, 2017).

Response Strategies for Crimes Motivated By Hate/Bias and Racial Profiling

Part Three presents content that deals with both implicit and explicit hate and bias, and broadly speaking, violations of a civil rights nature. The focus is on both crimes committed by individuals toward others, and on racial profiling by officers. The term "biased-based policing" refers to intentional and unintentional acts of biased decision making and police action, where the administration of justice results in racial profiling.

Chapter 11 contains information on policies, practices, and procedures for responding to hate crimes or incidents. In this chapter, the focus is primarily on hate crimes and incidents wherein the motivation is related to the victim's race, ethnicity, national origin, religion, or sexual orientation. (The examples do not convey the breadth of hate crimes against all "protected" and vulnerable groups; space limitations allow for examples of selected groups only.) The chapter presents the reasons for collecting data on crimes and incidents motivated by hate/bias committed by individuals or organized groups. The chapter ends with examples to help students, members of the criminal justice system, and the community to develop sensitive and effective programs for handling these crimes and incidents. The policies, training, practices, and procedures outlined in this chapter are recommended by the U.S. Department of Justice's Community Relations Service, and are currently in operation in most law enforcement agencies across the nation.

Chapter 12 provides detailed information on racial profiling, including historical background, the illegitimate use of race and ethnicity in police stops, and strategies for the prevention of racial profiling by law enforcement officers. This chapter discusses police and citizens' perceptions of racial profiling as well as covers when profiling, as a legal tool, is justified by law enforcement. Chapter 12 will help law enforcement professionals gain a solid working knowledge of guidelines to prevent racial profiling.

Each chapter ends with summary points, discussion questions, and a list of references.

- Appendix E, *Organized Hate Groups*, corresponds to content in Chapter 11.

- Appendix F, *Resources for Hate/Bias Crimes Monitoring*, corresponds to content in Chapter 11.

11

Hate/Bias Crimes

LEARNING OBJECTIVES

After reading this chapter, you should be able to:

- Describe the scope of the hate crime problem, including historical perspectives, and the nationwide reporting system for hate crime data collection.
- Define and differentiate between hate crimes and hate incidents.
- Explain the need for standardized and comprehensive statistics for the analysis of trends related to hate crimes and bias.
- Explain hate crime and incident source theories.
- Discuss response strategies to hate crimes and appropriate victim assistance techniques.
- Identify hate crimes related to anti-Semitism, anti-Arab/Muslim, sexual orientation and gender identity, race, ethnicity, and national origin.
- Identify extremist hate groups, and the organizations that monitor them.
- Explain hate crime laws, investigative procedures, and offender prosecution.

OUTLINE

- Introduction
- The Hate/Bias Crime Problem
- Definition of Hate/Bias Crime and Hate/Bias Incident
- Hate/Bias Crime Source Theories
- Jews and Anti-Semitism
- Anti-Arab/Muslim Victimization
- LGBTQ and Gender Identity Victimization
- Organized Hate Groups
- Hate/Bias Crime and Incident Investigations
- Hate/Bias Crime/Incident Control and Prosecution
- Law Enforcement Response Strategies
- Hate/Bias Crime and Incident Victimology
- Summary
- Discussion Questions and Issues
- References

INTRODUCTION

The term, "hate crime" was introduced in the mid-1980s to identify crimes motivated by hate or bias (Jacobs & Potter, 1998). Crimes motivated by hate/bias have occurred in the United States for generations and have victimized most of the immigrant groups in the country, including the Irish, Italians, Chinese, Polish, and Puerto Ricans. Even though they are indigenous peoples, Native Americans have not been immune to hate crimes. In addition, African Americans continue to be victims of bias, discrimination, and crimes motivated by hate.

Data must be collected at local levels and sent in a standardized fashion to state and national clearinghouses so that proper resources may be allocated to hate/bias crime prevention, education, investigations, prosecutions, and victim assistance. Such a system provides information necessary not only to the criminal justice system, but also to public policymakers, civil rights activists, legislators, victim advocates, and the general public. The data, if comprehensive and accurate, provide a reliable statistical picture of the problem. Agencies collecting data have also been able to use the statistics to strengthen their arguments and rationale for new hate crime penalty enhancements. In addition, the information collected is used in criminal justice training courses and in educating communities on the impact of the problem. Another, and possibly the most important, rationale for expending energy on tracking, analyzing, investigating, and prosecuting these crimes is that a single incident can be the tragedy of a lifetime to its victim and may also be the spark that disrupts an entire community.

Increased public awareness of and response to such crimes have largely been the result of efforts by community-based organizations and victim advocate groups. By documenting and drawing public attention to acts of bigotry and violence, these organizations have laid the groundwork for the official action that followed. It is extremely important that hate groups across the United States be monitored by criminal justice agencies. Documenting and publicizing a problem does not guarantee it will be solved, but is a critical part of any strategy to create change. It also raises consciousness within the community and the criminal justice system. It is a simple but effective first step toward mobilizing a response. U.S. Federal Bureau of Investigation (FBI) former director, James Comey, during a 2014 speech to the Anti-Defamation League said that "we need to do a better job of tracking and reporting hate crimes to fully understand what is happening in our communities and how to stop it" (U.S. Federal Bureau of Investigation, 2016). This chapter includes general information on hate crimes and also focuses on anti-Semitic, anti-Arab/Muslim as well as sexual/gender identity hate crimes to illustrate the nature of hate crimes. (See Chapters 5–9 for additional specific information on hate crimes against cultural, national, racial, and ethnic groups.)

THE HATE/BIAS CRIME PROBLEM

The criminal justice system as well as communities whose members are victims must address the problem of hate/bias crimes. Victims of hate/bias crimes are particularly sensitive and unsettled because they often feel powerless to alter the situation, since they cannot change their color, racial, ethnic, religious background, gender, gender identity, or sexual orientation. Furthermore, the individual involved is not the sole victim, because fear of similar crimes often affects an entire group of citizens. A physical attack on a person because of race, religion, ethnic background, sexual orientation, gender, or gender identity is a particularly insidious form of violent behavior. Verbal assaults on persons because of others' perceptions of their "differences" are equally distressing to both the victim and to society. The ripple effect of bias crime is shown in Exhibit 11.1.

Unfortunately, these kinds of incidents can also occur in the law enforcement workplace among coworkers. When law enforcement treats such occurrences seriously, it sends a message to community members that the local police agency will protect them. Doing the same within the law enforcement organization and correctional system sends a vitally important message to all employees. The criminal justice system, and especially local law enforcement agencies, will become the focus of criticism if attacks are not investigated, resolved, and

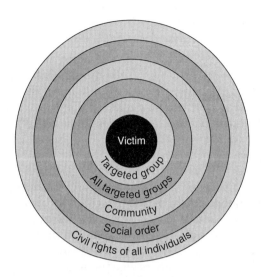

EXHIBIT 11.1 The Ripple Effect of Bias Crime

Source: "Responding to Hate Crime: A Multidisciplinary
Curriculum." National Center for Hate Crime Prevention.
U.S. Department of Justice. Retrieved from www.hhd.org/
sites/hhd.org/files/Responding%20to%20hate%20crime%20
-%20A%20multidisciplinary%20curriculum.pdf

prosecuted promptly and effectively. A hate/bias crime can send shock waves through the community at which the act was aimed. Law enforcement and corrections personnel must have an understanding on both the global and the local situation when it comes to hatred and bias within the population they serve or within which they work. Criminal justice professionals must be aware of ongoing world conflicts that have had and still have repercussions in the United States.

Studies over the years have shown that numerous perpetrators of hate crimes are motivated by the desire for excitement, and that as many as 60 percent of offenders commit crimes for the thrill associated with victimization (National Institute of Justice, 2008). The second most common group responsible for hate crimes includes people who feel that *they* are responding to an "attack" of an emotional or psychological nature by the individuals who they (the perpetrators) have victimized. Hate crime perpetrators may feel that their victims have infringed on their rights simply because the victims:

- look different because of ethnicity or race,
- have religious beliefs that differ from those of the offender,
- are of a sexual orientation that differs [or appears to differ] from that of the perpetrator, or
- represent some other facet of diversity not shared with the offender. (Davis, 2017; McDevitt, 2017)

Hate crime perpetrators may also feel defensive and threatened by those who differ from them, and commit crimes against perceived outsiders in order to "protect" their neighborhood (ibid.).

The least common perpetrators are hard-core fanatics who are driven by racial or religious ideology or ethnic bigotry. These individuals are often members of or potential recruits for extremist organizations discussed later in this chapter and Appendix E. Some perpetrators of hate crimes live on the U.S. border and are extremely fearful of Mexicans, South and Central Americans, Cubans, and others who enter the United States both legally and illegally. They feel that their militant rhetoric and violence is necessary to keep even more immigrants from coming into the country. Mexicans are the largest immigrant group in the United States and thus, often the victims of hate crimes.

Community awareness of hate violence grew rapidly in the United States during the late 1980s and the 1990s. Many states commissioned special task forces to recommend ways to control such violence, and new legislation was passed. Despite many who have spoken out against bigotry and hate violence, few communities have utilized an integrated approach to the problem. There are many effective programs that deal with particular aspects of bigotry or hate in specific settings; however, few models weave efforts to prevent hate violence into the fabric of the community.

Hate crimes are the most extreme and dangerous manifestation of racism. Criminal justice professionals, including neighborhood police officers (a key source of intelligence information) must be aware of the scope of the hate/bias crime problem from both historical and contemporary perspectives. The same is true of the correctional officers who work directly with the inmate population.

Purpose of Hate/Bias Crime Data Collection

Establishing a good reporting system by law enforcement agencies is essential in every area of the country. Hate/bias crime data are collected to help law enforcement:

- Identify current and potential problems (i.e., trends)
- Respond to the needs of diverse communities
- Recruit a diverse force
- Train criminal justice personnel on the degree of the problem and the reasons for priority response

When law enforcement has information about crime patterns, they are better able to direct resources to prevent, investigate, and resolve problems pertaining to them. Tracking hate/bias incidents and crimes allows criminal justice managers to deploy their resources appropriately when fluctuations occur. Aggressive response, investigation, and prosecution of these crimes demonstrate that police are genuinely concerned and that they see such crimes as a priority. As departments show their commitment to addressing hate/bias crime, the diverse communities they serve will be more likely to see police as responsive to their concerns. A secondary benefit for a responsive agency is minorities, including women, would be more apt to consider law enforcement as a good career opportunity.

The Scope of Hate Crimes Nationally

The federal Hate Crime Statistics Act of 1990 encourages states to collect and report hate crime data on crimes committed because of the victim's race, religion, disability, sexual orientation, or ethnicity to the FBI (H.R. 1048, 1990). The FBI, in partnership with state and local law enforcement agencies in 1992, began collecting that data pertaining to hate/bias incidents, offenses, victims, offenders, and motivations. In 2009, the Matthew Shepard Hate Crimes Prevention Act became law which expanded existing U.S. federal hate crime law to apply to crimes motivated by a victim's actual or perceived gender, sexual orientation, gender identity, or disability. The legislation ended the prerequisite that the victim be engaged in a federally protected activity (S.909, 2010).

The FBI publishes an annual report as part of the Uniform Crime Reporting (UCR) Program, which collects data for crimes motivated by biases against race, religion, sexual orientation, ethnicity/national origin, gender and gender identity, and disability. Each bias type is then broken down into more specific categories. For example, when a law enforcement agency determines that a hate crime was committed because of bias against an individual's race, the agency may then classify the bias as anti-white, anti-black, anti-American Indian/Alaskan Native, anti-Asian/Pacific Islander, or anti-multiple races, which describes a group of victims in which more than one race is represented. Most hate/bias crime statistics are, by definition, "single-bias incidents" (that is, those that involve one type of bias). Multiple-bias incidents are those that involve two or more offense types motivated by two or more biases. In August 2013, the U.S. Department of Justice (DOJ) announced that several additional groups would be included in the national program that tracks hate crimes. These groups include individuals from South Asia who are living in the United States, such as Arabs, Sikhs, and Hindus, as well as Buddhists, who are from all parts of Asia.

The UCR Program is a nationwide cooperative statistical effort of city, county, state, federal, tribal, university, and college law enforcement agencies. The collection of hate crime information reported in the UCR is voluntary, however, and not all agencies gather or submit data to the FBI. During 2015 (the most recent year for which data are available),

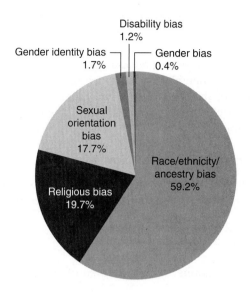

EXHIBIT 11.2 Hate in 2015

Source: https://www.fbi.gov/news/stories/2015-hate-crime
-statistics-released; https://ucr.fbi.gov/hate-crime/2015/
home/topic-pages/incidentsandoffenses_final

the UCR recorded 5,818 single-bias incidents involving 7,121 victims (see Exhibit 11.2). Of those victims:

- 59.2 percent were targeted because of a race/ethnicity/ancestry bias
- 19.7 percent because of a religious bias
- 17.7 percent because of sexual-orientation bias
- 1.7 percent because of a gender identity bias
- 1.2 percent because of a disability bias
- 0.4 percent because of a gender bias

Of the hate crimes due to religious bias, there were 695 anti-Jewish incidents with 731 victims, and 257 anti-Islamic incidents with 307 victims. The total numbers for both anti-Jewish and anti-Islamic hate crimes are much higher than those for any other group. Of the 5,493 known offenders:

- 48.4 percent were white
- 24.3 percent were African American
- 16.2 percent were of unknown race (U.S. Federal Bureau of Investigation, 2016)

However, because many hate crimes go unreported, the statistics do not represent the real picture and this is discussed later in this chapter.

The 2015 Hate Crime Statistics report, for the first time, included "... seven additional religious anti-bias categories (anti-Buddhist, anti-Eastern Orthodox, anti-Hindu, anti-Jehovah's Witness, anti-Mormon, anti-Christian, and anti-Sikh), as well as an anti-Arab bias motivation" (ibid.).

THE FBI UCR PROGRAM VERSUS THE NATIONAL CRIME VICTIMIZATION SURVEY (NCVS) The FBI's annual hate crime report is an essential tool for understanding our nation's hate crime problem; however, it alone does not provide a clear picture of the extent and nature of this type of crime. This is because of the voluntary nature of the reporting system on the part of law enforcement agencies and the failure of many victims to report crimes to police. Thus, although the report gives some insight into the trends in hate crimes, it does not entirely reflect the total problem. The data in the FBI annual report, a summary-based system, provide little information about the characteristics of crimes, victims, offenders, or arrests. Recognizing these deficiencies, the FBI created the National Incident-Based Reporting System (NIBRS).

The new system requires electronic submission of data from a records management system at the local agency level to a state system, and ultimately to NIBRS. This reporting system results in more details on additional categories of crime, including concurrent offenses, weapons, injury, location, property loss, and characteristics of the victims, offenders, and arrestees, including their gender, race, and age. The information is analyzed annually and becomes the NCVS report.

The information is combined with the statistics collected by the FBI as part of the UCR Program and results in a more thorough report and analysis of the data. To make the data comparable between the UCR Program and the NCVS, only those crimes in which an individual was the victim are included. A comparison of UCR and NCVS data reveals some striking similarities but also some major differences between the two. In February of 2016, then FBI director, James Comey, approved a recommendation to phase out the FBI UCR reporting system by January 2021 and establish NIBRS as the national standard for crime reporting (U.S. FBI, 2015).

Underreporting of Crime

Nearly two of three hate crimes go unreported to the police, according to the DOJ. A report by that agency indicates that "the percentage of all hate crime victimizations reported to police declined from 46 percent in 2003–06 to 35 percent in 2007–11" (U.S. Department of Justice, 2013). The report, the most recent, indicates that despite growing awareness of hate crimes, reporting has decreased over the years because victims of violent attacks doubt the police can or will help. The study determined the following based upon surveys covering the time period 2007 to 2011:

- 24 percent of hate crime victims said they did not report the crime because they believed that the police could not or would not help.
- 15 percent of hate crime victims stated that fear of reprisal or getting the offender in trouble was the reason not to report the crime to police.
- 23 percent of hate crime victims did not report the crime because they felt it was a private or personal matter or dealt with the crime in another way. (Ibid.)

Another study by a task force of the Crime Victims Center involved feedback from and interviews with victims of hate crimes. The finding was that victims do not report due to:

- Lack of knowledge about what constitutes a hate crime, how the laws are applied, and the overall criminal justice process;
- Lack of knowledge of crime victims' rights and available support services;
- Fear of retaliation by the perpetrator for reporting;
- Fear of being re-victimized by the criminal justice process, especially those immigrants who had been terrorized at the hands of military personnel and/or corrupt police in their countries of origin;
- Lack of English language proficiency or knowledge of the mechanisms available to report hate crimes;
- Fear of being identified as an undocumented immigrant and being deported;
- A belief, whether real or perceived, that law enforcement does not want to address hate crimes;
- Shame or embarrassment for being a victim of any crime, especially a hate crime;
- Cultural or personal beliefs that one should not complain about misfortunes and handle problems on one's own;
- Fear of being exposed as gay, lesbian, bisexual, or transgendered to one's family, employer, friends, or the general public and the potential ramifications of exposure;
- Fear of retaliation on the part of the elderly or persons with disabilities who have emotional and/or life-supporting dependence upon someone who has or is committing hate crimes against them; and
- The inability of some people with disabilities to articulate that they have been victims of hate crimes. (Ahearn, 2011)

Growth of Online Racism

On the one hand, racial insults and epithets are generally not as overt as in the days of the Civil Rights era. However, bigots can now express their intolerance and prejudice insidiously, anonymously, and sometimes openly. The World Wide Web is full of racist Web sites; furthermore, readers can freely comment on articles with race-related content. Daily, there are vicious remarks about a multitude of targeted groups, including immigrants, gays, blacks, Jews, and Muslims. Such comments often do not end up being removed from chat threads and their existence suggests that while overall progress has been made with respect to equal rights, there is still deep societal racism. However, efforts to remove hate speech have often clashed with those who argue that it's a form of free speech. Intolerance expressed online can and does incite violence just like face-to-face verbal manifestations of hate, and remains a major race relations challenge.

DEFINITION OF HATE/BIAS CRIME AND HATE/BIAS INCIDENT

Hate Crime

Under Title 18 U.S.C. Section 249, a hate crime is "a criminal offense committed against a person, property, or society that is motivated, in whole or in part, by the offender's bias against a race, color, religion, disability, sexual orientation or gender identity, or ethnicity/national origin" (U.S. Department of Justice. The Matthew Shepard and James Byrd, Jr., Hate Crimes Prevention Act of 2009). Definitions of hate crime often incorporate not only violence against individuals or groups but also crimes against property, such as arson or vandalism, those directed against government buildings, community centers, or houses of worship. As it is sometimes difficult to determine the offender's motivation, bias is to be reported only if an investigation establishes sufficient objective facts "to lead a reasonable and prudent person to conclude that the offender's actions were motivated, in whole or in part by bias" (ibid.).

Hate Incident

Hate incidents involve behaviors that, though motivated by bias against a victim's race, religion, ethnicity, gender, gender identity, disability, or sexual orientation, are not criminal acts. Hostile or hateful speech, or other disrespectful or discriminatory behavior, may be motivated by bias, but is not illegal. Such incidents become crimes only when they directly incite perpetrators to commit violence against persons or property or if they place a potential victim in reasonable fear of physical injury.

Definitions for Hate Crime Data Collection

To ensure uniformity in reporting, the following definitions have been adopted by the U.S. Federal Bureau of Investigation Uniform Crime Reporting Program:

Bias—A preformed negative opinion or attitude toward a group of people based on their race, religion, disability, sexual orientation, ethnicity, gender, or gender identity.

Bias Crime—A committed criminal offense that is motivated, in whole or in part, by the offender's bias(es) against a race, religion, disability, sexual orientation, ethnicity, gender, or gender identity; also known as Hate Crime. Note: Even if the offender was mistaken in his or her perception that the victim was a member of the group he or she was acting against, the offense is still a bias crime because the offender was motivated by bias against the group.

Bisexual—Of or relating to people who are physically, romantically, and/or emotionally attracted to both men and women.

Disability Bias—A preformed negative opinion or attitude toward a group of persons based on their physical or mental impairments, whether such disability is temporary or permanent, congenital or acquired by heredity, accident, injury, advanced age, or illness.

Ethnicity Bias—A preformed negative opinion or attitude toward a group of people whose members identify with each other, through a common heritage, often consisting of a common language, common culture (often including a shared religion), and/or ideology that stresses common ancestry. The concept of ethnicity differs from the closely related term race in that "race" refers to grouping based mostly upon biological criteria, while "ethnicity" also encompasses additional cultural factors.

Gay—Note: Generally, word is used to refer to gay men, but may also be used to describe women; the term "gay" is preferred over the term "homosexual." For the FBI UCR Program purposes, however, if reporting an antigay bias, the victim should be a male.

Gender—This term is used synonymously with sex to denote whether a newborn is male or female at birth, for example, "it's a boy" or "it's a girl."

Gender Bias—A preformed negative opinion or attitude toward a person or group of persons based on their actual or perceived gender, for example, male or female.

Gender Identity—A person's internal sense of being male, female, or a combination of both; that internal sense of a person's gender may be different from the person's gender as assigned at birth. Note: A transgender person may express their gender identity through gender characteristics, such as clothing, hair, voice, mannerisms, or behaviors that do not conform to the gender-based expectations of society.

Gender Identity Bias—A preformed negative opinion or attitude toward a person or group of persons based on their actual or perceived gender identity, for example, bias against transgender or gender nonconforming individuals.

Gender Nonconforming—Describes a person who does not conform to the gender-based expectations of society, for example, a woman dressed in traditionally male clothing or a man wearing makeup. Note: A gender nonconforming person may or may not be a lesbian, gay, bisexual, or transgender but may be perceived as such.

Hate Crime—Bias Crime.

Hate Group—An organization whose primary purpose is to promote animosity, hostility, and malice toward persons of or with a race, religion, disability, sexual orientation, ethnicity, gender, or gender identity that differs from that of the members or the organization. Examples include the Ku Klux Klan and the American Nazi Party.

Heterosexual—Of or relating to people who are physically, romantically, and/or emotionally attracted to people of the opposite sex. Note: The term straight is a synonym.

Homosexual—Of or relating to people who are physically, romantically, and/or emotionally attracted to people of the same gender. Note: Some people consider this to be an outdated and derogatory term, but it depends on the context in which it is used. Current journalistic standards restrict the usage of this term. "Lesbian" and/or "gay" are the currently accepted terms for referring to people who are attracted to others of the same sex.

Lesbian—Of or relating to women who are physically, romantically, and/or emotionally attracted to other women. Note: Some lesbian women prefer to be described as gay women. For FBI UCR Program purposes, however, if reporting an antigay bias, the victim should be a male.

LGBT—Common abbreviation for "lesbian, gay, bisexual, and transgender," used here to refer to community organizations or events that serve lesbian, gay, bisexual, transgender, and gender identity people. (LGBTQ, defined in Chapter 2 is also used in this textbook.)

Racial Bias—A preformed negative opinion or attitude toward a group of persons who possess common physical characteristics, such as color of skin, eyes, and/or hair, facial features, and so forth, genetically transmitted by descent and heredity, which distinguish them as a distinct division of humankind, for example, Asians, blacks or African Americans, and whites.

Religious Bias—A preformed negative opinion or attitude toward a group of people who share the same religious beliefs regarding the origin and purpose of the universe and the existence or nonexistence of a supreme being, for example, Catholics, Jews, Muslims, Protestants, and atheists.

Sexual Orientation—The term for a person's physical, romantic, and/or emotional attraction to members of the same and/or opposite sex, including lesbian, gay, bisexual, and heterosexual (straight) individuals. Note: Avoid the offensive terms "sexual preference" or "lifestyle."

Sexual-Orientation Bias—A preformed negative opinion or attitude toward a person or group of persons based on their actual or perceived sexual orientation.

Transgender—Of or relating to a person who identifies as a different gender from their gender as assigned at birth. Note: The person may also identify himself or herself as "transsexual." A transgender person may outwardly express his or her gender identity all of the time, part of the time, or none of the time; a transgender person may decide to change his or her body to medically conform to his or her gender identity. Avoid the following terms: "he-she," "she-male," "tranny," "it," "shim," "drag queen," "transvestite," and "cross-dresser."

Source: Adapted primarily from U.S. Federal Bureau of Investigation Uniform Crime Report Program: "Hate Crime Data Collection Guidelines and Training Manual," 2012.

HATE/BIAS CRIME SOURCE THEORIES

Introduction

Hate crime has been studied over the past three decades by criminologists, sociologists, and others, but there is no single conclusion about its causes. Although the reader should understand there are sometimes social forces, described later, that are offered as the reason for hate crime, the individual committing such a crime is still responsible for his or her action and should be punished. Among the community characteristics that have been cited as contributing to hate crime are density and overcrowding, clustering, move-in violence, inequality, and economic deprivation, each of which will be discussed more fully later in this chapter. The intent of providing the following descriptions of hate crime source theories is that by understanding them, there is the potential for government and community agencies to change the social conditions that have the potential to breed hate.

Urban Dynamics and Other Theories

IMMIGRANT CLUSTERING   Hate incidents and crimes often do not occur in a vacuum, but are part of a larger social and economic interchange, one aspect of which is immigration. Newly arrived immigrants who are not trained professionals (e.g., those in the high-tech field) tend to locate or cluster where immigrants of their own ethnic or racial background are already established, called an ethnic enclave. They tend to congregate in the same areas of the country or within a city to be near relatives or friends, to have assistance in finding housing and jobs, to cope with language barriers, and to find the security of a familiar religion and social institutions. This is true of both undocumented and documented immigrants, and has a long history resulting in neighborhoods ranging from Little Italy and Greektown to Spanish Harlem and Koreatown. According to Steven Wallace, professor and chair of the Department of Community Health Sciences at the UCLA, members of an ethnic community provide a sense of continuity for each other, and, accordingly, ease subsequent generations into American values and society. According to Wallace,

> An ethnic enclave represents a place where immigrants can associate with others like themselves and provides a safe place to speak a language other than English, and maintain some of the traditions and customs that provide comfort in a new culture. The resulting social and economic supports are one explanation for the observation that immigrants living in ethnic enclaves tend to have better health than similar immigrants living outside the enclaves. (Wallace, 2017)

It is common for first-generation immigrant communities to be in low-rent districts: these core urban areas are typically where low-socioeconomic-class minorities from all backgrounds live, because of inexpensive or government subsidized housing (ibid.). Employment or welfare services are available, and there is a measure of comfort derived from living with people of one's own race or culture. These areas are often impoverished with substandard, older housing, and are frequently overcrowded, with a high incidence of social conflict and crime, including drug and gang activity. As new immigrants and members of varied racial and cultural groups move into the core area, they come into conflict with existing members of that community—a phenomenon that has been going on for generations. The newcomers and the established community members often compete for housing, jobs, health services, and education. When there is a collapse of affordable health services, lack of affordable housing, and reductions in benefits (cuts in social programs by federal and state authorities), as occurred in the 1990s, 2003, and again from 2008 to 2013, conflicts escalate between racial and ethnic groups. As these circumstances intensify, incidents of discrimination, bias, and hate violence increase. Those who are better-off want to move out, not just to improve their lot but also to escape the conflict. Although Wallace published his initial findings in the 1980s, he does not think that "the basic theories [about social causes] have changed much over the past 30 years, though the details have" (ibid.).

THE ECONOMY AND HATE VIOLENCE   A poor economy contributes greatly to hate violence. In many areas of the country, when major industries have downturns, go out of business, or relocate, the likelihood of economic distress among low-skilled and unskilled workers increases. Between 2007 and 2013, during an economic crisis worldwide, several large American cities, such as Detroit, filed for bankruptcy. Detroit had been in financial chaos

Mini Case Study: Immigrants from Asia Settle in Long-Established Neighborhoods

Read the following description and then discuss your responses to the questions below:

Attacks against elderly and vulnerable Asian Americans in an affordable urban area (historically, a primarily black neighborhood) resulted in a wedge between Asian- and African Americans. Asian immigrants held rallies at City Hall complaining that they were targets of racially motivated violence. Per police investigations, the perpetrators were primarily black teenagers. Many black residents of the area and activists expressed their displeasure at the Asian immigrants' protests, saying that this sort of violence had been happening to African American seniors for a long time; thus, anyone moving into a neighborhood where there is violence can become a victim. These tensions were exacerbated by economic stresses at the time as well as deep language and cultural barriers between the Asian immigrants and black neighbors.

1. What steps could and should the police department have taken in order to plan for the demographic change that took place in this neighborhood?
2. What community programs might be utilized to reduce crimes against seniors in this neighborhood for both groups?
3. How could community networking between the police department and national, regional, state, and/or local organizations and the neighborhood have been employed?
4. How could community educational programs via the media and schools have been used?
5. What other steps would you take if it were your responsibility to bring harmony to and fewer attacks against the citizens of the neighborhood?
6. What community policing resources could be used to prevent, investigate, and resolve the issue of any citizen in the neighborhood becoming the victim of crime?

after experiencing a decline in population over the years, prompted by the shutdown of automobile manufacturing plants. Following the closures, crime there skyrocketed and the city experienced the highest murder rate since the 1970s (Damron, 2012; Fisher, 2012). The distress that accompanies unemployment and poverty is often directed toward immigrants and minorities and manifests itself as harassment and violence. There are examples, during the same period, of the same happening in the suburbs as poverty in those communities grew, in some cases, twice as fast as in the cities (ibid.). The stresses associated with these economic challenges can give rise to increased incidents of violence.

MOVE-IN VIOLENCE Move-in violence can occur when people of one ethnicity or race move into a residence or open a business in a neighborhood composed of people from a different race or ethnicity. Changing demographics can have a significant impact on a community because of hostility based on both perceived and real group differences. However, the presence of new migrants or immigrants in a racially or ethnically different neighborhood does not automatically result in intergroup conflict or violence.

Historically, most cases of move-in violence have involved black, Hispanic, or Asian victims who locate housing or businesses in previously all-white suburbs or neighborhoods. Whites have not been the sole perpetrators, however; they have also been victims. Other cases of conflict have involved communities with new immigrants from the Middle East and South Asia. In some of these new mixed neighborhoods, community members have perceived that their concerns are being ignored.

Trend Monitoring in Multicultural Communities

Monitoring conditions in a community provides useful information for forecasting potential negative events and preparing accordingly. Evaluating predictions should include an analysis of economic circumstances, social/cultural conditions, as well as the political environment within the community. Often, there is a connection between these elements and social unrest, including hate speech, incidents and crimes

ECONOMIC CIRCUMSTANCES Crime, social unrest, riots, and disturbances occur during depressed economic times. Waves of immigrants (both documented and undocumented) also add to the scramble for available jobs and services. Internationally, poverty, overcrowding, and wars have been pressuring more people to migrate than ever before. Many areas experienced real conflict as established residents who were already struggling now had masses of people competing with them for services and jobs. California continually experiences legal and illegal immigration from Mexico and Central and South America. The new immigrants (the weakest group) become the target for people's frustrations as their own sense of well-being decreases. The established ethnically and racially mixed groups in neighborhoods see what they perceive as preferential treatment for the newcomers and react accordingly.

Federal decisions that lead to settlement of immigrants into economically depressed communities have frequently been made without regard to the adequacy of local resources to handle the influx. Police and community problems can evolve because of these well-intentioned national policies that have not been thoroughly worked through. Tracking influxes of immigrants into communities, plus an awareness of political decisions, should keep law enforcement executives and officers alert to relocation and acculturation problems of newcomers in their communities, and increasing anti-immigrant attitudes. Tracking also provides an opportunity to work with the community to develop transition management plans as well as preventive programs for keeping the peace. National immigration policies and politics have a tremendous impact on cities and counties, and therefore criminal justice agencies must monitor them and plan accordingly.

Urban issues, as discussed, can lead to conditions that are ripe for hate crimes. The following, from a Police Executive Research Forum publication from over two decades ago, clearly holds true today:

> Urban tensions are fueled by a combination of...wealth disparity and the pressures of large scale migration, which are present not only in American cities, but in cities worldwide... [Robin] Wright notes, "tensions in cities are often complicated by another dimension—racial or ethnic diversity." Minorities are increasingly left stranded in urban outskirts—slums or squatter camps—and excluded politically and financially. Their ensuing frustrations contribute to the volatility of urban life. (DeGeneste & Sullivan, 1997)

Conflicts, including riots resulting from urban decay, overcrowding, poor social services, and ethnic tension have occurred in cities worldwide and can be expected to continue, particularly as swelling migrant populations flock to cities (ibid.).

However, a 2011 survey by the Pew Research Center revealed that conflict between rich and poor now eclipses racial strain and friction between immigrants and native-born as the greatest source of tensions in American society. About two-thirds of Americans believe there are "strong conflicts" between rich and poor in the United States (Morin, 2012).

POLITICAL ENVIRONMENT Executives of criminal justice agencies must monitor legislation, sensitive court trials, and political events that affect not only the jurisdictions they serve, but also the nation and the world. Often what goes on outside of the United States has an impact on local populations. Law enforcement must be aware of foreign political struggles and their potential to polarize ethnic and racial groups in the local community, leading to conflict. Police must have the ability to recognize potential problems and strive to prevent or mitigate intergroup conflict. Only by acknowledging their primary role in preventing and mediating conflict in the community can peace officers begin to remediate long-standing and emerging tensions. During the contentious presidential debates in 2016 and the new administration of Donald Trump, there were many political environment examples within the United States and Europe of events that needed to be monitored. The criminal justice system operates within the larger political context.

SOCIAL AND CULTURAL CONDITIONS Typically, poverty and frustration with the system, the perception of racism, and unequal treatment are conditions for social unrest. Diverse peoples living in close proximity can also create potentially unstable social conditions. Furthermore, on the familial level, a decline in the cohesiveness of the nuclear family adds to stresses within societal micro units. Unemployment, especially among youth, is another social condition with potentially dangerous consequences.

Finally, gangs and the use of illegal drugs and their impact on neighborhoods lead to social and cultural conditions ripe for explosive events and hate/bias crimes. None of these elements alone, however, account for community violence. All of these factors, in combination with political and economic conditions, contribute to discontent. Officers often find themselves frustrated because they cannot undo decades of societal precursors that set the stage for upheavals.

Targets of Hate Crimes and Incidents

The psycho-cultural origin of hate crimes stems from human nature itself. People are culturally conditioned to hate those who are different from them because of their places of origin, looks, beliefs, or preferences. As the musical *South Pacific* says, "You've got to be taught to hate and fear/You've got to be taught from year to year." Crimes and acts of hate serve as frightening reminders to vulnerable citizens that they may not take safety for granted. Collectively, they begin to develop a mentality that hate crimes can take place anywhere—in streets, in neighborhoods, at workplaces, and even in their homes. Not all crimes and incidents that look like they are motivated by prejudice or bias involve hate per se. For example, many nonviolent incidents are committed impulsively, or as acts of conformity or mental instability, or as deliberate acts of intimidation.

There are innumerable examples of hate/bias crimes that have victimized blacks, Asians, Hispanics, and whites as well. Clearly, such hate goes back for many generations. Examples of these are included in Part Two, "Cultural Specifics for Law Enforcement." The following sections address Jews, Arab/Muslim and LGBTQ and gender identity people as victims of hate or bias crimes.

JEWS AND ANTI-SEMITISM

Jews

As of 2013, per the Pew Research Center, American Jews comprised approximately 2 percent of the adult American population (Lipka, 2013). Jews belong to a religious and cultural or ethnic group, although they have sometimes been incorrectly labeled as a racial group. Jews have experienced discrimination, persecution, and violence throughout history because their religious beliefs and practices often set them apart from the majority. Even when they were totally assimilated (integrated into society), as was true in Germany in the early twentieth century, they were still not accepted as full citizens and eventually experienced the ultimate hate crime—genocide. The term *anti-Semitism* means "against Semites," which literally includes Jews and Arabs. Popular use of this term, however, refers to anti-Jewish sentiment.

European anti-Semitism had religious origins: Jews did not accept Jesus Christ as the son of God and were portrayed as betrayers and even killers of Christ. This accusation gave rise to religious anti-Semitism and what Christians saw as justification for anti-Jewish acts. In the past half century, there have been great strides made by religious leaders to eliminate centuries of prejudice. For example, a 1965 Roman Catholic decree (the *Nostra Aetate*) stated that the church did not hold Jews responsible for the death of Christ. The decree, written by the Second Vatican Council under the leadership of the pope, encouraged people to cease blaming Jews and instead work for stronger links and increased understanding between the religious groups. But despite some progress in ecumenical relations, there are still individuals who, 2,000 years after the birth of Christ, believe that Jews of today are responsible for Christ's death, even though he was a Jew himself. Abraham Foxman, national director of the Anti-Defamation League (ADL) from 1987 to 2015, has expressed his great concern about two different types of "insidious anti-Semitism." One emanates from the incorrect belief that Jews are more loyal to Israel than to the United States. The other relates to the belief that Jews killed Christ (AICE, 2011). No other group in the history of humankind has been accused of killing the God of another religious group; this religious dimension may explain the virulence and long history of anti-Semitism.

Nationwide surveys by the ADL over the years have revealed trends regarding American views of Jews and anti-Semitic attitudes. The most recent poll was in October of 2016 and it discovered that 14 percent of the population, approximately 34 million American adults, holds anti-Semitic beliefs (ADL, New York, 2017). Public opinion surveys by the ADL in January and February of 2017 reveal

> ... that while anti-Semitic attitudes in the United States have increased slightly to 14 percent, the vast majority of Americans hold respectful opinions of their Jewish neighbors. However, for the first-time ADL found a majority of Americans (52 percent) saying that they are concerned about violence in the U.S. directed at Jews, and an even a higher percentage (76 percent) concerned about violence directed at Muslims. More than eight in 10 Americans (84 percent) believe it is important for the government to play a role in combating anti-Semitism, up from 70 percent in 2014. (Ibid.)

Historically, a nationwide survey in 2011 by the ADL found that 15 percent (nearly 35 million adults) of American people had "deeply" anti-Semitic attitudes, which was an increase from 12 percent in 2009. However, this was a dramatic decline since their initial survey in 1964, when 29 percent of Americans were found to hold anti-Semitic attitudes. The ADL attributed the increase from 2009 to 2011 to the "the impact of broader trends in America—financial insecurity, social uncertainty, the decline of civility and the growth of polarization" (ADL, 2011). The report suggests that in times of high unemployment and economic problems, age-old myths and/or stereotypes about Jews and money, influence, and power in business become even more prevalent and negative. Jews remain the religious/ethnic group most likely to be targeted in hate crimes, per current statistics. However, Muslims have seen an alarming rise in hate crimes in the past few years; this topic is discussed in detail later in this chapter as well as in Chapter 8.

Another type of anti-Semitism falls under what some would label as anti-Zionism (i.e., against the establishment of the state of Israel as a homeland for Jews). Although politically oriented, this type of anti-Semitism still makes references to "the Jews" and equates all Jews with the suppression of the Palestinian people. Police officers must be aware of the potential fallout in the United States when conflicts arise in the Middle East, particularly between Israelis and Palestinians. Anti-Semitic attitudes are sometimes expressed as anti-Zionist sentiments, even though Jewish political identification with Israel varies greatly. Over the years there have been synagogues and other Jewish institutions tagged with anti-Israel and anti-Semitic graffiti, in apparent response to the Palestinian–Israeli conflict (see Chapter 8 for further information).

Prevalence of Anti-Semitic Crimes

The ADL produces an annual report on the number of anti-Semitic incidents, which is compiled from official crime statistics from all states and the District of Columbia as well as information provided to ADL's regional offices by victims, law enforcement officials, and community leaders. The numbers consistently exceed those collected by the FBI for the UCR report produced each year, and identify both criminal and noncriminal incidents of harassment and intimidation, including distribution of hate literature, threats, and slurs. It includes incidents such as physical and verbal assaults, harassment, property defacement, vandalism, and other expressions of anti-Jewish sentiment.

In 2017, the ADL's annual audit of Anti-Semitic incidents recorded 1,266 anti-Semitic incidents in 2016 that targeted Jews and Jewish institutions, a 34 percent year-over-year increase in incidents—assaults, vandalism, and harassment. "While anti-Semitic incidents in the United States are still low compared to previous decades, the number of violent assaults jumped dramatically in the last year and the first quarter of 2017" (ADL, 2017).

In the beginning of 2017, there was a surge of hate attacks and graffiti directed against Jews not only in the United States, but also Canada and Europe. The April 2017 ADL report indicated, that in the first quarter of 2017, preliminary reports of the 541 anti-Semitic incidents included the following (see Exhibit 11.3):

- 380 harassment incidents, including 161 bomb threats, an increase of 127 percent over the same quarter in 2016;
- 155 vandalism incidents, including three cemetery desecrations, an increase of 36 percent; and
- Six physical assault incidents, a decrease of 40 percent. (Ibid.)

Note: Since the 2017 ADL report was published, it was determined that many of the bomb threats were actually hoaxes committed by two different people (Chan, 2017; Rayman, Alcorn, McShane, 2017).

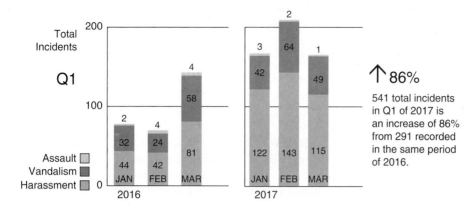

EXHIBIT 11.3 First Quarter Comparison, Anti-Semitic Incidents: United States
Source: ADL. www.adl.org/news/press-releases/us-anti-semitic-incidents-spike-86-percent-so-far-in-2017

The ADL first quarter report continued,

> The 2016 presidential election and the heightened political atmosphere played a role in the increase. There were 34 incidents linked to the election. For example, in Denver, graffiti posted in May 2016 said, "Kill the Jews, Vote Trump." In November, a St. Petersburg, Fla., man was accosted by someone who told him "Trump is going to finish what Hitler started." (Ibid.)

As indicated above, some believe that the increase was due to the contentious presidential 2016–2017 campaign; anti-Semitic hate crimes began to increase in 2014.

Anti-Semitic Groups and Individuals

Several different varieties of groups in the United States have exhibited anti-Semitic attitudes, and some of the most extreme groups have committed hate crimes against Jews. According to the Southern Poverty Law Center (SPLC), there are 917 active hate groups in the United States, and 521 of them are significantly hostile toward Jews (SPLC, 2017d). These organizations include white supremacist groups, such as the Ku Klux Klan (KKK), Aryan Nations, White Aryan Resistance (WAR), Posse Comitatus, and neo-Nazi skinheads (discussed further in Appendix E). These groups tend to hate all who are different from them but focus a great deal of attention on blacks and Jews. The two states with the most anti-Semitic hate groups are Texas (62) and California (31) (ibid.).

Those who argued that it was United States' support of Israel that led to the 9/11 attacks have demonstrated another aspect of anti-Semitism. Some hate groups used this argument to stir up anti-Jewish feelings and to erode sympathy and support for Jews and for Israel at their organizations' rallies and within the general public. In addition, those who are vehemently against the existence of the state of Israel may exhibit strong anti-Jewish attitudes. While it is not as common for anti-Zionist attitudes to result in acts of violence against Jews in the United States as it is in Europe, Jewish Americans, like Arab Americans, can nevertheless become targets during Middle Eastern crises. Finally, in times of recession, Jews are often blamed for the economic decline, and the notion of Jewish "influence" (that is, the baseless charge that Jews control the media, the banks, and even the world economy) provides a convenient scapegoat. It is not within the scope of this section to delve into these myths; however, there is widespread harmful misinformation about Jews that anti-Semites continue to spread.

Synagogues are not the only targets of anti-Semitism. In 2011, for example, "an Oregon white supremacist and his girlfriend, linked to four slayings in three states, were driving to Sacramento to 'kill more Jews' when they were arrested by police" (SPLC, 2012). In 2017, a neo-Nazi march was planned for Martin Luther King Day in the town of Whitefish, Montana (population 7,000). For many years, there has been what has been described as a battle between neo-Nazi extremists and the residents, especially those opposed to the group. Those in opposition, including elected officials and human rights groups, planned and mobilized a large group of counter protesters. Montana is an "open carry" state where permits are not needed for guns, and both sides planned to bring weapons to the neo-Nazi march. Ultimately, the neo-Nazis called off the march and the nonviolent opposition achieved a victory that could be considered a good case study (Beckett, 2017; Julian, 2017).

Jewish Community Concerns

Around the holiest days of the Jewish year (Rosh Hashanah and Yom Kippur, usually occurring in the early fall), there may be heightened anxiety among some community members regarding security. Indeed, many synagogues hire extra security during times of worship over this 10-day holiday period. Acts of defilement can occur in synagogues and other Jewish institutions at random times as well. These acts of prejudice bring back painful memories for Jews who experienced violent expressions of anti-Semitism in other countries, especially for those who lived through the Holocaust; some of the memories and fears have been passed on to subsequent generations. A swastika painted by teenagers on a building does not necessarily precede any acts of anti-Jewish violence, yet it can evoke fear among many Jewish community members, especially older Jews, because of the historical significance of the symbol.

Police officers must understand that different segments of the Jewish community feel vulnerable to anti-Semitism, and therefore officers are advised to listen to and take seriously community members' expressions of concern and fear. At the same time, officers can explain that acts of vandalism are sometimes isolated or random, and are not targeting any group in particular. Finally, police officers should be aware that anti-Semitism has a long and active history, and even if some fears appear to be exaggerated, they are grounded in the Jewish experience. Therefore, officers who take reports from citizens should reassure them that their local law enforcement agency views hate crimes and incidents seriously and that extra protection will be provided if the need arises.

What Law Enforcement Can Do

Officers can take the following steps to establish rapport and provide protection in Jewish communities when the need arises:

1. When an officer hears of an act that can be classified as a hate crime toward Jews, it should be investigated, tracked, and dealt with as such. Dismissing acts of anti-Semitism as petty crime will result in a lack of trust on the part of the community.
2. When hate crimes and incidents are perpetrated against other groups in the community (e.g., gay, African American, Asian American groups), officers should alert Jewish community leaders immediately. Their institutions may be the next targets.
3. Officers should be aware of groups and individuals who distribute hate literature on people's doorsteps or vehicle windshields. Even if no violence occurs, the recipients of such hate literature become very fearful.
4. In cooperation with local organizations such as the Jewish Community Relations Councils (JCRC) or regional offices of the ADL (Anti-Defamation League), officers can provide information through joint meetings on ways that individuals can heighten the security of Jewish institutions (such as information on nonbreakable glass, lighting of facilities in evenings).
5. Law enforcement officials should be familiar with the important dates of the Jewish calendar, especially when the High Holidays (Rosh Hashanah and Yom Kippur) occur. (Note that the Jewish holiday cycle is based on the lunar calendar, thus the holiday dates vary from year to year.) Safety and protection can be even more important during events at which large groups of Jews congregate.
6. Finally, officers should contact Jewish umbrella organizations in the community and ask for assistance in sending necessary messages to local Jewish institutions and places of worship. Two examples include: the JCRC and the ADL. Both JCRC and the ADL have representative organizations in almost every major city in the United States. These organizations as well as Jewish federations can greatly assist law enforcement in disseminating information to community members.

Because of Jewish history, anti-Semitic incidents do not come as a surprise to many Jews. An officer's ability to calm fears as well as to investigate threats thoroughly will result in strong relations between law enforcement officials and Jewish community members.

ANTI-ARAB/MUSLIM VICTIMIZATION

Arabs and Muslims

The number of Muslims living in the United States is estimated at 3.3 million, according to the Pew Research Center, or just 1 percent of the country's population. Despite their small numbers, Muslims have been disproportionately affected by hate crimes, especially in the aftermath of September 11, 2001; in 2001, incidents targeting people, institutions and businesses associated with the Muslim faith went from 28 in 2000 to 481, a rise of 1,600 percent, according to the FBI (U.S. Federal Bureau of Investigation, 2001). Hate crimes against American Muslims spiked again as both a backlash against terrorist attacks around the world and in reaction to highly divisive language (e.g., references to "Muslim ban.") during the U.S. presidential campaign, beginning in 2015. Americans, once again, saw an exponential leap in hate crimes and much anti Muslim/anti-Arab sentiment expressed openly (see Exhibit 11.4). According to FBI findings, the true number of hate crimes against people of Middle Eastern descent is believed to be much higher than published statistics, given that many are not reported to the authorities. According to the Council on American-Islamic Relations (CAIR), a national Muslim civil rights and advocacy group, the number of hate crimes and "anti-Muslim" incidents reported by American Muslims exceeded 1,700 for the same time frame, ranging from public harassment, hate mail, bomb threats, physical assault, property damage, and murder.

Arab and Muslim Identities and Misidentification

Arabs and Muslims of Middle Eastern descent have lived in the United States for hundreds of years, although conflicts in the Middle East in recent years have caused an increase in immigrants from the region. Others come to the United States to study or pursue professional opportunities and become permanent residents or naturalized citizens (see Chapter 8 for further information). Yet, Middle Eastern immigrants and established Americans from the Middle East are often the victims of hate speech and hate crimes, targeted by people who make the assumption that all Middle Easterners are immigrants or Muslims. Established Arab Americans can be second, third or even fourth generation and may have very little, if any, connection to their countries of origin. It is equally important to understand that there are differences among people from the Middle East, an area that includes 17 countries, not including the Palestinian Authority, also referred to as Palestine. Most are Arab, although not all. Iranians are not Arabs, and Israel, while located in the Middle East, is a Jewish-majority country. Likewise, all Arabs are not necessarily Muslim, and a considerable number of Arabs are actually from North Africa or East Africa. Anti-Arab/Muslim victimization can affect most of these groups and even others appearing to be "Arab" or "Muslim." Male followers of the Sikh religion, who wear turbans and are not allowed to cut their beards, are often

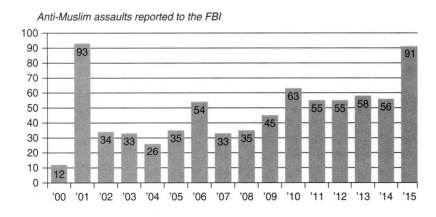

EXHIBIT 11.4 Anti-Muslim Assaults at Highest Level since 2001

Source: www.pewresearch.org/fact-tank/2016/11/21/anti-muslim-assaults-reach 911-era-levels-U.S. Federal Bureau of Investigation-data-show/

mistaken for Muslims. Chapter 5, focusing on Asian Americans, presents examples of South Asian victims of hate crimes because they were wrongly assumed to be Muslim or Arab or simply "immigrants" who did not belong.

Prevalence of Anti-Arab/Muslim Crimes

Broadly speaking, Islamophobia is defined as a fear or hatred of Islam and Muslims. According to CAIR, "this phenomenon promotes and perpetrates anti-Muslim stereotyping, discrimination, harassment, and even violence. It negatively impacts the participation of American Muslims in public life" (CAIR, 2015). A few features of Islamophobia include:

- The view that Muslim cultures and Islam are monolithic and unchanging.
- The view that Muslim cultures are wholly different from all other cultures.
- That Islam is inherently threatening and should not be allowed or at most, limited, in the United States. (CAIR, 2015; Runnymeade Trust, 1996)

Islamophobia goes through cycles of intensity in the United States and prior to the recent surge of hate/bias crimes against Arabs, Muslims, and those who appear to be of Middle Eastern descent. In 2010, a controversial plan to build a mosque and Islamic cultural center in lower Manhattan, located within blocks of the former World Trade Center, spurred massive opposition and led to a backlash against proposed construction or expansion of Islamic places of worship around the country (CAIR, 2015).

As anti-Muslim hate crimes surged, so did the number of anti-Muslim hate groups in the United States (see Exhibit 11.5). The largest grassroots anti-Muslim group, according to the SPLC, is said to be ACT for America, billed by the group itself as the National Rifle Association (NRA) of national security (SPLC, 2017a).

After leveling off for several years following the September 11 terrorist attacks, hate crimes against Muslims have again surged. These have coincided with the United States' wars in Iraq and Afghanistan, and later the Syrian refugee crisis, prompted by a civil war, which has sent millions of Muslims in search of new homes in Europe, the United States, and Canada. The pressure on countries to accept Muslim refugees, as well as numerous incidents of terrorist attacks in Europe and the United States committed by people of Muslim faith, resulted in a climate of growing fear and suspicion and increased anti-Muslim rhetoric and

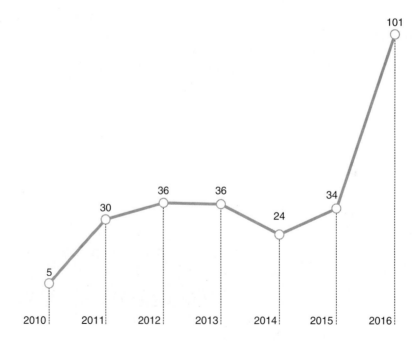

EXHIBIT 11.5   Anti-Muslim Groups 2010–2016

Source: The Southern Poverty Law Center. www.splcenter.org/fighting-hate/extremist-files/ideology/anti-muslim

hate crimes. In 2015, 257 hate crime incidents against Muslims were recorded, according to the FBI, the highest since 2001 and a 67 percent increase over the 154 incidents reported in 2014 (FBI:UCR, 2015a).

Hate crimes continued to rise during 2016, a year marked by an unusually bitter presidential campaign marked by then candidate Donald Trump's calls to monitor mosques, create a database of Muslims, which some compared to the yellow stars Jews were made to wear in Nazi Germany in an effort to closely monitor activity, and a travel ban on travelers from some Muslim countries. According to the SPLC, a group that tracks extremist groups, Trump's comments emboldened people who already feeling anger or suspicion toward Muslims (Abdelkader, 2016; SPLC, 2016). Examples of attacks include a Muslim woman's hijab, or traditional head covering favored by many conservative Muslim women, was lit on fire by a man as she shopped in fall 2016 (Hawkins, 2016; Moore, 2016). In August of 2016, an imam in Queens and his assistant were shot and killed execution-style on the sidewalk. Earlier that year, a man shouting obscenities about Islam, shot two men in traditional Muslim religious garb in Minneapolis, and in St. Louis, a man was arrested after he pointed a gun at a Muslim family that was out shopping and told them they "all should die" (Lichtblau, 2016). Another example of a hate crime targeting Muslims occurred in Garden City, Kansas, in 2016. Three men were arrested before they could carry out their plan to detonate truck bombs around an apartment complex where Muslims from Somalia lived and worshipped. The men were members of a militia group called the Crusaders. The group is known for its anti-immigrant, anti-Muslim, and antigovernment ideology (U.S. Department of Justice, 2016).

Arab/Muslim Community Concerns

Throughout the history of the United States, the vast majority of extremist or terrorist violence in the United States has been committed by white supremacists (Craven, 2015; Ybarra, 2015). However, in recent years, violence carried out in the name of Islam has been prevalent, creating the stereotype of the "violence-prone" or "terrorist Muslim." It has also led to a false perception that Middle Easterners are not patriotic and do not have the United States' best interests at heart. A 2016 Pew Research Center survey found that almost half of American adults (49 percent) think at least "some" Muslims in the United States are anti-American, including 11 percent who think "most" or "almost all" are anti-American (Kishi, 2016). Another survey from about the same time found that 46 percent of Americans thought Islam was more likely than other religions to encourage violence.

Muslim groups, such as CAIR, have worked to dispel this perception by pointing out that the Qur'an condemns violence and regards the unjust taking of someone's life or property as a criminal behavior and great sin. Other stereotypes include that Islam oppresses women and forces them to wear a headscarf as a sign of submission, which Muslim leaders say is not based on facts. Muslim women in the United States can decide how to interpret the various teachings of the Qur'an, and while many women in Muslim countries do face oppression, it is caused by cultural traditions, not Islamic law, according to the SPLC's Teaching Tolerance project (SPLC). "Honor killings" of girls, for example, a practice mainly associated with the Middle East, North Africa (as well as South Asia), comes from deeply embedded traditions associated with "cultures of honor" rather than "cultures of law" (Department of Justice [Canada], 2016).

What Law Enforcement Can Do

Negative experiences Muslims may have had with police in their countries of origin, as well as a fear that they will be wrongly suspected of crimes based on their religious or ethnic affiliation, have resulted in a fear of dealing with law enforcement authorities, according to CAIR. This, in turn, can manifest as a lack of willingness to report hate crimes. Police can work to dispel mistrust by showing that they are knowledgeable about and respectful of Muslim practices and customs. Discussed in further detail in Chapter 8, these include removing shoes when entering a mosque or a home, and not extending a hand to a person of the opposite sex, since religious Muslims abstain from touching anyone of the opposite sex to whom they are not related. In such cases, it may be helpful to send an officer of the same sex as the person seeking to be interviewed. Additionally, Arab culture values respect and "saving face," so police officers may have more success if they interview people apart from their families. Law enforcement should also work to forge alliances with local and regional Muslim organizations and investigate all crimes against Muslims as potential hate crimes.

More information can be found in the "Law Enforcement Official's Guide to the Muslim Community" booklet, available on the Council of American-Islamic Relations Web site (CAIR, 2005).

CAIR in April of 2017 reported

> Preliminary data reveals that cases of U.S. Customs and Border Protection (CBP) profiling accounted for 23 percent of all Council on American-Islamic case intakes in the first three months of 2017. This represents a 1035 percent increase in CBI typed cases in 2017 over the same period in 2016. Of the 193 CBP cases recorded from January–March 2017, 181 were reported after the January 27 signing of the Executive Order "Protecting the Nation from Foreign Terrorist Entry into the United States," also known as the Muslim Ban. (CAIR, 2017)

LGBTQ AND GENDER IDENTITY VICTIMIZATION

The abbreviation, "LGBTQ" has, in some instances, replaced "LGBT," the latter standing for "lesbian, gay, bisexual, and transgender" (see p. 000 for full definitions of these terms and Chapter 2). As mentioned in Chapter 2, there is no across-the-board agreement as to what the "Q" stands for in LGBTQ. One meaning is "questioning," which implies that individuals are unsure of their orientation, and are not comfortable with the existing, established categories (i.e., LGBT). Most millennials define the "Q" as, "Queer," which at one time was a highly derogatory word, signifying homosexual. "Queer" for many younger people has lost the derogatory connotations it once had.

According to Ken Carlson, sergeant with the Concord (California) Police Department, who is gay, all words for homosexuals and homosexuality were derogatory for many years. The term "homosexual" was actually listed as one type of diagnosis for psychiatric illness by the American Psychiatric Association, until 1993. Gay leaders later introduced the term "homophile" and later "gay," while homosexual women began calling themselves "lesbian" to set themselves apart. As other LGBT people sought to be represented and protected, the terms "bisexual" and "transgender" were also added.

In discussing anti-LGBTQ attitudes, it is important to understand the word, *phobia*, which is defined "as an irrational, excessive, and persistent fear of some particular thing or situation," *Homophobia*, for example, is an "irrational hatred or fear of homosexuals or homosexuality" (Collins English Dictionary online). Sometimes, homophobia results in homophobic acts, which can run the full spectrum from antigay jokes to physical battery resulting in injury or death. In this text, as in government reporting systems, homophobic acts are referred to as antisexual orientation or gender identity bias incidents and offenses. Hate crimes targeting LGBTQ individuals are distinct from other bias crimes because they target a group made up of every other category discussed in this textbook. The membership of LGBTQ organizations in the United States includes people of all ethnicities, races, nationalities, and religions.

Hate Crime Laws Specific to Sexual Orientation and Gender Identity

Every year, thousands of LGBTQ individuals in the United States are harassed, beaten, or murdered solely because of their sexual orientation or gender identity. Prosecution is for the most part left to the states, since most crimes are investigated by state or local police. It was only in 2009 that the Matthew Shepard and James Byrd, Jr., Hate Crimes Prevention Act, named for the 21-year-old Wyoming student who was tortured and murdered because of his sexual orientation, was passed. The Act provides for the following:

- Extend existing federal protections to include "gender identity, sexual orientation, gender, and disability"
- Allow the Justice Department to assist in hate crime investigations at the local level when local law enforcement is unable or unwilling to fully address these crimes
- Mandate that the FBI begin tracking hate crimes based on actual or perceived gender identity, sexual orientation, gender, and disability

- Remove limitations that narrowly define hate crimes as violence committed while a person is accessing a federally protected activity, such as voting or going to school
- Require the FBI to track statistics on hate crimes against transgender people (Legislative Digest, 2009)

Hate crime laws can vary widely from state to state, and some do not have hate crime laws at all. As of 2017, 17 states and the District of Columbia have laws specific to crimes directed against LGBTQ persons because of their sexual orientation and gender expression. Thirteen states have laws that cover only sexual orientation, and 16 states do not have hate crime laws that cover sexual orientation or gender identity (Movement Advancement Project, 2017).

LGBTQ Victims of Hate/Bias Incidents and Offenses

Those in favor of the expansion of hate crime laws to cover LGBTQ people say that doing so is important because hate crimes are much more egregious than regular crimes since they target an entire group of people versus an individual. Hate crimes are motivated by prejudice and take longer for victims to recover from, emotionally and psychologically, leading to a higher rate of depression, anxiety, and post-traumatic stress (Carlson, 2017).

THE SCOPE OF LGBTQ VICTIMIZATION The FBI UCR hate crime report covering 2015, the most recent available, indicates that there were 5,818 single-bias incidents reported, of which 1,030 (17.7 percent) were based on sexual-orientation bias and 99 (1.7 percent) motivated by gender-identity bias (FBI, 2016). The 2015 data reveal that anti-LGBTQ hate crimes rose about 5 percent over the 2014 level. Hate violence specifically against transgender people rose by 13 percent between the two years (ibid.). However, the UCR statistics, as in previous years, continue to fall well short of the number of incidents and offenses reported to the National Coalition of Anti-Violence Programs (NCAVP) and other such organizations. The NCAVP is a network of over 35 antiviolence organizations that monitor, respond to, and work to end incidents of hate and domestic violence and other forms of violence affecting LGBTQ communities. The coalition produces a report each year documenting the number of bias-motivated incidents targeting LGBTQ individuals in the United States.

Because the number of LGBTQ victims reporting bias-motivated incidents to the NCAVP is significantly higher than to the FBI, researchers and gay rights groups question the validity, findings, and implications of the FBI UCR reports. Law enforcement compliance with the Hate Crime Statistics Act of 1990 is voluntary and many agencies in the United States do not report hate/bias incidents and offenses to the FBI. Thus, the LGBTQ hate crimes reported in the FBI UCR likely represents a fraction of the cases.

Increases in bias crimes based on sexual orientation or gender identity occurred during the years when gays and lesbians were trying to gain marriage and adoption rights, which resulted in movements in some states to block these efforts. Because of the prominence of these issues, LGBTQ persons and communities gained more visibility, both positive and negative. Both statistical and anecdotal evidence have demonstrated that when LGBTQ issues are in the limelight, LGBTQ communities and individuals are more likely to be targeted for violence.

LGBTQ VICTIM PROFILES Per the NCAVP, across various demographics, whites represented the largest proportion of LGBTQ victims of hate crimes (45 percent). The race/ethnicity of victims for the year 2011 is displayed in Exhibit 11.6.

Anti-LGBTQ murders are often distinguishable from other murders by the level of brutality involved. In 2016, 50 people were killed and 53 more injured at a nightclub frequented by individuals from LGBTQ communities in Orlando, Florida, when a lone gunman opened fire on the crowd. It was called the deadliest attack involving a single gunman and the deadliest targeting of the LGTBQ community in the United States (Alvarez, Perez-Pena, & Hauser, 2016; Hayes, Lotan, Cherney, Miller, Lomongello, & Rodgers, 2016). LGBTQ people of color are far more likely to be targets of hate violence-related homicides. In 2015, 50 percent of LGBTQ victims of homicides were black; 12 percent Latino/a, and 38 percent white (Prakash, 2016).

See Exhibit 11.7 for a year-to-year analysis of known anti-LGBT murders from 2006 to 2015 (Prakash, 2016).

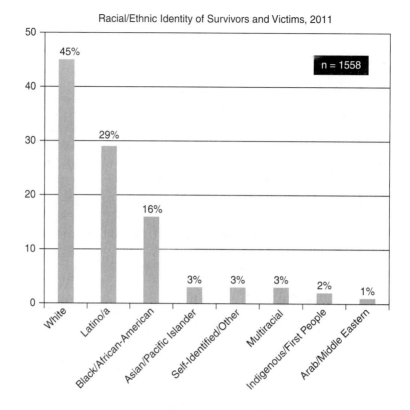

EXHIBIT 11.6   Racial/Ethnic Identity of Victims 2011

Source: "Hate Violence against Lesbian, Gay, Bisexual, Transgender, Queer and HIV-affected Communities in the U.S. in 2011." Retrieved from www.avp.org/storage/documents/Reports/2012_NCAVP_2011_HV_Report.pdf

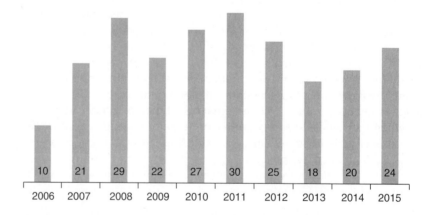

EXHIBIT 11.7   Number of Hate Violence Homicides per Year since 2006

Source: National Coalition of Anti-Violence Programs (NCAVP) 2015 LGBTQ and HIV-Affected Hate Violence Report, http://avp.org/wp-content/uploads/2017/04/ncavp_hvreport_2015_final .pdf (accessed September 18, 2017)

The number of homicides against LGBTQ people more than doubled since 2006. Victims of anti-LGBTQ bias hesitate to report their experiences, either to police or to organizations within their own community. The reasons include:

- fears of reprisal from the offender(s)
- fears of embarrassment or abuse from police
- fear of ostracism from family, friends, or coworkers and possible loss of employment, custody of children, or housing
- urging by family members, friends, and coworkers not to report the incident
- trauma from the incident that results in a desire to "forget" it and "move on"

- blame themselves for being in the "wrong" place, saying the "wrong" thing, or acting or dressing in the "wrong" way
- believing that nothing can be done or that police won't do anything
- dismissing hate incidents as not being serious enough to report
- not being aware of national or local antiviolence organizations and intake centers (such as Lesbian and Gay Community Centers) or other programs that provide alternatives to the police, or believing these organizations won't help without an official police report (NCAVP, 2010)

Differences in culture and language, along with gender, age, and class, often lead to perceptions that advocacy organizations may not be sensitive to the victim's own background. The NCAVP strongly believes that the incidence of anti-LGBT bias crime affecting younger and older people, immigrants, people of color, people in the military, and those within other marginalized populations is grossly underreported (NCAVP, 2012).

According to a 2015 report, "FBI Anti-LGBT Hate Crime Statistics Point to Reporting Problem":

> When it comes to gay friendly states, California, Massachusetts, and New York are...among the top ten states with the highest rates of anti-gay hate crimes. The study makes the assumption from facts that LGBTQ hate crimes are more prevalent in gay friendly states because there are more targets and victims believe that the police won't be hostile or harassing, thus they make a report. So, by virtue of their thriving gay scenes and more sympathetic police departments, states like California and New York are both more likely to provide opportunities for anti-gay hate crimes to happen and to foster reporting of those incidents. ... But this doesn't necessarily mean that more hate crimes are occurring in those places. (Clark-Flory, 2015)

TRANSGENDER VICTIMS OF SEXUAL ORIENTATION HATE CRIMES People who identify as transgender are more likely to experience physical violence than gay men and lesbians who are gender conforming in appearance (Bolles, 2012). Not only are transgender women more likely to experience violent hate crimes, those hate crimes are more likely to result in death. In the first 10 months of 2015, "the number of transgender homicide victims in the U.S. hit a historic high ... 21.... There are now more transgender homicide victims in 2015 than in any other year that advocates have recorded" (Kellaway & Brydum, 2015; Stafford, 2015).

Sexual Orientation Hate/Bias Crimes and School Campuses

Every two years, the Gay, Lesbian, & Straight Education Network (GLSEN) surveys schools to assess the experience of LGBTQ students from 50 states and the District of Columbia. Some of the key findings from its 2015 report include:

- 85 percent of LGBTQ students reported being verbally harassed (e.g., called names or threatened), 27 percent reported being physically harassed (e.g., pushed or shoved), and 13 percent reported being physically assaulted (e.g., punched, kicked, injured with a weapon) at school in the past year **because of their sexual orientation**.
- 71 percent of LGBTQ students reported being verbally harassed (e.g., called names or threatened), 20.3 percent reported being physically harassed (e.g., pushed or shoved), and 9.4 percent reported being physically assaulted (e.g., punched, kicked, injured with a weapon) at school in the past year **because of their gender expression**.
- 49 percent of LGBTQ students experienced electronic harassment in the past year (via text messages or postings on Facebook), often known as cyberbullying.
- 60 percent of LGBTQ students were sexually harassed (e.g., unwanted touching or sexual remarks) in the past year at school.
- 60 percent of LGBTQ students who were harassed or assaulted in school did not report the incident to school staff, most commonly because they doubted that effective intervention would occur or thought the situation could become worse if reported. (GLSEN, 2016)

Campus police need to be aware that many states have enacted "Safe Schools" laws mandating that campus environments be free of harassment, bullying, and discrimination, where no student is subjected to abuse or a hostile learning environment.

A study by the U.S. Department of Health and Human Services in 2016 determined suicide is the second leading cause of death among young people ages 10 to 24, and that:

- The rate of suicide attempts is four times greater for LGBTQ youth and two times greater for questioning youth than straight youth.
- Suicide attempts by LGBTQ youth and questioning youth are four to six times more likely to result in injury, poisoning, or overdose that requires treatment from a doctor or nurse, compared to their straight peers. (CDC, 2016)

"Cyberbullying," which is the use of the Internet and social media to harm other people, primarily fellow students, in a deliberate, repeated, and hostile manner, has become so common that it is one of the most frequent issues being addressed by school administrators and legislators. Because of bullying in schools, law enforcement agencies, particularly campus police or school resource officers, are becoming more involved in campus situations such as sexual-orientation bias crimes and bullying. They are expected to complete official documentation regarding alleged violations and physical assaults based on a student's perceived or actual sexual orientation or gender identity. It is particularly important for campus police to be vigilant because most LGBTQ teens do not report bias incidents or crimes at school out of fear that school officials will tell their parents about their real or perceived sexual orientation and/or that school officials will not do anything to stop the abusers.

Police Relations with LGBTQ Communities

> Improved policing comes from having a diverse police force. So, if you want to be able to address some of the unique issues—whether they be hate crimes or some other issue—within the gay community, it's good to have officers who are at least culturally competent. And if you can get gay and lesbian officers, all the better. (Colvin, 2013)

Historically, in most cities and counties in the United States, relations between the police and the LGBTQ communities have been strained, sometimes due to how residents, as individuals or as a certain group, have been mistreated by law enforcement officers. Many LGBTQ people believe that police regard them as deviants, criminals, and second-class citizens who are unworthy of protection or equal rights. Because of this perception, many gay and lesbian victims do not report crimes to the police or cooperate with investigations (Copple & Dunn, 2017). Even though negative attitudes and stereotypes will probably continue, modern police agencies have found that communication and mutual respect between the department and gay and lesbian communities are in the best interests of all concerned. "There has been 50 years of activism between gay and lesbian communities and the police and great strides have been made," says Sergeant Carlson, of the Concord (California) Police Department. "Police departments need to be at the forefront of LGBTQ issues...and more proactive" (Carlson, 2017).

Examples of police departments in which outreach and communication have resulted in cooperation between the agencies and the gay community include the San Francisco, San Diego, Portland, Boston, and Philadelphia police departments. As a result, these agencies have observed a noticeable difference in such things as increased reporting of hate crimes and incidents by lesbian and gay crime victims, fewer complaints of police abuse, and a general improvement in relations between law enforcement and LGBTQ communities.

It is also important that community-based policing principles and protocol be utilized in LGBTQ communities. Officers should recognize issues and concerns not only about sexual-orientation bias crimes but also about domestic violence within the LGBTQ community. According to Roddrick Colvin, associate professor at John Jay College of Criminal Justice, one of the keys to good relations between law enforcement agencies and the LGBTQ community is regular, institutionalized communication at the department, in committees and councils, and in public forums. Other suggestions include:

1. Task forces and councils to establish ongoing dialogue and networking on important issues.
2. Public forums that allow police officials to meet the LGBTQ community and help officials to recognize that they are a constituency with legitimate needs and concerns.

3. The appointment of a police official to be a liaison with the LGBTQ community to respond to complaints and requests.
4. The involvement of prosecutors in the development of policies, procedures, communications, and awareness training to improve relations between the criminal justice system and LGBTQ groups and individuals. (Colvin, 2013)

Federal Hate Crime Laws

Federal laws provide criminal and civil causes of action for victims of hate crimes in the United States, regardless of whether they are citizens. Federal law does not prohibit all acts of hate violence, however. Federal statutes forbid violence by private parties only when there is intent to interfere with a federally protected right—that is, one specifically guaranteed by a federal statute or by the U.S. Constitution. Such activity includes voting, serving on a jury, going to work, or enrolling in or attending public school. Nevertheless, these rights are broadly interpreted when a perpetrator's motive is tainted by racial hatred. For additional information pertaining to federal laws, see previous discussion of the Matthew Shepard Act in this chapter under the heading "The Scope of Hate Crimes Nationally."

A victim of a hate/bias crime that violates a federal law can initiate criminal prosecution by reporting the crime to the local FBI office, which assigns an investigator to the case. A victim may also contact the local U.S. attorney's office or the criminal section of the Civil Rights Division at the DOJ in Washington, D.C. In general, federal criminal statutes are intended to supplement state and local laws. Procedurally, the DOJ will not become actively involved in prosecuting a particular action until local authorities have concluded their case. After a person is convicted or acquitted in state courts, the DOJ evaluates the result before determining whether to prosecute under federal statutes.

Why Special Laws and Penalty Enhancements?

There are those, including some law enforcement leaders, who argue that there is no need for special laws dealing with hate/bias crimes because there are already statutes covering specific crimes. For example, an assault by one person on another is prosecutable in all jurisdictions. Therefore, the argument runs, why would such an assault be prosecuted differently even if it is motivated by a person's hate or bias toward victims because of their color, ethnic background, religion, sexual orientation, gender, gender identity, or disability?

There are several responses to this critique. First, if incidents were not classified by racial, ethnic, sexual orientation, gender, gender identification, disability, or religious motivation, it would be virtually impossible to tabulate acts of hate violence, spot trends, perform analyses, or develop response strategies. Second, an inaccurate characterization of certain types of hate violence crimes would occur. For example, in the past, cross burnings were variously classified as malicious mischief, vandalism, or burning without a permit, and swastikas painted on buildings were often classified as graffiti incidents or malicious mischief.

There are also some key differences that make hate/bias crimes more serious than standard offenses, justifying the establishment of special laws and sentence enhancements. "Hate crimes differ from other forms of interpersonal violence in three important ways. They are more vicious, extremely brutal, and frequently perpetrated at random on total strangers, commonly a single victim by multiple offenders and predominately male teenagers and young adults" (Christie, Wagner, & Winter, 2001). Crimes of this sort deny the free exercise of civil rights, sometimes frightening the victim out of exercising freedom of speech, association, and assembly. Often, the attacks are acts of terrorism intended to punish the victim for being visible (i.e., a person who looks or acts different from others is easy for a bigoted person to single out). Finally, these acts against individuals are also often meant to terrorize entire communities.

Hate/bias crimes require more police resources for investigation, community response, and victim assistance than most other crimes. There is a national consensus that such crimes justify special laws and enhanced penalties for offenders. They send a clear message to the perpetrator and the public that these crimes will not be tolerated and will be treated as serious offenses. Sometimes, it is not just an individual perpetrator, but an organized group that commits crimes against members of the LGBTQ and gender identity community.

ORGANIZED HATE GROUPS

The number of organized hate groups in the United States increased from 784 in 2014 to 917 in 2016, according to the SPLC. As mentioned earlier, the most striking was the near tripling of anti-Muslim hate groups, which grew in number from 5 in 2010 to 101 in 2016 (SPLC, 2017c). On the other hand, the Ku Klux Klan has been steadily losing members over the years (AP, 2016). The SPLC estimates the Klan has about 190 chapters nationally with somewhere between 5,000 and 8,000 members identifying as Klan, but often representing groups in conflict with each other (SPLC, 2017e). In the 1920s, it is estimated the Klan had 2 million to 5 million members (ibid.) Law enforcement representatives need to be aware that the KKK, as splintered as it is in its current state, is attempting to rebrand itself with toned down language. It is reported to have a "rule against violence aside from self-defense" (AP, 2016), and is backing off from the use of the word "white supremacist," asserting, instead that members believe in their race, or with some saying that they are "white separatists" (AP, 2017). The hate organization's rebranding began following a number of members' going to prison for bombings, beating, shootings, and arson attacks (AP, 2016). The number of organized, patriot antigovernment groups, also called militias, fluctuated greatly in the last two decades, peaking in 2012 with 1,360 groups and totaling approximately 623 in 2016 (SPLC, 2017b).

Knowledge of hate groups is essential when policing in a multicultural society. It is imperative for the criminal justice system to investigate (using methods including informants, surveillance, and infiltration) and control organized hate groups. Aggressive prosecution and litigation against these groups is also important. White supremacist groups such as Neo-Nazis, the Ku Klux Klan, Skinhead, Aryan Nations, National Alliance, World Church of the Creator, and other hate groups are discussed in Appendix E.

Hate Groups Monitoring and Community Resources

Monitoring extremist groups is an important obligation for law enforcement. See Appendix F for information about government and nongovernment organizations that monitor extremist groups in the United States. Included in the appendix is a list of resources and programs, available in most communities, to reduce and control hate/bias crimes perpetrated by individuals and extremist groups.

Trends and Predictions for Organized Hate Groups

Some experts predict that white supremacists will continue to commit traditional crimes (such as cross burnings and vandalism) but will also venture into high-tech activities such as computer hacking and electronic sabotage. Their political activism will include "white rights" rallies, protests, and demonstrations; election campaigns by racist candidates; and legislative lobbying. These activities are expected to incite counter movements and will create very labor-intensive situations for law enforcement to handle.

Observers of hate groups have also noted the shift in tactics of white supremacists in the United States. Discovering that supremacists could no longer effectively recruit members using the ideology of open racism with the focus on persons of color, Jews, immigrants, and the like, they are now targeting lesbians and gays. According to those who study hate groups, supremacists find that while many whites may share their racial, religious, and ethnic prejudices, most are no longer willing to act on them openly. Thus, a new strategy is being employed that combines old hatreds with new rhetoric. This new approach does not imply that supremacists no longer hate people of color, Jews, and other non-white citizens. Rather, it means they are refocusing their energies to include not only homophobia but also so-called "pro-family," "pro America" values that include opposition to abortion and immigration, in addition to traditional racist and anti-Semitic beliefs. Ross says the broadening of issues and the use of conservative buzzwords have attracted the attention of whites who may not consider themselves racist but do consider themselves patriotic Americans concerned about the moral decay of the country (Ross, 1995).

Organizations and officials tracking hate groups have offered other predictions on the evolution and future of hate groups. These experts believe groups that have traditionally shunned or actively opposed each other for ideological reasons will join forces against their "common enemies." For one example among many, although neo-Nazis have long despised

Arabs and Muslims, they have increasingly allied with Arab and Muslim extremists against common enemies, most often Jews. American neo-Nazis have also been increasingly cooperating with their counterparts in Europe.

The Internet and Hate Groups

One disturbing trend is observed in the age and gender of new members of supremacist groups: There is a larger number of younger members than in the past (including teenagers), and many are young women. Organized hate is no longer the exclusive domain of white men over 30 years of age. As noted previously, the Internet, including Facebook, Twitter, and the like, has become the medium of choice for recruiting young members to hate groups and for disseminating hate dogma and racist ideology. The Internet enables people to spread racist ideology around the world instantaneously, in a cheap, easy, and anonymous manner. The medium provides hate groups the ability to send unsolicited mass e-mails, some of them seeking to recruit today's affluent and educated youth to their cause. Their Web sites, in the hundreds, or possibly thousands, entice viewers with online games, comic strips, and music, or simply a friendly pitch from another kid. College and university sites are being bombarded with messages and lures from hate groups. In some areas, the Internet is also being used to provide tips on how to target opponents of such groups with violence. Internet providers must work with the police, within the realm of freedom-of-speech requirements, to enforce their own standards and to block hate dogma Web sites or hate e-mail within their system.

First Amendment versus Hate Speech

The sight of members of the Westboro Baptist Church of Topeka (Kansas) picketing outside military funerals has provoked outrage across the United States. The unaffiliated church, which consists primarily of members of one family, believes that military deaths are God's punishment for U.S. tolerance of homosexuality. The members hold signs with offensive, antigay messages such as "God Hates You" and "God Hates Fags" not only at funerals, but also at other events that attract a lot of people, such as football games and concerts. Members travel nationally to picket funerals of LGBTQ victims of murder or those who have died from AIDS. The church has been described as a hate group and is monitored by the SPLC and the ADL. The United States Supreme Court, in a free-speech ruling that challenged popular opinion, ruled that even deliberately obnoxious funeral protests are protected by the First Amendment (*Snyder v. Phelps*, 2011).

HATE/BIAS CRIME AND INCIDENT INVESTIGATIONS

Criminal justice agencies must make hate/bias crimes a priority for response, from the initial report through prosecution. To ensure that all personnel treat such crimes seriously, each agency must have written policies and procedures that establish protocol for a quick and effective response. Only when such policies and procedures, as well as feasible community programs, are in place, will the number of hate crimes start to decrease.

Law enforcement agencies must provide investigators with training that includes such critical elements as understanding the role of the investigator, identifying a hate/bias crime, classifying an offender, interviewing a victim, relating to a community, and prosecuting an offender. When hate/bias crimes occur, they require investigators' timely response, understanding, and vigilance to ensure a careful and successful investigation. Investigators must have a comprehensive knowledge of the general elements and motivations behind hate/bias crimes and must recognize the potential of these crimes to affect not only the primary victim, but also the victim's family, other members of the victim's group, and the larger community.

There are general and specific procedures and protocols that should be used in response to crimes and incidents motivated by the victim's race, religion, ethnic background, or sexual orientation (RRES). These include actions to be taken by each of the following categories of personnel:

- Assigned officer/first responder
- Patrol field supervisor
- Watch commander

- Assigned investigator or specialized unit
- Crime prevention, community relations, or specialized unit
- Training unit

The actual guidelines may vary among jurisdictions, but the basics are the same. Specific guidelines are available from federal and state organizations or police and sheriffs' departments.

Models for Investigating Hate/Bias Crimes

The following are suggested guidelines for law enforcement agencies without standardized protocol for follow-up of hate/bias crimes and incidents. The suggested formats are based on the size of the department. However, regardless the size of the agency, an established protocol between law enforcement and emergency medical services personnel who respond to the crime scene is recommended. This will benefit the victim and the overall outcome of the investigation.

SMALL DEPARTMENT (AGENCIES OF 1 TO 100 SWORN) A small department may not have the staffing to have a specialized unit or investigator who can deal solely with hate crimes. Officers in small departments are usually generalists, meaning that they carry any type of case from the initial report through the investigation and submission to the district attorney. Therefore, all personnel should receive awareness training on cultural and racial issues and learn the requirements of handling crimes and incidents motivated by hate. The officer who takes the crime or incident report must have it approved by his or her supervisor. Some small departments have allowed patrol officers to specialize in the investigation of certain crimes; they might be involved in either providing advice and direction or taking the case and handling it to its conclusion. These officers are usually the ones allowed to attend training and conferences that will teach and update them on the investigations of these crimes and incidents. Some departments have a patrol supervisor perform the follow-up investigation and submit the case to the prosecutor's office. It is important that the officer and his or her supervisor keep command officers informed of major cases. Small agencies with a follow-up investigations unit must make sure that unit members are trained in aspects of dealing with crimes motivated by hate.

MEDIUM-SIZED DEPARTMENT (AGENCIES OF 100 TO 500 SWORN) For medium-sized departments with a crimes-against-persons investigations unit and an administration unit responsible for community relations or affairs, the following protocol is recommended: The responding patrol officer takes the initial report, decides if what occurred could be considered a crime or incident motivated by hate or bias, and then completes a preliminary investigation. Then the officer documents the findings on the department offense report form and follows the policy and procedure as established by the agency. The officer's supervisor and watch commander approve the report (which may or may not already be classified as a hate/ bias or civil rights violation, depending on department policy). It is then forwarded to the investigations unit (usually crimes-against-persons), which typically follows up on such cases. The investigations unit supervisor reviews the report and again evaluates whether a hate/bias crime or incident took place. If it is decided that it is a hate/bias crime, the report is assigned to a crime-against-persons investigator who specializes in this type of investigation.

A copy of the report is also forwarded (through the appropriate chain of command) to the administration or community relations unit for follow-up. The staff of the latter unit is also trained to handle hate/bias and civil rights violations investigations and to provide victim assistance. The administrative follow-up includes:

- Investigations required
- Referrals and support for the victim
- Conducting of public meetings to resolve neighborhood problems
- Liaison with the diverse organizations in the community and victim advocates

Some cases may require that the criminal investigator and the administrative officer work jointly to resolve the crime or incident under investigation.

LARGE DEPARTMENTS (AGENCIES OF 500-PLUS SWORN) Most large departments have enough staff that they can have a specialized unit that focuses on crimes motivated by hate/bias or civil rights violations. There are many advantages to having such a unit. The investigators become familiar and experienced with the law and special procedures required and can handle more complex, sensitive cases. Investigators who are allowed to specialize can form networks with victim advocate organizations, other police agencies, and community-based agencies. They work closely with the district attorney's office (probably with a special bias unit within that agency), establishing the working relationships and rapport important to successful prosecutions. Since the primary function of the unit is hate/bias crime investigations, officers can sometimes develop knowledge of individuals and groups that commit such offenses and become more aware of where the incidents occur. Specialized units can evaluate the field performance of the patrol officers who have handled such crimes and can provide suggestions for improvement or commendations when the response has been effective or innovative.

There are also disadvantages to specialized units. Detectives who handle a multitude of cases do not have the time to track and monitor these crimes and therefore may not spot trends. The officer takes reports and then passes it on to another department, therefore removing him or herself from responsibility for seeing the incident through to prosecution or closure. Patrol officers may also be unaware of what resources are being marshaled to resolve it unless there is effective communication between them and the members of the specialized unit. These disadvantages can be dealt with through more communication among agency units and with the community.

Hate crimes that fit certain criteria are investigated at the federal level by the FBI's Bias Crimes Unit, the Bureau of Alcohol, Tobacco and Firearms (ATF), and church arson and explosives experts. ATF investigators also focus on regulating the illegal sale to and possession of firearms by potential perpetrators of hate crimes.

HATE/BIAS CRIME/INCIDENT CONTROL AND PROSECUTION

Hate/bias crimes and incidents can be controlled only through the combined efforts of the community (schools, private organizations, government agencies, churches, service organizations, and families), federal and state legislatures, and the criminal justice system—a holistic approach. It is important to study communities to determine whether they are at risk of strife or conflict caused by the social, economic, and environmental conditions that can result in hate crimes and incidents. Refer to Appendix F for information about hate crime and incident monitoring and control.

District Attorneys' or Prosecutors' Offices

Many district attorneys' offices in the United States now have attorneys and/or units that specialize in hate crime prosecution. These agencies have established policies and procedures designed to prosecute such crimes effectively and efficiently. There are compelling reasons for district attorneys to devote special attention and resources to these crimes. A prosecutor has discretion to influence, if not determine, what might be called the public safety climate that citizens in the communities he or she serves will experience. Establishing a public safety climate that fosters the full enjoyment of civil and political rights by the minority members of our communities requires a focused political will directed to that end, as well as resources and capacity. The most effective and successful approaches to building a climate of public safety have been those that:

- establish specialized hate crimes or civil rights violations units
- create standardized procedures to prosecute hate crime cases
- appoint attorneys to serve as liaisons with various ethnic, racial, religious, and sexual minority groups in the community
- provide all attorneys on staff with cultural awareness or sensitivity training
- provide alternative sentencing programs aimed at rehabilitating individuals who commit hate-motivated crimes.

District attorneys can play a major role in educating judges on the nature, prevalence, and severity of hate crime and in encouraging effective sentences for this offense. They can also be very effective in their working relationships with and encouragement of police officers investigating these crimes. The effort involves each member of the criminal justice system, but the prosecutor has one of the most important roles.

Special Problems in Prosecuting Hate/Bias Crimes

Prosecutors confront an array of issues when considering a potential hate crime. Determining the real motivation for someone's behavior is difficult, and proving that a person took an action because of hate can be an arduous task. Hate crime charges are the only ones for which proving motive becomes as important as proving modus operandi. Juries can often find it impossible to conclude with certainty what was going on in a defendant's mind during the crime. Attorneys who handle hate/bias crimes indicate that there are four potential obstacles to successful prosecutions:

1. Proving the crime was motivated by bias
2. Uncooperative, complaining witnesses
3. Special defenses
4. Lenient sentences

Given these obstacles, prosecutors sometimes have difficulty deciding whether to file hate crime charges. It is often difficult to accurately identify hate-motivated crimes or incidents. Usually, no single factor is sufficient to make the determination, and sometimes the perpetrator disguises the incident so that it does not appear to be a hate/bias crime. Even cases that have been well investigated may lack sufficient evidence to prove that the crime was motivated, beyond a reasonable doubt, by hate or bias. Generally, prosecutors follow established guidelines for determining whether a crime was bias-related. Their criteria include the following:

- Common sense
- Perceptions of the victim(s) and witnesses about the crime
- Language used by the perpetrator
- Background of the perpetrator
- Severity of the attack
- Lack or presence of provocation
- History of similar incidents in the same area
- Absence of any apparent motive

The American Prosecutor's Research Institute (APRI) developed a comprehensive desk manual for prosecutors for identifying, responding to, and preventing hate violence. The manual, titled *A Local Prosecutor's Guide for Responding to Hate Crimes*, contains information about working with outside agencies and organizations, case screening and investigation, case assignment and preparation, victim and witness impact and support, trial preparation, sentencing alternatives, and prevention efforts. The publication can be useful in designing a training curriculum specifically for prosecutors.

Objective Evidence: Bias Motivation

It is important that first responders and investigators properly identify and classify bias-motivated crimes. Officers unsure about identifying a potential hate/bias crime should consult with a supervisor or internal or external expert on the topic. To help investigators determine whether an incident meets sufficient objectively determined criteria to be classified as a hate/bias crime, the DOJ developed a document, "Hate Crime Data Collection Guidelines and Training Manual" (U.S. Department of Justice, 2015), which contains a series of examples related to the reporting of hate crime incidents. These examples are intended to ensure uniformity in reporting data to the state and the FBI's Uniform Crime Reporting Section. The most recent guidelines can be found on the DOJ Web site.

Training is available from the DOJ to help criminal justice agency personnel make decisions regarding hate/bias crimes. The Office for Victims of Crime (OVC), the Bureau of Justice Assistance (BJA) and the Office of Juvenile Justice and Delinquency Prevention (OJJDP) all sponsor grants to fund the development of programs, and provide training seminars and technical assistance to individuals and local agencies regarding hate crimes. OVC is working to improve the justice system's response to victims of hate crimes; OJJDP funds agencies to develop training for professionals and to address hate crimes through preventive measures and community resources. BJA has a training initiative for law enforcement agencies designed to generate awareness and to help in identifying, investigating, and taking appropriate action for bias crimes, as well as arming agencies with tools for responding effectively to incidents.

The following Mini Case Studies require that you decide how the investigating officer should report the incident using the UCR Hate Crime Data Collection Guidelines from the FBI UCR training manual (FBI:UCR, 2015b). Answers to the four questions can be found on pp. 329, following the chapter summary.

Mini Case Study #1

Someone throws a rock and breaks a window in a Syrian-owned convenience store. The store has signs written in Arabic displayed in the window and outside the store. The rock, which has a disparaging message about the owner's Arab ancestry, strikes the owner in the head, causing a gash that requires medical attention.

Mini Case Study #2

Unknown people enter a synagogue overnight and destroy many religious objects, draw swastikas on a door, and write "Death to Jews" on a wall. There are many items of value in the synagogue, but none are stolen.

Mini Case Study #3

Late in the night, a group of individuals break into a local LGBTQ community center. The group paints well-known and recognized LGBTQ epithets on the walls and steals the gay pride rainbow flag flown above the front door of the center.

Mini Case Study #4

A man wearing a "tilak" (a sacred Hindu mark worn on the forehead) is assaulted by two men with baseball bats. During the assault, the men scream at the victim to "clean" the mark off his head. When taken into custody, the suspects say they assaulted the man because they want the Hindus to go back to where they came from.

Source: (FBI:UCR, 2015b). "Hate Crime Data Collection Guidelines and Training Manual." Law Enforcement Support Section and Crime Statistics Management Unit.

LAW ENFORCEMENT RESPONSE STRATEGIES

Public confidence and trust in the criminal justice system, and law enforcement in particular, are essential for effective response to hate/bias crimes. Residents in communities where people of a race, ethnic background, religion, or sexual preference different from their own reside must be able to trust that they will be protected. They must believe that the police are not against them, that prosecutors are vigorously prosecuting, that judges are invoking proper penalties, and that parole, probation, and corrections are doing their share to combat crimes motivated by hate or bias. If people believe that they cannot count on law enforcement to protect them, the result can often culminate in rising tensions, communication breakdowns, and vigilante justice as people take the law into their own hands.

EDUCATING THE PUBLIC AT LARGE Prejudice and bias, which can ultimately lead to violence, are often the result of ignorance. In many cases the bias may be due to learned stereotypes and negative media images, with the perpetrator having little or no firsthand exposure to the targeted group.

One key to combating ignorance is to educate the public as well as criminal justice system employees about the history, diversity, cultures, languages, and issues of concern of the various groups within the community. This can be accomplished through neighborhood forums, workshops, and speakers' bureaus featuring people who are well versed on the issues. Criminal justice employees should be trained in the workplace and/or through in-service or academy-based training courses. Most cities and counties have organizations that represent community groups that can assist in developing and implementing such education at local elementary and secondary schools, in churches, and on college and university campuses. To check the accuracy of material presented, organizers of educational programs should have at least two or three minority community members provide input on the content of the program to be delivered. Preferably, they would represent the different subgroups within the community. Neighborhoods and community residents should be encouraged to observe their various heritages through the celebration of holidays and other special days via fairs and festivals. Calendars show that there are more holidays for different religions and cultures in the United States than anywhere else in the world.

ORGANIZATIONAL NETWORKING National and local organizations must network to share information, resources, ideas, and support regarding crimes motivated by hate. The list of potential organizations would include the National Association for the Advance of Colored People (NAACP), the Anti-Defamation League (ADL), the Committee Against Anti-Asian Violence, the National Gay Lesbian Task Force, and the Southern Poverty Law Center (SPLC), a group that tracks hate groups around the country.

Such advocacy organizations can construct an invaluable bridge to victim populations and assist in urging citizens to come to the police with information about hate crimes. Most of these organizations have publications and reports covering such topics as how to respond to bigotry, trends in racism, and community organizing. Through networking, organizations, or groups learn who their allies are, increase their own resources and knowledge about other minority groups, and form coalitions that make a greater impact on the community and the criminal justice system. They can also assist criminal justice agencies in dealing with community reactions to hate violence and help the victims of violence cope with the experience.

MONITORING THE MEDIA Minority organizations and the criminal justice system must monitor the media, which should be used strategically for education and publicity about hate/bias crimes and incidents, about multicultural and multiracial workshops, and about festivals and other cultural events. The media must also be monitored in terms of accuracy of reporting and must be asked to publish corrections when warranted. Negative editorials or letters to the editor pertaining to an affected group should be countered and rebutted by an op-ed piece from within management of the involved criminal justice agency. Organization leaders or their designated spokespersons should make themselves available as the primary sources of information for reporters to contact.

FEDERAL, STATE, AND COUNTY PROGRAMS Police executives should seek out every source of federal, state, and county law enforcement assistance programs and make the information available to investigators and/or task forces investigating or preventing hate crimes.

CHURCHES, MOSQUES, AND SYNAGOGUES Where the usual support organizations (such as the American Civil Liberties Union [ACLU], NAACP, and ADL) do not exist, and sometimes even where they do, churches, mosques, and synagogues often are advocates for people facing discrimination and/or who are victims of a hate incident or crime.

HATE/BIAS CRIME AND INCIDENT VICTIMOLOGY

Meaningful assistance to victims of major crimes became a priority only in the 1980s. The growth of a body of "victimology" literature (President's Task Force on Victims of Crime created by President Ronald Reagan in 1982; the Omnibus Victim and Witness Protection Act of 1982; and the Comprehensive Crime Control Act of 1984, to name a few) and the emergence of numerous victim advocate and rights organizations began at about that time, reflecting a growing concern about victims of crime and their treatment by the criminal justice system. The perception was that the defendant's rights were a priority of the system, while the victim was neglected in the process. Because of the task force recommendations, state and federal legislation, and research by public and private organizations (most notably the National Institute of Justice), improvements were made in victim services and treatment as well as in the criminal justice system.

Law Enforcement and the Victim

In the law enforcement field, courses in recruit academies and advanced in-service officer programs typically include training about victimization that covers such topics as socio-psychological effects of victimization, officer sensitivity to the victim, victim assistance and advocacy programs, and victim compensation, restitution criteria, and procedures for applying. Classes normally stress the importance of keeping victims informed of their case status and of the criminal justice process. How patrol officers and investigators of such crimes interact with victims affects the victims' immediate and long-term physical and emotional recovery. Proper treatment of victims also increases their willingness to cooperate in the total criminal justice process. Because of such training programs, the victims of hate crimes began receiving special attention and assistance in progressive cities and counties all over the country.

Victims of hate/bias violence generally express three needs: (1) to feel safe, (2) to feel that people care, and (3) to get assistance. To address the first two needs, law enforcement agencies and all personnel involved in contacts with victims must place special emphasis on victim assistance to reduce trauma and fear. Such investigations sometimes involve working with people from diverse ethnic backgrounds, races, and/or sexual orientation. Many victims may be recent immigrants with limited English and unfamiliar with the American legal system, or may be afraid of the police, courts, or government rooted in negative experiences from their countries of origin.

Therefore, the officer or investigator must be not only a skilled interviewer and listener but also sensitive to and knowledgeable about cultural and racial differences and ethnicity. He or she must have the ability to show compassion and sensitivity toward the victim and his or her plight while gathering the evidence required for prosecution. As when dealing with other crime victims, officers involved in the investigation must:

- approach victims in an empathic and supportive manner as well as demonstrate concern and sensitivity;
- attempt to calm the victim and reduce the victim's fear;
- reassure the victim that every available investigative and enforcement tool will be utilized by the police to find and prosecute the person(s) responsible for the crime;
- consider the safety of the victim by recommending and providing extra patrol and/or providing prevention and precautionary advice;
- provide referral information to entities such as counseling and other appropriate public support and assistance agencies;
- advise the victim of criminal and civil options.

The stress experienced by victims of hate/bias crime or incidents may be heightened by a perceived level of threat or personal violation. Just like victims of rape or abuse, many become traumatized when they must recall the details of what occurred. Sometimes victims even transfer their anger or hostility to the officer—a psychological reaction called *transference*. The officer must be prepared for this reaction and must be able to defuse the situation professionally without resorting to anger. It is imperative that investigators and officers make every effort to treat hate crime victims with dignity and respect so that they feel that they will receive justice. Insensitive, brash, or unaware officers or investigators may not only alienate victims, witnesses, or potential witnesses, but also create additional distrust or hostility and cause others in the community to distrust the entire police department.

Addressing the victim's need to get assistance requires that the community provide resources that can assist the victim and the victim group. Few communities have the resources necessary to offer comprehensive victim services. Even where resources are available, victims are often unaware of them because of poor public awareness programs or the failure of the criminal justice system to make appropriate referrals due to lack of training or motivation. A key resource is the availability of interpreters for non-English-speaking victims and witnesses. Ideally, jurisdictions with large populations of non-English-speaking minorities should recruit and train an appropriate number of bilingual employees. If the jurisdiction does not have an investigator who speaks the same language, an interpreter system should be in place for immediate callout.

Readers wishing additional information about how to deal with victims can refer to *Bringing Victims into Community Policing*, developed by the National Center for Victims of Crime (NCVC) and the Police Foundation. The publication, available on the NCVC Web site, provides guidelines for dealing with specific types of crime victims. Another publication containing multiple sources for victim assistance can be found on the Web site of the OVC, a component of the Office of Justice Programs.

Law Enforcement and the Community

When it comes to hate/bias crimes, it is essential that law enforcement work with the community to:

- Reduce fears
- Stem possible retaliation
- Prevent additional bias incidents
- Encourage other victimized individuals to come forward and report crimes
- Condemn the bigotry that leads to violence
- Provide an outlet for collective outrage
- Create public awareness of the scope of bias crimes and prevention strategies
- Control rumors (National Center for Hate Crime Prevention, 2000)

Summary

- The federal Hate Crime Statistics Act of 1990 encouraged states to collect and report hate crime data to the FBI. The FBI, in partnership with local law enforcement agencies, collects data on hate/bias incidents, offenses, victims, offenders, and motivations and publishes an annual report as part of the Uniform Crime Reporting (UCR) Program.
- Standardized and comprehensive statistics for hate/bias crimes provide information to law enforcement agencies so they can monitor and respond to trends. The tracking of these crimes allows criminal justice managers to deploy their resources appropriately when fluctuations occur. Aggressive response, investigation, and prosecution demonstrate that police are genuinely concerned and that they see such crimes as a priority.
- In the United States, crimes motivated by hate have historically been directed against immigrant groups. Other victims include Native Americans, African Americans, and Jews; as well as Arabs, Muslims from multiple geographic regions, East Asians, South Asians such as Sikhs, as well as gays, lesbians, and bisexual and transgender individuals, and they continue to be victims of bias, discrimination, and crimes motivated by hate.
- The federal definition of hate crime falls under Title 18 U.S.C. Section 249. Although state definitions and statutes vary, in general a hate crime is a criminal act, or attempted act, against a person, institution, or property, that is motivated in whole or in part by the offender's bias against a race, color, religion, gender, ethnic/national origin group, disability status, gender or gender identity, or sexual-orientation group.
- The criminal justice system must be proactive and react swiftly to crimes by hate groups. This lets the hate groups know that their actions will result in apprehension and prosecution. Proactive enforcement also means that other community members are more likely to be sensitive to the impact of hate/bias crimes on victims and the criminal justice system's response. When community members see a law enforcement agency that responds quickly to hate crimes, it can serve to encourage blacks, Asians, Hispanics, Native Americans, lesbians, gays, women, and any other historically marginalized group to consider law enforcement as a good career opportunity.
- Knowledge of hate groups is essential when policing in a multicultural society. It is imperative that organized hate groups be investigated, monitored, and aggressively prosecuted. It is equally important that criminal justice agencies develop a method for networking to share information about hate groups.
- Extremist hate groups are categorized as Ku Klux Klan, Neo-Nazi, Racist Skinhead, Christian Identity, Black Separatist, Neo-Confederate, and Other. The

"Other" category includes groups, vendors, and publishing houses that endorse racist doctrines.

- Jews belong to a religious and cultural group that has experienced discrimination, persecution, and violence throughout history because their religious beliefs and practices often set them apart from the majority.
- "LGBTQ" refers to lesbian, gay, bisexual, transgender people and queer/questioning. Hate crimes targeting LGBTQ individuals are distinct from other bias crimes in that they target a group that is made up of every other category discussed within this textbook. Every year, thousands of LGBTQ persons are harassed, beaten, or murdered solely because of their sexual orientation or gender identity.
- Criminal justice agencies must make hate/bias crimes a priority for response, from the initial report through prosecution. Law enforcement agencies must provide all responders and investigators with training on the various protocols relating to hate/bias crimes. It is often necessary for the agency to establish liaisons with diverse organizations in the community and with victim advocates.
- District attorneys' offices have established policies and procedures designed to prosecute hate/bias crimes effectively. This is necessary to establish a public safety climate that fosters the full enjoyment of civil and political rights by minority members of communities.
- Meaningful assistance to victims of hate/bias crimes should be a priority for members of the criminal justice system that investigate and prosecute perpetrators. Perpetrators of hate crimes commit them to intimidate a victim and members of the victim's community. Criminal justice agency employees dealing with the victims of hate/bias crimes must be aware of and sensitive to the socio-psychological effects of victimization.

Answers to Mini Case Studies (from pp. 325):

Mini Case Study 1: Offenses—Aggravated Assault and Destruction/Damage/Vandalism of Property. This incident should be reported with an Anti-Arab Race/Ethnicity/Ancestry Bias since the evidence indicates the victim was targeted due to his ancestral descent.

Mini Case Study 2: Offenses—Burglary and Destruction/Damage/Vandalism of Property. This incident should be reported with an Anti-Jewish Religious Bias because the offenders destroyed priceless religious objects and left anti-Semitic words and graffiti behind, and theft did not appear to be the motive for the burglary.

Mini Case Study 3: Offenses—Burglary and Destruction/Damage/Vandalism of Property. This incident should be reported with an Anti-Lesbian, Gay, Bisexual, or Transgender (Mixed Group) Sexual-Orientation Bias based on the offender's intent; the property crime was clearly meant to intimidate the employees and patrons of the center.

Mini Case Study 4: Offense—Aggravated Assault. This incident should be reported as an Anti-Hindu Religious Bias because the evidence indicates the motivation of the attack was due to the victim's religious symbols (the tilak) and the offenders' derogatory comments about the Hindu community.

Source: (FBI:UCR, 2015b). "Hate Crime Data Collection Guidelines and Training Manual." Law Enforcement Support Section and Crime Statistics Management Unit.

Discussion Questions and Issues

1. *Hate/Bias Crimes and Incident Reduction.* Design a community-based program to reduce the number of hate/bias crimes and incidents in your area. What elements should it include?
2. *Move-in Violence.* In a group setting, discuss what strategies might be used by a community to reduce the impact of move-in violence on a new immigrant.
3. *Hate Crimes Monitoring Systems:* Does your law enforcement agency have a system in place for monitoring hate/bias crimes and incidents? If yes, obtain a copy of the statistics for at least the past five years (or for as many years as are available) of the hate/bias crimes and determine the following:
   a. What trends are noticeable in each category?
   b. Do the categories measure essential information that will assist your law enforcement agency in recognizing trends?
   c. What would improve the data collection methods to make them more useful in measuring trends and making predictions?
   d. Has your law enforcement agency used data to track the nature and extent of such crimes and incidents? Did it deploy resources accordingly? Provide examples.
4. *Role of Your District Attorney's Office:* Assess the role of your district attorney's or prosecutor's office by determining the following:
   a. Does it have a special hate crimes or civil rights unit?
   b. Do hate crime cases receive special attention?
   c. Are misdemeanor and felony hate crimes prosecuted differently?
   d. How does the office determine if it will prosecute a hate crime case?
   e. What types of training do assistant district attorneys receive regarding hate crimes?
   f. What types of community outreach does the district attorney's office provide regarding hate crimes?
5. *Victims of Hate/Bias Crimes or Incidents.* Have you been the victim of a hate/bias crime or incident? Share the experience with others in a group setting, including the circumstances, the feelings you experienced, how you

responded, and what action was taken by law enforcement and a community-based agency or organization, if relevant.

6. *Victim Resources.* Find out what resources exist in your community to assist victims of hate/bias crimes.
    a. Which groups provide victim assistance?
    b. Does your state have a crime victims' assistance program? Does it offer victim compensation? What about a victim's bill of rights?

c. What services does the local department of mental health staff offer?
d. Do any community groups, rape crisis centers or crime victim services agencies in the area offer counseling to hate crimes victims?
e. Are any mental health care professionals willing to donate their services to victims of hate crimes?

References

Abdelkader, Engy. (2016). "When Islamophobia Turns Violent: The 2016 U.S. Presidential Election." Immigration Research and Information. www.bridge.georgetown.edu/wp-content/uploads/2016/05/When-Islamophobia-Turns-Violent.pdf (accessed April 26, 2017).

ADL. (2011). "ADL Poll Finds Anti-Semitic Attitudes on Rise in America." November 3. Anti-Defamation League. www.archive.adl.org/PresRele/ASUS_12/6154_12.htm (accessed August 22, 2013).

ADL, New York. (2017). "In First, New ADL Poll Finds Majority of Americans Concerned about Violence against Jews and Other Minorities, Want Administration to Act." April 6. www.adl.org/news/press-releases/in-first-new-adl-poll-finds-majority-of-americans-concerned-about-violence (accessed April 26, 2017).

ADL. (2017). "U.S. Anti-Semitic Incidents Spike 86 Percent so Far in 2017 after Surging Last Year, ADL Finds." April 24. Anti-Defamation League. www.adl.org/news/press-releases/us-anti-semitic-incidents-spike-86-percent-so-far-in-2017 (accessed April 24, 2017).

Ahearn, Laura. (2011, April). "Why Are Hate Crimes Not Reported in the United States and in Suffolk County?" Crime Victims Center Hate Crime Task Force Recommendations. www.parentsformeganslaw.org/export/sites/default/Megans_proj/jsp/public/CRIMEV_x007E_2.PDF (accessed August 2, 2013).

AICE. (2011). "Abraham 'Abe' Foxman." Jewish Virtual Library; A Project of AICE (ADL Audit of Anti-Semitic Incidents of 2011). www.jewishvirtuallibrary.org/abraham-quot-abe-quot-foxman (accessed April 30, 2017).

Alvarez, Lizette, Richard Perez-Pena, and Christine Hauser. (2016). "Orlando Gunman Was 'Cool and Calm' after Massacre, Police Say." New York Times, June 13. www.nytimes.com/2016/06/14/us/orlando-shooting.html?action=click&contentCollection=U.S.&module=RelatedCoverage&region=EndOfArticle&pgtype=article (accessed April 14, 2017).

AP. (2016). "At 150, KKK sees Opportunities in U.S. Political Trends." July 4. Associated Press (Ryan Phillips Associated Press Writer/Contributor). www.latimes.com/nation/nationnow/la-na-ap-kkk-20160630-snap-story.html (accessed April 28, 2017).

AP. (2017). "KKK Disavows White Supremacist Label; Experts Say Group Trying to Make Racism More Palatable." http://www.chicagotribune.com/news/nationworld/ct-kkk-white-supremacist-label-20161210-story.html (accessed May 24, 2017).

Beckett, Lois. (2017). "Whitefish Neo–Nazi March." The Guardian, February 5. www.theguardian.com/us-news/2017/feb/05/richard-spencer-whitefish-neo-nazi-march (accessed April 14, 2017).

Bolles, Alexandra. (2012). "Violence against Transgender People and People of Color Is Disproportionately High, LGBTQH Murder Rate Peaks." June 4. GLAAD Organization. www.glaad.org/blog/violence-against-transgender-people-and-people-color-disproportionately-high-lgbtqh-murder-rate (accessed August 27, 2013).

CAIR. (2015). "Challenging Islamophobia Pocket Guide." Council on American-Islamic Relations. https://www.cair.com/images/pdf/Islamophobia-Pocket-Guide.pdf (accessed March 30, 2017).

CAIR. (2017). "The Evolving Muslim Ban." April 25. Council for American-Islamic Relations. www.islamophobia.org (accessed April 16, 2017).

Carlson, Ken. (2017). Sergeant, Concord, California Police Department, personal communication, January 30.

CDC. (2016). *Sexual Identity, Sex of Sexual Contacts, and Health-Risk Behaviors among Students in Grades 9–12: Youth Risk Behavior Surveillance.* Atlanta, GA: U.S. Department of Health and Human Services. www.cdc.gov/healthyyouth/disparities/smy.htm (accessed May 5, 2017).

Chan, Melissa. (2017). "What to Know About Juan Thompson, the Man Accused of Threatening Jews to Frame His Ex-Girlfriend." *Time,* March 3. time.com/4690400/juan-thompson-jewish-center-bomb-threats-arrest/

Christie, Daniel J., Richard V. Wagner, and Deborah D. Winter (Eds.). (2001). *Peace, Conflict, and Violence: Peace Psychology for the 21st Century.* Englewood Cliffs, NJ: Prentice-Hall. academic.marion.ohio-state.edu/dchristie/Peace%20Psychology%20Book.html (accessed August 27, 2013).

Clark-Flory, Tracy. (2015). "U.S. Federal Bureau of Investigation Anti-LGBT Hate Crime Statistics Point to Reporting Problem." June 22. www.vocativ.com/culture/lgbt/U.S.-Federal-Bureau-of-Investigaton-anti-lgbt-hate-crime-statistics-point-to-reporting-problem/ (accessed January 3, 2017).

Collins English Dictionary online. www.collsdictionary.com/dictionary/english. (accessed July 26, 2013).

Colvin, Roddrick A. (2013). *Gay and Lesbian Cops: Diversity and Effective Policing.* Boulder, CO: Lynne Rienner Publishers.

Copple, James and Patricia Dunn. (2017). "Gender, Sexuality, and 21st Century Policing: Protecting the Rights of the LGBTQ+ Community." January 19. U.S. Department of Justice. Product ID: COPS-W0837. https://ric-zai-inc.com/ric.php?page=detail&id=COPS-W0837 (accessed June 20, 2017).

Craven, Julia. (2015). "White Supremacists More Dangerous to America than Foreign Terrorists, Study Says." *The Huffington Post*, June 24. www.huffingtonpost.com/2015/06/24 /domestic-terrorism-charleston_n_7654720.html (accessed February 17, 2017).

Damron, Gina. (2012). "Detroit Homicide Rate Nears Highest in 2 Decades." *Detroit Free Press*, December 28. www .datadrivendetroit.org/files/2013/01/Detroits-homicide -rate-nears-highest-in-2-decades-_-City-of-Detroit -_-Detroit-Free-Press-_-freep.pdf (accessed May 5, 2017).

Davis, Daryl. (2017). "Hate Crimes." April 13. National Save. http://nationalsave.org/chapter-tools/resources/hate -crimes/ (accessed May 13, 2017).

DeGeneste, Henry I. and Sullivan, John P. (1997, July). "Policing a Multicultural Community." *Fresh Perspectives.* Washington, D.C.: Police Executive Research Forum.

Department of Justice [Canada]. (2016). "Preliminary Examination of So-Called 'Honour Killings' in Canada." December 30. www.justice.gc.ca/eng/rp-pr/cj-jp/fv-vf /hk-ch/p3.html (accessed April 13, 2017).

FBI:UCR. (2015a). "2015 Hate Crime Statistics." Federal Bureau of Investigation. www. ucr.fbi.gov/hate-crime/2015 /tables-and-data-declarations/1tabledatadecpdf (accessed April 17, 2017).

FBI:UCR. (2015b). "Hate Crime Data Collection Guidelines and Training Manual." February 27. https://ucr.fbi.gov/hate -crime-data-collection-guidelines-and-training-manual.pdf (accessed April 17, 2017).

Fisher, Daniel. (2012). "Detroit Tops the 2012 List of Most Dangerous Cities." *Forbes*, October 12. www.forbes.com /sites/danielfisher/2012/10/18/detroit-tops-the-2012 -list-of-americas-most-dangerous-cities/#d4916852931c (accessed May 5, 2017).

GLSEN. (2016). "2015 National School Climate Survey— LGBTQ Students Experience Pervasive Harassment and Discrimination, But School Based Supports Can Make a Difference." Lesbian, & Straight Education Network. www.glsen.org/sites/default/files/GLSEN% 202015%20National%20School%20Climate%20Survey%20 %28NSCS%29%20-%20Executive%20Summary.pdf

Legislative Digest. (2009). "H.R. 1913, Local Law Enforcement Hate Crimes Prevention Act of 2009." Digest for H.R. 1913, 111th Congress, 1st Session. www.GOP.gov/bill/111/1 /hr1913 (accessed July 24, 2013).

Hawkins, Derek. (2016). "Muslim woman set on fire on New York's Fifth Avenue in Possible Hate Crime, Police Say." September 13. www.washingtonpost.com/news /morning-mix/wp/2016/09/13/muslim-woman-set-on -fire-on-new-yorks-fifth-avenue-in-possible-hate-crime -police-say/?utm_term=.d10701a57775 (accessed April 21, 2017).

Hayes, Christal, Gal Lotan, Elyssa Cherney, Naseem Miller, Stephen Lomongello, and Bethany Rodgers. (2016). "Orlando Shooting Victims Remembered in Vigils across City, Nation and World." June 12. Orlando Sentinel. www.orlandosentinel.com/news/breaking-news/os -orlando-shooting-pulse-nightclub-story.html (accessed April 14, 2017).

Heller, Aron. (2017). "Israel Indicts Hacker Allegedly Linked to Threats on US Jewish Centers." *WESH2 News*, April 24. www.kcci.com/article/israel-indicts-hacker-allegedly -linked-to-threats-on-us-jewish-centers/9551029 (accessed April 14, 2017).

H.R. 1048. (1990). "H.R. 1048—Hate Crime Statistics Act." April 23. 101st Congress. https://www.congress.gov/bill/101st -congress/house-bill/1048 (accessed May 4, 2017).

Jacobs, James B. and Kimberly Potter. (1998). *Hate Crimes: Criminal Law & Identity Politics*. New York, NY: Oxford University Press.

Julian, Hana. (2017). "Neo-Nazi 'March on Jew' Planned for Jan. 15 in Whitefish, Montana." *Jewish Press*, January 5. www .jewishpress.com/news/breaking-news/neo-nazi-march-on -jews-planned-for-jan-15-in-whitefish-montana /2017/01/05/ (accessed April 14, 2017).

Kellaway, Mitch and Sunnivie Brydum. (2017). "The 21 Trans Women Killed in 2015." February 23. Advocate. www .advocate.com/transgender/2015/07/27/these-are-trans -women-killed-so-far-us-2015 (accessed April 14, 2017).

Kishi, Katayoun. (2016). "Anti-Muslim Assaults Reach 9/11 -Era Levels, U.S. Federal Bureau of Investigation Data Show." November 21. Pew Research Center. www.pewresearch .org/fact-tank/2016/11/21/anti-muslim-assaults-reach 911-era-levels-U.S. Federal Bureau of Investigaton-data -show/(accessed April 13, 2017).

Lichtblau, Eric. (2016). "Hate Crimes against American Muslims Most since Post-9/11 Era." *The New York Times*, September 18. www.nytimes.com/2016/09/18 /us/politics/hate-crimes-american-muslims-rise.html (accessed February 17, 2017).

Lipka, Michael. (2013). "How many Jews are there in the United States?" October 2. Pew Research Center. www .pewresearch.org/fact-tank/2013/10/02/how-many-jews -are-there-in-the-united-states/ (accessed March 14, 2017).

Moore, Tina. (2016). "Muslim Woman in Religious Garb Set on Fire While Shopping." September 12. www.http://nypost .com/2016/09/12/muslim-woman-in-religious-garb-set -on-fire-while-shopping/ (accessed April 21, 2017).

Morin, Rich. (2012). "Rising Share of Americans See Conflict between Rich and Poor." January 11. Pew Research Center. http://www.pewsocialtrends.org/2012/01/11/rising -share-of-americans-see-conflict-between-rich-and-poor / (accessed April 21, 2017).

Movement Advancement Project. (2017). "Hate Crime Laws." www.lgbtmap.org/equality-maps/hate_crime_laws (accessed April 14, 2017).

National Center for Hate Crime Prevention. (2000). "Responding to Hate Crime: A Multidisciplinary Curriculum." Web posted at www.hhd.org/sites/hhd .org/files/Responding%20to%20hate%20crime%20-%20A (accessed August 30, 2013).

National Institute of Justice. (2008). "What Motivates Hate Offenders." January 9. www.nij.gov/topics/crime/hate -crime/motivation.htm (accessed August 3, 2013).

NCAVP. (2012). "Hate Violence against Lesbian, Gay, Bisexual, Transgender, Queer, and HIV-affected Communities in the United States in 2011." The National Coalition of Anti-Violence.

Prakash, Nidhi. (2016). "Hate Violence against LGBT People Is on the Rise and Fewer People Are Reporting It to Police." June 13. NCAVP. fusion.net/hate-violence-against-lgbt -people-is-on-the-rise-and-fe-1793857470 (accessed April 14, 2017).

Rayman, Graham, Chauncey Alcorn, and Larry McShane. (2017). "Disgraced Reporter Cuffed for String of Anti-Semitic Bomb Threats." *New York Daily News*, March 4. www.nydailynews.com/new-york/disgraced-writer-juan-thompson-arrested-anti-semitic-threats-article-1.2987823

Runnymeade Trust. (1996). Islamophobia: A Challenge for Us All. Report of the Runnymede Trust: Commission on British Muslims and Islamophobia. Chair of the Commission, Professor Gordon Conway. www.runnymedetrust.org/companies/17/74/Islamophobia-A-Challenge-for-Us-All.html (accessed May 1, 2017).

S.909. (2010). "S.909—Mathew Shepard Hate Crimes Prevention Act." 111th Congress. https://www.congress.gov/bill/111th-congress/senate-bill/909/text (accessed May 4, 2017).

Snyder v. Phelps. (2011). Supreme Court of the United States. No.09-751. www.supremecourt.gov/opinions/10pdf/09-751.pdf (accessed April 17, 2017).

SPLC. "Debunking Misconceptions about Muslims and Islam." Teaching Tolerance. A Project of the Southern Poverty Law Center. Tolerance. www.tolerance.org/sites/default/files/general/tt_debunking_misconceptions_0.pdf (accessed April 17, 2017).

SPLC. (2012). "Racist Couple Could Face Death in West Coast Murder Spree." Southern Poverty Law Center. www.splcenter.org/fighting-hate/intelligence-report/2011/racist-couple-could-face-death-west-coast-murder-spree (accessed April 14, 2017).

SPLC. (2016). "Update: More Than 400 Incidents of Hateful Harassment and Intimidation since the Election." November 15. www.splcenter.org/hatewatch/2016/11/15/update-more-400-incidents-hateful-harassment-and-intimidation-election (accessed April 17, 2017).

SPLC. (2017a). "ACT FOR AMERICA." Southern Poverty Law Center. www.splcenter.org/fighting-hate/extremist-files/group/act-america (accessed June 20, 2017).

SPLC. (2017b). "Antigovernment Movement." www.splcenter.org/fighting-hate/extremist-files/ideology/antigovernment (accessed April 17, 2017).

SPLC. (2017c). "Hate Groups Increase for Second Consecutive Year as Trump Electrifies Radical Right." February 15. www.splcenter.org/hate-map (accessed June 20, 2017).

SPLC. (2017d). "Hate Groups, State Totals." Southern Poverty Law Center. www. https://www.splcenter.org/hate-map (accessed April 17, 2017).

SPLC. (2017e). "Ku Klux Klan." Southern Poverty Law Center. https://www.splcenter.org/fighting-hate/extremist-files/ideology/ku-klux-klan (accessed May 24, 2017).

Stafford, Zach. (2015). "Transgender Homicide Rate Hits Historic High in US, Says New Report." *The Guardian*, November 13. www.theguardian.com/us-news/2015/nov/13/transgender-homicide-victims-us-has-hit-historic-high (accessed April 14, 2017).

U.S. Federal Bureau of Investigations. (2001). Hate Crime Stats–2001. https://ucr.fbi.gov/hate-crime/2001 (accessed April 17, 2017).

U.S. Federal Bureau of Investigation. (2015). "The Expansion of NIBRS." Uniform Crime Reporting Program—National Incident-Based Reporting System. https://ucr.fbi.gov/nibrs/2015/resource-pages/the-expansion-of-nibrs-2015_final-1.pdf (accessed April 24, 2017).

U.S. Federal Bureau of Investigation. (2016). "Latest Hate Crime Statistics Released." November 14. www.fbi.gov/news/stories/2015-hate-crime-statistics-released (accessed March 13, 2017).

U.S. Department of Justice. "The Matthew Shepard and James Byrd, Jr., Hate Crimes Prevention Act of 2009." The United States Department of Justice. www.justice.gov/crt/matthew-shepard-and-james-byrd-jr-hate-crimes-prevention-act-2009-0 (accessed April 24, 2017).

U.S. Department of Justice. (2013, March). "Hate Crime Victimization." Justice Statistics Special Report. www.bjs.gov/content/pub/pdf/hcv0311.pdf (accessed May 8, 2013).

U.S. Department of Justice. (2015). "Hate Crime Data Collection Guidelines and Training Manual." February 27, 2015. https://ucr.fbi.gov/hate-crime-data-collection-guidelines-and-training-manual.pdf (accessed April 17, 2017).

U.S. Department of Justice. (2016). "Three Kansas Men Charged with Plotting a Bombing Attack Targeting the Local Somali Immigrant Community." October 14. www.justice.gov/opa/pr/three-kansas-men-charged-plotting-bombing-attack-targeting-local-somali-immigrant-community (accessed May 23, 2017).

Wallace, Steven P. Dr. (2017). Professor and Chair of the Department of Community Health Sciences, UCLA Fielding School of Public Health, personal communication, June 24.

Ybarra, Maggie. (2015). "Majority of Fatal Attacks on U.S. Soil Carried out by White Supremacists, Not Terrorists." *The Washington Times*, June 24. www.washingtontimes.com/news/2015/jun/24/majority-of-fatal-attacks-on-us-soil-carried-out-b/ (accessed February 17, 2017).

12   Racial Profiling

LEARNING OBJECTIVES

After reading this chapter, you should be able to:

- Explain the historical background of the term *racial profiling* in law enforcement.
- Define *racial profiling* and explain the problems associated with using inconsistent definitions.
- Explain the challenges involved in the use of profiling in the war on terrorism.
- Identify seven approaches used by police departments to prevent racial profiling.
- Discuss the rationale for and against collection of racial profiling data.
- Explain the differences between "racial profiling" and the legitimate use of "profiling" in law enforcement.

OUTLINE

- Introduction
- Definitions
- Historical Background of the Term Racial Profiling
- Profiling Challenges and Terrorism
- Police and Citizens' Perceptions of Racial Profiling
- Profiling as a Legal Tool of Law Enforcement
- Controversy around Racial Profiling and the "War on Terrorism"
- Prevention of Racial Profiling in Law Enforcement
- Professional Police Traffic Stops
- Data Collection on Citizens' Race/Ethnicity
- Summary
- Discussion Questions and Issues
- References

INTRODUCTION

Racial profiling is a significant issue in law enforcement today. Actual or perceived racial profiling by law enforcement officers disproportionately affects African Americans, Hispanics, Arab Americans, and other minority groups from every walk of life and every level of the socioeconomic ladder. The extent to which race, ethnicity, and/or national origin can be used as factors in targeting suspects for stops, searches, and arrests has been a concern to citizens and law enforcement for some time. This concern became even more critical since the "War on Terrorism" began on September 11, 2001. Racial profiling is illegal and a violation of the Fourteenth Amendment. It also prevents some communities from working with law enforcement and can easily escalate an encounter into racially motivated violence. Despite all this, there are still some people who feel it is necessary.

Racial profiling, as a policy, is not just a "politically incorrect" or racially insensitive practice, but one that can have destructive results, and is ultimately an ineffective law enforcement technique, according to Dr. Tom Head, a civil rights activist and author of books about human rights. Law enforcement needs to look at the impact of racial profiling and understand what can be done to prevent it (Head, 2017).

The President's Task Force on 21st Century Policing report released in 2015 included a recommendation that law enforcement agencies adopt and enforce policies prohibiting profiling and discrimination based on race, ethnicity, national origin, religion, age, gender, gender identity/expression, sexual orientation, immigration status, disability, housing status, occupation, or language fluency (U.S. Department of Justice, 2015). The study was commissioned by President Obama following officer-involved shooting deaths of black men in 2014, followed by protests and violence in the cities where they occurred.

DEFINITIONS

Since the issue of racial profiling came to the attention of the public and to law enforcement in the 1990s, it has been discussed and defined in hundreds of articles and publications. However, no single definition of racial profiling has dominated the national conversation. The debate troubled not only those involved in the criminal justice system, but also concerned citizens and communities, scholars, researchers, civil rights organizations, and legislators. With no agreed-upon criteria for what does or does not constitute racial profiling, it was difficult to clarify, address, and develop approaches to prevent the practice. Variation among definitions means interested parties are often talking at cross-purposes, unwittingly discussing different types of police practices, behavior, and stops. For this reason, proposals to prohibit racial profiling were difficult to develop and carry out. Eventually, the U.S. government, federal and state legislatures, law enforcement organizations, and community advocacy institutions addressed the problem of definition and reached some agreement. A newer term is now being used, "bias-based policing," which includes racial profiling, but incorporates other prejudices based on gender, sexual orientation, economic status, religious beliefs, and age. The term racial profiling continues to be used throughout the textbook as it is more common. See definitions that follow.

Bias-Based Policing

Bias-based policing refers to intentional and unintentional acts of applying or incorporating personal, societal, or organizational biases and/or stereotypes in decision-making, police actions, or the administration of justice. It is the inappropriate consideration of specified characteristics (i.e., race, ethnicity, national origin, gender, gender identity, sexual orientation, socioeconomic status, religion, disability, and/or age) in carrying out duties when making law enforcement decisions.

Bias-based policing is often misinterpreted as pertaining only to racial profiling. An example of gender bias would include an officer who would not give, in most cases, a ticket to a female, but the officer would give one to a male for the same violation. An example of economic bias would be an officer's not giving a ticket to someone who appears that he or she couldn't afford it, but would give one to someone for the same violation who looks as if he or she could. If an older person is not ticketed, but a teenager is, this is an example of bias.

Another example of bias is an officer who would not give a ticket to an off-duty police officer, but would to a civilian for the same violation.

Racial Profiling

The authors will use the definition developed by the U.S. Department of Justice and the National Organization of Black Law Enforcement Executives (NOBLE). According to these organizations, racial profiling is any police-initiated action that relies on the race, ethnicity, or national origin rather than on the behavior of an individual or on information that leads the police to a particular individual who has been identified as being, or having been, engaged in criminal activity. Racial profiling, also known as "Driving While Black or Brown" (DWB), has been ruled illegal by the courts and is considered improper police practice by law enforcement officers and agencies.

Profile: Formal and Informal

A *formal profile* is typically a document containing explicit criteria or indicators issued to officers to guide them in their decision-making. It is often based on data collected and interpreted to signify a trend or suggest that given behavioral or situational commonalties, a person could believe that something may result. It can be an outline or short biographical description, an individual's character sketch, or a type of behavior associated with a group. Officers use behavioral or situational indicators to develop reasonable suspicion or probable cause to stop subjects. A profile is a summary of data that also relies upon expert advice about "average" or "typical" appearance that can *potentially* identify perpetrators of criminal activities. An *informal profile* represents the "street sense," personal experiences, and strongly held beliefs that officers use to evaluate people or situations. Informal profiles are more common in law enforcement than formal ones.

Profiling

The term *profiling*, also known as criminal profiling, refers to any police-initiated action that uses a compilation of the background, physical, behavioral, and/or motivational characteristics for a type of perpetrator to identify a particular individual as being, having the potential to be, or having been engaged in criminal activity. Criminal profiling is a legitimate investigative instrument that can be used by law enforcement officers.

Minority

The terms *minority* or *minorities* are used within the text to describe groups of individuals who represent a numeric minority within a racial or ethnic population.

Reasonable Suspicion

A police officer may briefly detain a person for questioning or request identification only if the officer has what is called a "reasonable suspicion" that the person's behavior is related to criminal activity. Reasonable suspicion requires that the officer have specific facts that must be articulated to support his or her actions; a mere suspicion or "hunch" is not sufficient. Reasonable suspicion can be based on the observations of a police officer combined with his or her training and experience, and/or reliable information received from credible outside sources. A police officer possesses reasonable suspicion if he or she has enough knowledge to lead a reasonably cautious person to believe that criminal activity is occurring and that the individual played some part in it. Reasonable suspicion is a level of belief that is less clear-cut than probable cause.

Probable Cause

Probable cause is a higher level of reasonable belief, based on facts that can be articulated, that is required to arrest a person and prosecute him or her in criminal court. Also, before a person or a person's property can be searched, police must possess probable cause, with some exceptions to be discussed later. All states have similar constitutional prohibitions against unreasonable searches and seizures.

Suspect-Specific Incident

An incident in which an officer is lawfully attempting to detain, apprehend, or otherwise be on the lookout for one or more specific suspects who have been identified or described in part by national or ethnic origin, gender, or race is called a "suspect-specific" incident.

HISTORICAL BACKGROUND OF THE TERM *RACIAL PROFILING*

During the 1990s, concerns about police use of racial profiling as a pretext to stop, question, search, and possibly arrest people became a major focus of minority individuals and communities, politicians, law enforcement administrators, scholars, and researchers. National surveys during that period revealed that most Americans, white as well as black, believed racial profiling was commonly used in the United States, but 80 percent of those surveyed opposed the practice. Survey results showed that people believed that officers were routinely guilty of bias in their treatment of racial and ethnic minorities, and that such behavior had been going on for a long time.

What is the source of racial profiling as both a term and as a law enforcement practice? Before addressing that question, it is useful to examine how people use prior events or information to make decisions in everyday life.

People routinely form mental images or tentative judgments about others and the surrounding circumstances or situation, both consciously and subconsciously, which is also a form of stereotyping. This sort of stereotyping, or looking for what one perceives to be indicators, provides a preliminary mental rating of potential risk to a person encountering an event or person.

This mental activity involves conscious and unconscious thought processes whereby an individual:

–makes observations and selects data born out of that person's past experiences
–adds cultural and personal meaning to what he or she observes
–makes assumptions based on the meanings that he or she has attributed to the observation
–draws conclusions based on his or her own beliefs, and,
–finally, takes action. (For a more detailed explanation, see Senge's "Ladder of Inference" on pp. 352–353).

This process comprises, for all people, basic decision-making in their lives, and it guides a person's interpretation of events. A person's socialization, including the person's upbringing by his or her parents, plays a major role in determining decisions and the actions taken because of these decisions in both professional and personal settings.

Profiling in law enforcement is used by officers to look for characteristics that indicate the probability of criminal acts, or factors that tend to correlate with dangerous or threatening behavior. For officers, most of these characteristics have been internalized based on experience and training. If they have had dangerous encounters while on duty, such experiences prepare them for similar future events—as the old saying goes, *better safe than sorry!* The professional training that leads to the development of indicators or common characteristics comes from many sources, beginning with the police academy and in-service training under the supervision of a field-training officer. Informal education may include mentoring by an older partner and pressure from peers on how to do the job, and more formal training continues via advanced officer courses on various subjects. All of these help establish the common practice of profiling. If an official profile of a suspect is used by an agency, and the perpetrator is caught, we say, "He or she fits the profile," thus validating this perspective.

When serial bombing suspect Eric Robert Rudolph was finally apprehended in June 2003, for example, FBI profiling experts immediately confirmed that the notorious fugitive did indeed "fit their profile." Training and experience provide officers with indicators to look for, not only to prevent harm to themselves, but also to identify those people or events that are suspicious and warrant closer attention. This attention then helps civilians and police officers decide what action is prudent to take when confronted by a similar person or situation. This does not necessarily mean the person using profiling in this way is biased or prejudiced. Writer Ira Straus suggests that some degree of profiling can be appropriate and even necessary if it is not abusive. In an article for United Press International, he uses the term *profiling* chiefly to mean stereotyping:

> Profiling is universal. Every person relies on it for a preliminary rating of their risks with each person they run into. If people do not profile explicitly, they do it implicitly. If they do not do it consciously, they do it unconsciously… Do police do it too? Of course they do. All police and investigative efforts involve working from two ends, direct and indirect. The direct end means following the trail of specific leads and informants. The indirect end means profiling; that is, finding a social milieu or pool to look in and ask around in—a milieu where there are more likely to be informants, leads, and criminals answering to that crime. To profile is morally risky… The dangers of unfair and unreasonable profiling—that is, profiling based on unfounded prejudices such as racism—are well known. (Straus, 2002)

Straus implies that profiling is not always based on accurate information or data. When the meanings placed on observations are faulty or biased, the assumptions and conclusions, therefore, may be incorrect, leading to inappropriate attitudes, behavior, and actions.

Law enforcement officers, airport security personnel, customs and border patrol agents, and members of some other occupations use profiles. In the absence of conclusive or specific details, it is the only way to narrow the amount of information from which to make decisions, including whether to stop a person for further investigation.

Although there are other historical examples of racial profiling, the first use of the term appears to have occurred in New Jersey, where troopers were trying to stem the flow of illegal drugs and other contraband into and across their state. In the early 1990s, the Drug Enforcement Administration (DEA) and the New Jersey State Police (NJSP) developed a relationship: the DEA provided training to the NJSP on what it had determined to be common characteristics of drug couriers along Interstate 95 from Miami through New Jersey. The characteristics included the types of cars preferred (Nissan Pathfinders), the direction of travel, and the use of rental vehicles from another state. In addition, it was common to find that a third party had rented the vehicle, that the driver was licensed in a state different from the one in which the rental took place, and that there were telltale behavioral cues (such as nervousness or conflicting stories). The profile also noted that the national origin of those involved in drug trafficking organizations was predominantly Jamaican, thus implying dark skin.

The NJSP used "pretextual stops" (i.e., using some legal pretext, such as failing to signal a lane change or having a missing license plate or faulty brake light) on I-95 to determine the potential criminality of a car's driver and occupants. The officer(s) would then attempt to establish a legal basis to search for illegal drugs. Many argued, and the courts agreed, that these pretextual stops were also based on the fact that the cars' drivers and occupants were black or dark-skinned. In other words, they had been racially profiled—targeted because of the color of their skin. The resultant studies determined that blacks and Hispanics on I-95 were stopped with a frequency disproportionate to their numbers on that road. Due to the controversy, and the subsequent court decision and punitive judgment against the NJSP, that organization no longer distributes a typical felony offender profile to their officers "because such profiles might contribute to what the state's attorney general called 'inappropriate stereotypes' about criminals" (Will, 2001). New Jersey, like other states, has also created legislation making racial profiling illegal, with criminal sanctions for officers practicing it.

PROFILING CHALLENGES AND TERRORISM

Prior to September 11, 2001, the use by law enforcement agencies of profiles that included race, ethnicity, or national origin, or the act of profiling using the same criteria, had come to be generally frowned upon, or even condemned, in the United States. But an attitude change occurred after the horrendous attacks on the World Trade Center in New York City and the Pentagon. One outcome of that event was the establishment of the U.S. Department of Homeland Security (DHS) and the attempt to coordinate law enforcement agencies and the military in defense of the nation's citizens and infrastructure. The scope of the state of emergency created by the hijackers altered both public opinion and government policy concerning profiles and profiling based on national origin and ethnicity, especially regarding both the legitimacy and necessity of the practices. Given the ongoing and complex conflicts in the Middle East, plus the global terrorist threat from al-Qaida, the Taliban, and other Islamist extremists, including ISIS, the issue became more charged and complicated. Police at the national and local level had to develop strategies for detecting and apprehending terrorists. Tentative profiles were quickly developed on the basis of obvious characteristics and experience.

Since all the terrorists involved in the 9/11 incidents were Islamic males from the Middle East, the issue became whether law enforcement and security personnel could target or profile suspicious men with similar backgrounds for stops, searches, or increased questioning. Profiling, using those criteria, began to be employed based on several factors common to these particular terrorists, who were:

- young males, Arab in appearance
- primarily citizens of Saudi Arabia
- trained in fundamentalist religious and/or al-Qaida training camps in Afghanistan or Pakistan
- adherents of Islam who had been inspired to religious extremism by fundamentalist clergy, especially about **Al-jihad**
- harboring a deep hatred, in general, of Western decadence, materialism, and immorality, which they perceived as undermining the values and stability of their societies, and of America for its interference in Middle Eastern affairs.

Al-jihad or Jihad   Struggle (literal translation of Arabic). The term has also been used by some to mean "holy war" against infidels or nonbelievers. This subject is covered in more detail in Chapter 8, Law Enforcement Contact with Arab Americans and Other Middle Eastern Groups.

Initially there was little outcry among the public against these actions. Prior to 9/11, 80 percent of Americans opposed racial profiling. Polls taken soon after the attack showed that 70 percent of Americans believed that some form of profiling was necessary, and acceptable, to ensure public safety. A McClatchy-Ipsos poll in 2009 determined that 51 percent of Americans agreed that "it is necessary to give up some civil liberties to make the country safe from terrorism," after an attempted terrorist attack set off a debate regarding full-body scans by the Transportation Security Administration (TSA) at airports (Thomma, 2010). At the time, it was apparent that some of the public was willing to give up certain freedoms in exchange for helping the government reduce the opportunity for terrorists to operate in the United States.

Members of the American Association for Public Opinion Research, at a May 2002 meeting, offered a historical perspective. They said that while civil liberties usually have broad public support, the public has been willing to tolerate substantial limits on those freedoms when there are serious threats to security and safety within the United States and to Americans abroad. Their report cited the decline in support for civil liberties after Pearl Harbor and again at the height of the Cold War. Other than the American Civil Liberties Union (ACLU) and the National Association of Arab Americans, there were few who spoke out against detentions of Middle Easterners and South Asians at security areas in airports and elsewhere after 9/11. These organizations questioned the use of what appeared to them to be racial profiling and abuse of civil rights, generally and specifically. However, many citizens argued that proactive law enforcement and enhanced security measures at airports were necessary to prevent or reduce the likelihood of terrorist acts and to investigate and bring to justice those involved. Discovering terrorists and their missions, prior to another attack, became a matter of urgency. The researchers added, however, that support for civil liberties has always resumed when the threat subsided. This certainly was the case as time passed after 9/11 without additional terrorist acts in the United States.

A Reason-Rupe Poll published in 2014 found that the majority of Americans oppose police use of racial profiling. (See Exhibit 12.1.)

It has been reported that some police officers stop motorists or pedestrians of certain racial or ethnic groups because the officers believe that these groups are more likely than others to commit certain types of crimes. Do you approve or disapprove of this practice by the police?

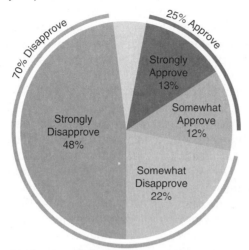

EXHIBIT 12.1 Strong Majority of Americans Oppose Police Use of Racial Profiling, but with Varied Intensity

Source: Ekins, Emily (2014). "Poll: 70% of Americans Oppose Racial Profiling by the Police." October, 2014. Reason-Rupe Poll. http://reason.com/poll/2014/10/14/poll-70-of-americans-oppose-racial-profi

Profiling by law enforcement, therefore, is a balancing act between efficiency, equality, liberty, and security concerns. It has the potential to affect millions of innocent people in the United States who are or may appear to be of Arab, Middle Eastern or South Asian descent and may or may not be Muslim or Sikh. It is important that law enforcement officials and security agents avoid hasty judgments and not condemn all Muslims or Middle Easterners for the crimes of a few. Officers, agents, and those who protect airports and other public facilities should seek to learn more about both Islam and Arab culture.

POLICE AND CITIZENS' PERCEPTIONS OF RACIAL PROFILING

Myth, Misperception, or Reality?

There are some police officers, government administrators, and others who maintain that racial profiling is a myth or a misperception. They argue that most officers do not stop or detain people based on their race, ethnicity, or national origin, but on their behavior, location, circumstances, and other factors. Officers contend that those who are stopped often do not understand police procedures or are overly sensitive, or are using the allegation that bias was involved in their stop, questioning, search, and/or arrest to get out of the situation.

There have been over two decades of reform measures carried out by agencies to eliminate racial profiling or the perception thereof. Sometimes the reforms were compelled by a class action lawsuit, court ordered federal oversight consent decrees, or legislation. It appears that despite laws, court orders, and agency policies and procedures that prohibit officers from using race or ethnicity as a decision-making factor, the practice still exists. However, it is difficult to analyze the degree to which this is the case, because the data collected by law enforcement agencies are often fraught with methodological problems. This is discussed later in this chapter.

As indicated, most police officers and city or county administrators deny the existence of racial profiling. They claim that those who believe they have been the victims of profiling may not be aware of other factors that the officer took into consideration. In a 2002 study, the findings of which are still relevant today, David and Melissa Barlow surveyed African American police officers in Milwaukee to determine whether they felt they had ever been racially profiled, and, if so, to what extent. The researchers wanted to learn how black officers felt about the legality of the circumstances under which they had been stopped by police. Because the subjects of the survey were themselves police officers, their views could not be easily dismissed.

The survey defined racial profiling as "when race is used by a police officer or a police agency in determining the potential criminality of an individual" (Barlow & Barlow, 2002). Of the 2,100 sworn personnel of the Milwaukee Police Department, 414 were African American. The response rate to this survey was 38 percent (158 officers). Over 99 percent were over 25 years of age and had been sworn police officers for at least one year. The percentage of male respondents was 83.5, while the percentage of female respondents was 16.5.

Exhibit 12.2 shows that most of those who responded to the survey believed that they had been racially profiled. Note that the percentages drop off rapidly as the survey proceeded from questions about being stopped and questioned to questions about being arrested. The researchers suggest that the numbers fall off rapidly because the officers would have identified themselves as such upon being stopped and thus avoided further action. It should be noted that some of those surveyed reported that they were on duty but in plain clothes when they were stopped. From their findings, the Barlows conclude that black men are more likely to be the victims of racial profiling than black women by a ratio of three to one.

In their research, the Barlows also asked the sworn police officers of the Milwaukee Police Department whether they personally used racial profiling in the performance of their job. They found that most (90 percent) of the respondents said that they do not use racial profiling nor believe it is a necessary or legitimate tool for law enforcement. The researchers concluded: "Although many white Americans, members of law enforcement, and government officials deny the existence of racial profiling or racially biased policing, the findings from the study suggest it is a reality" (ibid.).

A traffic stop is the most common situation leading to complaints of racial profiling. A 2011 nationwide survey by the Department of Justice regarding police contact with the public established that speeding was the most common reason for being pulled over, representing about half of drivers stopped. The survey revealed:

- Relatively more black drivers (13 percent) than white (10 percent) and Hispanic (10 percent) drivers were pulled over in a traffic stop during their most recent contact with police.
- In instances where the driver and the officer were of the same race, 83 percent of drivers believed that the reason they were pulled over was legitimate, compared to 74 percent of drivers who believed the officer had a legitimate reason to pull them over if they were of a different race than the officer.
- White drivers were both ticketed and searched at lower rates than black and Hispanic drivers. (Langton & Durose, 2013)

	Yes (%)	No (%)
Stopped	69	31
Questioned	52	60
Searched	19	81
Ticketed	21	79
Arrested	7	93

EXHIBIT 12.2   Racial Profiling Survey

Question: In your professional opinion, do you believe you have ever been stopped, questioned, searched, ticketed, or arrested because of racial profiling?

Source: Barlow & Barlow, 2002, p. 14.

Another study by law students at Seton Hall University, New Jersey, of three communities, in proximity to each other, took place between September 2014 and August 2015 (Owen, 2016). The research was to determine whether tickets were being issued disproportionately to black or Latino drivers within the Bloomfield Township. The Bloomfield Township is a predominately white suburb with neighboring communities, East Orange, over 88 percent black, and Newark, which is 53 percent black and 34 percent Latino.

> The researchers found that black and Latino drivers were being disproportionately ticketed, accounting for 78 percent of court appearances for traffic violations despite comprising roughly 43 percent of Bloomfield's population. Drawing on a database of tickets issued by Bloomfield Police [during the time period], they determined that almost 84 percent of 7,110 traffic tickets with verifiable addresses had occurred in the areas around East Orange and Newark. (Ibid.)

They saw a pattern as their study found that a higher number of traffic tickets were written on specific routes entering Bloomfield. The routes were coming from East Orange and Newark, thus … are effectively deterring African Americans and Latinos from entering Bloomfield. The argument was put forth that the higher numbers of traffic tickets given to minority drivers did not occur because of racial profiling, but rather because of where officers were deployed, which was based on where the crime was taking place (ibid.).

Discretionary decision-making of individual officers is a subject that has long been the object of study by criminal justice researchers and is inextricably linked to racial profiling.

Police Perceptions

What are the police officers' perceptions of allegations that all race-based decision-making by them is motivated by their own prejudice? Most law enforcement officers would maintain that they are not biased, prejudiced, or using racial profiling in their policing methods. Proactive policing sometimes involves using legitimate profiling based on officer experience and training or using profiles provided by their agency. Sometimes, however, officer experience can mean a lot of things. If the experience leads to faulty assumptions and conclusions, then the officer might engage in inappropriate behavior and take the wrong action. (See the section "Education and Training" in this chapter for a discussion of the sources of officers' beliefs and attitudes.)

Officers use profiling (behavioral commonalities or indicators) or written profiles to identify those whom they should investigate to determine if they are committing or about to commit a crime. Profiling or criminal profiling is done daily by police officers, not just in high-crime areas where gangs congregate or highway corridors where drug runners operate, but in all communities. It also takes place in predominantly white communities when officers see out-of-place or suspicious-looking members of minority groups. The officer in this situation would argue that he or she would find reason to check out anyone, regardless of color, who did not seem to fit the area or time of day, especially if he or she were acting suspiciously. Profiling also takes place when an officer sees a white person in a predominantly minority area, especially if the area is one in which drug sales or prostitution takes place. The officer checks out the individual if reasonable suspicion is present that a crime might be taking place. Most officers would emphatically deny they are biased or prejudiced when using such profiling.

Officers also insist that both their agency and the community in which they work pressure them to reduce crime in the neighborhoods, and that profiling (not racial profiling) is a tool to accomplish a reduction in some crimes. Also, if officers believe that their agency supervisors and managers want them to be aggressive on the streets by stopping vehicles and pedestrians to determine if there is potential criminal activity, officers will do so, especially if this behavior is rewarded within their organization. Reward structures within agencies include such things as favorable evaluations, shifts and assignments, and even promotions. Another reason for officers to make such contacts is if they didn't, it would likely draw the attention of the supervisor and result in a negative performance evaluation. Unfortunately, if officers come to believe that minority citizens are more likely to be involved in criminal activity of some sort and that aggressively stopping their vehicles will result in more searches and arrests, they are more likely to stop them (referred to as the expectancy theory), especially if the department encourages and rewards the practice.

Two examples of law enforcement agencies encouraging their officers to use proactive, and sometimes aggressive, techniques to reduce crime took place over a period of years in New York City and Baltimore, Maryland. The approaches were used predominately in inner city, high-crime areas. New York City named their program the "Stop-and-Frisk" (also known as "Stop, Question, Frisk") campaign. Baltimore used "Zero-Tolerance" policing. Similar programs were used in other major cities. A statistical analysis of the data collected in both cities suggested that the proportion of African Americans and Latinos/as stopped for questioning was much greater than that of whites. Many argued that there was no credible evidence that the approaches were responsible for reductions in crime experienced while others argued that the strategies were effective.

Ultimately in New York, the stop-and-frisk program became controversial and political during the mayoral campaign in 2012–2013. The New York Civil Liberties Union criticized the stop-and-frisk policy saying "… it was applied heavily to communities of color. More than half of those detained and searched … were black, and nearly a third were Latino" (Bump, 2016; Tracy & Rayman, 2016). The program was challenged in court and a U.S. District judge ruled that the stop-and-frisk practice was unconstitutional. Per a report on stop-and-frisk by the ACLU in New Jersey,

> Stop-and-frisk—if applied in accordance with the Constitution—is not inherently discriminatory. But the way police use stop-and-frisk today all too often does not comport with the reasons the courts originally permitted it. In New York City, a federal judge found the NYPD violated the constitutional rights of people of color because police routinely stopped and frisked residents based on their race, not on whether reasonable suspicion existed. (ACLU of New Jersey, 2013)

Ultimately, the use of the stop-and-frisk approach to reduce crime declined in New York and eventually was phased out.

The Baltimore Police Department use of zero-tolerance techniques also came under fire not only from civil rights organizations and citizens, but also from the Justice Department. The criticism was, as in New York City, that the policy unfairly targeted blacks, especially in the inner city. In a 2016 report, the U.S. Department of Justice wrote about a black man in his mid-50s who was stopped 30 times in less than four years, none of which led to a citation or criminal charge. African American residents attributed for 95 percent of the 410 individuals stopped at least 10 times in the five-and-a-half years of data reviewed, according to the report (U.S. Department of Justice, 2016).

Meanwhile, Baltimore's policy of focusing on small infractions to prevent bigger crimes resulted in the police making a high number of stops, searches, and arrests for minor offenses. In both New York City and Baltimore, the programs created tensions with minority communities and they were not considered successful crime fighting strategy. The experience of these and other large cities struggling with crime showed that this is an ongoing issue and that there is an inherent tension between investigation and fighting crime in high-crime neighborhoods and respecting the rights of residents who may have had nothing to do with a particular incident but fit "the profile."

The Police Executive Research Forum (PERF) undertook an extensive study of racial profiling, noting that there were a variety of terms and definitions used (and still are). In their report, the authors chose to avoid the term *racial profiling*, preferring *racially biased policing*. They indicate (Fridell, Lunney, Diamond, & Kubu, 2001) that racial profiling was often so narrowly defined, that it did not adequately communicate the concerns of both police and citizens.

In the PERF study, staff conducted focus groups around the country with citizens as well as police line and command staff regarding occurrences and perceptions of biased policing. The meetings revealed that the *police* were using the narrow definition of racial profiling (stops based *solely* on race or ethnicity) and thus could declare vehemently that police actions based solely on race, national origin, or ethnicity were quite rare. The *citizens* in the study, however, were using a broader definition, one that included race as one among several factors impacting inappropriately on law enforcement actions.

> Many of our law enforcement participants did express skepticism that "racial profiling" was a major problem, exacerbating some citizens' frustration. It became clear to staff that these differing perceptions among citizens and police regarding racial profiling's pervasiveness were very much

related to the respective definitions they had adopted. The citizens equated "racial profiling" with all manifestations of racially biased policing, whereas most of the police practitioners defined "racial profiling" as stopping a motorist based *solely* on race. Presumably, even officers who engage in racially biased policing rarely make a vehicle stop based *solely* on race (often ensuring probable cause or some other factor is also present). (Ibid.)

Even a racially prejudiced officer is likely to use more than just race when making a decision in the line of duty. This may include decisions based on the neighborhood someone lives in, the age of the car they drive and their gender, combined with their race to make a determination about how to proceed with their police work. Activities based on considerations other than just race would therefore not be strictly defined as "racial profiling." The citizens in the study, however, were using a broader definition, one that included race as one among several factors leading up to the stop of the individual. The mismatch between how law enforcement viewed the issue and the views of citizens, who were likely to equate "racial profiling" with all manifestations of racially biased policing views, led to frustration among citizens.

OTHER FACTORS IN POLICE STOPS   When a stop or detention by officers is not self-initiated, it was most likely to have been initiated because a witness or victim had provided a description, sometimes by a 911 call, of a person or event that they felt required police action— a suspect-specific incident or one due to computer-generated information. This is the case in most contacts police make with citizens. If the complainant describes a suspect of a certain race, ethnicity, or national origin, that is what the officer will search for. For example, if police receive a report of possible criminal activity, and reliable information indicates that he is 5-feet-8-inches tall, lean, long-haired, and Asian, then "Asian" may be considered, along with the other descriptors, in developing reasonable suspicion or probable cause to detain. If, however, the citizen is reporting the activity of a minority because of his or her own biases, the police should attempt to ensure the legitimacy of the complaint and not be an agent of what might be racially charged paranoia.

Some allegations of racially motivated stops are clearly not reasonable. In some cases, officers cannot discern the race or ethnicity of the driver and/or occupant(s) prior to the stop. For example, some cars have tinted or darkened windows or a head rest on the back of the seat, making it impossible to determine the race, ethnicity, or even gender of the occupant(s). When officers use radar, it is the electronic device that determines which vehicle to stop, and not the race, ethnicity, or national origin of the driver. Obviously at nighttime, it is challenging to identify drivers or passengers in detail. (To test this assertion, readers should try to describe the occupants of a vehicle in front of them, especially at night.)

One example of many of urban policing using race-neutral, data-driven technology and methods is New York's innovative **CompStat**—or COMPSTAT—(short for **Comp**uter **Stat**istics or COMParative STATistics) program. CompStat is the New York Police Department's personnel and resource management system, the purpose of which is crime reduction. It uses Geographic Information Systems (GIS) technology to map crime and identifies problems in the city. Crime data are forwarded every week to the chief of the department's CompStat Unit. Based on this information, precinct commanders and members of top management deploy people and other resources to most effectively reduce crime and improve police performance. Officers are held accountable for reducing specific crime in targeted areas. If robberies are up in a certain precinct, officers are deployed to locate and arrest those responsible. If the neighborhood to which officers are assigned is a minority part of the city, then the people they contact will likely be members of that minority group. Race is irrelevant to this sort of policing.

Victim and Civil Rights Advocates' Perceptions

The claims and counterclaims about the existence and prevalence of racial profiling have been made for years, and they should not be dismissed as misperceptions or misunderstandings. We have to regard them as indicators of a very real social phenomenon. Court and U.S. Department of Justice decisions have upheld claims of targeting, harassment and intimidation by law enforcement officers in various jurisdictions in the United States.

Blacks are not the only Americans who say they have been the targets of racial or ethnic profiling by law enforcement. Studies have concluded that Hispanic men report being more likely than white men to question why they were stopped and how they were treated. Just as "DWB" (Driving While Black or Brown) has been used by civil rights advocates to demonstrate racial profiling of African Americans or Hispanics, in recent years, "flying while Arab" has been used to describe the targeting of Arabs, South Asians, and Middle Easterners. These complaints of racial profiling are most often heard at airports and other places where there is a concern about the potential for terrorist attack. Civil rights advocates say that Arabs, South Asians, and Middle Easterners, most of them loyal American citizens, have become victims of the new war on terrorism. It is a difficult issue and one in which officers and security agents are damned if they do and damned if they don't. Minorities complain that they are not only more likely to be stopped than whites, but they are also often pressured to allow searches of their vehicles.

The following mini case studies involve descriptions of fictional events but are based upon actual occurrences. The issues and implications of each should be discussed in class, especially the question of whether the police behavior is proper, justified, legal, or necessary.

PROFILING AS A LEGAL TOOL OF LAW ENFORCEMENT

How does law enforcement balance the need to reduce crime, especially in the inner cities, against the potential for accusations of discrimination, bias-based policing, and stereotyping? It is a challenging and complex problem for officers, especially for those strongly committed

---

Mini Case Studies: Culture and Crime

You Decide—Racial Profiling?

Mini Case Study 1

A well-dressed young Hispanic male is driving through a predominantly white community early in the morning on his way to work in a new BMW. He is pulled over for speeding and the officer, instead of simply asking for a driver's license and writing a speeding ticket, calls for backup and is joined by another officer. The young man is told to leave his vehicle and the officers search it. "Hey, where did you get the money for something like this?" one officer asks mockingly as he starts going through every inch of the BMW. One of the officers pulls off an inside door panel, and more dismantling of the vehicle follows. They say they are looking for drugs, but in the end, find nothing. After ticketing the driver for speeding, the two officers drive off.

1. While Hispanic officers might have stopped the same speeding driver, do you think they would have treated the driver in the same manner?
2. Is there any indication of probable cause in the example that would lead the officers to such a search?
3. Do you believe police officers do in fact pull over and search the vehicles of minorities at rates that are disproportionate to their numbers?
4. Should profiling only include the actions, behavior, and activities of the person(s) observed by the officer?
5. How can law enforcement leadership and trainers teach officers to distinguish between behavioral profiling and racial profiling?

Mini Case Study 2:

An Arab American was traveling from Washington, D.C., to Detroit. At the airport, he was pulled out of the security line, questioned, and searched. He reported that this was done in front of everyone else in line and was humiliating. He thought that the authorities at the airport were doing this so non-Arab Americans could see that something was being done about security. He felt he had been racially profiled.

1. Passengers who appear "Arab-looking," a category that has included South Asians and Latinos, have been asked by airline officials to leave airplanes because fellow passengers and crew members refuse to fly with them. How can airline security and management justify these actions?
2. Should Sikh men be denied the right to board aircraft because they refuse to fly without their turban, which equates to asking an individual to fly without a basic article of clothing?
3. Has the war on terrorism or the conflicts in the Middle East provided the opportunity for officers and security personnel to use racial profiling tactics?
4. What options are available for officers and security personnel to provide security and safety to the public they serve?

to nonbiased practices and the belief in proactive policing. The real questions associated with any type of law enforcement profiling are as follows:

- Who is doing the profile construction and on what basis?
- Does that person have some expertise (e.g., in behavioral science)?
- Is the profile creator objective, unbiased, and nonjudgmental in formulating a particular profile?
- Who is interpreting the profile?
- Is that person sufficiently trained in its application?
- Is the officer who is using profiling doing so legally?
- Is it based on departmental policy rather than on his or her personal biases, attitudes, and beliefs?

Criminal justice agencies face major challenges regarding the issue and impact of the use of profiles and profiling. Law enforcement personnel are entrusted with (1) protecting the rights of those who are the subject of stereotyping, harassment, and discrimination (i.e., those who are misidentified as a result of profiles or profiling); (2) identifying and bringing to justice those who are terrorists or criminals (i.e., those who are correctly identified); (3) identifying terrorists and/or criminals who do not fit a particular profile or stereotype; and (4) not being so hampered by their personal stereotypes, attitudes, beliefs, perceptions, and knowledge (or lack thereof) that innocent people are detained and terrorists are not apprehended in the course of law enforcement.

Profiling and profiles have long been used as legitimate law enforcement tools to look for signs of potential criminal activity in almost every country in the world, although the people profiled will vary by country. In Israel, for example, police have profiles of Palestinian terrorists. Now the criminal justice community in many parts of the world is using profiles to locate and arrest members of al-Qaida and allied radical Islamist groups. In the United States, a potential terrorist's profile used by airport and homeland security agents might include such factors as (1) a man in his 20s or 30s who comes from Saudi Arabia, Egypt, or Pakistan (2) who is probably living in one of six states: Texas, New Jersey, California, New York, Michigan, or Florida; and (3) who is likely to have engaged in some sort of suspicious activity, such as taking flying lessons, traveling in areas of possible targets, or getting a U.S. driver's license. Meeting some of these criteria—not necessarily having a certain skin color— is enough to instigate questioning by law enforcement authorities.

The PERF created policy intended for police departments across the nation that defines legal profiling. Because the Fourth Amendment to the Constitution protects citizens against unreasonable search and seizure, the policy mandates that officers shall *not consider* race/ethnicity to establish reasonable suspicion or probable cause except under specific circumstances. The policy:

- disallows use of race as a general indicator for criminal behavior
- disallows use of stereotypes/biases
- allows for the consideration of race *as one factor* in making law enforcement decisions if it is based on trustworthy and locally relevant information that links specific suspected unlawful activity to a person(s) of a particular race/ethnicity
- relies on *descriptions* of actual suspects, not general *predictions* of who may be involved in a crime.

In the PERF publication, *Racially Biased Policing: A Principled Response* (Fridell et al., 2001), the authors advised that the following principle be applied: "Race/ethnicity should be treated like other demographic descriptors. Police can use race/ethnicity as one factor in the same way that they use age, gender and other descriptors to establish reasonable suspicion or probable cause." The authors recommended that the best "litmus test" for officers to use includes two questions: (1) Would I be engaging this particular person if this person were white? (2) Would I be asking this question of this person if this person wasn't [fill in the demographic descriptor]? (FIP Web site, 2017a; Fridell et al., 2001).

What is necessary in assessing the use of profiles and profiling is a combination of common sense and fairness, a balance between effective law enforcement and protection of civil liberties. The authors believe that profiles and profiling will not upset such a balance if they are used judiciously, fairly, and within the law. Most officers understand that profiling, not racial profiling, is an acceptable form of proactive law enforcement, and the courts agree. The U.S. Customs Service, the U.S. Border Patrol, and the DEA have long used profiles as a tool to detain and investigate persons fitting the "drug courier profile." Such a profile is based on behaviors, actions, traits, demeanor, intelligence information, carrier routes, statistical evidence, and other factors—not just a single characteristic like race or ethnicity. The U.S. Border Patrol obviously, links ethnicity to incidence of crime on the border with Mexico. It is only logical to assume that most people attempting to enter the country illegally from Mexico are of Hispanic/Latino or Mestizo descent. The use of profiles in this context appears to be legal and acceptable. A border patrol profile, however, not only includes the ethnicity of the individual but also such factors as their proximity to the border, erratic driving, suspicious behavior, and the officers' previous experience with alien traffic.

CONTROVERSY AROUND RACIAL PROFILING AND THE "WAR ON TERRORISM"

The subject of racial profiling, which began to receive a great deal of attention following the terrorist attacks of September 11, 2001, continues to be one of the most significant civil rights issues today. There is a great deal of controversy as to whether racial profiling is taking place in the name of the "War on Terrorism" at airports and the borders. Airport police and security agents (i.e., the TSA), and the U.S. Border Patrol and Immigration officers within the DHS use profiles to try to identify those who might be a threat to security in their respective jurisdictions. When a person books a plane ticket, certain identifying information is collected by the airline, including name, birth date, address, and phone number. If an international flight is involved, a passport number is also required. This information is checked against other data such as the TSA's No-Fly list and the FBI's 10 most wanted fugitive list. (The no-fly list, established following the September 11, 2001 attacks, is designed to prevent air travel to or from the United States by those whom the government suspects of having ties to terrorism.) The traveler is then assigned a terrorism "risk score." High scores require the airline to conduct extended baggage and/or personal screening, and, where appropriate, to contact law enforcement. Passengers are also screened based on their destination and how they purchased their tickets—not on how they looked. None of the profile information specifically involves the race, ethnicity, or national origin of the persons checked.

In 2009, TSA implemented Secure Flight, which ultimately passed tests for accuracy and privacy protection. All flights into, out of, or within the United States had the Secure Flight program in place by December 2010.

TSA also uses race- and ethnicity-neutral techniques to screen passengers. That is, everyone boarding an airplane in the United States is treated the same way, regardless of age, disability, appearance, nationality, race, or ethnic group. If metal detector, full-body scan, or pat-down discovers a discrepancy, extra scrutiny is triggered. Some flyers have voiced resentment to this intrusion. Some argue that TSA should be allowed to profile travelers, as their resources are wasted on screening low-risk passengers.

Legitimate Use of Race/Ethnicity

An important question is whether race can *ever* be a valid consideration when conducting law enforcement activity. In the *United States v. Travis* opinion, the Sixth Circuit Court of Appeals ruled that "race or ethnic background may become a legitimate consideration when investigators have information on this subject about a particular suspect" (*U.S. v. Travis*, 62 F.3d 170, 1995). Simply put, the suspect described and being sought is of a certain race or ethnicity (refer to the definition of suspect-specific incident in this chapter). Court decisions have allowed officers to consider the totality of the circumstances surrounding the subject of their attention in light of their experience and training, which may include "instructions on a drug courier profile" (*Florida v. Royer*, 460 U.S. 491, 1983). Many courts have upheld the use of drug courier profiles as the sole determinant of a stop or cause for suspicion. Therefore, profiles combined with other facts and circumstances can establish reasonable suspicion or probable cause. Race or color may be a factor to consider during certain police activity (*U.S. v. Brignoni-Ponce*, 442 U.S. 837, 887, 1975). The *Whren* (*Whren v. United States*, 517 U.S. 806, 1996) decision by the Supreme Court enhanced the already extensive power of police to detain individual citizens under the banner of the war on drugs by allowing pretext stops through the "objective" standard test.

Some see the *Whren* decision "objective" standard (defined as a standard that is based on factual measurements, in the absence of a biased judgment or analysis) ruling as opening the door for police abuse. They argue that in the *Whren* case, it did not matter to the court that the officers lied about their intent, that they were violating departmental policy to make the stop, or that they really wanted to stop the car because it contained two African American men who sat at a stop sign for 20 seconds in an area known for drug dealing. They are concerned that the *Whren* decision clearly opens the door for racial profiling because it allows police officers to stop anyone without reasonable suspicion or probable cause, thus providing a mechanism for circumventing the Fourth Amendment requirements of the U.S. Constitution. Because minor traffic violations are numerous, they argue, to limit stops to the observation of traffic violations is no limitation at all. If a police officer wants to stop a car but does not have the legal authority to do so, all the officer has to do is to follow it until the driver gets nervous and at some point, turns right without a turn signal, drifts across the center line, or simply fails to come to a complete stop at a stop sign. Upon observing a minor traffic violation, the police officer can stop the driver and attempt to pressure him or her into giving consent for the car to be searched.

It is important to note that the Court's decision in *Whren* did not create the practice of pretextual stops. Instead it validated these long-standing police practice that is even encouraged by police administrators. Neither was the *Whren* decision unpredictable. The courts said the burden that "brief detentions" place on law-abiding minority citizens is a minor and necessary inconvenience in the war on crime, suggesting that little damage is done by the practice of profiling. However, those who advocate making the standard for brief detentions more restrictive insist that these court decisions have failed to acknowledge that these detentions grow into regular occurrences, breeding resentment and anger both in the citizens stopped and in the police officers who confront hostile persons of color. Police officers who use race, ethnicity, gender, sexual orientation, or national origin as a factor in criminal profiling based on presumed statistical probabilities then contribute to the very statistics upon which they rely.

The Supreme Court has made it clear that if the government can show that police searches and seizures are objectively reasonable (i.e., based on probable cause or reasonable suspicion, defined earlier in this chapter), then they do not violate the Fourth Amendment (see shaded area in the following text), regardless of the officer's subjective (actual) motivation for the search or seizure. That does not mean, however, that objectively reasonable searches and seizures can never violate the Constitution. Officers motivated by prejudice who lawfully search or seize only members of certain racial, ethnic, religious, or gender groups are still subject to claims of constitutional violations (i.e., racial profiling).

"The right of the people to be secure in their persons, houses, papers, and effects against unreasonable searches and seizures shall not be violated, and no warrants shall issue but upon probable cause supported by oath or affirmation, and particularly describing the place to be searched, and the persons or things to be seized." United States Constitution, Amendment IV

Police officers who undertake searches of persons or vehicles not incident to an arrest must have reasonable suspicion or probable cause to perform such a search. An officer who does not have reasonable suspicion may ask for consent to search (except in those states or localities where it is illegal) and even have the motorist sign a waiver to that effect. Sometimes, however, evidence of racial bias may be discovered when there is a repeated pattern of minorities being subjected to consent searches much more often than whites. Law enforcement agencies must monitor the data they collect on discretionary consent searches to ensure that the discretion is not applied more often to minorities. One explanation for the disparity, per some researchers, is that minorities may be more nervous around police and officers may misinterpret that as suspicious behavior.

Far-reaching authority for searches was granted to law enforcement when, in 2001, President George W. Bush signed the USA Patriot Act into law. The law gave sweeping new powers to both domestic law enforcement and international intelligence agencies. The provisions of the law, aimed at terrorism, expanded surveillance capabilities (in effect, searches) and allowed for nationwide wiretaps under certain circumstances. Many aspects of the new law were questioned by those concerned about the potential for government intrusion into the lives and civil rights of innocent people. The Patriot Act expired on June 1, 2015 and a modified version, now called the USA Freedom Act of 2015, was renewed by Congress on June 2, 2015. The Freedom Act will be in place through 2019 (U.S. House of Representatives, 2015).

There are exceptions to the general rules that require that searches must be based on reasonable suspicion or probable cause. Courts have ruled in favor of routine searches at airports, mass transit sites and entrances to courts and other official buildings. These screenings or searches are called the "special needs" exception to the Fourth Amendment requirements, and are permitted only in limited circumstances or situations. The purpose of such searches or screening is not primarily to detect weapons or explosives or to apprehend those who carry them, but to deter such persons from carrying banned items into the area being protected. The court considers such screening a legitimate means of implementing counterterrorism measures while at the same time expecting that the intrusion to the public and their privacy is minimal. It is also expected that such administrative programs are an effective deterrent to a terrorist attack or the bringing of contraband or restricted items into a controlled area. The Supreme Court ruled in *Navarette v. California* in 2014 that officers can stop cars and question their drivers even though the officer didn't witness the driving. The court ruled that:

> After a 911 caller reported that a vehicle had run her off the road, a police officer located the vehicle she identified during the call and executed a traffic stop. We hold that the stop complied with the Fourth Amendment because, under the totality of the circumstances, the officer had reasonable suspicion that the driver was intoxicated. (U.S. Supreme Court 572 U.S., 2014)

Illegitimate Use of Race/Ethnicity

Courts have held that matching a profile *alone* is not the equivalent of the reasonable suspicion or probable cause necessary to conduct an investigative detention or arrest (see, for example, *Reid v. George*, 448 U.S. 438, 1980, and *Royer* at 525, note 6). There are no circumstances under which officers may stop citizens based solely on their race, ethnicity, gender, religion, national origin, or any other demographic feature. Officers must base their stops of persons, whether in a vehicle or on foot, on reasonable suspicion or probable cause that a violation of the law has been or is about to be committed based on facts and information that they can articulate.

Some states, via legislation, have banned consent searches where there is no clear reason for suspicion. The mere nervousness of the motorist or occupant(s) is not sufficient reason to ask for a consent search. The Fourth and the Fourteenth (equal protection under the law) Amendments to the U.S. Constitution provide a framework for the protection of drivers from being indiscriminately targeted by the police via traffic stops. To prove an allegation of being indiscriminately targeted, the claimants must produce facts or statistics showing that they were targeted solely because of their race, ethnicity, gender, religion, or national origin. The police officer must then provide evidence that he or she did not act solely on any of these factors.

In 2003, the U.S. Department of Justice banned all racial profiling by federal agents performing law enforcement activities, except for those working national security cases, in a directive entitled "Guidance Regarding the Use of Race by Federal Law Enforcement Agencies." However, the directive only applied to race and ethnicity and not religion, gender, national origin, sexual orientation, or gender identity (U.S. Department of Justice, 2003). Attorney General Eric Holder corrected this in 2014 when he updated the directive to prevent the FBI, and other federal agents, from considering gender, national origin, religion, sexual orientation and gender identity, in addition to race and ethnicity, during enforcement activities. The regulations apply to the security operations of the DHS, which includes Immigration and Customs Enforcement, U.S. Coast Guard, and Border Patrol enforcement activities not near the border. The rules also apply to DHS officers protecting government buildings and federal air marshals. An exemption is that Customs and Border Protection federal agents are still allowed to use profiling when conducting screenings and inspections at U.S. ports of entry. The rules do not apply to local, county, or state law enforcement officers. The Secret Service is also exempt from the regulations (U.S. Department of Justice, 2014). The United States Congress has considered various pieces of legislation that would ban state and local law enforcement agencies from using racial profiling over the years; however, they have never been passed (ibid.). As of 2011, 28 U.S. states had enacted laws related to racial profiling (Glaser, 2014).

PREVENTION OF RACIAL PROFILING IN LAW ENFORCEMENT

To formulate measures to prevent the practice of racial profiling and inappropriate behavior and actions on the part of officers, the criminal justice system should consider the following six areas:

- Accountability and supervision
- Self-assessment
- Agency policies to address racial profiling
- Recruitment and hiring
- Education and training
- Minority community outreach

Accountability and Supervision

Preventing the use of racial profiling or biased policing in law enforcement is critical. Police executives must reflect seriously on this and respond to both the reality and the perceptions of biased policing. Law enforcement executives, managers, and supervisors must send a clear message to all personnel that using race, ethnicity, or national origin alone as the basis for any investigative stop is not only unacceptable conduct, but also illegal. It can lead to termination from employment and possibly to prosecution. If convicted, the officer(s) could be fined and/or incarcerated depending on the laws of the state.

Police managers and supervisors, in order to identify officers who might be biased, should monitor such indicators as: (1) high numbers of minority citizen complaints; (2) high numbers of use-of-force or resisting incidents involving minorities; (3) large numbers of arrests not charged because prosecutors find improper detentions and/or searches; (4) perceptible negative attitude toward minorities; and (5) negative attitudes toward training programs that enhance police–community relations or cultural awareness.

Prevention of racial profiling also involves other components of the criminal justice system, such as prosecutors and courts. Legislators are also an integral part of the process. Supervision, legislation, and documentation of the race/ethnicity of drivers stopped alone will not root out rogue officers who use racial profiling tactics. A program that reviews other contacts officers have with residents should also be instigated to help reduce such incidents. Law enforcement agencies must convey to their communities that they, the citizens, will be protected from such abuses and that abuse is not tolerated or advocated. Preventing the use of racial profiling by law enforcement officers not only is crucial to maintaining credibility within the community, but also reduces exposure to civil liability for departments and officers. Law enforcement managers might use the following self-assessment to evaluate their agency's policies and practices to determine if any of them could lead to a negative image of the department in the community or possible civil liability.

Self-Assessment

1. Has your law enforcement agency taken a proactive stance regarding bias-based traffic law enforcement?
2. How many civil rights complaints has your department received during the past year? What percentage is related to traffic stops?
3. Has your department been negatively portrayed in the media regarding community relations or bias-based traffic enforcement?

4. Do you collect data on the race, ethnicity, gender, and national origin of those your agency's officers have stopped, detained, searched, and arrested?
5. Have you authorized department-wide use of in-car video systems or body cameras?
6. Is there an effective citizen complaint system in place and is the department responsive?
7. Do you have supervisory control that can identify (early alert) officers who may have patterns of bias-based traffic enforcement?
8. Does your agency have disciplinary policies and training established for officers with patterns of using racial profiling or bias-based policing traffic enforcement?
9. Has your agency instituted proactive measures to build positive relations with the minority community (e.g., meetings with community leaders and neighborhood associations) before problems surface? (Jackson, 2003)

Most law enforcement officers, supervisors, and managers within agencies across the country are committed to serving all members of our communities with fairness and respect. These professionals know racial profiling is unacceptable and conflicts with the standards and values inherent in ensuring all people are treated equally regardless of their race or ethnicity. They know racial profiling can expose a police department to costly lawsuits and ruin relations with communities of color. They are intolerant of the use of racial profiling and willingly partner with their communities to address the issues involved. These professionals develop approaches to eradicate both confirmed acts of racial profiling and the perception that it is taking place within their agency or jurisdiction.

Agency Policies to Address Racial Profiling

Law enforcement agencies must have clear policies and procedures to address racial profiling and the perceptions thereof. Many departments in the United States have developed such general orders to cover not only traffic stops, but also the temporary detentions of pedestrians and even bicyclists. The policies usually address the Fourth Amendment requirement that investigative detentions, traffic stops, arrests, searches, and property seizures by officers must be based on a standard of reasonable suspicion or probable cause that officers can support with specific facts and circumstances. The policy must include the following: (1) no motorist, once cited or warned, shall be detained beyond the point where there exists no reasonable suspicion of further criminal activity and (2) no person or vehicle shall be searched in the absence of probable cause, a search warrant, or the person's *voluntary* consent. The policy should specify that in each case where a search is conducted, this information shall be recorded, including the legal basis for the search and the results. It is strongly recommended that consent searches be conducted only with written consent utilizing the agency forms provided. Some agencies now require that an officer's verbal request for consent to search an individual or vehicle be documented by a video or audio recording at the scene.

Per the International Association of Chiefs of Police (IACP), departments without a policy should look at as many models addressing racial profiling as possible before they create one that meets their needs. Agencies should also involve community members, especially minorities and civil rights advocates, in the development and implementation of the policy. The policy must communicate a clear message to law enforcement personnel and the people they serve that racial profiling and other forms of bias-based policing are not acceptable practices. The statement should include what discipline (including criminal prosecution where such laws exist) could result if officers violate the provisions of the policy.

The San Francisco Police Department created a general order that outlines their policy for policing without racial bias. It states that the department has always "striven to gain the trust of the community. To maintain that trust, it is crucial for members of our Department to carry out their duties in a manner free from bias and to eliminate any perception of policing that appears racially biased." The general order clarifies the circumstances under which officers can consider race, color, ethnicity, national origin, gender, age, sexual orientation, or gender identity when making law enforcement decisions.

Policy: Investigative detentions, traffic stops, arrests, searches, and property seizures by officers will be based on a standard of reasonable suspicion or probable cause in accordance with the Fourth Amendment of the U.S. Constitution. Officers must be able to articulate specific facts and circumstances that support reasonable suspicion or probable cause for investigative detentions, traffic stops, arrest, nonconsensual searches, and property seizures. Department personnel may not use, *to any extent or degree*, race, color, ethnicity, national origin, age, sexual orientation, or gender identity in conducting stops or detentions, or activities following stops or detentions *except* when engaging in the investigation of appropriate suspect-specific activity to identify a particular person or group. Department personnel seeking one or more specific persons who have been identified or described in part by any of the above listed characteristics may rely on them in part only in combination with other appropriate identifying factors. The listed characteristics should not be given undue weight:

- Except as provided above, officers shall not consider race, color, ethnicity, national origin, gender, age, sexual orientation, or gender identity in establishing reasonable suspicion or probable cause.
- Except as provided above, officers shall not consider race, color, ethnicity, national origin, gender, age, sexual orientation, or gender identity in deciding to initiate even those consensual encounters that do not amount to legal detentions or to request consent to search. (San Francisco Police Department General Order 5.17, 2011)

Another example of an agency proactively dealing with racial profiling is the Portland Police Bureau. In 2009, the department actively worked with the community to develop a plan to address the issue of racial profiling. The plan, which can be seen on the agency's Web site, emphasizes the following strategic priorities:

- Work with the Human Rights Commission and Office of Human Relations, among others, to create opportunities for officers to engage with communities of color.
- Develop a plan to reduce the number of unsuccessful searches by improving officers' ability to accurately identify individuals likely to carry weapons and/or contraband (i.e., improving their "hit" rate on searches)—thereby reducing disparate treatment among Caucasians, African Americans, and Latinos.
- Inventory the Bureau's training and supervision on issues of professionalism and respect, with the goal of improving customer service.
- Develop and improve partnerships with other agencies engaged in reducing racial disparities in our work. (Portland Police Bureau, 2009)

In 1979, the IACP, NOBLE, the National Sheriffs' Association, and PERF created the Commission on Accreditation for Law Enforcement Agencies (CALEA). The primary purpose of the Commission is to improve law enforcement service by creating a national body of standards developed by law enforcement professionals. Furthermore, it recognizes professional achievements by establishing and administering an *accreditation* process through which a law enforcement agency can demonstrate that it meets those standards. "Participation in the CALEA accreditation program is voluntary, but successful completion provides a law enforcement agency with a nationally recognized award of excellence and professional achievement. Additional benefits of obtaining CALEA accreditation may include more favorable liability insurance costs and increased governmental *and community support*" (see CALEA Web site: www.calea.org).

In 2001, CALEA issued Standard 1.2.9 regarding bias-based profiling. The standard requires that CALEA-accredited agencies have a written policy governing bias-based profiling and, at a minimum, include the following provisions: (1) a prohibition against biased profiling in traffic contacts, in field contacts, and in asset seizure and forfeiture efforts; (2) training agency enforcement personnel in bias-based profiling issues including legal aspects; (3) corrective measures if bias-based profiling occurs; and (4) an annual administrative review of agency practices, including citizen concerns. CALEA does not require mandatory collection of traffic stop data even though there is a growing demand for such action. The Commission's position is that not all law enforcement agencies must collect traffic stop data when other successful measurement systems are in use and/or the situation in the community served does not indicate that there is a concern about police bias.

Recruitment and Hiring

Police agencies can reduce racial bias by recruiting and hiring officers who can police in a professional way. Within legal parameters, the department should hire a workforce that reflects the community's racial and ethnic demographics. Those hired should be expected to carry out their duties with fairness and impartiality. Having such a workforce increases the probability that, as a whole, the agency will be able to understand the perspectives of its racial/ethnic minorities and communicate with them effectively.

The officers that departments should be recruiting are those who are aware of and capable of managing their own ethnic, racial, and cultural stereotypes and biases in a professional way. These qualities are essential to reducing bias in policing. The multiple testing stages that applicants for law enforcement positions go through help weed out those who are unable to control their biases. Interviews, polygraphs, psychological tests, and background investigations are all intended to identify those who are biased to the point that they might act based on their prejudices (see Chapters 1 and 3). It should be noted that the possibility of bias is not limited to white officers. Members of minority groups can also have biases against white people, against members of other minority groups, or even against members of their own race/ethnic group. There have been numerous studies that have determined that minority officers can be just as tough as whites on minority drivers, and sometimes tougher. Police recruitment messages, verbal and written, must emphasize that those who are prejudiced, regardless of their race or ethnicity, and who cannot distinguish between appropriate and inappropriate behavior and actions, will not be hired. As mentioned earlier in this chapter, no one is completely free of bias, but the recruitment effort should be targeted at those who understand and control their biases.

Education and Training

Law enforcement agencies need to provide training and education to enable officers to utilize legal enforcement tools so they can perform their work professionally and effectively within today's multicultural communities. Some departments have used interactive simulation training exercises to train officers on professional traffic stop procedures, especially those involving agitated citizens. Clearly, most law enforcement officers know not to act based on the prejudices and stereotypes they might hold. However, the nature of prejudice is such that some people are not aware of their own prejudices or biases. Therefore, they make inferences and take actions toward certain groups based on these unrecognized biased perceptions. Training that provides accurate information concerning groups about which officers might have prejudices and stereotypes is one of the approaches police departments should use to prevent racial profiling.

What is the mental process that takes place when an officer makes a stop based on race, ethnicity, or national origin? Officers who have a biased belief system observe and collect certain data that in turn reinforce that belief system. Meanings are added to make sense of the observations ("I notice minorities more and stop them more because of my biased beliefs about them"). Based on these meanings, assumptions are made that fill in for missing data ("This motorist is carrying drugs on him"). The officer draws conclusions (based on beliefs) and then takes action (decides to stop African American and Hispanic motorists much more frequently than whites). These steps in our thinking take place very quickly. Most of us are not aware that this process goes on all the time (see the section in Chapter 1 on "Prejudice and Bias in Law Enforcement").

In their book *The Fifth Discipline Fieldbook: Strategies and Tools for Building a Learning Organization*, management specialist Peter Senge and his coauthors provide a clear and simple model called the "Ladder of Inference," which illuminates most people's typical patterns (and flaws) of thinking. Using the ladder, the authors discuss thinking and decision-making processes to describe, from the bottom up, how people select data, add meanings, make assumptions, draw conclusions, adopt beliefs, and ultimately act (see Exhibit 12.3). They maintain that:

> We live in a world of self-generating beliefs that remain largely untested. We adopt those beliefs because they are based on conclusions, which are inferred from what we observe, plus our past experience. Our ability to achieve the results we truly desire is eroded by our feelings that:

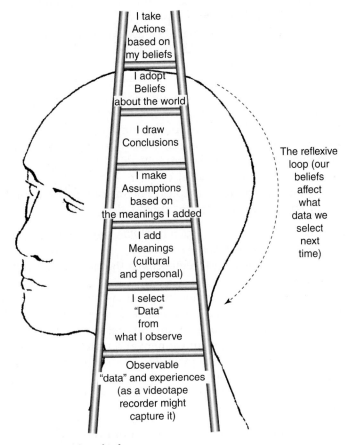

I take
Actions
based on
my beliefs

I adopt
Beliefs
about the world

I draw
Conclusions

I make
Assumptions
based on
the meanings I added

I add
Meanings
(cultural
and personal)

I select
"Data"
from
what I observe

Observable
"data" and experiences
(as a videotape
recorder might
capture it)

The reflexive
loop (our
beliefs
affect
what
data we
select
next
time)

EXHIBIT 12.3 Ladder of Inference
Source: Senge et al., 1994, pp. 242–246. Reproduced with permission of Peter Senge.

- Our beliefs are the truth.
- The truth is obvious.
- Our beliefs are based on real data.
- The data we select are the real data. (Senge, Kleiner, Roberts, Ross, & Smith, 1994)

The authors explain that most people no longer remember where their attitudes and beliefs came from (i.e., what data or experiences led to their assumptions and conclusions). Therefore, they may not understand the basis of the actions they take. Senge and his coauthors discuss "leaps of abstraction" in which:

> Our minds literally move at lightning speed…because we immediately "leap" to generalizations so quickly that we never think to test them… [L]eaps of abstraction occur when we move from direct observation (concrete "data") to generalization without testing. Leaps of abstraction impede learning because they become axiomatic. What was once an assumption becomes treated as a fact. (Ibid.)

The authors go on to say that we then treat generalization as fact:

> How do you spot leaps of abstraction? First, by asking yourself what you believe about the way the world works… Ask "what is the 'data' on which this generalization is based?" Then ask yourself, "Am I willing to consider that this generalization may be inaccurate or misleading?" It is important to ask this last question consciously, because, if the answer is no, there is no point in proceeding. (Ibid.)

In intensive training conducted by Senge, police and other corporate executives can learn about the models above and relate them to issues and challenges in their own organizations. The models provide insight into what may be going on in officers' minds as they stop members of minority groups. Thus, the models can help officers better understand their actions vis-à-vis racial profiling. It is natural for people to substitute assumptions for what is not known, but in the case of racial profiling, this is a very dangerous proposition. Officers should recognize when they are converting their biases into "facts" and when their assumptions substitute for real data.

Training and education provide departments an opportunity to inform officers of the penalties for not adhering to policies and laws on the subject. Many state legislatures have created laws barring law enforcement officers from engaging in racial profiling. Such legislation also requires that every law enforcement officer participate in expanded training regarding racial profiling. This training is typically coordinated, monitored, and controlled by the Commission on Peace Officer Standards and Training (POST), an agency that is found in every state. These state commissions should, if they haven't already, integrate the topic of racial profiling into their diversity training for both entry-level and in-service programs. Law enforcement agencies should consult local chapters of their community's minority group organizations to obtain accounts and examples of actual or perceived racially biased policing for use in training programs. Such programs should also cover:

1. Definitions of key terms involved, such as *profile, profiling, racial profiling, racially biased policing, probable cause,* and *reasonable suspicion.*
2. Identification of key indices and perspectives that signal cultural differences among residents in a local community.
3. The negative impact of biases, prejudices, and stereotyping on effective law enforcement, including examination of how historical perceptions of discriminatory enforcement practices have harmed police–community relations.
4. History and role of the civil rights movement and its impact on law enforcement.
5. Specific obligations of officers in preventing, reporting, and responding to discriminatory or biased practices by fellow officers.
6. Various perspectives of local groups and race relations experts regarding cultural diversity and police–community relations.

Training on avoiding racial profiling should be part of every state's POST academy as well as in service training programs. Training should include constitutional law, ethics, communications skills (respectful stops, and especially skills in de-escalating a situation that has potential for conflict or confrontation. For example, how should an officer on either a traffic or pedestrian stop respond if the person detained says, "You stopped me because I'm …" (see Chapter 4 [communication for de-escalation and responses to allegations of racial profiling] and the racial profiling section in Chapter 6).

Every state has different training requirements regarding racial profiling, either in class or online, and of varying durations. The POST Commission of Missouri requires training for peace officers with authority to make traffic stops. Following are some stipulations of the training:

1. All commissioned peace officers with the authority to enforce motor vehicle/traffic laws, regardless of whether they actually make traffic stops, must attend racial profiling training.
2. Peace officers who have no authority to make traffic stops are exempt from this training requirement.
3. All racial profiling training used to meet this requirement must either be obtained from a licensed/approved provider of continuing education, a training provider that has obtained a POST control number, or from a law enforcement agency that has had their Center for Law Enforcement Education (CLEE) course preapproved and assigned a control number.
4. The mandated statutory learning objective for racial profiling is as follows: "The training shall promote understanding and respect for racial and cultural differences and the use of effective, non-combative methods for carrying out law enforcement duties in a racially and culturally diverse environment." The training can be tailored for patrol officers, first-line supervisors, command staff officers or top administrators.
5. The racial profiling training requirement is part of the CLEE training requirement, not in addition to it. Depending on how the course is constructed, it may also be used to meet the core CLEE requirements of legal studies, interpersonal perspectives, technical studies or skill development. The certificates of completion will reflect this two-part usage (Missouri Department of Public Safety, 2017).

The Department of Justice, in collaboration with Dr. Lorie Fridell, former PERF director of research, produced multilevel training for law enforcement agencies, entitled, "Fair and Impartial Policing" (FIP Web site, 2017a). The comprehensive training series, also referenced in Chapters 1 and 6, includes recommendations for police executive management:

- …hire diverse personnel and people who can police in an unbiased fashion.
- …create meaningful policies that tell officers when they can and cannot use race and ethnicity (and other demographics) to make law enforcement decisions.
- …design effective academy and in-service training on the ways that racial and other biases might manifest in any department.
- …put accountability mechanisms in place to promote professional behavior, promoting fair and impartial policing.
- …ensure that there are ongoing efforts to strengthen relationships between departments and diverse communities.
- …assess the costs/benefits of collecting (vehicle/pedestrian) stop data.
- Make an INFORMED decision regarding whether to include data collection as part of its response. (Ibid.)

A publication by the IACP, "Protecting Civil Rights: A Leadership Guide for State, local, and Tribal Law Enforcement," references exemplary policies and practices of departments promoting civil rights protections. The content includes a discussion of consent decrees and memorandums of agreement that individual police agencies have signed with the U.S. Department of Justice. Law enforcement leaders should review the publication for recommendations pertaining to community partnerships in ways that both protect and promote civil rights (IACP, 2006).

First-Line Supervisor Training topics should include:

- How bias manifests in even well-intentioned people
- Science of bias
- How to identify officers who may be manifesting bias (What are they looking for? What are potential information sources?)
- Difficulty of identifying biased behavior
- How to intervene with officers when they have concerns about bias
- How might bias manifest in their own work/decisions
- How to talk about bias with individuals (officers, community members), community groups, media (Ibid.)

Command-Level Training should be composed of small classes that might involve ranking officers from other agencies plus leaders in the minority community. Topics should include:

- "Re-thinking biased policing"
- The social science of human bias and the implications for policing
- The benefits and elements of a comprehensive program to produce fair and impartial policing
- How to implement a comprehensive program (Ibid.)

The law enforcement community is more capable now than ever before of effectively addressing biased policing. In the past few decades, there has been a revolution in the quality and quantity of police training, the standards for hiring officers, and accountability.

Minority Community Outreach

Every police–community interaction requires a strong, ongoing link to community groups and civil rights organizations. Links might be established when community policing, which became popular in the 1990s, is used to address neighborhood problems. A link is also established when community task forces are assembled to address issues, especially racial profiling, both, real or perceived. These steps demonstrate respect for communities of color and create shared responsibility for whatever action is taken. The police hold primary responsibility for community outreach on every level, but the community is also responsible for becoming involved in activities that form positive relationships with the police. Policing within the community can function only in an environment of mutual engagement and respect. In the context of racial profiling or biased policing, outreach to the community is imperative. For constructive dialog to take place, therefore, police executives must remain open to discussions of racial profiling or the perception thereof within their jurisdictions. Sometimes, data on traffic stops and people searched can be used as a springboard for dialog and communications between law enforcement and the community. It is an opportunity for the clarification and open discussion of the raw data. An individual who has been trained in the analysis of such data and the use of appropriate statistical benchmarks should moderate the discussions.

PROFESSIONAL POLICE TRAFFIC STOPS

The reason for every stop made by a law enforcement officer must be legally defensible and professional. Professional traffic stops involve four key elements:

- *Organizational/agency policy:* Agencies must develop a well-structured policy concerning professional traffic stops, outlining the conduct of officers and the prohibition of discriminatory practices.
- *Officer training:* Agencies should include a component on racial profiling into existing in-service training programs. Special workshop discussions on the issue of racial profiling can also be scheduled.
- *Data collection:* Agencies must collect traffic stop data when the situation in the community served indicates that there is a concern about police bias.
- *Accountability/supervision:* Law enforcement supervisors and managers must hold officers accountable for adhering to the policy. Managers must personally take the message to employees, as well as to the public, that biased policing will not be tolerated and could result in discipline, possibly including prosecution or termination. Managers, supervisors, and the entire workforce must embrace and adhere to the policy.

Former deputy chief Ondra Berry (Reno, Nevada, Police Department), advises officers to ask themselves if there is any possibility that they are making an assumption about a driver based on race? Another question to ask is: "Am I moving from my own personal 'data' and making a leap of extraction about this vehicle or about this person?" At the same time it's important to realize that most people have unbalanced views about people who are different from them (Berry, 2017).

In Chapter 6, Law Enforcement Contact with African Americans, we emphasize the need for officers to slow down their thinking processes and challenge some of their personal biases when considering stopping an individual when there are no obvious signs of wrongdoing. To review, officers would be well advised to go through the following mental steps before acting on racial biases and prejudices (clearly, this does not suggest that all officers act on racial biases and prejudices):

> *If I see an individual simply walking down the street, let me first acknowledge to myself that I am not sure whether there is any reason to stop this person. I will ask myself the following questions:*
>
> *"Why do I think this person should be stopped?"*
>
> *"What is this person doing that makes me think he/she is suspicious?"*
>
> *"Could this person be lost or in the need of help?"*
>
> *"Is this person's race a part of the reason why I want to stop them?"*

If I decide that I should, for whatever reason, stop this individual, would there be merit in my saying something like:

> "There has been a robbery in the neighborhood and I want you to be aware of the potential dangers. You look a little lost, so I was wondering if you need any help or directions." (This only applies if there have been recent robberies in the neighborhood. If the person lives in that neighborhood, being dishonest can negatively affect the officer's credibility.)

In the process of slowing down one's mental processes, the officer makes a conscious decision to recognize potential bias if it is there, and refrains from making inferences or jumping to conclusions based on racial bias or prejudice. Officers can increase cooperation with respectful communication, and, at the same time, assess the **behavior** of the person they are stopping.

The IACP, after significant study, identified the components that constitute a "professional traffic stop." The organization's "Recommendations from the First IACP Forum on Professional Traffic Stops" should be referred to for additional information (International Association of Chiefs of Police, 2001).

DATA COLLECTION ON CITIZENS' RACE/ETHNICITY

Some also require data be collected for pedestrian stops. In October 2015, California Governor Jerry Brown signed Assembly Bill 953, known as the Racial and Identity Profiling Act, into law. The legislation requires police to keep records of car and pedestrian stops. The information collected includes the race or other identifier of the individual, the reason for the stop, how the person was treated and whether an arrest or citation resulted (State of California Department of Justice, 2015). The purpose of collecting data is to address racially biased policing and the perceptions thereof and to determine whether it is taking place. The use of data collection requires officers to complete a form following each traffic stop.

Research by PERF examined the arguments for and against data collection:

Arguments in Favor of Data Collection

Data collection helps agencies:

1. Determine whether racially biased policing is a problem in the jurisdiction
2. Convey a commitment to unbiased policing
3. Take a proactive approach toward rooting out racial profiling
4. Effectively allocate and manage department resources

Collecting data and interpreting it, if done correctly, reflects accountability and openness on the part of the agency and improves police–community relations. Departments that do so can identify problems and search for solutions. In addition, the data can be informative to department management about what types of stops and searches officers are making. Managers and supervisors can then decide not only whether these practices are the most efficient allocation of department resources, but also whether biased policing is taking place. Without the collection and analysis of data, departments can have a difficult time defending their practices if challenged in court.

Arguments against Data Collection

1. Data collection does not yield valid information regarding the nature and extent of racially biased policing.
2. Data could be used to harm the agency or its personnel.
3. Data collection may impact police productivity, morale, and workload.
4. Police resources might be used to combat racially biased policing and the perceptions thereof in more effective ways. (Fridell et al., 2001; Fridell, 2017)

Many departments still resist record keeping. They argue, for one, that the mere collection of "racial" statistics may imply that biased policing is taking place. These agencies maintain that the raw data, when first collected and before analysis and comparison with benchmarks, could reinforce or increase the public's negative perceptions of the agency at the cost of both the morale and the effectiveness of officers. At the same time, some departments have expressed concern that any data they collect can be used against them in court. These law enforcement executives question the ability of data collection systems to provide valid answers about the nature and extent of racially biased policing within their departments. The simple collection of data will neither prevent racial profiling nor accurately identify if it is taking place. The process alone does not protect agencies from public criticism, scrutiny, and litigation because the data collected is open to interpretation.

The raw data collected represents meaningless numbers unless put into relevant context using statistical benchmarks (discussed later) to provide a legitimate means of comparison. The data collected can be used to make or defend any position that someone may adopt about racial profiling. Law enforcement agencies, therefore, must take additional steps to ensure that the numbers they collect accurately reflect reality. Each department must evaluate its specific circumstances. For agencies that have had no community complaints and/or already closely monitor officer behavior in other ways, undertaking data collection may not be the most efficient use of resources.

Another argument used against data collection has been the observation that, within some law enforcement agencies, officers discontinued or reduced the number of self-initiated traffic stops and pedestrian contacts they made when data collection became a requirement. Officers resentful or concerned about being monitored ceased to initiate stops to avoid the possibility of being perceived as racially biased. Some agencies do not require the officer to reveal his or her identity on the data form. There is also a concern among city and county administrators and law enforcement executives about the time and costs associated with the collection and analysis of data.

Thus, data collection has its advantages, disadvantages, and limitations. PERF recommends that police agency executives, in collaboration with citizen leaders, review the pros and cons of the practice. They must factor in the agency's political, social, organizational, and financial situation to decide whether to either initiate data collection or allocate available resources to other approaches to address racially biased policing and the perceptions thereof.

DATA COLLECTION ELEMENTS The basic elements for data collection that both the U.S. DOJ Resource Guide and PERF recommend to law enforcement agencies are:

- Date/time/location
- Characteristics of the individual(s): Age/gender, race/ethnicity/national origin
- Reason for stop: penal or vehicle code violation or infraction; reactive (call for service) or self-initiated
- Search or no search: if search, the search authority (including consent, if consent involved) and results (what, if anything, was recovered)
- Disposition: arrest, citation, verbal warning, written warning, or no action

There is a rationale and justification behind each of the recommended elements. They are designed to determine not only who the police are stopping, but also the circumstances and context of the stops. "In effect, we are trying to collect 'circumstantial' data to tell us the real reasons citizens are being stopped—which should reflect the motivations of the officers and/or the impact of agency policies and practices" (Fridell et al., 2001). In completing the section of the form pertaining to race, ethnicity, or national origin, officers are expected to use their best judgment, based on their observations, training, and experience, and not ask the person detained. PERF, COPS, and the DOJ have developed protocols and guidelines for the collection, analysis, and interpretation of vehicle stop data. These detailed how-to guides should be referred to by those involved in developing a system or method of tracking vehicle stops and trying to measure racial bias in policing. The materials available from these agencies provide information on what activities to target for data collection.

Most agencies collect data only on traffic stops (moving or mechanical violations) because of their frequency and because that is where there is the greatest potential for police racial bias (or perception thereof) to occur. Another source of data is vehicle stops or general investigative stops of drivers. This sort of stop involves officer discretion (wherein the officer should have reasonable suspicion or probable cause to conduct an investigative stop) and is also an important source of information to analyze. Collecting data on *detentions* encompasses not only traffic and vehicle stops, but also pedestrian or bicyclist stops. A fourth source of data is *nonconsensual encounters*, in which an officer is not detaining the citizen, but is questioning him or her. PERF recommends that agencies collect data on all vehicle and traffic stops. Their recommendation does not include pedestrian stops or nonconsensual encounters that do not amount to detentions.

Data collection would be different for municipal and highway policing. The job of city police and county sheriffs is mostly responsive in nature in that they answer to calls for service from victims or witnesses to events. The officers' enforcement patterns depend on the character of the neighborhoods in which they serve, and thus the race/ethnicity of the persons they contact will vary accordingly. This must be considered during data analysis and interpretation. Comparative benchmarks must be utilized for each differing community and area of the city or county. Highway policing, in contrast, involves more self-initiated activity and more discretion on the part of officers.

STATISTICAL BENCHMARKS Statistical benchmarks are the comparative populations or groups against which the data collected are going to be analyzed and interpreted. In other words, they are the estimates of the proportions of individuals available to be stopped by race or ethnicity within the area studied. Racial profiling analysis requires developing and using an appropriate benchmark. The selection and development of benchmarks is a very complicated process often requiring the assistance of specialists in the field so the correct interpretation of the data is achieved. There are different types of benchmarks, but three are most common:

1. *Resident population or census of the community* that is policed by the department under consideration; that is, the demographics of the geographic area to be studied. This method is probably the most commonly used.
2. *Field observation of drivers* at randomly selected sites during randomly selected times. Normally field observers attempt to identify the race or ethnicity and approximate age of each driver.
3. *Accident records for not-at-fault drivers* to estimate the qualitative features (e.g., racial composition) of actual roadway users. Information arising from accident statistics is commonly used by traffic engineers to develop qualitative benchmarks of motorists.

There are advantages and disadvantages to each type of benchmark, and there is no agreement among experts on which is the most reliable. None of these benchmarks is universally adaptable to every racial profiling evaluation, and the positive and negative aspects of each must be taken into consideration when deciding which one to use. The benchmarks selected must be able to help measure whether individuals are being stopped because of bias on the part of the officer due to the person's race, ethnicity, national origin, sexual orientation, gender, gender identity, or any of the other categories covered under bias-based policing. One question to be asked is, in a similar situation, would a person who was not a member of a minority group have been stopped? In other words, the correct comparison is not to the people living in the neighborhood or driving on the highway who did not engage in the same conduct as the person stopped, but to those who did engage in the same conduct but were not stopped because they were not of a minority race (Ramirez, McDevitt, & Farrell, 2000). One can see how difficult a task it is to develop statistical benchmarks.

Most research and analysis of collected data on traffic and field interrogation stops (detentions) does not take into consideration the decision-making processes of the officers involved. Distinguishing between low- and high-discretion stops may prove useful for data collection and analysis. Most data collection efforts have neglected the need to explain how and why officers make decisions pertaining to traffic or other stops when studying racial profiling. Research designs should allow for the investigation of officers' decision-making after stops have been initiated (Engel, Calnon, & Bernard, 2002). One strategy recently developed to do this is the Internal Benchmarking method, which involves conducting routine, ongoing racial profiling surveillance of certain law enforcement officers and comparing their behavior or performance with similarly situated peers. The term *similarly situated* refers to officers who work the same assignment (e.g., patrol), in the same geographical area, and during the same time. An agency using the Internal Benchmark strategy to determine if a suspected officer is using racial profiling practices would also incorporate other performance indicators into the investigation. For example, is the officer receiving an above-average number of citizen complaints or excessive-force allegations?

Unfortunately, no benchmarking strategy has proven to be universally acceptable, and there is considerable disagreement amongst practitioners, scholars, and researchers on their reliability and validity. In general, benchmarking strategies fail to completely measure the population of individuals who are observed by the police but not stopped. At best, benchmarks estimate the population of individuals who *might* or *should* be observed by the police, and thus available to be stopped (Withrow, 2007). The benchmark sets the stage for responding to the most important question asked in a racial profiling study: Do the police stop a disproportionate number of racial and ethnic minorities? "Inevitably, the answer to this question comes from comparing a numerator (the proportion of individuals stopped by race or ethnicity) with a denominator (the proportion of individuals estimated to be available to be stopped by race or ethnicity)" (Withrow, Dailey, & Jackson, 2008).

DATA ANALYSIS AND INTERPRETATION Once data have been collected, what do they show? The most difficult part of the process is the analysis and interpretation of the statistics compiled. As researcher Robin Engel and her colleagues reported:

> Ultimately, the problem with interpreting results is that the traffic and field interrogation data have been collected without the guidance of any theoretical framework. Researchers have simply counted things—the number of traffic stops, citations, and searches conducted by police against white and nonwhite suspects. Instead, the research should be conducted under the larger theoretical context of *explaining* behavior. Problems with the interpretation of empirical data are due partially to data collection efforts that have not addressed *why* officers might engage in decision-making based on citizens' race. (Engel et al., 2002)

Engel and her coauthors suggest that research on racial profiling should include consideration of three dependent variables:

1. *The behavior of the individual police officer:*
   a. Why do police officers in general stop more black citizens than white citizens? How and why do officers make decisions?
   b. Why do some officers exhibit more racial disproportionality, while others exhibit less?
   c. Have there been changes in racial disproportionality over time?
2. *The behavior of different police departments:* Do some police departments have high rates of racial profiling and others have low rates? If so, what explains these differences?
3. *The aggregate rates of officer and departmental behavior:* Has race-based decision-making been transformed in the past 40 years from one based primarily on individual racial prejudice to one based mainly on race-based departmental policies? (Ibid.)

As explained, statistical benchmarks must be developed for comparison with raw data collected by agencies. Among the decisions that must be made are:

1. Are the statistics collected compared with the city's racial makeup as determined by the nationwide census?
2. Are they compared with licensed drivers living in the city's jurisdiction?
3. Are they compared with the racial composition of the drivers on the roads, if that could be determined?
4. Are situational characteristics (e.g., suspects' characteristics, characteristics of the police–citizen encounter, and legal characteristics) considered and collected?
5. Are officers' characteristics (e.g., sex, race, experience, and attitudes) considered and collected?
6. Are organizational characteristics (e.g., formal and informal policies and attitudes and preferences of administrators and first-line supervisors) considered and collected?
7. Are community characteristics (e.g., demographic, economic, and political) considered and collected?

Data interpretation can be done internally by the law enforcement agency involved if the community political climate is good and there is trust that the analysis will be credible. However, since a positive community political climate is not usually the case, and to avoid the perception that the findings are suspect, most agencies obtain the services of an independent analyst. It is important that the analyst not only have some general knowledge of law enforcement procedures, but also be knowledgeable on the selection and development of statistical benchmarks or base rates. COPS, in conjunction with the DOJ, has produced a document entitled "How to Correctly Collect and Analyze Racial Profiling Data: Your Reputation Depends on It." This provides recommendations on the methodology for data collection and analysis. This 2002 document can be downloaded from the COPS Web site. Also, published by PERF in 2005 (FIP Web site, 2017b) in collaboration with COPS and DOJ, is "Understanding Race Data from Vehicle Stops: A Stakeholder's Guide," by Lorie Fridell. *By The Numbers* (Fridell, 2004) presents the same subject matter, but significantly more expanded. Both of these can be found on the PERF Web site.

According to a National Institute of Justice (NIJ) article on racial profiling and traffic stops, minorities are disproportionately stopped more often than whites (National Institute of Justice, 2013). It has also been established by a great deal of social science research that bias exists (see Chapters 1 and 6 for specifics). Bias exists in the society at large, and therefore police are not immune to it. The NIJ article also reports that researchers are attempting to determine the percentages of disproportionate stops due to prejudice or bias on the part of the officer and those due to other factors, such as:

- **Differences in driving patterns.** The representation of minority drivers among those stopped could differ greatly from their representation in the residential census. Naturally those driving on the road, particularly major thoroughfares, could differ from those who live in a particular neighborhood. As a result, social scientists now disregard comparisons to the census for assessing racial bias.
- **Differences in exposure to the police.** If minority drivers tend to drive in communities where there are more police patrols, then the police will be more likely to notice any infractions the black drivers commit. Having more intense police patrols in these areas could be a source of bias or it could simply be the police department's response to crime in the neighborhood.
- **Differences in offending.** Seatbelt usage is chronically lower among black drivers. If a law enforcement agency aggressively enforces seatbelt violations, police will stop more black drivers. (Ibid.)

WHAT happens *during* the stop is as important as the reason for it. So, in addition to questions about bias in the decision to initiate a stop, other factors such as the length of the stop, the decision to cite, search or use force also need to be examined (ibid.).

COMMUNITY TASK FORCES FOR DEVELOPMENT AND IMPLEMENTATION   Citizen input is critical to the success of data collection and interpretation. Community group representatives reflecting the diversity of the community must be involved with police personnel of all ranks to form a task force. The task force members, including in most cases an independent analyst, work together to decide: (1) if data will be collected about the race/ethnicity of persons contacted by officers, (2) the design of benchmarks to utilize in the interpretation of the data, and (3) the response or action to be taken based on the interpretation. Police departments should take the input of the task force and implement the appropriate recommendations in subsequent phases of the project. Task forces and community policing are beneficial to a department's efforts to investigate and solve problems associated with allegations of racial profiling. Task forces not only help ensure that the process addresses specific concerns of the community, but also help improve police–community relations. With respect to beginning the process, the authors of "Racially Biased Policing: A Principled Response" suggest the following (Fridell et al., 2001):

1. Unless mandated, decide, with citizen input, whether data collection should be a component of the jurisdiction's overall response to racially biased policing.
2. Communicate with agency personnel as soon as a decision is made to start collecting data. The executive should provide a rationale for data collection and address anticipated concerns.
3. Set up a process for listening to the concerns of personnel, and have personnel help to develop constructive ways to address them.
4. Develop a police–citizen group to serve in an advisory capacity.
5. Develop the data collection and analysis protocol. Ensure that the interpretations will be responsible, based on sound methodology and analysis.
6. Field test the data collection system for three to six months, and use that test to make modifications before implementing the system jurisdiction-wide.

UNINTENDED RESULTS OF DATA COLLECTION   In some agencies, such as Houston and Cincinnati, when mandatory data collection was instituted, the number of traffic tickets dropped precipitously as officers, wary of being accused of racial profiling, stopped fewer people. In other agencies, officers refused to fill out the forms or made mistakes, which made the data unusable. The officers complained that the collection process was a waste of time and that data collected might be used against them. Some argued that officers who use racial profiling because they are prejudiced will never fill out the form. There are examples of cities in which police officers are so fearful of the possibility of being accused of being racist if they stop a person of color that they avoid making contact even if a violation or minor crime is being committed. If accusations begin to control policing, public safety suffers. Some agencies have equipped their patrol vehicles with video cameras and audio recording devices to provide evidence of the actions of their officers in the event of complaints.

Summary

- Although the term *racial profiling* was first used in association with the New Jersey State Police stopping individuals along Interstate 95 in the early 1990s, there have been complaints about this practice for decades in the United States.
- When the issue of racial profiling came to the attention of the public and law enforcement in the 1990s, there was no agreement on a definition, so it was difficult to develop approaches to prevent the practice. A term is now being used, "bias-based policing," which includes racial profiling but incorporates other prejudices based on gender, sexual orientation, economic status, religious beliefs and age.
- Prior to September 11, 2001, use of profiles that included race, ethnicity, or national origin were condemned by most U.S. citizens, but this attitude changed after the attacks on the World Trade Center and the Pentagon, and after subsequent attempted attacks. As time, has passed since those events, a strong majority of Americans again oppose profiling by police.
- Some police officers, government administrators, and others maintain that racial profiling is a myth or a misperception. But there is much evidence, including government reports, organizational studies, and statistics, that indicates that the racial profiling of African Americans, Latinos, Native Americans, Arabs, Sikhs, and some other races and ethnicities persists, however, despite efforts to end the phenomenon.
- Racial profiling is illegal and a violation of the Fourteenth Amendment; prevents some communities from working with law enforcement; can easily escalate an encounter into racially motivated violence; is morally wrong, yet there are still some that feel it is necessary.
- Many police and sheriffs' departments across the nation as well as federal law enforcement agencies have adopted policies that address racial profiling. These policies cover accountability and supervision; recruitment and hiring; education and training; outreach to the minority community; professional traffic stops; and data collection on race and ethnicity.
- To be legally defensible and professional, traffic stops must be part of a well-structured organizational policy that prohibits discriminatory practices; officer training must include a component on racial profiling; traffic stop data must be collected if there is a community concern about police bias; and officers must be held accountable by their supervisors. Any data collected must be analyzed using appropriate benchmarks.
- An analysis of the New York City police stop-and-frisk campaign and the Baltimore, Maryland zero tolerance approach to policing determined that African Americans and Latinos/as were stopped, both as drivers and pedestrians, disproportionately to whites. Many argued that there was no credible evidence that the approaches were responsible for reductions in crime experienced while others argued that the strategies were effective.
- Citizen discontent and lawsuits can originate because of racial profiling or the use of any profiling that appears to have been based on bias. Law enforcement professionals must be critical and introspective when analyzing the problem of racism and prejudice in the profession, and must be aware of the strong feelings the topic of profiling engenders.

Discussion Questions and Issues

1. *Law Enforcement Agency Policy on Racial Profiling.* The student can determine if a police department in the area meets recommended standards regarding policies pertaining to racial profiling in the following manner:
   a. Does the policy clearly define acts constituting racial profiling using the definition provided at the beginning of this chapter?
   b. Does the policy strictly prohibit peace officers employed by the agency from engaging in racial profiling?
   c. Does the policy provide instructions by which individuals may file a complaint if they believe they were victims of racial profiling by an employee of the agency?
   d. Does the agency provide public education relating to the complaint process?
   e. Does the policy require appropriate corrective action to be taken against a peace officer employed by the agency who, after an investigation, is shown to have engaged in racial profiling in violation of the agency's policy?
   f. Does the agency require the collection of data relating to traffic stops in which a citation is issued and to arrests resulting from those traffic stops, including information relating to:

      1. The race or ethnicity of the individual detained?
      2. Whether a search was conducted and, if so, whether it was based on the consent of the person detained?

g. Does the agency's policy require it to submit a report on the findings and conclusions based on the data collected to a governing body of the county or state for review and monitoring purposes? What benchmarks are utilized and who interprets the data?

2. *Actual Incident for Discussion.* In a city in Indiana, an African American police officer driving an unmarked police car was pulled over by an officer not from his agency. The officer was wearing his uniform at the time, but he was not wearing his hat, which would have identified him as a police officer when viewed from outside the car. Per a complaint filed, the trooper who pulled the man over appeared shocked when the officer got out of the car. The trooper explained that he had stopped the man because he had three antennas on the rear of his car. Discuss the following:

a. Do you think the officer who pulled over a colleague was guilty of racial profiling?

b. Do you think the officer was being honest when he said the reason for the stop was the multiple antennas? Is having multiple antennas a crime?

c. Can complaints of being racially profiled be dismissed as the exaggerations of hypersensitive minorities or people who do not understand the job of a police officer?

3. *President's Task Force on 21st Century Policing.* Determine if the local, county or state law enforcement agency in which you live or work have adopted and enforce policies prohibiting profiling and discrimination by officers based on race, ethnicity, national origin, religion, age, gender, gender identity/expression, sexual orientation, immigration status, disability, housing status, occupation, or language fluency as recommended in the 21st Century Task Force report released in 2015.

References

ACLU of New Jersey. (2013). "Stop-and-Frisk: The Facts." February 25, 2014. The American Civil Liberties Union New Jersey. www.aclu-nj.org/theissues/policepractices/newark-stop-and-frisk-data/stop-and-frisk-facts/(accessed March 1, 2017).

Barlow, David E. and Melissa H. Barlow. (2002). "Racial Profiling: A Survey of African American Police Officers." *Police Quarterly, 5*, 334–358.

Berry, Ondra. (2017). Retired deputy chief, Reno, NV, Police Department, personal communication, January 19.

Bump, Phillip. (2016). "The Facts about Stop-and-Frisk in New York City." *The Washington Post*, September 26. www.washingtonpost.com/news/the-fix/wp/2016/09/21/it-looks-like-rudy-giuliani-convinced-donald-trump-that-stop-and-frisk-actually-works/?utm_term=.a7-ddd5d1088a (accessed March 1, 2017).

Ekins, Emily. (2014, October). "Poll: 70% of Americans Oppose Racial Profiling." Reason-Rupe Poll. http://reason.com/poll/2014/10/14/poll-70-of-americans-oppose-racial-profi (accessed February 13, 2017).

Engel, Robin S., Jennifer M. Calnon, and Thomas J. Bernard. (2002). "Theory and Racial Profiling: Shortcomings and Future Directions in Research." *Justice Quarterly, 19*(2), 249–273.

FIP Web site. (2017a). "Fair and Impartial Policing." USDOJ COPS supported training programs for Law Enforcement (*Command Level, Supervisor, Patrol and Train the Trainer*) developed between 2008–2014; (2017 update FIP, LLC) http://fairandimpartialpolicing.com/docs/stakeholders .pdf (accessed December 15, 2016).

FIP Web site. (2017b). "Understanding Race Data from Vehicle Stops: A Stakeholder's Guide." *DOJ/COPS*. Washington, D.C.: Police Executive Research Forum, 2005. http://fairandimpartialpolicing.com/docs/stakeholders.pdf (accessed April 21, 2017).

Fridell, Lorie. (2004). "By The Numbers: A Guide for Analyzing Race Data from Vehicle Stops." *DOJ/COPS*. Washington, D.C.: Police Executive Research Forum. www.policeforum.org/assets/docs/Free_Online_Documents/Racially-Biased_Policing/by%20the%20numbers%20-%20a%20guide%20for%20analyzing%20race%20data%20from%20vehicle%20stops%202004.pdf (accessed April 21, 2017).

Fridell, Lorie. (2017). *Producing Bias-Free Policing: A Science-Based Approach*. New York, NY: Springer Publishers.

Fridell, Lorie, Robert Lunney, Drew Diamond, and Bruce Kubu. (2001). "Racially Biased Policing: A Principled Response." Washington, D.C.: Police Executive Research Forum.

Glaser, Jack, Katherine Spencer, and Amanda Charbonneau. (2014). "Racial Bias and Public Policy." *Goldman School of Public Policy. Behavioral and Brain Sciences, 1*(1), 88–94. https://gspp.berkeley.edu/assets/uploads/research/pdf/GlaserSpencerCharbonneau_for_PIBBS_2014.pdf (accessed May 18, 2017).

Head, Tom. (2017). "Why Racial Profiling Is a Bad Idea." *About News*, February 19. http://civilliberty.about.com/od/lawenforcementterrorism/tp/Against-Racial-Profiling.htm (accessed April 15, 2017).

International Association of Chiefs of Police. (2001). "Recommendations from the First IACP Forum on Professional Traffic Stops." www.theiacp.org/PublicationsGuides/ResearchCenter/Publications/tabid/299/Default.aspx?id=119&v=1 (accessed January 19, 2009).

International Association of Chiefs of Police. (2006, September). "Protecting Civil Rights: A Leadership Guide for State, Local, and Tribal Law Enforcement." www.theiacp.org/portals/0/pdfs/PCR_LdrshpGde_Part1.pdf

Jackson, V.K. (2003). "Understanding Bias-Based Traffic Law Enforcement." National Highway Traffic Safety Administration. www.nhtsa.gov/people/injury/enforce/biasbased03/trafficenforcement.htm (accessed January 19, 2009).

Langton, Lynn and Matthew Durose. (2013). Bureau of Justice Statistics. www.bjs.gov/index.cfm?ty=pbdetail&iid=4779 (accessed February 13, 2017).

Missouri Department of Public Safety. (2017). "Racial Profiling Training Requirements for Peace Officers." www.dps.mo.gov/dir/programs/post/racialprofiling.php (accessed February 21, 2017).

National Institute of Justice. (2013). "Racial Profiling and Traffic Stops." www.nij.gov/topics/law-enforcement/legitimacy/pages/traffic-stops.aspx (accessed February 21, 2016).

Owen, Tess. (2016). "Driving While Black: Cops Target Minority Drivers in This Mostly White New Jersey Town." *VICE News.* www.news.vice.com/article/driving-while-black-cops-target-minority-drivers-mostly-white-new-jersey-town (accessed February 13, 2017).

Portland Police Bureau. (2009, August). "Police Plan to Address Racial Profiling." www.portlandoregon.gov/police/article/230887 (accessed February 29, 2017).

Ramirez, Deborah, Jack McDevitt, and Amy Farrell. (2000, November). "A Resource Guide on Racial Profiling Data Collection Systems: Promising Practices and Lessons Learned." U.S. Department of Justice. NCJ 184768. www.ncjrs.gov/pdffiles1/bja/184768.pdf (accessed February 13, 2013).

San Francisco Police Department. General Order 5.17. (2011). https://sanfranciscopolice.org/sites/default/files/FileCenter/Documents/27231-DGO%205.17%20-%20rev.%2005-04-11.pdf (accessed February 21, 2017).

Senge, Peter, Art Kleiner, Charlotte Roberts, Richard Ross, and Bryan J. Smith. (1994). *The Fifth Discipline Fieldbook: Strategies and Tools for Building a Learning Organization.* New York, NY: Currency Doubleday.

State of California Department of Justice. (2015). AB 953: The Racial and Identity Profiling Act of 2015. www.oag.ca.gov/ab953 (accessed February 27, 2017).

Straus, Ira. (2002). "Commentary: Profile to Survive." October 19. United Press International. www.upi.com/Top_News/2002/10/19/Commentary-Profile-to-Survive/UPI-41611035051600/(accessed January 19, 2004).

Thomma, Steven. (2010). "Poll: Most Americans Would Trim Liberties to Be Safer." January 12. McClatchy DC Bureau. http://www.mcclatchydc.com/news/nation-world/national/article24570223.html (accessed May 17, 2017).

Tracy, Thomas and Graham Rayman. (2016). "Crime, Stop and Frisk Drop in NYC in First Half of 2016: NYCLU."

New York Daily News, October 11. www.nydailynews.com/new-york/crime-stop-frisk-drop-nyc-months-2016-article-1.2826671 (accessed March 1, 2017).

U.S. Department of Justice. (2003). "Guidance Regarding the Use of Race by Federal Law Enforcement Agencies." www.justice.gov/sites/default/files/crt/legacy/2010/12/15/guidance_on_race.pdf (accessed March 8, 2017).

U.S. Department of Justice. (2014). "Guidance for Federal Law Enforcement Agencies Regarding the Use of Race, Ethnicity, Gender, National Origin, Religion, Sexual Orientation, or Gender Identity." www.justice.gov/sites/default/files/ag/pages/attachments/2014/12/08/use-of-race-policy.pdf (accessed February 20, 2017).

U.S. Department of Justice. (2015). "President's Task Force on 21st Century Policing." www.themarshallproject.org/documents/2082979-final-report-of-the-presidents-task-force-on#.vUnDUGJmC) (accessed December 23, 2016).

U.S. Department of Justice. (2016). "Investigation of the Baltimore City Police Department." August 10. www.justice.gov/opa/file/883366/download (accessed March 1, 2017).

U.S. House of Representatives. (2015). "H.R. 2048—USA FREEDOM Act of 2015" www.congress.gov/bill/114th-congress/house-bill/2048 (accessed February 20, 2017).

U.S. Supreme Court. *United States v. Brignoni-Ponce*, 422 U.S., 873. (1975). www.supreme.justia.com/us/422/873/ (accessed April 14, 2009).

U.S. Supreme Court 572 U.S. (2014). Opinion of the Court. *Navarette v. California*. April 22. supreme.justia.com/cases/federal/us/572/12-9490/(accessed March 8, 2017)

Will, George F. (2001). "Exposing the 'Myth' of Racial Profiling." *Washington Post*, p. A19.

Withrow, Brian L. (2007). "When Whren Won't Work: The Effects of a Diminished Capacity to Initiate a Pretextual Stop on Police Officer Behavior." *Police Quarterly, 10*(4), 351–370.

Withrow, Brian L., Jeffrey D. Dailey, and Henry Jackson. (2008). "The Utility of an Internal Benchmarking Strategy in Racial Profiling Surveillance." *Justice Research and Policy 10*(2), 19–47.

APPENDIX A

General Distinctions among Generations of Immigrants
(See Descriptions of Types Below)

Type	Description	Behavioral Differences
Type I	Recently arrived adult immigrant or refugee (fewer than five years in the United States)	Survival needs; often living within ethnic enclaves
Type II	Recently arrived adolescent teen or immigrant refugee (fewer than five years in the United States)	Adjusting and "fitting in"; identity is a combination of new and former cultures
Type III	Adult immigrant or refugee, five or more years in the United States	Preserving culture of origin, or aspects thereof, while still striving to adapt
Type IV	Second-generation individual (U.S.-born offspring of immigrants or refugees)	Straddling two cultures; significantly more assimilated than parents
Type V	Third-generation (and beyond)	Fully or nearly fully assimilated; may choose to identify bi-culturally

DESCRIPTIONS OF TYPES

Type I

The behavior of the most recent immigrant and refugee groups centers around survival. Some people in this category have had interactions with corrupt law enforcement officials in their countries of origin; these officials were very likely aligned with a repressive government and the military. The focus of these newcomers is on building the basics of a new life, often starting from nothing. The survival focus of refugees, in particular, is frequently compounded by the traumatic ordeals that they faced before and during their journeys to the United States. Police officers may observe that recently arrived immigrants or refugees from certain countries may react fearfully, based on their experiences with police in their countries of origin (e.g., refusing to speak English or not producing identification; blindly saying "Yes, I understand," without fully responding or cooperating).

Type II

Young immigrants or refugees, whose major life experience has taken place in the United States, focus a great deal of energy on striving to "fit in" socially (i.e., assimilate), which can result in conflicts with their parents and their cultural values. However, at the same time, many of these young newcomers feel torn. They may appreciate and wish to retain many elements of their parents' culture, which can lead to confusion about identity. For these young immigrants and refugees, reactions to law enforcement officials vary depending on when they immigrated and their socioeconomic level. Immigrant children, whose parents are very absorbed with survival, can be vulnerable to adverse external influences.

Type III

The behavior of adult refugees or immigrants with five or more years in the United States largely centers around the desire to preserve the culture of origin, while still trying to adapt and assimilate. Given that they have spent much of their lives outside the United States, many of these individuals attempt to hold on to the values and traditions of their home cultures. Intergenerational conflicts tend to occur within this group (i.e., adults with their elderly parents and/or with their own teen and young adult children). Many individuals are working hard at balancing, i.e., attempting to adapt while holding on to certain aspects of their cultures of origin. Other individuals continue to keep to their ethnic communities (e.g., Chinatowns) and, generally, try to avoid contact with law enforcement.

Type IV

Many second-generation (i.e., U.S.-born) individuals work hard to assimilate into society in order to become part of "mainstream" America. Among some groups, immigrant parents' expectations are often very high, with parents sacrificing so that their offspring will succeed. Some individuals in this category interact primarily with nonimmigrants and internalize many of the values and norms of U.S. culture. Despite these individuals' efforts to become like the mainstream, they may continue to be viewed as outsiders, particularly by those who hold biases against immigrants. Results from a 2013 Pew Research poll revealed that the crime rate increases as the second-generation of immigrants assimilate, explained in part by feeling "caught between two conflicting worlds—the old world of their parents and the new world of their birth."[*]

Type V

By the third or fourth generation, individuals are fully assimilated, and identification with the culture of origin varies. Some may be completely assimilated. Others may choose to be bicultural, selecting activities, values, norms, and lifestyles that blend traditions and customs of their families' country of origin with American culture. Many do not speak their grandparents' and great-grandparents' native languages as well as they do English, and rely on English as their primary or only language (thus, someone can be bicultural, but not bilingual). Contact by members of this group with law enforcement personnel is expected to be the same as contact with other Americans.

---

[*]Morin, Rich. (2013). "Crime Rises among Second-Generation Immigrants as They Assimilate." October 15. Pew Research Center. http://www.pewresearch.org/fact-tank/2013/10/15/crime-rises-among-second-generation-immigrants-a (accessed February 5, 2017).

APPENDIX B

Cross-Cultural Communication Skills Assessment for Law Enforcement Professionals

Self-awareness is a key factor in the development of an effective professional communication style and the sharpening of your cross-cultural communication skills. As you answer the following questions, think about cross-cultural communication both with citizens/noncitizens you encounter as well as coworkers in your department. Consider having a coworker fill out the assessment for you to the extent possible, and then compare your responses with his or hers.

While the following assessment focuses on cross-cultural skills, some of the categories also pertain to communication with people from the same background as oneself. Many of these topics are discussed in Chapter 4 of this text.

Instructions: Answer using the following ratings:

Usually   Sometimes   Seldom

---

1. I exhibit patience when communicating with individuals for whom English is not their first language. _____

2. I make a point of simplifying my language and refraining from using slang and idioms with people for whom English is not their mother tongue. _____

3. (Except in emergency situations) I refrain from filling in words for individuals trying to communicate with me. _____

4. When using an interpreter, I maintain eye contact with the individual I am questioning or with whom I am interacting (i.e., rather than focusing on the interpreter). _____

5. I spend extra time explaining police procedures to new immigrants where required. _____

6. I am aware of the cultural "baggage" that some new immigrants carry with them related to fear or distrust of police, and make efforts to communicate in a supportive, nonthreatening manner. _____

7. I am familiar with culturally different beliefs around eye-contact related to respect and authority. _____

8. To check understanding, I restate, paraphrase, or summarize what an individual has said in order to allow him or her the opportunity to correct/confirm my understanding. _____

9. I am aware of my biases toward groups from different backgrounds, and I make an effort to communicate professionally with all people, in spite of these biases. _____

10. I make an effort not to let citizens/coworkers push my "hot buttons" so that my communication remains non-defensive and professional. _____

11. When speaking with individuals from groups that speak English differently from the way I do, I try not to imitate their manner of speech in order to be "one of them." _____

12. With nonnative speakers of English, I try not to speak in an excessively loud voice in an attempt to make myself clear. _____

13. I encourage people to let me know when they have not understood something I have communicated. _____

14. I make it a point to convey respect to all citizens while on duty, regardless of their race, color, gender, religion, or any other dimension of diversity. _____

15. With all channels of communication and vis-à-vis all groups (i.e., face-to-face with co-workers, agency online communication, social media), I avoid any derogatory remarks that can result in the breaking of trust. _____

APPENDIX C

Listing of Selected Gangs and Identifying Characteristics

Sources:

- 2009 National Gang Threat Assessment (National Drug Intelligence Center/National Drug Intelligence Center) https://www.fbi.gov/file-repository/stats-services-publications -national-gang-threat-assessment-2009-pdf/view
- 2011 National Gang Threat Assessment: https://www.fbi.gov/stats-services/ publications/2011-national-gang-threat-assessment (*click on "view printable version" link*)

The following information lists selected national and regional gangs and specific characteristics for the three major types of gangs presented in Chapter 10:

Section I: Street Gangs

Section II: Prison Gangs

Section III: Outlaw Motorcycle Gangs.

This appendix is not an exhaustive list of all gangs in the United States. Individual state, county, and city law enforcement agencies should be contacted for information on local and regional gangs in their jurisdictions.

This listing was adapted and reproduced from the National Drug Intelligence Center of which the *National Gang Threat Assessment for the National Gang Intelligence Center* is a part. Both centers are part of the United States Department of Justice. Published in 2009, this information is believed to be current as of the writing of this text's seventh edition.

Information on immigrant gangs, from the 2011 National Gang Threat Assessment, can be found on pp. 375–377 of this appendix.

SECTION I: STREET GANGS

18th Street (National)

Formed in Los Angeles, 18th Street is a group of loosely associated sets or cliques, each led by an influential member. Membership is estimated at 30,000 to 50,000. In California, approximately 80 percent of the gang's members are illegal aliens from Mexico and Central America. The gang is active in 44 cities in 20 states. Its main source of income is street-level distribution of cocaine and marijuana and, to a lesser extent, heroin, and methamphetamine. Gang members also commit assault, auto theft, carjacking, drive-by shootings, extortion, homicide, identification fraud, and robbery.

Almighty Latin King and Queen Nation (National)

The Latin Kings street gang was formed in Chicago in the 1960s and consisted predominantly of Mexican and Puerto Rican males. Originally created with the philosophy of overcoming racial prejudice and creating an organization of "Kings," the Latin Kings evolved into a criminal enterprise operating throughout the United States under two umbrella factions—Motherland, also known as KMC (King Motherland Chicago), and Bloodline (New York). All members of the gang refer to themselves as Latin Kings and, currently, individuals of any nationality are allowed to become members. Latin Kings associating with the Motherland faction also identify themselves as "Almighty Latin King Nation (ALKN)," and make up more than 160 structured chapters operating in 158 cities in 31 states. The membership of Latin Kings following KMC is estimated to be 20,000 to 35,000. The Bloodline was founded by Luis Felipe in the New York State correctional system in 1986. Latin Kings associating with Bloodline also identify themselves as the "Almighty Latin King and Queen

Nation (ALKQN)." Membership is estimated to be 2,200 to 7,500, divided among several dozen chapters operating in 15 cities in 5 states. Bloodline Latin Kings share a common culture and structure with KMC and respect them as the Motherland, but all chapters do not report to the Chicago leadership hierarchy. The gang's primary source of income is the street-level distribution of powder cocaine, crack cocaine, heroin, and marijuana. Latin Kings continue to portray themselves as a community organization while engaging in a wide variety of criminal activities, including assault, burglary, homicide, identity theft, and money laundering.

Asian Boyz (National)

Asian Boyz is one of the largest Asian street gangs operating in the United States. Formed in southern California in the early 1970s, the gang is estimated to have 1,300 to 2,000 members operating in at least 28 cities in 14 states. Members primarily are Vietnamese or Cambodian males. Members of Asian Boyz are involved in producing, transporting, and distributing methamphetamine as well as distributing MDMA and marijuana. In addition, gang members are involved in other criminal activities, including assault, burglary, drive-by shootings, and homicide.

Black P. Stone Nation (National)

Black P. Stone Nation, one of the largest and most violent associations of street gangs in the United States, consists of seven highly structured street gangs with a single leader and a common culture. It has an estimated 6,000 to 8,000 members, most of whom are African American males from the Chicago metropolitan area. The gang's main source of income is the street-level distribution of cocaine, heroin, marijuana and, to a lesser extent, methamphetamine. Members also are involved in many other types of criminal activity, including assault, auto theft, burglary, carjacking, drive-by shootings, extortion, homicide, and robbery.

Bloods (National)

Bloods is an association of structured and unstructured gangs that have adopted a single-gang culture. The original Bloods were formed in the early 1970s to provide protection from the Crips street gang in Los Angeles, California. Large, national-level Bloods gangs include Bounty Hunter Bloods and Crenshaw Mafia Gangsters. Bloods membership is estimated to be 7,000 to 30,000 nationwide; most members are African American males. Bloods gangs are active in 123 cities in 33 states. The main source of income for Bloods gangs is street-level distribution of cocaine and marijuana. Bloods members also are involved in transporting and distributing methamphetamine, heroin, and PCP (phencyclidine), but to a much lesser extent. The gangs also are involved in other criminal activity including assault, auto theft, burglary, carjacking, drive-by shootings, extortion, homicide, identity fraud, and robbery.

Crips (National)

Crips is a collection of structured and unstructured gangs that have adopted a common gang culture. Crips membership is estimated at 30,000 to 35,000; most members are African American males from the Los Angeles metropolitan area. Large, national-level Crips gangs include 107 Hoover Crips, Insane Gangster Crips, and Rolling 60s Crips. Crips gangs operate in 221 cities in 41 states. The main source of income for Crips gangs is the street-level distribution of powder cocaine, crack cocaine, marijuana, and PCP. The gangs also are involved in other criminal activity such as assault, auto theft, burglary, and homicide.

Florencia 13 (Regional)

Florencia 13 (F 13 or FX 13) originated in Los Angeles in the early 1960s; gang membership is estimated at more than 3,000 members. The gang operates primarily in California and increasingly in Arkansas, Missouri, New Mexico, and Utah. Florencia 13 is subordinate to the Mexican Mafia (La Eme) prison gang and claims Sureños (Sur 13) affiliation. A primary source of income for gang members is the trafficking of cocaine and methamphetamine. Gang members smuggle multikilogram quantities of powder cocaine and methamphetamine obtained from supply sources in Mexico into the United States for distribution. Also, gang members produce large quantities of methamphetamine in southern California for local distribution. Florencia members are involved in other criminal activities, including assault, drive-by shootings, and homicide.

Fresno Bulldogs (Regional)

Fresno Bulldogs is a street gang that originated in Fresno, California, in the late 1960s. Bulldogs are the largest Hispanic gang operating in central California, with membership estimated at 5,000 to 6,000. Bulldogs are one of the few Hispanic gangs in California that claim neither Sureños (Southern) nor Norteños (Northern) affiliation. However, gang members associate with Nuestra Familia (NF) members, particularly when trafficking drugs. The street-level distribution of methamphetamine, marijuana, and heroin is a primary source of income for gang members. In addition, members are involved in other criminal activity, including assault, burglary, homicide, and robbery.

Gangster Disciples (National)

The Gangster Disciples street gang was formed in Chicago, Illinois, in the mid-1960s. It is structured like a corporation and is led by a chairman of the board. Gang membership is estimated at 25,000 to 50,000; most members are African American males from the Chicago metropolitan area. The gang is active in 110 cities in 31 states. Its main source of income is the street-level distribution of cocaine, crack cocaine, marijuana, and heroin. The gang also is involved in other criminal activity, including assault, auto theft, firearms violations, fraud, homicide, the operation of prostitution rings, and money laundering.

Latin Disciples (Regional)

Latin Disciples, also known as Maniac Latin Disciples and Young Latino Organization, originated in Chicago in the late 1960s. The gang is composed of at least 10 structured and unstructured factions with an estimated 1,500 to 2,000 members and associate members. Most members are Puerto Rican males. Maniac Latin Disciples are the largest Hispanic gang in the Folk Nation Alliance. The gang is most active in the Great Lakes and southwestern regions of the United States. The street-level distribution of powder cocaine, heroin, marijuana, and PCP is a primary source of income for the gang. Members also are involved in other criminal activity, including assault, auto theft, carjacking, drive-by shootings, home invasion, homicide, money laundering, and weapons trafficking.

Mara Salvatrucha (National)

Mara Salvatrucha, also known as MS 13, is one of the largest Hispanic street gangs in the United States. Traditionally, the gang consisted of loosely affiliated groups known as cliques; however, law enforcement officials have reported increased coordination of criminal activity among Mara Salvatrucha cliques in the Atlanta, Dallas, Los Angeles, Washington, D.C., and New York metropolitan areas. The gang is estimated to have 30,000 to 50,000 members and associate members worldwide, 8,000 to 10,000 of whom reside in the United States. Members smuggle illicit drugs, primarily powder cocaine and marijuana, into the United States and transport and distribute the drugs throughout the country. Some members also are involved in alien smuggling, assault, drive-by shootings, homicide, identity theft, prostitution operations, robbery, and weapons trafficking. (See Chapter 1, page 19 for information on MS13 in Central American countries.)

Sureños and Norteños (National)

As individual Hispanic street gang members enter prison systems, they put aside former rivalries with other Hispanic street gangs and unite under the name Sureños or Norteños. The original Mexican Mafia members, most of whom were from southern California, considered Mexicans from the rural, agricultural areas of northern California weak and viewed them with contempt. To distinguish themselves from the agricultural workers or farmers from northern California, members of Mexican Mafia began to refer to the Hispanic gang members who worked for them as Sureños (Southerners). Inmates from northern California became known as Norteños (Northerners) and are affiliated with Nuestra Familia. Because of its size and strength, Fresno Bulldogs are the only Hispanic gang in the California Department of Corrections (CDC) that does not fall under Sureños or Norteños but remains independent. Sureños gang members' main sources of income are retail-level distribution of cocaine, heroin, marijuana, and methamphetamine within prison systems and in the community as well as extortion of drug distributors on the streets. Some members have direct links to Mexican DTOs and broker deals for Mexican Mafia as well as their own gang. Sureños gangs also are involved in other criminal activities such as assault, carjacking, home invasion, homicide, and robbery. Norteños gang members' main sources of income are the retail-level distribution of cocaine, heroin, marijuana, methamphetamine, and PCP within prison systems and in the community as well as extortion of drug distributors on the streets. Norteños gangs also are involved in other criminal activities such as assault, carjacking, home invasion, homicide, and robbery.

Tango Blast (Regional)

Tango Blast is one of largest prison/street criminal gangs operating in Texas. Tango Blast's criminal activities include drug trafficking, extortion, kidnapping, sexual assault, and murder. In the late 1990s, Hispanic men incarcerated in federal, state, and local prisons founded Tango Blast for personal protection against violence from traditional prison gangs such as the Aryan Brotherhood, Texas Syndicate, and Texas Mexican Mafia. Tango Blast originally had four city-based chapters: Houstone, Houston, Texas; ATX or La Capricha, Austin, Texas; D-Town, Dallas, Texas; and Foros or Foritos, Fort Worth, Texas. These founding four chapters are collectively known as Puro Tango Blast or the Four Horsemen. From the original four chapters, former Texas inmates established new chapters in El Paso, San Antonio, Corpus Christi, and the Rio Grande Valley. In June 2008, the Houston Police Department (HPD) estimated that more than 14,000 Tango Blast members were incarcerated in Texas. Tango Blast is difficult to monitor. The gang does not conform to either traditional prison/street gang hierarchical organization or gang rules. Tango Blast is laterally organized, and leaders are elected sporadically to represent the gang in prisons and to lead street gang cells. The significance of Tango Blast is exemplified by corrections officials reporting that rival traditional prison gangs are now forming alliances to defend themselves against Tango Blast's growing power.

Tiny Rascal Gangsters (National)

Tiny Rascal Gangsters are one of the largest and most violent Asian street gang associations in the United States. It is composed of at least 60 structured and unstructured gangs, commonly referred to as sets, with an estimated 5,000 to 10,000 members and associates who have adopted a common gang culture. Most members are Asian American males. The sets are most active in the southwestern, Pacific, and New England regions of the United States. The street-level distribution of powder cocaine, marijuana, MDMA, and methamphetamine is a primary source of income for the sets. Members also are involved in other criminal activity, including assault, drive-by shootings, extortion, home invasion, homicide, robbery, and theft.

United Blood Nation (Regional)

Bloods is a universal term that is used to identify both West Coast Bloods and United Blood Nation (UBN). While these groups are traditionally distinct entities, both identify themselves by "Blood," often making it hard for law enforcement to distinguish between them. United Blood Nation (UBN) started in 1993 in Rikers Island GMDC (George Mochen Detention Center) to form protection from the threat posed by Latin Kings and Ñetas, who dominated the prison. United Blood Nation (UBN) is a loose confederation of street gangs, or sets, that once were predominantly African American. Membership is estimated to be between 7,000 and 15,000 along the U.S. eastern corridor. UBN derives its income from street-level distribution of cocaine, heroin, and marijuana; robbery; auto theft; and smuggling drugs to prison inmates. UBN members also engage in arson, carjacking, credit card fraud, extortion, homicide, identity theft, intimidation, prostitution operations, and weapons distribution.

Vice Lord Nation (National)

Vice Lord Nation, based in Chicago, is a collection of structured gangs located in 74 cities in 28 states, primarily in the Great Lakes region. Led by a national board, the various gangs have an estimated 30,000 to 35,000 members, most of whom are African American males. The main source of income is street-level distribution of cocaine, heroin, and marijuana. Members also engage in other criminal activity such as assault, burglary, homicide, identity theft, and money laundering.

SECTION II: PRISON GANGS

Aryan Brotherhood

Aryan Brotherhood, also known as AB, was originally ruled by consensus but is now highly structured with two factions—one in the CDC and the other in the Federal Bureau of Prisons (BOP). The majority of members are white males, and the gang is active primarily in the southwestern and Pacific regions. Its main source of income is the distribution of cocaine, heroin, marijuana, and methamphetamine within prison systems and on the streets. Some AB members have business relationships with Mexican DTOs that smuggle illegal drugs into California for AB distribution. AB is notoriously violent and is often involved in murder for hire. Although the gang has been historically linked to the California-based Hispanic prison gang Mexican Mafia (La Eme), tension between AB and La Eme is increasingly evident, as seen in recent fights between whites and Hispanics within CDC.

Barrio Azteca

Barrio Azteca is one of the most violent prison gangs in the United States. The gang is highly structured and has an estimated membership of 2,000. Most members are Mexican national or Mexican American males. Barrio Azteca is most active in the southwestern region, primarily in federal, state, and local corrections facilities in Texas and outside prison in southwestern Texas and southeastern New Mexico. The gang's main source of income is derived from smuggling heroin, powder cocaine, and marijuana from Mexico into the United States for distribution both inside and outside prisons. Gang members often transport illicit drugs across the U.S.-Mexico border for DTOs. Barrio Azteca members also are involved in alien smuggling, arson, assault, auto theft, burglary, extortion, intimidation, kidnapping, robbery, and weapons violations.

Black Guerrilla Family

Black Guerrilla Family (BGF), originally called Black Family or Black Vanguard, is a prison gang founded in the San Quentin State Prison, California, in 1966. The gang is highly organized along paramilitary lines, with a supreme leader and central committee. BGF has an established national charter, code of ethics, and oath of allegiance. BGF members operate primarily in California and Maryland. The gang has 100 to 300 members, most of whom are African American males. A primary source of income for gang members comes from cocaine and marijuana distribution. BGF members obtain such drugs primarily from Nuestra Familia/Norteños members or from local Mexican traffickers. BGF members are involved in other criminal activities, including auto theft, burglary, drive-by shootings, and homicide.

Hermanos de Pistoleros Latinos

Hermanos de Pistoleros Latinos (HPL) is a Hispanic prison gang formed in the Texas Department of Criminal Justice (TDCJ) in the late 1980s. It operates in most prisons and on the streets in many communities in Texas, particularly Laredo. HPL is also active in several cities in Mexico, and its largest contingent in that country is in Nuevo Laredo. The gang is structured and is estimated to have 1,000 members. Members maintain close ties to several Mexican DTOs and are involved in trafficking quantities of cocaine and marijuana from Mexico into the United States for distribution.

Mexikanemi

The Mexikanemi prison gang (also known as Texas Mexican Mafia or Emi) was formed in the early 1980s within the Texas Department of Criminal Justice (TDCJ). The gang is highly structured and is estimated to have 2,000 members, most of whom are Mexican nationals or Mexican American males living in Texas at the time of incarceration. Mexikanemi poses a significant drug trafficking threat to communities in the southwestern United States, particularly in Texas. Gang members reportedly traffic multikilogram quantities of powder cocaine, heroin, and methamphetamine; multiton quantities of marijuana; and thousand-tablet quantities of MDMA from Mexico into the United States for distribution inside and outside prison. Gang members obtain drugs from associates or members of the Jaime Herrera-Herrera, Osiel Cárdenas-Guillén, and/or Vicente Carrillo-Fuentes Mexican DTOs. In addition, Mexikanemi members maintain a relationship with Los Zetas, a Mexican paramilitary/criminal organization employed by the Cárdenas-Guillén DTO as its personal security force.

Mexican Mafia

The Mexican Mafia prison gang, also known as La Eme (Spanish for the letter M), was formed in the late 1950s within the CDC. It is loosely structured and has strict rules that must be followed by the 200 members. Most members are Mexican American males who previously belonged to a southern California street gang. Mexican Mafia is primarily active in the southwestern and Pacific regions of the United States, but its power base is in California. The gang's main source of income is extorting drug distributors outside prison and distributing methamphetamine, cocaine, heroin, and marijuana within prison systems and on the streets. Some members have direct links to Mexican DTOs and broker deals for themselves and their associates. Mexican Mafia also is involved in other criminal activities, including controlling gambling and homosexual prostitution in prison.

Ñeta

Ñeta is a prison gang that began in Puerto Rico and spread to the United States. Ñeta is one of the largest and most violent prison gangs, with about 7,000 members in Puerto Rico and 5,000 in the United States. Ñeta chapters in Puerto Rico exist exclusively inside prisons; once members are released from prison they are no longer considered part of the gang. In the United States, Ñeta chapters exist inside and outside prisons in 36 cities in nine states, primarily in the Northeast. The gang's main source of income is retail distribution of powder and crack cocaine, heroin, marijuana and, to a lesser extent, LSD, MDMA, methamphetamine, and PCP. Ñeta members commit assault, auto theft, burglary, drive-by shootings, extortion, home invasion, money laundering, robbery, weapons and explosives trafficking, and witness intimidation.

SECTION III: OUTLAW MOTORCYCLE GANGS

Bandidos

Bandidos Motorcycle Club, an OMG with 2,000 to 2,500 members in the United States and 13 other countries, is a growing criminal threat to the nation. Law enforcement authorities estimate that Bandidos is one of the two largest OMGs in the United States, with approximately 900 members belonging to more than 88 chapters in 16 states. Bandidos is involved in transporting and distributing cocaine and marijuana and producing, transporting, and distributing methamphetamine. Bandidos is most active in the Pacific, southeastern, southwestern, and west central regions and is expanding in these regions by forming new chapters and allowing members of support clubs to form or join Bandidos chapters. The members of support clubs are known as "puppet" or "duck" club members. They do the dirty work of the mother club.

Hells Angels

Hells Angels Motorcycle Club (HAMC) is an OMG with 2,000 to 2,500 members belonging to more than 250 chapters in the United States and 26 foreign countries. HAMC poses a criminal threat on six continents. U.S. law enforcement authorities estimate that HAMC has more than 69 chapters in 22 states with 900 to 950 members. HAMC produces, transports, and distributes marijuana and methamphetamine and transports and distributes cocaine, hashish, heroin, LSD (lysergic acid diethylamide), MDMA, PCP, and diverted pharmaceuticals. HAMC is involved in other criminal activity, including assault, extortion, homicide, money laundering, and motorcycle theft.

Mongols

Mongols Motorcycle Club is an extremely violent OMG that poses a serious criminal threat to the Pacific and southwestern regions of the United States. Mongols members transport and distribute cocaine, marijuana, and methamphetamine and frequently commit violent crimes, including assault, intimidation, and murder, to defend Mongols territory and uphold its reputation. Mongols has 70 chapters nationwide, with most of the club's 800 to 850 members residing in California. Many members are former street gang members with a long history of using violence to settle grievances. Agents with the ATF have called Mongols Motorcycle Club the most violent and dangerous OMG in the nation. In the 1980s, the Mongols OMG seized control of southern California from HAMC, and today Mongols club is allied with Bandidos, Outlaws, Sons of Silence, and Pagan's OMGs against HAMC. The Mongols club also maintains ties to Hispanic street gangs in Los Angeles.

Outlaws

Outlaws Motorcycle Club has more than 1,700 members belonging to 176 chapters in the United States and 12 foreign countries. U.S. law enforcement authorities estimate that the Outlaws have more than 94 chapters in 22 states with more than 700 members. The Outlaws are also known as the American Outlaws Association (A.O.A.) and Outlaws Nation. Outlaws are the dominant OMG in the Great Lakes region. Gang members produce, transport, and distribute methamphetamine and transport and distribute cocaine, marijuana and, to a lesser extent, MDMA. Outlaws members engage in various criminal activities, including arson, assault, explosives operations, extortion, fraud, homicide, intimidation, kidnapping, money laundering, prostitution operations, robbery, theft, and weapons violations. It competes with HAMC for membership and territory.

Sons of Silence

Sons of Silence Motorcycle Club (SOSMC) are one of the largest OMGs in the United States, with 250 to 275 members among 30 chapters in 12 states. The club also has five chapters in Germany. SOSMC members have been implicated in numerous criminal activities, including murder, assault; drug trafficking, intimidation, extortion, prostitution operations, money laundering, weapons trafficking, and motorcycle and motorcycle parts

IMMIGRANT GANGS—SELECTED CHARACTERISTICS

Source: National Gang Intelligence Center: 2011 National Gang Threat Assessment; Emerging Trends.

Asian Gangs

- Asian gangs, historically limited to regions with large Asian populations, are expanding throughout communities nationwide. Although often considered street gangs, Asian gangs operate similar to Asian Criminal Enterprises with a more structured organization and hierarchy.

- They are not turf-oriented like most African-American and Hispanic street gangs and typically maintain a low profile to avoid law enforcement scrutiny. Asian gang members are known to prey on their own race and often develop a relationship with their victims before victimizing them.

- Law enforcement officials have limited knowledge of Asian gangs and often have difficulty penetrating these gangs because of language barriers and gang distrust of non-Asians.

- Asian gangs are involved in a host of criminal activities to include violent crime, drug and human trafficking, and white collar crime. Asian gang members in New England and California maintain marijuana cultivation houses specifically for the manufacturing and distribution of high potency marijuana and pay members of the Asian community to reside in them, according to 2010 NDIC and open source reporting.

East African—Somali Gangs

- Somali gang presence has increased in several cities throughout the United States. Somali gangs are most prevalent in the Minneapolis-St. Paul, Minnesota; San Diego, California; and Seattle, Washington areas, primarily as a result of proximity to the Mexican and Canadian borders, according to ICE, NGIC, and law enforcement reporting. (Somali gang activity has also been reported in other cities throughout the United States such as Nashville, Tennessee; Clarkston, Georgia; Columbus, Ohio; East Brunswick, New Jersey; and Tucson, Arizona.)

- Unlike most traditional street gangs, Somali gangs tend to align and adopt gang names based on clan or tribe, although a few have joined national gangs such as the Crips and Bloods. NGIC reporting indicates that East African gangs are present in at least 30 jurisdictions, including those in California, Georgia, Minnesota, Ohio, Texas, Virginia, and Washington. Somalian gangs are involved in drug and weapons trafficking, human trafficking, credit card fraud, prostitution, and violent crime.

- Homicides involving Somali victims are often the result of clan feuds between gang members.

- Sex trafficking of females across jurisdictional and state borders for the purpose of prostitution is also a growing trend among Somalian gangs.

- In November 2010, 29 suspected Somalian gang members were indicted for a prostitution trafficking operation, according to open source reporting. Over a 10 year period, Somalian gang members transported underage females from Minnesota to Ohio and Tennessee for prostitution.

- The Somali youth may emulate the local gangs, which frequently leads to friction with other gangs, such as Bloods and Crips, as well as with Ethiopian gangs.

East African—Sudanese Gangs

- Sudanese gangs in the United States have been expanding since 2003 and have been reported in Iowa, Minnesota, Nebraska, North Dakota, South Dakota, and Tennessee.

- Some Sudanese gang members have weapons and tactical knowledge from their involvement in conflicts in their native country.

- The African Pride (AP) gang is one of the most aggressive and dangerous of the Sudanese street gangs in Iowa, Minnesota, Nebraska, and North and South Dakota.

Caribbean—Dominican Gangs

- Although largely confined to the East Coast, Caribbean gangs, such as Dominican, Haitian, and Jamaican gangs, are expanding in a number of communities throughout the United States.

- The Trinitarios, the most rapidly expanding Caribbean gang and the largest Dominican gang, are a violent prison gang with members operating on the street. The Trinitarios are involved in homicide, violent assaults, robbery, theft, home invasions, and street-level drug distribution.

- Dominicans Don't Play (DDP), the second largest Dominican gang based in Bronx, New York, are known for their violent machete attacks and drug trafficking activities in Florida, Michigan, New Jersey, New York, and Pennsylvania. An increase in the Dominican population in several eastern U.S. jurisdictions has resulted in the expansion and migration of Dominican gangs such as the Trinitarios. This has led to an increase in drug trafficking, robberies, violent assaults in the Tri-state area.

Haitian Gangs

- Haitian gangs, such as the Florida-based Zoe Pound, have proliferated in many states primarily along the East Coast in recent years according to NGIC reporting.

- According to NGIC reporting, Haitian gangs are present in California, Connecticut, Florida, Georgia, Indiana, Maryland, Massachusetts, New Jersey, New York, North Carolina, South Carolina, and Texas.

- The Zoe Pound gang, a street gang founded in Miami, Florida by Haitian immigrants in the United States, is involved in drug trafficking, robbery, and related violent crime. In February 2010, 22 suspected Zoe Pound members in Chicago, Illinois, were charged with possession of and conspiracy to traffic powder and crack cocaine from Illinois to Florida, according to FBI reporting.

- The Haitian Boys Posse and Custer Street Gang are involved in a myriad of criminal activities including drug and weapons trafficking, robberies, shootings and homicides along the East Coast.

Jamaican Gangs

- Traditional Jamaican gangs operating in the United States are generally unsophisticated and lack a significant hierarchical structure, unlike gangs in Jamaica.

- Many active Jamaican gangs operating in the United States maintain ties to larger criminal organizations and gangs in Jamaica, such as the Shower Posse or the Spangler Posse.

- Jamaican gang members in the United States engage in drug and weapons trafficking.

APPENDIX D

Resources for Law Enforcement: Gangs and Human Trafficking

The following valuable resources provide an understanding of and strategies to mitigate the threat of gangs and human trafficking:

- COPS. (2017). "Gangs Toolkit." Community Oriented Policing Services. https://cops.usdoj.gov/default.asp?Item=1309
- G.R.E.A.T. (2017). "What is G.R.E.A.T.? Welcome." Gang Resistance Education and Training. www.great-online.org/GREAT-Home
- NGC. (2017). "About the National Gang Center." National Gang Center. www.nationalgangcenter.gov/About
- OJJDP. (2017). "Model Programs Guide." Office of Juvenile Justice and Delinquency Prevention. www.ojjdp.gov/mpg/
- PAL. (2017). "About Us." Police Athletic League. www.nationalpal.org/
- OVC. (2017). "Faces of Human Trafficking Video Series." Office for Victims of Crime. https://ovc.ncjrs.gov/humantrafficking/publicawareness.html
- U.S. Department of Homeland Security. (2017). "Law Enforcement Support." www.dhs.gov/blue-campaign/law-enforcement-support
- National Center for Missing & Exploited Center. (2016). "Resources for Law Enforcement." www.missingkids.com/LawEnforcement

U.S. DEPARTMENT OF JUSTICE OFFICE OF COMMUNITY ORIENTED POLICING

The community oriented policing (COPS) Office report that street gangs can take on many forms. To address the specific types of crimes committed by gangs, it offers the COPS Gangs Toolkit, consisting of resources for law enforcement officials, educators, and parents. These resources address community-policing solutions to youth crime and school violence. The COPS Office encourages law enforcement agencies to analyze their local gang problem and use these resources when appropriate. The following publications can be downloaded or requested from the COPS Web site (COPS, 2017):

1. Bullying in Schools
2. Disorderly Youth in Public Places
3. Drive-By Shootings
4. Drug Dealing in Open-Air Markets
5. Graffiti
6. Gun Violence among Serious Young Offenders
7. Juvenile Runaways
8. Solutions to Address Gang Crime CD-ROM
9. Street Gangs and Interventions: Innovative Problem Solving with Network Analysis
10. Witness Intimidation

GANG RESISTANCE EDUCATION AND TRAINING (G.R.E.A.T.) PROGRAM

The G.R.E.A.T. program is a school-based, law enforcement officer-instructed classroom curriculum. The program's primary objective is prevention, designed to assist young people avoid delinquency, youth violence, and gang membership. G.R.E.A.T. develops partnerships with the Boys & Girls Clubs of America and the Police Athletic League. It also has five regional training centers to train police officers across the United States (G.R.E.A.T., 2017).

NATIONAL GANG CENTER—LAW ENFORCEMENT ANTI-GANG TRAINING

The National Gang Center (NGC), part of the Office of Juvenile Justice and Delinquency Prevention, under the control of the Bureau of Justice Assistance of the U.S. Department of Justice, offers four classes for law enforcement—Advanced Gang Investigations, Basic Training for Street Gang Investigators, Gang Unit Supervision, and an Anti-Gang Seminar for Law Enforcement Chief Executives. These classes are provided on a regional basis to include participants from all law enforcement agencies (police and sheriff) within a geographical region. NGC also offers general consultations to assist communities in formulating strategies and programs that address their gang-related problems (National Gang Center, 2017).

The NGC features the latest research about gangs for state, local, and tribal jurisdictions, serving researchers, policymakers, direct service providers, criminal justice practitioners, and other community members through peer-to-peer information exchange and mentoring, training, and on-site and off-site technical assistance. NGC activities contribute to reductions in gang-related crime and violence and gang activity by juveniles and adults (National Gang Center, 2017).

OFFICE OF JUVENILE JUSTICE AND DELINQUENCY PREVENT—MODEL PROGRAMS GUIDE

The Office of Juvenile Justice and Delinquency Prevention's (OJJDP's) Model Programs Guide contains information about evidence-based juvenile justice and youth prevention, intervention, and re-entry programs. It is a resource for practitioners (i.e., law enforcement, courts, and corrections) and communities about what works, what is promising, and what does not work in juvenile justice, delinquency prevention, and child protection and safety The OJJDP is a component of the Office of Justice Programs of the U.S. Department of Justice (OJJDP, 2017).

POLICE ATHLETIC LEAGUE

The purpose of the National Police Athletics/Activities Leagues Inc. is to prevent juvenile crime and violence by providing civic, athletic, recreational and educational opportunities and resources to Police Athletic League (PAL) chapters. The National PAL organization provides its chapters with resources and opportunities to operate their own programs and enhance the quality of their employee and volunteer services (PAL, 2017).

OFFICE FOR VICTIMS OF CRIME

The Office for Victims of Crime (OVC) provides "Faces of Human Trafficking" video series. The series is intended to be used for outreach and education efforts of service providers, law enforcement, prosecutors, and others in the community. The series includes information about sex and labor trafficking, multidisciplinary approaches to serving victims of human trafficking, effective victim services, victims' legal needs, and voices of survivors. Accompanying the video series is a discussion guide, fact sheets, and posters. The videos and training tools are downloadable (Office for Victims of Crime, 2017).

U.S. DEPARTMENT OF HOMELAND SECURITY

The U.S. Department of Homeland Security (DHS) provides 24-hour operational support to law enforcement officials who may encounter a potential victim of human trafficking in the course of their duties. In addition, DHS offers online interactive human trafficking awareness training for first responders and law enforcement plus, other resource tools (U.S. Department of Homeland Security, 2017).

NATIONAL CENTER FOR MISSING & EXPLOITED CHILDREN

The National Center for Missing & Exploited Children provides valuable resources and technical assistance to law enforcement as they work to find missing children and combat child sexual exploitation. Some of these services to law enforcement include: searching for missing children, training, on-site assistance, child victim identification, assistance to identify and recover child victims of sex trafficking, and victim and family support (National Center for Missing & Exploited Children, 2016).

APPENDIX E

Organized Hate Groups

The information in this appendix has been extracted and/or adapted from the Southern Poverty Law Center (SPLC), and the Anti-Defamation League (ADL), two organizations fighting hate. For more information, see their Web sites:

www.splcenter.org/issues/hate-and-extremism

www.splcenter.org/fighting-hate/extremist-files/ideology

www.adl.org/

THE WHITE SUPREMACIST MOVEMENT

The white supremacist movement is composed of dozens of organizations and groups, each working to create a society totally dominated by white Christians, where the human rights of LGBTQ individuals and members of other minority groups are denied. Some groups seek to create an all "Aryan" territory; others seek to re-institutionalize Jim Crow segregation. While most of these organizations share a common bigotry based on religion, race, ethnicity, and sexual orientation or gender identity, they differ in many ways. They range from seemingly innocuous religious sects or tax protesters to openly militant, even violent, neo-Nazi skinheads and Ku Kluxers. No single organization or person dominates this movement. Frequently, individuals are members of several different groups at the same time. The supremacists have historically targeted blacks, Jews, and LGBTQ individuals, but in recent years have focused on Latino immigrants, particularly, the undocumented. These hate groups have exploited the controversy surrounding illegal immigration to recruit more members, especially in the states bordering Mexico.

Additionally, in recent years there has been a steady rise of anti-Muslim groups, one of those being ACT for America. ACT for America makes the claim on its website as being the "National Rifle Association (NRA) of national security." The Southern Poverty Law Center has designated this organization to be the largest grassroots anti-Muslim group in the U.S.

HOW HATE GROUPS ARE CATEGORIZED

Hate groups are categorized by the SPLC as Ku Klux Klan (KKK), Neo-Nazi, Racist Skinhead, Christian Identity, Black Separatist, Neo-Confederate, Patriot, Anti-Muslim Hate Groups, and Other. The "Other" category includes groups, vendors, and publishing houses endorsing a mixture of racist doctrines. The following is a partial list of hate groups with brief descriptions and ideology. Groups' membership and activities fluctuate for a variety of reasons.

Neo-Nazis and Klans

The reason for concern about the activities of neo-Nazis and Klans is obvious from their history of criminal activities, and their plots to launch race wars and kill officials who oppose them.

The largest of the neo-Nazi and Klan groups include the following:

Neo-Nazi-Type Groups	Klan-Type Groups
Aryan Nations	Alabama White Knights of the KKK
Knights of Freedom	America's Invisible Empire Knights of the KKK
National Alliance	American Knights of the KKK
Nationalist Socialist Movement	Imperial Klans of America
Creative Movement	Invincible Empire Knights of the KKK
	Knights of the White Kamellia
	New Order Knights of the KKK
	White Shield Knights of the KKK

The ideology of Klan members, neo-Nazis, and other white supremacists has been clear since the formation of these groups. They commonly advocate white supremacy, anti-Semitism, homophobia, racism, and sentiments against undocumented immigrants.

The most violent groups are the neo-Nazis; their movements are growing in the United States and in countries such as Germany and Austria. Young people between the ages of 13 and 25 who wish to join these organizations are required to commit a hate crime as part of the induction process. They openly idealize Hitler, and have committed murders and hundreds of assaults as well as other violent crimes; most of their victims are African Americans, Latinos, Asian Americans, gays, lesbians, bisexuals, transgender individuals, and even the homeless.

The World Church of the Creator (WCOTC), classified as a neo-Nazi-type group, was founded in 1973 by Ben Klassen, who wrote the organization's manifesto, *The White Man's Bible.* The organization's existence ended in mid-1990, following the suicide of Klassen and the imprisonment of other leaders. In 1996, however, the WCOTC was reborn under the leadership of Matt Hale. The group's rallying cry is "Rahowa," which stands for Racial Holy War. The group is also violently anti-Christian. A judge of the U.S. District Court in Chicago ruled in December 2002 that the WCTOC, founded in Illinois, would have to surrender the name because an Oregon-based religious group already had a trademark on it. The group now calls itself the Creativity Movement and makes a concerted effort to encourage women and children to become members. Matt Hale is serving a 40-year prison sentence and not expected to be released until 2037. According to the SPLC, his followers (The Creative Movement) scattered into small groups around the country.

ARYAN NATIONS The group Aryan Nations was formed in the early 1970s by Richard Butler. The organization virtually collapsed when he died in 2004, but under his leadership it was America's most notorious neo-Nazi group. Although there are still small factions in some states, Aryan Nations is no longer considered powerful as it was. The organization preaches that God's creation of Adam marked "the placing of the White Race upon this earth, that all nonwhites are inferior, and that Jews are the 'natural enemy' of our Aryan (white) race."

THE NATIONAL ALLIANCE The neo-Nazi group National Alliance (NA) believes it is subject to nature's laws only; therefore, members can determine their own destiny regardless of laws imposed by the government. They profess that those who believe in a divine control over mankind absolve themselves of responsibility for their fate. They also believe they are members of the Aryan (or European) race and are superior to other races. The NA is headquartered in Hillsboro, West Virginia. For many years, it was the largest and best-organized neo-Nazi group in the United States.

Racist Skinheads

Racist skinheads are considered the most dangerous radical-right threats facing law enforcement today. They are known for being hard to track because they are organized into small, mobile "crews" that move around frequently and without warning. They can act independently of other members or network in their verbal and physical attacks, sometimes violent, upon the persons or property of Jews, blacks, Hispanics, immigrants, gays, lesbians, and others.

Racist skinheads are often easily recognized because a significant part of their subculture is their dress and appearance. They typically have closely shaven heads, many visible tattoos and piercings, and skinhead-related garb such as work boots (with red laces) and suspenders. It is noteworthy, however, that some influential white supremacists have advocated that their members try to blend in more with the community. Some followers heeded the advice by growing out their hair, covered or removed their tattoos, and acquired legitimate jobs, thus enabling them to carry out their racist activities more covertly. As a result, not every skinhead fits the stereotypical profile. Some skinheads are transient and do not join groups. Because of this, the SPLC indicates that their numbers are hard to assess.

The influence of adult white supremacist groups on racist skinheads and neo-Nazi skinheads has been substantial, since the adult hate groups seek to replenish their membership ranks from the younger groups.

Christian Identity

Christian Identity describes a movement that is fundamentally racist, anti-Semitic, and anti-homosexual. According to the SPLC, the active Identity groups across the United States are organized under different names but with similar ideologies. The goal of these groups is to broaden the influence of the white supremacist movement under the guise of Christianity. They form their views of diverse people based on a particular interpretation of the Bible. The movement takes the position that white Anglo-Saxons—not Jews—are the real biblical "chosen people," and that blacks and other nonwhites are "mud people" on the same level as animals and therefore are without souls. Identity followers believe that the Bible commands racial segregation, interpreting racial equality as a violation of God's law.

POSSE COMITATUS   Another Identity group is Posse Comitatus, which means "power of the country" in Latin. The group is antitax and anti–federal government. Members of the Posse believe that all government power is vested in the county rather than at the federal level.

Black Separatists

The black separatist groups are active in the United States under two different names: The House of David and the Nation of Islam. Black separatist groups are organizations whose ideologies include tenets of racially based hatred. Black separatist followers share the same agenda as white supremacists: racial separatism and racial supremacy. The two movements also share a common goal of racial purity and a hatred of Jews. Despite the differences and mutual contempt between black extremist and white supremacist groups, and their mutual contempt, these groups join rhetorical forces to demean and slander Jews.

Patriot Groups

Patriot groups used to be referred to as militia groups; they define themselves as opposed to the "New World Order." They advocate or adhere to extreme anti-government doctrines. Some groups advocate or engage in violence or other criminal activities, or are racist.

Anti-Muslim Hate Groups

All anti-Muslim hate groups exhibit extreme hostility toward Muslims. The organizations portray those who worship Islam as fundamentally alien and attribute to its followers an inherent set of negative traits. Muslims are depicted as irrational, intolerant and violent, and their faith is frequently depicted as sanctioning pedophilia, coupled with intolerance for homosexuals and women. Anti-Muslim hate groups also broadly defame Islam, which they tend to treat as a monolithic and evil religion. These groups generally hold that Islam has no values in common with other cultures, is inferior to the West and is a violent political ideology rather than a religion.

APPENDIX F

Resources for Hate/Bias Crimes Monitoring

MONITORING HATE GROUPS

Law enforcement agencies must actively work to fight and control organized hate groups, tracking their activities, establishing when they are responsible for crimes, and assisting in their prosecution. Intelligence gathering is crucial to the efforts to reduce and prevent hate/bias crimes. Equally important is networking and sharing hate group information with other criminal justice agencies. Many have called this approach a cross-disciplinary coalition against racism. It involves statewide and regional commitments by criminal justice agencies to work with other public and private entities, including the Internal Revenue Service. All the institutions jointly develop and implement components of multitiered intervention strategies targeting enforcement, education, training, victim assistance, media relations, political activism and advocacy, and ongoing self-evaluation. A few of the hate/bias crimes monitoring, nongovernmental organizations include:

Southern Poverty Law Center: The nonprofit Southern Poverty Law Center (SPLC), located in Montgomery, Alabama, monitors and investigates organizations and individuals whom it deems "hate groups" and "extremists" and publishes a quarterly *Intelligence Report*. The organization considers the monitoring of white supremacist groups on a national scale and the tracking of hate crimes among its primary responsibilities. The SPLC also offers free legal services to victims of discrimination and hate crimes. The organization publishes e-mail newsletters "Hatewatch Weekly," "Mix It up Monthly," "Tolerance.org," and "Teaching Tolerance," and "Immigration Watch" to report on and monitor hate and extremism in the anti-immigration movement.

Anti-Defamation League: The Anti-Defamation League (ADL) was founded to expose and combat anti-Semitism, and to secure justice and fair treatment for all citizens alike. The ADL has been a leader of national and state efforts in the development of legislation, policies, and procedures to deter, investigate, and counteract hate-motivated crimes. The organization is also respected for its research publications and articles dealing with such crimes. The ADL developed a recording system that has served as a model of data collection nationwide.

National Gay and Lesbian Task Force and NGLTF Policy Institute: The National Gay and Lesbian Task Force (NGLTF) works to eradicate discrimination and violence based on sexual orientation and Human Immunodeficiency Virus (HIV) status.

Simon Wiesenthal Center: The Simon Wiesenthal Center, based in Los Angeles, is a human rights group named after the famed Nazi hunter. It monitors the Internet worldwide for tactics, language, and symbols of the high-tech hate culture. The center shares its information with affected law enforcement agencies. The organization, in some states, also operates Holocaust exhibits that are used as shocking examples of atrocities committed against Jewish people during World War II. Police academies and in-service, advanced officer training courses often use the exhibits for training on hate violence.

ONLINE MANUALS AND RESOURCES

Bureau of Justice Administration (BJA): The Bureau of Justice Administration (BJA) prepared a document entitled "Addressing Hate Crimes: Six Initiatives That Are Enhancing the Efforts of Criminal Justice Practitioners." The document describes six BJA-funded projects that involve efforts of local, state, and federal law enforcement agencies in combating bias-motivated crime. The paper identifies projects that support police and prosecutorial agencies in responding to hate crimes and supplies sources for additional information. The monograph (NCJ 179559) produced in 2000, can be found on the Web site (https://www .ncjrs.gov/pdffiles1/bja/179559.pdf) of the National Criminal Justice Reference Service.

Criminal Justice Information Services (CJIS) Division – Uniform Crime Reporting Program: The Law Enforcement Support Section of the Crime Statistics Management Unit prepared a document entitled "Hate Crime Data Collection Guidelines and Training Manual." The publication is intended to assist law enforcement agencies in establishing an updated hate crime training program so their personnel can collect and submit hate crime data to the FBI UCR (**Uniform Crime Reporting**) Program. In addition to providing suggested model reporting procedures and training aids for capturing the new bias motivations, the manual is written to raise law enforcement officers' awareness of the hate crime problem. The publication, dated February 27, 2015, can be found on their Web site (https://ucr.fbi .gov/hate-crime-data-collection-guidelines-and-training-manual.pdf).

SELECTED EXAMPLES OF COMMUNITY RESOURCES

Some jurisdictions have used a community approach to decrease the number of crimes and incidents of all types, including those motivated by hate/bias. Some exemplary programs include the following:

- *Town Watch Integrated Services:* Operation Town Watch is an organization located in the City of Philadelphia, which is dedicated to the development and promotion of organized, law enforcement-affiliated crime and drug prevention programs. Members include: Neighborhood, Crime, Community, Town and Block Watch Groups; law enforcement agencies; state and regional crime prevention associations; and a variety of businesses, civic groups, and concerned individuals working to make their communities safer places to live and work. The organization promotes neighborhood safety through community policing and support services.

- *Task Force on Police—Asian Relations:* In localities that have large Asian populations, task forces have been created that consist of criminal justice professionals, educators, victim/refugee advocates, volunteer agency representatives, and representatives from each Asian group living or working in the community. The purposes are several: to train criminal justice employees on communication techniques that improve relations and make them more effective in dealing with the Asian community; to prepare Asians on what to expect from the various criminal justice components, especially the police; to open lines of communication between law enforcement and Asians; and to encourage Asians to report crimes and trust the police. These task forces could certainly be adapted to other ethnic and racial groups as well. The city of Boston and other cities have effectively used the task force approach to resolve neighborhood problems, and have found them to be effective for exchanging information and curtailing rumors; identifying problems and working on solutions; and, perhaps most important, allowing citizens to help with and approach problems on a joint basis. Boston also has the Asian Task Force against Domestic Violence, which provides resources, a newsletter, tips, and links to receive assistance.

- *School Programs:* Some schools, with the help of the U.S. Department of Justice, Bureau of Justice Administration, uses teams of students and faculty members to promote awareness of bias and prejudice in its public high schools, middle schools, and elementary schools. Their stated mission is that no students in the state should have to experience anxiety, fear, or terror in school because of their color of the skin, religion, gender, sexual orientation, or disability, or any other aspect of themselves that makes them different from other students. Law enforcement works together with teachers and administrators to empower students to stand up for civility and respect. Typically, teams are made up of three or four students per grade, plus two or three faculty advisers. The teams have two formal responsibilities: (1) to promote awareness of bias and prejudice within their schools and (2) to organize forums for students to talk about harassment. If a team receives information about harassment, it is charged with forwarding that information to a responsible teacher or administrator.

- *Places of Worship:* Churches, synagogues, temples, and mosques can play a vital role in reducing violence in neighborhoods, schools, and the workplace. Interfaith coalitions in which multiple communities are represented can form vital partnerships with law enforcement with the objective of combatting hate in the community.

GENERIC COMMUNITY RESOURCES AND PROGRAMS

Neighborhoods (citizens and all local institutions encompassed by the term) working together with the police provide the best means of hate/bias incident control. Officers and citizens meet to discuss neighborhoods' most serious problems and work together to resolve them.

Community policing encourages officers to delve into observations and feelings to determine not only what is happening, but also who is involved, what their motivation is, and where they are from. Officers should consider themselves as first-line intelligence assets for their community. For example, they should watch for graffiti and/or other materials posted on walls, fences, telephone poles, and buildings. These markings could signal a racist operation in progress or a locally active hate group. In addition, to be effective, officers who patrol highly diverse areas must have some degree of cultural awareness and ability to engage in cross-cultural communication. It has been said that if officers are scrambling to understand communities only after a crime is committed, it is a terrible indictment of their lack of professionalism.

In addition, officers must know neighborhood leaders and ways to locate them quickly if they are needed to provide general assistance or to help control rumors or people. Neighborhood leaders can also provide invaluable help when it comes to dealing with victims who distrust police. A problem-focused approach provides officers with a solid understanding of social, economic, and environmental problems in the community. There are limits to what the police can do without community help. In many communities, however, police first must overcome their traditional role identification as crime fighters independent of the community before they can become an integral part of a team that works together to solve local problems. When officers patrol neighborhoods daily, they can interact with citizens to engender trust and can monitor their activities. Police officers and their department are better able to view and monitor what is taking place within the community they serve than any other government agency. Thus, officers and law enforcement agencies are in a better position to recognize the mood and tensions within the community.

Community resources and programs that are available or can be established include:

- *Victims' Hotline:* Like those available for domestic violence and rape victims, and suicide prevention. The staff is trained to provide victim assistance in terms of compassion, advice, referrals, and a prepared information package.

- *Human Relations Commission:* The staff aids victims of hate crimes or incidents, holds hearings, and provides recommendations for problem resolution.

- *United States Department of Justice Community Relations Service:* The CRS, with headquarters in Washington, D.C., has regional and field offices and provides services to every state. The Justice Department has trained staff who, when notified of a problem, will participate in and mediate community meetings to resolve conflicts. Many states have similar justice agencies that perform these services. The CRS created an excellent resource: *Understanding Bias: A Resource Guide* (Community Relations Services Toolkit for Policing). It is designed to help people in towns, cities or counties resolve tensions arising from community perceptions of bias or the lack of cultural competency among police officers. The CRS Toolkit for Policing is available at their Web site (www.justice.gov/crs/file/836431/download).

- *Conflict Resolution Panels:* Specially trained staff of a city or county who can assist agencies and/or victims (including groups) in the resolution of conflict, such as that caused by hate or bias.

- *The Media:* Cooperation in building public awareness of the problem of hate/bias violence via articles on causes and effects, resources, and legal remedies is essential.

- *Multilingual Public Information Brochures:* These can be provided by government agencies on the rights of victims, services available, and criminal and civil laws related to hate and bias.
- *Police Storefronts:* Police substations, established in the neighborhoods of communities with high concentrations of ethnic minorities, which are staffed by bilingual officers and/or civilians. The staff takes reports and aids the members of that community.

Community Resource List: List of organizations that specialize in victim assistance:

- American-Arab Anti-Discrimination Committee (ADC)
- Anti-Defamation League (ADL)
- Black Families Associations
- Japanese American Citizens League (JACL)
- Asian American Justice Center (AAJC)
- Coalition against anti-Asian Violence (CAAAV)S
- Congress of Racial Equality (CORE)
- Gay & Lesbian Alliance against Defamation (GLAAD)
- National LGBTQ Task Force
- Museum of Tolerance
- The National Association for the Advancement of Colored People (NAACP)
- National Black Parents' Association
- National Conference for Community Justice (NCCJ)
- National Congress of American Indians (NCAI)
- National Organization for Women (NOW)
- Arab American Institute (AAI)
- Council on American-Islamic Relations (CAIR)
- National Council of La Raza (NCLR)
- The Mexican American Political Association (MAPA)

GLOSSARY

Acculturation: The process of becoming familiar with and comfortable in another culture. The ability to function within that culture or environment, and retain one's own cultural identity.

Affirmative action: Legally mandated programs whose aim is to increase the employment or educational opportunities of groups that have been disadvantaged in the past.

African American Vernacular English: (AAVE) considered to be a dialect of English by some and a language by others; AAVE meets all the requirements of a language; it possesses a coherent system of signs; it has a grammar of elements and rules; and it is used for communication and social purposes. The terms African American Vernacular English and Ebonics are often used interchangeably.

Alien: Any person who is not a citizen or national of the country in which he or she lives.

Al-Jihad: Struggle (literal translation in Arabic). The term has also been used by some to mean "holy war" against infidels or nonbelievers.

Al-Qaida: Also spelled al-Qaeda. An international terrorist network consisting of loosely affiliated cells of operatives around the globe; the organization provides money, logistical support, and training to a variety of Islamist terrorist groups, and carries out attacks and bombings in order to disrupt the economies and influence of Western nations.

Alzheimer's disease: The most common type of dementia. "Dementia" is an umbrella term describing a variety of diseases and conditions that develop when nerve cells in the brain (called neurons) die or no longer function normally. The death or malfunction of neurons causes memory loss, erratic behavior and lessens one's ability to think clearly. In Alzheimer's disease, these brain changes eventually impair an individual's ability to carry out such basic bodily functions as walking and swallowing. Alzheimer's disease is ultimately fatal.

Anti-semitism: Latent or overt hostility toward Jews, often expressed through social, economic, institutional, religious, cultural, or political discrimination and through acts of individual or group violence.

Assimilation: The process by which ethnic groups that have emigrated to another society begin to lose their separate identity and culture, becoming absorbed into the larger community.

Asylum seeker (also asylee): A foreign-born individual in the United States or at a port of entry who is found to be unable or unwilling to return to his or her country of nationality, or to seek the protection of that country, because of persecution or a well-founded fear of persecution. Persecution or the fear thereof must be based on the individual's race, religion, nationality, membership in a particular social group, or political opinion (U.S. Citizenship and Immigration Services [USCIS], 2013).

At-risk communities: Communities having a high level of criminal activity or disorder and usually a higher number of incidents of civil rights violations—hate/bias crimes, discrimination, racism, and bigotry.

Awareness: Bringing to one's conscious mind that is only unconsciously perceived.

Bias: A preformed negative opinion or attitude toward a group of people based on their race, religion, disability, sexual orientation, ethnicity, gender, or gender identity.

Bias-based policing: Intentional and unintentional acts of applying or incorporating personal, societal, or organizational biases and/or stereotypes in decision-making, police actions, or the administration of justice; the inappropriate consideration of specified characteristics in carrying out duties (i.e., race, ethnicity, national origin, gender, gender identity, sexual orientation, socioeconomic status, religion, disability, and/or age) when making law enforcement decisions.

Bias Crime: A committed criminal offense that is motivated, in whole or in part, by the offender's bias(es) against a race, religion, disability, sexual orientation, ethnicity, gender, or gender identity; also known as Hate Crime.

Bigot: A person who steadfastly holds to bias and prejudice, convinced of the truth of his or her own opinion and intolerant of the opinions of others.

Bisexual: Of or relating to people who are physically, romantically, sexually, and/or emotionally attracted to both men and women.

Blue Code of Silence: The unspoken rule said to exist in police culture, resulting in officers not reporting the misconduct, errors, or crimes of fellow officers.

Communication Context: The "environment" in which communication takes place. It includes the circumstances of the communication, the relationships involved as well as cultural and social influences. These factors constitute the **context of the communication,** impacting *how* people communicate. For example, the fear of deportation impacts the way an undocumented immigrant will respond to questions by a police officer. Cultural influences can also have a bearing on indirectness, directness, and specificity with officers. In all cases where any variables within the **context** inhibit individuals (such as fear or high power distance relationships), officers will have to work harder at establishing rapport and building trust to open the communication.

Community policing: A partnership between the police and the local community that identifies strategies to reduce crime, increase traffic safety, and deal with all other public safety problems.

Community profiling: Demographic analysis of a community with regard to the ethnicity/national origin, race, religion, and sexual orientation of groups whose members work or reside there.

Consent Decree: Upon finding that a police agency has a "pattern or practice" of biased policing, the Department of Justice will reach a legal agreement with that agency, designed to bring about positive change in the areas of recruiting, training, use of force, and discipline. Consent decrees are enforceable by the courts.

Criminalizing homelessness: Referring to homeless people's being subject to arrest by police officers for violating city ordinances such as trespassing, disorderly conduct, sleeping in certain public places, or other life-sustaining behaviors.

Cross-cultural: Involving or mediating between two cultures.

Culture: Beliefs, values, habits, attitudes, patterns of thinking, behavior, and everyday customs that have been passed on from generation to generation. Culture is learned rather than inherited and is manifested in largely unconscious and subtle behavior. Culture is passed on from generation to generation.

Cultural competence: A developmental process in which individuals gain awareness, knowledge, and skills that enable effective organizational work across cultures and equitable cross-cultural and cross-racial treatment of all citizens. A "culturally competent organization" is one that has developed and adheres to a set of principles, attitudes, and policies that enable all individuals in an organization to work effectively and equitably across all cultures and ethnicities.

Department of Homeland Security (DHS): The cabinet-level federal agency responsible for preserving the security of the United States against terrorist attacks. This department was created as a response to the 9/11 terrorist attacks.

Disability bias: A preformed negative opinion or attitude toward a group of persons based on their physical or mental impairments, whether such disability is temporary or permanent, congenital or acquired by heredity, accident, injury, advanced age, or illness.

Discrimination: Action based on prejudiced thought and biases; the denial of equal treatment to individuals or groups because of their age, disability, employment, language, nationality, race, ethnicity, sex, gender and gender identity, sexual orientation, religion, or other form of cultural identity. "Racial" and "ethnic" discrimination are sometimes used interchangeably.

Diversity: The term used to describe a vast range of cultural differences that have become factors needing attention in living and working together. It is often applied to organizational and training interventions having to do with the interface of people who are different from each other. Diversity (and "diverse groups") includes race, ethnicity, gender, disability, sexual orientation, age, class, and educational background.

Dominant culture: Refers to the value system that characterizes a particular group of people that dominates the value systems of other groups or cultures. (See also majority cultural group.)

Ebonics: At its most literal level, Ebonics simply means "black speech" (a blend of the words ebony "black" and phonics "sounds"). The term was created in 1973 by a group of black scholars who disliked the negative connotations of terms like "Nonstandard Negro English" that had been coined in the 1960s when the first modern large-scale linguistic studies of African American speech-communities began. (See also African American Vernacular English.)

Economic Migrant: Generally referring to people fleeing devastating poverty from third world countries, who are not able to survive in their own countries.

Émigré: An individual forced, usually by political circumstances, to move from his or her native country and who deliberately resides as a foreigner in the host country.

Ethnic group: Group of people who conceive of themselves, and who are regarded by others, as alike because of their common ancestry, language, and physical characteristics.

Ethnicity: Refers to the background of a group with unique language, ancestral, often religious, and physical characteristics. Broadly characterizes a religious, racial, national, or cultural group.

Ethnicity bias: A preformed negative opinion or attitude toward a group of people whose members identify with each other, through a common heritage, often consisting of a common language, common culture (often including a shared religion), and/or ideology that stresses common ancestry. The concept of ethnicity differs from the closely related term *race* in that "race" refers to grouping based mostly upon biological criteria, while "ethnicity" also encompasses additional cultural factors.

Ethnocentrism: An attitude of seeing and judging other cultures from the perspective of one's own culture; using the culture of one's own group; using the latter as a standard for judging others, or thinking of it as superior to other cultures that are merely different; an ethnocentric person would say there is only one way of being "normal" and that is the way of his or her own culture.

Explicit bias: Conscious negative feelings toward a particular group.

Foreign-born: Refers to an individual who is not a U.S. citizen at birth or who is born outside the United States, Puerto Rico, or other U.S. territories, and whose parents are not U.S. citizens. The terms "foreign born" and "immigrant" are used interchangeably. The term includes naturalized U.S. citizens, legal permanent residents, temporary migrants (e.g., foreign students), humanitarian migrants (refugees), and unauthorized migrants. (U.S. Census Bureau, State and Country Quick Facts: Foreign-Born Persons, 2010)

Formal profile: Typically, a document containing explicit criteria or indicators issued to officers to guide them in their decision-making. It is often based on data collected and interpreted to signify a trend or suggest that given behavioral or situational commonalties, a person could believe that something may result. It can be an outline or short biographical description, an individual's character sketch, or a type of behavior associated with a group. Officers use behavioral or situational indicators to develop reasonable suspicion or probable cause to stop subjects. A profile is a summary of data that also relies upon expert advice about "average" or "typical" appearance that can *potentially* identify perpetrators of criminal activities.

Gang: The definition of a gang varies among most law enforcement agencies and jurisdictions at the federal, state, and local levels in the United States. The following five criteria are widely accepted and recognized among researchers for classifying groups as gangs (*Source:* National Gang Center, 2011):

1. The group has three or more members, generally aged 12–24 (particularly common with street gangs).
2. Members share an identity, typically linked to a name, and often have shared symbols, such as style of clothing, graffiti, tattoos, and hand signs.
3. Members view themselves as a gang, and are recognized by others as a gang.

4. The group has some permanence and a degree of organization.
5. The group is involved in an elevated level of criminal activity.

Gay: A male homosexual. Generally, this word is used to refer to gay men, but may also be used to describe women; the term "gay" is preferred over the term "homosexual."

Gender: Refers to an individual's sexual identity, or socially constructed characteristics.

Gender bias: A preformed negative opinion or attitude toward a person or group of persons based on their actual or perceived gender, for example, male or female.

Gender identity: A person's internal sense of being male, female, or a combination of both; that internal sense of a person's gender may be different from the person's gender as assigned at birth. Note: A transgender person may express their gender identity through gender characteristics, such as clothing, hair, voice, mannerisms, or behaviors, that do not conform to the gender-based expectations of society.

Gender identity bias: A preformed negative opinion or attitude toward a person or group of persons based on their actual or perceived gender identity, e.g., bias against transgender or gender nonconforming individuals.

Gender nonconforming: Describes a person who does not conform to the gender-based expectations of society, for example, a woman dressed in traditionally male clothing or a man wearing makeup. Note: A gender nonconforming person may or may not be a lesbian, gay, bisexual, or transgender person but may be perceived as such.

Glass ceiling: An invisible and often perceived barrier that prevents some ethnic or racial groups and women from becoming promoted or hired.

Hate crime: A criminal offense committed against a person, property, or society that is motivated, in whole or in part, by the offender's bias against a race, religion, disability, sexual orientation, or ethnicity/national origin (FBI, 2015).

Hate group: An organization whose primary purpose is to promote animosity, hostility, and malice toward persons of or with a race, religion, disability, sexual orientation, ethnicity, gender, or gender identity that differs from that of the members or the organization. Examples include the Ku Klux Klan and the American Nazi Party.

Hate incident: Incidents involving behaviors that, though motivated by bias against a victim's race, religion, ethnicity, gender, gender identity, disability, or sexual orientation, are not criminal acts. Hostile or hateful speech, or other disrespectful or discriminatory behavior, may be motivated by bias, but is an "incident," and not "crime."

Heterogeneity: Dissimilarity; composed of unrelated or unlike elements. A heterogeneous society is one that is diverse, and frequently refers to racial and ethnic composition.

Heterogeneous: Dissimilar, or composed of unrelated or unlike elements.

Heterogeneous society: A society that is diverse, and frequently refers to racial, ethnic, religious, and linguistic composition.

Heterosexual: Of or relating to people who are physically, romantically, and/or emotionally attracted to people of the opposite sex. Note: The term *straight* is a synonym.

Hierarchy: A deeply embedded system of societal structure whereby people are organized according to how much status and power they have. Hierarchical societies have specific and defined ways in which people must behave toward those lower and higher on the hierarchy. Communication is restricted in hierarchical societies, and people are always aware of where they stand in terms of status and power vis-à-vis other individuals.

High-Context/Low-Context Communication: Frameworks of communication, largely influenced by culture, related to how much speakers rely on messages other than from words to convey meaning; explicit and specific communication is valued in the low-context style; conversely, a relatively indirect style with less reliance on the spoken word characterizes high-context communication.

Holistic: View that the integrated whole has a reality independent and greater than the sum of its parts.

Homeland security: Federal and local law enforcement programs for gathering, processing, and application of intelligence to provide the United States with a blanket of protection against terrorist attacks.

Homeless adult person: (1) An individual or family who lacks a fixed, regular, and adequate nighttime residence; (2) an individual or family who resides in a public or private place not designed for or ordinarily use as a regular sleeping accommodation for human beings, including a car, park, abandoned building, bus or train station, airport or camping ground; (3) an individual or family living in a supervised publicly or privately operated shelter designed to provide temporary living arrangements paid for by Federal, State, or local government programs for low-income individuals or by charitable organizations, congregate shelters, and transitional housing; (4) an individual who resided in a shelter or place not meant for human habitation and who is exiting an institution where he or she temporarily resided. (*Source:* Subchapter 1: General Provisions Section 11302, U.S. Code, 2010)

Homeless children and youth: Have similar residency and shelter/transitional housing as a homeless adult, but includes sharing the housing of other persons due to loss of housing; living in motels, hotels, trailer parks, or camping grounds; or abandoned in hospitals; or are awaiting foster care placement. (*Source:* Subchapter VI: Education and Training, Part B: Education for Homeless Children and Youth, Section 11434a, U.S. Code, 2010)

Homophile: Relating to homosexuals.

Homosexual: Of or relating to people who are physically, romantically, and/or emotionally attracted to people of the same gender. Note: This is an outdated term considered derogatory and offensive by many people.

Human trafficking: The transportation of persons for sexual exploitation, forced labor, or other illegal or criminal activities.

Human trafficking/commercial sex acts: Inducing a person by force, fraud, or coercion to participate in commercial sex acts, or in which the person induced to perform such act(s) has not attained 18 years of age. (*Source:* FBI: UCR, 2016c)

Human trafficking/involuntary servitude: The obtaining of a person(s) through recruitment, harboring, transportation, or provision, and subjecting such persons by force, fraud, or coercion into involuntary servitude, peonage, debt bondage, or slavery (not to include commercial sex acts). (*Source:* FBI: UCR, 2016c)

Hybrid gangs: Nontraditional gangs with multiple affiliations and ethnicities.

Immigrant: Any individual admitted to the United States as a lawful permanent resident; also referred to as "permanent resident alien." (*Source:* Department of Homeland Security, Definition of Terms, 2013)

Implicit bias: Unconscious biases, held by all people, that can potentially influence judgements and actions; implicit bias results in an automatic association between groups of people and stereotypes about those groups.

Informal profile: Represents the "street sense," personal experiences, and strongly held beliefs that officers use to evaluate people or situations.

Indian country: "All land within the limits of any Indian reservation under the jurisdiction of the United States Government; …, all dependent Indian communities within the borders of the United States whether within the original or subsequently acquired territory thereof, and whether within or without the limits of a state, and all Indian allotments, the Indian titles to which have not been extinguished…" (*Source:* U.S. Code, 2007)

Indian tribe: Any Indian or Alaska Native tribe, band, nation, pueblo, village, or community that the Secretary of the Interior acknowledges to exist as an Indian tribe. (*Source:* U.S. Code, 2012b)

Informal networks: A system of influential colleagues who can, because of their position or power within an organization, connect the employee with information, resources, or other contacts helpful to his or her promotion or special assignment prospects.

Institutional racism: The failure of an organization (public or private) to provide goods, services, and opportunities to people because of their color, culture, ethnic origin.

Internalized racism: In general terms, the personal conscious or sub-conscious acceptance of the dominant society's views, stereotypes, and biases of ethnic, racial, and other protected classes of people.

IPV—Intimate Partner Violence: Domestic violence by a spouse or partner in an intimate relationship against the other spouse or partner or former partner; the violence can be physical, verbal, emotional, economic, and/or sexual.

Islamophobia: Fear or hatred of Islam and Muslims.

Jihad: See **Al-Jihad.**

Justice-based policing: Strategy to improve the quality and outcome of interactions between police and citizens while improving officer safety; over time and across multiple interactions, it strengthens community trust and confidence in the police and increases future cooperation and lawful behavior by citizens.

Juvenile gangs: The terms *youth* and *street gang* are commonly used interchangeably; however, the use of the term *street gang* for *youth gang* often results in confusing youth gangs with adult criminal organizations. (*Source:* NGC, 2013). To eliminate confusion, street gangs are composed of juveniles and young adults.

Leadership: Exercised when one takes initiative, guides, or influences others in a particular direction.

Legal immigrant: An individual granted legal permanent residence; granted asylum; admitted as a refugee; or admitted under a set of specific authorized temporary statuses for longer-term residence and work. This group includes "naturalized citizens," legal immigrants who have become U.S. citizens through naturalization; "legal permanent resident aliens," who have been granted permission to stay indefinitely in the United States as permanent residents, asylees, or refugees; and "legal temporary migrants," who are allowed to live and, in some cases, work in the United States for specific periods of time (usually longer than one year).

Lesbian: A homosexual woman. Some lesbian women prefer to be described as gay women and others as lesbians; both terms are preferred over the term "homosexual."

LGBT: Common abbreviation for "lesbian, gay, bisexual, and transgender," used to refer to community organizations or events that serve lesbian, gay, bisexual, transgender, and "allies," or those who support them.

LGBTQ: In recent years, the "Q" has been added to LGBT by some individuals, organizations, and publications, signifying "questioning" or "queer" (there is not across the board agreement). (See definitions of "Queer" and "Questioning" in this glossary.)

Machismo: Literally, maleness, manliness, and virility; a strong and sometimes aggressive sense of pride and power

Majority cultural group: The group within a society that is largest and/or most powerful. This power usually extends to setting cultural norms for the society as a whole. The term majority is falling into disuse because its connotations of group size are inaccurate in certain cities or regions of the country.

Mental illness: A mental, behavioral, or emotional health disorder which can range from no or mild impact to a serious impairment, affecting one or more major life activities; and meets the diagnostic criteria specified with the 4th edition of the Diagnostic Statistical Manual of Mental Disorders.

Mentor: "A trusted counselor or guide." (*Source:* Webster's New World Dictionary.) A mentor is usually a more experienced person who helps a less experienced one. The mentor provides information, advice, support, and encouragement to someone who is usually an apprentice, protégé, or a less experienced person. It involves leading, developing, and guiding by example in his or her area of success.

Millennial: The term usually applies to individuals who reached adulthood around the turn of the twenty-first century; members of the millennial generation were born (approximately) between 1977 and 1994.

Minority: The terms *minority* or *minorities* are used within the text to describe groups of individuals who represent a numeric minority within a racial or ethnic population.

Minority group: Refers to a category of people differentiated from the social majority; part of the population that differs in certain ways from the majority population and is sometimes subjected to differential treatment; a demographic group that is smaller in number than the majority cultural group.

Multiculturalism: The existence of diverse groups within one society; those groups maintain their unique cultural identities while accepting and participating in the larger society's legal and political system.

Order maintenance: The police handling of incidents that are not crimes, but public nuisance matters about which the police officer uses discretion to decide a course of action.

Outlaw Motorcycle Gangs: Gang members must possess and be able to operate a motorcycle to achieve and maintain membership with the group. The gangs of three or more persons engage in a pattern of criminal conduct.

Paradigm shift: What occurs when an entire cultural group begins to experience a change that involves the acceptance of new conceptual models or ways of thinking and results in major societal transitions (e.g., the shift from agricultural to industrial society).

Parity: The state or condition of being the same in power, value, rank, and so forth; equality.

Personally mediated racism: Explicit and overt racism, including specific attitudes based on stereotypes, biases, beliefs, practices, and behaviors leading to acts of prejudice and discrimination directed toward others.

Pluralistic: The existence within a nation or society of groups distinctive in ethnic origin, culture patterns, religion, or the like. A policy of favoring the preservation of such group with a given nation or society.

Power Distance: Refers to the way that power is viewed and distributed, with significant variations across cultures. Behavior and communication in "higher power distance" cultures vary, depending on an individual's place in the hierarchy; in "lower power distance" cultures, there is an appearance of equality, with behavior and communication consistent across power distances, and markedly less emphasis on status differences.

Prejudice: A judgment or opinion formed before facts are known, usually involving negative or unfavorable thoughts about groups of people.

Profiling (also known as criminal profiling): refers to any police-initiated action that uses a compilation of the background, physical, behavioral, and/or motivational characteristics for a type of perpetrator to identify a particular individual as being, having the potential to be, or having been engaged in criminal activity.

Prison gangs: Prevalent throughout the federal and state prison system in the United States, these are highly structured and organized networks, having an influence in prison operations and in street gang crime. Prison gangs are controlled by established internal rules and codes of conduct that are strictly enforced by gang leaders. (*Source:* National Gang Intelligence Center, 2013)

Probable cause: Probable cause is a higher level of reasonable belief, based on facts that can be articulated, that is required to arrest a person and prosecute him or her in criminal court. Also, before a person or a person's property can be searched, police must possess probable cause. All states have similar constitutional prohibitions against unreasonable searches and seizures.

Professionalism: Approach to one's occupation or career, with a sense of dedication and expertise.

Profile: A "profile" is typically a document that contains explicit criteria or indicators issued to officers to guide them in their decision making. It is usually based on data collected and interpreted to signify a trend or suggest that, given a particular set of characteristics (behavioral or situational commonalties), a person could believe that something may result based on that particular cluster of characteristics. A profile relies on using expert advice provided to law enforcement agencies to identify perpetrators of criminal activities. It can be an outline or short biographical description, an individual's character sketch, or a type of behavior associated with a group. It is a summary of data presenting the average or typical appearance of those persons situations under scrutiny. Officers use these indicators of physical, behavioral, or situational commonalties to develop reasonable suspicion or probable cause to stop subjects.

Profiling: Any police-initiated action that uses a compilation of the background, physical, behavioral, and/or motivational characteristics for a type of perpetrator that leads the police to a particular individual who has been identified as being, could be, or having been engaged in criminal activity.

Protected Classes: Refers to groups of people protected by law against illegal discrimination. Protected classes include people who cannot be targeted for discrimination for reasons of age, disability, religion or religious beliefs, pregnancy, national origin, race, ethnic background, sexual orientation or gender identity. The law also includes "retaliation," meaning that it protects people who assert "their rights to be free from employment discrimination including harassment."

Psychotic episode: The period of time when a person with a serious mental illness is impaired and at risk of endangering himself or herself, or others.

Queer: An umbrella term for LGBTQ individuals; no longer considered to be a derogatory term by certain segments of the population. The word has come to be an umbrella term for individuals who do not see themselves in fixed categories, such as male or female, gay or lesbian (sometimes referred to as "genderqueer").

Questioning: The questioning of one's gender, sexual identity, sexual orientation, or all three by people who may be unsure or exploring, and resistant to applying a social label (e.g., LGBTQ) to themselves.

Race: A group of persons of (or regarded as of) common ancestry. Physical characteristics are often used to identify people of different races. These characteristics should not be used to identify ethnic groups, which can cross racial lines.

Racial bias: A preformed negative opinion or attitude toward a group of persons who possess common physical characteristics, such as color of skin, eyes, and/or hair, facial features, and so forth, genetically transmitted by descent and heredity, which distinguish them as a distinct division of humankind, for example, Asians, blacks or African Americans, whites.

Racially biased policing: Occurs when law enforcement inappropriately considers race or ethnicity in deciding with whom and how to intervene in an enforcement capacity.

Racial profiling: Any police-initiated action that relies on the race, ethnicity, or national origin rather than the behavior of an individual or information that leads the police to a particular individual who has been identified as being, or having been, engaged in criminal activity.

Racism: Total rejection of and discrimination against others for reason of race, color, and sometimes cultural background.

Racist: One with a closed mind toward accepting one or more groups different from one's own origin in race or color.

Refugee: Any person who is outside his or her country of nationality who is unable or unwilling to return to that country because of persecution or a well-founded fear of persecution. Persecution or the fear thereof must be based on…race, religion, nationality, membership in a particular social group, or political opinion. People with no nationality must generally be outside their country of last habitual residence to qualify as a refugee. (*Source:* Department of Homeland Security, Definition of Terms, 2013.) Economic refugee generally refers to people fleeing devastating poverty from third world countries, who are not able to survive in their own countries.

Religious bias: A preformed negative opinion or attitude toward a group of persons who share the same religious beliefs regarding the origin and purpose of the universe and the existence or nonexistence of a supreme being, for example, Catholics, Jews, Muslims, Protestants, and atheists.

Reasonable suspicion: A police officer may briefly detain a person for questioning or request identification only if the officer has what is called a "reasonable suspicion" that the person's behavior is related to criminal activity. Reasonable suspicion requires that the officer have specific facts that must be articulated to support his or her actions; a mere suspicion or "hunch" is not sufficient. Reasonable suspicion can be based on the observations of a police officer combined with his or her training and experience, and/or reliable information received from credible outside sources. A police officer possesses reasonable suspicion if he or she has enough knowledge to lead a reasonably cautious person to believe that criminal activity is occurring and that the individual played some part in it. Reasonable suspicion is a level of belief that is less clear-cut than probable cause.

Sanctuary city, county, or state: There is no official definition for "sanctuary" as applied to cities, counties, and states. However, it is a term that is applied by some to localities that have adopted policies designed to protect unauthorized immigrants by not prosecuting them solely for violating federal immigration laws.

Scapegoat: Falsely blame the failures and shortcomings of an individual, organization, cultural/racial group, etc. on other often innocent people.

Sexual orientation: The term for a person's physical, romantic, and/or emotional attraction to members of the same and/or opposite sex, including lesbian, gay, bisexual, and heterosexual (straight) individuals. Note: Avoid the offensive terms "sexual preference" or "lifestyle."

Sexual-orientation bias: A preformed negative opinion or attitude toward a person or group of persons based on their actual or perceived sexual orientation.

Stereotype: To believe that people conform to a pattern or manner with all other individual members of a specific group. People who are prone to stereotyping often categorize the behavior of an entire group based on limited or no experience with people in that group. The characteristics ascribed to others are mostly negative; this negative stereotyping classifies people in the targeted group by the use of slurs, innuendoes, names, or slang expressions, depreciating the group as a whole as well as individuals in it.

Street gangs: National, regional, and local street gangs, represented in urban, rural, and Indian Country, are the largest types of gangs and control the greatest geographic areas; while, the majority of gang members identified by law enforcement agencies are 18 years and older; juveniles also comprise a percentage of street gang membership, and actively participating in criminal behavior and violence.

Subculture: A group with distinct, discernible, and consistent cultural traits existing within and participating in a larger cultural grouping.

Suspect-specific incident: An incident in which an officer lawfully attempts to detain, apprehend, or otherwise be on the lookout for one or more specific suspects identified or described, in part, by national or ethnic origin, gender, or race.

Transgender: Of or relating to a person who identifies as a different gender from their gender as assigned at birth. Covers a range of people, including heterosexual cross-dressers, homosexual drag queens, and transsexuals who believe they were born in the wrong body, and may take hormones or undergo a sex change operation to alter their gender.

Unauthorized/Undocumented immigrant: All foreign-born noncitizens residing in the country who are not "legal immigrants" and who entered the country without valid documents or arrived with valid visas but stayed past their visa expiration date or otherwise violated the terms of their admission. (*Source:* Passel and Cohn, 2011 [Chapter 1].) Although the term "unauthorized immigrant" is increasingly in use, it has not entirely replaced the term "undocumented immigrant."

U.S.-born: Describes those who are U.S. citizens at birth, including people born in the United States, Puerto Rico, or other U.S. territories, as well as those born elsewhere to parents who are U.S. citizens.

Verbal De-Escalation: Refers to the act of decreasing the intensity, volume or magnitude of a conflict or confrontation through a communication style that deflects anger and calms a potentially aggressive or violent situation.

White supremacist group: Any ongoing organization, association, or group of three or more persons, whether formal or informal, having as one of its primary activities the promotion of white supremacy through the commission of criminal acts.

INDEX

Note: The 'b' and 'e' following the locators refer to boxes and exhibits cited in the text.